The Effective Teaching of Language Arts

FOURTH EDITION

The Effective Teaching of Language Arts

Donna E. Norton
Texas A&M University

Merrill, an imprint of
Macmillan Publishing Company
New York

Maxwell Macmillan Canada
Toronto

Maxwell Macmillan International
New York   Oxford   Singapore   Sydney

Macmillan Publishing Company
866 Third Avenue
New York, NY 10022

Macmillan Publishing Company is part of the Maxwell Communication Group of Companies.

Maxwell Macmillan Canada, Inc.
1200 Eglinton Avenue East, Suite 200
Don Mills, Ontario M3C 3N1

Library of Congress Cataloging-in-Publication Data

Norton, Donna E.
    The effective teaching of language arts / Donna E. Norton.—4th ed.
        p.   cm.
    Includes bibliographical references and index.
    ISBN 0-02-388310-3
    1. Language arts (Elementary) I. Title.
LB1576.N84 1993
372.6'044—dc20   92-31177
                                            CIP

Printing: 1 2 3 4 5 6 7 8 9   Year: 3 4 5 6 7

Editor: Linda James Scharp
Production Editor: Mary Harlan
Photo Editor: Anne Vega
Text Designer: Anne Flanagan
Cover Designer: Cathleen Norz
Cover art: Tom Post
Production Buyer: Patricia A. Tonneman

This book was set in Leawood by Carlisle Communications, Ltd. and was printed and bound by R.R. Donnelley & Sons Company. The cover was printed by Lehigh Press, Inc.

Photo Credits: All photos copyrighted by the individuals or organizations listed. Andy Brunk: 449, 485. Andy Brunk/Macmillan: 476. Ben Chandler/Macmillan: 218. Robert Finken: 6, 9, 10, 23, 72, 74, 96, 124, 129, 137, 146, 188, 253, 273, 276, 315, 339, 386, 435, 456, 469, 488. Kevin Fitzsimmons/Macmillan: 532. Jean Greenwald/Macmillan: 522. Jean-Claude LeJeune: 28, 59, 83, 221, 330, 347, 363, 390, 395, 431. John McNamara: 178, 181. Mark Madden/Macmillan: 1, 248, 355, 471. Charles Quinlan: 283. Barbara C. Schwartz/Macmillan: 119, 197, 215, 374, 411, 425, 438, 517. Michael Siluk: 92, 167, 257, 297, 421, 479, 482, 524. David Strickler/Strix Pix; 45, 232, 304. Anne Vega/Macmillan: 31, 243, 361. Cynda Williams/ Macmillan: 267. Gale Zucker: 12.

*F*ollowing the completion of her doctorate at the University of Wisconsin, Madison, Donna E. Norton joined the College of Education faculty at Texas A&M University where she teaches courses in children's literature, language arts, and reading. Dr. Norton is the 1992 recipient of the Virginia Hamilton Essay Award. She is listed in *Who's Who of American Women, Who's Who in America*, and *Who's Who in the World*.

Dr. Norton is the author of three books in addition to this volume: *Through the Eyes of a Child: An Introduction to Children's Literature*, 3d ed., *Language Arts Activities for Children*, 2d ed., and *The Impact of Literature-Based Reading*. She is on the editorial board of several journals and is a frequent contributor to journals and presenter at professional conferences. The focus of her current research is multicultural literature, comparative education, and literature-based reading programs. The multicultural research includes a longitudinal study of multicultural literature in classroom settings. This research is supported by grants from the Meadows Foundation and the Texas A&M Research Association. In conjunction with the research in comparative education, she developed a graduate course that enables students to study children's literature and reading instruction in England and Scotland and is evaluating educational programs in several Asian and European countries. She currently has a grant from GTE Foundation to develop institutes in children's literature and literacy.

Prior to her college teaching experience, Dr. Norton was an elementary teacher in River Falls, Wisconsin and in Madison, Wisconsin. She was a Language Arts/Reading Consultant for federally funded kindergarten through adult basic education programs. In this capacity she developed, provided in-service instruction, and evaluated kindergarten programs, summer reading and library programs, remedial reading programs, learning disability programs for middle school children, elementary and secondary literature programs for the gifted, and diagnostic and intervention programs for reading disabled adults. Dr. Norton's continuing concern for literature programs results in frequent consultations with educators from various disciplines, librarians, and school administrators and teachers.

Preface

*E*ffective teaching of language arts requires commitment to excellence on the part of classroom teachers. The language arts include speaking, listening, reading, and writing. Excellence cannot be attained without thorough knowledge of the language arts and understanding of methods that develop language arts abilities in children.

Diagnostic procedures are suggested for evaluating children's strengths, weaknesses, and interests. Because teachers are accountable to the children they teach, to the administrators of the school, and to the parents, they must have accurate knowledge about their students.

Diagnosis is worthless, however, without research-based knowledge about learning environments, motivation, objectives, instructional procedures, grouping, and teacher effectiveness. Because effective teaching is built on a solid knowledge base, more than 160 new research citations have been added to this edition. In addition, examples of lesson plans, instructional/thematic units, and learning centers demonstrate how theory can inform classroom practice. The successful use of these ideas with children is indicated by the inclusion of examples of children's oral and written responses.

For preservice teachers to experience planning lessons, evaluating language arts abilities, or teaching a lesson, reinforcement activities are included throughout each chapter and at the conclusion of each chapter. All the reinforcement activities have been used with college language arts classes or as inservice presentations with experienced teachers. The professor and the students may choose as many of these reinforcement activities as they wish in order to develop the objectives of the chapter and to explore effective teaching strategies.

Each chapter in this text contains features geared to the development of effective language arts instruction. At the beginning of each chapter, chapter objectives are listed to provide an overview of content, preview the materials to be covered, and stress the major concepts to be mastered.

The chapters on tools for writing—grammar and mechanics, handwriting, and spelling—have been maintained and updated. Three types of grammar are presented: traditional, structural, and transformational.

Other major changes for the fourth edition of *The Effective Teaching of Language Arts* include:

- *Attention to the expanded role of children's literature.* Current educational practice emphasizes the role of children's literature in all phases of the language arts. Consequently, this edition of the text includes an increased emphasis on children's literature. By referring to the combined information in chapters 11 and 12, you will be able to develop a literature-based language arts and reading program. Many of the "For Your Plan Book" features are based on children's books. This edition contains more than 190 new children's literature references.
- *Special focus on cultural diversity.* Because we can *expect* cultural diversity in the classrooms of the 1990s, special attention was given to the revision of chapter 5, "Linguistically Different Children and Multicultural Education." Included are discussions of assessment issues, characteristics of effective intervention programs, and educational implications and approaches. Also, guidelines are presented for selecting multicultural literature and identifying values embodied in traditional literature from a variety of cultural groups.
- *Expansion of "For Your Plan Book" features.* These features, which are identified by a special symbol in the margin, are actual lesson or unit plans that can be used immediately. Assessment strategies are part of each plan book feature.
- *Integration of computer and media coverage.* The use of computer technology in the classroom is addressed in special sections in chapter 9, "Computers and writing and editing," and chapter 12, "Computers and reading." Special coverage of media can be found in chapters 4 (critical listening) and chapter 13, "Library and reference skills."
- *Increased emphasis on children's "talk" and listening.* Intentional use and development of children's oral language abilities are essential for effective language arts classrooms today. Reader's theatre, choral reading, and critical listening strategies are discussed. "For Your Plan Book" features on critical evaluation of advertising and propaganda suitable for both upper elementary and middle school students can be found in chapter 4.
- *Suggestions for assessment, including informal assessment strategies.* Specific ideas for assessment are discussed whenever major teaching strategies are covered. Each lesson or unit plan contains specific assessment suggestions. Informal assessment techniques that classroom teachers can use and interpret easily are stressed.

The goal of this text is to provide support, motivation and knowledge for the classroom teacher who is responsible for the effective teaching of *all* children. This goal can be achieved if we can instill in teachers a commitment to excellence.

ACKNOWLEDGMENTS

The methods development of a language arts text would be impossible without the enthusiasm, critical evaluation, and suggestions of many individuals. My special appreciation is extended to the many language arts students and teachers who have tried specific methods and strategies in their classrooms, shared stimulating experiences, and criticized sections of this text. Outstanding teachers have shared their experiences with me by suggesting lesson examples, units, and learning centers that have been used successfully in their classrooms. Both undergraduate and graduate language arts classes read the text to ensure understanding of the content. The enthusiasm and sincerity of these students are appreciated.

My thanks go to Editor-in-Chief Jeff Johnston, editor Linda James Scharp, and production editor Mary Harlan. In addition, the text has benefited from the copy-editing expertise of Charlene Rundo and Ann Mirels.

Contents

FOR YOUR PLAN BOOK

Chapter One

After completing this chapter, you will be able to:

1. *Describe the contents and importance of the language arts curriculum.*
2. *Describe the format of this textbook.*
3. *Identify current issues and trends that affect language arts instruction.*
4. *Evaluate elementary language arts textbooks based on national guidelines for judging and selecting these textbooks.*

Introduction to the Language Arts

L anguage is the most important form of human communication. Language communication includes speaking, writing, listening, and reading and as such, it is the most important, as well as the most exciting, part of the elementary curriculum. Its importance is reflected in estimates that the average person listens to the equivalent of a book each day, talks the equivalent of a book each week, reads the equivalent of a book each month, and writes the equivalent of a book each year. It is your responsibility as a language arts teacher to promote the ability to communicate effectively. The purpose of this textbook is to provide you with effective methods for developing language arts skills in all children.

THE LANGUAGE ARTS CURRICULUM

A brief overview of the language arts curriculum reinforces the suggestion that the language arts are both important and exciting. In an elementary school where learning is taking place, the teachers use language arts in all areas of the curriculum.

Because oral language is a vital form of human communication, effective teachers provide many opportunities for oral language development and do not assume that oral language skills cannot be improved. Good oral questioning strategies focus on an initial question, extend information and understanding, clarify facts, and raise the comprehension levels of children. Exciting discussions take place in all subject areas when teachers use oral questioning strategies that encourage children to develop their individual thought processes. Discussions are also extended through such techniques as buzz sessions, roundtable and panel discussions, and debates.

Original drama is an extremely exciting method for developing creative thinking and oral language skills. In a stimulating elementary school, children are presenting puppet plays, doing improvisations, using creative play activities, pantomiming characters and objects, role-playing experiences, and doing choral poetry reading. Children in such an environment are involved in all aspects of oral language, and the teachers increase the participation of students in oral language as well as evaluate and improve it.

The teachers in this environment recognize that effective oral language instruction requires an audience, and that this audience needs to refine its listening skills. Research shows that listening skills can be improved through instruction, although both evaluation and instruction are complicated. Listening includes hearing; auditory discrimination; literal, interpretational, critical, and evaluational comprehension; and appreciation. Effective language arts teachers recognize the importance of each aspect of listening. They use audiometers to screen children suspected of hearing loss; auditory discrimination tests to identify students who have problems with auditory perception; informal tests to identify children who have problems with achievement due to inattentive listening; and listening comprehension tests to evaluate the ability of students to restate, interpret, and critically evaluate what they hear.

Teachers use the information obtained through evaluation to provide exciting and effective learning activities. To develop auditory awareness, have young children listen to and describe sounds they hear in their environment. Have them listen to music, rhymes, and limericks to become aware of the lovely sounds in our language. To improve auditory discrimination, have them listen to and describe likenesses and differences in sounds, words, and rhymes. Many of these discrimination activities can take the format of games. To develop attentive listening skills, help children set purposes for listening, provide opportunities for children to give as well as follow directions, and provide instruction that requires children to listen for specific purposes. Many stimulating methods can help children develop listening comprehension. In one class, children might listen to a taped conversation between two famous people for the purpose of identifying the individuals. Another class might listen to the beginning of a story and then predict its outcome. Students can listen to commercials and critically evaluate the propaganda techniques or develop appreciative listening skills by listening to poetry, music, or literature for pure enjoyment.

Teachers in an effective language arts curriculum provide many opportunities for children to develop their writing skills. Such teachers should keep folders of each child's writing so that the student and teacher can evaluate growth in writing. The environment is critical in developing writing skills. Stimulate, react to ideas, confer with the writer, listen to and read the writing, and provide opportunities for sharing writing, rather than merely assign projects and provide group instruction. Stimulation is essential. Before children write poetry, let them go out into a field or the woods to experience nature; before they write a creative story let them listen to music or discuss a thought-provoking item or picture. Have the children in this environment experience the development of a composition by identifying their audience and purpose, deciding on the subject, and organizing their ideas. Also have them write a great deal—biographies, classroom newspapers, and creative stories.

Effective language arts curriculums also include the more mechanical aspects of written and oral language. Young children experience readiness activities for handwriting. First-grade children are usually instructed in manuscript printing. About third grade, children receive instruction in switching from manuscript to cursive writing. Numerous writing activities in the classroom offer opportunities to use and improve handwriting skills. Because the study of modern grammar stresses that children should understand their language, effective language arts teachers use activities such as sentence-pattern exploration, sentence combining, sentence expansion, and sentence transformation to allow children to explore language and discover how it works. Children also examine appropriate levels of usage. They learn that different levels of usage are appropriate for different audiences and purposes. Instruction is flexible and increases the levels of usage available to the children. Effective teachers assess spelling levels and provide instruction at the appropriate level for each child.

Literature is a dynamic part of effective language arts classrooms. Books are everywhere. Effective teachers read to the students and allow them many opportunities to read for enjoyment and to discuss the books they read with other children. The teachers model behavior and help children through the decision-making process as they approach various literary elements in literature. A classroom where literature is important should contain a colorful library corner with attractive and comfortable places for children to read. Children should share their books through creative oral, written, and art ideas.

Most important, teachers should read and tell stories to the students so that the students know storytelling is a wonderful experience. Use literature to stimulate research and interest in social studies and science subjects. A class studying the westward expansion, for example, may be adding to its knowledge of frontier life by reading the Little House books by Laura Ingalls Wilder. A class studying science may learn more about a famous scientist by reading a biography or autobiography. In this environment, teachers evaluate the interests of the students in literature as well as ability to read and use this information to help the children find books to read and enjoy.

Tchudi (1986) maintains that literature and reading materials are excellent sources for extending the curriculum into multicultural reading, multidisciplinary reading, and multimedia studies. Multicultural reading includes infusion of black and ethnic literature into all language arts classes. Multidisciplinary reading emphasizes that literature from a wide variety of disciplines and genres is appropriate in language arts classes. Likewise, quality literature is appropriate in other disciplines, such as science, mathematics, history, and social studies. Multimedia studies include television and other media as integral parts of the curriculum.

Language arts instruction that utilizes the various media can be highly motivating for many children. Creative teachers use television to motivate reading, to develop discussion skills, and to develop critical thinking. Commercial films and filmstrips can add visual interpretations to books, stimulate creative writing, and stimulate oral expression. A visit to an effective language arts class might find the students actively involved in making their own film, providing a musical background for it, and showing the finished product to an appreciative audience. Another class might be developing critical evaluation skills by studying propaganda techniques used in newspaper, television, and radio commercials. The students can distinguish fact from opinion in newspapers or write their own newspaper ads, news stories, or special features. A class-produced newspaper, television show, radio program, or film is an exciting culminating activity for a study of media.

The subjects covered in the language arts curriculum are obviously important. Effective language arts teachers must be able to provide instruction in each of these subject areas—oral language, listening, written composition, handwriting, grammar, usage, literature, reading, media, and using references—to a wide variety of children. This text is designed to prepare prospective teachers for this exciting work.

This text includes several features to help preservice and in-service teachers become effective language arts teachers. Look at each feature to see how it can improve understanding of and instruction in the language arts.

Chapter Objectives

Each chapter includes a list of objectives. This list provides an overview of the chapter as well as a means of evaluating your learning after having completed the chapter.

Diagnostic Procedures

Effective language arts teaching combines children in small groups, large groups, or individually, according to each child's strengths and weaknesses. For this reason, many chapters describe both formal and informal diagnostic procedures for assessing children's abilities.

Informal assessment techniques are especially valuable in language arts. Because many of the standardized tests given in elementary schools do not adequately assess language arts skills, teachers cannot use the information gained from these tests to improve instruction. Assessment of oral language is an example. Group-administered, standardized tests do not have oral language components. If oral language is a vital part of language arts instruction, then assessment techniques must allow for observation and evaluation of each child's total language apparatus under many different circumstances.

This text includes checklists for immediate use by teachers. Examples include an individual student profile to accompany oral language evaluation; an auditory inventory; a listening comprehension inventory; a handwriting analysis checklist; a writing evaluation checklist; a usage, punctuation, and capitalization inventory; an interest inventory for literature; and a library reference skills checklist. Teachers must avoid repeating skills a child has already mastered. Spelling is one example. Without assessment of spelling levels, a child may be receiving instruction on words he or she already knows, which is boring for the child and a waste of valuable instructional time. It is equally wasteful to provide spelling instruction at a level so difficult that it frustrates the child. Diagnostic procedures include an emphasis on the portfolios that are especially helpful when assessing literature-based instruction.

Reinforcement Activities and Plan Book Features

People learn and retain knowledge by becoming actively involved in their own education. This is particularly true in an educational methods course such as language arts. To thoroughly understand assessment techniques, you must use them with children or adults. Likewise, to develop skills in teaching various language arts subjects, you must design lessons and teach them, either to children or to peers. Each chapter includes reinforcement activities so that you can immediately apply a language arts assessment or instructional technique. In Chapters 3 through

Effective language arts teachers understand the individual needs of children.

13, there are also field-tested, exemplary lesson or unit plans for you to try. The "Plan Book" features are listed in a separate table of contents to help you locate them quickly.

Research

Teachers of language arts are fortunate in that a great deal of research has been done in most areas of the language arts. This is important because sound instructional practices are based on research. This text includes reviews of research that provide rationales for suggestions concerning diagnosis and instruction. This research may also be used for further study in that area of language arts. Research findings have changed some of the instructional emphases in language arts and have explored the most effective roles for teachers. Researchers such as Flower and Hayes (1978), Graves (1981), Applebee (1984), Britton et al. (1979), and Hillocks (1986) develop foundations for effective instruction or practices that improve students' abilities to respond during different phases of the writing process. Likewise, research in modeling and implications from schema theory improve instruction in literature and reinforce the strong connections between literature and reading. Summaries of reading comprehension, such as those written by Dole, Duffy, Roehler, and Pearson (1991), provide insights for effective instruction in literature and reading.

The various topics covered in the recently published *Handbook of Research on Teaching the English Language Arts* (Flood, Lapp, Jensen, & Squire, 1991) illustrate the importance of research in the area of language arts. According to Hoffman (1991), the handbook "synthesizes a formidable body of knowledge derived from scientific investigations. We can speak today with some confidence regarding literacy acquisition and literacy teaching" (p. 61). Hoffman expresses concern, however, that the knowledge gained from research is not applied in many classrooms: "Although our knowledge of the language arts has grown enormously through research, the day-to-day teaching of literacy in schools has remained remarkably unchanged over the decades. In fact, the insights gained from research regarding effective practices appear to be grossly at odds with the 'typical' instruction offered on a day-to-day basis in classrooms across the country. How do we explain the ever-widening gap between knowledge and practice? Why aren't teachers using what researchers have found to be effective in instruction? Where has the system broken down?" (p. 61). Hoffman maintains that illiteracy could be eradicated in the next century if only we could find a way to bridge the gap between research and practice. Such an effort would require the combined efforts of researchers, teacher educators, administrators, and business people.

Research from cognitive psychology is also important in language arts teaching. Cognitive mapping or webbing strategies now enhance all areas of language arts. Research shows that use of creative and critical thinking skills increases students' interactions and understandings in all content areas. In 1986, the National Council of Teachers of English Committee on Classroom Practices in Teaching English identified development of creative and critical thinking skills in students as the current major concern for English language arts teachers. Undoubtedly, this will be an area of research concern for the next decade.

Developmental Instruction

After diagnosis, the next step is to provide the most effective language arts instruction for each child. This instruction encompasses the learning environment, motivation, objectives, instructional procedures, and teacher effectiveness. None of these elements can be ignored in an effective language arts classroom. Notice these essential elements as students proceed from a motivation for writing, to consideration of a topic, to a tentative approach for writing, to gathering materials, to organizing ideas and materials, to writing first drafts, to reviewing and rereading drafts, to revising and making changes in the content, to proofing and editing, and to sharing the works with the intended audiences. Such various prewriting, writing, and postwriting activities encourage interactions between students as well as between students and teachers. This text explores instructional interactions in a chapter on the writing process and a chapter on developing expressive, poetic, and expository writers.

Researchers such as Roehler and Duffy (1984) and Gordon (1985) developed instructional approaches that place teachers in active learning roles with students and that show students how teachers approach thought processing before the students are expected to perform similar tasks. Effective modeling approaches proceed from identifying skill requirements, to providing examples showing that skill, to identifying why the skill is important to students, to identifying text samples, to developing questions, to considering the answers to the questions, to citing the evidence that supports the answers, and to thinking through the reasoning process used to acquire the answers. As modeling progresses, the approach proceeds from total teacher modeling, to gradual student interaction, to total student responses. Several chapters demonstrate modeling, including those on oral language, grammar, and literature.

This book includes examples of lesson plans, instructional units, and learning centers to help you visualize instructional procedures and to give you ideas for developing similar lessons. Lesson plans include language experience chart stories, expressive writing, vocabulary webs, manuscript writing, sentence transformations, usage, and modeling of various literary elements and cohesive devices. Units include a puppetry project, a proofreading unit, a folktale unit, a composition approach to biography, a literary approach to biography, a filmmaking project, an advertising unit for critical evaluation of propaganda techniques, and a library reference unit. Learning centers include a listening learning center and a newspaper learning center. These lesson plans, units, and learning centers have been used effectively with children.

Where feasible, examples of products from a lesson are included. The examples, many of which are in creative poetic writing, range from first grade through middle school and illustrate the results of instruction.

Developmental instruction is not accomplished in isolation. Any language arts topic requires interaction and integration of numerous areas. For example, a series of language arts lessons based on folktales may require development of critical and appreciative listening, analysis of literary elements, comparison of folklore types, creation of a play or oral storytelling based on folktales, and creative writing that follows similar forms. Consequently, such lessons require integration of listening, literature, reading, oral language, writing, and social studies. In addition, a film or filmstrip may supplement folklore references selected from the school media center. Integration of such language arts subjects and various content areas is emphasized throughout the text.

The Literature Connection

The role of primary literature sources in the language arts and reading curriculum is receiving renewed interest. There are two types of considerations. First are those for using literature to motivate students to read and to appreciate literature. Second are those for instructional approaches to encourage understanding of various genres, story structures, literature elements, and reading improvement.

Two chapters within this text emphasize the roles of pleasure and understanding. The literature chapter focuses on selection of literature from various genres, identification of students' interests that relate to literature, stimulation of interest and appreciation of literature, and methodologies that help students understand particular genres and literary elements within books. The literature and reading chapter emphasizes additional methodologies that you may use in the

Effective language arts teachers use literature to motivate children to read and foster an appreciation of literature.

reading program. To help you increase the use of primary sources within all areas of language arts, chapters on oral language, listening, writing, and multicultural education include strong literature components.

Linguistically Different Children and Multicultural Education

Many children in our schools do not speak and read the language of the classroom and the teacher, and as a result, these children are frequently unsuccessful in our schools. The chapter on linguistically different children stresses research that classroom teachers can use to improve instruction, techniques effective for diagnosing language arts needs of linguistically different children, and factors influencing performance. It describes programs that have been successful with speakers of black English and with Mexican-American children. It also places special stress on evaluation of literature for and about linguistically different children.

Many different languages and cultures are represented in today's classrooms, and effective teachers adapt teaching techniques to meet the needs of all students.

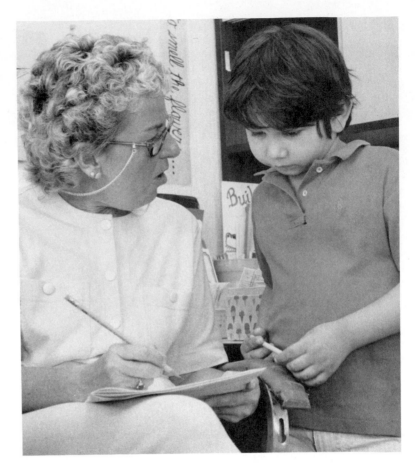

Summaries

A summary at the end of each chapter reviews the most important information presented in the chapter. As with the chapter objectives, you can read all the summaries before you read the text to obtain a quick overview of the information covered. You should also read the summary after completing each chapter to reinforce the important concepts.

REINFORCEMENT ACTIVITY

Preview this language arts text. Read the objectives at the beginning of each chapter and the summaries at the end of each chapter. Locate the sections containing diagnostic procedures; briefly glance over the informal checklists. Read the reinforcement activities; they provide another overall view of the information covered in the text. Look for research pertaining to a language arts subject. Find a lesson plan, unit, or learning center that illustrates developmental instruction. In class, or with a group of teachers, discuss the scope and importance of the subject matter covered in the language arts.

CURRENT ISSUES AND CONCERNS

Many of the issues that surround education in general and language arts instruction in particular can be classified under either control of our profession from the outside or improvement of our profession from within. College students, college professors, and classroom teachers are affected by these influences.

Control of the profession from the outside includes legislative mandates, public opinion responses to studies on education, and censorship attempts by various interest groups. For example, states such as Illinois and Texas have mandated language arts objectives to be taught and assessed. In 1985, Illinois Public Act 84-126 amended the School Code of Illinois to include specific goals and objectives for reading, listening, writing, oral communication, literature, and language functions. Likewise, Texas law includes detailed objectives for language arts teaching and assessment. Many states across the country either have similar mandates or are in the process of developing or considering such mandates.

Responses of school districts to these mandates reflect both negative and positive reactions. Negative responses include minimal individualization and teaching to the assessment instruments. In schools where such practices are common, teachers lose control over curricular development. In contrast, positive responses include using the mandates to identify knowledge areas that should be improved through varied types of instruction. This positive response views mandates as minimal requirements. Within this attitude, educators search for ways to improve instruction based on sound theory and practice. Throughout this text are methodologies that show teachers how to both improve language arts instruction and meet legislative mandates.

Public responses to national studies, evaluative reports, and critical statements affect language arts instruction at all levels of education and cause local school districts and colleges of education to evaluate their programs. Newspapers and television and radio broadcasts across the nation highlight such reports and frequently analyze the efforts of local school districts to overcome cited deficiencies. For example, results from a recent study by the National Endowment for the Humanities, a report requested by the U.S. Congress, were highlighted on September 1, 1987, by the CBS News. The same study was reported as the lead front page headline in *The Dallas Morning News*. The headline read, "Teens Know Little about America's Past, Report Says." The secondary headline stated, "Public schools faulted for failing to teach literary classics, history" (Holloway, 1987, p. 1A). The news story reported that a majority of seventeen year olds do not know when the signing of the Constitution occurred or when the Civil War took place, do not recognize works of authors such as Nathaniel Hawthorne and Herman Melville, and do not know literary classics and history because "Our system of elementary and secondary education stresses skills rather than knowledge" (p. 1A). After reporting these national findings, the news article continued with interviews with local educators and descriptions of programs such as magnet schools and pro-

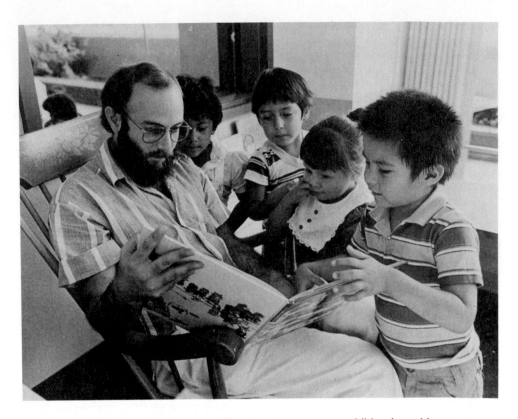

Effective language arts teachers use literature to encourage children's oral language development.

posed new programs designed to increase knowledge of literature and history. Results of national testing of students also generate a variety of responses. For example, Harry Smith, reporting the latest SAT scores on "Sunday Morning News" (1991) suggested that the drop in the scores would lead to two classes of students in the United States: the elite who could read, write, and do math and the others who could not.

Other national reports and articles in professional journals emphasize lack of critical thinking skills among students and provide suggestions for remedying this lack. Reporting on the National Assessment of Educational Progress, Petrosky (1982) stated that students' responses "requiring explanations of criteria, analysis of text, defense of judgments, or points of view were in general disappointing. Few students could provide more than superficial responses to such tasks, and even the better responses showed little evidence of well-developed problem-solving strategies or critical thinking skills" (p. 10). Petrosky provided several recommendations for improving critical thinking skills that relate to language arts instruction. First, students should be required to use their knowledge and conceptual strategies to make interpretations that they can substantiate with evidence from texts and their own values and ideas. Second, critical thinking skills should be stressed across the content areas. Third, teachers should examine classroom practices to make sure that there is opportunity for student involvement in genuine problem-solving discussions and writing tasks that focus on the students' interpretations and their use of evidence to support and criticize their interpretations.

Educators and researchers such as Petrosky recommend reading and writing assignments that allow students to use critical thinking and problem-solving abilities. Unfortunately, studies show that even college students are not required to do many higher level writing assignments. In an analysis of the writing assignments of elementary education majors, Pearce (1990) found only a very small percentage of assignments in which students were required to "synthesize, analyze, or explore course concepts in a coherent and systematic way" (p. 65).

Language arts educators and researchers are not alone in requesting more opportunities for developing critical thinking abilities. For example, O'Reilly (1991) argues for in-depth study of history and other social studies areas that promotes critical thinking. In writing about the lack of science literacy among young people, Steen (1991) decries passive learning through memorization and emphasizes the need to develop critical thinking skills by encouraging students to explore, use, revise, test, modify, and finally accept through a process of active investigation, argument, and participation. Steen also maintains that "students must be encouraged to make connections—whether to social, historical, or personal contexts, to scientific and social phenomena, or to elegant argument and compelling logic" (p. 12). Notice how Steen's recommendations cross the language arts curriculum and require speaking, listening, reading, and writing.

A third type of control from outside forces includes organized group efforts to censor children's literature and school textbooks. Certain groups believe that some books are capable of subverting children's religious, social, or political beliefs and that teachers should not be allowed to use the materials in the classroom. According to a survey by People for the American Way, censorship attempts "increased by 20 percent during the 1986–87 school year and by 168 percent in the last five years" (Wiessler, 1987, p. 1). A report by Dronka (1987) indicates that organized groups are increasing their sponsorships of censorship. According to Dronka, 17 percent of the censorship incidents in 1982–83 were linked to organizations. By 1985–86, 43 percent were associated with organized group efforts. Currently, there is considerable controversy over tradebook and textbook censorship. As schools increase their use of primary sources of literature and literature anthologies containing uncut material, selections are subject to increased scrutiny by various groups. According to Russ (1991), literature-based programs in general have come under attack by special-interest groups. For example, O'Neal (1990) describes challenges to such books as Mary Rayner's *Mr. and Mrs. Pig's Evening Out*, Rumer Godden's *The Battle of the Villa Fiotita*, and Katherine Patterson's *The Bridge to Terabithia* and *The Great Gilly Hopkins*. Hicks (1991) reports challenges to Frank Baum's *The Wizard of Oz* and to other books that describe witches. Gregory (1991) answers a criticism that a book of nursery rhymes, Wallace Tripp's *Granfa Grig Had a Pig and Other Rhymes Without Reason from Mother Goose*, should be censored because the book includes comic illustrations of devils. Meade (1990) describes controversy in a California community as parents debate the content of a literature anthology: "Depending on your point of view, [the anthology] is either a treasure-trove of children's literature or a passport to perdition" (p. 38).

Various organizations have provided guidelines and suggestions for responding to censorship attempts. For example, The International Reading Association's Delegates Assembly passed the following resolution on textbook and reading program censorship:

1. The Association should commend those state, provincial, and local bodies that consistently support teachers' professional judgment even when "self-appointed censors" try to restrict students' freedom to read.
2. The Association should condemn attempts by those with narrow interests who try to deprive students of quality reading programs.
3. The Association should condemn efforts to prevent or disrupt objective discussions on issues related to reading materials and school reading programs. (Russ, 1991, p. 1)

The forces concerned with improving our profession from within include resolutions by professional societies, studies conducted by respected language arts authorities and studies and recommendations by university groups. Issues related to both control and improvement of the curriculum are found in the resolutions adopted by the National Council of Teachers of English (Maxwell and Allen, 1986). For example, NCTE (1986) responded to legislative controls with this resolution:

RESOLVED, that the National Council of Teachers of English affirm that as professional practitioners English language arts teachers are best qualified to decide what constitutes informed practice and curriculum content; that NCTE urge legislative bodies and the agencies that regulate education to directly involve professional language arts organizations in the development of all legislation, regulations, and guidelines governing English language arts practice and curriculum; and that NCTE oppose the imposition by mandate of curriculum and practice that have not been developed with the involvement of professional language arts teachers. (pp. 101–2)

Resolutions of NCTE geared toward instructional improvement emphasize integration of accounts of racial and ethnic minorities and their contributions to American history and literature; recommend discontinuance of isolated grammar and usage exercises not supported by theory and research; and endorse inclusion of meaningful listening, speaking, reading, and writing activities at all levels of language arts instruction.

Studies by Durkin (1986) analyze classroom practices, classroom textbooks, and college-level methodology textbooks. Durkin's studies question the quality and quantity of comprehension instruction provided in both public school classes and college methods courses. After evaluating the quality of comprehension instruction in college-level reading methodology textbooks, Durkin concluded that the specific suggestions for teaching comprehension are brief and meager, that suggestions for assessing comprehension are falsely identified as methods for teaching comprehension rather than testing comprehension, that textbooks underemphasize the need for text-based comprehension instruction, and that instructors of methods courses need to supplement textbooks with specific instructions in how to teach comprehension. (This textbook includes methodologies for teaching comprehension through listening [Chapter 4], through literature [Chapters 10 and 11], and through media [Chapter 12]).

As more school districts emphasize literature-based programs and use literature across the curriculum, the quality of the literature available to teachers and students becomes an even greater issue. Teachers, librarians, and students face problems of selecting literature from the thousands of books that are published each year. Nilsen (1991) argues that "good books are still being published. It's just harder to find the wheat because there's now twice as much chaff" (p. 181). Because of the proliferation of mediocre literature, Nilsen reinforces the need to teach individuals how to carefully evaluate literature and how to use the variety of excellent books available.

This concern for quality of literature is an issue not only for language arts teachers but for other teachers as well. According to Millhouser (1991), adults use science to explore and explain the unknown and good books are children's first step toward this lifelong process. Unfortunately, she concludes that there is currently a trend to flood the market with children's books "no matter what the quality" (p. 47). This question of poor-quality science books is addressed in an analysis of the qualifications of authors who write science trade books for children (Broadway & Howland, 1991). Findings indicated that only 19 percent of the authors of science books for children selected topics on the basis of their own expertise or experience. As stated by Broadway and Howland "the findings suggest an insufficient concern about the qualifications and authority of those who write science and technology books for children and adolescents. Perhaps too many publishers and authors may believe that writing ability and interest qualify authors to write science books for children, regardless of credentials in a particular subject" (p. 38). They recommend that teachers and students be taught how to evaluate and select nonfiction and to be concerned with the accuracy of the author's documentation. They conclude: "We must insist that publishers require authors to demonstrate their authority in the subject areas in which they write. Certainly, education, experience, and interest in a topic are three manifestations of authority. Well-documented research is another barometer of authority that is needed in children's books. As long as we accept and purchase the hundreds of only fair-to-good books that are issued each year, publishers and authors will have less incentive to produce more excellent informational books for young people" (p. 38).

With reference to the social studies curriculum, Lee (1991) argues that teachers in early childhood education use too many outdated materials that teach children outdated concepts. She maintains that concepts such as milkmen delivering milk to the door should be placed in a historical context; they should not be used to suggest contemporary lifestyles. Again, this concern indicates that teachers must carefully evaluate the books that will be used in the various curricula areas.

Other researchers are exploring issues related to improving textbook writing and illustrating. For example, Beck, McKeown, Sinatra, and Loxterman (1991) report that texts that have been revised to include findings from cognitive theory and research are better understood by fourth- and fifth-grade students than the original texts. Graves, Prenn, Earle, Thompson, Johnson, and Slater (1991) point out the need to consider both the development of cognitive abilities and positive attitudes among readers; consequently, they explore the need for texts to be vivid, lively, and interesting as well as to reinforce cognitive theory. In a study by Purnell and Solman (1991), it was found that quality illustrations increase comprehension in geography. Writing style, textbook design, and graphics are currently receiving a lot of attention and are pointing up the need for high-quality classroom materials.

As an answer to declining SAT scores, many authorities recommend the development of national standards and national examinations. Wolk (1991), the editor of *Teacher*, states that "the big education story this summer was the bill

President Bush sent to Congress calling for a national examination system'' (p. 5). As one might expect, there are differences of opinion about national standards and examinations. There are also numerous issues related to their development. Marchese (1991), the editor of *Change,* writing from the perspective of higher education, states: "We're witnessing . . . a sea change in thought about education reform, coming together in a movement that wants systematic change and is unafraid of radical strategies. What's afoot is a national system of education, driven by national goals, anchored to national standards, monitored by national tests—the latter explicitly intended to drive instruction. The plan is nothing if not bold; it will know no boundaries between school and college; it is too important a development to sit out" (p. 4)

Marchese also points to the need to consider several important questions as the process develops. For example, What will the goals demand of students, teachers, and institutions? Who will write the tests? Is there a test that can serve for both public reports and for improvement of learning? Will the new tests be the same old multiple-choice exams, or the more authentic, performance-based exams aimed at higher literacies? After the results are reported, where will we get the ideas, programs, and resources that will enable all students to meet higher standards?

Educators in all academic areas are discussing issues related to standards, testing, and evaluation. The following examples from social studies and language arts reflect some of the concerns related to testing. The position statement of the National Council for the Social Studies (1991) provides guidelines for testing and evaluation in the social studies. The recommendations state that "evaluation in social studies should be based on clearly formulated curriculum objectives that social studies professionals have developed and adopted. . . . Social studies teachers, curriculum developers, supervisors, and methods professors, as well as scholars in history and the social sciences, must influence testing and evaluation programs through the curriculum materials used in classrooms and through consultation on the content and behavioral dimensions of social studies tests and other assessment instruments" (p. 285). The recommended guidelines are as follows:

> Evaluation instruments should:
>   focus on stated curriculum goals and objectives
>   be used to improve curriculum and instruction
>   measure both content and process
>   be chosen for instructional, diagnostic, and prescriptive purposes
>   reflect a high degree of fairness to all people and groups
> Evaluations of student achievement should:
>   be used solely to improve teaching and learning
>   involve a variety of instruments and approaches to measure students' knowledge, skills, and attitudes
>   be congruent with both the objectives and the classroom experiences of the students examined
>   be sequential and cumulative (pp. 285–86)

Writing in *Language Arts,* a professional journal for language arts educators, O'Neal (1991) identifies both limitations and recommendations associated with large-scale testing in the language arts. In the area of limitations she states that (1) tests are imperfect and therefore misleading as single measures of individual performance, (2) some tests are unfair to individuals and groups, (3) students are already subjected to too much standardized testing, (4) some testing practices are undermining important social policies, and (5) tests have become instruments of public policy without sufficient public accountabilities. O'Neal then makes the following three predictions for testing in the language arts by the year 2000. First, although large-scale testing will probably increase, accountability will require that school districts increase student performance on some type of outcome measure. She believes that accountability will replace the regulations that surrounded the reforms of the 1980s. Second, the nature of large-scale testing will change as leaders in language arts curriculum and instruction demand tests that are more compatible with what is known about reading, writing, listening, and speaking. She maintains that "reading tests, such as those developed in the last decade by the National Assessment of Educational Progress and the state-wide efforts in Michigan and Illinois will . . . be the blueprints for virtually all large-scale reading testing in the country" (p. 72). She warns, however, that such testing procedures may become a burden for the teacher. Consequently, "teaching time may be infringed upon and safeguards must be built in to protect teacher–student instructional time" (p. 72). Third, O'Neal predicts that language arts classrooms will engage in constant data collection for all students.

REINFORCEMENT ACTIVITY

As you read Marchese's questions about standards and testing, the guidelines from the National Council for the Social Studies, and O'Neal's concerns for and predictions about evaluation in the language arts, try to answer the questions and consider the issues from the perspective of a language arts educator. What are your recommendations for meaningful evaluation of programs and assessment of students' progress in the various areas of the language arts?

Trends in Language Arts

A review of the literature shows that educators are emphasizing several areas that will influence the language arts in the next decade. Trends include changing attitudes toward assessment, increasing teacher empowerment, developing and expanding literature-based instruction through integration of content areas, and narrowing the gap between research and practice.

The preceding discussion of national standards and tests also emphasized trends in language arts assessment. Of special interest are O'Neal's (1991) predictions that reading and writing testing will more closely measure the goals of language arts instruction and that data collection for all students will be on an ongoing basis. Trends in assessment are also reflected in such sources as the "Assessment" column published each month in *The Reading Teacher.* A few examples of these columns are "The Assessment of Reading: A Time for Change" (Pikulski, 1989), "Alternative Assessment: Separating the Wheat from the Chaff" (Valencia, 1990), and "Assessment of Emergent Literacy: Storybook Reading" (Sulzby, 1991). Educators usually emphasize the need to assess three important areas: the instructional environment, the students, and the total program (Norton, 1992). Newer approaches for assessing the language arts, such as the portfolio approach, are advocated by many educators (Valencia, 1990). Throughout this text we will emphasize these important trends in assessment.

Increasing teacher empowerment is mentioned by many educators as a way to improve instruction and increase accountability. Educators emphasize the role of teachers in developing goals and creating instruction that meets the individual needs of the students. Teacher empowerment may include numerous types of collaborative efforts. For example, Templeton (1990) cites potential for collaborative efforts between media specialists and teachers. She predicts that this collaboration will embrace empowerment as teachers and media specialists take "control from within rather than simply responding to dictates from above" (p. 778). Hoffman (1991) states that there are four critical conditions for teacher empowerment: "choice, knowledge, access, and accountability" (p. 63). In the area of choice, teachers need to be able to make critical decisions about both learners and teaching. Hoffman argues that while choice usually generates the most discussion, the other critical conditions are of extreme importance. In his view, teachers must have increased knowledge if they are to enjoy full empowerment. This means that teachers must begin to see themselves as producers of knowledge about teaching. In addition, they must have access to quality options in choosing materials. Researchers must become actively involved in developing instructional materials and teachers must demand materials that respect their roles as decision-makers. Teacher empowerment also increases as they become involved in the research process. Ahuna-Ka'Ai'Ai', Wong-Kam, and Au (1991) review several publications that explore the role of the teacher as colleague, researcher, and change agent. Finally, teachers must accept responsibility for the decisions they make. They must document responses to instruction, provide rationales for instructional decisions, and draw on research and theory in literacy education. Hoffman states that "teachers must be prepared to demonstrate the ways in which their ongoing instructional decision making takes into account the information gathered through assessment" (p. 65). Throughout this text we will focus on helping teachers make choices, increase knowledge, improve access to effective instructional materials, and provide accountability for their actions.

A trend for creating literature-based programs is becoming increasingly evident in the 1990s (Norton, 1992). Research by Hiebert, Mervar, and Person (1990) shows how children's selection of and discussion about books improves after they have been involved with literature-based programs. Other educators emphasize the importance of integrating literature throughout the content fields. For example, Barnes (1991) advocates using children's literature in the early anthropology curriculum and Diakiw (1990) recommends its use for developing global education. Each year the April/May issue of *Social Education* features "Notable Children's Trade Books in the Field of Social Studies." Articles in the journal frequently discuss integrating literature into the social studies curriculum. In 1991, an institute was developed at Texas A&M University to instruct teachers of geography on the use of literature in their classrooms. The institute was partially funded by the National Geographic Society. This text will continue to emphasize the importance of literature within the language arts; the integration of speaking, listening, writing, and reading through literature; the importance of increasing connections between reading and writing; and the integration of the various content areas.

1. Language arts textbooks should center on children's language. Lessons should help teachers focus on students' real purposes for communication. Textbooks should supplement and enrich students' active use of language through listening, speaking, reading, and writing.
2. Language arts textbooks should emphasize activities that focus on social uses of language. The lessons should help students value their own speaking and writing efforts and help them learn to develop clear and appropriate communication.
3. Language arts textbooks should reflect the integrated nature of listening, speaking, writing, and reading. Lessons should include provocative literature and language activities.
4. Language arts textbooks should recognize broad patterns of developmental language growth. Students should learn to use their knowledge, skills, strategies, and awareness with increasingly complex samples of language and in more sophisticated contexts.
5. Language arts textbooks should help teachers assess students' use of language. Textbooks should guide teachers in developing assessment procedures for the major goals in the language arts curriculum and should provide help in interpreting observations of students' daily use of language for a variety of purposes.
6. Language arts textbooks should stimulate children's and teachers' thinking. Textbooks need to promote inquiry about language: its purposes, its origins, its growth and change.
7. Language arts textbooks should be equity balanced. Textbooks should help students become aware of the cultural aspects of their own language and help them achieve a sensitivity toward and understanding of the cultural aspects of the language of others.
8. Language arts textbooks should reflect the centrality of listening, speaking, writing, and reading for learning in all subject areas. Examples and suggested activities in the textbooks need to be selected from a variety of subject areas.

FIGURE 1–1
Evaluation criteria for elementary language arts textbooks

Judging and Selecting Elementary Language Arts Textbooks

The Committee on Elementary Language Arts Textbooks of the National Council of Teachers of English (1991) has published a list of guidelines for you to use when judging and selecting elementary language arts textbooks (see Figure 1–1). Notice how these guidelines reflect all areas of the language arts, including reading, writing, speaking, and listening. Also, think about how you might incorporate some of the guidelines into your total language arts curriculum, whatever methods and materials you may be using now.

SUMMARY

Effective teaching of language arts includes assessment of all areas of the language arts. The language arts curriculum includes instruction that fosters development of oral language, listening, handwriting, creative writing, written composition, grammar, usage, and spelling. This curriculum also allows children to develop an appreciation for literature and other media.

Language arts classrooms must accommodate children who demonstrate various needs and ability levels. In addition to serving children who acquire the various language arts skills without undue difficulties, the classrooms must serve children who require slower-paced instruction and those who demonstrate various learning disabilities.

Control of the profession from the outside includes legislative mandates, public opinion responses to studies on education, and censorship attempts by various interest groups. The forces concerned with improving our profession from within include professional societies and university groups.

Recent trends in language arts include reexamining the area of assessment, increasing teacher empowerment, expanding literature-based instruction, and narrowing the gap between research and practice.

In judging and selecting elementary language arts textbooks, national guidelines reflecting all areas of the language arts curriculum are now available to assist teachers.

BIBLIOGRAPHY

Ahuna-Ka' Ai' Ai', J.; Wong-Kam, J.; and Au, K. "Reviews and Reflections: The Teacher as Colleague, Researcher, and Change Agent." *Language Arts* 68 (1991): 328–32.

Applebee, Arthur N. "Writing and Reasoning." *Review of Educational Research* 54 (Winter 1984): 577–96.

Barnes, B. "Using Children's Literature in the Early Anthropology Curriculum." *Social Education* (1991): 17–18.

Beck, I.; McKeown, M.; Sinatra, G.; and Loxterman, J. "Revising Social Studies Text from a Text-Processing Perspective: Evidence of Improved Comprehension." *Reading Research Quarterly* 26 (1991): 251–76.

Britton, James; Burgess, Tony; Martin, Nancy; McLeod, Alex; and Rosen, Harold. *The Development of Writing Abilities (11–18).* Schools Council Research Studies, London: Macmillan, 1979.

Broadway, M., and Howland, M. "Science Books for Young People: Who Writes Them?" *School Library Journal* 37 (1991): 35–38.

Committee on Elementary Language Arts Textbooks. "Guidelines for Judging and Selecting Elementary Language Arts Textbooks. *Language Arts* 68 (1991): 253–54.

Diakiw, J. "Children's Literature and Global Education: Understanding the Developing World." *The Reading Teacher* 43 (1990): 296–300.

Dole, J.; Duffy, G.; Roehler, L.; and Pearson, P. "Moving from the Old to the New: Research on Reading Comprehension Instruction." *Review of Educational Research* 61 (1991): 239–64.

Dronka, Pamela. "Forums for Curriculum Critics Settle Some Disputes: Clash Persists on Students' Thinking about Controversy." *Update* (March 1987): 1, 6, 7.

Durkin, Dolores. "Reading Methodology Textbooks: Are They Helping Teachers Teach Comprehension?" *The Reading Teacher* 39 (January 1986): 410–17.

Flood, J.; Lapp, D.; Jensen, J.; and Squire, J. *Handbook of Research on the Teaching of English Language Arts.* New York: Macmillan, 1991.

Flower, Linda, and Hayes, John. "The Dynamics of Composing: Making Plans and Juggling Constraints." In *Cognitive Processes in Writing,* edited by Lee W. Gregg and Erwin R. Steinberg. Hillsdale, N.J.: Lawrence Erlbaum Associates, 1978.

Gordon, Christine J. "Modeling Inference Awareness across the Curriculum." *Journal of Reading* 28 (February 1985): 444–47.

Graves, Donald. *A Case Study Observing the Development of Primary Children's Composing, Spelling, and Motor Behaviors during the Writing Process.* Final Report, NIE Grant No. G-78-0174. Durham, N.H.: University of New Hampshire, 1981.

Graves, M.; Prenn, M.; Earle, J.; Thompson, M.; and Slater, W. "Improving Instructional Text: Some Lessons Learned." *Reading Research Quarterly* 26 (1991): 110–12.

Gregory, Helen. "A Tale of Granfa Grig." *School Library Journal* 37(1991):32.

Hicks, R. "The Devil in the Library." *School Library Journal* 37 (1991): 53.

Hiebert, E.; Mervar, K.; and Person, D. "Research Directions: Children's Selection of Trade Books in Libraries and Classrooms." *Language Arts* 67 (1990): 758–63.

Hillocks, George. *Research on Written Composition: New Directions for Teaching.* Urbana, Ill.: National Conference on Research in English, 1986.

Hoffman, J. "Research Directions: Literacy in the 21st Century: Who Can Prevent It?" *Language Arts* 68 (1991): 60–66.

Holloway, Karel. "Teens Know Little about America's Past, Report Says." *The Dallas Morning News.* August 31, 1987, pp. 1A, 6A.

Lee, M. "The Milkman Doesn't Come to My Door: Teaching about Family Service Providers." *Social Education* 55 (1991): 307–10.

Marchese, T. "National Goals." *Change* 23 (1991): 4.

Maxwell, John C., and Allen, Diane. "NCTE to You." *Language Arts* 63 (January 1986): 99–106.

Meade, J. "A War of Words." *Teacher Magazine* (November–December 1990); 36–45.

Millhouser, F. "Beautiful Science: Books That Cash in on Children's Curiosity." *School Library Journal* 37 (1991): 47–48.

National Council for the Social Studies. "Testing and Evaluation of Social Studies Students." *Social Education* 55 (1991): 284–86.

NCTE Committee on Classroom Practices in Teaching English. *Activities to Promote Critical Thinking.* Urbana, Ill.: National Council of Teachers of English, 1986.

NCTE Committee on Elementary Language Arts Textbooks. *Guidelines for Judging and Selecting Elementary Language Arts Textbooks.* Urbana, Ill.: National Council of Teachers of English, 1991.

Nilsen, A. "Speaking Loudly for Good Books: Promoting the Wheat and Winnowing the Chaff." *School Library Journal* 37 (1991): 180–83.

Norton, D. E. *The Impact of Literature-Based Reading.* New York: Merrill/Macmillan, 1992.

O'Neal, S. "Leadership in the Language Arts: Controversial Books in the Classroom." *Language Arts* 67 (1990): 771–75.

———. "Leadership in the Language Arts: Student Assessment in the Present and Future." *Language Arts* 68 (1991): 67–73.

O'Reilly, K. "The Commission Report and Critical Thinking: A Defense." *Social Education* 55 (1991): 298.

Pearce, D. "An Examination of the Writing Required in an Elementary Education Degree Program." *Action in Teacher Education* 12 (1990): 61–67.

Petrosky, A. "Reading Achievement." In *Secondary School Reading: What Research Reveals for Classroom Practice,* edited by A. Berger and H. A. Robinson. Urbana, Ill.: ERIC Clearinghouse on Reading and Communication Skills and the National Conference on Research in English, 1982.

Pikulski, J. "The Assessment of Reading: A Time for Change." *The Reading Teacher* 43 (1989): 80–81.

Purnell, K., and Solman, R. "The Influence of Technical Illustrations on Students' Comprehension in Geography." *Reading Research Quarterly* 26 (1991): 277–99.

Roehler, Laura, and Duffy, G. "Direct Explanation of Comprehension Processes." In *Comprehension Instruction,* edited by Gerald G. Duffy, Laura R. Roehler, and Jana Mason. New York: Longman, 1984, pp. 265–80.

Russ, W. "Controversy Continues over Reading Textbook Censorship." *Reading Today* 8 (1991): 1, 5.

Smith, H. "Sunday Morning News, CBS, September 1, 1991."

Steen, L. "Reaching for Science Literacy." *Change* 23 (1991): 11–19.

Sulzby, E. "Assessment of Emergent Literacy: Storybook Reading." *The Reading Teacher* 44 (1991): 498–500.

Tchudi, Stephen N. "Reading and Writing as Liberal Arts." *Convergencies: Transactions in Reading and Writing,* edited by Bruce T. Peterson. Urbana, Ill.: National Council of Teachers of English, 1986, pp. 246–59.

Templeton, Shane. "New Trends in an Historical Perspective: Children, Librarians, and Language Arts Educators." *Language Arts* 67 (1990): 776–79.

Valencia, S. "Alternative Assessment: Separating the Wheat from the Chaff." *The Reading Teacher* 44 (1990): 60–61.

———. "A Portfolio Approach to Classroom Reading Assessment: The Whys, Whats, and Hows." *The Reading Teacher* 43 (1990): 338–40.

Wiessler, Judy. "Book Censorship Attempts Are Soaring, Group's Survey Says." *Houston Chronicle* (August 28, 1987): 1–8.

Wolk, R. "A Need for Revolutionary New Schools." *Teacher* (August 1991): 5.

Chapter Two

After completing this chapter on language and cognitive development, you will be able to:

1. Describe the behaviorist theory of language acquisition and analyze instructional outcomes according to this view.
2. Describe a genetic theory of language acquisition and analyze instructional outcomes according to this view.
3. Describe a sociocultural theory of language acquisition and evaluate the impact of sociocultural research on language acquisition.
4. Relate a child-development-oriented philosophy to an instructional program.
5. Compare the role of teacher and the role of student in a program with a behaviorist perspective and in a program with a child-development perspective.
6. Describe the sequence of language development in preschool and early-elementary-age children.
7. Understand that all children go through approximately the same stages of language development but the rate of development varies from child to child; relate this understanding to instructional practice.
8. Describe some implications for language study developed from linguistic investigations.
9. Describe some implications for language study developed from psycholinguistic investigations.
10. Understand the importance of cognitive development and describe some instructional activities that stimulate cognitive development.

Language and Cognitive Development

*I*f someone asks you to name the most important means of communication, what will you answer? Most of you will probably respond, "Language." Language is the key to human communication. We can use written language to convey information or to read the vast accumulation of knowledge available to us.

The spoken and written language that separates us from the animal kingdom is made up of sounds and symbols that are grouped into words. Although words are the fundamental units of language, they must be placed within the structure of a sentence to convey complete meaning. For example, if you see the word *wind*, can you even pronounce the word correctly without knowing the sentence context in which it is to be placed? This isolated word may refer to a breeze, as in the sentence "The wind blew the kite up into the sky." In contrast, the same word may refer to an action, as in "You must wind the clock." The identical spellings have two pronunciations and two meanings. They are different parts of speech, depending on the surrounding sentence. Every language has sounds, or *phonemes*, that combine to form words. The words are put into certain sequences to comprise grammatical forms that are structured within the language (syntax).

THEORIES OF LANGUAGE ACQUISITION

How do children acquire language? This question has fascinated people since the early days of recorded history. According to Herodotus, as early as 600 B.C. Egyptian King Psammetichus I tried to answer this question by having two children actually raised in a speechless environment. Although modern experimenters dispute both the scientific and ethical status of such research, they are still trying to answer the same question.

The last fifty years have produced many changes in language study. Early studies often took the form of diary investigations, in which investigators listened to young children and recorded their language as the children progressed through the various stages of language development. The 1930s and 1940s produced a movement calling for scientific rigor in research. During this time, researchers considered earlier studies by parents suspect, because they assumed that parents would show bias in their recordings. The concern for rigorous scientific experimentation led to language studies with large groups of children. These studies described properties of children's speech, such as the average length of utterance, parts of speech used, and number of different words spoken by a child during a specific period of time. Madorah Smith (1933) was one of the earliest researchers to conclude that the language of children is systematic and rule-governed.

It was in the 1950s that language researchers began to investigate what children know about language. They stressed systematic study of fewer children over longer periods of time. The studies, summarized by Ervin-Tripp (1966), concluded that children learn an underlying linguistic system rather than all of the sounds or words in the language. These studies also implied that children's language is systematic and rule-governed.

In the late 1950s and in the 1960s, researchers sought to describe rule systems that could account for children's use of sentences. Language investigators developed theories about how children acquire language. Researchers such as Lawton (1968) from England and Poole (1976) from Australia investigated the linguistic strategies of working-class and middle-class subjects and added to the increasing body of research in language development.

As researchers began to use computer analysis and electronic recording to systematically investigate language in the 1970s and 1980s, their investigations became more sophisticated. These researchers also considered the social context in which children develop language.

As might be expected from the changes in research, theories about language acquisition have changed over time. According to Menyuk (1991), "one of the more dramatic changes occurred some 30 years ago. This was the advent of transformational or, more accurately, generative grammar. Previously language theories were influenced by behaviorists' theories of learning. Language was described as a set of learned habits and was acquired . . . through stimulus, response, and reward conditions. Generative theories hold that language knowledge is represented in the mind as a system of rules, and that language is acquired by an active learner" (p. 24).

Menyuk maintains that only the influences of this generative theory in its various forms are now considered relevant for understanding language acquisition. She states: "The aspects of current linguistic theory most germaine to the teaching of the language arts are theoretical positions now held about the nature of language knowledge and its acquisition, about the process of language acquisition and application of linguistic knowledge in learning, and about how differing socio-cultural experiences can affect what the child knows when entering school. These aspects are studied by linguists, psycholinguists and sociolinguists" (p. 24).

We will now briefly examine the various theories of language acquisition. Not only will we see how theories have changed over time, we will also see how theories influence instruction in the language arts.

The Behaviorist Theory

The behaviorist theory of education is believed to have emerged with B. F. Skinner's article "The Science of Learning and the Art of Teaching," published in 1954. Although the early behaviorists, represented by Pavlov, worked primarily with conditioning behavior in laboratory settings, modern behaviorists place major emphasis on the application of laboratory implications to human learning and educational settings. Skinner saw a strong parallel between his activities in the laboratory and practices that he felt would improve education. Thus, we now hear of and use such concepts as imitation, reinforcement, successive approximation, and shaping. These concepts are also used to explain language acquisition and development (Staats, 1964, 1968). Behaviorists believe that young children learn language through the process of imitating the language of other speakers in the environment and that language is not instinctive. Behaviorists explain language learning in terms of reinforcement of the imitated language. Consequently, language that is positively reinforced is learned, whereas language that is negatively reinforced is not learned. If the behavior, in this case language, increases in frequency, behaviorists believe the behavior is positively reinforced. Jenkins and Palermo (1964) believe the babbling of an infant becomes infant speech because parents or other adults reinforce speech sounds close to adult speech. The reinforcement may be in the form of paying attention to the child, talking to the child, responding with a smile, providing food, or holding the child.

Behaviorists believe that as children grow older, they modify their behavior because they are rewarded for successive approximations of both adult pronunciation and grammar. Rewards may include wishes granted and even answers to questions. Such modification of behavior by rewards is called *shaping*—one of the most important features of behaviorist technology. Eachus (1971) contends that teaching is a continuous process of shaping behavior.

The DISTAR Language Program is a result of the behaviorist theory of language acquisition. The program uses both imitation and reinforcement to develop language. Engelmann (1974) describes a fast-paced verbal instruction program that uses similar techniques to teach reading and arithmetic. In this program instruction includes patterning in sequence in order to train children to pay attention. All of the instruction demands that the children pay close attention and respond correctly. According to Engelman, during one lesson the children sat directly in front of the teacher. The pace was quite rapid as the teacher asked every child to do exactly what she did. This teacher did some patterned clapping activities, then had the students repeat exactly the same patterns. The group of five-year-olds worked on sentence patterns by answering questions posed by the teacher. For example, the teacher showed a picture of a ball on a table and asked the children, "Where is the ball?" The children replied in unison, "The ball is on the table." This activity continued with a number of different pictures and more sentence responses in unison from the children. The teacher responded with praise for correct answers, using such sentences as "You did it right" and "That was good remembering." She also provided raisins to reward hard work. The half hour of language instruction required close attention and identical responses by every child.

Some child development and early childhood educators have expressed concern about some aspects of such highly structured, intense programs as the one just described. These programs are very different from the enrichment approach used in many nursery school and kindergarten classrooms.

The Genetic Theory

While behaviorists look upon language learning as behavior that can be explained by the conditioning processes of imitation, reinforcement, and shaping, other researchers believe that children possess innate, or instinctive, language ability.

According to this theory, language learning is largely instinctive rather than imitative. All children are thus believed to be born with the ability to use language; they start with a language of their own and amend their language to conform to adult language.

Researchers such as Carol Chomsky (1969) argue that imitation theories of language acquisition do not explain how children create sentences they have never heard. Language acquisition studies reinforce this viewpoint. For example, a study by Menyuk (1963) found that preschool children develop a grammar that differs from the adult model. Ervin-Tripp (1964) provides additional insights into the role of imitation and innate ability. She asked children to repeat sentences such as "Mr. Miller will try." Young children who were speaking at the two-word level responded with "Miller try" rather than the longer adult sentence. Ervin Tripp concluded that children imitate only the language structures that already appear in their speech.

A rule-learning theory began to emerge as researchers investigated children's grammatical structures. Researchers such as Slobin and Welsh (1973) and Cazden (1972) added to the knowledge about syntactic development in children. Slobin and Welsh asked two- and three-year-old children to repeat sentences. They found that children repeat sentences according to their own levels of grammatical development. Likewise, Cazden concluded that the language of children is rule-governed. Consequently, children process language data around them, draw rules that they test, and revise rules based on feedback they receive. In this way, children's speech gradually approaches adult speech.

The Sociocultural Theory

Language acquisition is probably neither totally genetic nor totally behavioristic. The sociocultural theory stresses the interactive reality of language acquisition. While many researchers in the sixties and seventies concluded that language is an innate capability triggered by the presence of language in the environment, other researchers in both America and England (Wells, 1979, 1981) considered the importance of the social environment in which language is acquired and the interaction that takes place between children and adults. Bruner (1978) describes a sociocultural viewpoint of language acquisition: Language is "encountered in a highly orderly interaction with the mother, who takes a crucial role in arranging the linguistic encounters of the child. What has emerged is a theory of mother–infant interaction in language acquisition—called the fine tuning theory—that sees language mastery as involving the mother as much as it does the child" (p. 44).

Support for a social context for language acquisition frequently relies on cases in which children do not interact with adults. For example, Moskowitz (1978) describes a boy with normal hearing who was raised by deaf parents. Although the child listened to television daily, by the age of three he could neither speak nor understand English. He was, however, fluent in his parents' sign language. Moskowitz concludes, "It appears that in order to learn a language a child must also be able to interact with real people in that language" (p. 94).

Snow (1977) and Lindfors (1987) suggest that adults play an important role in the socialization process. Snow studied the interactions between infants and their mothers. She found that mothers adjust their speech to meet the conversational skills of their children. Likewise, Lindfors found that adults adjust their language to

Cooperative learning activities in small groups allow children to test hypotheses and enrich language development.

fit the oral language skills of their children. Consequently, early conversations include shorter sentences characterized by considerable contextual support, repetitions, and exaggerated intonational patterns. The goal of these early conversations is apparently a meaningful exchange of language.

Conversational skills apparently develop quite early in infants. Shugar (1978) found that the interchange of conversation appears before very young children are able to speak in two-word utterances. She maintains that the initial burden for oral interaction rests upon the adults, who identify the children's meanings and build conversations upon those meanings. During these interactions, socialization also occurs.

Language acquisition research has changed since the sixties. Following a review of language research, Fox (1983) states: "The current attention of child language researchers has shifted from rate and stages of acquisition to variations of language use. This change has focused upon interactional language and the social settings in which it takes place, a direction which limits the number of subjects involved. The role of interaction in language learning begins practically at birth. It seems that, almost instinctively, mothers recognize the need to establish meaning with their infants through negotiation" (p. 237).

A study by Shatz and Ebeling (1991) reflects this change in emphasis. These researchers focused on the conversations of six children from age two to two years, six months as they interacted with parents and siblings at home. Revisions in the speech of these children usually involved grammatical changes. Shatz and Ebeling concluded that the spontaneously initiated speech of these children "adds support to the arguments and evidence presented by researchers over the years that children work actively at language learning during the third year of life" (p. 307). In another recent study, Akhtar, Dunham, and Dunham (1991) examined how mothers use language to direct their young children's attention. They found that mothers who followed their children's attention during their conversations, rather than trying to change the focus of this attention, had beneficial effects on their children's subsequent vocabulary development. In still another study, Sorsby and Martlew (1991) analyzed mothers' conversations with their four-year-old children during picturebook reading and during play-doh modeling. They found that the mothers' conversations were on a higher level of abstraction and the accuracy and the children's responses were superior during the reading activity.

Some researchers focus attention on children's language interactions during play. For example, Pellegrini, Galda, Dresden, and Cox (1991) studied the influence of specific types of language used during play on early literacy. They used audio-tapes and behavior notes to collect language samples from which they obtained "symbolic play scores." They found that these scores could be used to predict the emergence of children's writing.

Research findings from investigations of the interactive nature of language are frequently used to support efforts to improve parent–child interactions and to increase play opportunities in early childhood education. Strickland and Morrow (1990) emphasize the importance of developing a "positive verbal interaction between parent and child during story readings." They then describe how such an environment can be created in the home. Likewise, Smith (1990) provides guidelines to help parents effectively interact with their children for the purpose of reading development. Morrow and Rand (1991) describe the need to recognize the importance of play when designing early childhood classroom environments that promote literacy. They, too, emphasize adult interactions with children during these play experiences: "Preschool and kindergarten children are likely to engage in more voluntary literacy behaviors during free-play periods when literacy materials are introduced and teachers guide children to use these materials" (p. 399).

Child-Development Theory

If you are aware of the teachings of Piaget, you are already familiar with the concept that interaction with the physical and social environment is critical to both intellectual and language development in children. Piaget related intellectual development to several stages of child development. Raven and Salzer (1971) developed some of the instructional implications of Piaget's theory. According to Raven and Salzer, during the sensori-motor period, from birth to about two years, children should manipulate objects and materials to enable them to develop images and to stimulate cognitive growth.

The second stage, the preconceptual period, is divided into two developmental phases. During the first phase, from two to four years, it is important to provide many varied concrete experiences. Sensory and motor activities are necessary for developing concepts and complex thinking, both of which are necessary for the development of advanced language art skills. The second phase, or preoperational period, is the intuitive phase from the ages of four through seven years. During this time, activity-oriented curriculums are desirable. Children should have chances to manipulate objects such as books and explore such skills as language and reading. This theory suggests that children in this stage should not be taught in a program that demands the mental gymnastics necessary for reading or spelling programs based on rules of grapheme–phoneme relationships.

During the third stage, the concrete-operational period from ages seven to eleven years, children have the ability to reason, but they can reason adequately only about direct experiences and not about abstractions. Because children are able to reason about what they read only if it relates closely to direct experience, the environment should enrich that direct experience. During the concrete-operational stage, students should have opportunities to combine sentence and word elements and to associate the elements in different ways. They should be encouraged to transform the word elements and observe the differences produced. Questioning techniques developed from the child's own experience should be used.

During the final stage hypothesized by Piaget, the formal-operational period that begins at eleven or twelve years of age, children have the ability to control formal logic. They can begin to deal with propositions and hypotheses that are not related to direct experience. During this period, instructional procedures should be structured so that students may analyze various logical relationships. Oral discussion, listening, and writing experiences allow children opportunities to deal with logic.

Educational strategies formulated from Piaget's beliefs include close observation of children, numerous opportunities for children to manipulate things in the environment and to work individually at tasks of their own choosing, and encouragement of oral language development through such activities as arguing and debating.

LANGUAGE DEVELOPMENT

Linguists have provided increasing knowledge about language development by asking such questions as: What features of phonological (sound), grammatical, and semantic (meaning) development seem to be universal? Why is one linguistic skill acquired before another? What is the nature of the child's linguistic ability during various stages of development? There appears to be more agreement about the sequence of language development than about language acquisition.

Early Development

The first few years of life produce dramatic changes in language ability. An infant begins communicating by crying, then progresses to cooing and babbling. Linguists have used several different terms to label the speech produced by children during the first year of life. *Infant vocalization, preverbal period,* and *prelinguistic vocalization* have been used to describe the early speech of babies. Researchers

During the preverbal period, children learn to exert increasing control over vocal production.

interested in this stage of language development have listened to young children and analyzed what they have heard.

In this early stage, infants show increasing control over vocal production. Fry (1966) describes this babbling stage:

> During the babbling stage, the child is doing two important things: he is trying out mechanisms that will be needed for speech, combining phonation with articulation and no doubt gaining a certain control of the respiratory system, and he is establishing the circuits by which motor activity and auditory impressions are firmly linked together. He is learning the acoustic effect of making certain movements and finding out how to repeat a movement, how to do it again and again to get more or less the same acoustic results. In one sense he is learning a trick, and the experience lasts him, so to speak, for the rest of his life. (p. 190)

During the first few years of life, children move from vocalizing to meaningful language use. When children produce and comprehend meaningful sentences they have never heard before, we say that they have learned the language. Linguists have studied the early speech of children in many different countries and have concluded that children throughout the world have the innate capacity to make the various speech sounds. The linguists believe that some of these universal sounds are encouraged by the specific language heard, and that others disappear from early language because they are not part of the child's environment. Consequently, each child learns a particular grammar, language, and phonological system. Linguists refer to this process as *internalizing*.

Language development is very rapid in most children, who usually speak their first word at about one year of age. As you know, this is an important occasion; your parents can probably remember your first word and when you said it. Early words probably mean more than the single word implies. For example, the child who says "mama" may mean "Mama come here," "Where is mama?" or "Mama pick me up." Linguists use the term *holophrastic* to describe this speech.

At about eighteen months, children usually begin putting two words together. According to Braine (1978), the number of different two-word combinations increases slowly, then shows a sudden upsurge around the age of twenty-three or twenty-four months. Braine recorded the speech of three children from the ages of eighteen months. The cumulative number of different two-word combinations for one child in successive months was 14, 24, 54, 89, 350, 1,400, 2,500+. Obviously, this is a rapid expansion of speech in such a short time.

The time when children put two words together for speech is also considered important by linguists. According to Slobin (1979), at this time a child's active grammar can be investigated. For example, Peterson and Dodsworth (1991) conducted a longitudinal study of the cohesive links used by children from age two to three years, six months. They found that young children do use cohesive devices and these cohesive devices increase with age. They conclude, "On average, the children linked successive utterances with approximately two cohesive ties and there is an increase in such linkage with age. Normal adults link their sentences with between three and four cohesive ties on average, so these children still have room for considerable improvement" (p. 409).

Brown (1973) conducted one of the most extensive longitudinal studies of early language acquisition. In this study, the speech of three children was recorded over a five-year period. Brown found that during approximately the first two years of life speech could be described as telegraphic. During this stage, speech was made up of content words belonging to the large open classes called nouns, verbs, and adjectives. The speech in this telegraphic period did not utilize function words such as prepositions, articles, auxiliary verbs, or pronouns. When children say such phrases as "pretty flower" or "allgone milk," they are using telegraphic speech.

Brown's research also provides valuable insight into the next stage of language acquisition. During this second stage, children acquire the ability to use grammatical morphemes, which are the smallest significant units of syntax. These units may be whole words, as in *came* to show the past tense of *come,* or only parts of words, as in *s* added to a word to form the plural (for example, *balls*) or possessive (for example, *baby's*).

In *A First Language/The Early Stages,* Brown analyzes the results of his longitudinal study and combines them with other early language studies to determine the order in which children acquire fourteen of the grammatical morphemes. This order is apparently consistent for most children. Table 2–1 shows this order of language acquisition and provides an example of each grammatical morpheme.

All children appear to go through the same stages of language development, although the rate of development varies from child to child. Even Brown's study showed great variance among the three children. For example, one child success-

Grammatical Morpheme	Example
1. Present progressive *-ing*	Jimmy eating
2. and 3. *in, on*	toy in box,
	Sally sit on bed
4. Plural *-s*	tables
5. Past irregular	came, went
6. Possessive	Sandy's chair
7. Uncontractible copula (linking verb)	am, is, are, be
8. Articles	the, a
9. Past regular *-ed*	Billy walked home
10. Third person regular *-s*	He plays
11. Third person irregular *-s*	He does
12. Uncontractible auxiliary *is*	This is going fast
13. Contractible copula (linking verb) = *s*	Billy's sleepy
14. Contractible auxiliary	He's flying

TABLE 2–1
The order of grammatical morphemes acquired in early stages of language

SOURCE: Roger Brown, *A First Language/The Early Stages.* (Cambridge, Mass.: Harvard University Press, 1973). Copyright © 1973 by the President and Fellows of Harvard College. Reprinted with permission.

fully used six grammatical morphemes by the age of two years, three months, while a second child did not master them until the age of three years, six months. The third child was four years old before reaching an equivalent stage in language development.

The children in any one nursery school, kindergarten, or elementary class are in various stages of language development. Because language is such a vital aspect of education and is basic to the skills of oral communication, listening, writing, and reading, teachers must understand the process of language development. Such knowledge is essential to diagnose oral language skills or to create an educational environment that will foster development of all the communication skills.

Development in the Elementary Grades

The most extensive study of language development in school-age children is a longitudinal study conducted by Loban (1976). In his study, Loban examined the language development of the same group of over 200 children from the ages of five to eighteen years. This study has numerous implications for language arts teachers, because Loban investigated stages of language development, identified differences between students who ranked high in language proficiency and those who ranked low, and stressed the use of taped oral language samples rather than published language tests.

What were the differences between children who ranked high in language proficiency and those who ranked low? First, students who demonstrated high language proficiency excelled in the control of expressed ideas. Both speech and writing showed unity and planning. They spoke freely, fluently, and easily; used a rich variety of vocabulary; and adjusted the pace of their words to their listeners. The high-proficiency group also used more words in each oral sentence. The difference in language development was so dramatic that the higher group had reached a level of oral proficiency in first grade that the lower group did not attain until the sixth grade. The lower group's oral communication was characterized by rambling and unpurposeful dialogue that showed a meager vocabulary.

In addition, in the area of writing, the high group was more fluent, used more words per sentence, showed a richer vocabulary, and was superior in using connectors such as *meanwhile* and *unless* in writing. This group also used more subordination in combining thoughts into complex forms. The high group again showed greater proficiency at a much younger age than did their peers; the fourth-grade level of proficiency shown by the high group was not shown by the low group until the tenth grade.

Moreover, the students who were superior with oral language also ranked highest on listening. They were both attentive and creative listeners. Children who were superior in oral language in kindergarten and first grade also excelled in both reading and writing in the sixth grade. In a recent review of the implications of language research, Loban (1986) concludes, "The awesome importance of oral language as a base for success with literacy is crystal clear" (p. 612). Consequently, children need oral language instruction to help them organize ideas and illustrate complex generalizations. Oral discussion should be a vital part of the elementary school program.

Young children apparently go through similar stages of language development, although the rate of development shows wide variations. This is seemingly true also for school-age children. Power over language increases through successive control over forms of language, including the ability to handle pronouns, to use appropriate verb tenses, and to use connectors. There is also steady growth in the average number of words per sentence and the average number of dependent clauses per sentence. Consequently, although language development is well advanced by the time children enter school, it is far from complete (Lamb, 1977). Carol Chomsky (1969) emphasizes the expanding acquisition of syntax in children ages five through ten years. Chomsky found that children in this age group are still acquiring syntactic structures. Language learning does not cease, nor is it limited to an expansion of previously acquired structures. Likewise, McGhee-Bidlack (1991) analyzed the ability to define nouns in students ages ten, fourteen, and eighteen years. She found that there are significant differences in the way concrete and abstract nouns are defined: "All three age-groups defined concrete nouns mainly by class and characteristic responses. But it was not until age 18 that abstract nouns were defined by class and characteristic responses. The development of abstract noun definitions follows the development of concrete noun definitions. The ability to define is dependent upon knowledge of the meaning of the word but it is also dependent upon implicit or explicit knowledge of the definitional form. The ability to define abstract nouns is a late developing metalinguistic skill" (p. 417).

Although the rate of language development differs, Table 2–2 may help you visualize the language acquisition stages common to many children at specific age levels. This table was compiled from studies by Brown (1973) and Loban (1976), and a report by Bartel (1986).

TABLE 2–2

A general overview of language development

Age	General Language Characteristics
3 months	Young children start with all possible language sounds and gradually eliminate the sounds that are not used around them.
1 year	Many children are speaking single words (for example, *mama*). Infants use single words to express entire sentences. Complex meanings may underlie single words.
18 months	Many children are using two- or three-word phrases (for example, "see baby"). Children are developing their own language rule systems. Children may have a vocabulary of about 300 words.
2–3 years	Children use such grammatical morphemes as plural suffix /s/, auxiliary verb *is* past irregular. They use simple and compound sentences. They also understand tense and numerical concepts such as "many" and "few." They have a vocabulary of about 900 words.
3–4 years	The verb past tense appears, but children may overgeneralize the *ed* and *s* markers. Negative transformation appears. Children understand numerical concepts such as *one, two,* and *three.* Speech becomes more complex, with more adjectives, adverbs, pronouns, and prepositions. Vocabulary is about 1,500 words.
4–5 years	Language is more abstract and children master most basic rules of language. Children produce grammatically correct sentences. Vocabularies include approximately 2,500 words.
5–6 years	Most children use complex sentences quite frequently. They use correct pronouns and verbs in the present and past tense. The average number of words per oral sentence is 6.8. Children understand approximately 6,000 words.
6–7 years	Children are speaking in complex sentences that use adjectival clauses. Conditional clauses beginning with *if* begin to appear. Language becomes more symbolic. Children begin to read and write and understand concepts of time and seasons. The average sentence length is 7.5 words.
7–8 years	Children use relative pronouns as objects in subordinate adjectival clauses. ("I have a cat, which I feed every day.") Subordinate clauses beginning with *when, if,* and *because* appear frequently. The average number of words per oral sentence is 7.6.
8–10 years	Children begin to relate concepts to general ideas through use of such connectors as *meanwhile* and *unless.* Fifty percent of the children correctly use the subordinating connector *although.* Present participle active and perfect participle appear. The average number of words in an oral sentence is 9.0.
10–12 years	Children use complex sentences with subordinate clauses of concession introduced by *nevertheless* and *in spite of.* The auxiliary verbs *might, could,* and *should* appear frequently. Children have difficulties distinguishing among past, past perfect, and present perfect tenses. The average number of words in an oral sentence is 9.5.

Listen to the oral language of several preschool children or elementary-age children. How does their oral language development compare to that found by Brown or Loban? Write some specific examples of speech found at a certain age level and share your findings with your classmates.

Linguistics

Linguists observe and record people to discover how language functions and how it is evolving. They use their data to draw conclusions and formulate generalizations about the nature of language. For communication to take place, both speakers and listeners must use the same code system. Linguists refer to several code signals, including phonology, morphology, syntax, and semantics.

Phonology is the sound system within a language. Each language has a set of sounds that provide meaningful differences within that language. The smallest distinctive unit of sound within the language is a *phoneme.* A phoneme is the minimal linguistic unit, and replacement of a phoneme can result in a meaning difference. For example, in the words *c/a/t* and *m/a/t,* the /c/ and the /m/ sounds are distinct phonemes. There are forty-four sounds in the English language that communicate such meaning. The written representations of the sounds are called *graphemes.* Because there are only twenty-six graphemes in English, some children have trouble relating the correct phoneme to the grapheme, especially in reading and spelling.

In an effort to limit the sound/symbol inconsistencies, some instructional systems present only consistent spellings in beginning materials. These materials present sentences such as "The cat sat on a bat." Another attempt to overcome inconsistencies is the *i/t/a* alphabet developed by Sir James Pitman. This alphabet has forty-four graphemes, one for each phoneme. Children learn to read and spell in this alphabet and then go through a transitional period in which they learn standard English spelling (Fink and Keiserman, 1969). Figure 2–1 illustrates the *i/t/a* alphabet.

The second code signal studied by linguists is *morphology,* or word structure. The smallest meaning-bearing units are called *morphemes.* Thus, *girl* is a morpheme, and it is also the smallest meaningful unit; if any of the graphemes are removed, the combination of letters does not mean *girl.* Because *girl* can also stand alone in meaning, it is called a *free morpheme.* If we add an *s* to *girl* to form *girls,* we have two small units of meaning. We still have the meaning *girl,* but the *s* has added the meaning of plurality. Because *s* cannot stand alone and still mean plurality, it is called a *bound morpheme.* Prefixes and suffixes have meanings, and also change the meaning of root words when they are added to the root.

Study of word changes attributable to bound morphemes helps children understand meaning and develop vocabulary. For example, consider the following list of free and bound morphemes. What happens to the meaning of the words when the prefix *un* is added?

Bound Morpheme	Free Morpheme
un	happy
un	done
un	desirable
un	domesticated

A third code signal is *syntax,* or how words are put together in meaningful order to form sentences. The study of syntax in school may be referred to as grammar. Grammar is either structural grammar, which looks at the grammatical structure of a sentence, or, more recently, transformational grammar, which looks at how meaning is communicated in sentences. According to many linguists, instruction should emphasize the systematic building of sentences according to certain patterns rather than the diagramming of sentences. Sentence building should also stress the functions of words in sentences rather than rigid categorizations. Consequently, the term *usage* is often preferred to *grammar.*

The final code signal usually studied by linguists is *semantics,* or the study of meaning, and is probably the most important code signal.

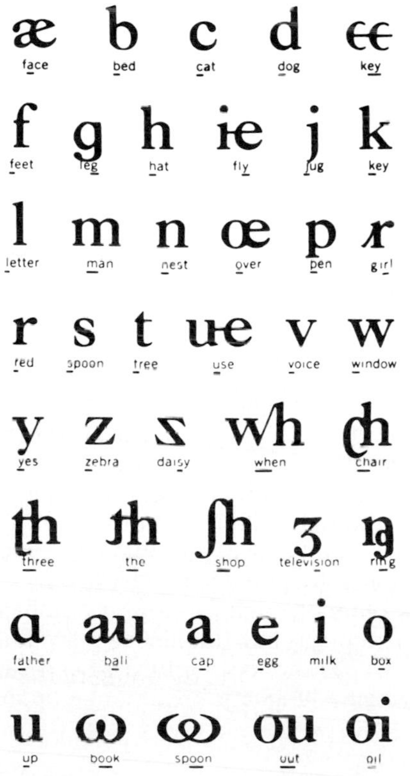

FIGURE 2–1

The *i/t/a* alphabet (Reprinted with the permission of Pitman Learning, 6 Davis Drive, Belmont, CA 94002)

Through the study of code signals, linguists present several conclusions about linguistic development in children. Lamb (1977) summarizes some of these conclusions:

1. Language development, although well advanced by the time children enter school, is far from complete.
2. Growth occurs in all of the areas identified—phonology, morphology, syntax, and semantics.
3. There are probably close corollaries between cognitive growth and linguistic development. (The stages identified by Piaget seem to be significant in language development.)
4. Teachers should adjust their expectations in terms of reading comprehension, skill in composition, and acquisition of phoneme–grapheme correspondence generalizations to account for the growth still occurring.

Psycholinguistics

Whereas linguists study the various code signals of language, including phonology, morphology, syntax, and semantics, psycholinguists stress the interdisciplinary study of psychology and linguistics. Psycholinguists, therefore, maintain that the various code signals of language cannot be studied independently of one another, nor can instruction be provided in one without looking at the total language system. Rayner and Pollatsek (1989) describe a psycholinguistic approach having three types of cues: graphophonic, syntactic, and semantic: "The graphonic cues represent rather general knowledge of spelling–sound relations; the syntactic cues are the reader's knowledge of syntactic patterns and the markers that cue these patterns (such as function words and inflectional suffixes); and the semantic system is everything else (such as the reader's knowledge of word meanings and knowledge of the topic)" (p. 351).

For an example of this interrelatedness, look at the letter *e*. In isolation, the letter may have several different sounds. Not until it appears in the context of a word may you know the correct pronunciation. Even in a sequence of letters, such as *read,* you may need to see the *e* in a sentence context. In "He read the book yesterday," the pronunciation and meaning are quite different from "Will you read the story tomorrow?" In this case, total meaning is not available until you utilize all of the code signals of language.

Roach Van Allen (1976) developed an excellent diagram of the interrelationship of these language signals and their relationship to reading, oral skills, environmental influences, and communication skills (Figure 2–2). In Figure 2–2, the language signals are interrelated. Strand 1 refers to experiencing communication, and it includes self-expression through talking, painting, singing, dancing, acting, and writing. Strand 2 refers to studying communication, including how language works, sound-symbol relationships, and vocabulary acquisition. Strand 3 refers to relating communication of others to oneself, and it emphasizes the influences of language and the ideas of others as individuals read, see and hear films, listen to records and music, or enjoy art prints and sculpture. Roach Van Allen uses this diagram as a rationale for employing language-experience approaches with children.

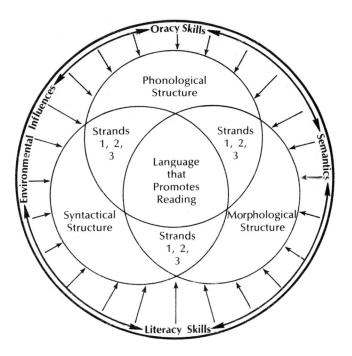

FIGURE 2–2
Psycholinguistic base for language instruction (Roach Van Allen, *Language Experiences in Communication.* Copyright © 1976 by Houghton Mifflin Co. Used with permission.)

Kenneth Goodman has conducted much psycholinguistic research. His theory of instruction is based on psycholinguistic principles, which he relates to reading. According to Goodman (1972):

1. Meaning must always be the immediate, as well as the ultimate, goal of reading.
2. Language systems are interdependent, so language cannot be divided into words for instructional purposes.
3. Children learning to read their native language must be competent language users.
4. Children find it easier to read language that is meaningful and natural to them.
5. Children must learn strategies for predicting, sampling, and selecting information; guessing, confirming, or rejecting guesses; correcting; and reprocessing.
6. Children need special reading strategies for reading special forms of language.
7. Readers must be able to relate their reading experiences to real experiences.

Psycholinguistic theory stresses that students need uninterrupted reading time in order to discover strategies for gaining meaning and they need opportunities to use the meaning and grammatical systems of language to predict an appropriate word. If you teach reading from a psycholinguistic perspective, you do not teach sounds or words in isolation. Instead, you teach in sentence contexts, so that children always have the support of the grammatical and meaning cueing systems in language.

COGNITIVE DEVELOPMENT

How important is an understanding of cognitive development? According to Morrow (1989), "Researchers investigating early childhood literacy development are bringing about changes in theory and practice. Generally, they base learning and instructional strategies on what is known about cognitive development" (p. 11). In an article describing research on reading comprehension, Dole, Duffy, Roehler, and Pearson (1991) emphasize important understandings about comprehension and instruction that have been gained from cognitive research: "In a cognitively based view of comprehension instruction, the teacher becomes a mediator who helps students construct understandings about: (a) the content of the text itself; (b) strategies that aid in interpreting the text; and (c) the nature of the reading process itself. Elements of this perspective are seen in virtually all comprehension instruction research. Taken as a whole, such instruction can be described as consisting of four kinds of instructional actions: planning, selecting academic work, providing information, and restructuring student understandings" (p. 252).

Cognitive psychologists study not only how information is presented to students but also how learners process the information. Within cognitive psychology, learning is considered a process in which learners actively participate in the teacher–learner act. Educational approaches include teaching students how to think, how to learn, how to remember, and how to motivate themselves. Weinstein and Mayer (1986) identify the following learning strategies under cognitive processes: (1) rehearsal strategies, such as repeating names in an ordered list and underlining pertinent information; (2) elaborative strategies, such as forming mental images, paraphrasing, and creating analogies; (3) organizational strategies, such as grouping, categorizing, and creating diagrams; (4) comprehension monitoring strategies, such as self-questioning and using guide questions to structure reading behavior; and (5) affective strategies, such as reducing external distractions by studying in a quiet place. Terminology frequently associated with cognitive processing includes *schema* (an individual's conceptual system or structure for understanding something), *metacognition* (an individual's knowledge of the functions of his or her own mind and conscious efforts to monitor or control those functions), and *semantic maps* or *webs* (diagrams that help individuals visualize the relationships of words or concepts to one another). The "Essentials of English" adopted by the National Council of Teachers of English (1983), emphasizes stimulating cognitive development. Child development authorities Mussen, Conger, and Kagan (1984) emphasize developing cognitive processes necessary for perception. They identify the following essential processes:

1. Perception—the deletion, organization, and interpretation of information.
2. Memory—the storage and retrieval of perceived information.
3. Reasoning—the use of knowledge to make inferences and draw conclusions.
4. Reflection—the evaluation of the quality of ideas and solutions.
5. Insight—the recognition of new relationships between two or more segments of knowledge.

What instructional strategies are recommended for developing cognitive processes? Interestingly, silence can be an important strategy. Allowing time to think about a discussion, to formulate questions, and to answer questions increases the cognitive level of both responses and questions. Tobin (1987) reviewed research that extended the average one-second wait time in discussions to between three and five seconds. He reported that such extensions cause teachers to repeat fewer questions, to ask higher level questions, and to ask more probing questions. Positive changes in student behavior included more responses, longer responses, increases in the cognitive levels of responses, greater initiation of discussions, more student-to-student interaction, decreases in confusion, and higher achievement. Tobin concludes "silence provides teachers with time to think and to formulate and use higher quality discourse that then influences the thinking and responding of students" (p. 87).

Dole et al. (1991) identify effective instructional actions related to cognitive development. First, teachers modify the instructional plan to accommodate students and to allow teachers to respond to students' emerging understandings. Second, teachers select academic work that provides appropriate experiences; that allows students to conclude that comprehension requires making predictions, asking questions, summarizing, and clarifying parts of the text; that focuses students' attention on the reasoning processes expert readers use when they read; and that allows students to apply the cognitive strategies that teachers model. Third, teachers provide students with information about the usefulness of what is being taught. Through modeling, they provide explicit, unambiguous information that allows students to understand the teachers' reasoning processes when approaching a task, solving a problem, and answering questions. Fourth, as the lessons progress, teachers obtain feedback from students so as to assess their understanding. On the basis of this informal assessment, "effective teachers spontaneously create instructional scaffolding—cuing, prompting, analogies, metaphors, questioning, elaborations, and remodeling—to provide students with the necessary information that will help them restructure their understandings" (p. 255). Gradually, teachers move from instruction in which they provide the scaffolding, to instruction in which students assume increasing responsibility. This instruction takes time, however. Brown, Dole, and Trathen (1990) report that it took four weeks of instruction using a variety of instructional activities before fifth-grade students could transfer a prior knowledge prereading strategy to independently read selections.

The literature provides numerous suggestions for ways to develop students' cognitive abilities. Myers (1983) suggests activities that encourage students to organize information into meaningful wholes. Myers also recommends semantic mapping strategies to help students visualize concepts and relationships. A similar approach for concept and vocabulary development is recommended by Johnson and Pearson (1984). Squire (1982) focuses instruction on language tasks that encourage analyzing, reporting, persuading, interpreting, reflecting, imagining, and inventing. Schmitt (1990) develops a questionnaire that measures students' awareness of the strategies they use. Flynn (1989) helps students analyze, synthesize, and evaluate ideas through cooperative problem solving. Stahl and Kapinus (1991) teach students to predict word meanings in content areas. Wade (1990) uses think-alouds to assess comprehension. Norton (1991) recommends literature-related oral activities to develop observing, comparing, classifying, hypothesizing, organizing, summarizing, applying, and criticizing.

The development of these important cognitive operations will be stressed throughout this text. Oral language activities as well as other language arts activities are especially beneficial for developing cognitive skills. Teachers may also base activities that encourage the development of these operations on the various content areas. Literature, history, geography, art, math, and science provide excellent sources. Oral language activities frequently precede or accompany written composition, listening, reading, and literature activities.

Basic Operations Associated with Thinking

As teachers use more literature-based instruction within their classrooms, they may easily use books to help focus students' attention on the basic operations associated with thinking. We will now recommend some language arts activities that focus attention on observing, comparing, classifying, hypothesizing, organizing, summarizing, and applying. Specific books to enhance these activities are mentioned.

Observing   Language arts teachers have many opportunities to develop observational skills. Teachers of young children may focus children's observations on concrete objects in the school, home, or neighborhood. Young children can describe the color, size, shape, and use of objects in their environment.

Colorful illustrations in picture books enhance observational skills as children identify objects and describe the content. Number and alphabet books are particularly good sources. For example, students can search for and describe the objects that illustrate each number in Jim Aylesworth's *One Crow: A Counting Rhyme* (1988). Olivier Dunrea's *Deep Down Underground* (1989) allows children to search for and describe various animals. Suse MacDonald's *Alphabatics* (1986) entices viewers to follow the illustrations and to describe the changes in each letter of the alphabet as the letter is transformed into an object that represents the letter. For example, *A* proceeds from a brown letter on a white background, to an angled *A* floating on blue water, to an upside down *A* on blue waves, to an ark shape on waves, to an ark filled with animals.

Books that encourage manipulation and searches for objects are also good sources for observation. Mitsumasa Anno's *Anno's Faces* (1989) encourages manipulation of various facial features placed on fruits and vegetables. Children can describe the fruits and vegetables and then describe the changes caused by frowning or smiling. In Millicent Selsam and Joyce Hunt's *Keep Looking!* (1989), the wildlife around a rural house in winter is identified. Children can locate the animals and describe them. They can also follow the instructions of the authors: "Now look down on the ground. Do you see juncos, or snowbirds, pecking at the seeds that the blue jay dropped? (p. 3, unnumbered). After children have observed and described what is in the illustrated environment, they can look closely at their own environment and describe what they observe. To relate the observations to writing and art, they can create their own book.

Older students can search for literary, art, or historical objects in Mitsumasa Anno's *Anno's U.S.A.* (1983) or in *Anno's Britain* (1982). They may observe and describe the various stories and geographical locations that inspire the boy's dream in David Wiesner's wordless book, *Free Fall* (1988). Teachers can enhance the science curriculum by having students observe and describe the illustrations in

Anne Ophelia Dowden's *The Clover & the Bee: A Book of Pollination* (1990). Different types of giraffes may be observed while reading Helen Roney Sattler's *Giraffes, the Sentinels of the Savannas* (1989). Both observation and knowledge of geography are enhanced as students use clues from illustrations to identify various locations in Edith Baer's *This Is the Way We Go to School: A Book About Children Around the World* (1990). Students may check the accuracy of their observations on a world map located at the back of the book.

Word association activities enhance observational skills, vocabulary development, and writing capabilities. These activities are appropriate for any age level, but you should change them to meet the developing language capabilities of children. Younger children may consider words that create strong emotions. You may ask, "What causes you to feel angry? How do you show your anger? How do other people or even animals display anger?" Similar discussions and observations may invoke students into thinking about feelings of love, happiness, and fear.

A verbal observation activity for older children may follow the format developed by Catherine Daughtery, a headmistress of a primary school in Scotland. In an effort to help children visualize and describe emotional experiences, she tells them a short story. For example, to enhance observations about misery, she tells children a story about a puppy lost in the snow after it is taken from its mother. She asks the children to describe orally their visual pictures. Next, they list words, mainly verbs and adjectives, that convey the emotional message of the story. Finally, each child provides one sentence, with carefully selected words, that describes a visual picture. This activity can expand as children first observe and then describe people in the environment, on film, or in pictures.

Daughtery maintains that oral language development is very important if children are to develop observational skills and imagination and use them in oral and written compositions. She states: "Broadly speaking, we must begin by training the children's observation of things which are to them commonplace and very often not worthy of notice. We must then explore the way in which they tell or write the results of their observations. Initially, these will be 'flat' matter-of-fact observations with no attendant aids from emotive language or imagery. The use of emotive language and imagery is not essentially instinctive unless to a particular gifted child, so a great deal of groundwork, including vocabulary building, must be done. The bulk of this work should be, in the initial stages, oral. Free expression and expansion of thought are inhibited by the superfluous process of recording at this level" (personal communication, June 20, 1983).

Comparing When children describe attributes of concrete objects, literary selections, or pictures, encourage them to make comparisons with those of other objects, literary selections, or pictures. For example, have children observe, describe, and compare real hats. Then, have them consider the attributes of hats illustrated in Stan and Janice Berenstain's *Old Hat, New Hat* (1970).

Readers can compare how a location might appear at different time periods in Jeannie Baker's *Where the Forest Meets the Sea* (1987). The story is set in the tropical rain forest between the Daintree River and Bloomfield in North Queensland, Australia, near the Great Barrier Reef. The collage illustrations show a contemporary boy and his father visiting the location and imagining what it might have looked like 100 million years ago. Careful observation reveals extinct and rare animals living in the forest and aboriginal children playing there. In the final illustration, the boy is visualizing what the same location might look like if the trappings of modern culture were to impinge.

Changes over time periods may be compared using John Goodall's *The Story of a Main Street* (1987), Renata Von Tscharner and Ronald Fleming's *New Providence: A Changing City Scape* (1987), and Gian Paolo Ceserani and Piero Ventura's *Grand Constructions* (1983). Goodall's illustrations portray the same English town from medieval through contemporary times. Students can compare buildings, transportation, clothing, and hairstyles. Von Tscharner and Fleming's text and illustrations follow a small town from 1910 through 1987. Geography teachers find this book exciting because students can search for changes in land use, transportation, and culture. The grand constructions in Ceserani and Ventura's text and illustrations range from Stonehenge to Versailles to contemporary architecture.

Some books emphasize changes that result from natural disasters. For example, students can use Carole Vogel and Kathryn Goldner's *The Great Yellowstone Fire* (1990) to compare the Yellowstone Park before and after the fire. Or, they can use Patricia Lauber's *Volcano: The Eruption and Healing of Mount St. Helens* (1986) to compare the area before, during, and after the volcanic eruption.

Older students may compare plots and characterizations in stories that have similar conflicts. For example, in Marion Bauer's *On My Honor* (1986), person-versus-self conflict results when a boy disobeys his father and swims in a river, resulting in the drowning of his best friend. In Paula Fox's *One-Eyed Cat* (1984), personal conflict results when a boy disobeys his father and shoots an air rifle, wounding a cat. Students can compare the plot development in the two stories, the ways in which conflict is portrayed, and how each character overcomes conflict. They can also compare their personal responses to the conflicts of the characters.

Different artists' renditions of the same story or of similar stories provide numerous opportunities for comparisons and critical evaluations. Multicultural components come into play with different versions of "Little Red Riding Hood." Four excellent choices would be the Brothers Grimm *Little Red Riding Hood* (1983), James Marshall's *Red Riding Hood* (1987), Charles Perrault's *Little Red Riding Hood* (1983) and Ed Young's *Lon Po Po: A Red-Riding Hood Story from China* (1989).

Interesting comparisons also may be made between original novels and movie or television adaptations. Students can consider the changes that were made, the reasons for the changes, and their personal responses to the two versions.

Classifying Children may describe and classify concrete objects in the environment according to shape, color, size, and use. Concept books that emphasize alphabetical order, colors, numbers, sizes, and shapes enhance classifying activities. For example, Anita Lobel's *On Market Street* (1981), an alphabetical trip through a market street of an earlier time, encourages children to add to various objects categorized in groups, such as apples, books, clocks, instruments, and toys. Elizabeth Cleaver's *ABC* (1985) provides a good beginning for classifying numerous objects alphabetically. Older students could use Eve Merriam's *Halloween ABC* (1987) as a model by which to categorize poems for an anthology. Tana Hoban uses colors to classify objects in *Of Colors and Things* (1989). Her numerous concept books on colors and shapes provide excellent sources for the classification activities of young children.

Picture books stimulate numerous discussions and applications related to classifying. Students can add their own sounds to those described in Rebecca

Classifying activities stimulate cognitive development in children.

Emberley's *City Sounds* (1989). Classifying words that rhyme could be stimulated by Bruce McMillan's *One Sun: A Book of Terse Verse* (1990). Ann Jonas's *Aardvarks, Disembark!* (1990) may stimulate a classification scheme for endangered and extinct animals.

Hypothesizing   Literature selections can encourage children to hypothesize about the language an author might use, about the plot from clues in the title, and about how the plot will develop. Rhyming patterns in books for younger children provide powerful language cues. Read such books as Jack Prelutsky's *Beneath a Blue Umbrella* (1990) and ask children to complete a missing word in these humorous rhyming poems. Debra and Sal Barracca's *The Adventures of Taxi Dog* (1990) encourages children to fill in rhyming words in a story about Maxie as he accompanies the driver around New York City. Let older children listen for and complete the rhyming elements in "The King of Cats" in Nancy Willard's *A Visit to William Blake's Inn* (1981). In addition, the poems in Jack Prelutsky's *The Random House Book of Poetry for Children* (1983) provide a rich source for rhyming activities.

Stories that use repetition of language or plot stimulate children to hypothesize about what will happen next. While listening to Mem Fox's *Hattie and the Fox* (1987), children can hypothesize about the language to be used and changes in the story. In a similar approach, students can provide the next lines in Michael Rosen's *We're Going on a Bear Hunt* (1989). This cumulative tale adds a new incident with each telling until the story is complete. Verna Aardema's *Why Mosquitoes Buzz in People's Ears* (1975), Janet Stevens's *The House That Jack Built* (1985), the "Gingerbread Boy," "Henny Penny," and "The Fat Cat" are other good examples of cumulative tales that encourage children to hypothesize and join in with appropriate words.

Illustrated texts such as Peter Newell's *Topsys and Turvys* (1893, 1988) and *Topsys and Turvys—Number Two* (1894, 1988) provide numerous opportunities for hypothesizing as students consider what might appear if the illustrations were turned upside down. Students may also choose to develop some of their own topsy turvys.

Descriptive and imaginative book titles, such as Judith Viorst's *Alexander and the Terrible, Horrible, No Good, Very Bad Day* (1972), James Stevenson's *The Wish Card Ran Out* (1981), Kit Pearson's *A Handful of Time* (1989), and Geraldine McCaughrean's *A Pack of Lies* (1988), encourage hypothesizing about story content. Chapter titles also can be used for this purpose.

Organizing   Picture books that develop stories using seasonal changes, such as Donald Hall's *Ox-Cart Man* (1979), can help children understand the time sequence in which events take place. Susi Gregg Fowler's *When Summer Ends* (1989) portrays a young child as she thinks about all the good experiences she has had through the various seasons of the year. Leo Buscaglia's *The Fall of Freddie the Leaf: A Story of Life for All Ages* (1982) follows the life cycle of a leaf from spring to summer to fall, and finally to a new beginning as the leaf becomes part of the nourishment for the tree during the following year. This book also has implications for all life and death.

Informational books for older students often follow a chronological order. Judith St. George's *The White House: Cornerstone of a Nation* (1990) discusses the changes and events that have occurred over the last two centuries. It begins in 1791 and progresses into the late 1900s. In Kathryn Lasky's *Sugaring Time* (1983), photographs and text describe the procedures used to collect sap from maple trees and process it into syrup.

Stories with strong sequential plots help children analyze plot structures. Flannel board presentations may be used to identify logical organization in these stories:

1. "The Three Little Pigs"—progressing from flimsiest to strongest building materials.
2. "The Little Red Hen"—following chronological order in the steps for preparing bread.
3. "The Three Billy Goats Gruff"—proceeding according to size from smallest to largest.

Summarizing Children should be given many opportunities to summarize the stories they hear or read, the content covered in course work, and the points made by visiting speakers. Summaries of a given story may vary. Some children may summarize the most exciting part; others, the funniest part; still others, the actions of the main character.

Applying Books that encourage children to observe, gather data, experiment, compare, and formulate hypotheses are excellent for cognitive development. For example, Sandra Markle's *Exploring Winter* (1984) includes numerous experiments that readers may perform. Questions about their observations are also included. Jim Arnosky's *Drawing from Nature* (1982), *Drawing Life in Motion* (1984), and *Sketching Outdoors in Summer* (1988) provide detailed drawings that show how to observe nature. Discussions between children and teachers about the children's readings or activities also stimulate crucial cognitive capabilities.

Semantic Mapping and Vocabulary Development

Semantic mapping and webbing, a method for graphically and visually displaying relationships between various ideas and concepts, emphasizes cognitive processes and encourages problem solving. Semantic mapping encourages higher thought processes, stimulates ideas, and promotes discussion between students and teachers. Semantic mapping procedures promote vocabulary development (Johnson & Pearson, 1984; Toms-Bronowski, 1983); enhance literary discussions that highlight plot, setting, characterization, and theme (Norton, 1991); improve reading comprehension (McNamara & Norton, 1987; Prater & Terry, 1985); enhance development of instructional units (Norton, 1982); stimulate the composition process (Myers & Gray, 1983); encourage interaction and understanding in various content areas (Heimlich & Pittelman, 1986); provide ways of assessing understanding of literature (Norton, 1991); stimulate the identification of background knowledge (Norton, 1991); and encourage the integration of reading, literature, writing, listening, and oral discussion within the language arts curriculum (McNamara & Norton, 1987).

Each of the objectives for the semantic mapping strategy uses slightly different procedures. An in-depth approach to each procedure is provided as it is developed within the appropriate chapters of this text. General procedures, however, usually begin with brainstorming activities in which teachers encourage students to verbalize associations or ideas while the teachers map the ideas on the chalkboard. The content of an initial map varies according to teaching and learning objectives and the subject matter being visualized. Semantic mapping may be an introductory activity to organize and extend previous knowledge or to explore various possibilities, a discussion activity to visualize relationships and promote understanding of content, or a follow-up activity to reinforce learning or even to test understandings. Semantic mapping strategies may help children identify words with similar meanings, expand vocabulary, understand multiple meanings for words, develop concepts, and perceive relationships between words and between ideas. The activities we will describe in this section can be stimulated through brainstorming and group or class discussion.

Similar meanings and semantic precision   Numerous words, such as *said* and *went,* are overused in speaking and writing. Helping children use words precisely will improve both their speaking and writing and stimulate their cognitive development. A fourth-grade teacher developed the following procedures using the word *went.* First, the teacher wrote and then read several sentences on the chalkboard. For example:

> Jackie *went* to the park to find a lost football.
> Mike *went* to the store to spend his birthday money.
> Sharon *went* to school to take a spelling test.
> Terry *went* to the park to play in the championship soccer game.

Next, the class identified the word *went* and discussed how well the word expressed the feelings and actions of the subjects. To illustrate different meanings, the teacher asked the students to dramatize each sentence. The students also dictated additional sentences in which *went* could be used but might not be appropriate. The teacher then led a brainstorming activity, encouraging the children to identify numerous words that could be used in place of *went.* The following is a partial list:

ran	jogged	hurried	strutted
marched	danced	pranced	promenaded
raced	flounced	dawdled	sauntered
ambled	swaggered	rambled	crawled
glided	drifted	skipped	bounced
wandered	staggered	bounded	meandered
strolled	dashed	trotted	hopped
hastened	shuffled	scampered	capered
lurched	stumbled	wobbled	tottered
swayed	moseyed	struggled	limped

In an effort to categorize meanings for *went,* the teacher and class identified happy meanings, tired meanings, slow meanings, fast meanings, proud meanings, frightened meanings, and sad meanings. Then, they used the meanings as subheadings in a web around the word *went* (see Figure 2–3).

Finally, the class considered the words on the list and placed them around the appropriate meaning or meanings. The children identified additional words as they considered each classification. They also discussed the relationships between words that had several meanings. Figure 2–4 represents a partial web developed by the class.

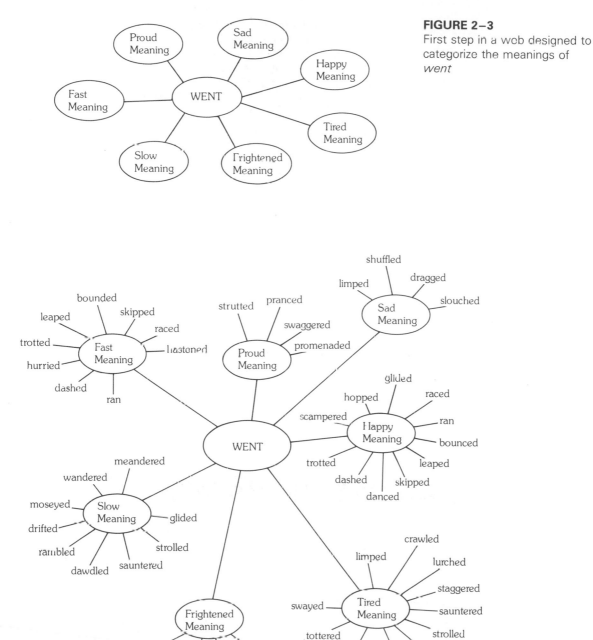

FIGURE 2–3
First step in a web designed to categorize the meanings of *went*

FIGURE 2–4
A web showing various meanings for the word *went*

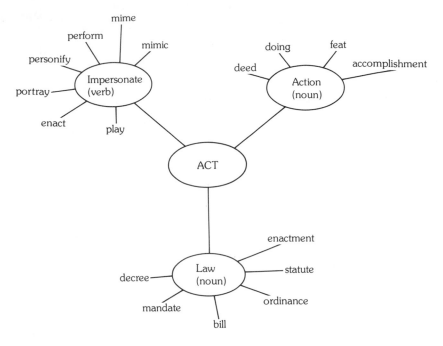

FIGURE 2–5
A map illustrating three meanings for the word *act*

Multiple meanings and different parts of speech   Even simple words may become difficult for children to understand if they are used in unfamiliar contexts or as previously unused parts of speech. Three meanings for the word *act* are illustrated in Figure 2–5, which was developed in an upper elementary social studies class.

Semantic maps representing concepts   Johnson and Pearson (1984) recommend developing semantic maps to illustrate class and property links that "capture the character of our intuitive notions about the similarities and differences among concepts" (p. 29). Figure 2–6 illustrates the concepts of *dog* and *cat* and some of the related concepts. (In this semantic map *is a* refers to class and *has, is,* or *does* refer to property.)

Semantic maps and story comprehension   Semantic maps help children understand stories and see relationships between various character traits, settings, and plots. In Chapter 4, "Listening," Figures 4–3 and 4–4 illustrate how these story elements are mapped.

Semantic maps and vocabulary development   Webbing can relate to the vocabulary of a single book or it can suggest related words in a unit or theme approach. A web can be drawn as a prereading vocabulary activity or it can be used in a follow-up approach. Students can exhibit prior knowledge about vocabulary

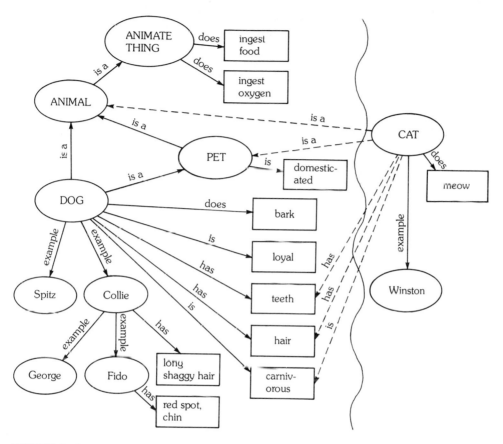

FIGURE 2–6

An incomplete map representation of the concepts *dog* and *cat* and related concepts, using substitutions for class, property, and example relationship terms (Adapted from *Teaching Reading Vocabulary,* 2d ed. by Dale D. Johnson and P. David Pearson. Copyright © 1984 by Holt, Rinehart & Winston. Reprinted by permission of the publisher.)

on the web before they read and then add to and even change the web after they have read a book. For example, to accompany Katherine Paterson's *The Tale of the Mandarin Ducks,* the teacher could draw a web on the board with *The Tale of the Mandarin Ducks* in the center. Words that have special relevance to the story would be placed on the branches of the web. In this case, the words might include *servant, lord, drake, samurai, manor, condemned, conspire, compassion,* and *customs.* The web shown in Figure 2–7 was developed with a group of middle elementary students.

A similar approach may be used when identifying important words in a unit. For example, in completing a unit on friendship, students could identify important characteristics associated with friendship. They could then brainstorm additional words relating to those characteristics.

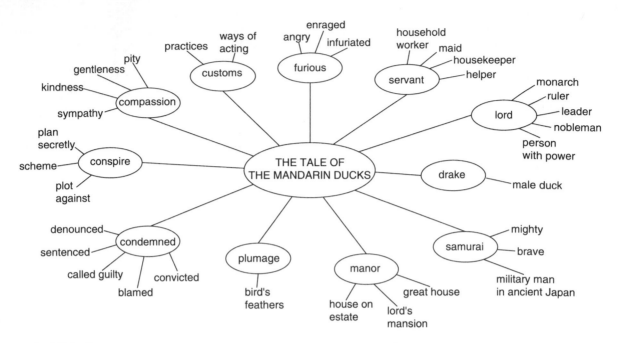

FIGURE 2–7
A web to accompany *The Tale of the Mandarin Ducks*. On the branches are words that are particularly meaningful for the story.

SUMMARY

Language is the basis of human communication. In fact, language is uniquely human, and it is the only form of communication that allows its users to devise theories about the language system itself. This chapter discusses three theories of language acquisition. Behaviorists believe that language is learned through imitation and, consequently, they relate language acquisition to such concepts as imitation, reinforcement, successive approximation, and shaping. These concepts have been used to teach language to young children, as illustrated in the DISTAR language program.

A contrasting theory of language acquisition, the genetic theory, states that language is not learned through imitation but is innate, or instinctive. Proponents of this theory believe all children are born with the ability to use language. They begin with a language of their own and amend it to conform to adult language. Linguists give three reasons to support the theory that language ability is biologically inherited: (1) there are many features common to all languages; (2) word patterns that children construct are not imitations of adult speech; and (3) the sequence of language development in children is orderly and systematic, related to the physical and motor aspects of development.

Although scholars disagree about theories of language acquisition, most agree about the sequence of events in language development. Research concludes that all children appear to go through approximately the same stages of language development, although the rate of development varies from child to child. Longitudinal studies by Brown and Loban provide educators with extensive knowledge about language development. Although language development is advanced by the time most children enter school, it is far from complete; thus, teachers should adjust their expectations in written and oral composition as well as in reading comprehension to the level of language development of each child.

This chapter also reviews a linguistic analysis of language and discusses some of its implications for instruction. Linguists investigate the code signals of language, including phonology (the sound system), morphology (meaning in relation to speech sounds), syntax (how words are put together to form sentences), and semantics (meaning).

Psycholinguistic research has developed knowledge about the interrelationships of the various linguistic code signals. From a psycholinguistic perspective, the various linguistic cues are so closely related that they should not be separated in providing language instruction. Psycholinguists consider meaning the core of language. The grammatical structure is fused to meaning, and the sound and written symbols are vehicles by which meaning is displayed.

Learning environments must stimulate cognitive development in children. Therefore, teachers should provide stimulating activities for students. Activities that encourage children to observe, compare, classify, hypothesize, organize, summarize, and apply what they have learned are important. Semantic mapping and webbing strategies emphasize cognitive processes and encourage problem solving.

ADDITIONAL LANGUAGE AND COGNITIVE DEVELOPMENT ACTIVITIES

1. Look at several different instructional materials used to develop language or reading skills with children. Do the materials fragment the instruction of the linguistic code into phonology, morphology, syntax, and semantics, or do they stress the interrelationship between the linguistic signals? Find some examples of each approach and share them with your class.

2. Visit several nursery school or kindergarten classrooms. Observe the environments and the instructional activities. Can you identify a theory of language acquisition supported by the instructional activities for each classroom?

3. Interview a professor of early childhood development, educational psychology, or special education. What is the professor's view on language acquisition? What type of learning environment and instructional activities does the professor recommend? Share the results of your interview with your language arts class. Do all of the professors agree on a theory of language acquisition and learning environments? Can you provide any reasons for differences of opinion?

4. Tape-record a conversation between a very young child and his or her parents. How does the parent adjust his or her language to the conversational skills of the child? How is meaning achieved?

5. Read a recent journal article or chapter in a text emphasizing language acquisition or development. What is the major emphasis of the author? What theory of language acquisition does the author support? What evidence does the author include? What implications for instruction are included or implied?

6. Read an article on cognitive development and identify an instructional application important in the language arts.
7. Select one of the cognitive operations discussed in the chapter. Develop a lesson plan to help children observe, compare, classify, hypothesize, organize, summarize, or apply.
8. Plan a lesson to encourage vocabulary development. With a group of children or your peers, develop a semantic map that identifies words with similar meanings, expands a precise vocabulary, or increases understanding of multiple meanings.

BIBLIOGRAPHY

Akhtar, N.; Dunham, F.; and Dunham, P. "Directive Interactions and Early Vocabulary Development: The Role of Joint Attentional Focus." *Journal of Child Language* 18 (1991): 41–49.

Allen, Roach Van. *Language Experiences in Communication.* Boston: Houghton Mifflin Co., 1976.

Bartel, Nettie. "Assessing and Remediating Problems in Language Development." In *Teaching Children with Learning and Behavior Problems,* 3d ed., edited by Donald Hammill and Nettie Bartel. Boston: Allyn & Bacon, 1986.

Braine, Martin D. S. "The Ontogeny of English Phrase Structure: The First Phase." In *Readings in Language Development,* edited by Lois Bloom. New York: John Wiley & Sons, 1978.

Brown, K. B.; Dole, J. A.; and Trathen, W. "A Comparison of Alternative Approaches to Prereading Instruction." Paper presented at the meeting of the National Reading Conference, Miami. 1990.

Brown, Roger. *A First Language/The Early Stages.* Cambridge, Mass.: Harvard Univ. Press, 1973.

Bruner, Jerome. "Learning the Mother Tongue." *Human Nature* 1 (September 1978): 42–49.

Cazden, Courtney B. *Child Language and Education.* New York: Holt, Rinehart & Winston, 1972.

Chomsky, Carol. *The Acquisition of Syntax in Children from 5 to 10.* Research Monograph 52. Cambridge, Mass.: The M.I.T. Press, 1969.

Dole, J.; Duffy, G.; Roehler, L.; and Pearson, P. "Moving from Old to the New: Research on Reading Comprehension Instruction." *Review of Educational Research* 61 (1991): 239–64.

Eachus, Herbert Todd. *In-Service Training of Teachers as Behavior Modifiers: Review and Analysis.* Washington, D.C.: Sponsoring Agency, Bureau of Educational Personnel Development, Division of Assessment and Coordination, September, 1971.

Engelmann, Siegfried. "The Effectiveness of Direct Verbal Instruction on IQ Performance and Achievement in Reading and Arithmetic." In *Control of Human Behavior,* edited by Roger Ulrich. Glenview, Ill.: Scott, Foresman & Co., 1974.

Ervin-Tripp, Susan. "Imitation and Structured Change in Children's Language." In *New Directions in the Study of Language,* edited by E. H. Lenneberg. Cambridge, Mass.: The M.I.T. Press, 1964.

_____ . "Language Development." In *Review of Child Development Research,* edited by L. Hoffman and M. Hoffman. New York: Russell Sage Foundation, 1966.

Fink, Rychard, and Keiserman, Patricia. *i/t/a. Teacher Training Workbook and Guide.* New York: Initial Teaching Alphabet Publications, 1969.

Flynn, L. "Developing Critical Reading Skills through Cooperative Problem Solving." *The Reading Teacher* 42 (1989): 664–68.

Fox, Sharon E. "Research Update: Oral Language Development, Past Studies and Current Directions." *Language Arts* 60 (February 1983): 234–43.

Fry, Denis B. "The Development of the Phonological System in the Normal and the Deaf Child." In *The Genesis of Language: A Psycholinguistic Approach,* edited by Frank Smith and George A. Miller. Cambridge, Mass.: The M.I.T. Press, 1966.

Goodman, Kenneth. "The Reading Process: Theory and Practice." In *Language and Learning,* edited by Richard Hodges and E. Hugh Rudorf. Boston: Houghton Mifflin Co., 1972.

Heimlich, Joan E., and Pittelman, Susan D. *Semantic Mapping: Classroom Applications.* Newark, Del.: International Reading Association, 1986.

Jenkins, J. J., and Palermo, D. S. "Mediation Processes and the Acquisition of Linguistic Structure." *Monographs of the Society for Research in Child Development* 29 (1964): 141–69.

Johnson, Dale D., and Pearson, P. David. *Teaching Reading Vocabulary.* 2d ed. New York: Holt, Rinehart & Winston, 1984.

Lamb, Pose. *Linguistics in Proper Perspective.* 2d ed. Columbus, Ohio: Merrill Publishing Co., 1977.

Lawton, Denis. *Social Class, Language, and Education.* New York: Schocken Books, 1968.

Lindfors, Judith W. *Children's Language and Learning.* 2d ed. Englewood Cliffs, N.J.: Prentice-Hall, 1987.

Loban, Walter. *Language Development: Kindergarten through Grade Twelve.* Urbana, Ill.: National Council of Teachers of English, 1976.

_____ . "Research Currents: The Somewhat Stingy Story of Research into Children's Language." *Language Arts* 63 (October 1986): 608–16.

McGhee-Bidlack, B. "The Development of Noun Definitions: A Metalinguistic Analysis." *Journal of Child Language* 18 (1991): 417–34.

McNamara, James, and Norton, Donna E. *An Evaluation of the Multiethnic Reading/Language Arts Program for Low Achieving Elementary and Junior High School Students, Final Report,* College Station, Tex.: Texas A&M University, 1987.

Menyuk, Paula. "Linguistics and Teaching the Language Arts." *Handbook of Research on Teaching the English Language Arts,* edited by J. Flood, J. Jensen, D. Lapp, and J. Squire, 24–29. New York: Macmillan, 1991.

_____ . "Syntactic Structures in the Language of Children." *Child Development* 34 (June 1963): 407–22.

Morrow, L. *Literacy Development in the Early Years.* Englewood Cliffs, N.J.: Prentice-Hall, 1989.

Morrow, L., and Rand, M. "Promoting Literacy during Play by Designing Early Childhood Classroom Environments." *The Reading Teacher* 44 (1991): 396–402.

Moskowitz, Breyne Arlene. "The Acquisition of Language." *Scientific American* (November 1978): 92–108.

Mussen, Paul Henry; Conger, John Janeway; and Kagan, Jerome. *Child Development and Personality.* 6th ed. New York: Harper & Row, 1984.

Myers, Miles. "Approaches to the Teaching of Composition." In *Theory and Practice in the Teaching of Composition: Processing, Distancing and Modeling,* edited by Miles Myers and James Gray. Urbana, Ill.: National Council of Teachers of English, 1983, pp. 3–43.

Myers, Miles, and Gray, James. *Theory and Practice in the Teaching of Composition: Processing, Distancing, and Modeling.* Urbana, Ill.: National Council of Teachers of English, 1983.

National Council of Teachers of English. "Forum: Essentials of English." *Language Arts* 60 (February 1983): 244–48.

Norton, D. "Developing Higher Cognitive Skills through Children's Literature." Address presented at Clemson University Reading Conference, Clemson, South Carolina, 1991.

_____ . *Through the Eyes of a Child: An Introduction to Children's Literature,* 3d ed. New York: Merrill/Macmillan, 1991.

_____ . "Using a Webbing Process to Develop Children's Literature Units." *Language Arts* 59 (April 1982): 348–56.

Pellegrini, A. D.; Galda, L.; Dresden, J.; and Cox, S. "A Longitudinal Study of the Predictive Relations among Symbolic Play, Linguistic Verbs, and Early Literacy." *Research in the Teaching of English* 25 (1991): 219–35.

Peterson, C., and Dodsworth, P. "A Longitudinal Analysis of Young Children's Cohesion and Noun Specification in Narratives." *Journal of Child Language* 18 (1991): 397–415.

Poole, Millicent E. *Social Class and Language Utilization at the Tertiary Level.* St. Lucia: University of Queensland Press, 1976.

Prater, D. C., and Terry, C. A. *The Effects of a Composing Model on Fifth Grade Students' Reading Comprehension.* Paper presented at the American Educational Research Association, 1985 (ERIC Document Reproduction Service No. ED 254 825).

Raven, Ronald J., and Salzer, Richard T. "Piaget and Reading Instruction." *Reading Teacher* 24 (April 1971): 630–39.

Rayner, K., and Pollatsek, A. *The Psychology of Reading.* Englewood Cliffs, N.J.: Prentice-Hall, 1989.

Schmitt, M. "A Questionnaire to Measure Children's Awareness of Strategic Reading Processes." *The Reading Teacher* 43 (1990): 454–61.

Shatz, M., and Ebeling, K. "Patterns of Language Learning-Related Behaviors: Evidence for Self-Help in Acquiring Grammar." *Journal of Child Language* 18 (1991): 295–313.

Shugar, G. W. "Text Analysis as an Approach to the Study of Early Linguistic Operations." In *The Development of Communication,* edited by Catherine Snow and N. Waterson. Chichester, England: John Wiley, 1978.

Slobin, Dan I. *Psycholinguistics.* 2d ed. Glenview, Ill.: Scott, Foresman & Co., 1979.

Slobin, Dan I., and Welsh, Charles A. "Elicited Imitation as a Research Tool in Developmental Psycholinguistics." In *Studies of Child Language Development,* edited by Charles A. Ferguson and Daniel I. Slobin. New York: Holt, Rinehart & Winston, 1973.

Smith, C. "Involving Parents in Reading Development." *The Reading Teacher* (1990).

Smith, Madorah. "Grammatical Errors in the Speech of Preschool Children." *Child Development* 4 (1933): 182–90.

Snow, Catherine E. "The Development of Conversation between Mothers and Babies." *Journal of Child Language* 4 (February 1977): 1–22.

Sorsby, A., and Martlew, M. "Representational Demands in Mothers' Talk to Preschool Children in Two Contexts: Picture Book Reading and a Modelling Task." *Journal of Child Language* 18 (1991): 373–95.

Squire, James R. "The Collision of the Basics Movement with Current Research in Writing and Language." In *The English Curriculum Under Fire: What Are the Real Basics?*, edited by George Hillocks, Jr. Urbana, Ill.: National Council of Teachers of English, 1982, pp. 29–37.

Staats, A. W. "A Case in and Strategy for the Extension of Learning Principles to the Problems of Human Behavior." In *Human Learning*, edited by A. W. Staats. New York: Holt, Rinehart & Winston, 1964.

_____ . *Learning, Language, and Cognition*. New York: Holt, Rinehart & Winston, 1968.

Stahl, S., and Kapinus, B. "Possible Sentences: Predicting Word Meanings to Teach Content Area Vocabulary." *The Reading Teacher* 45 (1991): 36–43.

Strickland, D., and Morrow, L. "Family Literacy: Sharing Good Books." *The Reading Teacher* 43 (1990): 518–19.

Tobin, Kenneth. "The Role of Wait Time in Higher Cognitive Level Learning." *Review of Educational Research* 57 (Spring 1987): 69–95.

Toms-Bronowski, S. "An Investigation of the Effectiveness of Selected Vocabulary Teaching Strategies with Intermediate Grade Level Students." *Dissertation Abstracts International* 1983, 44, 1405 A (University Microfilms No. 83-16, 238).

Wade, S. "Using Think-Alouds to Assess Comprehension." *The Reading Teacher* 43 (1990): 442–51.

Weinstein, Claire E., and Mayer, Richard E. "The Teaching of Learning Strategies." In *Handbook of Research and Teaching*, 3d ed., edited by Merlin C. Wittrock. New York: Macmillan, 1986, pp. 315–27.

Wells, Gordon. "Describing Children's Linguistic Development at Home and at School." *British Educational Research Journal* 5 (1979): 75–98.

_____ . ed. *Learning through Interaction: The Study of Language Development*. London: Cambridge University Press, 1981.

CHILDREN'S LITERATURE REFERENCES

Aardema, Verna. *Why Mosquitoes Buzz in People's Ears*. New York: Dial Press, 1975.

_____ . Anno, Mitsumasa. *Anno's Britain*. New York: Philomel, 1982.

_____ . *Anno's Faces*. New York: Philomel, 1989.

_____ . *Anno's U.S.A.* New York: Philomel, 1983.

Arnosky, Jim.. *Drawing from Nature*. New York: Lothrop, Lee & Shepard, 1982.

_____ . *Drawing Life in Motion*. New York: Lothrop, Lee & Shepard, 1984.

_____ . *Sketching Outdoors in Summer*. New York: Lothrop, Lee & Shepard, 1988.

Aylesworth, Jim. *One Crow: A Counting Book*. Illustrated by Ruth Young. New York: Lippincott, 1988.

Baer, Edith. *This Is the Way We Go to School: A Book about Children around the World*. Illustrated by Steve Bjorkman. New York: Scholastic, 1990.

Baker, Jeannie. *Where the Forest Meets the Sea*. New York: Greenwillow, 1987.

Barracca, Debra, and Barracca, Sal. *The Adventures of Taxi Dog*. Illustrated by Mark Buehner. New York: Dial Press, 1990.

Bauer, Marion. *On My Honor*. New York: Houghton Mifflin Co., 1986.

Berenstain, Stan, and Berenstain, Janice. *Old Hat, New Hat*. New York: Random House, 1970.

Buscaglia, Leo. *The Fall of Freddie the Leaf: A Story of Life for All Ages*. Thorofare, N.J.: Slack, 1982.

Ceserani, Gian Paolo. *Grand Constructions*. Illustrated by Piero Ventura. New York: Putnam's, 1983.

Cleaver, Elizabeth. *ABC*. New York: Atheneum Pubs., 1985.

Dowden, Anne Ophelia. *The Clover & the Bee: A Book of Pollination*. New York: Crowell, 1990.

Dunrea, Olivier. *Deep Down Underground*. New York: Macmillan, 1989.

Emberley, Rebecca. *City Sounds*. Boston: Little, Brown & Co., 1989.

Fowler, Susi Gregg. *When Summer Ends*. Illustrated by Marisabina Russo. New York: Greenwillow, 1989.

Fox, Mem. *Hattie and the Fox*. Illustrated by Patricia Mullins. New York: Bradbury, 1987.

Fox, Paula. *One-Eyed Cat*. Scarsdale, N.Y.: Bradbury Press, 1984.

Goodall, John. *The Story of a Main Street*. New York: Macmillan, 1987.

Grimm, Brothers. Retold by Trina Schart Hyman. *Little Red Riding Hood*. New York: Holiday, 1983.

Hall, Donald. *Ox-Cart Man*. New York: Viking Press, 1979.

Hoban, Tana. *Of Colors and Things*. New York: Greenwillow, 1989.

Jonas, Ann. *Aardvarks, Disembark!* Greenwillow, 1990.

Lasky, Kathryn. *Sugaring Time.* Photographs by Christopher G. Knight. New York: Macmillan Co., 1983.

Lauber, Patricia. *Volcano: The Eruption and Healing of Mount St. Helens.* New York: Bradbury, 1986.

Lobel, Anita. *On Market Street.* New York: Greenwillow, 1981.

McCaughrean, Geraldine. *A Pack of Lies.* New York: Oxford University Press, 1988.

McMillan, Bruce. *One Sun: A Book of Terse Verse.* New York: Holiday, 1990.

MacDonald, Suse. *Alphabatics.* New York: Bradbury Press, 1986.

Markle, Sandra. *Exploring Winter.* New York: Atheneum, 1984.

Marshall, James, retold by. *Red Riding Hood.* New York: Dial Press, 1987.

Merriam, Eve. *Halloween ABC.* Illustrated by Lane Smith. New York: Macmillan, 1987.

Newell, Peter. *Topsys and Turvys.* Century Co., 1893, Rutland, Vermont, 1988.

_____ . *Topsys and Turvys—Number Two.* Century Co., 1894, Rutland, Vermont, 1988.

Paterson, Katherine. *The Tale of the Mandarin Ducks.* Illustrated by Leo and Diane Dillon. New York: Lodestar, 1990.

Pearson, Kit. *A Handful of Time.* New York: Viking, 1989.

Perrault, Charles. *Little Red Riding Hood.* Illustrated by Sarah Moon. Mankato, Minn.: Creative Education, 1983.

Prelutsky, Jack. *Beneath a Blue Umbrella.* Illustrated by Garth Williams. New York: Greenwillow, 1990.

_____ , ed. *The Random House Book of Poetry for Children.* New York: Random House, 1983.

Rosen, Michael. *We're Going on a Bear Hunt.* Illustrated by Helen Oxenbury. New York: Macmillan, 1989.

St. George, Judith. *The White House: Cornerstone of a Nation.* New York: Putnam's, 1990.

Sattler, Helen Roney. *Giraffes, the Sentinels of the Savannas.* Illustrated by Christopher Santoro. New York: Lothrop, 1989.

Selsam, Millicent, and Hunt, Joyce. *Keep Looking!* Illustrated by Normand Chartier. New York: Macmillan, 1989.

Stevens, Janet. *The House That Jack Built.* New York: Holiday, 1985.

Stevenson, James. *The Wish Card Ran Out!* New York: Greenwillow, 1981.

Viorst, Judith. *Alexander and the Terrible, Horrible, No Good, Very Bad Day.* New York: Atheneum Pubs., 1972.

Vogel, Carole, and Goldner, Kathryn. *The Great Yellowstone Fire.* San Francisco: Sierra Club, 1990.

Von Tscharner, Renata, and Fleming, Ronald. *New Providence: A Changing City Scape.* Illustrated by Denis Orloff. San Diego: Harcourt Brace Jovanovich, 1987.

Wiesner, David. *Free Fall.* New York: Lothrop, 1988.

Willard, Nancy. *A Visit to William Blake's Inn.* San Diego: Harcourt Brace Jovanovich, 1981.

Young, Ed, retold by. *Lon Po Po: A Red-Riding Hood Story from China.* New York: Philomel, 1989.

Chapter Three

After completing the chapter on oral language development, you will be able to:

1. *State the objectives of oral language instruction.*
2. *Design a stimulus for eliciting an oral language sample.*
3. *Evaluate a child's oral language after administering several informal tests.*
4. *Describe several instructional practices that help to build an environment in which oral language flourishes.*
5. *Describe how oral communication skills may be developed through conversation, storytelling, and oral discussion.*
6. *Describe and demonstrate the sequential development of questioning strategies designed to develop students' higher level thought processes.*
7. *Demonstrate the use of pantomime as a basic dramatic technique.*
8. *Describe the five steps to guide children in dramatization.*
9. *Develop a puppetry activity.*
10. *Describe and demonstrate the major types of choral speaking arrangements.*
11. *Describe the use of oral reading and reader's theater.*

Oral Language Development

*O*ral language is basic to learning in all disciplines because it is a primary means of communication. Through oral language, children develop self-identity and shape their experiences and knowledge. Conclusions from Pinnell and Jaggar's (1991) review of research associated with oral language, both speaking and listening, emphasize the importance of developing a language arts program that provides many opportunities for oral language interaction. Pinnell and Jaggar conclude that language arts instruction should (1) offer students many opportunities to engage in talking during real social situations, (2) provide students with opportunities to engage in many kinds of talking and listening situations, (3) guarantee opportunities for students to develop the skills necessary to use language for the full range of social and intellectual functions, (4) create a rich classroom environment that fosters language development, and (5) allow students to participate in oral language activities and display their competence.

OBJECTIVES OF INSTRUCTION

Educators emphasize the importance of both providing many opportunities for language interactions and developing a rich environment for oral language. A joint statement prepared by the Early Childhood and Literacy Development Committee of the International Reading Association (1986) emphasizes a learning environment that permits children to build on already existing knowledge of oral and written language and that encourages them to develop positive attitudes toward themselves and toward language and literacy. In reference to oral language instruction, the committee recommends that instructional activities focus on meaningful language and experiences rather than on isolated skill development; respect the language children bring to school and use it as a base for language and literacy activities; help children see themselves as people who enjoy exploring language; foster affective and cognitive development by encouraging oral communication; encourage children to be active participants in the learning process; and provide opportunities for them to experience a wide variety of poetry, fiction, and nonfiction.

The "Essentials of English" adopted by the National Council of Teachers of English (1983) provides excellent objectives in the areas of speaking and creative thinking. Both areas are closely related to the development of effective oral communication. For speaking, students should learn

- to speak clearly and expressively about their ideas and concerns.
- to adapt words and strategies according to varying situations and audiences, from one-to-one conversations to formal, large-group settings.
- to participate productively and harmoniously in both small and large groups.
- to present arguments in orderly and convincing ways.
- to interpret and assess various kinds of communication, including intonation, pause, gesture, and body language that accompany speaking. (p. 246)[1]

In a rapidly expanding knowledge base, knowing how to think creatively, logically, and critically is essential. Ability to analyze, classify, compare, formulate hypotheses, make inferences, and draw conclusions is crucial for all adults. Early and continuous stimulation is necessary, however, if these important cognitive skills are to develop. Notice how many of them can be enriched through oral language. The National Council of Teachers makes the following recommendations:

In the area of creative thinking, students should learn

- that originality derives from the uniqueness of the individual's perception, not necessarily from an innate talent.
- that inventiveness involves seeing new relationships.
- that creative thinking derives from their ability not only to look, but to see; not only to hear, but to listen; not only to imitate, but to innovate; not only to observe, but to experience the excitement of fresh perception.

In the area of logical thinking, students should learn

- to create hypotheses and predict outcomes.
- to test the validity of an assertion by examining the evidence.
- to understand logical relationships.
- to construct logical sequences and understand the conclusions to which they lead.
- to detect fallacies in reasoning.
- to recognize that "how to think" is different from "what to think."

In the area of critical thinking, students should learn

- to ask questions in order to discover meaning.
- to differentiate between subjective and objective viewpoints; to discriminate between opinion and fact.
- to evaluate the intentions and messages of speakers and writers, especially attempts to manipulate the language in order to deceive.
- to make judgments based on criteria that can be supported and explained. (p. 247)[2]

ASSESSMENT OF ORAL LANGUAGE

Much of the assessment connected with oral language development relies on informal techniques for eliciting and evaluating language. Loban (1976) recommends that "because no published tests measure power over the living language, the spoken word, [teachers should] devise ways of assessing oral language using cassettes,

---

[1] From the National Council of Teachers of English, "Forum: Essentials of English," *Language Arts* 60 (February 1983): 244–48. Copyright © 1983 by the National Council of Teachers of English. Reprinted by permission of the publisher and author.
[2] Ibid.

tape recorders, and video tapes" (p. 1). Goodman (1985) states that assessment is an ongoing activity and that "informal, naturalistic observation is the most effective way to learn about children's language and their ways of learning" (p. 8). According to Goodman, teachers should evaluate ability to adjust language to meet the demands of new situations and settings. Consequently, during evaluation, teachers should observe children using language to explore concepts in a variety of areas — art, social studies, math, and physical education, for example.

Results of current research indicate the importance of adding oral interview techniques to paper-and-pencil tests when analyzing students' understanding of a topic. For example, Valencia, Stallman, Commeyras, Pearson, and Hartman (1991) used both interview techniques and paper-and-pencil tests to assess students' topical knowledge. They found that interview techniques pointed up individual differences more dramatically than recognition tests. They concluded: "If one's goal is to obtain a fairly complete picture of a person's topical knowledge, then both interview and recognition measures seem appropriate. If the goal is to assess only a specific body of information, then a recognition measure might suffice. And if the goal is to open a broader window on a student's knowledge, then an interview seems preferable" (p. 204). Oral interviews are possible within any content area and add considerable information about each student's language and knowledge.

Otto and Smith (1980) promote using informal approaches to assess the oral language of disabled learners. They believe that standardized instruments for diagnosing speaking deficiencies are often based on language standards that are more contrived than real and that standardized instruments generally do not yield any more information than do informal assessments. Moreover, they feel that teachers must carefully observe total language in order to formulate the best instructional approach for each child. This observation should consider the child's effectiveness of communication in terms of purpose, message, and audience. In addition, they recommend that all diagnoses of speaking deficiencies be constructed in a highly personal way and that teachers avoid measuring a disabled student's performance on a standardized scale. Of course, in order to do this, teachers need sufficient background in language development. This section reviews some techniques to elicit oral language from children for the purpose of assessment.

Language Experience Stories

A dictated story, or language experience, may be used to evaluate language informally. This approach may be as simple as asking a child to draw or paint a picture and tell the story to a teacher or an aide, who writes down the story as it is dictated. The completed story provides the teacher with information about both language and thought processes of the child. (See the reinforcement activity on pages 68–69 for an appropriate chart.)

A more structured language experience approach for evaluating language is recommended by Dixon (1977). She states: "The ease with which the language experience stories can be obtained and their reflection of the uniqueness of each child, make their use as informal diagnostic–evaluative tools worth further consideration" (p. 501). Dixon distinguishes between three types of information that can be obtained from the language experience. First is observable behavior, which includes watching as words are written, pacing dictation, pausing at the end of a phrase or sentence, providing an appropriate title, and attempting to read back the story. Second is global language usage, which includes dictating complete sentences and using a variety of words. Third is refined language usage, which includes counting the number of adjectives, adverbs, prepositional phrases, and embedded sentences.

Dixon uses a puppet from the Peabody Language Development Kit to motivate the language experience story. She allows a child to feel and manipulate the puppet while discussing it. She asks questions, such as What does it look like? How does it feel? What color is it? What do you think it is? Then, she asks the child to tell a story about the puppet and writes a two minute sample. Following the dictation, she gives the child an opportunity to "read" the story with her and scores the language sample according to the checklist shown in Figure 3–1.

Dixon suggests that a weighted score is the most desirable because it allows equal value within categories of the checklist. She believes that a low score in the first category may imply a need for more language enrichment activities and exposure to stories before normal reading instruction because a child who does not watch or pace dictation while words are being written may not be aware that the words being written are the same as those being spoken. A low score in the second category may indicate that language enrichment and development activities should be a large part of the instructional program. A low score in the final category may imply a need for vocabulary development and language refinement activities as part of the language arts program.

Story Retelling

Story retelling is a means of evaluating the ability of a child to perceive and recall events. Pickert and Chase (1978) state that "early assessment of children's ability to comprehend, organize, and express language, followed by appropriate education based on this assessment, may be the key to student success in school" (p. 528). They recommend the use of story retelling because the organization, comprehension, and sentence structures of a student are not biased by prestructured teacher questions.

For this assessment, a teacher tells a short story individually to a student, asks the student to retell the story, and tape records the student's version. The story selected should have a plot simple enough for the age of the child but too long for memorization. Pickert and Chase feel that story retelling affords the following information:

1. Comprehension—Does the child comprehend the grammatical forms of the sentences and the meaning of the vocabulary? Children who do not understand sentence structures, words, or concepts may give the story a different but plausible ending.
2. Organization and recall of information—Does the child organize information and recall it in a logical manner? Are events left out, is the order confused, or is the task impossible to perform?
3. Fluency—Does the child express the story in fluent, connected sentences, using correct grammatical forms? If you understand the differences that age, experience, culture, and individual learning styles have on children's

I. Observable Behaviors:			
1. Watches when words are written down	(usually)	(sometimes)	(seldom)
2. Paces dictation	(usually)	(sometimes)	(seldom)
3. Pauses at end of phrase or sentence	(usually)	(sometimes)	(seldom)
4. Appropriate title	(very)	(acceptable)	(poor)
5. Attempts to read back	(most)	(some)	(none)
II. Global Language Usage:			
1. Complete sentences	(all)	(some)	(none)
2. Total words	(31 +)	(16–30)	(0–15)
3. Total different words	(30 +)	(15–29)	(0–14)
III. Refined Language Usage:			
1. Number of adjectives	(9 +)	(4–8)	(0–3)
2. Number of adverbs	(3 +)	(1–2)	(0)
3. Number of prepositional phrases	(4 +)	(1–3)	(0)
4. Number of embedded sentences	(2 +)	(1)	(0)
Total	____3X	____2X	____1X
Total points	____	____	____
Grand total ____			

FIGURE 3–1
Language experience checklist (Carol N. Dixon, ''Language Experience Stories as a Diagnostic Tool,'' *Language Arts* 54 [May 1977]. Copyright © 1977 by the National Council of Teachers of English. Reprinted by permission of the publisher and the author.)

performance, you can use retelling to learn more about the children in their classroom and also learn which errors are typical of young children and which suggest more severe language disturbance.

Unaided Recall

Another evaluative measure is unaided recall of a story. You can use this technique to assess a child's oral ability in placing materials in logical order; presenting main ideas, important details, and cause-and-effect relationships; analyzing characters;

defending a viewpoint; and using oral vocabulary and language structures. This approach differs from retelling because the child reads the selection rather than listens to it.

The child first reads a selection that tells a complete story. *Reader's Digest Skill Builders* are good for this activity, because they have short, interesting stories ranging in reading difficulty from first through eighth grade. The following is an example of a retelling activity for third-grade students. The three students in this example all have high reading ability.

First, each student reads a selection from a fifth-grade *Reader's Digest Skill Builder* entitled, "Mustang's Last Stand." After the reading, each child tells the story individually. The unaided recall is taped. In addition, each child is asked, "Why did the author write this story for us to read?" and "How did the story make you feel?" After the taping, the unaided-recall stories are transcribed from the tape and analyzed for understanding of characters, logical outline of the story, grasp of main ideas and important details, and level of oral language development. In order to rate ability to present the story in logical organization, a list of characters and an outline of the story are developed and each student's number is placed by the list and outline if he or she recalls the item in its proper order. The format is as follows:

Mustang's Last Stand

Student Number   *Characters*

Student Number			Characters
1	2	3	Mustangs—One was called ghost
1	2	3	Cowboys
1	2	3	Hunters
1	2		Man who wanted to save the mustangs

Outline

Student Number			Outline
1		3	1. Mustangs were plentiful in the West in the 1800s.
1	2		2. Mustangs were trapped, broken for saddle horses, and used by farmers.
1	2	3	3. Some mustangs were too swift to be caught: ghosts.
1	2	3	4. Some mustangs when trapped jumped into the mud and suffocated.
	2		5. Ranchers disliked mustangs eating the grass they wanted for their cattle.
1	2	3	6. Many mustangs were killed from planes for sport.
1	2	3	7. Not many mustangs are left.
1			8. Some friends of mustangs have succeeded in a few states in getting laws passed to protect the mustangs. In other states, wild horses are still being killed.
1			9. In stories of the West, cowboys say thunderstorms are the rumbling hooves of mustangs running across pastures in heaven.

Why did the author write this story for us to read?

Student 1: "The author wrote the story in order to tell us what is actually happening in the world to mustangs today. He wants us to help him get a law through all the states that will prohibit the killing of mustangs. If we don't, they'll become extinct. Our next generation won't know anything about mustangs."

Student 2: "To make us think about horses. To think about stop killing them. They are starting to be extinct (sort of). He wants us to tell someone to do something about it."

Student 3: "So we would know about the mustangs. There aren't many left."

How did the story make you feel?

Student 1: "I felt sad about all of the mustangs who have been killed. There used to be millions, now there are only about 20,000."

Student 2: "Sort of in between. I like cattle better than horses and horses are eating too much of the grass and there isn't enough for the cattle and then they would die off."

Student 3: "Sad."

As you can see, even high-ability students demonstrate differences in abilities to develop an outline sequentially and to form opinions based on facts. Students 1 and 2 demonstrate the highest ability in retelling the story, formulating and supporting an opinion with facts, and level of oral vocabulary development. In contrast, student 3 misses several important details, misses the real purpose of the story, and does not substantiate opinions with facts; such skills can be improved with instruction. Many low-ability students find this task difficult, and cannot perform the activity without numerous structured questions.

Other Techniques

Puppets are excellent motivational devices, and you can use them in several different ways. First, a child who is reluctant to talk to an adult may speak without hesitation to a hand puppet. You can use a hand puppet to carry on a conversation with the child in order to collect a language sample and other information about the child. Puppets of familiar characters are good for this purpose. For prekindergarten language screening, you can use Winnie-the-Pooh puppets because children respond well to Pooh Bear. With first-grade children, a hand puppet of the elephant Dumbo is a great success. He has great big ears, which are ideal for listening to children's speech, and he has such a good memory that he can remember everything about the child. He is also a baby elephant, and needs to have many questions answered about the world around him!

A second way to use puppets for evaluation is to have a child manipulate the puppet and tell a story to you or to classmates. Evaluate the story according to some of the same criteria used for storytelling or language experiences.

One of the easiest ways to elicit a language sample is to show a child an interesting picture or series of pictures in a wordless book and encourage the child to tell you about the picture or to tell you a story suggested by the wordless book. Frame your introduction to the picture or book so that you provide the child with a language activity rather than a set of factual questions. Responses to certain questions may require only one or two words and therefore will not provide an accurate impression of the child's language. For example, use any of the illustrations in Chris Van Allsburg's *The Mysteries of Harris Burdick* (1984). Choose an illustration and read the accompanying title and the first line of a proposed story. Then, ask a child to tell you the story he or she believes could accompany the illustration, the title, and the sentence.

SOCIAL FUNCTIONS OF LANGUAGE

Educators are increasingly interested in helping children use language effectively during a wide range of functions. These functions range from satisfying basic needs and interacting on social levels, to acquiring knowledge and communicating information. Pinnell (1985) maintains that "teachers need ways of assessing language that will help them to monitor the child's growing ability to use language skillfully in the social milieu" (p. 60), to assess the language environment within the classroom, and to change the environment—if necessary, in order to encourage and to develop a greater variety of language functions.

Pinnell's framework for oral language observation is based on Halliday's (1973) seven functions for language. These functions include:

1. Instrumental language—the language used by young children to satisfy needs and desires and to make requests or by older children to persuade.
2. Regulatory language—the language used to control the behavior of others or to get others to do what one wants.
3. Interactional language—the language used to establish and define social relationships. The maintenance language used in group situations that include negotiation, encouragement, and expressions of friendship.
4. Personal language—the language used to express feelings, opinions, and individuality.
5. Imaginative language—the language used to create a world of one's own, and to express fantasy through drama, poetry, and stories.
6. Heuristic language—the language used to explore the environment, to investigate, and to acquire knowledge and understanding; the language of inquiry.
7. Informative language—the language used to communicate information, to report facts, to synthesize material, and to draw inferences and conclusions.

Pinnell (1985) developed the observational form shown in Figure 3–2. She recommends that you use this form for two purposes. First, to assess individual students, you should record oral language samples during different types of formal and informal activities. You should gather these samples periodically to note progress. Second, to assess the total language environment, you should record class and small-group responses during different activities and at different times of the day. Use the results from the observations to analyze the types of language demonstrated by individual children as well as by the entire class.

Provide individual opportunities or change the total classroom environment if you have trouble observing a range of oral language functions. Pinnell recommends that you stimulate instrumental language by teaching children how to state requests effectively, give help and directions to peers, and analyze advertising and propaganda techniques. Enhance regulatory language by allowing children to be in charge of groups and by teaching them appropriate regulatory language. Improve interactional language by creating situations in which students work and plan together in small groups that encourage discussion and interaction. Increase personal language by encouraging children to share personal thoughts and opinions and by listening to children's conversations during cafeteria and playground duty. Stimulate imaginative language through creative drama, role-playing, stories that foster imagination, and art. Stimulate heuristic language by structuring classroom experiences to arouse interest and curiosity, creating problems to solve, and developing projects that require inquiry. Develop informative language by planning activities that require students to observe objectively and to summarize and draw conclusions, to keep records and draw conclusions, to use questioning techniques, and to use reporting techniques that encourage discussion and feedback.

Name: _____
        (individual, small group, large group observed)

Time: _____
        (time of day)

Setting: _____
         (physical setting and what happened prior to observation)

Activity: _____
          (activity, including topic/subject area)

_____

Language Function	*Examples*
Instrumental	
Regulatory	
Interactional	
Personal	
Imaginative	
Heuristic	
Informative	

Note: Check each time a language function is heard and/or record examples.

FIGURE 3–2

Functions of language observation form (From "Ways to Look at the Functions of Children's Language" by Gay Su Pinnell, 1985, p. 67. In *Observing the Language Learner,* A. Jaggar and M. T. Smith-Burke, editors. Reprinted with permission of Gay Su Pinnell and the International Reading Association.)

REINFORCEMENT ACTIVITY

Use the following student profile when demonstrating the kinds of evaluative information that can be obtained from a dictated story. After you have looked at the profile, read the language experience story "Our Hunting Trip." Then, using the student profile, evaluate the language ability of this student. Finally, collect language samples from a student using two or three of the different methods described in this section. Evaluate the oral language information that you gain from the samples.

Student Profile to Accompany a Language Experience Evaluation

Name _____ Date _____
Grade _____ Motivation _____
Average number of words per sentence _____

		Yes	Some-times	No
1.	Dictates complete sentences	_____	_____	_____
	Example: _____			
2.	Uses good sequential order	_____	_____	_____
3.	Demonstrates rich vocabulary	_____	_____	_____
4.	Indicates grasp of main idea	_____	_____	_____
5.	Is confident during the dictation experience	_____	_____	_____
6.	Indicates a background of experiences	_____	_____	_____
7.	Shows a consistency in noun–verb agreement in sentences	_____	_____	_____
8.	Uses pronouns correctly	_____	_____	_____
9.	Arranges words coherently	_____	_____	_____
10.	Includes all words needed for understanding	_____	_____	_____

The following language experience story was dictated by a second grade boy. Read the story and list some of the information you now have about his language ability:

Our Hunting Trip

Yesterday my friend Brian and I went hunting with my brother's pellet gun. I got two mallard ducks. They were sitting down in our pond. My dog Laddie was with me. He brought the ducks out of the pond. Laddie is my friend, I can really count on him. It was a happy day and it was my eighth birthday.

CLASSROOM ENVIRONMENTS THAT PROMOTE ORAL LANGUAGE DEVELOPMENT

If oral language is to develop in the classroom, there must be ample opportunity for children to practice oral communication. Just as you cannot become an accomplished tennis player without practice and feedback, you cannot become an effective oral communicator without instruction and opportunity to develop communication skills. King (1985) emphasizes that "it is the obligation of the school to extend the opportunities for children to use language for an ever increasing range of purposes—especially to use it to learn" (p. 37).

According to Squire (1991), there is an emerging interest in oral language as it influences literacy across the curriculum. The development of a positive environment that encourages oral language is especially important for at-risk students. Squire states that the discovery that "at-risk children frequently lack opportunity in school or out of school to exchange ideas orally with others seems to be leading to a new emphasis in our classrooms" (p. 11). Brophy and Good (1986) found that young children with below-average ability benefit from active engagement. Menyuk's (1991) summary of research about language development concludes that "communication interaction between the child and more mature users of the language is vital for such growth" (p. 28). She maintains that children should be asked to actively think and talk about language.

Teachers must also be aware of the types of experiences that will help develop oral communication skills. Loban (1976) is critical of oral language instruction that merely stresses "talk and chatter." He maintains that oral language instruction should focus on thinking and organizing ideas. Helping students organize their thoughts is as important for high school students as it is for those in lower grades. Curry (1987) found that an approach using lecture, small-group work, and class discussion was most effective in improving high school students' ability to make inferences.

Research on communication between parents and their children often generates interesting suggestions for instructional environments. For example, Edelsky (1978) drew several inferences from studying the home environment. First, parents do not sequence or partition oral language (that is, phonics one day and syntax the next). Thus, classrooms should use more whole-language activities, including real projects that stress the use of oral language. Second, parents interact with learners. In order to meet this requirement, the classrooms should provide opportunities for interactions of teachers and students—in pairs, in small groups, and in large-group situations. Third, parents use language for nonlinguistic purposes—for instance, to correct ideas rather than language form. Classrooms, too, should examine childrens' ideas and ask for clarification, elaboration, and justification. Classrooms should provide an atmosphere in which children may explore and struggle with ideas. To achieve this objective, involve children in planning, decision making, and problem solving. Fourth, parents talk to children about things they can see or are actually attending to. Teachers should also notice what children are focusing on and supply language labels for what the children are actually doing. Finally, parents expect success and delight in progress. Teachers should also delight in children's progress in both language and thinking.

Research conducted with parents also shows that children's oral language ability improves if the parents receive instruction. For example, Whitehurst, Falco, Lonigan, Fischel, DeBaryshe, Valdez-Menchaca, and Calfield (1988) found that children whose parents received instruction in how to do effective picture-book reading with their children scored higher on expressive language ability.

Some educators emphasize the quality of the physical environment. According to Morrow and Rand (1991), "the role of a classroom's physical environment in learning is typically overlooked. Most educators focus on pedagogy, content, and interpersonal dynamics, giving little formal consideration to the physical contexts in which teaching and learning occur" (p. 396). These educators present evidence that an environment for young children that encourages dramatic play and storytelling and that organizes space so that children can select reading and writing materials and produce creative art and written products enhances the development of oral language. Morrow and Rand's research also indicates the importance of adult guidance. They conclude: "Preschool and kindergarten children are likely to engage in more voluntary literacy behaviors during free-play periods when literacy materials are introduced and teachers guide children to use those materials" (p. 399).

ORAL LANGUAGE ACTIVITIES

In concluding their review of oral language research, Pinnell and Jaggar (1991) state that the most effective techniques for promoting oral language development include small-group discussions and projects, informal conversations, storytelling, creative dramatics, and role playing and improvisation. In this section we will consider the development of oral language through such activities as conversation, storytelling, oral discussion (including modeling), creative dramatics (including pantomime and puppetry), choral speaking and reading, and reader's theater. As you will see, speaking, listening, writing, and reading interact closely in many of these activities. Theme approaches are excellent; they develop serious explorations of content and encourage purposeful speaking, listening, reading, and writing.

Instructional units that develop various aspects of oral communication have always been extremely popular with both undergraduate and graduate students. One student titled her oral language unit "Life in the Himalayas—or how a group of intractable 4th- and 5th-graders can be made to clamber up the mountain, converse with the Sherpas, and tame the abominable snowman." You may wonder how she approached such a formidable project. She began by introducing various communication modes such as discussion, mime, oral story development, and creative dramatics. This student not only enjoyed teaching, but also helped children learn a great deal about oral language.

Conversation

In the early primary grades and especially in kindergarten, children spend much time developing oral conversation skills. Kindergarten teachers must frequently work hard toward developing the confidence of young children to the point that they feel at ease conversing with either teachers or fellow classmates. Children need opportunities to communicate their ideas to each other and to realize that they have information worth sharing with someone else. Conversation is a more informal activity than discussion. It allows children to move more freely from one topic to another. Morrow and Rand (1991) found that even conversations during free-play periods are improved when literacy materials are introduced and teachers have guided children in the use of those materials. Show and tell and telephone conversations are two good activities for developing oral conversation skills.

Show and tell This activity is almost a daily part of many kindergarten and first-grade classrooms. Teachers find that allowing children to talk about something familiar to them both stimulates conversation and builds confidence in speaking. Show and tell also provides a vital link between the home, where children

Conversations can help children realize that their ideas are worth sharing.

may feel very confident, and the school, where they may be shy and reserved. Show and tell also provides listeners for the conversational experience. Children learn to ask appropriate questions and to respond to other children in a group. During a show and tell experience, children talk about an activity or show an object that they have brought to school. (A circular or semicircular arrangement, with children sitting in chairs or on the floor, allows more interaction than do rows.) The children voluntarily take turns talking about their objects or activities.

Teachers have a definite role during show and tell. When you first initiate show and tell, you may have to lead some of the conversation by asking questions that provide structure for the conversation and cues for the children to elaborate. Ask questions that provide models for appropriate questions, but encourage other children to ask questions, too. In addition, model attentive listening and prevent other children from interrupting the speakers. Finally, offer enthusiastic responses to all children.

One effective kindergarten teacher asked children to bring one of their favorite toys to class. She asked the children to join her in the conversation circle, and the children began to tell about their toys individually. One little girl showed her toys and said, "This is my panda." At that point, the child could not think of anything else to say, but the teacher carefully prompted her with remarks such as "Oh what a nice panda, we would like to know his name"; "Who gave you the panda?"; "Where does the panda sleep when he's at home?"; "What games does the panda play with you?"; and "Have you ever seen a real panda?"

Teachers may specialize show and tell and its resulting conversation by asking children to bring something they made, something they drew, something that illustrates a season of the year, and so forth. Having difficulty encouraging some of her kindergarten children to take part in show and tell, one student teacher asked them to bring a picture of their family and tell the rest of the class something special about the family. (The picture could be either a snapshot or a picture drawn by the child.) She was amazed when every child wanted to share. They held their pictures confidently and talked about something very precious to them. Another student teacher asked first-grade children to bring something small enough to fit in a paper sack. She asked the children not to tell anyone what was in their sacks. The children took turns describing the objects and allowing the other children to guess what was in the sack. This activity also assisted in vocabulary development, as the children (frequently encouraged by the teacher) discovered the importance of words indicating size, shape, color, and use.

After children are competent in conversation during show and tell, you may divide the group into smaller conversation circles and allow children to lead.

Telephone conversations Play telephones in elementary classrooms provide opportunities for children to develop a specific type of conversation. With telephones, children learn about the importance of the quality of their speaking voices, to take turns during conversation, and to respond appropriately to another speaker. Through role playing, they may learn how to use the telephone for reaching the fire or police departments. During role playing, let one child assume the role of a person who needs assistance and another child assume the role of the person at the desired location. Children discover the necessity for giving exact directions or details, and learn procedures to use in real emergencies. Other role playing with telephone conversations includes calling a grocery store to place an order, calling a friend to ask about his weekend trip, or calling Grandmother to wish her happy birthday.

Wordless Books

The illustrations in books encourage students to respond in a variety of ways. According to Cianciolo (1990), artists "can stimulate the reader to extract from the images new meanings about aspects of the human condition that the author or illustrator chooses to represent in the images created through carefully selected words or pictures" (p. 26). Books that encourage aesthetic responses and stimulate intellectual development are important in elementary classrooms. Wordless books—picture books in which the illustrations tell a story without words—provide excellent frameworks for various responses and for oral storytelling. Even young children can describe their responses to the characters and situations depicted. Strong story lines develop the ability to interpret sequential plot development. Detailed illustrations encourage observational capabilities and descriptive vocabu-

A play telephone in the classroom motivates role playing.

laries. Emily Arnold McCully's *New Baby* (1988), *School* (1987), and *Picnic* (1984) have easily followed plots, familiar environments, and problem-solving situations. Mercer Mayer's humorous wordless books are especially appealing to primary children. The antics of a boy, a dog, and a frog stimulate oral interpretations in *A Boy, A Dog, and a Frog* (1967), *Frog, Where Are You?* (1969), *A Boy, a Dog, a Frog, and a Friend* (1971), and *Frog Goes to Dinner* (1974). The appealing characters and plot ideas in Peter Collington's *On Christmas Eve* (1990) and *The Angel and the Soldier Boy* (1987) encourage children to respond to fantasy and to problem solving. Henrik Drescher's *The Yellow Umbrella* (1987) allows children to follow the plot line and predict what they think will happen.

Wordless books are not just for very young children. Older children respond quite differently to books such as David Wiesner's *Free Fall* (1988) than do very young ones. Younger children may give more of a literal interpretation of the illustrations. Older children frequently respond to and interpret the story according to their background knowledge of the various characters and settings developed through the illustrations. Mitsumasa Anno's rich details and intricate drawings in *Anno's Journey* (1978), *Anno's Italy* (1980), and *Anno's Britain* (1982) encourage older children to journey through European countries and identify landmarks, sculptures, paintings, and well-known literary characters.

Because wordless books differ so greatly, you should consider the following questions when choosing books to promote oral language development:

1. Is there a sequentially organized plot that provides a framework for children who are just developing their own organizational skills?
2. Is the depth of detail appropriate for the children's age level? (Too much detail will overwhelm younger children, while not enough detail may bore older ones.)
3. Do the children have enough experiential background to understand and interpret the illustrations? Can they interpret the book or would adult interaction be necessary?
4. Is the size of the book appropriate for the purpose? (Larger books are necessary for group sharing.)
5. Is the subject one that will appeal to children? (Norton, 1991, p. 185)

The following lessons show how you may develop various responses with wordless books. The first lesson encourages children to make personal responses to several wordless books.

1. After looking at and talking about Collington's *On Christmas Eve,* ask the students to assume the role of the little girl. If they were the girl, what would they be thinking about as mother and father kissed them goodnight? What feelings would they have? Then, ask them to assume the role of the fairy. How would they try to solve the problem of not having a fireplace in the house? Next, ask them to assume the role of Santa Claus. What reactions would they have when they saw the line of lights leading up to the house? Finally, ask them to assume the role of the girl on Christmas morning. Ask them to describe their feelings as they woke up.
2. After looking at and talking about Wiesner's *Free Fall,* ask the students to describe their emotional responses to the book. Ask, "What colors or techniques did the artist use to make you feel that way?" Ask the students to use their imaginations and put themselves into one of the pictures in *Free Fall.* How will they respond? How might experience with literature influence what they do in this situation? Ask the students to pretend they are having a dream that is influenced by what they were reading or doing before they went to bed. Ask them to describe their dream.
3. After looking at and talking about McCully's *New Baby* or *School* ask the students to describe their feelings about the little mouse child and the mouse family. Ask them to assume the role of the mouse child. What feelings would they have when they looked at the new baby or watched their brothers and sisters go off to school? Ask, "In your opinion are the little mouse child's feelings and actions believable?"

The next two lessons show how the same wordless book, in this case Emily Arnold McCully's *Picnic* (1984), may enhance oral language development in early-elementary and upper grades. *Picnic* has a sequentially developed plot. In the book, a mouse family prepares for a picnic, proceeds to the picnic grounds, unknowingly loses a child on the way, plays games, discovers the child is missing, and searches for the child. The detailed illustrations flash back and forth between the actions of the picnickers and the locations of the lost mouse child.

A lesson to encourage younger children to observe illustrations, describe actions, expand vocabulary, and create sequential narrative includes the following steps and discussions:

1. Ask the students to look carefully at the first double page. Ask them the following questions: Who is the story about? Look at each of the mice. How would you describe the mice? (Encourage expansion of descriptions to include color, size, emotions, and relationships within the family.)

2. Ask the students to look at the same pictures again. Ask them the following questions: What do you believe the mice are planning to do? Choose one of the characters and explain what you think the mouse is going to do. How will you know if you are right? What should we see on the next few pages?

3. Tell the students: All stories take place in some setting. Ask them: What is the setting on this first page? Look carefully at the picture. Describe the woods and the house. What setting do you expect for the remainder of the story? Why?

4. Continue an in-depth discussion of each double-page illustration focusing on descriptions of actions, characters, and setting.

5. Ask the students to retell the sequence of the story.

Older students may use the same book to enhance the development of language skills and to build an understanding of specific literary skills. The following lessons highlight setting, characterization, and point of view:

1. Setting—Discuss the importance of setting for developing geographic location and for identifying when the story takes place—past, present, or future. Have the students look at the illustrations and create descriptions that provide an accurate geographical location, that set the mood for the story, and that set the time for the story. Have the students compare the settings in which the young mouse is lost and the settings in which the other mice are joyfully picnicking. Ask them to describe one setting so that the setting causes problems for the character (setting as antagonist) and to describe the other setting so that the setting enhances a happy, carefree mood. Ask the students to consider the importance of the words they use in describing each setting. Help them experiment with the impact of various descriptive adjectives, harsh verbs, and figurative language such as similes, metaphors, and other comparisons.

2. Characterization—Discuss the importance of characterization for developing characters who seem lifelike and who develop throughout the story. Share with the students that authors promote understanding of characters by describing appearance, feelings, actions, attitudes, strengths, and weaknesses. Have the students select one of the characters in the book and describe that character to provide a better understanding of the character. Expand this activity to teach or reinforce the ways that authors reveal character. For example, have students create conversations through dialogue, such as between mother and father mouse before and after they discover the missing mouse child or between the mouse and mother before and after the incident to reveal family

relationships and feelings. Have the students tell about the characters through oral narrative. Have them describe the thoughts of the characters. The inner thoughts of the lost mouse child should reveal both his fears and his self-determination, while the thoughts of brothers and sisters and of mother and father should reveal various attitudes toward the lost mouse. Finally, have the students describe actions revealing both the physical and emotional changes in the lost mouse or in the other mice toward the mouse.

3. Point of view—Discuss the importance of developing a story line from a specific point of view. Explore the impact of how a story might change if a different character tells the story. Have the students choose a character in the story and tell the story from that viewpoint. Examples include mother mouse, father mouse, the lost mouse, and any of the other children.

You may use this format with any wordless book that contains a story line and includes enough information to develop characterization, setting, and point of view. You can extend the activity to include the development of conflict and the exploration with various literary styles.

Discussion

The goal of the discussion activities in this section is the development of higher level thought processes as well as the development of oral language; consequently, the time spent on these activities may be some of the most rewarding in the elementary classroom. It is through open discussion that children learn to express themselves clearly and convincingly, to share ideas, to appreciate others' opinions, and to cooperate in problem solving. The instructional environment should allow children to become involved in many different types of discussions. The activities we will highlight include teacher modeling, questioning strategies, and grouping techniques for discussion.

Teacher modeling   Researchers such as Roehler and Duffy (1984) and Gordon (1985) have developed approaches that allow teachers to interact actively with students and show them how to approach thought processing. According to Dole, Duffy, Roehler, and Pearson (1991), modeling is one of the most effective ways of increasing students' higher thought processes and comprehension abilities. In a modeling approach, teachers explain the mental reasoning involved in performing various tasks. The goal is not to have students replicate the teacher's thinking, but to have teachers provide enough background so that learning takes place. Dole et al. identify three factors that improve the effectiveness of modeling. First, the information presented should be explicit. Second, the modeling should be flexible to allow teachers to adjust to cues. Third, the modeling should explain the reasoning employed to answer the questions. Without exploring the reasoning phase, many students have difficulty understanding how questions are answered.

Although modeling may be used with any subject, it is an excellent way to help students understand literature, especially in areas such as inferring characterization and understanding an author's use of figurative language. Making in ferences about the characters through their actions, dialogues, and thoughts is difficult for many students. You can help students understand the often complex nature of inferences by modeling activities in which they analyze evidence from the text and speculate about the characters or other literary elements. The following steps are particularly useful in modeling understanding of various literary elements:

1. Identify the skill that you plan to teach and analyze the requirements for effective reasoning within that skill. Ask yourself, What do the students need to know to be successful? What types of cognitive processes are needed? Decide how you will introduce the particular skill.

2. Make sure that the students understand why this skill is important to them. Ask yourself, Why is this important to the students? How and when will they use the skill?

3. Develop the model and the lesson. This includes identifying examples from the literature, stipulating questions that will be asked following the reading of each example, developing answers that typify the types of answers that students might give, identifying evidence from the text and other sources that supports the answer, and thinking through the reasoning used to reach the answer.

4. Introduce the subject and the literature selection. Review what the students know that is important to both the skill to be taught and to the literature selection. Provide any new information.

5. Teach the model. As part of the teaching, introduce the subject and the book and explain what the lesson will include. It is important that students understand terms such as *evidence* and *reasoning.* They should also understand that reasoning is a very personal part of the model. The students may draw on their background experience and knowledge as they explore their own reasoning processes. You then teach the model by completing the first series in which you read the example, ask the question, answer the question, provide the evidence, and explain how you reasoned out the answer. As part of the reasoning, be sure that students understand that you used your previous knowledge about the subject and any personal responses to the literature. After you have completely modeled the first example, make sure that students understand the process. If they do not, completely model another example. As soon as they understand the process, bring the students into the discussion as they answer questions, provide evidence, and explore their reasoning. Older students can take notes to use during the discussions.

6. Conclude the lesson by asking the students to summarize what they have learned and to consider what they would still like to know about the skill or the literature subject.

The following example shows how to develop and teach a modeling lesson using Patricia MacLachlan's *Sarah, Plain and Tall.* This is an excellent source for modeling inferential reasoning because some of the characterizations are stated, whereas others are merely implied. Students frequently need considerable help in analyzing and understanding implied characterizations.

FOR YOUR PLAN BOOK
A Modeling Lesson Using *Sarah, Plain and Tall*

Requirements for effective inferential reasoning: Effective inferential reasoning requires that readers go beyond the information an author provides in a book. Readers must use clues from the text to hypothesize about a character's emotions, beliefs, actions, hopes, and fears. Readers must also be aware that authors develop characters through dialogue, narration, a character's thoughts or the thoughts of others about the character, and the character's actions.

Introduction to inferential reasoning: Review characterization by asking students to identify how authors develop three-dimensional, believable characters. Share examples of each type of characterization as part of this review. Also explain to students that in this modeling activity they will listen to you ask a question, answer the question, provide evidence from the story that supports the answer, and share the reasoning process that you used to reach the answer. Tell them that after they have listened to you proceed through the sequence, they will use the same process to answer questions, identify evidence, and explore their own reasoning processes. As part of this introduction, discuss the meanings of the terms *evidence* and *reasoning*. Encourage the students to identify evidence about a character in literature and to share how they would use this evidence.

The importance of inferential reasoning: Ask students to explain why it is important to be able to make inferences about characters in literature. Encourage them to discuss how understanding characterization makes a story more exciting, enjoyable, and believable. Also encourage them to think about when they could use inferences about characterization in their own writing.

An introduction to the story: There are two important settings in *Sarah, Plain and Tall:* (1) the pioneer setting in one of the prairie states and (2) the pioneer setting in Maine. To identify their understandings of these locations and time periods, ask students to pretend they are sitting on the front porch of a cabin in one of the prairie states in the 1800s, to look away from the cabin, and to describe what they see. Make sure that they describe prairie grass, wheat fields, a scarcity of trees, a dirt road, and flat or gently rolling land. Ask them to tell the colors they see. Then ask them to turn around and describe what they see through the open door of the cabin. Again, make sure that they describe a small space, a fireplace, and characteristic furnishings, such as wooden chairs and a wooden table.

The Maine setting is also important to this story because Sarah's conflict results from love of a very different setting. Ask the students to pretend that they are sitting on the coast of Maine, to look out at the ocean, and to describe what they see. Ask them to turn toward the land and describe the setting. Ask them to discuss the differences between the prairie and the Maine coast and to consider whether these differences could cause conflicts for a character.

This discussion provides numerous opportunities for students to bring in their background knowledge. If it is necessary to provide additional background information, share and discuss pictures showing the two areas. Also, show the locations on a map.

The first modeling example: Read orally from the beginning of the book through the line, "That was the worst thing about Caleb," on page 5. Ask, "What was Anna's attitude toward her brother Caleb when he was a baby?" Answer, "I think Anna disliked her brother a great deal. We might even say she hated him." Provide the evidence. Say, "Anna thinks that Caleb is homely, plain, and horrid smelling. Anna associates Caleb with her mother's death." Provide the reasoning that you used to reach the answer. For example, explain, "The words Anna uses, especially horrid, are often associated with things we do not like. I know from my own experiences that I would use those words about something I do not like. I know from the reference to the happy home that Anna loved her mother. When she says her mother's death was the worst thing about Caleb, I believe that she blamed him for the death." (Notice that you can encourage students to use both efferent and aesthetic responses as they describe their reasoning processes. Including both types of responses in the modeling lessons encourages students to respond with their own feelings and emotions.)

The second modeling example: At this point, verify that the students understand the procedure. If they do not, continue by completely modeling another example. If the students understand the process, let them join the discussion by providing an answer, the evidence, and the reasoning. It is advisable to have the students jot down brief answers to the questions, evidence, and reasoning; these notes will enhance the quality of the discussion that follows each question.

The next logical discussion point occurs at the bottom of page 5. Read through the line, "And Papa didn't sing." Ask, "What is Anna really telling us about her inner feelings?" The students will provide answers similar to this one: She believes that nothing can replace her lost mother and that the home will not be happy again. Ask the students to provide evidence; for example: The author tells us that the relatives could not fill the house; The days are compared to long, dark winter days; The author states that Papa did not sing. Ask the students to provide reasoning; for example: The author created a sad mood. We see a house filled with relatives that do not matter to Anna; I know what long, dark winter days are like; I can feel and visualize a house without singing; I think Anna is very unhappy and it may take her a long time to get over her loss; I wanted to cry when Anna described the setting and her feelings.

Continue this process, having the students discuss the many instances of implied characterization in the book. The letters written by Sarah to Mr. Wheaton (p. 9), to Anna (pp. 9–10), and to Caleb (p. 11) are especially good for inferring what the characters are like because students must infer what was in the letters written by Anna and Caleb. To help the students infer the contents of the letters, ask them to write the letters themselves.

Long stories, such as *Sarah, Plain and Tall,* lend themselves to discussions built around chapters. Students may read and discuss several chapters each day. After each session, however, ask the students to summarize what they know about Sarah, Anna, Caleb, and Papa. Ask, "What do you want to know about these characters?"

Additional examples from the remainder of the book: Chapters 3 and 4: Read through page 17, "Caleb slipped his hand into mine as we stood on the porch, watching the road. He was afraid." Ask, "Why was Caleb afraid? What does this fear reveal about Caleb's character?" Students may answer: Caleb was afraid because Sarah was coming; Caleb was afraid he might disappoint Sarah and she would not stay; Caleb was afraid of the unknown; Caleb, a young child, was unsure of himself; Caleb really longed for a mother. Ask students to cite evidence; for example: The text tells that Caleb did his chores without talking; The text tells that Caleb stood for a long time holding his sister's hand and watching the road; The text tells that he asked many questions about what Anna thought about Sarah and he worried whether Sarah would like him. Ask the students to explore their reasoning; for example: Caleb longed for a mother during the first two chapters—his actions now show that he is afraid that Sarah will not like him or that she will not be nice; I know from my own experiences that I may be very quiet if I am afraid; I know from my own experiences that I worry about unknown people and experiences; I know from my own experiences that I go to someone like an older sister if I am frightened; Caleb's actions let me know that he is close to his sister, that he wants a mother, and that he is afraid that his dreams will not come true; I think Caleb shows the needs of a little boy; I think that is how I would act if I were Caleb.

Continue following a similar approach with Chapters 3 and 4, stopping at the inference about Sarah's strong personality as reflected in her statement on page 19: "The cat will be good in the barn," said Papa. "For mice." Sarah smiled, "She will be good in the house too"; the inference about Anna's and Sarah's characterization in Anna's statement, "I wished we had a sea of our own" (p. 21); the characterization inferred by the flower-picking incident on page 23; the characterization of Papa inferred by the hair-cutting incident on page 25; and the inference about Sarah's conflicting emotions in the discussion of seals and singing on page 27.

Chapters 5 and 6: After the sheep incident on page 28, ask, "What type of a person is Sarah? Do you believe that she will make a good mother for Caleb and for Anna? Why or why not?" Students may respond in the following ways: Sarah is a warm, tender person who likes animals and wants to protect Caleb and Anna from a sad experience; I think Sarah would make a good mother because she cares about people and about animals; I think Sarah would take good care of Caleb and Anna and bring laughter back into the house. Ask students to cite the evidence; for example: The text describes Sarah as naming the sheep after her favorite aunts, as smiling when she looks at and talks to the sheep, as crying when a lamb dies, as protecting the lamb from buzzards, and as not letting Caleb and Anna near the dead lamb. Previous descriptions in the text describe Sarah as caring for the children and being interested in what they do and feel. The students then explore their reasoning processes; for example: I think that Sarah's actions during the lamb incident indicate that she cares about animals; I know from my own experiences that I name things I like after favorite people; I know from my own experiences that if I like an animal I cry when it dies; I know from my own experiences that I want a mother who protects me and who demonstrates love; I like Sarah—I would like that kind of a person for my mother.

Continue reading Chapters 5 and 6, emphasizing the implications of the haystack incident and the comparison to sand dunes on page 32 and the inferences gained from Anna's dream described on page 37.

Chapters 7, 8, and 9: Stop after reading the description of a squall and the family's reactions to the storm on page 49. Ask, "What do Sarah's actions and her statement, 'We have squalls in Maine too. Just like this. It will be all right, Jacob,' tell you about Sarah's character? What do you believe Sarah has decided to do?" Students may respond with the following statements: Sarah is finally satisfied to live on the prairie. She sees that storms in Maine and storms on the prairie are alike. She has changed her opinion about the importance of living near the sea and appears to be happy on the prairie. She may be saying that her life in the new family may sometimes be rough like a storm, but in the end everything will be fine. Sarah is a strong person who can live with hardships. I believe that Sarah has decided to stay on the prairie. Ask the students to cite the evidence; for example: The text tells us that she watched the storm for a long time and that she compared what she saw on the prairie to what she had experienced in Maine; This time Sarah touches Papa's shoulder and tells the family that everything is going to be all right; It sounds as if Sarah has finally made up her mind and that she will stay on the prairie even though it may sometimes be rough. Ask the students to discuss their reasoning; for example: I know from other chapters that Sarah was always making comparisons between Maine and the prairie—some of the comparisons showed a desire to return to Maine; This time, Sarah touches the family members and says that everything will be all right; I know from my own experiences that I may be silent for a long time when I am making important decisions; Incidents in the book show that Sarah is a strong person who is willing to defend her beliefs and the people and things she loves; I feel that Sarah is now ready to love the family more than she loves her former home; I put myself in the place of Sarah as she watched the storm and finally touched the family. When I did that, I could feel the love within the family and I knew that if I were Sarah I would stay.

Continue reading the book, stopping to discuss the inference drawn from the reactions of the children when Sarah rides to town alone on page 52 and the inference drawn from Anna's comparison of Sarah's driving away in the wagon by herself to her mother leaving in a pine box (p. 54).

REINFORCEMENT ACTIVITY

Choose a skill that you can develop through modeling. Choose a book in which students must apply that skill. Identify the requirements for the skill, develop an example showing that skill, identify why it is important to students, identify the text samples, develop the questions, consider the answers, cite the evidence that supports the answers, and think through your own reasoning process used to acquire the answers. Present your modeling lesson to your language arts class. The following lesson plan may be used for this activity:

Modeling for _____

Requirements for understanding:
Example showing this skill:
Why is _____ important for students to understand and to use:

Text Examples:	Questions:	Answers:	Evidence Cited:	Reasoning Processes:

Questioning strategies   Research findings indicate that many of the questions asked of students are at the simplest, literal level of comprehension; thus, they

Effective teachers ask questions that require students to analyze and evaluate what they read.

make the least demand on reasoning. Although there is certainly nothing wrong with asking literal questions, which demand comprehension prerequisite for higher levels of learning, this type of question should not dominate education.

Taba (1964) provides a framework for asking questions that will lead to higher reasoning abilities. In fact, Taba maintains that a teacher's way of asking questions is by far the single most influential teaching art. She believes that the teacher's questions define the mental operations that students can perform and determine which points they can explore and which modes of thought they learn. According to Taba, the steps in the cognitive operations are hierarchical; some operations represent a lower level of abstraction, and the mastery of a higher level task requires the ability to perform tasks at the lower level.

Taba studied the questioning–response pattern of elementary-school social studies classes in the United States. She investigated whether the teacher questions and student responses focused the thought, extended the thought on the same cognitive level, or lifted the thought to a higher level. Taba concluded that only when students had first been involved at the lower levels of cognition could the discussion be lifted and continued at a higher level. The most important conclusion for teachers is that questions must be sequenced from less to more abstract in order to get students to operate at higher thought levels. Taba also found that she could instruct teachers in this sequential development.

TABLE 3–1
Grouping and processing data

Ultimate Goal: Labeling Categories of Transportation	
Levels of Abstraction	Example
1. Data gathering—differentiating the specific properties of things, listing specific examples	1. Listing, gathering, and describing various ways of travel. Look at concrete objects and discuss their properties (for example, cars, trucks, airplanes, sailboats, helicopters, submarines). Ask questions to help children discover properties of each item.
2. Data processing—grouping related items	2. Have children group items that are related. Ask questions and emphasize how these items are alike and how they are different. Help children discover that there are different ways to relate items, such as by color, shape, size, or use, and that sometimes one type of arrangement is more useful than another.
3. Abstracting—labeling each category that has been distinguished	3. Use questioning and discussion to lead to labeling: car, bus, truck—transportation that moves on land; sailboat, submarine—transportation that travels in the water; airplane, helicopter— transportation that travels in the air.

Sequential development must progress from data gathering (the lowest level), to data processing, and, finally, to abstraction (the highest level). Tables 3–1 and 3–2 present the sequencing in grouping and processing data, interpreting data and making inferences, and applying previous knowledge to new situations. Each table includes examples of the steps as they might be used to develop thought processes with elementary children.

As seen in Table 3–1, the teacher's questions and class discussion allow the students time to explore the data thoroughly before they must provide abstract labels. The activity may be as complicated as the ability level of the children and subject matter. A kindergarten teacher may lead children through an activity in which they gather data, process and label objects according to shape, or label types of clothing, such as warm-weather clothing, cold-weather clothing, and rainy-weather clothing. A science class may progress through a similar sequence in order to categorize machines, plant families, or animal families.

In Table 3–2, the teacher encourages development of the ability to interpret data and to make inferences and generalizations. Students begin by assembling the data—the specifics on which a generalization will be based. They handle specific items cognitively before they develop the relationships and formulate generalizations. Table 3–2 follows a sequence that might be used to teach the generalization that when the letter *c* is followed by either *e, i,* or *y,* the *c* usually has the soft, or *s,* sound.

TABLE 3–2
Interpreting data and making inferences

Ultimate Goal: Stating the *Ce, Ci,* and *Cy* Generalization	
Levels of Abstraction	Example

1. Data gathering—assembling, describing, and summarizing the data. What do we need to know before we can make a decision?	1. Present sentences such as the following: "The *ceilings* in the house are eight feet high." "*Cider* is a drink made from apples." "A *cyclone* is a bad windstorm." Help students read the sentences. Ask for other words that have a beginning sound like *ceiling, cider,* and *cyclone.* Let the class provide other examples and place them under appropriate columns.
	
	    ce *ci* *cy* *s*
	  cement cinder cycle seam
	  cellar city cypress (words that
	                              do not fit)

2. Data processing—relating aspects within the data. How is one item like another item? Is there any item that is different? Why does _____ happen?	2. Ask the students to look carefully at each word in the row and decide if there is anything similar about all the words in the first row, etc. Ask the students to listen carefully as they say each word. Is there anything similar about their sounds?
3. Abstracting—forming generalizations and inferences	3. Help the students put together, in their words, a generalization incorporating the principles discovered. Ask, "What generalization could we make about these letters?" When *c* has an *e, i,* or *y* after it, the *c* usually has the sound of *s.*

The sequence of development described in Table 3–2 is extremely useful in all subject areas. You may develop scientific principles through experimentation and formulating a final generalization. Also, you may approach the meanings of prefixes, suffixes, and vocabulary words in this way.

Table 3–3 illustrates the steps used to help students apply previous knowledge to new situations (deduction). The activity is appropriate to use with children after they have read a literature selection. Have the children apply knowledge they have previously developed about the characteristics of a good plot and story (accomplished through inductive thinking activities) to a new story, decide whether the story can be judged as excellent literature, and defend their decision.

The sequential questioning and discussion approach helps students formulate opinions and value judgments. For example, one social studies teacher used this technique to have children reach an opinion about the question "Should the government allow industrial expansion and other types of development in the Everglades? Why or Why not?" The teacher first designed an activity in which the

TABLE 3–3
Applying previous knowledge to new situations—deduction

Ultimate Goal: Making a Decision Whether a New Literature Selection Should Be Judged Outstanding Literature	
Levels of Abstraction	Example
1. Data gathering—assembling related information and establishing the conditions under which to make predictions. What information do we need? What are the characteristics of the new example? What information do we already have that relates to the new situation?	1. Have the students gather information and examples about plot and character development, development of theme, the author's use of language, and development of an appropriate and realistic setting. Use questions and discussion to expand the base of critical data before you ask the students to make a judgment.
2. Data processing—relating the new situation to the previously stated generalization. How is the new situation like the one in the original generalization? How is it different? Does the generalization still apply?	2. Have the students compare their information about the story, plot, characterization, theme, language use, and setting with the set of criteria previously developed for evaluating literature. Do the criteria apply to the new story? If they do, why are they still applicable; if they are not, why are our criteria inappropriate?
3. Abstracting—applying the generalization. Supporting the prediction.	3. Let the children make a final decision as to whether they consider the new story an outstanding literature selection. Make them defend their decision with explanations.

class identified the data required to reach an intelligent judgment. (This is an open-ended question, so there may be no "correct" answer.) The class listed, with the teacher's assistance, the questions they would have to answer before making a decision; for example: "What animals, plants, and people now live in the Everglades?" "Are any of the inhabitants endangered species?" "What conditions do the inhabitants need for survival?" "How would different kinds of development affect the Everglades (such as, housing, airports, plastics industry, nuclear power plant)?" "How necessary is each kind of development to the economy?" The class investigated these questions, brought their data together, and discussed their findings.

Because students were expressing differences of opinion regarding the effects of development, the teacher next allowed the class to debate the issue. Some students supported ecology; some supported development. The class formed several teams for debate, so everyone had an opportunity to participate. Students who were not debating at a particular time acted as an audience for the others and were responsible for comparing the different points of view and substantiation of the views. The teacher encouraged the audience to ask questions. Discussion was lively because each child had previously investigated and discussed the pertinent data. When the teacher asked the final question, the students were able to provide answers demonstrating higher levels of thinking.

It is also important in the sequential questioning process to provide students with opportunities to ask appropriate questions. According to Hennings (1975), students must assume the role of questioner for the teacher to be sure that they can carry on the cognitive operations independently. The teacher in the Everglades example allowed the children to ask many appropriate questions. You can plan activities with student questioning as the major goal. In these activities, present the group with the ultimate question, and have the students, individually or in groups, list pertinent questions. Obviously, some students will require considerable assistance, whereas others will be able to work independently.

REINFORCEMENT
ACTIVITY

Choose one of these sequential development areas: grouping and processing data; interpreting data and making inferences; or applying previous knowledge to new situations. You may use any part of the curriculum (science, social studies, literature, etc.) to design sequential activities that progress from data gathering to data processing to abstraction. Outline the activities you will use and provide examples of questions for each level.

If you are a student teacher or classroom teacher, use your activity with children and tape the activity for later evaluation. Listen to the tape and evaluate the effectiveness of your activities, your questions, and the children's interaction. Were the students able to progress from data gathering to processing to abstraction? Did any steps need to be improved? If you are not teaching children at this time, share the activities you have developed with your language arts class, and discuss the probable effectiveness of each activity.

Grouping techniques The second responsibility of teachers in effective oral discussion is to manage the environment so that discussion can take place. Some discussion activities may take place in a total classroom setting, whereas others may be more effective in smaller groups. Several discussion techniques may stimulate group interaction. During a brainstorming activity, have the children rapidly present as many ideas on a subject as they can think of; accept all ideas uncritically during the brainstorming experience. Also, let the students add to the ideas of others. Let a class secretary write down all the ideas as they are presented. The chalkboard or an overhead projector works well for this, because the class will need a copy of the ideas generated during the brainstorming. Brainstorming stimulates creative thought, and it can be the first step in a more detailed problem-solving or creative-writing activity—for example, thinking of all of the ways a class might raise money for a class trip or listing all words that can be used in place of *said*.

A discussion technique similar to brainstorming requires dividing the class into smaller groups, called buzz groups. During the buzz session, give the students limited time in which to generate a number of ideas or to solve a problem. You may wish to model brainstorming activities before using the small-group activity so that students will understand what they are to do in the buzz grouping.

An elementary class thought of all the ways you can prevent your dog from going under a fence during a five-minute buzz session. Another group used buzz sessions to solve such problems as "You have a poisonous spider in the terrarium and you want to get rid of the spider without killing the plants" and "Your mother put the paper boy's money on a high shelf in the kitchen. The paper boy came while she was out and you could not reach the money." The teacher gave the children a few minutes to think of as many solutions as they could and to talk about the pros and cons of each solution.

Two other discussion formats are effective in the classroom. A roundtable discussion includes a moderator and three to eight participants. The group deals with a problem or shares ideas informally. The moderator, who may also be a student, guides the group and assists it in summarizing conclusions. A roundtable discussion may also have an audience. You may divide the class into several small groups, or let one group participate in the discussion while the rest of the class listens. Activities that develop thinking and questioning strategies are prerequisites to effective roundtable discussions because skills in asking questions as well as in answering them are necessary for successful interaction in group discussions.

A more formal small-group discussion technique is panel discussion. During a panel discussion, make each member of the panel responsible for a particular aspect of the subject. Each member must be knowledgeable enough in the subject to present information and answer questions raised by the audience.

Many of the successful panel discussions used with upper-elementary children may also use role playing. For example, one science class pretended to be well-known scientists in the area of solar power and presented a panel discussion on the advantages and disadvantages of using solar energy. Classroom discussions can motivate interest, develop higher reasoning abilities, and provide opportunities for oral language development in children.

Creative Dramatics

Probably no other areas of language arts stimulate children's imaginations and language abilities as much as do the various forms of drama. Children can explore real-life situations through role playing; they can learn physical control and ways to express emotions confidently through pantomime; they can learn to interpret literature and to develop creative presentations through puppetry. Dramatic interactions provide purposes for children to use their oral language and develop crucial thought processes. Petty and Jensen (1980) maintain that "creative dramatics fosters creativity in language, thinking, uses of the voice, and body movement" (p. 308). Drama allows each child to develop the ability to use language independently and creatively.

Drama for younger children usually deals with imagined characters based on fantasy or on reality. Older children usually incorporate real-life situations into the content of drama activities. Such real-life situations often have a sense of struggle and excitement. Children seem to want to imagine themselves experimenting with courage and loyalty and solving difficult problems.

According to Siks (1983), the drama curriculum should be a planned sequence of learning experiences. It should be geared to the developmental level, in which the children explore and apply the following concepts: (1) relaxation, concentration, and trust; (2) body movement; (3) use of the five senses; (4) imagination; (5) language, voice, and speech; and (6) characterization. Students should progress from these concepts related to the player, to playmaking and considerations of the audience. Siks suggests developing these concepts in varying time periods. For example, because children seem to learn player skills in short, concentrated experiences, you may devote fifteen minutes per day to exploring those concepts. However, when the children progress to playmaking, they need longer periods to explore the player, playmaker, and audience concepts. The longer periods might consist of several thirty-minute periods a week, or a one-hour period weekly.

Pantomime   Pantomime is the creative drama in which actors play parts with gestures and actions without the use of words. Pantomime develops a sense of movement and helps children interpret situations. The following pantomime activities are from several undergraduate- and graduate-student experiences.

1. The warm-up—Even though the warm-up takes only a few minutes, it is essential to the rest of the session. If the students are not relaxed and comfortable, they will not get the most they can from the period. The warm-up also sets the mood, so that children know what to expect and what structure they must work within. Exercises that stretch and relax muscles are good.

2. The glob—This exercise is a warm-up for the mind. It's an imagination game in which a pretend glob is passed around a circle. Ask each individual to do something with the glob and to pass it on. This activity will stimulate the imagination when one child perceives the glob as hot, another cold, another sticky, and so forth. The activity also tells something about the abilities and inhibitions of the group.

3. Ball tossing—This exercise is similar in its level to the previous one. Students stand in a circle and throw a pretend ball around. They begin to watch their bodies as they throw and to see what movements they make when throwing a ball. They also begin working with focus, because they must watch the path of the pretend ball to know who will catch it. It's a good idea to change the size and weight of the pretend ball. You may begin by pretending to throw a volleyball, then a beach ball, then a bowling ball or football.

4. Mirrors—This is a great exercise for cooperation and concentration. Two students face each other with their legs crossed. One is the leader, and the other is to imitate the leader's movements as if he or she were a mirror image. They begin with large, slow movements. Later, if they are adept, they may add facial expressions to mimic also.

5. Occupation and sport games—There are many games to play with pantomime. One of the most enjoyable is to guess the occupation or sport being pantomimed. Each student performs a short pantomime activity and the others guess what it is. The first to guess in any pantomime activity performs the next one. Perhaps your biggest responsibility is to establish a trusting and open atmosphere. Be sure that the students do not laugh at or make fun of other students.

6. People machine—This is a common dramatic game. The students construct a working, interacting, and spontaneous machine. One person begins, and the others attach themselves wherever they see a possible position. Machinelike sounds help them to get into the activity and realize these positions. Usually students attempt an assembly-line

machine, but it is best to encourage a conglomerate of interacting parts. For example, if the students choose a tractor, four students can be wheels, one the steering wheel, and others the body.

7. Role playing—Role playing works best with a more mature and experienced group. It is fascinating to watch, and the students learn from it. Start by giving the students a situation—something they can easily relate to. For example: The older daughter is setting the table, the younger daughter comes in and knocks a plate off the table and breaks it, and the mother blames the older. Explain the situation to each player, including the reasons for their actions. Tell the mother that she is tired from working all day; she thinks the younger daughter is too young to do much work; she feels the older daughter is often lazy and disobedient. Tell the older daughter that she feels she must do all the work while the younger daughter gets away with everything. Tell the younger daughter she is afraid of the mother because she is not in a good mood and does not want to take the blame.

8. Imitation game—This game is based on the game "telephone." Choose one child to perform a short pantomime with large motions. It should be something that all the students will be familiar with, such as getting ready for bed or making cookies. The other students can't watch when you watch the student for the first time. Then, the students come out one at a time; the first one watches, then must try to imitate the first student exactly. While the second student tries, the third one watches, and so forth. Each child gets only one chance to watch before he or she performs the pantomime, but after he or she performs the pantomime, the child may watch all the rest. This is an exercise in observation, but it is also fun to observe the mutations.

9. Slow motion—Any game in slow motion is good. The students learn how they use their bodies, and they must concentrate on what they are doing. They might all do a different sport simultaneously, or they can form pairs and guess what the other is performing.

10. Actions and emotions—Ask children to pretend to be a giant striding, a hobbled prisoner, someone pulling a sled, someone drinking something unpleasant. An individual pantomime game may be played by writing an emotion on paper, giving each child a different emotion, and having the child act out the emotion while the others guess. Include such emotions as anger, hunger, sadness, happiness, and gleefulness.

11. Visiting the beach—Ask students to lie comfortably on their backs. Tell them to clear their minds and concentrate on their breathing. Then tell them to react to what they hear, and take them to the beach through your voice. The students slowly "go to the beach," seeing things, hearing things, smelling things; the sun gets hot, the sun goes behind clouds, it becomes hot again, the students want to go for a swim. Suddenly rain clouds gather and your voice brings them quickly back to the cars. The students will react to your voice if it is sincere and descriptive. You can evaluate their involvement by their movements. Does the breathing slow down in places? Does it quicken in others? Do the children squirm in the sand? Do they shade their eyes from the sun? Do they pretend to swim?

12. Sense memory—This exercise is only for an experienced and trusting group. It is a way to teach emotional expression, and it must be handled with skill. Ask the students to relax on the floor, preferably not close to anyone else. First, tell them to concentrate on their breathing, focusing their attention on themselves. Again, your voice leads them into their memories. Ask the students to recall a time when they felt extremely happy or maybe silly. This memory can be any emotion, but it is usually better to start with a happy feeling that is easy to remember. Later, you might ask for anger, loneliness, frustration, and so forth, but children must first learn to deal with the emotions and how to rid themselves of undesirable feelings after the exercise is completed. Ask them questions about the experience, such as, Where were you? Who else was there? What were you doing? What did it look like? Were there any sounds? Guide them through the memory with your voice. Afterward, gather them into a group and talk about the experience. Don't ask them what the experience was, because it may be too personal to share; but if the children wish to talk about the experience, let them.

13. Narration—Narrate or read a story aloud, giving children time to pantomime each new act and to be each new character. Have the children pantomime all the roles, including the inanimate objects. Folktales such as "The Three Little Pigs" and "The Three Billy Goats Gruff" are appropriate for younger children. Children in the third and fourth grades enjoy pantomime scenes from "The Twelve Dancing Princesses" and the Jewish tale "Mazel and Shlimazel." Older children enjoy scenes from Greek and Norse mythology.

14. Object game—Write names of objects on separate pieces of paper. Have each student choose a paper and portray that object, allowing the rest of the class to guess the object. You might include a light bulb, an alarm clock, the sun rising, and the wind in a tree.

REINFORCEMENT
ACTIVITY

You will feel comfortable with the kind of movement and pantomime activities discussed in this section only if you actually try the activities. First, form a group of your peers and experiment with the activities. Take turns leading the activities. After you feel comfortable as part of this group, select several pantomime and movement activities and present them to a group of children. If you are a student teacher or a classroom teacher working with upper-elementary or middle-school children, you may wish to try some of the exercises in Tanner's (1979) book, *Basic Drama Projects*.

Playmaking Experiences that allow children to experiment with movement and to pantomime interpretations of characters and emotions provide foundations for other dramatic activities, whether acting in original plays or interpreting literature selections read by or to the children. During the process of acting out a

Retelling a story is often the beginning of creative dramatics.

role, the children develop new insights and are able to identify with the role. If children wish to share their performances with another group, they may use more elaborate settings, costumes, or masks to define the characters. Young children respond well when they are allowed to take on a character by dressing in appropriate costumes.

Both creative dramatics and improvisation are ways to develop creative thinking. To meet this goal, they must be open-ended, develop divergent-thinking abilities, and result in creative products.

McIntyre (1974) separates improvisation from dramatization by stating that in improvisation, children develop dramatic experiences out of their own ideas, whereas in dramatization, they use the work and ideas of others to expand and develop their own ideas. Improvisation places upon the teacher a guiding rather than a directing responsibility. As an example of improvisation, one group of third-grade children were motivated to act out a play after watching the television production "It's the Great Pumpkin, Charlie Brown" by Charles Schulz. The following day at school, the students were talking about what would happen if there really were a great pumpkin and it visited Linus in the pumpkin patch. The teacher allowed the children an opportunity to discuss what they felt would happen in those circumstances. There was enough difference of opinion that several groups were formed to further the discussion. These groups met and then presented their interpretations to the rest of the class.

Many ideas for dramatization come from story selections. McIntyre offers several criteria for selecting a story appropriate for dramatization.

1. The idea should have worth, and the story should be carefully written.
2. The story should involve conflict.
3. There should be action in the development of the plot, and it should be action that can be carried out satisfactorily.
4. The characters should seem real, whether they are human or animal.
5. The situations should call for interesting dialogue.

Numerous literature selections meet these criteria. For example, many of the folktales by the Brothers Grimm develop humorous conflict, easily identifiable characters, and plots that encourage dialogue. Stories such as *The Bremen Town Musicians* (1988) create interesting dialogue as the animals use their vocal talents to frighten the robbers. Stories that include twists that are motivated by folktales also encourage children to try their own interpretations. Alix Berenzy's *A Frog Prince* (1989) provides such motivation as the frog rethinks his choice of a bride. John Steptoe's *Mufaro's Beautiful Daughters: An African Tale* (1987) develops conflict between the selfish, spoiled daughter and the kind, considerate daughter. Janet Stevens's expanded version of the Aesop fable *The Tortoise and the Hare* (1984) stresses humorous action and dialogue among the various characters who try to help the tortoise or hinder the hare. Arthur Yorinks's *Hey, Al* (1986) involves conflict between a life with struggle and a life of endless leisure. Yorinks's book encourages expanded dialogue as students consider the consequences of each life style.

Even after the story is selected teachers have a responsibility to give more guidance than they did in improvisation. In an earlier writing, Siks (1958) suggests five steps that teachers should follow in guiding children in story dramatization:

1. Motivate the children into a strong mood.
2. Present the story, poem, or idea from which the children are to create.
3. Guide the children in planning.
4. Guide the children in playing.
5. Guide the children in evaluating their own work.

One second-grade teacher used the story "Stone Soup" as a literature selection to motivate dramatization. In order to accomplish the first step in dramatization, motivating the children into a strong mood, the teacher placed a large soup kettle and a stone in the front of the classroom. As the children entered the class room, they asked many questions. The teacher replied with a motivating question: "If you were hungry, could you get a meal out of a stone?"

To meet the second guiding step, the teacher told the story of "Stone Soup" to the class. While telling the story, she used as props the soup kettle, the stone, water, and the numerous soup ingredients the villagers were finally coaxed into bringing out from hiding. The class showed interest during the storytelling, and a desire to become involved in the presentation.

After hearing the story, the children talked about their favorite characters and scenes in the story. The teacher allowed them to improvise the actions of their favorite characters, such as a farmer hiding his barley from the soldiers, a hungry soldier marching into town, or a sly soldier stirring a stone into water to make soup. The class then discussed which characters should be in the play. They expanded the story with additional villagers that they felt should be in the play. They discussed how the mayor of the town, a baker, or a soldier might talk and act. They discussed a sequence of scenes, and decided they would use the soup kettle, the stone, and soup ingredients for props. The only costuming they considered necessary were single items for each person—an apron for a woman peasant, a badge for the mayor, a cardboard rifle for the soldier, a hat for the baker.

Next, the class acted out the story. The teacher added suggestions by becoming a character in the story. This was necessary at times to bring the story back to the discussed sequence. The children acted out the story several times so they could play different characters.

After acting out the story, the children, guided by the teacher, discussed and evaluated what had happened during the presentation. The teacher guided questions so that the class talked first about what was good about the play; for example, "How did the villagers show that they did not trust the soldiers?" "What did the baker do so you knew he was trying to hide the food?" "How did you know which actor was the leader of the soldiers?" After several questions, the children suggested ways they could improve the play another time.

Teachers play an important role in stimulating the drama experience. O'Neill (1989) identifies some of the tasks performed by an effective teacher. These tasks include encouraging student interaction and decision making, establishing the context for learning, taking risks with materials, working with a focus, tolerating ambiguity, devising fruitful encounters, and giving power to students.

You may wish to investigate the playmaking process further by developing activities that allow children to explore elements of plays such as plot, character concepts, theme, and language. For example, you can lead children to discover that plot provides the framework for the play, that there is a beginning, in which the conflict is introduced; a middle in which there is a struggle, which also moves the action toward a climax; and an ending, which brings a resolution to the conflict. An excellent source for a thorough study of playmaking is "Playmaking," Chapter 11 in Geraldine Siks's (1983) *Drama with Children.* Kukla (1987) and Booth (1985) present additional ideas for dramatization based on story texts. Both authors emphasize the role of story drama in expanding imaginations, stimulating feelings, enhancing language, and clarifying concepts.

Purves, Rogers, and Soter (1990) recommend that teachers enhance responses to literature by having students use their imaginations to role play interesting and challenging situations from literature. In addition, they suggest that students perform poetry readings with various interpretations and feelings. Then, the students decide which interpretations they believe are the most effective. Segedy and Roosevelt (1986) recommend that teachers adapt a courtroom trial format in working with certain types of literature. This approach combines reading, writing, speaking, and listening as students analyze the characters and situations, develop courtroom proceedings, use the writing process to develop summations to the jury, link and express their ideas through oral debate, and interact with each other. Books such as Elizabeth George Speare's *The Witch of Blackbird Pond* (1958) provide an exciting context for developing trials.

As children move from player to playmaker and present dramas to others, they learn that the audience also has a purpose. Children need experiences being audience members as well as actors. Siks maintains that in the role of audience children learn the responsibility of both listening and responding to peers with honest feedback about an activity. In this interactive process, which is extremely affective in nature, children gain respect and value for the efforts, imagination, and integrity of peers.

You should provide experiences for children to be audience members in both small and large groups. You can ask the audience to provide responses by asking, "What did you see that made you believe . . . ?" "How did you feel when . . . ?" "How did you know the players were in . . . ?"

One of the best ways for children to understand the role of the audience is for them to see excellent drama. When appropriate children's theater comes to your city, arrange trips, or have drama groups or puppeteers give presentations at your school. In addition to being marvelous opportunities for positive audience response, excellent presentations motivate child-produced drama.

*REINFORCEMENT
ACTIVITY*

Choose a literature selection you consider appropriate for dramatization. Does the selection contain McIntyre's five criteria for dramatizing a literature selection? Describe how you would develop the drama according to these five steps: (1) motivating the children, (2) presenting the story, (3) guiding the planning, (4) guiding the playing, (5) guiding the evaluation.

If you are a student teacher or a classroom teacher, develop your drama activity with a group of children. If you are not teaching, share your drama activity with your language arts class. If you are not teaching, try to visit a class in which drama is part of the curriculum. Try to evaluate the teacher's use of Siks's five guiding steps.

*REINFORCEMENT
ACTIVITY*

The National Association of Teachers of English publication *Talking to Learn: Classroom Practices in Teaching English* (1989) includes articles such as "Talking to Expand Understanding of Literature" and "Talking to Develop Self-Confidence in Communication."
With a group of your peers or a group of students, develop an activity that is motivated by one of these classroom practices.

Puppetry   What do you visualize when you hear "Punch and Judy" or "The Muppets"? Most of us associate these terms with a form of creative dramatics that has brought pleasure to both children and adults for many centuries. In Europe, puppet theaters are so elaborate that entire operas are performed by marionettes. The Japanese Bunraku puppets perform classical drama, and the puppeteers in Thailand perform in the temple courtyards. How many of you have observed children watching the Muppets on "Sesame Street" or the puppets in the Land of Make Believe on "Mr. Rogers's Neighborhood"? If you have watched children during a live puppet presentation, you know how responsive and attentive they become.

Puppets can encourage enthusiastic oral and written responses.

Young children need many experiences for developing their imaginations. Puppetry provides opportunities for children to develop the communication skills. When children present a play, they are developing oral language and drama skills; when they write their own plays, they are developing creative writing skills; when they retell literature stories, they are developing interpretive and comprehension skills, as well as other reading skills; when they design sets and puppets, they are learning about art and the theater; and when they become the audience, they are developing appreciative listening skills.

Use puppets in prekindergarten and kindergarten programs for developing language skills. It is truly exciting to hear a young child who does not normally speak in the classroom respond to puppetry. Also use puppets in remedial reading and language classes to encourage reading and communication skills with older children.

Although puppetry is highly motivating and enjoyable, some authorities in children's drama are critical of the ways puppetry is often used in classrooms. Discussing puppetry, Siks (1983) stresses: ''Many projects initiated in the class-room are less than successful because they are never really brought to a satisfac-

FIGURE 3–3
Paper plate puppets

Folded Plate Puppet   Whole Paper Plate Puppet

tory close. They stop with the making of the puppet. . . . A puppet is an extension of a human being who seeks another way to communicate. Puppet and child are one and the same. Serve one well and you serve both."

Introducing puppets. Children often respond to a puppet as if it were a real person or animal. Introduce children to puppetry by showing them puppet play and presenting several puppets to them. Some puppets lend themselves better to certain types of drama. Let children manipulate various types of puppets to discover the limitations and possibilities of each. Encourage children to explore some of the history of puppets; even young children can acquire information from pictures.

Initial puppet projects. After you have introduced puppetry and the children have experimented with the puppets, begin a puppet project. Many puppets are simple enough for even young children to make. The producer of the Valentinetti Puppeteers, Aurora Valentinetti (1977) suggests that in elementary classrooms, beginning puppet projects should be simple enough to be completed and given "life" within an hour. An early feeling of accomplishment is particularly desirable for children in the primary grades.

Good beginning projects include paper-plate puppets (Figure 3–3). Children can make the puppets by folding paper plates in the center, partially cutting eyes (so they stand up), and adding features. Children can manipulate these simple puppets to "talk" by folding and unfolding the paper plates. With unfolded paper plates, children can make an elephant by cutting out a round circle for the trunk, gluing on cardboard ears, and adding eyes. A puppeteer wearing a gray stocking on his or her hand can put the stocking through the circle in the plate to maneuver the hand as a trunk and communicate.

Another simple hand puppet is the paper-bag puppet (Figure 3–4). For this puppet, children draw features on a paper bag, allowing the mouth opening to fall on the fold of the bag. They can make features more lifelike by adding hair made from strips of paper, yarn, or felt. A scarecrow from *The Wizard of Oz* might even have real straw for the hair. Pieces of cloth add authenticity to the clothing.

Bring these first projects to life by having the puppeteers improvise short dialogues or present rhymes or riddles using the puppet. After the children share their puppets, have them gather in small groups and improvise short scenes with the puppets.

FIGURE 3–4
Paper bag puppets

Extending puppet projects. The next step is to select a play to present. Valentinetti recommends that children begin developing puppetry plays by working with literature because literature provides a foundation of plot and character upon which children can build. Learning principles of plot and character through the use of familiar stories also makes the transition to original work easier.

When helping children choose appropriate literature for puppetry, follow Briggs and Wagner's (1979) suggestions:

1. Stories should have briskly moving action that can be shown through the movements and voices of the puppet characters.
2. Selections should be interesting to children, well-liked, and easily understood.
3. Characters in the stories should present challenging, imaginative subjects that are not too difficult to construct.
4. The number of characters in a scene should be determined by the size of the puppet stage; consequently the story should not have more characters than can be accommodated by the restrictions of the puppet theater.

In addition, it is helpful if the story has dialogues or speeches that children can convert easily into their own words. If sets are to be added to the puppet theater, the story should require only a few simple sets.

Many fairy tales and folktales meet the preceding criteria and offer enjoyable projects for kindergarten and early-primary students. Some favorites are "Three Billy Goats Gruff," "The Three Bears," "Henny Penny," "Jack and the Beanstalk," "Bremen Town Musicians," "The Three Little Kittens," "Rumpelstiltskin," "Hansel and Gretel," "The Three Little Pigs," and Mother Goose verses. Also useful for puppetry are more contemporary stories such as *Winnie the Pooh* (1954) by A. A. Milne; *Where the Wild Things Are* (1963) by Maurice Sendak; and Rosemary Wells's *The Little Lame Prince* (1990).

Stories suitable for the intermediate grades include folktales and fairy tales as well as contemporary and historical fiction. Fairy tales such as "Aladdin and the Lamp" make excellent puppet productions. You also can use children's classics, such as Robert Louis Stevenson's *Treasure Island* (1911), Howard Pyle's *The Merry Adventures of Robin Hood* (1883, 1946), and Rudyard Kipling's *Just So Stories* (1902, 1987). Charlotte, Wilbur, and the rest of the delightful characters from E. B. White's *Charlotte's Web* (1952) can come to life through puppetry. The Paul Bunyan and Mike Fink tall tales provide plenty of action. Children can dramatize the Revolutionary War period in connection with *Johnny Tremain* (1943) by Esther Forbes.

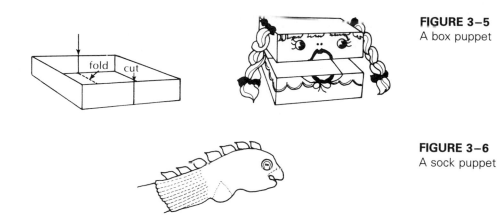

FIGURE 3–5
A box puppet

FIGURE 3–6
A sock puppet

To give each child an opportunity to become involved in puppetry, perform several plays or have the children take turns performing various roles. As we have mentioned, children need experience both as actors and audience. Read the literature selections to the children or let the children read the selections themselves, depending on the reading ability of the group. Encourage the children to discuss the story freely in order to see how they might interpret it for puppet theater. This is a time for building imagination. As the plans of the children progress, you can refine them. Prepare an outline of the plot, characters, and scenes of the play, but keep in mind that improvisation and free interpretation are preferable to memorization.

Hand puppets. Because hand puppets are easy to manipulate, they become part of the puppeteer. Hand puppets are useful for dialogue because children can make many puppets appear that they are speaking. Hand puppets also require less time and skill to make and perform with than do marionettes. Besides paper-plate puppets and paper-bag puppets, hand puppets include box puppets, sock puppets, cylinder puppets, molded-head puppets, and rod puppets.

Children can make a box puppet (Figure 3–5) by cutting the sides of a rectangular box so that it will fold or by lapping two boxes together so that the openings of the boxes face the puppeteer. Paint a face on the boxes so that the top half of the mouth is on the top box and the lower half of the mouth is on the lower box. Cut features from construction paper, cloth, or other scraps to give a three-dimensional effect. A puppeteer manipulates the puppet by placing fingers in the top box and thumb in the lower box; the puppet "talks" when the mouth of the box opens and closes.

Make a sock puppet (Figure 3–6) by placing a stocking over your hand and manipulating the hand so the puppet moves and talks. The elephant's trunk is an example of this type of puppet. Make features for sock puppets by adding buttons or felt for eyes, yarn for hair, and so forth.

Construct a puppet from a cardboard cylinder by adding facial features to the front of the cylinder (Figure 3–7). This puppet will be more elaborate and lifelike if you form a papier-mâché head around the top of the cylinder. Paint on features for the face and add paper, yarn, or felt hair. Make clothing from felt or another material. Manipulate the puppet by placing your fingers inside the cylinder.

FIGURE 3–7
A cylinder puppet

FIGURE 3–8
A molded-head puppet

Make more lifelike puppets by molding the head around a clay form, a balloon, or a Styrofoam ball (Figure 3–8). Mold a clay ball or blow a balloon to the desired size. (If you use clay, grease it with vaseline.) Dip paper strips into wallpaper paste and place layers over the head mold. Form the desired features. When the head is dry, pop the balloon, or remove the clay by cutting the head in half. If you cut the head, papier-mâché the two halves together. Cut and sew a cloth costume that will go over the hand, and place the head on top of the costume. Manipulate the puppet by placing a finger inside the head and in each of the costume armholes.

Rod puppets (Figure 3–9) are easy to construct and manipulate. Draw pictures of animals, people, and so forth on stiff paper, or cut pictures from magazines, coloring books, or old storybooks, and tape or glue them to cardboard. Then, attach the drawn or pasted character to the top part of a dowel, straw, or tongue depressor. Maneuver the puppet by grasping the lower end of the rod and moving the puppet across the stage so the audience sees only the puppet.

Humanette puppets. Humanette puppets (Figure 3–10) are large puppets that do not need a puppet stage. For this puppet, draw a large cardboard shape of a

FIGURE 3–9
A rod puppet

FIGURE 3–10
A humanette puppet

person, animal, or plant. Cut openings in the cardboard figure so the puppeteer's face is visible and the puppeteer can use his or her arms. The children themselves become the puppets.

Puppet stages. Puppet theaters (Figure 3–11) can be simple or elaborate. Make a stage by cutting an opening in a very large box, such as a refrigerator box, and decorating it. Design an instant stage by turning a rectangular table on its side, or by placing the puppeteers behind a large desk. Turn an open doorway into a puppet theater by placing a length of material (with an appropriate opening cut out) across it. Construct a portable puppet theater out of light-weight wood framing covered with burlap. This puppet theater folds for easy storage.

Puppet drama. Rehearse each puppet scene so the children can practice manipulating their puppets while speaking their parts. As indicated, improvising and interpreting a story freely is better than memorizing. Children will want to work with their puppets to develop character voices and to give the puppets life. When the children present a puppet drama to an audience, have the puppets exchange some dialogue with the audience. This involves the audience in the play and provides more opportunities for creative discussion. You can also add sound effects, light-

FIGURE 3–11
A folding puppet stage

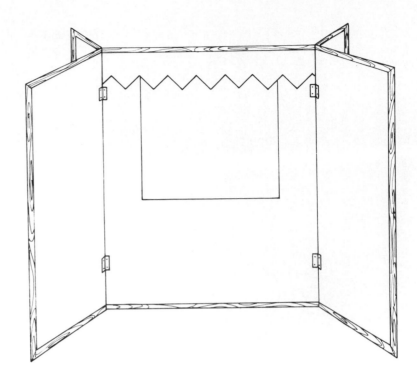

ing, and scenery to your puppet production. One student teacher even had the children write commercials, which different puppets presented between the acts of a formal puppet drama when they presented it for an audience! When children have learned some of the principles of puppet drama, have them create their own plays.

FOR YOUR PLAN BOOK
A Puppet Project: Helping Freddie Frog—
Second-grade Level

A teacher developed the following example of a creative writing and puppet project for a group of second-grade students. The objectives of this project were:

1. To use a puppet to motivate interest and response.
2. To help the children learn to work together—in composing their script, designing a cover for the puppet program, and designing scenery.
3. To reinforce creative abilities, including singing, drawing, oral expression, and drama.
4. To help the children put expression and emotion into their reading.
5. To give the children the experience of performing before the class.
6. To develop personal concern in the children for the problem of pollution, by writing a letter to their class, making posters, and by putting on the puppet show for others.

The teacher made the puppet Freddie Frog from a folded paper plate. He was green and had bulging eyes made from ping pong balls. After the teacher introduced the puppet to the group, he delivered the following letter to each child:

Dear _____ ,

My name is Freddie Frog and I hopped over here today to ask you to help me out. You see, I am in two storybooks that have only pictures in them—no words. Can you imagine that? A book that you can't read?

I know how well you can write stories, so I wondered if you could write one of these stories. Please write sentences that tell what happens to me, and also draw pictures so that the other boys and girls in second grade can see what is happening.

First, I want you to look through the books very carefully. Then I will ask you questions to see if you will be able to write the story for me.

Well, what do you think? I hope you can help me. Imagine that! You can be the writer and illustrator of your very own book!

Thanks so much!

Your friend,
Freddie Frog

After looking through two picture books by Mercer Mayer: *A Boy, a Dog and a Frog* (1967) and *Frog, Where Are You?* (1969), the children wrote their stories, copied them into their booklets, and illustrated each page. After the children finished their booklets, Freddie Frog gave each child another letter. Freddie again requested help from the children. Many of his friends and relatives were sick from drinking the polluted water in their pond. Could the children put on a puppet show in which the forest animals would clean up the pond and save their water friends? Freddie Frog presented the following letter:

Hi _____ ,

I hopped over here today to see if you can help me. You see, I am very sad today because my wife, Fanny Frog, and my little son, Frankie Frog, are very sick. The water around our log and lily pads is polluted, so every time we take a drink of water, we get tummy aches.

And do you know what else? My friend Farley Fish can't even swim around in our stream without bumping into pop cans, bottles, and old tires. He is very thin now because he can't eat green plants without swallowing oil and acids in the water. Our other forest friends, Cubby Bear, Pudgy Porcupine, and Randy Racoon can't even play tag in the water because it is full of garbage.

So do you see how much I need your help? Our pond and stream need to be cleaned up so that everyone will be well again and so we can have fun swimming in clear, clean water. I thought that if you put on a puppet show for the rest of the second-grade boys and girls, they might help stop some of the litterbugs who throw paper and pop bottles on the ground and in the water. Maybe after seeing your puppet show, the children will tell everyone to be helpers, and we can save the lives of the many little fish, turtles, and frogs like me, who die because of the dirty water.

I know how well you can write stories and draw pictures, so I think you can put on a very good puppet show. You could make puppets of our forest friends and water friends, and act out a story about how they decide to go swimming and what happens when they see the stream full of trash. What will they do to solve the problem?

Thanks so much for helping Farley Fish, Fanny and Frankie Frog, and all our other forest friends!

Your friend,
Freddie Frog

After reading the letter and discussing the problem, the children listened to a story from *Ranger Rick* magazine, "How Rick's Rangers Came to Be." This story gave them additional ideas for their puppet show. The children chose specific characters and made up dialogue. The teacher recorded this conversation and typed a script from the tape.

The children made their own puppets out of paper plates. In addition, the children wrote letters about pollution to their classmates, including some of the letters in the puppet-show program that they distributed to the audience. They worked together in designing a cover for the program and a background mural for the puppet show. They also made pollution posters, which they showed and explained to the audience after the puppet show. They incorporated music into the program with a rendition of "A Little Green Frog," making several changes in the song so the frog could sing, "He swallowed some water and he said, 'I'm sad, 'cause I'm a little sick frog swimming in the water. Glumph! Glumph! Glumph!' " The children presented the original puppet play, "The Bubbling Pond," to an appreciative audience and enjoyed positive experiences in creative writing, drawing, singing, and creative dramatics.

Choral speaking and reading   Choral speaking is the interpretation of poetry or literature by two or more voices speaking as one. Choral speaking and reading allow children to respond to and enjoy rhymes and poetry in new ways. Children discover that speaking voices can be combined as effectively as singing voices in a choir. Young children who are not yet able to read can enjoy this activity by reciting memorized rhymes and verses. Older children can select anything suitable that is within their reading ability.

Choral speaking and reading synchronize the three language elements of listening, reading, and speaking. They help children develop interpretive skills, and heighten their appreciation of poetry and literature. Choral speaking can also improve children's speech. Teachers of remedial reading and learning disability classes find that choral reading provides repeated reading practice and develops a realization that reading can be fun. Because choral speaking is a group activity, it builds positive group attitudes and realization that some activities are better if they are performed cooperatively. This realization can be beneficial to shy children as well as the aggressive ones. Kay (1991) also maintains that choral reading is an excellent approach for increasing children's interaction with literature both at school and at home.

According to McIntyre (1974) teachers must understand the phases through which to guide children before they attempt this instructional method. McIntyre identifies three phases. The first is understanding of rhythm and tempo. Young children are not interested in words or meaning—the rhythm or flow of words delight them. Consequently, explore rhythm by allowing children to clap or beat out the rhythm of verses. Children may suggest ways to express rhythm, and should experience fast and slow rhythms as well as happy and sad ones.

During this initial phase, plan activities in which the children can sense the rhythm and tempo of music and poetry with their whole bodies. Have them react to different tempos played on the piano or on a record. Rhythm instruments, such as bongo drums or rhythm sticks, help children appreciate rhythm. Experiment with rhythm and tempo by accompanying a selection with a bongo or stick beat. The children realize how a slow tempo creates one meaning, a fast tempo another.

The second phase is understanding the color and quality of the voices available to a choral-speaking choir. Four terms describe the voice presentation of a selection: *inflection* is the rise or fall within a phrase; *pitch* is the highness or lowness of sound; *emphasis* is the verbal pointing of the most important word; and *intensity* is loudness or softness of the voices. While you and the children learn about voice color and quality, experiment with the facets of an effective choral chorus. Children learn to be sensitive to inflection, pitch, emphasis, and intensity by listening to and experimenting with simple but exciting materials.

Furthermore, children must understand the different ways in which choral arrangements can be expressed. Choral speaking is not merely the unison presentation of a poem. In fact, if that were the sole way, choral presentations would be extremely dull. It is of more value if children and teachers develop their own arrangements, rather than simply using those suggested by a text. To arrange choral presentations successfully, teachers and students need to know the various alternatives available. Following are five different types of presentation, with an example of each using a well-known Mother Goose rhyme.

1. Refrain arrangement—In this type of choral speaking, a teacher or child reads or recites the body of a poem, and the rest of the class responds in unison with the refrain, or chorus. Three poems with refrains are Maurice Sendak's "Pierre: A Cautionary Tale," Robert Louis Stevenson's "The Wind," and Jack Prelutsky's "The Yak." This example is based on the Mother Goose rhyme "A Jolly Old Pig."

   Leader:　A jolly old pig once lived in a sty,
   　　　　　And three little piggies had she,
   　　　　　And she waddled about saying,
   Group:　"Grumph! grumph! grumph!"
   Leader:　While the little ones said,
   Group:　"Wee! wee!"
   Leader:　And she waddled about saying,
   Group:　"Grumph! grumph! grumph!"
   Leader:　While the little ones said,
   Group:　"'Wee! wee!"

2. Line-a-child or line-a-group arrangement—In this arrangement, one child or a group of children read one line, another child or group read the next line, and a third child or group read the third line, and so forth. Poems that can be used for line arrangements are Clyde Watson's "One, One," Carl Sandburg's "Arithmetic," and Eleanor Farjeon's "Geography." This example is "One, Two, Buckle My Shoe."

   Group A:　One, two, buckle my shoe;
   Group B:　Three, four, shut the door;
   Group C:　Five, six, pick up sticks;
   Group D:　Seven, eight, lay them straight;
   Group E:　Nine, ten, a good fat hen.

3. Antiphonal, or dialogue, arrangement—This choral speaking arrangement involves alternate speaking by two groups. You may balance boys' voices against girls' voices, high voices against low voices, and so forth. Poems in which one line asks a question and the next answers it work well for dialogue arrangements. Christina Rossetti's "Who Has Seen the Wind?" A. A. Milne's "Puppy and I," and Rose Pyleman's "Wishes" are dialogue poems. One you may want to try is the Mother Goose rhyme "Pussy-Cat, Pussy-Cat."

Group A: Pussy-cat, Pussy-cat, where have you been?
Group B: I've been to London to visit the Queen.
Group A: Pussy-cat, Pussy-cat, what did you there?
Group B: I frightened a little mouse under the chair.

4. Cumulative arrangement—This arrangement, also called crescendo arrangement, is used when a poem builds to a climax. One group reads the first line, the first and second groups read the second line, and so forth, until the poem reaches its climax, at which time all the groups read together. Two examples of cumulative poems are Edward Lear's "The Owl and the Pussy-Cat" and James Tippett's "Trains." This example is "There Was a Crooked Man."

Group A: There was a crooked man, and
                  he went a crooked mile,

Groups A,B: He found a crooked sixpence
                  against a crooked stile;

Groups A,B,C: He bought a crooked cat, which
                  caught a crooked mouse,

Groups A,B,C,D: And they all lived together in a
                  little crooked house.

5. Unison arrangement—In unison arrangement, an entire group or class presents a whole selection together. This kind of presentation can be difficult because it often produces a singsong effect. Sandburg's "Fog" and Hugo's "Good night" are suitable for unison arrangements. An example for you to try with a group is "A Big Black Cat," by second-grade authors.

Whole Group: A big black cat walks down the street,
                  meow, meow, meow.
               A big black cat with a long black tail,
                  meow, meow, meow.
               He growls.
               He spats.
               He arches his back.
               The big black cat walks down the street,
                  meow, meow, meow.

To stimulate poetry and literature interpretations, encourage older children to experiment with the effects of grouping their voices according to light, medium, and dark voices. Tanner (1979) recommends experimentation to allow children to discover that light voices can effectively interpret happy, whimsical, or delicate parts; medium voices can add to descriptive and narrative parts; while dark voices can interpret robust, tragic, and heavier material. The following example is one way that Robert Louis Stevenson's "From a Railway Carriage" (1883) can be interpreted:

(Light)   Faster than fairies, faster than witches,
(Medium)   Bridges and houses, hedges and ditches;
(Dark)   And charging along like troops in a battle,
(Medium)   All through the meadows the horses and cattle;
            All of the sights of the hill and the plain

(Dark)	Fly as thick as driving rain;
(Light)	and ever again, in the wink of an eye,
	Painted stations whistle by.
(Medium)	Here is a child who clambers and scrambles,
(Dark)	All by himself and gathering brambles;
(Medium)	Here is a tramp who stands and gazes;
(Light)	And here is the green for stringing the daisies!
(Dark)	Here is a cart runaway in the road
	Lumping along with man and load;
(Light)	And here is a mill and there is a river;
(All)	Each a glimpse and gone forever!

Following are general guidelines for choral speaking and reading:

1. When selecting materials for children who cannot read, choose poems or rhymes that are simple enough to memorize easily.
2. Choose material that will interest children. Young children like nonsense and active words, so you may find it advantageous to begin with a humorous poem. Remember that choral speaking should be fun.
3. Especially for younger children, select poems or rhymes that use refrains. These are easy for nonreaders to memorize and result in rapid participation from each member of the group.
4. Let the children help select and interpret poetry. Allow them to experiment with the rhythm and tempo of a poem, improvise the scenes of the selection, and try different voice combinations and various choral arrangements before they decide on the best structural arrangement.
5. Allow children to listen to each other as they try different interpretations within groups.

REINFORCEMENT
ACTIVITY

First, with a group of your peers, practice until you feel confident with the different approaches. Second, select several pieces of poetry, rhymes, or short literary selections that you think are appropriate for choral speaking. Third, instruct a group of children using choral speaking or present the choral speaking or reading activity to your peers.

Reader's theater   Reader's theater differs from oral reading in that several readers take the parts of the characters in a story or play. Reader's theater is not a play with memorized lines, detailed actions, or elaborate stage sets. Instead, it is an oral interpretation of literature, a dramatic reading for an audience who imagines the setting and the action. Consequently, reader's theater includes oral language, listening, literature, and writing. The actors are motivated to read, think, enjoy literature, and express themselves orally. If they develop or adapt their own materials, they enhance creative writing. Working together fosters teamwork and pride in accomplishment. The audience benefits through improved listening skills, literary enjoyment, and motivation for reading literature. The literary selections provide language models for both performers and audience.

Children's literature provides many excellent sources for reader's theater. Folktales originally told through the oral tradition, picture books designed to be read orally to children, and poetry are good sources for younger elementary children. Realistic stories, plays, and narrative poems are good for older students. Sloyer (1982) provides criteria for selecting materials. First, the story should be suspenseful, with a well-designed plot. It should be imaginative, presenting characters in a series of events complicated by problems. The action should turn on a dramatic moment and the ending should be clear and satisfying. The characters should be compelling and understandable quickly through the dialogue. The text should have sufficient dialogue or passages that can be changed into dialogue. Although narrative lines should be brief, they may introduce characters and setting or enhance plot development. Finally, repetitive words and phrases should produce rhythm patterns enjoyed by children and should encourage audience participation.

Examples of literature appropriate for younger children include Sarah Hayes's *Bad Egg: The True Story of Humpty Dumpty* (1987), Margaret Mahy's *17 Kings and 42 Elephants* (1987), Mem Fox's *Hattie and the Fox* (1987), Dayal Kaur Khalsa's *I Want a Dog* (1987), and Eve Bunting's *Ghost's Hour, Spook's Hour* (1987). More experienced readers can interpret Bill Martin, Jr., and John Archambault's *Knots on a Counting Rope* (1987), William Hooks's *Moss Gown* (1987), folktales such as the Grimms' "Rumpelstiltskin," and myths such as "Cupid and Psyche."

Before sharing an oral reading, readers must understand what they read. Because readers interpret the materials according to their experience, they benefit from discussion prior to the oral presentation. Accelerated students usually enjoy in-depth study of a selection, and research allows them to build a background of knowledge about the theater and literary selections. During an instructional sequence, have the children discuss theater-related experiences. Emphasize similarities and differences between reader's theater and other types of theater. Next help the students select and analyze literature for their presentation. Tanner (1979) developed nine points to use when analyzing a reader's theater selection prior to oral reading:

1. "What do any unfamiliar words mean?" Learn their meanings and pronunciations from a dictionary. One word may be the key to understanding a whole selection.
2. "Who is speaking?" Is it the author, a main character, a minor character, etc.?
3. "Who is listening?" Is the selection geared to a general audience, or to a specific listener?
4. "Where and when does the action take place?" Is it in modern times, some time in history, or in the future? This question may demand research to ascertain a correct interpretation.
5. "What happens?" What is the plot? What actions occur?
6. "When does the climax occur?" The climax is the most exciting part of the selection. Identify the exact lines.
7. "What is the basic mood in the selection?" Is it joyfulness, fright, sadness, bitterness, sarcasm, etc.? How is the mood achieved?

8. "What is the theme?" The theme is the basic idea that runs underneath the action.

9. "How does this selection keep you in touch with life right now? What in your background gives you appreciation for this literature?"[3]

For an oral reading, let the students choose a poem, short story, or portion of a story that both interests and excites them. Have the students read the selection silently and respond to the mood, style, and plot. Then, have the students study the selection in order to answer the questions just listed. Help the students prepare a brief introduction to attract the attention of the audience and provide background information to let the audience understand what it is about to hear. The introduction should set a proper mood for the oral reading. Finally, have the students rehearse both the introduction and the selection orally until they are familiar with it. The readers should appear animated in face, voice, and body.

Reader's theater allows an audience to enjoy many types of literature, and allows the participants to interpret creatively such diverse scripts as poetry, short stories, radio scripts, and essays. Tanner (1979) identifies two basic principles of reader's theater. First, allow the children to explore different ways of presenting the literature. There is no one correct way to perform reader's theater. Use guidelines, but let the material shape the method. Second, help children learn to stimulate the audience intellectually and emotionally by breathing life into the literature. They will be able to do this when they understand the literature and become excited about it.

Henning (1974) describes procedures for adopting reader's theater in the classroom. A simplified reader's theater involves three steps. First, read the selection silently. Each child does the first silent reading individually. Do the second reading orally in a group. Let the children choose parts, or designate which part each child will read. Children learn to compromise, because they are not always able to read their favorite parts. Children also learn to listen during this first oral reading. The third reading is also an oral reading, but this time the children act it out. The director, who may be the teacher, reads the title, the cast of characters, and descriptions of the setting or action. The players walk through the action as they read their parts. Add suggestions when a player has problems. There may be a fourth reading in front of an audience. Again, read the title, cast of characters, setting, and descriptions of actions. There may also be a short musical introduction and simple scenery, but avoid having the play become too elaborate. After several such readings, many children wish to write original plays or adaptations of literature.

REINFORCEMENT ACTIVITY

Choose a selection you feel would be appropriate for an oral reading or a reader's theater production. Answer the nine questions proposed by Tanner about the selection. Try the oral reading or reader's theater activity with a group of children or form a group and do the same activity with a group of your peers.

---

[3] Quoted material from Fran Tanner, *Creative Communication, Projects in Acting, Speaking, Oral Reading* (Pocatello, Idaho: Clark Publishing Co., 1979). Reprinted by permission.

MAINSTREAMING AND ORAL LANGUAGE

Many of the oral language activities developed in this chapter are excellent for handicapped children who have been mainstreamed into the regular classroom. Table 3–4 identifies specific characteristics of learning disabled children that might interfere with oral language development and lists teaching techniques recommended by research studies and/or authorities who work with these children. Table 3–5 provides the same information and guidelines for mentally handicapped children.

TABLE 3–4

Mainstreaming and oral language development of learning disabled children

Characteristics of Learning Disabled Children	Teaching Techniques for Language Arts Instruction
1. Problems in language and thought development characterized by poor or repetitive speech, or in comprehending or remembering spoken language (Bryan & Bryan, 1986; Lyon & Watson, 1981; Sapir & Wilson, 1978).	1. Use praise, flexible verbal behavior, effective questioning strategies, and acceptance of students' feelings to encourage academic growth (Smith, 1980). Try creative dramatics (Taylor, 1980). Use the language experience approach to focus the children's attention on the purpose of language: to communicate (Hall & Ramig, 1978). Try the neurological impress method, in which you sit slightly behind the child and read directly into his or her ear while the child either reads along or trails slightly in pronunciation (Bader, 1980; Cook, Nolan, & Zanotti, 1980).
2. Inability to follow directions (Hallahan & Kauffman, 1985).	2. Enhance the stimulus value of teaching materials; encourage children to rehearse academic tasks verbally; provide explicit, clear verbal directions; use concrete examples (Hallahan & Kauffman, 1985).
3. Inability to understand abstract words, form abstractions, acquire and use information, or demonstrate competencies essential to problem solving and reasoning (Fisher, 1980; Johnson & Morasky, 1980; Kavale, 1980; Sapir & Wilson, 1978).	3. Provide instruction in multiple meanings of words, relate unknown words to meaningful experiences, and emphasize vocabulary development within all content areas (Wallace & McLoughlin, 1988). Develop questioning strategies that encourage children to focus their attention on the purpose for an oral discussion or the problem to be resolved, extend their information on a subject, and clarify their knowledge by explaining or redefining previous information before they respond to questions that require inferential information, abstractions, and problem solving (Ruddell, 1978).
4. Disability in comprehending information signaled by grammatical morphemes (Fay, Trupin, & Townes, 1981).	4. Emphasize the comprehension information carried by function words, word endings, and word stem changes (McClure, Kalk, & Keenan, 1980). Use pictures to help children build morphological generalizations (Lerner, 1985).

Speech is a primary means of human communication. Linguists emphasize a need for classroom instruction to encourage oral language development and use of evaluation techniques based on actual language samples. Because most published tests do not assess oral language, you should use informal ways to evaluate it. Use language experience stories, story retelling, unaided recall of stories, puppetry, and wordless books to elicit language samples.

TABLE 3–4

Continued

Characteristics of Learning Disabled Children	Teaching Techniques for Language Arts Instruction
5. Deficiencies in cognitive processes, especially at the higher cognitive levels of imagery, verbal processing, and concept formation (Cohen & Plaskon, 1980).	5. Use semantic mapping or webbing strategies to help children visualize concepts and relationships (Cohen & Plaskon, 1980; Johnson & Pearson, 1984; Myers, 1983; Norton, 1977). Increase involvement time in content areas such as science laboratories and decrease textbook-oriented presentations to improve positive attitudes toward class, laboratory, and teachers (Milson, 1979). Develop cognitive processes through oral language activities accompanying children's literature: observing, comparing, classifying, hypothesizing, organizing, summarizing, applying, and criticizing (Norton, 1991).
6. Lack of linguistic sophistication, characterized by sentences that are shorter and simpler than sentences developed by age-level peers (Fisher, 1980).	6. Encourage sentence expansion using descriptive words and phrases; transformations of kernel sentences; and meaningful oral language activities, such as role playing, show and tell, puppetry, choral speaking, interviewing, and storytelling (Lerner, 1985).
7. Difficulties understanding concepts related to time, quantity, and space (Fay, Trupin, & Townes, 1981; Kavale, 1982).	7. Provide children with visible, tangible cue systems illustrating chronological order, quantity, and space relationships (Jordon, 1977).
8. Deficiencies in memory and the development of memory strategies (Bryan & Bryan, 1986; Torgesen, 1979).	8. Help children select and organize materials in logical order. Use repetition and frequent reviews. Organize materials to increase chunking of material into already existing memory units. Help children relate what they are learning to what they already know. Encourage children to use or develop mnemonic strategies. Use flannel boards to help children remember cues for a story. Teach nursery rhymes, poems, and finger plays that encourage auditory memory (Lerner, 1985).

TABLE 3–5

Mainstreaming and oral language development of mentally handicapped children

Characteristics of Mentally Handicapped Children	Teaching Techniques for Language Arts Instruction
1. Below-average language ability when compared with age-level peer group (Gearheart, Weishahn, & Gearheart, 1988).	1. Emphasize cognitive processes, problem-solving tactics, and motivation to improve mental abilities of twelve- to fifteen-year-old disadvantaged and socially backward students (Rand, Tannenbaum, & Feuerstein, 1979). Give directions in clear, simple language and use vocabulary that is within the understanding of the children (Hart, 1981). Provide many language experiences tied to meaningful situations. Create opportunities for verbal expression, reuse words in numerous contexts, and relate new ideas to concrete rather than abstract ideas (Gearheart, Weishahn, & Gearheart, 1988).
2. Poor self-concept and low self-esteem due to past failures in academic and social situations (Gearheart, Weishahn, & Gearheart, 1988).	2. Encourage children to discuss issues that are important to them (Hart, 1981). Praise students for small accomplishments and work well done (Gearheart, Weishahn, & Gearheart, 1988).
3. Below-average ability to generalize and see commonalities between similar situations as well as to generalize one set of conditions or rules to another similar situation (Gearheart, Weishahn, & Gearheart, 1988).	3. Integrate mechanical and conceptual skills into the lessons whenever possible and point out how one principle may apply to other academic or social situations (Gearheart, Weishahn, & Gearheart, 1988).

A positive classroom environment is critical to the development of oral language skills. Teachers must (1) have the knowledge necessary for eliciting oral language; (2) be able to evaluate each child's oral language; (3) use projects such as puppetry to provide an environment conducive to developing oral language; (4) provide opportunities for children to interact in pairs, small groups, and large groups; and (5) develop critical thinking and reasoning skills through activities that allow children to progress from the concrete to the abstract.

Several instructional approaches can improve oral language skills. Conversation, especially through show-and-tell and telephone activities, can promote self-confidence in children as speakers.

To develop discussion skills, use modeling strategies to accompany oral discussion of characterization in books. Second, emphasize the development of oral interchange through questioning strategies. Use questioning and discussion that progress from data gathering (the lowest level of abstraction) to data processing, and finally to abstraction. Use question and discussion techniques to help students group and process data, interpret data and make inferences, and apply previous knowledge to new situations. Third, manage the environment in such a way that children can participate in discussion groups. Use brainstorming, buzz groupings, roundtable discussions, and panel discussions.

Under the category of creative dramatics, develop students as players with such activities as movement and pantomime. Next, consider improvisation and dramatization. Your role in story dramatization includes motivating children; presenting the story; and guiding the children in planning, playing, and evaluating. Puppetry is an excellent means for children to utilize all of the communication skills. The activity should not end with making the puppet; rather, it should go on to include dramatic techniques. To use the method effectively, you must be familiar with the background of puppetry and know how to initiate the activity. Choral speaking and reader's theater synthesize three language elements—listening, reading, and speaking. Choral speaking arrangements include refrain, line-a-child, antiphonal, cumulative, and unison arrangements.

ADDITIONAL ORAL LANGUAGE ACTIVITIES

1. Identify a group of wordless books appropriate for younger children and another group appropriate for older children. Evaluate the books according to the criteria on page 75. Share one of the books with a child or your language arts class.
2. Plan an oral language activity that encourages children to use brainstorming, buzz sessions, roundtable discussion, or panel discussion.
3. Identify a story appropriate for reader's theater. With a group of your peers or a group of children, adapt the selection for an oral presentation and present it to an audience.
4. Develop a file of literature selections appropriate for choral speaking arrangements. Provide some recommendations for the types of choral arrangements.
5. Develop a file of literature selections appropriate for puppetry. Provide some recommendations for puppetry characters and types of puppetry construction.
6. Develop a dramatization activity based on reader's theater.

BIBLIOGRAPHY

Bader, Lois A. *Reading Diagnosis and Remediation in Classroom and Clinic.* New York: Macmillan Co., 1980.

Booth, David. "Imaginary Gardens with Real Toads: Reading and Drama in Education." *Theory into Practice* 24 (1985): 193–98.

Briggs, Nancy E., and Wagner, Joseph A. *Children's Literature through Storytelling and Drama.* Dubuque, Iowa: Wm. C. Brown, 1979.

Brophy, J., and Good, T. L. "Teacher Behavior and Student Achievement." *Handbook on Research on Teaching,* edited by M. C. Wittrock. New York: Macmillan, 1986, pp. 328–75.

Bryan, Tanis H., and Bryan, James H. *Understanding Learning Disabilities.* Sherman Oaks, Calif.: Alfred Publishing Co., 1986.

Cianciolo, P. *Picture Books for Children,* 3d ed. Chicago: American Library Association, 1990.

Cohen, Sandra B., and Plaskon, Stephen P. *Language Arts for the Mildly Handicapped.* Columbus, Oh.: Merrill Publishing Co., 1980.

Cook, Jimmie E.; Nolan, Gregory A.; and Zanotti, Robert J. "Treating Auditory Perception Problems: The NIM Helps." *Academic Therapy* 15 (March 1980): 476–81.

Curry, J. E. "Improving Secondary School Students' Inferential Responses to Literature." *Dissertation Abstracts International* 48 (1987): 11A.

Dixon, Carol N. "Language Experience Stories as a Diagnostic Tool." *Language Arts* 54 (May 1977): 501–5.

Dole, J.; Duffy, G.; Roehler, L.; and Pearson, P. D. "Moving from the Old to the New: Research on Reading Comprehension Instruction." *Review of Educational Research* 61 (1991): 239–64.

Early Childhood and Literacy Development Committee of the International Reading Association. "Joint Statement on Literacy Development and Pre-First Grade." *The Reading Teacher* 39 (April 1986): 819–21.

Edelsky, Carole. "Teaching Oral Language." *Language Arts* 55 (March 1978): 291–96.

Fay, Gayle; Trupin, Eric; and Townes, Brenda D. "The Young Disabled Reader: Acquisition Strategies and Association Deficits." *Journal of Learning Disabilities* 14 (January 1981): 32–35.

Fisher, Dennis F. "Compensatory Training for Disabled Readers: Research to Practice." *Journal of Reading Disabilities* 18 (March 1980): 25–31.

Gearheart, Bill R.; Weishahn, Mel; and Gearheart, Carol J. *The Exceptional Student in the Regular Classroom,* 4th ed. Columbus, Oh.: Merrill Publishing Co., 1988.

Goodman, Yetta M. "Kidwatching: Observing Children in the Classroom." In *Observing the Language Learner,* edited by Angela Jaggar and M. Trika Smith-Burke. Urbana, Ill.: National Council of Teachers of English, 1985, pp. 9–18.

Gordon, Christine J. "Modeling Inference Awareness across the Curriculum." *Journal of Reading* 28 (February 1985): 444–47.

Hall, Mary Anne, and Ramig, Christopher, J. *Linguistic Foundations for Reading.* Columbus, Oh.: Merrill Publishing Co., 1978.

Hallahan, Daniel P., and Kauffman, James M. *Introduction to Learning Disabilities: A Psycho-Behavioral Approach.* Englewood Cliffs, N.J.: Prentice-Hall, 1985.

Halliday, M. A. K. "The Functional Basis of Language." In *Class, Codes, and Control, Vol. 2, Applied Studies toward a Sociology of Language,* edited by B. Bernstein. London and Boston: Routledge & Kegan Paul, 1973.

Hart, Verna. *Mainstreaming Children with Special Needs.* New York: Longman, 1981.

Henning, Kathleen. "Drama Reading, an On-Going Classroom Activity at the Elementary School Level." *Elementary English* 51 (January 1974): 48–51.

Hennings, Dorothy. *Mastering Classroom Communication.* Pacific Palisades, Calif.: Goodyear, 1975.

Johnson, Dale D., and Pearson, P. David. *Teaching Reading Vocabulary,* 2d ed. New York: Holt, Rinehart & Winston, 1984.

Johnson, Stanley, and Morasky, Robert L. *Learning Disabilities,* 2d ed. Boston: Allyn & Bacon, 1980.

Jordon, Dale R. *Dyslexia in the Classroom.* Columbus, Oh.: Merrill Publishing Co., 1977.

Kavale, Kenneth A. "A Comparison of Learning Disabled and Normal Children on the Boehm Test of Basic Concepts." *Journal of Learning Disabilities* 15 (March 1982): 160–61.

_____ . "The Reasoning Abilities of Normal and Learning Disabled Readers on Measures of Reading Comprehension." *Learning Disability Quarterly* 3 (Fall 1980): 34–45.

Kay, R. "Commentary: Singing the Praises of Choral Reading." *Reading Today* 8 (1991): 12.

King, Martha L. "Language and Language Learning for Child Watchers." In *Observing the Language Learner,* edited by Angela Jaggar and M. Trika Smith-Burke. Urbana, Ill.: National Council of Teachers of English, 1985, pp. 19–38.

Kukla, Kaile. "David Booth: Drama as a Way of Knowing." *Language Arts* 64 (January 1987): 73–78.

Lamb, Pose. *Linguistics in Proper Perspective,* 2d ed. Columbus, Oh.: Merrill Publishing Co., 1977.

Lerner, Janet W. *Children with Learning Disabilities,* 4th ed. Boston: Houghton Mifflin Co., 1985.

Loban, Walter. *Language Development: Kindergarten through Grade Twelve.* Urbana, Ill.: National Council of Teachers of English, 1976.

Lyon, Reid, and Watson, Bill. "Empirically Derived Subgroups of Learning Disabled Readers: Diagnostic Characteristics." *Journal of Learning Disabilities* 14 (May 1981): 256–61.

McClure, Judith; Kalk, Michael; and Keenan, Verne. "Use of Grammatical Morphemes by Beginning Readers." *Journal of Learning Disabilities* 13 (May 1980): 34–49.

McIntyre, Barbara M. *Creative Drama in the Elementary School.* Itasca, Ill.: F. E. Peacock Publishers, 1974.

Menyuk, P. "Linguistics and Teaching the Language Arts." *Handbook of Research on Teaching the English Language Arts,* edited by J. Flood, J. Jensen, D. Lapp, and J. Squire. New York: Macmillan, 1991, pp. 24–29.

Milson, James L. "Evaluation of the Effect of Laboratory-Oriented Science Curriculum Materials on the Attitudes of Students with Reading Difficulties." *Science Education* 63 (January 1979): 9–14.

Morrow, L., and Rand M. "Promoting Literacy during Play by Designing Early Childhood Classroom Environments." *The Reading Teacher* 44 (1991): 396–402.

Myers, Miles. "Approaches to the Teaching of Composition." In *Theory and Practice in the Teaching of Composition: Processing, Distancing and Modeling,* edited by Miles Myers and James Gray. Urbana, Ill.:

National Council of Teachers of English, 1983, pp. 3–43.

National Council of Teachers of English. "Forum: Essentials of English." *Language Arts* 60 (February 1983): 244–48.

Norton, Donna E. *The Impact of Literature-Based Reading.* New York: Merrill/Macmillan, 1992.

_____ . *Through the Eyes of a Child: An Introduction to Children's Literature,* 3d ed. New York: Merrill/Macmillan, 1991.

_____ . "A Web of Interest." *Language Arts* 54 (November/December 1977): 928–33.

O'Neill, C. "Dialogue and Drama: The Transformation of Events, Ideas, and Teachers." *Language Arts* 66 (1989): 528–40.

Otto, Wayne, and Smith, Richard. *Corrective and Remedial Teaching.* Boston: Houghton Mifflin Co., 1980.

Petty, Walter T., and Jensen, Julie M. *Developing Children's Language.* Boston: Allyn & Bacon, 1980.

Pickert, Sarah M., and Chase, Martha L. "Story Retelling: An Informal Technique for Evaluating Children's Language." *Reading Teacher* 31 (February 1978): 528–29.

Pinnell, Gay Su. "Ways to Look at the Functions of Children's Language." In *Observing the Language Learner,* edited by Angela Jaggar and M. Trika Smith-Burke. Urbana, Ill.: National Council of Teachers of English, 1985, pp. 57–72.

Pinnell, G., and Jaggar, A. "Oral Language: Speaking and Listening." *Handbook of Research on Teaching the English Language Arts,* edited by J. Flood, J. Jensen, D. Lapp, and J. Squire. New York: Macmillan, 1991, pp. 691–720.

Purves, A.; Rogers, T.; and Soter, A. *How Porcupines Make Love II: Teaching a Response-Centered Literature Curriculum.* New York: Longman, 1990.

Rand, Yáacou; Tannenbaum, Abraham, J.; and Feuerstein, Reuven. "Effects of Instrumental Enrichment on the Psychoeducational Development of Low-Functioning Adolescents." *Journal of Educational Psychology* 71 (December 1979): 751–63.

Roehler, Laura, and Duffy, Gerald G. "Direct Explanation of Comprehension Processes." In *Comprehension Instruction,* edited by Gerald G. Duffy, Laura R. Roehler, and Jana Mason. New York: Longman, 1984, pp. 265–80.

Ruddell, Robert B. "Developing Comprehension Abilities: Implications from Research for an Instructional Framework." In *What Research Has to Say about Reading Instruction,* edited by Samuels. Newark, Del.: International Reading Association, 1978, pp. 109–20.

Sapir, Selma, and Wilson, Bernice. *A Professional's Guide to Working with the Learning Disabled Child.* New York: Brunner/Mazel, 1978.

Segedy, M., and Roosevelt, C. "Adapting the Courtroom Trial Format to Literature." *Activities to Promote Critical Thinking: Classroom Practices in Teaching English.* Urbana, Ill.: National Council of Teachers of English, 1986, pp. 88–92.

Siks, Geraldine. *Creative Dramatics: An Art for Children.* New York: Harper Brothers, 1958.

_____ . *Drama with Children.* New York: Harper & Row, 1983.

Sloyer, Shirlee. *Reader's Theatre: Story Dramatization in the Classroom.* Urbana, Ill.: National Council of Teachers of English, 1982.

Smith, Christine C. "The Relationship between Teacher-Pupil Interaction and Progress of Pupils with Reading Disabilities." *Reading Improvement* 17 (Spring 1980): 53–65.

Squire, J. "The History of the Profession." *Handbook of Research on Teaching the English Language Arts,* edited by J. Flood, J. Jensen, D. Lapp, and J. Squire. New York: Macmillan, 1991, pp. 3–17.

Taba, Hilda; Levine, Samuel; and Elzey, Freeman F. *Thinking in Elementary School Children: Cooperative Research Project Number 1574.* Washington, D.C.: Research Program of the Office of Education, U.S. Department of Health, Education, and Welfare, 1964.

Tanner, Fran Averett. *Creative Communication, Projects in Acting, Speaking, Oral Reading.* Pocatello, Idaho: Clark Publishing Company, 1979.

Taylor, Gail Cohen. "Creative Dramatics for Handicapped Children." *Language Arts* 57 (January 1980): 92–97.

Torgesen, Joseph K. "Factors Related to Poor Performance on Memory Tasks in Reading Disabled Children." *Learning Disability Quarterly* 2 (Summer 1979): 17–23.

Valencia, S.; Stallman, A.; Commeyras, M.; Pearson, P. D.; and Hartman, D. "Four Measures of Topical Knowledge: A Study of Construct Validity." *Reading Research Quarterly* 26 (1991): 204–33.

Valentinetti, Aurora. "Discovering the World of Puppets." In *Drama with Children,* edited by Geraldine Siks. New York: Harper & Row, 1977.

Wallace, Gerald, and McLoughlin, James A. *Learning Disabilities: Concepts and Characteristics,* 3d ed. Columbus, Oh.: Merrill Publishing Co., 1988.

Whitehurst, C. J.; Falco, F. L.; Lonigan, C. G.; Fischel, J. E.; DeBaryshe, B. D.; Valdez-Menchaca, M. C.; and Calfield, M. "Accelerating Language Development through Picture Book Reading." *Developmental Psychology* 24 (1988): 552–59.

CHILDREN'S LITERATURE REFERENCES

Anno, Mitsumasa. *Anno's Britain*. New York: Philomel, 1982.

_____ . *Anno's Italy*. Ontario, Canada: Collins, 1980.

_____ . *Anno's Journey*. New York: Philomel, 1978.

Berenzy, Alix. *A Frog Prince*. New York: Henry Holt, 1989.

Bunting, Eve. *Ghost's Hour, Spook's Hour*. Illustrated by Donald Clark. New York: Clarion, 1987.

Collington, Peter. *The Angel and the Soldier Boy*. New York: Knopf, 1987.

_____ . *On Christmas Eve*. New York: Knopf, 1990.

Drescher, Henrik. *The Yellow Umbrella*. New York: Bradbury, 1987.

Forbes, Esther. *Johnny Tremain*. Boston: Houghton Mifflin Co., 1943.

Fox, Mem. *Hattie and the Fox*. Illustrated by Patricia Mullins. New York: Bradbury, 1987.

Grimm, Brothers, retold by Josef Palecek. *The Bremen Town Musicians*. Saxonville, M. A.: Picture Book Studio, 1988.

Hayes, Sarah. *Bad Egg: The True Story of Humpty Dumpty*. Illustrated by Charlotte Voake. Boston: Little, Brown & Co., 1987.

Hooks, William H. *Moss Gown*. Illustrated by Donald Carrick. New York: Clarion, 1987.

Khalsa, Dayal Kaur. *I Want a Dog*. New York: Potter, 1987.

Kipling, Rudyard. *Just So Stories*. New York: Macmillan Co., 1902; Viking, 1987.

McCully, Emily Arnold. *New Baby*. New York: Harper & Row, 1988.

_____ . *Picnic*. New York: Harper & Row, 1984.

_____ . *School*. New York: Harper & Row, 1987.

MacLachlan, Patricia. *Sarah, Plain and Tall*. New York: Harper & Row, 1985.

Mahy, Margaret. *17 Kings and 42 Elephants*. Illustrated by Patricia MacCarthy. New York: Dial Press, 1987.

Martin, Bill, Jr., and Archambault, John. *Knots on a Counting Rope*. Illustrated by Ted Rand. New York: Holt, Rinehart & Winston, 1987.

Mayer, Mercer. *A Boy, a Dog, and a Frog*. New York: Dial Press, 1967.

_____ . *A Boy, a Dog, a Frog, and a Friend*. New York: Dial Press, 1971.

_____ . *Frog Goes to Dinner*. New York: Dial Press, 1974.

_____ . *Frog, Where Are You?* New York: Dial Press, 1969.

Milne, A. A. *Winnie the Pooh*. New York: E. P. Dutton, 1926, 1954.

Pyle, Howard. *The Merry Adventures of Robin Hood*. New York: Charles Scribner's Sons, 1946 (1883).

Sendak, Maurice. *Where the Wild Things Are*. New York: Harper & Row, 1963.

Speare, Elizabeth George. *The Witch of Blackbird Pond*. Boston: Houghton Mifflin Co., 1958.

Steptoe, John. *Mufaro's Beautiful Daughters: An African Tale*. New York: Lothrop, Lee & Shepard, 1987.

Stevens, Janet. *The Tortoise and the Hare*. New York: Holiday, 1984.

Stevenson, Robert Louis. *Treasure Island*. New York: Charles Scribner's Sons, 1911.

Van Allsburg, Chris. *The Mysteries of Harris Burdick*. Boston: Houghton Mifflin Co., 1984.

Wells, Rosemary, adapted by. *The Little Lame Prince*. Based on a story by Dinah Maria Mulock Craik. New York: Dial, 1990.

White, E. B. *Charlotte's Web*. New York: Harper & Row, 1952.

Wiesner, David. *Free Fall*. New York: Lothrop, Lee & Shepard, 1988.

Yorinks, Arthur. *Hey, Al*. New York: Farrar, Straus & Giroux, 1986.

Chapter Four

After completing this chapter on listening, you will be able to:

1. *Develop a comprehensive definition of listening.*
2. *Appreciate the importance of motivation and child involvement to listening improvement and describe classroom conditions and teacher behaviors conducive to good listening.*
3. *Evaluate students' ability to select and to use effective listening strategies.*
4. *Understand the importance of auditory discrimination.*
5. *Understand the importance of attentive listening, demonstrate several ways to diagnose a child's ability to listen attentively, and plan a series of lessons for improving attentive listening.*
6. *Evaluate listening comprehension tests, diagnose a student's level of listening comprehension, and develop directed listening for a specific purpose.*
7. *Develop activities that increase appreciative listening.*

Listening

*R*ecent research indicates that elementary children spend over 50 percent of their classroom time listening. According to Strother (1987), teachers expect children to listen 60 percent of the day, and half of that time listening to the teacher. Authorities stress, however, that children do not automatically learn the varied skills necessary for comprehensive listening. In addition, in a society where children are bombarded by the mass media, instruction in critical listening is vital to minimize conformity, misconceptions, prejudices, and stereotypes. In developing effective curriculums, teachers must understand the components of listening, how to assess listening abilities, and how to use instructional strategies that improve listening ability in children.

There is a strong relationship between the instructional strategies discussed in the previous chapter on oral language and those in this listening chapter. Listening, oral language, literature, and writing are all closely related. For example, the modeling activity described in Chapter 3 (pp. 79–82) includes choosing an appropriate literature selection; listening to the story; writing short responses; and discussing answers, evidence, and reasoning. Responding to the story requires analyzing content and describing personal feelings and background knowledge. As we develop the strategies in this listening chapter, you will notice these close relationships.

Listening is a complex topic. In fact, even education authorities do not fully agree on a definition of listening. For example, various studies define listening as ability to hear sounds (hearing), ability to distinguish differences in the sounds heard (auditory perception), ability to concentrate on what is heard (attentive listening), ability to comprehend and critically evaluate what is heard (listening comprehension), and ability to appreciate what is heard (appreciative listening). Obviously, all of these definitions are useful, but the teaching purposes, classroom environments, and assessment strategies associated with each one may differ. In this chapter we will describe listening assessment and instruction encompassing hearing, auditory perception, attention and concentration, listening comprehension, and listening appreciation. Assessment will focus on informal strategies that teachers develop themselves.

The various listening categories imply that students listen for a variety of reasons. It follows that the ways in which students approach listening tasks should change depending on the listening situation and the purpose for listening. Educators who are interested in the process approaches to instruction and self-monitoring strategies emphasize a need to teach appropriate listening strategies.

CLASSROOM ENVIRONMENTS THAT PROMOTE LISTENING

In order to teach some types of listening, visual and auditory distractions must be kept to a minimum. For example, a teacher of a group of open-classroom first graders found that he had to find a quiet and less visually distracting environment for both assessing and teaching the auditory discrimination skills that were recommended in his teacher's manual before the introduction of vowel sounds. This teacher used movable bookshelves and screens to create a small area in the classroom where there would be few distractions. Another teacher in an open classroom moved to the gym to present the rhythms and movements of a listening experience. For students with hearing loss, special seating arrangements may be required to put them close to the sound source.

In a review of research on developing listening abilities, Funk and Funk (1989) provide the following guidelines:

1. Teachers and students should state the purpose for listening. Students should be given specific purposes for each listening experience. They should approach listening differently depending on the purpose; for example, listening for a main idea, differentiating fact from opinion, or visualizing and responding to vivid language in a literature selection or to pleasing passages in music.

2. Teachers and students should set the stage for listening. This requires a classroom atmosphere conducive to listening for the intended purpose. Teachers may need to provide interesting lead-up activities as well as create the atmosphere.

3. Follow-up activities should be used to help achieve listening goals and encourage students to apply their new information and techniques. Art projects, writing assignments, library research, and choral arrangements are a few possibilities.

4. Teachers should use instructional techniques that promote and develop positive listening habits. The techniques should include many different types of listening experiences, for example, listening to and responding to stories, poetry, and music. Critical analysis can be fostered by having students listen to determine a speaker's intention or bias. Students should be involved in strategies that improve listening comprehension as well as reading comprehension.

Lundsteen's (1979) review of listening research adds several suggestions to the preceding guidelines. She recommends that teachers select and develop listening materials at the appropriate levels of difficulty, appreciate why listening instruction is important and guide children toward this realization, avoid needless repetition, encourage children to expect meaning from what they hear, and help children transfer listening ability to new contexts.

Listening is an active rather than passive activity. You should encourage students to participate in improving their abilities by asking them to restate questions, directions, and explanations. You should also develop their abilities through a variety of activities in which they see the consequences of their listening. Can they see that they enjoy listening to a story, to a good television show, or to a musical selection? Can they see that they enjoy playing a game when they have understood the directions? Can they see that they understand a subject better if they have participated in the class discussion? Can they see that they may lose some freedom of choice if they are not able to evaluate critically and act on what they hear?

You can improve a student's listening skills through specific instruction. Also, you may teach listening as part of many content areas, such as reading, literature, music, social studies, and science. Help students develop their own effective listening goals. If students do not see the necessity for and benefits of improved listening, they will not be motivated toward better listening and will not reach the desired level of competence.

Some student teachers have been disappointed in their listening lessons when they have not included their students in the initial planning. For example, one student teacher asked third graders to listen to a story record, then asked them specific questions about the content. She had not adequately prepared the class for the listening activity, and was disappointed in the results. She realized her problem and approached the next lesson quite differently. This time, she asked children to list the various listening activities they performed in a day. Then, they listened to several quite different activities, including specific oral directions for a worksheet, a short story for pleasure, and a short oral presentation on brushing their teeth. The class discussed the purposes for listening in each situation and the students included the consequences of good and poor listening for each activity. Finally, they set up guidelines to utilize in improving their own listening ability, including the following:

1. I will get ready for listening by getting rid of distractions.
2. I will know my purpose for listening.
3. I will concentrate on the listening activity.
4. I will expect to get meaning from the listening activity.
5. I will try to see in my mind what I hear.
6. If I am listening to a speaker, I will ask myself:
   a. Did I know the speaker's purpose for speaking?
   b. Did I know my purpose for listening?
   c. Did the speaker back up his or her ideas?
   d. Did I ask intelligent questions?
   e. Can I retell in my own words what the speaker said?

Guidelines developed by students are stronger instructional motivators than are guidelines developed by teachers. The teacher in the preceding example learned that using their own guidelines, the students in the class could judge their own behavior based on their own recommendations.

HEARING

Hearing without distortion is prerequisite to listening. The term *auditory acuity* is usually applied to hearing, and the lack of this acuity is deafness. In school settings, nurses and trained teachers usually administer hearing tests. However, teachers should also observe children informally for indications of hearing problems. If a child frequently asks for directions to be repeated, rubs his or her ears, or does not speak clearly, the child may have hearing loss and should be referred for further testing and, if necessary, diagnosis by a hearing specialist.

Children listen under such diverse circumstances and for such different purposes that it is impossible to evaluate listening ability through the administration of only one hearing test. You may evaluate listening informally in the course of many of the activities recommended in this chapter. Lundsteen (1979) maintains that evaluation of listening requires live listening situations involving a wide range of activities.

Auditory Perception

Auditory perception may also be a prerequisite for effective listening. Auditory perception tests evaluate such factors as (1) whether children recognize that different sounds have different meanings; (2) whether children are able to distinguish one sound from another (auditory discrimination); (3) whether children are able to blend sounds together to form words (auditory blending); and (4) whether children are able to hear sounds, remember the sounds, and repeat them in the same sequence they hear them (auditory sequential memory). Children with auditory perception problems may have difficulty with reading or spelling approaches that rely heavily on sound and letter relationships. As shown in the following examples, children are likely to enjoy auditory perception activities, which are often developed in the form of games.

Auditory Awareness

Auditory awareness is a fundamental skill. It requires that children hear and discriminate among sounds in the classroom, the home, and the rest of their environment. An instructional activity might consist of listening to and identifying sounds in a barnyard, on a street, at an airport, and so forth. One kindergarten teacher handled such an activity successfully by having the class walk around inside and then outside the school building. The children stopped periodically to close their eyes and listen to the sounds around them. They discovered, among other things, the difference between kitchen and playground sounds. After several experiences with sound awareness, the teacher taped sounds from different locations. The children listened to the tapes, identified the sounds, and classified them according to their locations.

You also can develop auditory awareness through the use of a sound box. Place several objects that have a characteristic sound on a box or tray. You might select a bell for ringing, a ball for bouncing, water for pouring, an egg beater for mixing, and a whistle for blowing. Using a screen to hide the objects, sound each object. Have the students listen carefully and identify the various sounds. Children can also bring in objects from home with which to try to mystify their classmates.

Other auditory awareness activities include imitation of animal sounds or other imitation sound games in which students or teachers present sounds for students to copy. Rhythm instruments and the piano are good props for sound awareness activities. Children can identify the sounds of rhythm sticks, blocks, triangles, and tambourines. They can imitate a pattern of sounds with these instruments, or can move—rapidly or slowly, sadly or joyfully—according to the rhythm of the instruments.

Listening to music, rhymes, and limericks helps children become aware of the lovely sounds in language. Older children can also listen to old radio broadcasts, available on records and tapes, and try to identify and duplicate the sound effects.

Auditory Discrimination

The most commonly evaluated auditory perception ability within classrooms is auditory discrimination, the ability to hear differences in letter sounds, words, and nonsense syllables. For example, can children discriminate between *bit* and *bet*? Most reading readiness programs include considerable work in auditory discrimination.

If auditory discrimination is a prerequisite skill for phonics, then, according to Harris and Sipay (1985), the most effective time to teach this skill is immediately before the corresponding discrimination is to be used in printed words. Thus, you must evaluate the sequence of the instructional program as well as assess the ability of the children to perform the required tasks.

Auditory discrimination can be measured by either standardized, norm-referenced tests or teacher-constructed informal approaches. The Wepman Audi-

Listening is an active, complex process.

tory Discrimination Test (1973) is the best-known standardized test of auditory discrimination. The test is designed to be used with children five through eight years old. The examiner reads two words to a child, who is positioned so that he or she cannot see the examiner's mouth. The child then states whether the words are alike or different. This individually administered test requires about five minutes for completion. Another type of auditory discrimination test for young children is part of the reading readiness test administered to many kindergarten and first-grade students.

Auditory discrimination of sounds, words, and rhymes   Auditory discrimination of likenesses and differences in sounds, words, and rhymes requires finer auditory perception than does auditory awareness. Provide opportunities for children to decide whether two musical sounds are the same or different. For example, play two notes on the piano and have the students say whether the notes are the same or different. Have them compare loudness and softness as well as high and low pitch.

Auditory discrimination activities can easily become games. Clap two patterns that may be either alike or different, and have the children tell whether the two patterns were the same or different.

If you consider auditory discrimination a reading readiness skill, then include activities in which the children discriminate between likenesses and differences in words. Carefully pronounce two words, such as *red* and *roll,* and have the children indicate whether they are the same or different. Have the children form a circle and close their eyes to listen carefully to the two words. If the words are the same, as, for example, *pet* and *pet,* have them raise their hands; if the words are different (for example, *mother* and *father*), tell them not to raise their hands.

Rhyming elements in words, nursery rhymes, jingles, and stories provide many opportunities to develop auditory discrimination and an awareness of the pleasure to be gained from word sounds. Dr. Seuss books are especially good for this activity. Read *The Cat in the Hat,* then reread it with the rhyming words deleted, to be supplied by the class. You also may utilize well-known nursery rhymes for this activity. For other rhyming activities, you can do the following:

1. Prepare two sentences in which the last words both rhyme. Read the sentences, omitting the final word, and ask the class to supply the missing rhyming word. (Several answers may be correct.)
    I just built a boat. I hope it will _____ . (float)
    The big black cat wore a funny yellow _____ . (hat)
    The robin built a nest. It was the very _____ . (best)
2. Use a series of pictures that have several rhyming elements, such as *sack, bat, cat, track, hat, black.* Have the pictures in random order and ask the students to put the rhyming pictures together. You can use a flannel board or bulletin board for this activity.
3. Read a sentence and ask the class to supply as many words as they can that rhyme with the final word of the sentence.
    We all went to the store with *Bill.* (*will, pill, kill, mill, hill, fill, still, Jill, shrill*)
    On her head, Mary wore a red *cap.* (*lap, map, gap, strap, trap, tap, clap, flap*)
    The baker made a chocolate *cake.* (*lake, bake, rake, snake, fake, brake, shake*)

Many interesting poems for older children contain lovely rhyming elements. "The Table and the Chair" by Edward Lear (1846, 1871, 1946) describes the adventures of a table and a chair when they decide to take a walk. The poem has such rhyming combinations as *heat-feet, walk-talk, air-chair, table-able, down-town, sound-round,* and *leetle-beetle.* Another comical rhyming poem is "The Plaint of the Camel" by Charles Edward Carryl. In this poem, the poor camel complains in rhyme about his food, his housing, his work loads, and his shape. Some of the rhyming elements are *feed-seed, crunch-lunch, able-stable, enclosed-exposed, noodles-poodles, treated-heated,* and *lumpy-bumpy-jumpy.* Because many of the rhyming words in this poem contain long and short vowels, this poem may also be used for a listening activity connected with medial vowels. The following books contain rhyming elements or repeated phrases and are excellent for auditory discrimination:

- Eve Merriam's *Halloween ABC* (1987)
- Arnold Lobel's *The Random House Book of Mother Goose* (1986)
- Jack Prelutsky's *Read Aloud Rhymes for the Very Young* (1986)
- Jane Yolen's *The Three Bears Rhyme Book* (1987)
- Nadine Westcott's *Peanut Butter and Jelly: A Play Rhyme* (1987)
- Reeve Lindbergh's *The Day the Goose Got Loose* (1990)

Auditory discrimination of beginning, ending, and middle sounds   Auditory discrimination of beginning and ending sounds is usually related to consonant sounds, whereas the auditory discrimination of middle sounds is usually associated with vowel sounds. Kindergarten and first-grade teachers often associate beginning sounds with the names of students in the class, or with common objects in the classroom. One successful first-grade teacher designed a sound board for her classroom. For example, if the letter *m* was being studied, children brought to school concrete examples of items beginning with the sound of *m.* Then, the class discussed and grouped these items on or under a bulletin board. Children also drew items to represent the sounds, such as mittens and monkeys.

Use listening activities in which children listen for and identify a beginning sound that is repeated frequently in a story, such as a writing-phonics review activity for second and third graders, and for an auditory discrimination activity for first graders. For a second/third-grade language arts class, review beginning consonant blends with the children and ask them to write stories that utilize a number of words containing the specific blend being reviewed. Have the second and third graders write these stories and then read them to the first graders. Have the first graders close their eyes, listen carefully, and raise their hands whenever they hear the specific sound in the story. The older children are motivated to write because they know they have an audience, and the first graders are interested in listening to stories written by children they know. Figure 4–1 shows an example of a *gr* story written by a third-grade girl.

Auditory discrimination also includes the ability to tell whether two words end with the same or different sounds. Rhyming activities require a child to listen to a group of sounds; now, ask children to discriminate between the ending consonants, which are usually harder to hear than rhyming sounds. Picture activities similar to those described for beginning sounds are appropriate. For example, show pictures of a mop, tub, cap, top, rug, and cup to the class. Ask the children to place all the pictures that end like *map* on a flannel board.

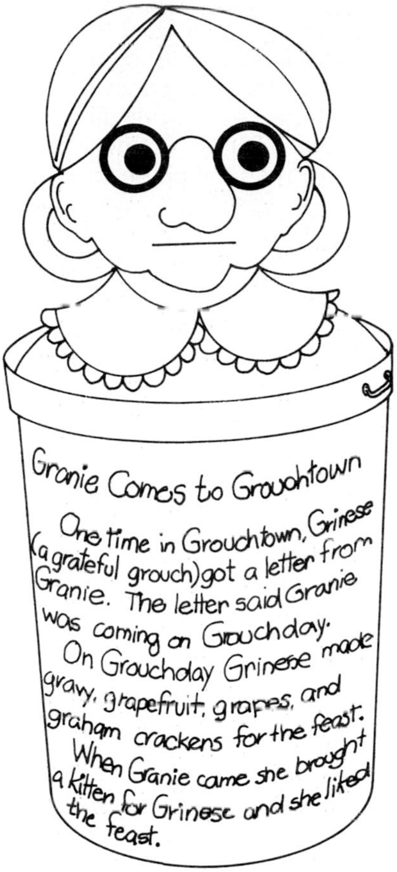

FIGURE 4–1
Gr story written by a third-grade girl

Granie Comes to Grouchtown

One time in Grouchtown, Grinese (a grateful grouch) got a letter from Granie. The letter said Granie was coming on Grouchday.
On Grouchday Grinese made gravy, grapefruit, grapes, and graham crackers for the feast.
When Granie came she brought a kitten for Grinese and she liked the feast.

For another word-ending auditory discrimination activity, pronounce pairs of words and ask the children to tell whether the words end with the same sound or different sounds. Examples include:

cot–cat	dump–clap	trunk–scat	Sam–tan
dad–tub	mail–will	flag–snug	jump–wag

Finally, auditory discrimination includes ability to discriminate between medial sounds. This may be the most difficult auditory discrimination task for many students. Some programs demand that the child master this skill at the beginning of first grade, whereas other programs do not require it until second grade.
Examples of useful words for medial auditory discrimination include:

let–pen	bug–bag	box–got
lift–pig	tap–cat	hug–but
hot–rat	plan–plane	read–red

Auditory Memory

Auditory memory activities include experiences in following and imitating sound, number, and sentence sequences. Auditory memory activities can be as simple as repeating a short, clapped rhythm pattern, or as difficult as repeating complex directions. For elementary children, many auditory memory activities can take the form of games. For example, play a rhythm on the piano or with rhythm sticks and have the class imitate the rhythm. Clap or rap rhythms, then have the class imitate them.

Children enjoy circle repetition games in which one child starts and each child has to repeat the same thing and add a new item. For example, the first child might say, "I'm going on a trip and I'm going to take an apple." The second child would say, "I'm going on a trip and I'm going to take an apple and a _____ ." This game may continue until it is impossible for anyone to remember the sequence of items. Adapt the game to have all items belong to a certain classification, such as food, toys, clothing; follow in alphabetical order, such as *apple, book, cat;* begin with the sound of *b,* such as *book, baby, bottle;* or contain the same vowel sound, such as *table, rake, pail, shape.*

Games of giving simple directions also provide practice in auditory memory. You or the children can present simple, two-part directions, such as "Jennifer, turn the light on and then go to your seat."

A trunk game also provides practice in following simple directions. For this activity, put a number of items, such as a ball, ruler, book, bat, picture, cap, game, toy, and glass, in a box or trunk. The leader names several items he or she would like from the box, and calls on another child to get the items. If the child responds correctly, he or she becomes the new leader and makes the next request.

ATTENTION AND CONCENTRATION

In order to reconstruct messages, listeners must be able to focus on speech sounds and select appropriate cues. Some students are unable to follow verbal instructions adequately because they are easily distracted by competing noises. This is especially true with certain learning-disabled children.

Listening is an active process. It requires participation on the part of the listeners. Poor communication results when students do not pay attention or are thinking about their responses rather than concentrating on what a speaker is saying. Inattentive students may not ask questions when they need clarification for understanding. Readers can stop and reread, but most listening situations do not permit listeners to go back and review what they hear. In addition, listening usually takes place in a public setting; consequently, students may be distracted by noise, mannerisms of a speaker, or actions of other listeners.

Testing for ability to pay attention is complicated by the fact that students may attend to a speaker without understanding. Thus, poor communication can be caused by either inadequate attention or poor ability to process ideas. Otto and Smith (1980) caution that a diagnostic procedure designed to assess attention should not be used to also assess ability to process ideas. These authors prefer informal measures for testing a student's attention.

Informal tests can be administered in many different classroom environments, whereas standardized listening tests are usually administered under con-

Research shows a strong correlation between attentive listening and achievement.

trolled conditions. For this reason, the results of a standardized listening test may not indicate how a student attends in an actual classroom setting. Students may demonstrate completely different attentive-listening responses when tested in an isolated testing room instead of informally during a class activity.

To find out how well children attend during class activities, assess them in various settings and do not inform them that they are being tested. In designing an attentive-listening task for average achievers, make the level of difficulty about the same as the independent reading level. Note however, that the listening ability of remedial students is usually greater than the reading ability.

Ability to follow oral directions explicitly demands attentive listening. You can give oral directions and see which students are able to complete the task, which ones cannot complete the task, and which ones ask you to repeat the directions. For example, a kindergarten teacher might say, "Take out your red crayon, your green crayon, and your brown crayon. Pick out your green crayon and show it to me." (Obviously, do not use this activity unless the children can already identify the colors.) An elementary teacher might say, "Put your spelling book and your arithmetic book on top of your desk. Place your spelling book on top of your arithmetic book so that I can see the spelling book when I walk around the room."

You can carry on this type of informal testing throughout a normal day and in the context of different instructional activities. During a social studies class, you might ask a question that has an easy and obvious answer but that is out of context with what you are discussing. For example, you could say, "Everyone who can tell me what two plus two is, please raise your hand." During a science class, you could read a short paragraph that presents the simple sequential steps of some logical process, then ask the students to summarize the order presented. For example, "Do you often wonder what causes a hard rock to split into several pieces? First, rain falls on the rock. Then, the water runs into cracks in the rock. When the weather is cold and the water freezes, the water expands into ice and widens the cracks. This process continues until the rock finally splits."

Although research has clearly defined the relationship between attention and achievement, it has not been as clear in identifying a methodology that effectively develops attentive listeners. Otto and Smith (1980) suggest the following four factors as causes of inattentiveness: (1) poor motivation to hear a speaker's message; (2) too much teacher talk; (3) excessive distractions; and (4) lack of mental set for anticipating the messages of speakers. Eliminating these four factors should, obviously, improve attentive listening behavior. Review the teacher behaviors essential for developing effective listeners to see how closely these behaviors also relate to developing attentive listening. Involving students in setting instructional listening goals helps overcome some of the problems of poor motivation.

Developing a mental set for purposeful listening may be more difficult than eliminating outside distractions. If students are not able to form mental sets for anticipating messages, they will have difficulty preparing for the types of listening the messages demand. Students who listen to complicated directions with the same mental set they use for listening to a musical recording will undoubtedly have difficulty attending in situations requiring strict accuracy of comprehension.

You may use a number of methods to help students develop the attentive listening required for directions. The school day lends itself to this type of instruction because directions are an essential part of all content areas. Some teachers tape a series of directions that children must follow explicitly. Taping has two advantages. First, it discourages students from asking that directions be repeated before they are given completely. Second, taping reduces excessive teacher talk. A math teacher who is reviewing shapes might, for example, tape the following directions: "Draw a red triangle near the top of your paper. Draw a blue rectangle under the triangle. Draw a green square on the bottom of your paper." After the class has completed the directions, the teacher may replay the tape to let the students verify how well they followed the directions. You may design similar activities around any content directions and be as complicated as is warranted by the ability level of the students.

Games reinforce the teaching of attentive listening to directions. An example of such a game is "Listen, Start, and Stop." To play the game, children form a long line, leaving plenty of room for movement. The leader gives a clear direction, such as "hop on your right foot," "walk using small steps," and "pat your head." Students continue one action until the leader tells them to stop or blows a whistle. Children must stop immediately and turn toward the leader to wait for the next direction. Children who fail to follow directions or to stop immediately are eliminated from the game. The game "Simon Says" is another good listening game.

You should also evaluate a student's ability to give clear directions and to follow oral directions. Pretending that a classmate is a stranger who needs directions to a specific location (principal's office, gym, etc.), have the remainder of the students prepare what they believe are explicit oral directions. Have a class member follow the directions to see if they are indeed adequate. Such an exercise evaluates both listening and oral directions.

Following are some additional activities for developing the ability to follow oral directions:

1. Have students write directions for a specific activity such as setting the table or washing a dog. Ask the students to read their directions without identifying the activity. Classmates must listen carefully and guess what the activity is as soon as they think they have enough clues.
2. Provide oral directions for making a simple object, such as a kite, and have the class make the object without telling them what the object will be.
3. Demonstrate the use of a camera, then ask a child to follow the exact directions to take a picture. This is especially good with instant cameras that provide an immediate picture.

Following directions may be more effective if students number the steps of the oral directions, then repeat the number of steps involved and relate each step to its corresponding number. Helping students map out listening strategies and providing guideposts prior to listening instruction is called ''applying advanced organizers.'' This strategy may be effective with all students, but it is especially appropriate for students with learning problems.

FOR YOUR PLAN BOOK
An Attentive-Listening Unit

The following attentive listening unit includes these objectives:

1. Following a motivational listening activity, the students will be able to realize the importance of attentive listening and develop their own guidelines for good listening.
2. The students will improve their listening skills through the use of listening games and other creative language arts activities.
3. The students will develop creative thinking through a variety of language arts activities, including oral communication, creative writing, and attentive-listening activities.

Use the following procedures to implement the objectives of the unit. First, ask the fourth-grade students to keep track of the approximate time they spend in one day on the following ways of communicating: speaking, listening, writing, and reading. The next day have them discuss their findings. They will find that a great deal of time was spent in listening. Present several types of listening activities, such as following directions, listening to records, and listening to stories, in order to answer specific questions. Have the students list the requirements for each type of listening and develop their own guidelines for listening behavior. (They may find that they are not very attentive listeners.)

Listening games and exercises prove very motivating, and also serve as excellent warm-up drills and challenges to fill free time before a first class period, lunch, and so forth. Listening warm-ups cover three broad areas: (1) reception of sounds, (2) comprehension of listening and understanding the purposes for listening, and (3) reaction to the ideas expressed. The procedures are sequential in nature, starting from simple games and drills and progressing to more challenging activities. Listening games include the following:

1. **Telephone game**—The purpose of this game is to send a secret message around the room, to test a student's ability to listen attentively and to speak clearly. One student starts the message, whispering it to the next student; the last person's response is matched with the beginning message.
2. **Recipe game**—The purpose of this game is to strengthen the ability of students to listen to and recite a sequential list of items. At first, students read recipes; later, they write their own.
3. **Direction game**—When a student reads a task, the remaining students test their ability to follow directions carefully. Students are not allowed to see the written directions.
4. **Morning sounds**—Students are assigned a specific time period and told to record all the sounds they hear during this period.
5. **Noise makers**—This activity uses a variety of sounds to test the aural perception abilities of students and their use of imagination. Students close their eyes and try to identify various noises. They use creative thinking to choose noises that will stump their classmates.

You may use many activities to stimulate creative thinking and listening, including role playing, which you can motivate by large action pictures of events common to most of the students, or hypothetical situations, in which students listen to a taped discussion, then role-play their reactions. Let other students listen to the role playing and discuss their reactions and the reasons for them. Have students write and tape many of the situations. Tapes of country sounds and city sounds provide opportunities to listen attentively, categorize the sounds, and specifically identify each sound. Let students listen to the beginning of a story and create an oral or written ending to the story. Finally, let students listen to television commercials and try to summarize what they hear. After the students listen to commercials, let them write their own commercials and present them to classmates, who, in turn, must listen attentively in order to summarize what they hear.

Following the completion of this listening unit, use the same types of listening experiences that you used to evaluate listening needs at the beginning of the unit. A majority of the students should improve in all types of listening. Informal observations should show that students require less repetition of directions and demonstrate greater accuracy in listening situations. In addition, speaking skills should improve.

Remember to involve students in setting their own goals. Remember also that listening improvement is a continuous activity.

LISTENING COMPREHENSION

Listening, or auditory, comprehension refers to the highly conscious seeking of meaning from a listening experience. Children may listen for factual or literal understanding, or they may reach the higher level of listening that Lundsteen

(1979) refers to as "thinking beyond listening." This level of listening involves such skills as classifying information, categorizing, indexing, comparing, defining, predicting, applying, seeing cause-and-effect relationships, critically evaluating, appreciating, and solving problems creatively.

Following a review of listening comprehension research, Pearson and Fielding (1982) draw the following conclusions about teaching listening comprehension:

1. Direct teaching of listening strategies appears to help children become more conscious of their listening habits than do more incidental approaches.
2. Listening training in the same skills typically taught during reading comprehension tends to improve listening comprehension (such as for main idea, inference, sequence).
3. Active verbal responses on the part of students during and following listening enhance listening comprehension.
4. Listening to literature tends to improve listening comprehension.
5. Instruction directed toward writing or reading comprehension may also improve listening comprehension.

These conclusions suggest ways to improve listening comprehension. They are also useful for developing assessment strategies that are closely related to curricular objectives. Furthermore, the conclusions indicate that listening comprehension may enrich the content areas. Carefully selected activities teach or reinforce content as well as enhance listening capabilities.

Assessing Listening Comprehension

Teachers frequently choose to include results from informal assessments for listening comprehension in the portfolios of students. One technique for measuring listening comprehension individually is administering an informal inventory. The inventory may be ready-made, or it may be developed by the teacher. Inventories that have been published usually have three forms, each of which includes paragraphs followed by comprehension questions for preprimary through eighth-grade levels. In order to test listening comprehension, read the paragraphs to the student. After each paragraph, ask the students to answer factual, vocabulary, and inference questions. The highest level at which a child correctly answers 90 percent of the oral comprehension questions is considered the independent level of listening comprehension. The level at which the student is able to answer 75 percent of the comprehension questions correctly is considered the instructional listening comprehension level.

One example of a listening comprehension inventory is the *Analytical Reading Inventory* by Woods and Moe (1989). This inventory has three forms, with paragraphs ranging in difficulty from primary through ninth grade. The paragraphs are followed by questions categorized according to main idea, facts, terminology, cause and effect, inferences, and conclusions. In addition to describing this inventory, Pikulski (1990) provides useful descriptions of three other IRIs: the *Basic Reading Inventory* (Johns, 1988), the *Classroom Reading Inventory* (Silvaroli, 1989), and the *Informal Reading Inventory* (Burns and Roe, 1989). Pikulski's chart allows teachers to compare the strengths and weaknesses of these inventories. If teachers choose to use ready-made reading inventories, they should analyze each and decide which one provides them with the most useful information. Such inventories enable teachers to analyze which types of questions are causing comprehension problems.

Tompkins, Friend, and Smith (1987) identify a series of questions that students should ask themselves as they select a listening strategy and monitor the effectiveness of their choice (see Table 4–1). Teachers may develop such a chart to help individual children evaluate their own listening strategies and to evaluate the effectiveness of listening behaviors and instruction.

Comprehension Strategies

Tompkins et al. (1987) differentiate between a practice approach and a strategies approach to listening instruction. In the practice approach, which frequently dominates classroom instruction, students listen to an oral presentation and then an-

TABLE 4–1
Selecting and evaluating effective listening strategies

I.	Before listening the student asks and answers the following questions:
	1. What is the speaker's purpose?
	2. What is my purpose for listening?
	3. What am I going to do with what I listen to?
	4. Will I need to take notes?
	5. Which strategies could I use?
	a. Imaging?
	b. Categorizing?
	c. Self-questioning?
	d. Discovering the organizational plan?
	e. Note-taking?
	f. Clues from the speaker?
	6. Which one [or ones] will I select?
II.	During listening the student asks and answers the following questions:
	1. Is my strategy still working?
	2. Am I putting information into groups?
	3. Is the speaker giving me clues about the organization of the message?
	4. Is the speaker giving me nonverbal cues such as gestures and varied facial expressions?
	5. Is the speaker's voice—pitch, speed, pauses, and repetitions—giving me other clues?
III.	After listening the student asks and answers the following questions:
	1. Do I have questions for the speaker?
	2. Was any part of the message unclear?
	3. Are my notes complete?
	4. Did I make a good strategy choice? Why or why not?

SOURCE: Numbered questions from "Listening Strategies for the Language Arts" (p. 39) by G. E. Tompkins, M. Friend, and P. L. Smith, 1987. In *Language Arts Instruction and the Beginning Teacher,* edited by Carl Personke and Dale Johnson, Englewood Cliffs, N.J.: Prentice-Hall. Reprinted by permission.

swer questions about the presentation. This approach assumes that students know what to do when they are given the listening assignment. Unfortunately, this may not be the case. In contrast, the strategies approach teaches strategies that students can use during a listening experience to make the message they receive clearer and easier to remember. The strategies approach helps students develop a repertoire of possible listening strategies, teaches students to make conscious choices when selecting appropriate strategies for specific listening situations, and teaches students to monitor the effectiveness of their choices. A listening strategy approach assumes that listening practice follows rather than precedes or replaces strategy instruction.

The listening strategies recommended by Tompkins et al. include imaging (teaching students to make pictures in their minds and to visualize details and descriptions), categorizing (teaching students to group or to cluster information), self-questioning (teaching students to monitor their own understanding by asking themselves such questions as "Could I explain this to someone else?"), discovering the organizational plan (teaching students to recognize and to use such patterns as comparison-contrast, problem-solution, cause-effect, description, and time-order when they are trying to comprehend and to remember oral presentations), note taking (teaching students to match their purposes for listening with the types of notes they take), and getting clues from the speaker (teaching students to recognize such clues as gestures, facial expressions, and written information on chalkboards that speakers use to convey important messages).

The strategies approach also benefits from the modeling approach. Within the modeling approach, teachers demonstrate what they expect students to do during listening instruction by discussing the requirements and purposes for each listening strategy, providing examples of that listening strategy, sharing their own thought processes as they approach and accomplish the listening task, and exploring the reasoning process used during that listening task.

Main ideas   You can incorporate listening for main ideas into any content area. One successful method of instruction is to have children identify their purpose for listening. During this activity, read a short story or several paragraphs aloud and then ask the children to supply a good title for the selection. The best titles usually contain the main idea of the selection. For example, a social studies teacher might read the following paragraph:

> Mount Everest in Tibet is the highest spot on earth and is a challenge to mountain climbers. From 1922 until 1952 many climbers tried to reach the top of Everest but all failed to reach the dangerous summit. In 1953 a British expedition tried again to reach the summit. Inch by inch the group struggled over the ice-packed surface. The air was so thin and cold that the climbers finally had to put oxygen tanks on their backs in order to breathe at such heights. Finally, on May 29, 1953, two members of the group, Edmund Hillary and Tenzing Norkey, reached the summit. At last, Everest had been conquered.

After the oral presentation, ask students to offer their ideas for the best title. Write the suggested titles on the chalkboard and let the students discuss and defend their appropriateness and completeness. Use simpler paragraphs for early-elementary classes.

Two other methods are useful in helping students listen for the main idea:

1. Before you read several paragraphs, have students listen to oral sub-headings. Ask them to turn the subheadings into questions to answer after listening to the selection. For example, a science subheading "The Shape of Molecules" could be changed to the question, "What is the shape of molecules?" This procedure helps students develop a purpose for hearing specific information.

2. Have children listen to a story. Stop periodically to have them summarize the main ideas of the selection up to that point.

Important details   Students often have trouble differentiating between important and insignificant details. For example, one student listening to a description about Henry Ford's invention of the Model T could remember only that the car was black. Although this was an interesting detail, it was not one of the most significant details of the selection. Listening for important details is closely related to listening for main ideas because important details support the main ideas.

Children can listen for supporting information as well as for the main idea in paragraphs such as that describing the dangerous conquest of Mt. Everest. Science books provide excellent sources for such material.

Briefly outlining an orally presented selection will also help students listen for both main ideas and supporting details. For example, a group of third graders listened to an introduction to the study of plants. The selection was called "Plants Are Important to People." The group first discussed the title and their purpose for listening to the selection. Next, the teacher asked for suggestions on how to turn the title into a question that would guide their selective listening. After writing the question on the chalkboard, the teacher read the selection to the class. Finally, the class developed an outline that answered their purpose question.

Why Are Plants Important to People?

A.   Plants give people oxygen to breathe.
B.   Plants give people food to eat.
C.   Plants like cotton give people clothes to wear.
D.   Trees are plants that give people houses.
E.   Plants decay and give people coal to burn.

This activity helped the students define their purpose for listening and organize the presentation logically. Following are some other activities for helping children listen for important details:

1. Present a selection orally and have students classify the details according to whether they are important, helpful, or unnecessary.

2. Read a descriptive selection to your class. Find a selection that mentions such characteristics as size, color, texture, and number. Have the class listen carefully for descriptive details, then draw a picture that accurately represents the details. Wordless books such as Pat Hutchins's *Changes, Changes* (1971) and Tana Hoban's *Round & Round & Round* (1983) can provide source material for descriptive text developed by teachers. Informational books such as Margery Facklam's *And Then There Was One: The Mysteries of Extinction* (1990), Helen Roney Sattler's *Giraffes, The Sen-*

Children need to learn to listen for important details that support main ideas.

tinels of the Savannas (1989), and Patricia Lauber's *Volcano: The Eruption and Healing of Mount St. Helens* (1986) provide detailed descriptions of science-related topics for older students.

3. Have students write detailed descriptions of characters in familiar stories. Have them read their descriptions to the class without naming the character. Let classmates try to identify the character and indicate which details were most helpful to them. Similar folktales from different cultures provide interesting sources for this activity. For example, have students describe the German Cinderella in a Grimms' version, the Vietnamese Cinderella from Ann Nolan Clark's *In the Land of Small Dragon* (1979), the Egyptian Cinderella in Shirley Climo's *The Egyptian Cinderella* (1989), and the Zuni version "Poor Turkey Girl" found in Virginia Haviland's *North American Legends* (1979). In these examples, cultural information adds to the descriptions.

4. While one child reads a detailed description, have another draw the character described without knowing the identity of the character. Then, have the partners compare the picture with the original description.

5. Tape imaginary or real conversations between two famous people in history, two people with different occupations, or two school employees. Have students listen carefully for details that suggest the identities of the individuals.

Sequences Point out to your students that both speakers and writers use signal words to help organize selections. Have students listen to oral presentations in which signal words are used. For example, have students listen to the following oral presentation to discover the usefulness of signal words:

> A moth that you see flying from plant to plant in the garden has not always been able to fly. In fact, there are four different stages in the life of that moth. The first stage in the life cycle of the moth is an egg. During the second stage the caterpillar hatches from the egg and starts to eat plants. After the caterpillar has been eating your garden plants for several weeks, he spins a cocoon of silk all around himself. During this third stage in the moth's cycle, he sleeps while his body actually changes. Finally, the cocoon breaks open and out flies the moth.

Which words in the preceding paragraph signal a sequence of events that actually took place? Help students discover the usefulness of the purpose statement "there are four different stages in the life of that moth" and that each cycle is identified with signal words—*first, second, third,* and *finally.*

Other useful sequential signal words and phrases are "to begin with," "at the same time," *before, after, previously,* "my next point," and "my final point." Signal words that emphasize a speaker's conclusion also deserve attention—"in conclusion," "in summation," *thus, consequently, therefore,* and *hence.*

Time lines are exceptionally appropriate devices to help students understand the sequences of orally presented selections. A group of fourth graders, interested in the study of aviation, developed the time line shown in Figure 4–2 after seeing and listening to several films and stories about aviation. Also, you can present this kind of time line before a listening activity as a visual advanced organizer for students who need more help than usual.

Other activities to help students listen for sequence include the following:

1. Cut up a story into paragraphs. Paste each paragraph on a piece of cardboard. Read the selection in proper sequence and have students place the mixed paragraphs into the right order.

2. Divide a sequentially developed paragraph into sentences. Paste the sentences on cardboard. Have students listen to the paragraph and place the sentences into proper sequence.

3. Comic strips work well for developing sequential skills. Have students listen while you read aloud a comic strip, then have them put individual panels into the right order.

4. A flannel board provides an excellent opportunity for children to listen to a story, hear its sequential organization, then retell the story in appropriate sequence.

1783 — World's first recorded balloon flight — passengers included a rooster, a
        duck, and a sheep
1900 — Zeppelin was developed in Germany
1903 — Wright brothers flew at Kitty Hawk
1927 — Lindbergh flew the *Spirit of St. Louis* across the Atlantic from New York to Paris
1932 — Amelia Earhart became the first woman to fly across the Atlantic
1937 — Hindenberg burned and crashed
1945 — Fighter planes used in World War II could go 450 miles per hour
1950 — American Air Force used mostly jets during Korean War
1970s — Space travel
1980s — Space shuttles

FIGURE 4–2
Aviation time line

Predicting outcomes   When children are asked to predict what happens next in
a story or speech, they draw on their ability to understand sequential relationships.
Predicting also requires children to listen carefully to the story so they can find out
whether or not their predictions were accurate. One useful technique is to have
students listen to the chapter titles of a book and predict what will be in each chapter.

For example, before reading *Runaway Slave—The Story of Harriet Tubman*, ask
third-grade children to listen to the title of each chapter and write a brief prediction
about what information they think will appear in the chapter. Writing involves each
student in making predictions. After reading and discussing the title so everyone
understands the time in which the book takes place, review the concept of slave.
Then, read each chapter title aloud, allowing enough time between titles for each
student to write a brief prediction. Have the class discuss their predictions and give
reasons for them. The chapter headings include: Who Was Harriet Tubman?; At
Miss Susan's; Follow the North Star; Trouble; I'm Going to Leave You; Harriet
Tubman, Conductor; Nighttime, Daytime; Go On—Or Die; A Sad Christmas; and
The War Years. After each chapter, have the students review the accuracy of their
predictions. This activity is also highly motivating because each child must listen
carefully to see if his or her predictions are correct.

Following are other activities for predicting outcomes:

1. Present a selection such as Mildred Pitts Walter's *Brother to the Wind* (1985)
   or Arthur Yorinks's *Hey, Al* (1986) orally and stop at an interesting point in the
   story. Have students tell or write how they think the story will end.
2. Orally present short descriptions of stories such as Hans Christian
   Andersen's *The Emperor's New Clothes* (1982), Michael Bond's *A Bear
   Called Paddington* (1960), Nathan Zimelman's *Treed by a Pride of Irate
   Lions* (1990), E. B. White's *Charlotte's Web* (1952), Caroline Arnold's *Saving the Peregrine Falcon* (1985), Jean Fritz's *Make Way for Sam Houston*
   (1986), and Colleen Bare's *Guinea Pigs Don't Read Books* (1985). Ask the
   children to predict whether the story will be fact or fantasy and to explain
   their decisions.

3. Films are also useful for predicting outcomes. Show a film until you reach an interesting point. Then, have students finish the story before they see the remainder of the film. You will note that many of the predicted endings may be as good or as logical as the actual endings.

Create a learning center for listening to find activities that will help develop listening for awareness, enjoyment, and specific purposes. The criteria for a listening learning center should include the following:

1. The activities should provide practice in developing one or more of the listening skills stated in the purpose.
2. The students should be able to work independently, either alone or in small groups. The listening material must be available on tape, and directions must be specific.
3. The activities should provide enough enjoyment to motivate without teacher assistance.
4. The activities should use a variety of skills and methods for responding.
5. The center should include activities geared to several ability levels.
6. The activities should be separate; thus, they should not require completion in a certain sequence.
7. The activities should be related to other school subjects and to the listening needs of the individual child.

Prepare the students by discussing the purposes for the activities in the center. Teach the students how to use the equipment in the center, and teach at least one activity to the whole class before students use the center individually. Instruct the students to prepare themselves mentally to concentrate on listening, as athletes concentrate on their sports. Instruct the students on ways to get rid of distractions, to close their eyes, to form a picture in their minds, and to pretend they and the voice or sound are all alone in the room. Specific activities, all on tape, may include:

1. A descriptive paragraph—Have students draw the picture described, then listen again, and correct or add to their pictures in another color.
2. A story—Have students divide their paper into four squares and draw four pictures to show the sequence of story events.
3. The story and poem, "The King's Breakfast"—Have students number in sequence printed sentences that describe the events in the story.
4. Mystery sounds (ball bouncing, blocks hitting together, water pouring, etc.)—Have students attempt to identify each sound.
5. Classmates' voices—Have students identify each voice.
6. Verbal descriptions of animals and their characteristics—Have the children listen to the tape and match the sounds to the appropriate picture.
7. Vivid verbal descriptions—Have students color a picture after listening to a description.
8. Poems that paint mental pictures, such as "Foul Shot," "Steam Shovel," and "Catalogue," which are all found in Stephen Dunning, Edward Lueders, and Hugh Smith's anthology *Reflections on a Gift of Watermelon Pickle . . . and other Modern Verse* (1967)—Have the students draw the pictures they see in their minds.

9. Pictures of a city street, a farm, a zoo, and a seashore—Have the students view the pictures and list the sounds they would hear if they were in the location of one of the pictures.
10. A funny short story with dialogue between characters, such as Steven Kellogg's *Tallyho, Pinkerton!* (1982)—Have the children listen to the tape and draw the sequences in cartoon style.
11. Several short stories—Have the children write a title for each selection.

Be sure that all activities are carefully planned so that the students can understand the purpose, order, content, and vocabulary of the exercises. Also, be sure to tell the students what to listen for. The best listening activities demand extensive student involvement.

Literature-Related Activities

Literature provides excellent listening materials that encourage active verbal responses, develop understanding of story structure, foster literacy appreciation, and teach reading. Activities that involve children during a story experience also foster language development and cognitive development. Books such as Arthur Geisert's *Pigs from A to Z* (1986) encourage children to interact with the text during a listening experience. Listening activities are also important for improving comprehension. For example, according to Vosniadou, Pearson, and Rogers (1988), students can detect inconsistencies better when listening to a story than when reading a story. When the topic is familiar, even first graders can detect inconsistencies during a listening experience.

As we have mentioned, listening, oral language, literature, and writing are closely related. The quality of literature read aloud to and discussed by students affects their writing. Discussion helps some students improve their writing if the discussion focuses on the techniques used by the authors and if it encourages the students to use those techniques in their own writing. Discussions that highlight aspects of the narrative structure also improve writing. Asking students to identify and discuss story elements in legends and fables improves students' writing. In a study conducted with fifth graders, Dressel (1990) reports that students who listened to and discussed high-quality literature produced better writing samples than did students who listened to and discussed literature of lower quality. Dressel emphasizes not only the quality of the literature but the quality of the oral discussion as she describes the study: "First, to avoid the 'reading difficulty' problem, the literature was read aloud. Second, since poetic language requires the reader/listener to consider the work as a whole . . . the text was respected and presented intact. Finally, since research indicates that sensitizing children to story elements as well as to the authors' craft helps them gain metacognitive control over comprehension and writing, a carefully designed program was implemented to encourage the children to examine the literature from the author's perspective" (p. 399).

There is also a close relationship between the quality of the stories heard and the quality of children's retellings. In a study by Hade (1988), for example, the richness of the original stories was reflected in the quality of the children's retellings.

Young children may become acquainted with story structure and language patterns by experiencing stories that have repetitive language patterns, such as "The Three Billy Goats Gruff," or repetitive or cumulative story events, such as "The Gingerbread Boy." Teachers frequently call such books predictable because the repetitive patterns encourage children to hypothesize about words that follow or events that happen next in the story. When using predictable books with children, present a series of activities during which children listen to a story and select the most useful phonemic, syntactic, and semantic information; predict the most probable language or happening; and confirm that their prediction was correct.

McCracken and McCracken (1986) describe a procedure in which they use simple stories to teach beginning reading to kindergarten and first-grade students. The stories they choose are either predictable because of the text or predictable because the children have previously memorized the text. During this type of activity, encourage children to memorize a story or the repetitive parts of a story by repeatedly reading the story to children and encouraging them to join in during the reading. Use pictures to help children follow the story sequence. Next, introduce the children to print by either printing the repetitive parts of the text on the chalkboard or placing accompanying word cards in a pocket chart. During this phase of the reading, point to the words as the class chants the lines. Next, have the children match the words on the word chart with a second identical set of word cards. If the words form a refrain, either place the whole refrain on the chart and have the children match the words by placing identical words on top of the cards or create the first line of the refrain and have the children reproduce the next lines. During this experience give children many opportunities to "read" the text. Next, place the story on phrase cards in a pocket chart. Have the children match these phrases to pictures representing appropriate parts of the story content or appropriate characters and their actions. Place these pictures in appropriate places on the pocket chart. Continue this type of activity, giving the children opportunities for individual and group practice until they can rebuild the entire story. By this time, many of the children will be able to read the completed story.

Tompkins and Weber (1983) provide a five-step teaching strategy that directs the attention of children to repetitive and predictable features of a book. First, read the title aloud, show the cover illustration, and ask the children what they believe the story is about. Second, read through the first set of repetitions and into the point where the second set of repetitions begins. Now, formulate questions that ask children to predict what will happen next or what a character may say. Third, ask the children to explain why they made their predictions. Fourth, read the next set of repetitive patterns to allow children to confirm or reject their predictions. Continue reading the selection as you repeat steps two, three, and four.

The following books contain predictable elements:

- Verna Aardema's *Bringing the Rain to Kapiti Plain* (1981)
- Maggie Duff's *Rum Pum Pum* (1978)
- Mem Fox's *Hattie and the Fox* (1987)
- Paul Galdone's *The Greedy Old Fat Man* (1983)
- Pat Hutchins's *Rosie's Walk* (1968)
- John Ivimey's *Three Blind Mice* (1987)
- Maurice Sendak's *Where the Wild Things Are* (1963)
- Janet Stevens's *The House That Jack Built* (1985)

Levesque (1989) describes a five-part read-aloud strategy, ELVES, designed to develop listening comprehension through the following sequence of activities:

1. Excite—focus the discussion on the listeners' experiences, the literary elements within the story, and predictions about the story.
2. Listen—have the students listen to verify predictions and to comprehend other story elements.
3. Visualize—have the listeners share their mental images.
4. Extend—have the students gain new understandings by relating previous knowledge and new knowledge.
5. Savor—have the students reflect on the story, verbalize their responses, and become involved with follow-up activities, such as writing or reader's theater.

FOR YOUR PLAN BOOK
Using **Owl Moon** to Develop the ELVES Strategy

The following example shows how the ELVES strategy could be developed with Jane Yolen's *Owl Moon* (1987):

Excite: Begin the discussion by posing questions that encourage the students to relate their own experiences to various elements within the story. For example, ask, "Have you ever been out on a winter night when there is a full moon? What could you see and hear?" "Pretend you are in the woods. What would you see and hear?" "Why would you want to go out into the woods on a cold winter night?" Ask questions that encourage students to make predictions about the title and the cover illustration. For example, "What do you think the author means by the title, *Owl Moon*?" "When you look at the cover, describe your feelings. Why do you have those feelings?" "Pretend you are the child on the cover. What are your feelings?" "What do you think will happen to the man and the child as they explore the night in *Owl Moon*?" "What kind of a mood do you think will be developed in the story?"

Listen: Now, read the story and ask the students to listen so that they can see whether their earlier responses and predictions were correct. The students might use signals in particular places in the story to show that they were right or wrong. In addition to having an interesting plot, this story uses vivid language. Encourage students to listen for language that is especially vivid, such as, "I could feel the cold, as if someone's icy hand was palm-down on my back" (p. 11, unnumbered). As you read, ask the students to try to visualize the story so they can describe the woodland setting and how the characters felt and reacted as they walked through the woods.

Visualize: Ask the students to describe their visual images. Pick out especially vivid sections and ask the students to close their eyes and describe what they see and feel as you read or reread these parts. For example, read, "We went into the woods. The shadows were the blackest things I have ever seen. They stained the white snow. My mouth felt furry, for the scarf over it was wet and warm. I didn't ask what kinds of things hide behind black trees in the middle of the night. When you go owling you have to be brave" (p. 13, unnumbered). Then, ask the students what they see and feel.

Extend: Lead a discussion in which students make connections between their previous knowledge and any new insights gained from listening to and experiencing this story. For example, ask, "How would the story change if the setting changed?" "Think about a story that might take place in the same location but in the daytime or in the summer." "What would happen if the story were set at night in a town or city?" "Think about the point of view of the story. How would it change if the story were told through the point of view of the owl?"

Savor: Have students savor the story by describing additional thoughts and feelings about it. As a writing activity, they could write personal responses to the characters of the child, the father, or the owl, or to the vivid language in the book. They could write a story from the owl's point of view, or pretend they are exploring a different setting and searching for something from nature. For a comparative-literature activity, they could compare the stories, the winter settings, and the points of view in *Owl Moon,* Tejima's *Fox Dream* (1987), and Jane Chelsea Aragon's *Winter Harvest* (1988). For oral language activities, they could develop a reader's theater production using *Owl Moon.* They could find poetry that explores winter settings and prepare the poems as choral reading arrangements. Various poems about winter in Jack Prelutsky's *The Random House Book of Poetry for Children* (1983) include A. A. Milne's "The More It Snows," N. M. Bodecker's "When All the World Is Full of Snow," Robert Frost's "Stopping by Woods on a Snowy Evening," Walter de la Mare's "The Snowflake," Jack Prelutsky's "The Four Seasons," John Updike's "January," Charles G. D. Roberts's "Ice," Langston Hughes's "Winter Moon," Kay Starbird's "Wendy in Winter," and Karla Kuskin's "Winter Clothes."

Story Structure

Traditional tales with easily identifiable conflicts, characters, settings, and plot developments are excellent sources for helping children understand story structure and story elements. The nature of the oral tradition makes it imperative that listeners be brought quickly into the action and identify with the characters. Consequently, tales such as "The Little Red Hen," "Puss in Boots," "Jack the Giant Killer," "Three Billy Goats Gruff," and "The Fisherman and His Wife" allow children to be immersed into the major conflict within the first few sentences, understand the nature and importance of the building conflict, identify the characters and character traits, identify the setting, and recognize major features in plot development. For example, the conflict in Paul Galdone's *The Little Red Hen* is between laziness and industriousness. The first sentence introduces the animals who live together. The second sentence introduces the conflict; that is, the cat, dog, and mouse are lazy. Next, the industrious hen is introduced. The remainder of the story develops conflict between lazy and industrious animals. The conflict is quickly resolved when the hen eats her own baking.

Drawing semantic maps and webs for characters, settings, and plot helps children visualize the relationships between these important elements. Two examples developed around traditional tales illustrate a simpler and a more complex folktale. The first, "Three Billy Goats Gruff," introduces characters and plot in a chronological order, proceeding from littlest to biggest (see Figure 4–3). Notice how the map illustrates the close relationship between the characters and plot.

The second example, the Grimms' "The Fisherman and His Wife," is more complex and more appropriate for older children (see Figure 4–4). The characters change as the tasks change, the setting becomes more turbulent as the demands of the characters increase, and the plot relates directly to changes in characters and setting. Developing a map following a listening activity vividly illustrates these relationships.

Evaluating What Is Heard

The final category of listening comprehension usually mentioned by authorities is the ability to evaluate what is heard. This subject lends itself well to listening to television and radio presentations and to listening to and reading newspaper advertisements and editorials.

FIGURE 4–3
Semantic web of "Three Billy Goats Gruff"

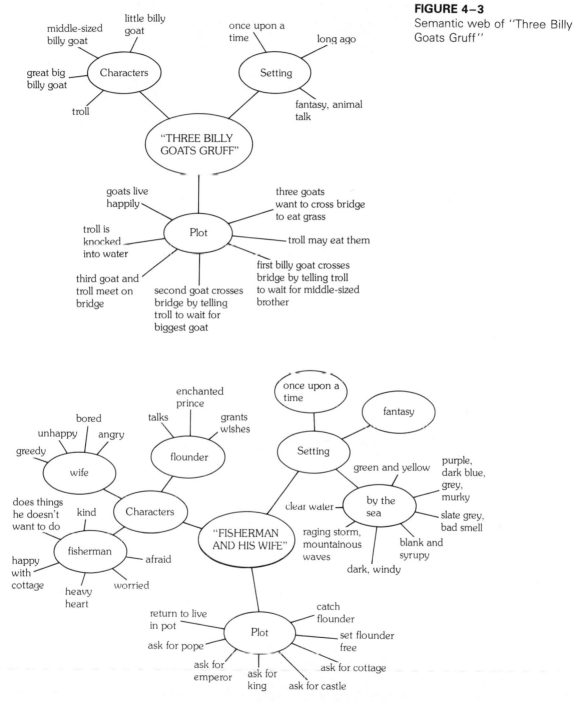

FIGURE 4–4
Semantic map for a book report

Functioning in this age of information requires learning to evaluate what is heard.

Critical Reading and Listening

Critical reading and listening demands careful evaluation. To determine what and whom to believe requires considerable judgment of the source. Critical reading and listening go beyond factual comprehension; they require weighing the validity of facts, identifying the real problem, making judgments, interpreting implied ideas, interpreting character traits, distinguishing fact from opinion, drawing conclusions, and determining the adequacy of a source of information.

Television, radio, and newspapers provide abundant material for teaching critical reading and listening skills. According to Arnold Cheyney (1984), students can learn many critical reading skills by carefully scrutinizing and questioning sources in newspapers. Cheyney provides a list of questions for teachers to put on charts for student referral when they read or discuss news items:

The Writer's Competency and Integrity
1. Is the writer an authority?
2. How does this writer know?
3. Does the writer make sense?

The Writer's Use of Sources and Evidence
4. What evidence is presented to document the assertions?
5. Is this fact or opinion?

6. Is anything missing?
7. What is the writer's purpose?
8. Does the writer have a hidden motive?

The Reader's Ability to Form, Revise, and Test Opinions

9. Are the premises valid?
10. Why are these facts important to me?
11. Do the conclusions necessarily follow?
12. What have others said about this topic?
13. Who stands to gain if I accept this without question?
14. Does my lack of knowledge keep me from accepting this?
15. Does my background make me intolerant of this point of view?
16. Is the information as true today as when it was written?
17. What more do I need to know before I come to my own conclusions?[1]

Fact versus opinion To answer critical questions about news items, students need assignments that require them to read and listen to a variety of news sources. One of the first skills is ability to separate fact from opinion. You can begin to help students understand the difference by reading them several paragraphs written around either fact or opinion; for example:

1. The grizzly bear lives in Alaska, Canada, and in the northern part of the United States. A big grizzly may weigh up to 1,000 pounds. The grizzly has a large hump above his shoulders; this makes it recognizable even at a distance. The grizzly likes to eat fish, fruit, and honey.
2. The grizzly bear is a cruel killer and should be outlawed in all parts of the United States. This killer not only attacks cattle, it also attacks and injures tourists in the national parks. The parks should be made safe for visitors, and they will not be safe for campers and hikers until this animal is removed.
3. The grizzly bear lived freely in the western part of the United States for hundreds of years. Humans have so infringed on the grizzly's hunting grounds that it now is found only in secluded areas of Alaska and Canada, and infrequently in the high country in the United States. The U.S. government must protect the grizzly and keep the tourists and ranchers out of the grizzly's territory. This powerful, beautiful animal deserves our best protection.

After reading paragraphs similar to these, ask students if they see any differences between the paragraphs. The conclusion should be that the first paragraph is based on facts and that the other two are based on opinions; it should also note that the two opinion paragraphs are trying to sway opinion.

Next, have the students formulate their own definitions of fact and opinion. Their definitions might resemble the following:

Fact = Statements that can be checked and proven to be true are facts.

Opinion = Statements that tell what someone thinks or believes to be true but cannot be proven are opinions.

---

[1] From Arnold B. Cheyney, *Teaching Reading Skills Through the Newspaper.* 2d ed. (Newark, Del.: International Reading Association, 1984). Reprinted with permission of Arnold B. Cheyney and the International Reading Association.

Allow the students to apply their knowledge of fact versus opinion and subsequently make judgments about new information. Have them search a newspaper for examples of factual writing and opinion writing. Make displays of the two kinds of writing and their characteristics. Students will find factual items in newspapers in the form of obituaries, birth notices, court announcements, and most news stories, although the latter may also include opinion. They will find personal opinion writing in editorials, advertisements, letters to the editor, and advice columns. Students can reinforce their skills by writing factual and opinion paragraphs to share with the class, and classmates can then make judgments about the paragraphs.

News coverage comparisons   Students can compare how television, radio, newspapers, and newsmagazines handle news. For stimulating discussions and learning experiences, assign children to report and analyze the various media presentations of an item reported in the news. For example, if your city has coverage on the three commercial television networks and an educational station, assign several students to watch the evening news on each channel. Have other students search newspapers for news stories, editorials, and editorial cartoons about the same subject. Have still other students listen to the news reports on the area radio stations. If possible, tape the television and radio segments for classroom listening and critical analysis. Have the students bring the newspaper items to the classroom for sharing and discussion. (Controversial news items that may result in editorial comment are especially interesting for this investigation.)

The following day, have the students share their reports of the news presentations; discuss differences resulting from media requirements; discuss bias noted in the various media or between networks; compare editorial comment in a paper with its news coverage; and discover words that might cause a biased reaction in readers or viewers. Have the students refer to Cheyney's list for evaluating the various news items. When they discuss media requirements, they should begin to see that television is primarily visual and presents brief coverage of a story. Radio relies entirely on words to develop images. Newspapers use both words and pictures and have room to discuss the who, what, when, where, why, and how of a story.

Advertising and propaganda   We are bombarded with advertising, visually and auditorially, during most of our waking hours. The morning newspaper often appears to be predominately advertising; the same is true for many magazines. Radio and television sometimes seem to be one long series of commercials, interrupted occasionally by programming. Presumably, adults have acquired enough critical listening and reading skills to enable them to judge the value, worth, honesty, and acceptability of ads that try to persuade them to invest in a product or vote a certain way in an election. There is a great deal of concern, however, for preschool and school-age children, who may be unduly influenced by messages ads put forth. Elizabeth Gratz and J. E. Gratz (1984) state that "those who sell products are influencing the cognitive and the affective development of children as well as contributing to changes in society" (p. 81). Although good commercials can raise the standards of civilization, bad commercials can distort reality and lead young people to think that what they see in television ads portrays real life, leading them to desire and expect the wrong things for the wrong reasons. Teachers should help students look closely at both the good and bad in advertising, so they can critically evaluate what they see and hear.

FOR YOUR PLAN BOOK
An Instructional Unit on Advertising

Two undergraduate elementary education majors developed the following unit to promote intelligent decision making among today's young consumers. They designed the three-week unit for fourth-grade students, incorporating art, consumer education, language arts, math, reading, and social studies activities around the theme of advertising. Their ideas should stimulate your own thinking about teaching through the medium of advertising.

Idea One: American audiences are continually exposed to advertising.

1. Have the students view or listen to a one-hour program of their choice on television or radio. Have them record the time devoted to commercials and compare the total commercial time to total program time by constructing a bar graph.
2. Have each student tabulate the number of advertising billboards, posters, and signs he or she sees from Monday through Friday.

Idea Two: Advertising influences the purchases of the American public.

1. Facilitate discussion about the influences of advertising by comparing two products—one that is advertised a great deal and one that is not advertised. Include the following questions:
   (a) Which product would you buy?
   (b) Have you ever switched brands after seeing an advertisement that compared the old and new brands?
   (c) What advertisements can you name that might influence your decision about buying food, clothing, toys, and so forth?
   (d) How do you feel about an advertisement that influences your decision to vote, purchase a product, or contribute to a charity fund?

Idea Three: Advertising is a multimillion dollar business in America.

1. Have the students choose a facet of the advertising industry that interests them. Possible choices include annual expenditure on advertising, central locations of the advertising industry, or in-depth exploration of advertising spending for a particular type of product. Have the students present their findings orally.

Idea Four: Advertisements appear in many of the media, including television, radio, newspapers, magazines, and billboards.

1. Utilize a guided discovery approach in a discussion of advertising media suitability. Topics include advertising cost, coverage, applicable regulations, using jingles and catchy phrases, company logos, and visual appeal.
2. Let each student choose a product, and decide whether the product is suitable for television or radio advertising. Have the student write a script to sell that product and tape an advertisement. The presentation should present characteristics suitable to television or radio.
3. Have the students use their imaginations to write an original classified advertisement to buy or sell an item or to gain employment.
4. Have each student compute the cost of placing his or her ad in a newspaper.

Idea Five: *Professional advertising opens many career options for today's young people.*

1. Present an expository lesson plan on a career in advertising. The lesson plan should cover such topics as jobs, training required for each job, related-interest fields, and salaries.
2. Have the students select a field in which they are interested or have special ability. Have each student research the chosen field and present a product representative of that field:
   (a) Drama—dramatic presentation for selling a product.
   (b) Speech—oral presentation of product, as on the radio with a microphone (disc jockey).
   (c) Art—drawing, sketching, painting.
   (d) Marketing—design package of product or catchy presentation of product.
   (e) Modeling—modeling clothes.
   (f) Journalism—written script and layout.
   (g) Photography—pictures of product.
   (h) Producing/directing—producing skits or slide shows.

Idea Six: *Some advertisements are designed especially to appeal to specific consumer groups.*

1. Videotape television commercials that attempt to appeal to specific groups. Discuss and categorize the intended groups with the students.
2. Have each student choose one commercial appealing to a specific group and write an adaptation of this commercial to appeal to another group, identifying the old and new groups.

Idea Seven: *Television advertisements attempt to appeal to different audiences during different times of the day or week.*

1. Conduct a guided discovery lesson on the influence that time of day or week has on the types of products advertised. Include such questions as these:
   (a) Who is most likely to be watching television during the day?
   (b) What products do you think would be advertised then?
   (c) How many of you watch the cartoons on Saturday mornings?
   (d) What kind of consumers watch television on Saturday morning?
   (e) What kinds of products are advertised then? Why?

Idea Eight: *Advertisements are used by cities and states to attract tourists.*

1. Tell the students that they have been chosen by the local Chamber of Commerce to write a description of their city in order to encourage people to visit. Tell them to make their city come alive with vivid verbs and descriptive adjectives.

Idea Nine: *Professional advertisers attempt to appeal to the five senses: (1) touch, (2) taste, (3) sight, (4) smell, and (5) hearing.*

1. Instruct the students to choose, cut out, and categorize magazine advertisements into the above categories, underlining key words.
2. Have each student create one original product appealing to at least two of the senses and write an advertisement for the product.

Idea Ten: ***Much advertising is propaganda, the purpose of which is to influence the audience to buy something.***

1. Have the students bring three newspaper or magazine ads and analyze each by answering the following questions:
   (a) What product is being advertised?
   (b) Has the advertiser used any tricks to attract you to the product and to make you think it is better or more popular than it actually is? Explain.
   (c) Are any definite claims cited by the manufacturers? If so, what are they?
   (d) Do you believe the ad? Why or why not?

2. Have the students orally present a sales pitch to their group, who will role-play the board of directors of an advertising firm. The salesperson will persuade the board of directors to sponsor the product. Visual aids are useful, and students should be as persuasive as possible.

Idea Eleven: ***Testimonial advertising quotes a favorable statement made about the product by a famous person.***

1. Have students identify and describe in writing at least one testimonial advertisement seen during afternoon or evening television viewing.

2. Have students list famous persons who have endorsed a product or participated in a testimonial advertisement, relying on past viewing experience.

Idea Twelve: ***Transfer advertising pictures a famous person or symbol with a product, although the person makes no statement about the product.***

1. Have the students search magazines and view television advertisements at home to find examples of the transfer propaganda technique.

2. Ask the students to think of a famous person in history whom they admire. Then, have the students write a transfer advertisement with that person using a product of their choice.

Culminating Activities:

1. Have the students advertise an upcoming school or community event. The event might be a book fair, carnival, Christmas program, band or choir presentation, or another type of assembly. The students should utilize as many forms of media as possible. Divide them into groups according to the medium each prefers. The advertisements should reflect the many forms and techniques studied during the unit.

2. Divide the students into several small groups. Have the groups take turns presenting several short skits with puppets. The groups not presenting a skit will present commercials between scenes and skits, so that each student will participate in both the commercials and puppet presentations. The commercials will be of the students' creation and should advertise imaginary products. The commercials, reviewed as a class effort, should reflect all of the advertising techniques learned in the unit.

Used with permission of Susan Watson and Sarah Wells, Texas A & M University.

FOR YOUR PLAN BOOK
An Instructional Unit on Propaganda Techniques in Advertising

To develop powers of critical evaluation, begin by studying the various propaganda techniques frequently used to sway public opinion. A fourth-grade teacher used such a study to help children listen to and read advertisements more critically. This study was so successful that the students afterward did not believe anything in an ad unless they had investigated its claims and evaluated how authorities in a field would feel toward the advertisement.

The teacher introduced this particular study by asking a parent who worked for an advertising agency to visit the class and talk about advertising. The guest speaker discussed the purpose of advertising and the money spent on it. Then, he showed the students some of the ways ads try to influence opinion about their products. Children saw examples of ads that used snob appeal, testimonials, transfer, glittering generalities, plain folks, bandwagon, and name-calling techniques to sway public opinion. They discussed the various methods and asked numerous questions. This guest speaker gave a highly motivating introduction to advertising, which enabled students to see that companies spend millions of dollars trying to win prospective buyers.

Next, the students studied in-depth the various propaganda techniques presented by the guest speaker. They listed characteristics of each technique, found oral and written examples of them, and compiled Table 1.

The students created several bulletin-board displays to illustrate the characteristics of the various propaganda techniques, with examples of newspaper and magazine advertisements and television and radio commercials. (They found that some advertising relied on more than one approach.) Next, the teacher taped commercials from television and radio. The students listened to them carefully and identified the different techniques and key words related to each selling approach.

After listening, identifying, and analyzing, the students chose a particular ad or commercial to research. They listed questions to answer before making an evaluative decision; for example, for a testimonial, the students tried to answer the following questions:

1. Who is the testimonial trying to persuade?
2. Who will benefit if I agree with the testimonial?
3. Who will be hurt if I agree with the testimonial?
4. Who is making the testimonial?
5. What is the credibility of this person in relation to the product or issue?
6. Who can make an honest appraisal of this product or issue?
7. What facts support the testimonial?
8. What facts disagree with the testimonial?

They asked similar questions for the remaining categories of advertising. The students presented their findings orally to the rest of the class and put their lists of answered questions next to the example of the advertisement or commercial on the bulletin board.

This advertising study concluded with an activity in which students divided into groups, wrote their own commercials, and presented them to the rest of the class. The class decided to write commercials on opposing issues, using the following four topics: (1) a commercial sponsored by an oil company that favored expansion and sale of oil and gasoline products, (2) an ecology commercial that opposed expanded use of oil and favored greater conservation of natural resources, (3) a commercial to sell big cars, and

TABLE 1

Characteristics and examples of propaganda techniques

Name	Characteristics	Example
1. Snob appeal	1. Makes us want a product because superior or wealthy people have it. Association with a small, exclusive group.	1. The jet set dine at _____, you should too. Drive a _____ like _____ .
2. Name-calling	2. Creates a feeling of dislike for a person or product by associating it with something disliked or undesirable. May appeal to hate and fear. Asks people to judge without first examining the evidence.	2. Congressman _____ associates with _____ . The mayor has dishonest friends.
3. Glittering generalities	3. Uses broad general statements, whose exact meanings are not clear. Appeals to emotions of love, generosity, brotherhood. Words suggest ideals such as truth, freedom, and the American way.	3. Your wildest dreams for adventure will come true if you sail on the _____ . Senator _____ will defend the American way.
4. Plain folks	4. Identifies the person or product with the average person. Politicians may try to win confidence by appearing to be like the good folks in your town.	4. For an honest used-car deal go to your friendly neighborhood _____ dealer. Senator _____ is a hometown boy who will vote for your interests.
5. Transfer	5. Creates a good or bad impression by associating a product or person with something respected or not respected. The feeling for the symbol is supposed to transfer to the new product or person.	5. _____ is as strong as Atlas.
6. Testimonial	6. A respected person, such as a movie star or athlete, recommends a product and suggests that you buy it because he or she uses it.	6. Lovely Lettie says, "I use Bright Hair shampoo because it leaves my hair silky and shiny."
7. Bandwagon	7. Follow the crowd and buy what everyone else is buying, or vote for the winner.	7. Everyone is rushing to _____ to buy the new _____ . If you want to belong to the "In" generation, drink _____ .

(4) a commercial to sell small cars. The students used any selling and propaganda techniques they wished, along with visual props, sound effects, and musical backgrounds. After each presentation, the remainder of the class identified the techniques in the commercial and discussed the truthfulness. (If the school has the equipment, videotape presentations and play them back as if they are commercials on a real television.)

REINFORCEMENT ACTIVITY

1. Look for examples of the propaganda techniques described in this section. How could you use these examples to develop critical evaluation skills with children? What questions should you ask for each example?
2. Develop an instructional lesson or series of lessons for improving children's critical thinking, listening, and reading skills. Build your lessons around television, radio, and newspapers. State your objectives, motivation, instructional procedures, and reinforcement or enrichment activities.

APPRECIATION

Sometimes teachers become so engrossed in teaching specific skills that they forget that enjoyment is one of the main purposes of listening. Appreciative listening includes listening to poetry, music, stories, plays, and sounds in nature. In fact, the development of appreciative listening skills can establish lifelong pleasure while it motivates the utilization of other language arts skills. Durkin (1966) found that young children whose parents read to them at home were also high achievers in reading at school. This listening experience apparently illustrates to the child the benefits of learning to read enjoyable books.

Various taxonomies offer some guidelines for developing appreciative listening with literature. Barrett's (1972) taxonomy of comprehension, for example, stresses the development of appreciative skills. Although this taxonomy was developed in relation to reading, it also has application for listening. According to Barrett, appreciation includes a student's awareness of literary techniques, forms and styles of literature, and structures an author uses to stimulate emotional responses. Barrett identifies four tasks that fall under this appreciation component: (1) emotional response to plot or theme, (2) identification with characters and incidents, (3) reactions to the author's use of language, and (4) reactions to the author's use of imagery.

To apply the emotional response task to a listening situation, require students to listen to a selection and determine how the author developed the plot or theme to elicit certain responses in the listener. Why did the listener feel excitement, happiness, or sadness? Emotional response is an individual matter, so not all children will respond in the same way to the same selection. Encourage children to respond through pantomime or other creative dramatics and then discuss how and why a selection made them feel a certain emotion.

Also, have students record their favorite stories or poems and then let the listeners discover the qualities in the stories and poems that have emotional appeal. One creative fourth-grade teacher asked her students to interview their parents. The students asked their parents to identify selections from poetry or stories they remembered from their childhood. Then, the teacher presented the most popular selections orally. The fourth graders listened to the selections and discussed their universal appeal.

The task of identification with characters and incidents on the appreciation taxonomy requires students to become aware of literary techniques that prompt them to sympathize with, empathize with, or reject a character. Have students listen to a selection to discover how the author presents a character, then ask what descriptive words influenced how they felt about the characters. Did the author use terms such as *heroic, shiftless, lazy, beautiful,* and *strong?* How does the author have other people describe the character? Does the character tell you his or her inner feelings? How do other people in the story react to the character? How does the character overcome adversity?

For the third task, reaction to the author's use of language, students must pay attention to how the writer uses such devices as figures of speech, similes, and metaphors. Authors frequently use similes and metaphors to create new relationships between unrelated things. A simile is an expressed comparison of two different things or ideas; a metaphor is an implied comparison. For example, in *Secret of the Andes* (1952), Ann Nolan Clark uses a number of similes. Listen to two examples and visualize how you would respond to these descriptions: "The boy's thoughts were whirling like the foaming rapids on the far side of the valley" and "He bore the proud look of the giant condor circling a cliff nest on a mountain crest." Let students search for similar devices and share them with the class.

Besides similes and metaphors, authors often use sentence length and structure to denote pace. Authors may change language patterns to help create the action of the story. Short, staccato sentences impart a feeling of mounting excitement; long, lazy sentences produce a feeling of relaxation. Robert McCloskey (1957) uses this technique in *Time of Wonder.*

> [I]n the afternoon, when the tide is out, they build a castle out of the rocks and driftwood below the spot where they had belly-whopped and dog-paddled during the morning . . . (p. 24)

> Suddenly the wind whips the water into sharp, choppy waves. It tears off the sharp tops and slashes them in ribbons of smoky spray. And the rain comes slamming down. The wind comes in stronger and stronger gusts. A branch snaps from a tree. (p. 44)

Read similar examples to children and see how their reactions change as sentence patterns vary.

The final appreciation-taxonomy task, reaction to the author's use of imagery, requires students to respond to an author's ability to paint word pictures. Can the students close their eyes and visualize the setting, a character, or a feeling? For example, when you listen to *Charlotte's Web,* can you visualize the barn that has such a peaceful feeling, as if nothing bad could ever happen again?

Sharing poetry with children is an excellent means for developing appreciative listening. Children's responses to Shel Silverstein's *Where the Sidewalk Ends* (1974) emphasize the importance of poetry. Poet José Garcia Villa (Cowen, 1983) maintains that children should be encouraged to enjoy poems for sound values, to hear the rhythm of language, and to be aware of the magic in a poetry line. While listening to poetry, children can sense and feel the meaning rather than explicitly state the meaning. Villa recommends that children listen to nursery rhymes and poems by Emily Dickinson, Robert Frost, e. e. cummings, Nathalia Crane, Lewis Carroll, and Edward Lear. For older children, Villa recommends poems by John Donne, Gerard Manley Hopkins, Dylan Thomas, Wilfred Owen, Elinor Wylie, and Marianne Moore. Villa believes that these poets help children discover the magic in poetry. He stresses "the magic to be found in poetry rather than its meaning which is what most educational programs and texts emphasize. Only after the older student or budding poet considers the magical elements inherent in such techniques as the importance of a vivid first line; the musicality, tension, and movement of language; the intricacies of versification; the richness of metaphor; the necessity of economy; the element of surprise; and the implosive drama of the last line, will the neophyte begin to understand the power and magnificence of poetry" (p. 84).

Teachers who want to encourage children to expand the imaginative quality of their minds and appreciate the various elements in poetry may share poems emphasizing such elements as rhythm, rhyme, sound patterns, repetitions, and figurative language. For example, David McCord uses rhythm in "The Pickety Fence" (*Far and Few: Rhymes of the Never Was and Always Is,* 1952) to suggest the sounds a stick makes as a child walks by the fence. Likewise, Robert Louis Stevenson relies on rhythm to suggest the dash and rattle of a train as it crosses the countryside in "From a Railway Carriage" (*A Child's Garden of Verses,* 1885).

The auditory pleasure of rhyming words is heard in Zilpha Snyder's "Poem to Mud" (*Today Is Saturday,* 1969) and Edward Lear's "The Owl and the Pussy Cat" (*The Nonsense Books,* 1946). Alliteration, the repetition of initial consonants to create sound patterns, creates strong sound patterns in Jack Prelutsky's "The Yak" (*A Gopher in the Garden,* 1966). Repetition in poetry may emphasize words, phrases, lines, or verses. Lewis Carroll's repetitive patterns in "Beautiful Soup" (*Alice's Adventures in Wonderland,* 1886, 1984) seem to recreate the marvelous sounds of rich, hot soup ladeled into a spoon and placed noisily into the mouth. Poets use figurative language to encourage their audiences to see things in new ways, to clarify, and to add vividness. Kaye Starbird's imagery in "The Wind" (*The Covered Bridge House and Other Poems,* 1979) depicts a wind that is sneaky, tricky, and full of life.

Music and literature also offer excellent connections for developing appreciative listening. Many picture storybooks may be used to stimulate interest in music and to motivate musical interpretations. Lamme (1990) describes an elementary music classroom in which students are involved with musical performances and picture books with musical content. During a thematic study of musical instruments, the teacher read Karen Ackerman's *Song and Dance Man* (1988), a story about a grandfather who relives his vaudeville experiences for his grandchildren, as well as other nonfiction and fiction books on musical instruments. Adults and students played various musical instruments for the class. As part of the unit, the students created a musical instrument museum, researched different types of instruments, and created a class book about music and instruments.

Additional nonfictional and fictional books that stimulate an interest in music include Jill Krementz's *A Very Young Musician* (1991), Dee Lilligard's *An Introduction to Musical Instruments: Strings* (1988), Tomi de Paola's *Sing, Pierrot, Sing* (1983), and Paul Fleischman's *Rondo in C* (1988).

In 1991, the bicentennial of Mozart's birth, it was particularly appropriate for students to listen to works such as "The Magic Flute" and to read and discuss books about Mozart's life. For example, Mozart's youth is explored in Catherine Brighton's *Mozart: Scenes from the Childhood of the Great Composer* (1990), F. N. Monjo's *Letters to Horseface: Young Mozart's Travels in Italy* (1975), and Lisl Weil's *Wolferl: The First Six Years in the Life of Wolfgang Amadeus Mozart, 1756–1762*

(1991). Information about his adult life and career is found in Julie Downing's *Mozart Tonight* (1991), Richard Tames's *Wolfgang Amadeus Mozart* (1991), and Wendy Thompson's *Wolfgang Amadeus Mozart* (1991). Elleman and LaBarbera (1991) recommend that students use the maps in Monjo's and Thompson's books to create their own maps, pinpoint important locations, and trace Mozart's travels.

MAINSTREAMING

Children with learning problems require more assistance in listening for a specific purpose than do children with no learning handicap. Ausubel (1960) stresses using advanced organizers in order to give students a sense of direction. (The use of advanced organizers is effective in listening for directions, as well as in listening for other specific information.) An advanced organizer for use with listening for directions might stress listening for key words in the directions, such as *first, second, third,* and *finally.* It helps students understand the purpose of the directions, the reason for each step, and the relation of each step to the set of directions.

One extremely useful technique is to ask students with learning problems to close their eyes and visualize themselves performing each step of a set of directions. You may want to try this activity with a pupil-motivated task, such as leaving the building when a fire alarm sounds. The purpose of an orderly, quick exit is easy to understand because the students are so vitally involved. Ask your students to close their eyes and visualize themselves doing each step of the following: "First, when you hear the fire bell, walk quickly to the classroom door. Second, form a line and turn to the right, walking close to the hall wall. Third, walk straight ahead and go out the double doors in the front of the building. Finally, line up outside the building next to the flagpole so I can count to make sure you are all safe." Ask the children to describe what they see and hear. After they have described each step, have them try to visualize the whole sequence. Then, have them physically perform the activity, comparing their visualizations with what they actually do. After this activity, some children claim they could even hear the bell and smell smoke!

Duker (1971) declares that probably no group in school has as much to gain from knowing how to listen well as children who have problems keeping pace with the normal curriculum. If these children are treated as if their only difficulty in language arts is reading, and it is taken for granted that they can listen without further instruction, they undoubtedly suffer. Duker concludes: "Such an approach is fallacious as much more often than not these children are suffering from a handicap in all communicative language arts skills. The fact that they perhaps listen better than they read does not justify the conclusion that they therefore listen well" (p. 217).

Many of the activities recommended in this chapter are good for children with special needs. To identify specific characteristics of children who might have difficulty during listening activities, see the charts that list characteristics that may be found in learning disabled children (Table 4–2) or in mentally handicapped children (Table 4–3). The techniques for language arts instruction are identified from research and authorities who work with mainstreamed children.

TABLE 4–2

Mainstreaming and listening development for learning disabled children

Characteristics of Learning Disabled Children	Teaching Techniques for Language Arts Instruction
1. Difficulty attending to task-relevant information and hyperactivity, impulsiveness, and distractibility (Bryan & Bryan, 1986; Hallahan & Kauffman, 1986; Samuels & Edwall, 1981; Sapir & Wilson, 1978; Swanson, 1980).	1. Use considerable positive reinforcement. (O'Connor, Stuck, & Wyne, 1979). Help children attend by providing a private space for learning; maintain a structured, well-organized environment; help the children focus on the task; provide immediate reinforcement; give several short assignments rather than one long assignment; let the children reduce stress by standing; provide quiet opportunities during the school day; and help children experience success (Stoodt, 1981). Read to children (Mandel, O'Connor, & Smith, 1990).
2. Auditory modality inferior to visual modality. Deficiencies in ability to blend sounds into words and difficulties in auditory closure related to problems in word analysis (Harber, 1979, 1980; Richardson, Di Benedetto, Christ, Press, & Winsberg, 1978; Swanson, 1980).	2. Provide practice in analyzing syllables and short words into phonemes and then blending phonemes into syllables and words (Williams, 1980). Focus on the order of sounds and letters in words, multisensory presentation of stimuli, considerable repetition, and varied materials (Wallace & Kauffman, 1986).
3. Difficulties comprehending main ideas in listening materials (Wong, 1979, 1980).	3. Precede a listening experience with questions focusing on the purpose for listening (Wong, 1979, 1980). Teach children to set purposes for listening; give them training in critical thinking through texts such as social studies and propaganda materials (Spache, 1981).

REINFORCEMENT ACTIVITY

This chapter discusses a number of methods, suggestions, and illustrative units for teaching attentive listening, listening for a specific purpose, and appreciative listening. Choose one of these topics and develop a lesson for fostering listening. If you are a student teacher or a classroom teacher, use your lesson with children. Allow the children to participate in developing their goals for the lesson and in evaluating their success. Share the activities with your language arts class. If you are not now teaching children, practice your listening lesson with a group of your peers.

Also, develop a learning center to teach some aspects of listening. Form a committee with a group of your classmates to determine objectives for the learning center and design appropriate activities for it. Use the learning center with children in a classroom, or demonstrate the use of the learning center to a group of your peers.

TABLE 4–3

Mainstreaming and listening development for mentally handicapped children

Characteristics of Mentally Handicapped Children	Teaching Techniques for Language Arts Instruction
1. Short attention span due to failure in past efforts, to inappropriate academic expectations, or to auditory or visual distractions in the classroom (Gearheart, Weishahn, & Gearheart, 1988).	1. Demonstrate consistency in classroom management techniques and model desired behaviors (Hart, 1981). It is easier to maintain attention and to recall later things that are concrete rather than abstract, familiar rather than remote, and simple rather than complex. Use language and ideas that are as concrete, familiar, and simple as possible. Eliminate visual and auditory distractions that might decrease the ability of students to attend (Gearheart, Weishahn, & Gearheart, 1988).
2. Below-average ability to generalize, conceptualize, and perform other cognitive-related tasks (Gearheart, Weishahn, & Gearheart, 1988).	2. Provide instruction that encourages cognitive development and improvement of listening comprehension by encouraging children to respond to inferential questions and to rephrase materials that they hear (Zetlin & Gallimore, 1980). Help children set their own purposes for listening by accompanying listening activities with a directed reading–thinking activity, in which children learn to make predictions based on a few cues, either pictorial or textual, then listen to confirm or disprove the prediction (Stauffer, Abrams, & Piluski, 1978). Use materials that are similar to those used for reading comprehension. Develop listening for main ideas, details, sequence of events, following directions, making inferences, drawing conclusions, and critical evaluation (Lerner, 1985).
3. Problems in auditory discrimination (Cook, Nolan, & Zanotti, 1980).	3. Try supplementing instruction with the neurological impress method, in which you and the student read aloud in unison (Cook, Nolan, & Zanotti, 1980). Encourage sensitivity to sounds by having the children listen with their eyes closed to environmental sounds, recorded sounds, and other teacher-made sounds. Encourage auditory attending to sounds by having the children listen to or repeat sound patterns. Encourage discrimination of sounds by having the children discriminate loud and soft sounds, high and low sounds, and near and far sounds. Encourage awareness of letter sounds by asking the children to identify words that begin with the same initial consonant or consonant blend, identify words that have the same endings or vowel sounds, and identify words that rhyme (Lerner, 1985).

SUMMARY

Listening is an important and complicated skill. It is an active rather than a passive activity, and one in which students participate in their own instructional improvement. They must help set goals for their listening instruction.

The units and lessons in this chapter will help you conceptualize the listening curriculum. Because listening relates to the total language arts program, it cannot be taught in isolation. It must be taught in classroom environments that reflect those outside the classroom. Listening also must be taught continually; it is part of everyone's experience from birth to adulthood.

A complete profile of the listening abilities of children requires understanding of and evaluation of several listening components. For example, tests for auditory acuity may be required because children cannot comprehend oral communication if they cannot hear. Even children who appear to hear well may still have weak auditory perception skills. Diagnosis of these skills may be critical for children who have difficulty recognizing sounds in a reading or spelling approach that relies on phonic analysis. There are several methods for developing the auditory perception skills necessary to distinguish differences in sounds and words.

There is a positive relationship between attentiveness and listening. Consequently, diagnosis of attentive listening skills may be crucial for a child's future achievement. A profile of listening ability includes how effectively children comprehend what they hear in a wide range of circumstances. You can use both standardized and informal tests for these diagnoses. Some of the informal tests devised by classroom teachers provide the best information for designing effective instructional programs. Develop the attentive listening skills necessary to follow directions and listen for specific purposes; for example, identifying main ideas, identifying important details and sequences, and predicting outcomes.

Critical reading and listening demand careful evaluation. In developing critical reading and listening skills in children, you will find that newspapers, television, and radio offer abundant material.

Finally, include listening for appreciation in your instructional planning. Use poetry, music, stories, and plays to develop appreciative listening.

ADDITIONAL LISTENING ACTIVITIES

1. Compile a list of children's books or poems and rhymes that contain rhyming elements or other interesting sound patterns such as alliteration.
2. Develop an advanced organizer that encourages children to listen for a specific purpose, such as following directions, paraphrasing the main idea of a selection, or identifying the sequential order in a paragraph or longer selection.
3. Create an auditory awareness tape that explores sounds such as nature sounds, animal sounds, street sounds, home sounds, or school sounds. Share the tape with a group of children. Ask them to identify the sounds, classify them according to location, and list other sounds that could be found in the same category.

4. With a group of children, develop a set of guidelines that will help them improve their listening ability. Ask them to identify different listening activities that occur in the day, their purpose for listening, and their requirements for that specific listening activity.

Listening Activity	Purpose	Requirements
Directions for assignments	Accurate, detailed information that I can follow	Attention to all information
Music	Entertainment and appreciation	Relaxed environment

5. Compile a list of predictable books that rely on repetitive language patterns or repetitive story events. Develop questions that direct children's attention to the repetitive or predictable features of a book. Share the book and questions with children.

6. Select a story or content area materials that provide practice gaining meaning from a listening experience (for example, summarizing, clarifying, predicting, and verifying). Identify appropriate places in the story where children should summarize what they hear, where they might benefit from a clarifying discussion of ideas or content, where they can predict what might happen next, and where they can verify predictions. Share the listening materials with a group of your peers. Evaluate the effectiveness of the listening experience.

7. Compile a card file of poems that allow children to hear the rhythm of language, that have rich metaphors, or that have elements of surprise that delight children.

8. Read a folktale to a group of children. Map or web the characters, settings, and plot.

9. Evaluate a listening learning center. Reinforce listening for the main idea, important details, sequence, and predicting outcomes by using the learning center. The listening center described in this chapter, developed by a group of student teachers, was used in both third and fourth grades. Look carefully at each component. What listening skill is being reinforced by each? How would you introduce the center to children? How would you assist children in using the center? Do you believe the purposes of the center were met? Would you add anything else to the center?

BIBLIOGRAPHY

Ausubel, D. P. "The Use of Advanced Organizers in the Learning and Retention of Meaningful Verbal Material." *Journal of Educational Psychology* 51 (1960): 267–72.

Barrett, Thomas C. "Taxonomy of Reading Comprehension." *Reading 360 Monograph.* Lexington, Mass.: Ginn & Co., 1972.

Bryan, Tanis H., and Bryan, James H. *Understanding Learning Disabilities,* 3rd ed. Mountain View, Calif.: Mayfield Pub., 1986.

Burns, P., and Roe, B. *Informal Reading Inventory,* 3d ed. Boston: Houghton Mifflin, 1989.

Cook, Jimmie E.; Nolan, Gregory A.; and Zanotti, Robert J. "Treating Auditory Perception Problems:

The NIM Helps." *Academic Therapy* 15 (March 1980): 473–81.

Cowen, John E. "Conversations with Poet José Garcia Villa on Teaching Poetry to Children." In *Teaching Reading Through the Arts,* edited by John E. Cowen. Newark, Del.: International Reading Association, 1983, pp. 78–87.

Dressel, J. H. "The Effects of Listening to and Discussing Different Qualities of Children's Literature on the Narrative Writing of Fifth Graders." *Research in the Teaching of English* 24 (1990): 397–414.

Duker, Sam. *Teaching Listening in the Elementary School: Readings.* Metuchen, N.J.: The Scarecrow Press, 1971.

Durkin, Dolores. *Children Who Read Early.* New York: Teachers College Press, 1966.

Elleman, B., and LaBarbera, K. *Book Links* 1 (1989): 38–42.

Funk, Hal, and Funk, Gary. "Guidelines for Developing Listening Skills." *The Reading Teacher* 42 (May 1989): 660–663.

Gearheart, Bill R.; Weishahn, Mel; and Gearheart, Carol J. *The Exceptional Student in the Regular Classroom,* 4th ed. Columbus, Oh.: Merrill Publishing Co., 1988.

Gratz, Elizabeth, and Gratz, J. E. "Who Is Controlling Children's Learning? Subliminals?" *Review Journal of Philosophy and Social Science* 9 (1984): 81–96.

Hade, D. D. "Children, Stories, and Narrative Transformations." *Research in the Teaching of English* 22 (1988): 310–325.

Hallahan, Daniel P., and Kauffman, James M. *Exceptional Children: Introduction to Special Education.* Englewood Cliffs, N.J.: Prentice-Hall, 1986.

Harber, Jean R. "Auditory Perception and Reading: Another Look." *Learning Disability Quarterly* 3 (Summer 1980): 19–29.

————. "Differentiating LD and Normal Children: The Utility of Selected Perceptual and Perceptual-Motor Tests." *Learning Disability Quarterly* 2 (Spring 1979): 70–75.

Harris, Albert J., and Sipay, Edward R. *How to Increase Reading Ability.* 8th ed. New York: Longman, 1985.

Hart, Verna. *Mainstreaming Children with Special Needs.* New York: Longman, 1981.

Johns, J. *Basic Reading Inventory,* 4th ed. Dubuque, Iowa: Kendall/Hunt, 1988.

Lamme, L. "Exploring the World of Music through Picture Books." *The Reading Teacher* 44 (1990): 294–300.

Lerner, Janet W. *Children with Learning Disabilities,* 4th ed. Boston: Houghton Mifflin Co., 1985.

Levesque, Jeri. "ELVES: A Read-Aloud Strategy to Develop Listening Comprehension." *The Reading Teacher* 43 (October 1989): 93–94.

Lundsteen, Sara W. *Listening: Its Impact on Reading and the Other Language Arts.* Urbana, Ill.: National Council of Teachers of English, 1979.

McCracken, Robert A., and McCracken, Marlene J. *Stories, Songs, and Poetry to Teach Reading and Writing: Literacy through Language.* Chicago: American Library Association, 1986.

Mandel, M., O'Connor, E., and Smith, J. "Effects of a Story Reading Program on the Literacy Development of At-Risk Kindergarten Children." *Journal of Reading Behavior* 22 (1990): 255–75.

Moss, J. F. *Focus Units in Literature: A Handbook for Elementary School Teachers.* Katonah, NY: Richard Owen, 1990.

Neilsen, Lorri. "Is Anyone Listening?" *The Reading Teacher* 44, (1991): 494–96.

O'Connor, Peter D.; Stuck, Gary B.; and Wyne, Marvin D. "Effects of a Short-Term Intervention Resource-Room Program on Task Orientation and Achievement." *The Journal of Special Education* 13 (Winter 1979): 375–85.

Otto, Wayne, and Smith, Richard. *Corrective and Remedial Teaching.* Boston: Houghton Mifflin Co., 1980.

Pearson, P. David, and Fielding, Linda. "Research Update: Listening Comprehension." *Language Arts* 59 (September 1982): 617–29.

Phillips, G., and McNaughton, S. "The Practice of Storybook Reading to Preschool Children in Mainstream New Zealand Families." *Reading Research Quarterly* 25 (1990): 196–212.

Pikulski, J. "Informal Reading Inventories." *The Reading Teacher* 43 (1990): 514–16.

Richardson, Ellis, Di Benedetto, Barbara; Christ, Adolph; Press, Mark; and Winsberg, Bertrand G. "An Assessment of Two Methods for Remediating Reading Deficiencies." *Reading Improvement* 15 (Summer 1978): 82–95.

Samuels, S. Jay, and Edwall, Glenance. "The Role of Attention in Reading with Implications for the Learning Disabled Student." *Journal of Learning Disabilities* 14 (June/July 1981): 353–61, 368.

Sapir, Selma, and Wilson, Bernice. *A Professional's Guide to Working with the Learning-Disabled Child.* New York: Brunner/Mazel, 1978.

Silvaroli, N. *Classroom Reading Inventory.* Dubuque, Iowa: William Brown, 1989.

Spache, George. *Diagnosing and Correcting Reading Disabilities.* Boston: Allyn & Bacon, 1981.

Stauffer, Russel G.; Abrams, Jules C.; and Piluski, John J. *Diagnosis, Correction, and Prevention of Reading Disability.* New York: Harper & Row, 1978.

Stoodt, Barbara D. *Reading Instruction.* Boston: Houghton Mifflin Co., 1981.

Strother, Deborah. "Practical Applications of Research on Listening." *Phi Delta Kappan* 68 (April 1987): 625–628.

Swanson, H. Lee. "Auditory and Visual Vigilance in Normal and Learning Disabled Readers." *Learning Disability Quarterly* 3 (Spring 1980): 71–78.

Tompkins, Gail E.; Friend, Marilyn; and Smith, Patricia L. "Listening Strategies for the Language Arts." In *Language Arts Instruction and the Beginning Teacher,* edited by Carl Personke and Dale Johnson. Englewood Cliffs, N.J.: Prentice-Hall, 1987.

Tompkins, Gail E., and Weber, Mary Beth. "What Will Happen Next? Using Predictable Books with Young Children." *The Reading Teacher* 36 (February 1983): 498–502.

Vosniadou, S.; Pearson, P. D.; and Rogers, T. "What Causes Children's Failures to Detect Inconsistencies in Text? Representation vs. Comparison Difficulties." *Journal of Educational Psychology* 80 (1988): 27–39.

Wallace, Gerald, and Kauffman, James A. *Teaching Students with Learning and Behavior Problems.* Columbus, Oh.: Merrill Publishing Co., 1986.

Wepman, Joseph M. *The Auditory Discrimination Test.* Chicago: Language Research Associates, 1973.

Wepman, Joseph M., and Morency, Anne. *The Auditory Memory Span Test.* Chicago: Language Research Associates, 1973.

Williams, Joanna P. "Teaching Decoding with an Emphasis on Phoneme Analysis and Phoneme Blending." *Journal of Educational Psychology* 72 (February 1980): 1–15.

Wong, Bernice Y. "Activating the Inactive Learner: Use of Questions/Prompts to Enhance Comprehension and Retention of Implied Information in Learning Disabled Children." *Learning Disability Quarterly* 3 (Winter 1980): 29–37.

_____ . "Increasing Retention of Main Ideas through Questioning Strategies." *Learning Disability Quarterly* 2 (Spring 1979): 42–47.

Woods, Mary Lynn, and Moe, Alden, J. *Analytical Reading Inventory,* 4th ed. Columbus, Oh.: Merrill Publishing Co., 1989.

Zetlin, Andrea G., and Gallimore, Ronald. "A Cognitive Skills Training Program for Moderately Retarded Learners." *Education and Training of the Mentally Retarded* 15 (April 1980): 121–31.

CHILDREN'S LITERATURE REFERENCES

Aardema, Verna. *Bringing the Rain to Kapiti Plain.* New York: Dial Press, 1981.

Ackerman, Karen. *Song and Dance Man.* Illustrated by Stephen Gammell. New York: Knopf, 1988.

Andersen, Hans Christian. *The Emperor's New Clothes.* Retold by Anne Rockwell. New York: Harper & Row, 1982.

Aragon, Jane Chelsea. *Winter Harvest.* Illustrated by Leslie Baker. Boston: Little, Brown and Co., 1988.

Arnold, Caroline. *Saving the Peregrine Falcon.* Photographs by Richard R. Hewett. Minneapolis: Carolrhoda, 1985.

Bare, Colleen. *Guinea Pigs Don't Read Books.* New York: Dodd, Mead & Co., 1985.

Bond, Michael. *A Bear Called Paddington.* Illustrated by Peggy Fortnum. Boston: Houghton Mifflin Co., 1960.

Brighton, Catherine. *Mozart: Scenes from the Childhood of the Great Composer.* New York: Doubleday, 1990.

Carroll, Lewis. *Alice's Adventures in Wonderland.* London, Macmillan Co., 1866, New York: Alfred A. Knopf, 1984.

Clark, Ann Nolan. *In the Land of Small Dragon.* Illustrated by Tony Chen. New York: Viking Press, 1979.

_____ . *Secret of the Andes.* New York: Viking, 1952.

Climo, Shirley. *The Egyptian Cinderella.* Illustrated by Ruth Heller. New York: Crowell, 1989.

de Paola, Tomi. *Sing, Pierrot Sing.* Orlando: Harcourt Brace Jovanovich, 1983.

Downing, Julie. *Mozart Tonight.* New York: Bradbury, 1991.

Duff, Maggie. *Rum Pum Pum.* New York: Macmillan Co., 1978.

Dunning, Stephen; Lueders, Edward; and Smith, Hugh. *Reflections on a Gift of Watermelon Pickle . . . and Other Modern Verse.* New York: Lothrop, Lee & Shepard, 1967.

Facklam, Margery. *And Then There Was One: The Mysteries of Extinction.* Illustrated by Pamela Johnson. Boston: Little, Brown, 1990.

Fleischman, Paul. *Rondo in C.* Illustrated by Janet Wentworth. New York: Harper & Row, 1988.

Fox, Mem. *Hattie and the Fox.* Illustrated by Patricia Mullins. New York: Bradbury, 1987.

Fritz, Jean. *Make Way for Sam Houston.* Illustrated by Elise Primavera. New York: G. P. Putnam's, Sons, 1986.

Galdone, Paul. *The Greedy Old Fat Man.* Boston: Houghton Mifflin Co., 1983.

———. *The Little Red Hen.* Minneapolis: Seabury, 1973.

Geisert, Arthur. *Pigs from A to Z.* Boston: Houghton Mifflin Co., 1986.

Haviland, Virginia. *North American Legends.* Illustrated by Ann Strugnell. New York: Philomel, 1979.

Hoban, Tana. *Round & Round & Round.* New York: Greenwillow, 1983.

Hutchins, Pat. *Changes, Changes.* New York: Macmillan, 1971.

———. *Rosie's Walk.* New York: Macmillan Co., 1968.

Ivimey, John. *Three Blind Mice.* Illustrated by Paul Galdone. New York: Clarion, 1987.

Kellogg, Steven. *Tallyho, Pinkerton!* New York: Dial Press, 1982.

Krementz, Jill. *A Very Young Musician.* New York: Simon & Schuster, 1991.

Lauber, Patricia. *Volcano: The Eruption and Healing of Mount St. Helens.* New York: Bradbury, 1986.

Lear, Edward. *The Complete Nonsense Book.* New York: Dodd, Mead & Co., 1946 (Original 1846, 1871).

Lilligard, Dee. *An Introduction to Musical Instruments: Strings.* Chicago: Children's Press, 1988.

Lindbergh, Reeve. *The Day the Goose Got Loose.* Illustrated by Steven Kellogg. New York: Dial, 1990.

Lobel, Arnold. *The Random House Book of Mother Goose.* New York: Random House, 1986.

McCloskey, Robert. *Time of Wonder.* New York: Viking, 1957.

McCord, David. *Far and Few: Rhymes of the Never Was and Always Is.* Boston: Little, Brown, 1952.

Merriam, Eve. *Halloween ABC.* Illustrations by Lane Smith. New York: Macmillan Co., 1987.

Monjo., F. N. *Letters to Horseface: Young Mozart's Travels in Italy.* Illustrated by Don Bolognese and Elaine Raphael. New York: Puffin, 1975.

Prelutsky, Jack. *A Gopher in the Garden.* New York: Macmillan Co., 1966.

———. Selected by. *The Random House Book of Poetry for Children.* Illustrated by Arnold Lobel. New York: Random House, 1983.

———. *Read-Aloud Rhymes for the Very Young.* Selected by Jack Prelutsky and illustrated by Marc Brown. New York: Alfred A. Knopf, 1986.

Sattler, Helen Roney. *Giraffes, the Sentinels of the Savannas.* Illustrated by Christopher Santoro. New York: Lothrop, Lee & Shepard, 1989.

Sendak, Maurice. *Where the Wild Things Are.* New York: Harper & Row, 1963.

Silverstein, Shel. *Where the Sidewalk Ends.* New York: Harper & Row, 1974.

Snyder, Zilpha. *Today Is Saturday.* New York: Atheneum Pubs., 1969.

Starbird, Kaye. *The Covered Bridge House and Other Poems.* New York: Four Winds, 1979.

Stevens, Janet. *The House That Jack Built.* New York: Holiday, 1985.

Stevenson, R. L. *A Child's Garden of Verses.* Longman, Green, 1885.

Tames, Richard. *Wolfgang Amadeus Mozart.* New York: Watts, 1991.

Tejima, Keizaburo. *Fox's Dream.* New York: Philomel, 1987.

Thompson, Wendy. *Wolfgang Amadeus Mozart.* New York: Viking, 1991.

Walter, Mildred Pitts. *Brother to the Wind.* Illustrated by Diane and Leo Dillon. New York: Lothrop, Lee & Shepard, 1985.

Weil, Lisl. *Wolferl: The First Six Years in the Life of Wolfgang Amadeus Mozart, 1756–1762.* New York: Holiday, 1991.

Westcott, Nadine. *Peanut Butter and Jelly: A Play Rhyme.* New York: E. P. Dutton, 1987.

White, E. B. *Charlotte's Web.* Illustrated by Garth Williams. New York: Harper & Row, 1952.

Yolen, Jane. *Owl Moon.* Illustrated by John Schoenherr. New York: Philomel, 1987.

———. *The Three Bears Rhyme Book.* Illustrated by Jane Dyer. San Diego: Harcourt Brace Jovanovich, 1987.

Yorinks, Arthur. *Hey, Al.* Illustrated by Richard Egielski. New York: Farrar, Straus & Giroux, 1986.

Zimelman, Nathan. *Treed by a Pride of Irate Lions.* Illustrated by Toni Goffe. Boston: Little, Brown, 1990.

Chapter Five

After completing the chapter on linguistically different children and multicultural education, you will be able to:

1. Describe the differences between a linguistically different and a linguistically deficient concept of language.
2. Understand the problems associated with the use of standardized tests when evaluating children who do not speak standard English.
3. Demonstrate an informal method for evaluating language usage.
4. Describe several factors, such as teacher attitudes and environment, that influence the performance of linguistically different children.
5. Describe how to utilize knowledge of the values and learning styles of Mexican-American children for effective education.
6. Describe the educational alternatives suggested by linguists and educators and the rationales for each approach.
7. Demonstrate the teaching of a language experience approach and understand its philosophy, its use with linguistically different children, and its integration of writing, oral discussion, and reading.
8. Describe several components of successful intervention programs for use with inner-city populations and preschoolers.
9. List criteria for evaluating multicultural literature.

Linguistically Different Children and Multicultural Education

A major issue facing educators is the low achievement of many black, Native-American, Mexican-American, inner-city, and poor rural children. Today's educators are increasingly emphasizing a need for educational excellence for minority students. For example, Kronkosky (1982), executive director of the Southwest Educational Development Laboratory, emphasizes reading and writing literacy, educational equity, computer literacy, and training and retraining of teachers. Likewise, Corrigan (1983) anticipates a minority school population that will exceed 50 percent in several southwestern states. High minority populations also exist in large urban school districts, such as New York, Detroit, Washington, D.C., Chicago, and Los Angeles. This concern in metropolitan Los Angeles was highlighted in a recent study analyzing achievement of high-school students. The study conducted by the University of Chicago (Daniels, 1987) found that reading, writing, and mathematics scores were lower for low-income-family black and Hispanic students. Dropout rates are also related to school achievement. A recent study by the National School Board Organization (National Public Radio, January 9, 1992) reported that dropout rates are 40 percent among Hispanic students. This is especially alarming because the same study reported that Hispanic populations have increased in schools by 103 percent.

Educators who are concerned with developing a quality educational system for all students face issues related to linguistically different speech patterns, non-English speech, and cultural diversity. A heightened sensitivity to the needs of all people in American society has led to the realization that language arts programs should heighten self-esteem and create a respect for the individuals, contributions, and the values of all cultures. This chapter considers the selection of literature that presents the values, diversity, and contributions of blacks, Native Americans, Hispanics, and Asians.

LINGUISTICALLY DIFFERENT CHILDREN

The term *dialect* is often used to describe linguistically different speech patterns, although everyone speaks some sort of dialect. Malmstrom (1977) defines dialect as "a distinct variety of a language used by a group of people who share interests, values, goals, and communication" (p. 67). Dialects differ from one another in pronunciation, grammar, and vocabulary. The United States contains a variety of regional dialects. One can often tell by listening to people whether they come from New England, the Midwest, the deep South, the Far West, and so forth. Farr (1991) expands the definition of dialect: "[It includes] either a regional variety of a language (e.g., Southern English in the U.S.) or a social variety of a language (e.g., African American vernacular English in the United States). Both kinds of varieties, of course, coexist with usually one 'official' or 'national' language of a country (in English-speaking countries, some form of 'standard' English). It is important to point out that standard, national languages often start out as regional dialects themselves, becoming the national standard because of social, economic, and political power of the region in which they are used" (p. 365).

Beginning in the 1960s, most American dialect studies began to examine the speech of urban centers, such as New York, Chicago, and Washington, D.C., investigating the influences of social class, urbanization, race, economic levels, and group values. Because the majority of people living in inner cities are black, this type of nonstandard English came to be referred to most commonly as "black English." Yet, the English spoken and taught in most American schools, and recognized by most American teachers, is standard English.

Many studies have focused on the low achievement of inner-city children. In 1969, Cohen reported that 83 percent of disadvantaged black children and 45 percent of disadvantaged white children in New York City were one to three years behind grade level in reading by third grade. Eisenberg's (1974) comparative study of metropolitan, commuter county, suburban, and independent schools showed that metropolitan schools had failure rates two-thirds higher than did the commuter county, three times higher than did the suburban schools, and more than fifty times higher than did the independent schools. Although the achievement of black students is still lower than the achievement of white students, there is a steady decline in the achievement differences between blacks and whites. For example, Burton and Jones (1982) analyzed data based on the National Assessment of Educational Progress in reading, writing, mathematics, science, and social studies. They concluded that achievement differences had lessened between 1970 and 1980. Increased understanding of linguistically different speech patterns may account for educational improvements.

Low socioeconomic levels, however, continue to be closely related to poor academic achievement. Chall and Curtis (1991) state that almost every study that relates socioeconomic status to school achievement finds that middle-class children are more advanced than children from low-income families. Following a study of the results reported in various National Assessment of Educational Progress reports, Chall and Curtis conclude: "In the United States, the relationship between socioeconomic status and reading and writing achievement is most clearly demonstrated by the results of the National Assessment of Educational Progress (NAEP). On each of its five assessments of reading, from 1971 to 1986, NAEP's results have shown a large gap between the achievement of disadvantaged urban children and their more advantaged age peers. Moreover, the longer that students are in school, the greater this gap becomes, such by age 17, low socioeconomic children read below the level achieved by advantaged 13-year-olds" (p. 349).

In searching for reasons why lower-class students have academic difficulties, many educators are now focusing on the ways in which various social and ethnic groups use oral and written language, their expectations and environments, and their knowledge about language and writing. In reviewing current attitudes toward the role of socioeconomic status in achievement, Chall and Curtis (1991) identify several class differences that may attribute to lower achievement. For example, many children from low-income families come from ethnic groups whose use of language differs from that practiced in schools. Consequently, some educators attribute low reading and writing achievement to a mismatch between the mainstream style of language used in school instruction and the various styles of language used in the group. Another view focuses on the kind of oral language environment that stimulates literacy development. In this view, children from low-income families do poorly because the kind of oral language environment that stimulates literacy development is not as prevalent in their homes as in the homes of middle-class children. Chall and Curtis argue that children from low-income families may go through the same stages of literacy development as their more advantaged peers, but that the growth in some aspect of low-income children's language or literacy development becomes delayed by conditions at home or experiences in school that affect their later development.

Two quite different theories have been proposed to explain the causes of low achievement by many black inner-city children. In the early 1960s, psychologists discovered that on standardized language tests, these children were unable to reach the standardized norms. Thus, psychologists such as Bereiter and Englemann (1966), Deutsch et al. (1967), and Bernstein (1961) argued that many black inner-city children lack a fully developed language system. They argued that black children often come to school with a language system that must be remediated if the children are to progress in school. Intensive language remediation programs such as Englemann's and Osborn's DISTAR reflect this view.

Other educators oppose this theory of language deficit. In the late sixties and seventies, linguists conducted much research pertaining to speakers of black English. They analyzed speech samples under various conditions, studied black dialects, and examined in great detail how those dialects differed from standard English dialects in terms of phonology (speech sounds); morphology (word forming, including inflection, derivation, and compounding); and syntax (the way words are put together to form phrases, clauses, and sentences). Extensive research by Labov (1969, 1970, 1971, and 1973) and by Baratz and Shuy (1969) demonstrated that children who speak black English have a system that is fully developed but different from that of standard English. These investigators disagree with the deficit theory, which stresses illogical grammatical structures in black English. In fact, these linguists maintain that black English is just as logical and consistent as standard English. Labov found that structures of black English function in ways similar to the structures in other languages. For example, the use of the double negative to signify negation, which appears in black English, also appears in French and German.

In one study, Baratz (1969) asked black-English-speaking children and standard-English-speaking children to repeat sentences read to them in both standard and nonstandard English. She found that black-English-speaking students had consistent verbal responses. For example, 97 percent of the black-English-speaking children responded in the same way to the sentence "I asked Tom if he wanted to go to the picture that was playing at the Howard." The black-English-speaking children responded with "I aks Tom did he wanna go to the picture that be playing at the Howard." Sixty percent of the black-English-speaking children responded to the sentence "Does Deborah like to play with the girl that sits next to her in school?" by repeating "Do Deborah like to play wif the girl what sit next to her in school?"

The white standard-English-speaking children also followed a definite pattern by translating black English back into standard English when they were asked to repeat sentences. Seventy-eight percent of the standard-English-speaking children repeated the sentence "I aks Tom do he wanna go to the picture that be playing at the Howard" as "I asked Tom if he wanted to go to the picture that was playing at the Howard." Likewise, 68 percent of the standard-English-speaking children repeated the sentence "Do Deborah like to play wif the girl what sit next to her at school" as "Does Deborah like to play with the girl that sits next to her at school?"

This study not only demonstrated the logic and consistency of speech patterns. According to Baratz, it also demonstrated that the dialect of black-English-speaking children interferes when these children attempt to use standard English. Problems as to how much interference results and how to provide effective education for speakers of nonstandard English have not as yet been resolved. According to Farr (1991), three positions (mostly politically motivated) relate to teaching students who are not in the language and cultural mainstream: (1) an eradication approach, which attempts to replace certain speech patterns with standard ones; (2) a biloquialism or biadialectism approach, which calls for learning new standard patterns without eliminating the old nonstandard ones or developing negative attitudes toward the nonmainstream cultures and dialects; and (3) an appreciation-of-differences approach that seeks to enlighten mainstream populations about variations in language rather than change any language spoken by various dialect populations. Farr states that debate about these positions has continued for two decades. She concludes that the second, or biloquialism, position is the most reasonable: "Since all speakers, mainstream and nonmainstream alike, shift among more or less formal styles, depending on context, to some degree, this position should be a relatively natural one. It also has the advantage of appearing to be the most reasonable position, presenting a compromise between the two more extreme positions of eradication and appreciation of dialect differences" (p. 366). Farr also maintains that the problems related to teaching standard English and literacy are more complicated than were originally thought.

According to linguist Guy Bailey, many unanswered questions are related to how or if oral language interferes with writing (personal communication, 1983). Bailey states: "Over the last decade an increasing number of scholars have suggested that students' oral language interferes with their writing: the syntactic structures and coherence devices characteristic of the oral code are used in lieu of those characteristics of the written code. This interference apparently involves both the intrusion of oral styles in writing (for example, failure to include explicit reference and coherence devices in compositions) and the influence of dialect (the absence of tense markers, for instance) or in some cases the student's first language. However, linguists have yet to specify the exact relationships between speech and writing because they lack comparable data from both modes" (p. 1).

Many linguists and educators believe that black English is systematically structured; therefore, it is different and not deficient. But even among those who agree on "different" versus "deficient," there is little agreement on the best educational approach to use to improve the school achievement of black-English-speaking children. Suggested educational alternatives include (1) contrastive analysis of black-English and standard-English sentence structures, (2) language experience approaches, (3) dialect reading and speaking of conventional instructional materials, (4) numerous opportunities for functional and interactive communication, and (5) abundant experiences with written texts. Evidence suggests that such factors as testing bias, teacher attitudes, early identification, parent involvement, early intervention, and long-term intervention programs can influence the achievement of linguistically different children.

ASSESSMENT ISSUES

Educators are concerned about the criticism that many commonly used standardized tests are both culturally and linguistically biased in favor of middle-class, standard-English-speaking children. In fact, Bartel, Grill, and Bryen (1973) went so far as to suggest that no standardized tests are appropriate for black-English-speaking children and that use of available tests may result in extreme errors in student placement.

Nontraditional Tests

Some educators suggest the use of nontraditional forms of assessment to measure cognitive ability and language. Adler (1973) recommends such tests for evaluating linguistically different children. He believes that language tests should consist of analysis of spontaneous speech in naturalistic settings. In fact, the best information about verbal capacity may be obtained by asking children questions that are interesting to them. For this reason, tests should encourage student involvement. For example, the Picture Story Language Test by Myklebust is designed to encourage the telling of a story. When administering any test to a linguistically different child, Adler urges examiners to repeat directions and use practice questions to ascertain whether the child actually understands what is expected. Examiners will probably need to use more oral directions and examples than are provided with the test manual and must be able to understand nonstandard speech.

Mantell (1974) made several suggestions for obtaining language samples and evaluating the language patterns of linguistically different children by nonstandardized methods. One device she recommends is photography of people or places familiar to the children. In this situation, a teacher would ask open-ended questions about the pictures, such as "What is the person in the photograph doing? Why is he doing that? How does the person look? How would he talk about himself? What would the person in the photograph do if . . . ?" Familiar photographs motivate children to talk about something they know and feel comfortable talking about.

A second device for obtaining language samples is what Mantell calls "The Faceless X." For this informal test, a teacher draws a circular face on a transparency. Students are asked to fill in expressions using eyebrows, mouth, hairstyle, skin color, headdresses, and so forth. The teacher then asks open-ended questions about the face. This activity can also provide insights into attitudes and biases of students.

As a third testing device, Mantell suggests role playing in order to analyze ability to alter language according to the requirements of a specific situation. Role-playing situations can be formal or informal. A student who role-plays an interview with the school principal for an article in the school paper or an interview with an employer for a part-time job displays an ability or inability to use more formal language. In contrast, role playing of an argument between a brother and sister over whose turn it is to do the dinner dishes allows analysis of the student's ability to use casual language. During role-playing situations, ask other students to watch for specific language usage. Note their ability to recognize various usage situations.

Several educators recommend modifying scoring procedures for reading tests so that errors attributable to dialect differences are not counted as reading errors. Hunt (1974) found that black, inner-city third- and fourth-graders scored significantly higher on the Gray Oral Reading Test when responses reflecting black English variations in language were not counted as errors than they did when the tests were scored according to the directions in the test manual. The Goodman Miscue Analysis also stresses the importance of recognizing dialect differences in reading. It suggests that dialect errors in oral reading not be counted as comparable to errors that change the meaning of the selection. In order to do this, of course, a teacher must be knowledgeable about the dialect.

Another researcher (Hutchinson, 1972) found that inclusion or deletion of dialect-related items in a word-discrimination test also influenced the grade-level scores of the students taking the test. When dialect-related items were included in the test, 40 percent of the black, inner-city, higher-ability third-graders scored below grade level; when the dialect-related items were removed, only 2.6 percent of these students scored below grade level. It is important, then, to examine tests for possible unintentional bias before administering them to linguistically different children.

Linguists have provided a great deal of knowledge about the differences between standard English and black English. They recommend that teachers become aware of these differences and utilize their knowledge to more fairly assess the achievement of a black-English-speaking child. Teachers need to become familiar with differences in both pronunciation and syntax. It is very important that teachers distinguish between differences in dialect pronunciation and erroneous interpretations of test material. Only a teacher familiar with the differences between black and standard English can accurately evaluate the language patterns of a black-English-speaking student and establish priorities for effective instruction in oral language, writing, and reading. Tables 5–1 and 5–2 provide guidelines for analysis of the major differences between pronunciation and syntax.

The type of informal testing recommended by many educators requires that teachers understand whatever linguistically different speech patterns the children use. The following resources will also be useful:

- "Major Differences Between Standard English and Black English," in *Reading and the Black English Speaking Child* (Harber and Beatty, 1978), pp. 46–47.
- "Black English: A Descriptive Guide for the Teacher," in *Black Dialects and Reading* (Fryburg, 1974), pp. 190–96.

TABLE 5–1
Phonological differences between standard English and black English

Feature	Standard English	Black English
Simplification of consonant	test	tes
clusters	past	pas
th sounds		
voiceless *th* in initial position	think	tink
voiced *th* in initial position	the	de
voiceless *th* in medial position	nothing	nofin
th in final position	tooth	toof
r and *l*		
in postvocalic position	sister	sistah
	nickel	nickuh
in final position	Saul	saw
Devoicing of final *b, d,*	cab	cap
and *g*	bud	but
	pig	pik
Nasalization		
ing suffix	doing	doin
i and *e* before a nasal	pen	pin
Stress—absence of the first syllable		
of a multisyllabic word when the		
first syllable is unstressed	about	'bout
Plural marker	three birds	three bird
	the books	de book
Possessive marker	the boy's hat	de boy hat
Third person singular marker	He works here	He work here
Past tense—simplification of	passed	pass
final consonant clusters	loaned	loan

SOURCE: Reprinted with permission of Jean R. Harber and Jane N. Beatty, and the International Reading Association, from *Reading and the Black English Speaking Child*. Newark, Del.: International Reading Association, 1978.

Informal Assessment: A Portfolio Approach

Many of the informal assessment techniques currently being recommended by educators are useful for teachers of linguistically or culturally different children. For example, Goodman (1991) recommends using such informal evaluations as portfolios, checklists, inventories, and observations. Particularly useful are individual portfolios in which teachers keep examples of each student's writing, interests, backgrounds, comprehension levels, processes for gaining comprehension, and responses to different types of literature and literacy activities (see Norton, 1992). Pikulski (1989) recommends this approach highly:

> One of the most dynamic assessment concepts currently being discussed in our field is that of a portfolio approach to the assessment of reading and literacy. Since there are no tests or test materials that are specifically associated with this approach, it has the potential for placing teachers and students—not tests and test scores—at the very center of the assessment process. (p. 81)

TABLE 5–2
Syntactic differences between standard English and black English

Feature	Standard English	Black English
Linking verb	He is going.	He goin' He is goin'
Pronomial apposition	That teacher yells at the kids.	Dat teachah, she yell at de kid.
Agreement of subject and third-person singular verb	She runs home. She has a bike.	She run home. She have a bike.
Irregular verb forms	They rode their bikes.	Dey rided der bike.
Future form	I will go home.	I'm a go home.
"If" construction	I asked if he did it.	I aks did he do it.
Indefinite article	I want an apple.	I want a apple.
Negation	I don't have any.	I don't got none.
Pronoun form	We have to do it.	Us got to do it.
Copula (verb "to be")	He is here all the time.	He be here.
Prepositions	Put the cat out of the house.	Put de cat out de house.
	The dress is made of wool.	De dress is made outta wool.

SOURCE: Reprinted with permission of Jean R. Harber and Jane N. Beatty, and the International Reading Association, from *Reading and the Black English Speaking Child*. Newark, Del.: International Reading Association, 1978.

Diverse samples of literacy events, which are collected as students interact with various aspects of the language arts, become what Pikulski refers to as "the fullest, most ecologically valid approach that can be taken to assessment" (p. 81).

When students are considering the development of a portfolio, have them imagine themselves in a profession in which portfolios are popular and extremely useful. For example, have them think of themselves as artists, photographers, or authors who want to demonstrate their talents and breadth of experience. They might ask, "What examples would best show our talents? What examples might show how we have progressed in our chosen fields?" Then, they can think about what might be included in a portfolio of language arts to illustrate their growing understanding of and appreciation for oral language, writing, listening, reading, and literature.

Valencia (1990) provides guidelines for development and management of portfolios, beginning with the selection of large expandable folders to hold samples of work that reflect the goals of the program. She recommends that states, school districts, or individual teachers develop goals for instruction and then decide what information would help to assess those goals. The folders usually include samples of work chosen by the teacher or the student, the teacher's observational notes, the student's self-evaluations, and the progress notes contributed collaboratively by student and teacher. The portfolio could also include results of classroom tests, various written responses, checklists, and audio or video tapes. The selections should relate closely to the goals and priorities for instruction. For example, by collecting both required evidence and supporting evidence that instructional goals are being achieved, teachers can look systematically at the progress of the students and the effectiveness of the language arts program. Valencia maintains that supporting evidence is especially important because it shows the depth and variety of a student's literacy abilities. In addition to collecting and assessing information in portfolios, Valencia recommends that teachers and students meet every few weeks to discuss progress, add notes, and decide what additional materials should be in the portfolios. At the end of the year, teachers and students can decide which materials will be taken home and which will be kept to show progress into the next year. The portfolios also can be used during conferences with parents and administrators.

REINFORCEMENT ACTIVITY

1. Review an often-used standardized test. Look at both the pictures and vocabulary. Find items that you feel might be biased because of a child's experience or English usage. Share your findings with your language arts class.
2. If you are teaching children, try one of the nonstandardized testing techniques suggested in this chapter. If you are not teaching at this time, develop a series of pictures and questions or a role-playing strategy, and present the informal techniques to a group of your peers.
3. Begin a portfolio by collecting the works of a student that include various examples of speaking, listening, writing, and reading. Assess changes in the student's ability as shown in portfolio examples over time. Which portfolio examples are the most useful? Why?

TEACHER ATTITUDES

Farr's (1991) review of research associated with dialects, culture, and teaching of English concludes that ethnosensitivity—the understanding that one's views of the world, or ways of using language, are not necessarily shared by others—is the most important principle of effective instruction for linguistically and culturally diverse students. Consequently, teachers must have a deep understanding of cultural and linguistic differences, especially among the students in their classrooms. This is especially important if teachers and students are from different cultural and ethnic groups.

The literature and research on teacher attitudes toward linguistically different children are quite startling. Teachers often not only react negatively toward students who speak nonstandard English but also rate them as lower in class, less intelligent, and less able to achieve academically than their standard-English-speaking peers. For example, Crowl and MacGinite (1974) audiotaped both black and white ninth-grade boys responding with identically worded answers to questions asked in school. Experienced white teachers were then asked to evaluate the appropriateness of the answers. The teachers assigned significantly higher grades to the answers given by the white students than to the identical answers given by the black students. Similar attitudes exist among elementary school teachers.

Watson-Thompson (1985) found that both black and white elementary school teachers expressed negative attitudes toward the use of black English.

There is no doubt that negative teacher attitudes affect the teaching that takes place in classrooms. This author has observed classrooms in which negative and positive attitudes toward linguistically different children have been openly displayed. One teacher of mostly black, lower-socioeconomic-class children, for example, mentioned that she taught her twenty-five students as one group because testing indicated they were all at a very low level of ability. She implied that one could not expect much from a class made up of mostly linguistically different students. In contrast, another teacher divided a similar group of linguistically different students into ability groups and taught highly motivating lessons. This teacher felt that the students had a great deal of potential that required exceptional teaching. She not only accepted nonstandard reading renditions from her black-English-speaking students, but also spoke Spanish for the benefit of her Mexican-American students. She encouraged her students to interact with other students during numerous oral and written activities. She praised them as she discussed their work and encouraged them to work cooperatively. The atmosphere in the room was so positive that one could almost feel the learning that was taking place.

Teacher attitudes about linguistically different speech also influence oral reading activities. A popular method of checking oral reading ability is to have a student read a selection to the teacher. In fact, this activity is duplicated millions of times each day in classrooms across the nation. During oral reading activities, teachers are not usually as concerned with correcting errors that do not change meaning as they are with correcting errors that do result in meaning change. However, in a study by Cunningham (1977), 78 percent of the teachers indicated that they would correct dialect errors that did not change meaning, whereas only 27 percent indicated that they would correct nondialect errors that did not change meaning. Consequently, Cunningham recommends that teacher training stress the meaning equivalence between standard and black English and the grammatical nature of black English. If a teacher spends a great deal of reading-instruction time correcting dialect, it is questionable that the children are receiving effective reading instruction.

It is clear that teacher attitudes are important to the achievement of students. To improve self-image and academic achievement, teachers need to expect more from students, to judge their capabilities independently of race and socioeconomic status, and to understand and respect their dialect and cultural background.

Overcoming long-standing attitudes and the effects of racism is a complex process. William Raspberry (1988), a syndicated columnist for the *Washington Post*, states that "the reasonable course for dealing with effects of racism is the course we are taking with AIDS: to learn as much as we can about how to cure it, how to immunize ourselves against it, and how to halt its tragic spread" (p. 6A).

REINFORCEMENT
ACTIVITY

1. Observe an elementary classroom that includes linguistically different children. Record in writing the questions asked by the teacher, the responses made by the students, and the responses made to the students by the teacher. Analyze

Interaction with teachers and in small groups is important for students with limited English proficiency.

the questions and responses. Does the teacher respond differently to children who speak black English as opposed to those who speak standard English?

2. Interview the children's teacher. Ask the teacher to identify which children he or she expects will do well in the class, and which ones he or she expects not to do well. Is there a relationship between the answers and the speech of the children? Discuss your findings in class. If negative attitudes exist, what is the implication for academic achievement? How will you make sure that all children in your classes receive a quality education?

ENVIRONMENTAL FACTORS

How important is the family environment for fostering student achievement? According to Brause and Mayher (1991), "family structures exert a powerful influence on our students' educational goals and their ability to participate in life at school. The size of the gap between the language and values of the school and those at home predicts the level of success the student is likely to achieve in school. Since the family experience has been such an important predictor of school success, it is essential that educators reconceptualize schooling so that all students, regardless of family background, will have not only access to a high-quality education, but be nurtured to succeed in such a setting" (p. 263). Consequently, successful programs bridge the gaps between experience and expectation.

An interesting study by Greenberg and Davison (1972) compares home environments of high-academic-achieving and low-academic-achieving black urban-ghetto children. Findings indicate that the high achievers had a more structured home life, more room, and more books than did low achievers. In addition, the parents of the high achievers showed more respect and concern for their children's education, used less punishment, offered more responses, and demonstrated broader social concerns than did the parents of the low-achieving children. Marzano (1991) points out that within any learning situation, the learner is concerned with environmental factors such as safety, order, and general level of comfort. He contends that "learners ask themselves such questions as whether they are safe and relatively comfortable, and whether the setting is orderly. Negative answers to these questions influence students' propensity to learn" (p. 572). According to Taylor and Dorsey-Gaines (1988) in a study of black families living below the poverty level, literacy interactions are difficult in many families because the families have to make concerted efforts just to survive.

The current emphasis on day-care centers and Head Start programs was instituted in response to a need for early stimulation of children. These programs try to provide stimulation that fosters responses through play materials, experiences, and interactions that help small children discover and manipulate auditory, visual, and tactile stimuli in the environment. Many educational authorities recommend both well-run day-care centers and parental education to help overcome environmental deficiencies.

The literature on linguistically different children often mentions that black, lower-socioeconomic-class children do not feel that they have as many opportunities as middle-class white or black children. It is frequently suggested that the educational environment of linguistically different children must build their self-esteem and use instructional materials that show minorities as contributing members of society.

CHARACTERISTICS OF EFFECTIVE INTERVENTION PROGRAMS

The educational environment is of critical concern for lower-socioeconomic-class children who may not have experienced the benefits of homes that foster academic advancement. Early intervention is particularly important for many children from low-income families. Juel (1988) found that children who enter school with little awareness about relationships between words, letters, and sounds experience problems in learning to read. Children who lack this readiness are more apt to become poor readers and writers by fourth grade. Juel contends that if one waits for readiness skills to emerge without intervening, children who are at risk will not succeed. Slavin and Madden (1989) state that the most important element for prevention of student failure is immediate and intensive assistance. They conclude: "Virtually all the programs found to be instructionally effective for students at risk assess student progress frequently and use the results to modify groupings or instructional content to meet students' individual needs" (p. 11).

In exploring the characteristics of effective elementary-school instruction for children considered at risk, Chall, Jacobs, and Baldwin (1990) analyzed the instruction provided for low-income children who were reading at or above grade level.

They found the following effective practices: (1) instruction was provided at or above the children's reading levels; (2) direct instruction was given in text comprehension in reading, social studies, science, health, and other content areas; (3) vocabulary was stressed during content-area, reading, and language arts instruction; (4) diverse materials were provided, including a wide range of reading levels; (5) field trips and other activities exposed students to new experiences and helped build background knowledge; (6) homework included workbooks in the early grades and trade books and content-area materials in the later grades; and (7) children's parents were in direct contact with their teachers. In a later study, Chall and Curtis (1991) found that effective instruction was characterized by "a good, strong start in the primary grades, followed in the intermediate and upper elementary grades by structured and challenging instruction in reading, writing, and vocabulary, opportunities for reading stimulating trade books that varied widely, and many opportunities to practice literacy skills" (p. 352).

BILINGUAL EDUCATION AND ENGLISH AS A SECOND LANGUAGE

Teachers are increasingly concerned with educating the diverse population of students in American schools. Statistics indicate that cities such as Los Angeles, New York, and Houston have high concentrations of children whose native language is not English; moreover, these populations are expected to grow.

Three terms are frequently used in reference to students whose native language is not English. One term, *limited English proficiency,* frequently abbreviated LEP, refers to students from any group who have not as yet mastered English. The other two terms, *bilingual* and *English as a second language* (ESL), are also common in the literature. Allen (1991) describes what a bilingual program involves: "The school programs designed to assist children who are in the process of acquiring English as their second language have been organized by focusing on the language in which instruction is delivered. Bilingual approaches involve the use of two languages for the instruction of language minority children. Transitional bilingual programs are ones in which children's first language is used as a medium of instruction until they become fluent enough to receive all their instruction in English. ESL is a part of such programs. It is expected that the amount of instruction offered in the child's native language will decrease as the child's ability to use English increases. Almost all bilingual programs in the United States would be identified as transitional programs" (p. 360).

Because considerable research has been done with Mexican-American students, we will focus on this population in the balance of this section. Clearly, there is reason for concern. According to Cortes (1986), about 45 percent of Hispanic students do not complete high school, with 40 percent dropping out of school before the tenth grade. In a comparative study of achievement, Maestas (1981) examined the effects of rural and urban backgrounds and ethnic differences on the achievement of high school seniors. He found that Mexican-American achievement, as measured by the Comprehensive Test of Basic Skills and the Iowa Test of Basic Skills, was lower than that of non-Mexican-Americans. Daniels (1987) also reported this finding in a study that analyzed achievement in Los Angeles.

Cultural values are instrumental in developing preferences for the type of learning environment that will be most rewarding.

Mexican-American children who have been raised during preschool years in the traditional culture of the Mexican-American community are required upon entering school to adjust to cultural values, language, and teaching styles that differ from anything they have previously experienced. Such children also must continue to function in their culture, so the adjustment problems for Mexican-American children are prodigious.

Freedman (1990) maintains that literacy is culturally framed and defined, and that members of different cultural groups differ in how they define literacy and what they view as literate behavior. It is important, therefore, to understand how culture shapes the behavior of individuals. Purves and Purves (1986) contend that teachers must investigate the extent to which reading, literature, and writing are valued by the culture. Cultural values and beliefs have deep historical and religious roots. Thus, these authors conclude: "When an individual is transplanted from one culture to another culture, the individual has a great deal both to unlearn and to learn if he or she is to be accepted as a writer in that culture. To some extent, it may be impossible for an individual thoroughly acculturated in one culture to become indistinguishable as a writer from members of another culture" (p. 194).

Critics of the educational system for Mexican-American children maintain that educators have created barriers between the culture of the children and that of the school and have often forced the children to choose between home and school. With the considerable information about the value systems, learning styles, and language of Mexican-Americans that has been gathered since the 1970s, teachers can now effectively improve the learning environment of such children.

Values

Ramírez and Castañeda (1974) identify four major Mexican-American value clusters. First, there are strong family ties in the Mexican-American culture; the needs and interests of the individual are considered secondary to those of the family. Because of these ties, the community and the total ethnic group become an extension of the family. This strong family and community identification contrasts with the stress on a child's separate identity and the development of self-awareness emphasized in most American schools.

Second, interpersonal relationships in Mexican-American communities are characterized by openness, warmth, and commitment to mutual dependence. Emphasis is on development of sensitivity to the feelings and needs of others. Achievements are considered the result of cooperative rather than individual effort. Ramírez and Price-Williams (1971) found that Mexican-American children in Houston scored higher than Anglo-American children on their need to cooperate with other children as well as on their need for sympathetic aid from another person. They also expressed greater need for guidance, direction, and support from authority figures. Consequently, Mexican-American children may achieve better in a cooperative rather than competitive atmosphere. This cultural characteristic of mutual dependence and cooperative achievement contrasts with the individual competition encouraged by American schools.

The third value cluster is role and status definition within the family and the community. Older people hold greater status, and children are expected to model themselves after their parents and other respected members of the community. Mexican-American children may produce higher levels of achievement if teachers take on the role of this status figure and provide a model for the children. The importance of this family and community value is shown in a study by McConnell (1989), who found that the school success of Spanish-speaking migrant children increased when there was interaction between the community and the school. In this program, parents became part of the teaching staff and teachers included people from the ethnic and language group.

The final value cluster is the support and reinforcement of the values provided by the Mexican-Catholic ideology. Emphasis on family ties is reinforced through religious commitment. Individuals are thus encouraged to be respectful of adults and social conventions and to be open to guidance.

Ramírez and Castañeda contend that development of understanding of Mexican-American values should be one of the primary concerns of educators, and educators have recently been taking this advice. Many school districts with predominately Mexican-American populations are providing in-service programs to help make the teachers aware of both the cultural characteristics and learning styles of Mexican-American students.

Learning Styles

Children develop their own styles of learning and means of assimilating information about their environments. The values and socialization styles of a culture affect the specific learning styles in children. Cultural values are instrumental in developing preferences for certain types of rewards, and for the type of learning environment that is most rewarding. Schools that recognize these preferences may utilize them in designing educational climates that are rewarding and produce higher achievement.

The motivational styles of Mexican-American children appear to be quite different from the motivational styles of Anglo-Americans. Kagan and Madsen (1971) found, as would be expected from Mexican-American values, that Mexican-American children are more highly motivated in a cooperative setting than in a competitive one. In contrast, Anglo-American children are more competitive.

Mexican-American children also show greater desire to interact with others and to belong to a social group (Ramírez & Price-Williams, 1974). Due to their orientation, Mexican-American children may do better when the curriculum has a human content and is closely related to the needs of others as well as to the family and community. Many of these features are found in a successful program described by Quintero and Huerta-Macias (1990) in which children and parents became part of a cooperative, relevant learning environment that included family teams.

EDUCATIONAL IMPLICATIONS FOR STUDENTS WITH LIMITED ENGLISH PROFICIENCY

Students with limited English proficiency face a formidable academic challenge in American classrooms. However, according to Ezer (1990), children can learn to read and write in two languages concurrently if the children have opportunities to interact in supportive environments. Wong-Fillmore's (1986) four-year study of the effects of instructional practices on the learning of English by students from Chinese and Hispanic backgrounds provides several educational implications. First, the research shows that students vary greatly in their ability to learn a second language. Whereas some students learn in just a few years, most students require from four to six years to achieve the proficiency needed for full participation in school. Furthermore, the research supports certain instructional practices. For example, Hispanic students gain in both production and comprehension skills if they have opportunities to use the new language while interacting with their peers. In contrast, interacting with peers has little value for Chinese students until they have enough proficiency in the new language to feel confident when using English with their classmates. For the Chinese students, close interactions with teachers and opportunities to use English during teacher-directed instructional activities relates to gains in oral language. Although both Chinese and Hispanic students gain from high-quality instruction and clear language usage, Hispanic students (mostly Mexican-Americans) do especially well when the instruction is clearly presented and well organized.

Wong-Fillmore is especially critical of the quality of much of the instruction. She states,

> I came to realize that what these LEP children generally get in school does not add up to a real education at all. Much of what they are being taught can be described as

"basic skills" rather than as "content." Instruction in reading, for example, is mostly focused on developing accuracy in reading rather than on understanding or appreciating textual materials. Writing focuses on accuracy in spelling, punctuation, the niceties of grammar rather than on communicating ideas in written form or on the development of sustained reasoning and the use of evidence in supporting written arguments. (p. 478)

Research by both Cumming and Genishi highlight the importance of encouraging communication within the environment. Cumming (1990) identifies three kinds of thinking strategies that are helpful to students while learning a second language: (1) searching out and assessing appropriate wording, (2) comparing cross-linguistic equivalents, and (3) reasoning about linguistic choices. Genishi (1989) observed a group of second-language learners and drew three conclusions pertaining to children, their teachers, and their learning. First, each child has his or her own approach to learning the second language. Teachers need to accept each child's approach and to encourage all attempts to communicate. Second, classrooms that have a variety of activities and people with many opportunities for oral language are best able to support the second-language learner. Third, effective teachers build on observations related to each child. They encourage oral language by providing a sensitive support system in which children are encouraged to use their new language. They observe when children look confused or interested, respond to nonverbal cues, allow friends to stay together, keep conversations alive, and record signs of children's learning.

Canadian educators provide additional guidelines for effective education. For example, Piper (1986) recommends using traditional stories and fables from various cultural sources and focusing on awareness of the different languages and different cultural backgrounds. He suggests that teachers compile lists of words that are the same across many languages, write signs in schools in several representative languages, explore emigration patterns of families within the classroom by using maps and family histories, and involve parents in the design and implementation of curricular materials. Sealey (1984) emphasizes that instruction should encourage students to accept and be sensitive to cultural diversity, understand that similar values frequently underlie different customs, have quality contact with people from other cultures, and role-play experiences with other cultures. The literature recommended later in this chapter and the activities that teach children how to identify values in the literature encourage cultural sensitivity.

Several educators have developed principles of effective second-language learning. For example, Early (1990) proposes the following:

1. Learning should build on the previous educational and personal experiences of ESL students, who should be encouraged to honor their cultural identities.
2. Developing proficiency in a language takes many years; it requires that language be used in such areas as learning, socializing, inquiring, imagining, and wondering.
3. Learning should allow for integration of language teaching into various academic content areas so that the ESL students experience continuing cognitive and academic growth.
4. Learning should allow ESL students to be involved with activities or tasks that encourage them to use language interactively across various situations, modes, and text types.

5. Learning should use multimedia approaches, such as drawing, writing, and talking, to make communication clearer and to lower the language barriers for students who are learning subject-matter in a second language.
6. Learning and social growth are increased when schools encourage parental participation.

Dixon (1976), who investigated the cultural values and learning styles of Mexican-American children, suggests the following teaching strategies:

1. Activities that emphasize improving skills of all members of a group may be more successful than activities that emphasize only individual improvement.
2. Activities that require cooperation rather than competition may be successful. The school environment should encourage cooperation by assigning tasks for small groups of children to work on together, and should encourage a cooperative attitude about classroom behavior.
3. Mexican-American children profit from educational experiences that allow them to interact with the teacher or other students.
4. Seeing other children in authority roles in the classroom may be natural and desirable as a result of the generalization from the home culture's use of other children as authority figures. Peer teaching is recommended for bilingual classes because the peer approach makes use of other children in authority roles and strengthens interpersonal relationships within the classroom. In peer teaching, a student who has a superior skill "teaches" or assists a child who needs help. The language experience approach is very good for bilingual children because the children can use both their own language and their cultural values.

According to Ramírez and Castañeda (1974), authorities on Mexican-American education, teachers should use many nonverbal indications of acceptance, including smiling, touching, allowing children to work next to the teacher, and sharing laughter and other warm experiences. These actions are reminiscent of the close family ties developed in the traditional Mexican-American culture. Teachers should also try to know the children as individuals and relate lesson material to their experiences whenever possible.

The close ties of the traditional Mexican-American family make it appropriate for teachers to work closely and cooperatively with families. Send notes to the family telling them how pleased you are with their child's progress. Notes accompanying excellent examples of student work are especially appropriate. Reward students with frequent reminders of how proud their families will be about their progress. Meet personally with and talk frequently to the families in order to develop a closer relationship.

As noted, researchers suggest that traditional Mexican-American children look up to an authority figure and model themselves after older, revered members of the community. Teachers may provide that model by having children repeat words after them in language instruction or by providing models of how to write, paint, or do other classroom activities. When trying to provide a positive model, show respect for the language of the children by using Spanish frequently during the school day. If the highly respected authority model uses a child's native language, it conveys the message that the language is to be respected. Teachers can also convey respect for the language by teaching Spanish songs and rhymes in addition to addressing Spanish-speaking children and adults in Spanish. Develop respect for the culture by studying famous Mexican-Americans and Mexican holidays and other celebrations.

Educators who use second-language techniques provide guidance for working with Mexican-American children who have limited skills in the English language. Carter's (1982) *Non-Native and Nonstandard Dialect Students: Classroom Practices in Teaching English, 1982–1983* describes current approaches in ESL classes. De Félix's (1982) language arts approach is based on the following basic principles: (1) fluency precedes accuracy, (2) students learn concepts and structures when they are ready to use them, (3) teachers should organize successively more challenging tasks, and (4) acquisition of the linguistic function precedes acquisition of the form. The ESL methods in the approach require teachers to slow the pace for students with limited English proficiency, introduce phonics after students have increased their vocabulary, build on children's native language, understand the nature of language strategies, and keep informed of new strategies. De Félix recommends the following five-step approach for working with ESL students:

1. *Develop comprehension.* Use a variety of resources, such as pictures, concrete materials, native language materials, community resources, pantomime, and peer tutors, to help students understand the concepts behind the language to be taught.
2. *Select and analyze for vocabulary, grammar, and linguistic function.* Analyze the materials to be used to help students integrate knowledge. For example, select vocabulary words that can be taught through concrete examples and experiences. When possible, expand this concrete understanding through categories. (If the word is *meat,* teach different kinds of meat or sample foods from different nutritional groups.) Next, select two or three types of sentences found in the lesson and extend the students' use of grammar and the target vocabulary. Construct sentences showing how the vocabulary fits into different sentence patterns. ("I like meat," "I like beef and ham," "Beef and ham are types of meat.") Finally, select linguistic functions to teach through the lesson; for example: phrases that justify actions or identify needs; phrases that direct students' actions; phrases or words that help students interpret materials by recognizing sequences, relationships, and causes; phrases that allow students to hypothesize, anticipate consequences, recognize problems, and predict solutions; experiences, such as puppetry, that allow students to explore language; and experiences, such as songs and games, that encourage students to have fun with language.
3. *Plan activities to meet students' needs.* Plan activities that consider individual needs, such as age, cultural background, and English proficiency.
4. *Present lessons by proceeding from the known to the unknown.* Present new information on the basis of prior knowledge and understanding of concepts to be acquired.
5. *Integrate and reaffirm skills.* Help students integrate concepts into their personal lives and school content areas, and help them reaffirm skills in various contexts.

If you have a bilingual class near your university or college, visit a classroom. Observe the children and describe some of the effective instructional techniques you see. (You may also observe some that are not effective. If this happens, see if you can decide why they are not effective.) If you do not have access to bilingual programs, read about an educational program for Mexican-American students. Is the program utilizing knowledge about learning styles as justified in the research?

INSTRUCTIONAL APPROACHES FOR LINGUISTICALLY DIFFERENT CHILDREN

In this section we will discuss some highly recommended instructional approaches for use with linguistically different students. Many of the approaches discussed in Chapters 2 and 3 are excellent for linguistically different students. Many of those we will now consider are useful for all populations; others are geared toward a specific group.

Contrastive Analysis

The aim of many educators who try to expand a child's language is improved oral and written communication in the classroom. Some programs stress teaching standard English before children learn to read; other programs teach standard English as an alternative dialect and a useful tool for school and society. This second approach usually teaches standard English usage while maintaining and respecting the original dialect. Thus, students theoretically have a choice: they may use whichever form of language is most useful for the specific occasion. This section looks at a program designed for early primary language expansion and another designed for the middle grades.

Cullinan, Jaggar, and Strickland (1974) developed a language expansion program for kindergarten through third-grade children attending predominately black public schools. The teachers in the program were trained to recognize the contrasts between standard English and black English so they could help children perceive the differences between the two forms of language. The program utilized literature selections read to the children daily. After hearing the selections, the children took part in activities that provided opportunities to expand oral language as well as to practice specific patterns of standard English.

The lessons included six different types of language expansion activities. The first activity utilized dramatization and puppetry. Students discussed a story, prepared the scenes to be dramatized, and presented the scenes to the class. The second activity was built on storytelling by the children. Students listened to a story, such as "Curious George," talked about the main character or the parts of the story that they most enjoyed and then told stories about the character in another situation. (For example, what would happen if George found himself locked overnight in a supermarket?) The third activity used book discussions, stressing various listening comprehension skills as well as clear expression of ideas. In the fourth

While some students acquire sufficient proficiency in English to become full participants in classroom activities quickly, other students may require four to six years to reach that goal.

activity, the children talked about the characters in a story and how the characters felt. They chose specific lines from the stories to illustrate a particular language pattern that needed practice. The students then role-played, using the specific sentence patterns from the story. The fifth activity used even more specific language patterns. Following a story and discussion, a puppet named "Peter Parrot" asked the children to repeat sentences from the story. Children repeated the sentences in unison and individually. The final activity, used after a literature selection, was choral speaking. After a story or poem was read to the children, they were divided into groups to perform the story or poem as a choral-speaking activity.

Mantell (1974) designed a language expansion program built on contrastive analysis (comparing the points of differences between two forms of language) for middle-grade black-English-speaking students. Mantell's program identified the most frequently used grammatical features of black English and then focused specifically on the features that most sharply separate one social group from other social groups. Mantell says it is most important to concentrate on features based on findings by Wolfram (1970). Wolfram plotted features of black English against the following five criteria: (1) sharpness of social stratification, (2) generality of application of the rule, (3) whether the rule is grammatical or phonological, (4) whether the significance is general or regional, and (5) frequency of occurrence of the feature. According to Wolfram, seven syntactic features of black English are important for students to control in respect to social prestige. These features, in the order ranked by Wolfram, include the following categories and examples:

1. *s* third person singular—he go
2. Multiple negation—didn't do nothing
3. *s* possessive—man hat
4. invariant *be*—he be home
5. copula absence—he nice
6. *been* auxiliary in active sentence—he been ate the food
7. existential *it*—it is a whole lot of people

The purpose of Mantell's program is to help middle-school children become aware of the syntactic differences and similarities between black English and standard English, as well as to test the appropriateness of each form of language. Language expansion activities include role-playing and games. Students listen to recorded samples of black English and standard English, and are then asked to isolate the differences on mimeographed copies of the recordings. Students are also asked to collect language samples showing how various people express possession, plurality, time, and negation. Other language expansion activities include providing short sentences as appropriate captions to photographs, storytelling, presenting eyewitness reporting of current or fantasy events for a news commentary, and role playing. In role-playing activities, a panel of students rates the appropriateness of language.

A final instructional approach in this program uses an incomplete sentence technique. The teacher provides the beginning of a sentence and asks students to complete it; for example, I . . . ; We . . . ; They . . . . This program does not use published materials. Rather, it uses drama, literature, and topics of interest to the students.

The Language Experience Approach

The language experience approach is highly recommended because it allows students to use and to expand on their own language and experiences. The approach may be structured to expand literature understanding, oral language development, development of abstract thinking, listening improvement, and written composition.

Batty and Batty (1985) recommend the language experience approach because it offers social and psychological benefits, eliminates the possible mismatch between language and print, allows children to incorporate their own experiences and thoughts into the reading program, personalizes instruction, and fosters positive attitudes toward reading. We will deal with the language experience approach in detail because it incorporates many language arts skills and is useful not only with linguistically different children, but with other children as well.

Philosophy   The title "language experience" provides a clue to the nature of the approach. This language-arts-oriented approach includes all of the communication skills—listening, speaking, reading, and writing. It emphasizes that the ideas of children are not only worth expressing, but also worth writing down and reading. This approach stresses a natural flow of language. First, art, literature, and other experiences stimulate oral expression. Then, written expression develops from the oral expression. Children are motivated to read because they see their own language in print. Finally, after reading their own language, children move naturally into reading the published works of others.

Practice   The language experience approach has been used for many years with linguistically and culturally diverse populations. As early as 1933, some educators advocated the use of this approach with Mexican-American children, whose language was different from that of the school. The students learned to read materials they dictated, so there were no problems with cultural or language interference.

Numerous programs have used language experience approaches with other linguistically or culturally diverse groups. For example, Hall (1965) developed a language experience approach for culturally disadvantaged black children in Washington, D.C. Her students made greater gains in reading readiness, word recognition, and sentence reading than did a group of students taught with traditional basal materials. Calvert (1973) used a language experience approach with middle-school Mexican-American students and found that his students made significant gains in writing, vocabulary, comprehension, and development of positive attitudes toward teachers.

Method   Language experience stimulates oral language and writing by providing opportunities for discussion, exploration of ideas, and expression of feelings. In turn, language experiences provide the content for group and individual stories composed by children and recorded by teachers. Many teachers introduce students to the language experience approach through a group chart story. This is possible with any age group, but it is frequently a readiness- or early-reading activity in kindergarten or first grade.

The motivational experience may be any activity that involves the group and encourages oral language. For example, one teacher brought a baby chick into the classroom. The first graders looked at and listened to the chick, carefully touched it, and fed and watered it. They discussed what they saw, heard, felt, and cared for. An excellent chart story resulted from each child's contributions. A third-grade remedial-reading teacher involved children in making pudding before they wrote an experience story. A seventh/eighth-grade learning-disabilities resource teacher read literature selections to her students. Then she had the class develop chart stories about the main characters. Other motivational materials and activities include trips, films, building projects, pictures, guest speakers, science experiments, puppet shows, music, and poetry. A room that offers a rich environment provides many motivational experiences for the chart story.

After a motivational experience and oral discussion, record the story exactly as each child says. You may record the story on a large piece of newsprint, on a posterboard chart, or on the chalkboard, from which it is reprinted onto a chart. Whichever means of recording you use, it is essential that children be seated so that they can see each word as it is written in the proper left-to-right sequence. Thus, children see that sentences follow a progressive pattern from the top of the page to the bottom and that sentences begin with capital letters and end with periods. As the children dictate the story, write each word, repeating the word aloud as you write. Following each sentence, read the whole sentence to the group, underlining the word being read with one hand. Ask the child who has dictated the sentence whether the sentence is correct.

After the chart story is complete, read the whole story. Then, have the students reread it with you. If the story does not have a title, have the class discuss an appropriate title. Some students may feel confident enough to try to read the selection individually, whereas other students may read only the sentence they dictated.

FOR YOUR PLAN BOOK
A Lesson Plan for Developing a Language Experience Chart Story

The objectives of the lesson are to (1) involve the students in a motivational activity that will result in oral discussion and a group-dictated chart story, (2) improve the ability of students to comprehend the sequential order of a selection, and (3) help the students increase the number of sight words they recognize. This lesson was developed with a group of learning-disabled third graders.

As a motivational activity, begin the discussion by asking the students to tell the group about their favorite desserts. Show a picture of a chocolate pie made from chocolate pudding and a graham cracker crust. Ask the students how many of them have helped make a pie like the one in the picture. Discuss how they think it would be accomplished. Ask them what they think they would need to make the pie in the picture. As they mention various items, remove them from a box and place them on the table (include instant chocolate pudding mix, milk, measuring cup, bowl, egg beater, spoon, and graham cracker crust). Explain to the students that you are not only going to make a pie but also eat the pie and then write a story about the experience in order to share it with the rest of the class and with their parents.

The procedures follow:

1. Lead an oral discussion about desserts, as described in the motivational activity.
2. Place the ingredients and utensils on the table. Clarify terms such as "instant chocolate pudding mix," "glass bowl," "measuring cup," "eggbeater," and "graham cracker crust" as you place each item on the worktable. Label each item so the students can visualize the printed term and associate it with the item.

3. Place the ingredients in the order the students believe is appropriate. Ask them how to verify whether the ingredients are in the proper order. A student may respond that you have to read a recipe. If no one does, tell the students what a recipe is.
4. Read the recipe to the group. As you read each step, have the students check to see if the ingredients and utensils are in the correct order.
5. Orally review the whole sequence, using the concrete items as reminders for the procedure.
6. Make the pie according to the recipe directions. Allow each child to take part in some portion of the pie-making activity.
7. Cut the pie and allow all of the children to have some.
8. Have the students dictate a chart story about the pie-making experience. Print the story on a large chart.

Children dictated the following story as a result of this lesson plan:

We Made a Chocolate Pie

We put chocolate pudding into a glass bowl. We poured milk into the bowl. We beat the milk and pudding with an eggbeater. The pudding got thick. We poured the pudding into a graham cracker crust. We ate the pie. It was good.

To reinforce this language experience activity:

1. Have students match the labels on the concrete examples with the same terms in the chart story.
2. Cut a duplicate chart story into sentences. Mix the sentences and have the students put them into the correct sequential order.
3. Duplicate the story. During the next class period, have the students read the story, underlining words they know. Test these words in isolation. If the students recognize the words the following day, place the words in the students' word bank.

Individualizing language experience   Teachers often use the language experience approach as an individualized approach, in which each student dictates a story to the teacher. Motivation is also essential for individual stories. A room that is rich with manipulative objects, pictures, animals, and learning centers motivates story dictation. A student's own artwork is often good motivation for language experience. The artwork is highly personal and requires complete involvement on the part of the child. Topics related to the children themselves, such as family, friends, school, and recreation, are frequently preferred by African-American inner-city students.

To develop an individual language experience lesson, let the children take turns dictating individual stories to you or an aide. Record the story on lined paper or on newsprint, or use a primer-size typewriter. Write the story exactly as the child dictates it. The dictation procedure is similar to the group chart story. As the child dictates the story, read back the words and sentences to the child to make sure that you have properly recorded them and to reinforce the development of the story. It is usually preferable that a beginning story be only a few sentences long.

FIGURE 5-1
A chart story dictated by an individual child

This owl <u>sitting</u> under <u>the</u> moon. <u>He</u> sitting on <u>a</u> branch. <u>He</u> sleep in <u>the</u> morning. <u>He</u> hunt at night.

After the dictation, have the child read the selection with your help. Have the child underline words that he or she knows in the story. For example, the story in Figure 5-1 was written about a child's drawing of an owl. The girl who dictated the story reread the story with the teacher's help and underlined each word she knew. The underlined words form a beginning for the child's word bank (words that are instantly recognized as sight words). The teacher gradually reduces the number of visible cues in order to help the child recognize the words not underlined. This gradual reduction includes the following steps:

1. Use the total story context to help the child read the story.
2. Point to individual words and ask the child to identify the words.
3. Use a window card to isolate words in the story sequence and ask the child to identify the words.
4. Use a window card to isolate words in the story in a random order and ask the child to identify these words. (You can construct a window card easily: Cut an opening large enough to show a word in a 3-by-5-inch file card [see Figure 5-2]. Move the card across the story and stop at individual words, testing whether a child can identify the words without the help of a total sentence.)

On a small card, print every word that a child still recognizes the second and third day after dictation. The card size should be about 3/8 of an inch by $1\frac{1}{2}$ inches. Place these cards in an individual file box labeled with the child's name. Use the cards for frequent review of words, sentence-building activities, word-recognition activities, development of alphabetizing skills, and creative writing.

FIGURE 5–2
A window card

come

Most children are motivated for further learning as they see their word banks grow. Children can construct many new sentences with the cards in a word bank. They can also experiment with sentence expansion (see Figure 5–3).

You may also use language experience stories and word banks for teaching phonics and structural analysis. Children can find all the words that begin with capital letters or all the words that end with *at,* such as *cat.* They can find all the words that have a certain word ending, such as *ed* in *walked.* After a number of words are in the word bank, the children may discover that they are difficult to find. This occasion provides a good opportunity to introduce alphabetizing. Have the students place small envelopes, one for each letter, inside their word boxes to facilitate the beginning of alphabetical instruction. This is also a logical time to introduce the use of a dictionary. Finally, a word bank provides a readily available source of words for creative writing.

FOR YOUR PLAN BOOK
A Language Experience Activity for Linguistically Different Children

The following activity was developed by Nancy Matula during a practicum experience with fifth-grade students, primarily African-American and Mexican-American students. (As you read the activity, try to see how Nancy motivated the students to write and used discussion as part of the experience. When you read about her results, note any examples of black dialect.) This is Nancy's activity described in her own words:

> The Language Experience activity I used with the fifth-graders dealt with biographies and autobiographies. To begin the activity, I read the students a relatively easy biography about Kit Carson. Following the reading, we discussed the book and talked about the specific type of book. The term *biography* was introduced, and students located the meaning of the word in the dictionary. Next, we discussed several characteristics of a biography. We discussed the fact that every one of us could have a biography written about us.
>
> After the discussion of biographies, I introduced the word *autobiography* to the class. We looked at several autobiographies and discussed the differences and similarities between biography and autobiography. We talked about and listed some of the things that could be included in an autobiography. Such items as birthplace, favorite colors, foods, sports, and pets, among other items, made up our list.
>
> At this point, I explained that we were going to write our own book. Because the book (constructed out of poster board held together by rings) had blank white pages, we needed to fill up the pages. Through discussion, it was suggested that we needed both words and pictures. We took both group pictures and individual pictures. It was decided that the group pictures would decorate the cover of our book and that each page would contain one student's picture. Beneath each person's picture would be his or her autobiography. Because we could not write our autobiographies on this same day, I asked the students to continue thinking about what they wanted to include in their autobiographies.
>
> During the following session, we reviewed what could go into our autobiographies. These items were written on the board for further reference. Next, we reviewed writing

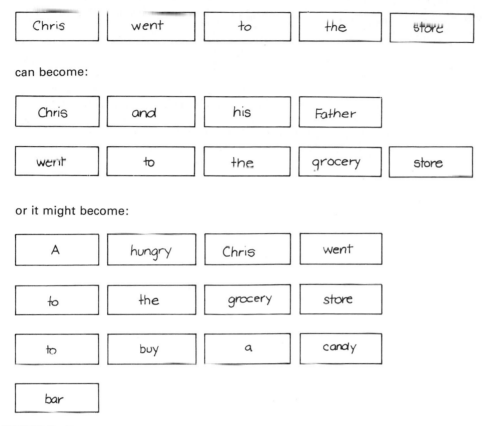

FIGURE 5–3
Sentence expansion with word cards

rules such as beginning sentences with capital letters and ending them with the correct punctuation. The students were off and running (or should I say some were off and walking). Many of the students had difficulty in beginning their writing. They needed assistance with spelling, and a few needed to dictate their stories orally.

Each student completed his or her autobiography and used the story for reading instruction. I also found they were highly motivated to read each other's autobiographies. The book is to be left in the classroom until the end of the school year, because everyone wants to read the whole book. At the end of the school year, each student can remove and keep his page from the book.

The students were extremely excited and happy with this writing experience. We all learned a great deal while writing about a subject we each know better than any other—ourselves.

The following autobiography was written by one fifth-grade boy:

I want to be a singer and a movie star. I have black and white eyes a black pupil, brown hair and afro. My favorite sport is basketball. My favorites singing group is the Jackson five. My favorites foods is hamburger, frenchfries, hot dog and green, green peas. My favorite music is hotline. My color is black.

Used with permission of Nancy Matula, elementary-school teacher.

REINFORCEMENT ACTIVITY

1. Choose a motivational activity to foster both discussion and writing. If you are teaching children, develop a language-experience chart story with a group. If you are not teaching, demonstrate your language experience activity with a group of your peers. Include a motivational activity, the writing of a dictated story, and a reinforcement activity.
2. Develop a language experience lesson plan such as one of those found in *Language Arts Activities for Children* (Norton & Norton, 1993).

MULTICULTURAL EDUCATION

America is a multicultural nation, including Europeans, Native Americans, African-Americans, Hispanics, and Asians. A heightened sensitivity to the needs of all people in American society has led to the realization that language arts programs should heighten self-esteem and create respect for the individuals, contributions, and values of all cultures. Unfortunately, literature and other language arts resources frequently ignore the needs of minority ethnic groups or present stereotypic images of ethnic groups.

Contemporary education, at both the university and public school levels, is beginning to stress the need for multicultural education. This section focuses on African-Americans, Native Americans, Hispanics, and Asians. Lewis and Doorlag (1987) present these reasons for developing multicultural education:

1. Commonalities among people cannot be recognized unless differences are acknowledged.
2. A society that interweaves the best of all of its cultures reflects a truly mosaic image.
3. Multicultural education can restore cultural rights by emphasizing cultural equality and respect.
4. Students can learn basic skills while also learning to respect cultures; multicultural education need not detract from basic education.
5. Multicultural education enhances the self-concepts of all students because it provides a more balanced view of American society.
6. Students must learn to respect others.

Positive multicultural literature has been used effectively to help children identify cultural heritages, understand sociological change, respect the values of minority groups, raise aspirations, and expand understanding of imagination and creativity. This author has found that positive multicultural literature and language art activities related to the literature also can improve reading scores and improve attitudes toward African-Americans, Native Americans, and Hispanics if the literature and literature-related activities are part of the curriculum and if teachers know how to select this literature and develop teaching strategies to accompany it (Norton, 1981, 1984, 1991). In contrast, merely placing the literature in the classroom without subsequent interaction does not change children's attitudes.

Multicultural literature helps children identify cultural heritage and appreciate diversity.

Selecting Multicultural Literature

Two selection problems face language arts teachers. First, although the number of books about African-Americans, Native Americans, Hispanics, and Asians is increasing, a disproportionately small number deal in any way with minorities. Second, books require careful evaluation to screen out stereotypic views of minority cultures and individuals. A brief review of children's literature written prior to the late 1960s suggests stereotypes for each minority. For example, books about blacks frequently characterized them as physically unattractive, musical, dependent on whites, and religious with superstitious beliefs. Native Americans were often characterized as savage, depraved, cruel or noble, proud, silent, and close to nature. Their culture was frequently portrayed as inferior and not worth retaining. Hispanic literature contained recurring themes related to poverty, intervention of Anglos in problem-solving situations, and superficial treatment of problems. Finally, Asian-American literature frequently suggested that Asians all looked the same, lived in quaint communities in the midst of large cities, and clung to outworn, alien customs.

Excellent criteria for evaluating books involving black people appear in Latimer's *Starting Out Right—Choosing Books About Black People for Young Children* (1972, pp. 7–12).[1] Latimer recommends the following criteria:

1. Has a black perspective been taken into consideration? There should be no stigma attached to being black, and the characters should not conform to old stereotypes. The dignity of the characters should be preserved.
2. How responsible is the author in dealing with issues and problems? Is the presentation honest, with problems presented clearly but not oversimplified? Must black characters exercise all the understanding and forgiveness?
3. Do the black characters look natural? This is especially crucial in picture books. Characters should not have exaggerated features.
4. Will young readers realize that they are looking at a black person, or do the characters look gray in appearance? ("Gray" refers to a merely darkened version of Caucasian-featured characters.)
5. Are the black characters unique individuals, or are they merely representative of a group?
6. Does clothing or behavior perpetuate stereotypes of blacks as primitive or submissive?
7. Are the characters glamorized or glorified, especially in a biography? Some situations may be glorified while others are ignored, resulting in an unbalanced presentation.
8. Are the settings authentic, so the children can recognize them as urban, suburban, rural, or fantasized?
9. Does the author have a patronizing tone?
10. Are black characters used as vehicles to get a point across so that they become tools of literary exploitation and acts artificial rather than real?
11. How are black characters shown in relationship to white characters? Is either placed in a submissive or inferior role without justification? Is a white person always shown as the benefactor?
12. If dialect is used, does it have a purpose? Does it ring true and blend naturally with the story, or is it used as an example of substandard English?
13. If the story deals with historical or factual events, how accurate is it?
14. If the book is a biography, does it show both the personality and accomplishments of the main character?

Well-written literary selections are excellent sources of materials for balancing the curriculum culturally. You may use them with any content area. For example, you may use books on African art or American black art in the art curriculum. You may add African myths to a literature study of mythology. Mythology provides an excellent source of materials for adding knowledge about a culture. You may add books of poetry from a specific culture to the study of literature. You may use biographies of great people from a culture to increase self-esteem and awareness.

---

[1] Used with permission of Wisconsin Department of Public Instruction, Madison, Wisconsin.

Native-American literature includes traditional tales, poetry, historical fiction, contemporary realistic fiction, and informational books. You may find the following criteria useful when evaluating Native-American literature:

1. Are the Indian characters portrayed as individuals with their own thoughts, emotions, and philosophies? The characters should not conform to stereotypes or be dehumanized.
2. Do the Indian characters belong to a specific tribe, or are they grouped together under one category referred to as Indian?
3. Does the author recognize the diversity of Indian cultures? Are the customs and ceremonies authentic for the Indian tribes?
4. Does the author respect the Indian culture? Or does the author present it as inferior to the white culture? Does the author believe the culture is worthy of preservation, or that it should be abandoned? Must the Indian fit into an image acceptable to white characters in the story?
5. Does the author use offensive and degrading vocabulary to describe the characters, their actions, their customs, or their life styles?
6. Are the illustrations realistic and authentic, or do they reinforce stereotypes or devalue the culture?
7. If the story has a contemporary setting, does the author accurately describe the life and situation of Native-Americans today?

Award-winning Hispanic literature for children tends to be about a small segment of the Spanish-American population, the sheepherders of Spanish Basque heritage, whose ancestors emigrated to regions of America before they became part of the United States. Award-winning picture storybooks tend to be about Christmas celebrations. Schon (1981) is critical because the "overwhelming majority of recent books incessantly repeat the same stereotypes, misconceptions, and insensibilities that were prevalent in the books published in the 1960s and the early 1970s" (p. 79). Schon supports this contention by reviewing books published in 1980 and 1981 that develop the stereotypes of poverty, embarrassment of children about their backgrounds, distorted and negative narratives about pre-Columbian history, and simplistic discussions of serious Latin-American problems.

There are not many books available for young readers about Hispanic cultures or Spanish-speaking regions of the world, and those that are available tend to go out of print rapidly (Norton, 1986). An analysis of two recent lists of notable books indicates the difficulty in finding multicultural material. Of the fifty-five titles on the "Best Books of the Year 1989" list, one centered on a black theme, one on a Native-American theme, and none on a Hispanic theme. Of the seventy-six titles on the "1990 Notable Children's Books" list, seven contained black themes, two contained Native-American themes, and none contained Hispanic themes (Norton, 1990). For those books that are available on Hispanic themes, you may want to use the following criteria:

1. Does the book suggest that poverty is a condition for all Hispanics? This is a negative stereotype suggested in some literature.
2. Are problems handled individually, allowing the main characters to use their efforts to solve their problems? Or are all problems solved through the intervention of Anglo-Americans?

3. Are problems handled realistically or superficially? Is a character's major problem solved by learning to speak English?
4. Is the cultural information accurate? Are Mexican-American, Mexican, or Puerto Rican cultures realistically pictured? Is the culture treated with respect?
5. Do the illustrations depict individuals, not stereotypes?
6. Is the language free from derogatory terms or descriptions?
7. If the author portrays dialects, are they a natural part of the story and not used to suggest a stereotype?
8. Does the book have literary merit?
9. If the author uses Spanish language, are the words spelled and used correctly?

There are also few highly recommended books written from an Asian-American perspective. The books by Lawrence Yep, who writes with a sensitivity about Chinese-Americans, have characters who overcome stereotypes associated with Asian-American literature. In addition, Yep's stories integrate information about the cultural heritage into the everyday lives of the people involved. Other authors are writing stories with settings in Vietnam and America. These stories frequently highlight difficulties associated with moving into a different culture. Historical fiction set in World War II tells about Japanese-American families placed in internment centers. Excellent traditional Asian tales also stress the traditional values.

The Council on Interracial Books for Children (1977, pp. 87–90) recommends the following criteria for evaluating Asian-American literature:

1. The book should reflect the realities and way of life of Asian-American people. Is the story accurate for the historical period and cultural context? Are the characters from a variety of social and economic levels? Does the plot exaggerate the exoticism or mysticism of the customs and festivals of the Asian-American culture? Are festivals in the perspective of everyday activities?
2. The book should transcend stereotypes. Do the Asian-American characters handle their own problems, or do they require benevolent intervention from a white person? Do the characters have to make a definite choice between two cultures, or is there an alternative in which the two cultures can mingle? Do the characters portray a range of human emotions, or are they docile and uncomplaining? Is there an obvious occupational stereotype—do all Asian-Americans work in laundries or restaurants?
3. The literature should seek to rectify historical distortions and omissions.
4. The characters in the book should avoid the model minority and super minority syndromes. Are the characters respected for themselves, or must they display outstanding abilities to gain approval?
5. The literature should reflect an awareness of the changing status of women in society. Does the author provide role models for girls other than subservient females?
6. The illustrations should reflect the racial diversity of Asian-Americans. Are the characters all look-alikes, with the same skin tone and exagger-

ated features, such as slanted eyes? Are clothing and settings appropriate to the culture depicted?

Books that meet the criteria for excellent multicultural literature are listed in the annotated bibliography at the end of this chapter. For additional books, see Chapter 11, "Multicultural Literature," in *Through the Eyes of a Child: An Introduction to Children's Literature* (Norton, 1991).

Understanding Traditional Values

In describing educational goals, Wong-Filmore (1986) emphasizes the desirability of teaching content and developing reasoning ability. Piper (1986) emphasizes the advantages of using traditional stories from various cultural sources. Sealey (1984) emphasizes the benefits of encouraging students to accept cultural diversity and understand that similar values frequently underlie different customs. Reading, analyzing, and discussing multicultural literature is one of the best ways to achieve all of these goals. Traditional literature (folktales, myths, and legends) provides excellent sources for exploring the traditional values of a culture. Students gain insights and hone their reasoning abilities as they analyze the values reflected in the stories, compare the values across cultures, consider whether the values are reflected in contemporary literature, and respond to whether the values are important in their own lives.

This type of activity can be applied to African, Native American, Hispanic, and Asian literature. It is especially beneficial with students in middle- and upper-elementary grades. In the following lesson plan, a Native-American folklore selection and an excerpt from a contemporary story by a Native-American author are compared with respect to the values they reflect. (See Norton & Norton [1993] for similar activities using African and Hispanic literature.)

FOR YOUR PLAN BOOK
Experiencing Traditional Native-American Values

Purpose

1. To develop an appreciation for a culture that places importance on oral tradition, respect for nature, understanding between animals and humans, wisdom of the elderly, folklore as a means of passing on culture and tribal beliefs, and diversity of Native-American folktales, cultures, and customs.
2. To listen for and to identify traditional values found in Native-American folklore.
3. To compare the traditional values in folklore and contemporary literature.

Sources

1. Tomie de Paola's *The Legend of the Bluebonnet* (1983)
2. White Deer of Autumn's *Ceremony—In the Circle of Life* (1983)

Procedures

1. Discuss ways in which students can identify traditional values found in folklore. For example, they can read the tales to discover answers to the following

TABLE 1
Folklore analysis

Comparisons	Folklore: *The Legend of the Bluebonnet*	Realistic Fiction: *Ceremony—In the Circle of Life*
What is the problem?	Drought and famine killed the Comanche	Humans are destroying the land
What do the characters desire?	To end drought and famine To save land and people	To comfort and honor Mother Earth To teach humans about Earth
What actions or values are rewarded or respected?	Sacrifice to save land and tribe Belief in Great Spirit	Honoring and caring for Mother Earth Living in harmony Knowledge, truth, belief
What actions are punished or not respected?	Selfishness Taking from Earth without giving back	Pollution and destruction of Earth
What rewards are given?	Bluebonnets, as a sign of forgiveness Rain, end of drought Name change	A living pipe, which symbolizes the vision of Earth New strength and knowledge Understanding
What are the personal characteristics of heroes or heroines?	Unselfish love of people and land Respect for the Great Spirit Willingness to sacrifice for benefits for all	Love of animals and land Respect for the Star Spirit and ways of the people Desire for knowledge and truth

questions and then analyze what those answers reveal about the values and the beliefs of the people:

   a. What is the problem the characters face?
   b. What do the characters desire?
   c. What actions or values are rewarded or respected?
   d. What actions are punished or not respected?
   e. What rewards are given?
   f. What are the personal characteristics of the heroes or the heroines?

2. Print each question on a chart. Allow room to include several tales. Use the chart to identify the answers to the questions and then to consider what these answers reveal about the beliefs and the values of the people (see Table 1). (Use the same chart form for different cultures to help students compare values.)

3. Introduce de Paola's *The Legend of the Bluebonnet.* Ask the students to listen for the answers to the questions printed on the chart.

4. After reading *The Legend of the Bluebonnet* aloud, have students identify the answers and place them on the chart. Discuss the implications for the various answers. How do these answers relate to possible values and beliefs of the people?

5. During another class, introduce White Deer of Autumn's *Ceremony—In the Circle of Life.* Tell the students that this is a contemporary story written by a Native-American author who wants to share his vision for the earth and his concerns with Native-American children and other children of the world. Ask the students to listen for the answers to the same questions, consider the possible implications of those answers, and compare the values reflected in the two books. Ask them to provide possible reasons for the similarities in values expressed in the two books.

6. During other class periods read other traditional literature from various Native-American tribes and other groups. Ask the children to consider what information they learn from these sources.

REINFORCEMENT ACTIVITY

Using Latimer's criteria for evaluating multiethnic books (or one of the other criteria for evaluating Native-American, Hispanic, or Asian-American literature), find several books that you feel are excellent examples of literature revealing an African-American, Native-American Hispanic, or Asian perspective. Find several books that violate these guidelines. Refer to specific examples in the books in order to substantiate your judgments.

SUMMARY

The issues relating to instruction of linguistically different children are complex. Because the majority of children classified as linguistically different have consistently made smaller academic gains than have children who speak standard English, the subject is of great concern to educators. If linguistically different children are to compete with speakers of standard English, then teachers must be specifically prepared.

Although the current viewpoint stresses the "linguistically different" rather than the "linguistically deficient" philosophy, there is not yet agreement about the best instructional procedures to use. This chapter reviews educational alternatives suggested by linguists and educators. Alternatives include oral language expansion programs, conventional materials read in dialect, and the language experience approach.

Investigators are concerned not only with the interference of black English in instruction with standard English materials but also with the problems of testing linguistically different children using tests written in standard English. Some educators suggest that if standardized tests are used, scoring procedures should be modified. For example, oral reading tests should be scored so that mistakes attributable to dialect differences are not counted as reading errors. Other educators recommend the use of nonstandardized tests. This chapter reviews some informal testing procedures, such as using pictures to elicit oral language samples and role-playing techniques. Teachers cannot provide evaluation unless they are familiar with differences between black English and standard English. In addition to bias within tests, teacher attitudes and environment also influence testing and academic results.

Characteristics of effective intervention programs for children from low-income families are also discussed. Language or literacy development of these children may be delayed by conditions at home. For students in bilingual programs, including English as a second language, recommendations for effective education emphasize interactions among students, teachers, and community, as well as relevant content for the students.

The chapter concludes with recommendations for developing course content relevant for linguistically different students. Teachers should evaluate multiethnic literature and balance their educational programs by selecting literature that both recognizes that Americans take pride in their ethnic background and helps students in their search for identity.

ADDITIONAL MULTICULTURAL EDUCATION ACTIVITIES

1. Informally interview a child who uses black English or listen to conversations on a playground (tape the conversations). Can you identify any of the phonological and syntactic features discussed in this chapter?

2. Read the contrasting viewpoints expressed by S. I. Hayakawa in "Why the English Language Amendment?" and Victor Villanueva, Jr., in "Whose Voice Is It Anyway? Rodriguez's Speech in Retrospect." Both articles are in the *English Journal* 76 (December 1987): 14–21. Discuss each of these viewpoints and then consider how the adoption of each one would influence language arts instruction.

3. Read and summarize the findings in three current journal articles that provide information on (1) teaching linguistically different children, (2) teaching bilingual classes, and (3) teaching English as a second language.

4. Compare the characteristics of Native-Americans in a book published before 1965 (for example, Walter Edmond's *The Matchlock Gun*) with the characteristics of Native-Americans in a book published after 1975 (for example, Brent Ashabranner's *Morning Star, Black Sun: The Northern Cheyenne Indians and America's Energy Crisis*). Find quotations that show stereotypic or nonstereotypic characterizations.

5. Read one of the books awarded The Coretta Scott King Award for portraying "people, places, things, and events in a manner sensitive to the true worth and value of things." Read one of the books that the Children's Literature Review Board does not recommend because of stereotypes, unacceptable values, or terms used. For example, David Arkin's *Black and White,* Florine Robinson's *Ed and Ted,* Shirley Burden's *I Wonder Why,* Anco Surany's *Monsieur Jolicoeur's Umbrella,* May Justus's *New Boy in School,* or William Pappas's *No Mules.* Develop a rationale for the recommendations for the King award and for the negative responses for the stereotypic books.

BIBLIOGRAPHY

Adler, Sol. "Data Gathering: The Reliability and Validity of Test Data from Culturally Different Children." *Journal of Learning Disabilities* 6 (August/September 1973): 429–34.

Allen, V. "Teaching Bilingual and ESL Children." In *Handbook of Research on Teaching the English Language Arts,* edited by J. Flood, J. Jensen, D. Lapp, and J. Squire. New York: Macmillan, 1991, pp. 356–64.

Baratz, Joan C. "A Bi-Dialectical Task for Determining Language Proficiency in Economically Disadvantaged Children." *Child Development* 40 (December 1969): 889–901.

––––––, and Shuy, Roger. *Teaching Black Children to Read.* Washington, D.C.: Center for Applied Linguistics, 1969.

Bartel, Nettie R.; Grill, Jeffrey, J.; and Bryen, Diane N. "Language Characteristics of Black Children: Implications for Assessment." *Journal of School Psychology* 11 (Winter 1973): 351–64.

Batty, Constance J., and Batty, Beauford R. "Teaching Minority Children to Read in Elementary School." In *Tapping Potential: English and Language Arts for the Black Learner,* edited by Charlotte K. Brooks. Urbana, Ill.: National Council of Teachers of English, 1985.

Bereiter, Carol, and Engelmann, Siegfried. *Teaching Disadvantaged Children in the Preschool.* Englewood Cliffs, N.J.: Prentice-Hall, 1966.

Bernstein, B. "Social Structure, Language, and Learning." *Educational Research* 3 (1961): 163–76.

Brause, R., and Mayher, J. "Our Students." In *Handbook of Research on Teaching the English Language Arts,* edited by J. Flood, J. Jensen, D. Lapp, and J. Squire. New York: Macmillan, 1991, pp. 259–72.

Burton, Nancy W., and Jones, Lyle V. "Recent Trends in Achievement Levels of Black and White Youth." *Educational Research* (April 1982): 10–14, 17.

Calvert, John D. *An Exploratory Study to Adapt the Language Experience Approach to Remedial Seventh and Tenth Grade Mexican American Students.* Doctoral dissertation, Arizona State University, 1973.

Carter, Candy, ed. *Non-Native and Nonstandard Dialect Students: Classroom Practices in Teaching English, 1982–1983.* Urbana, Ill.: National Council of Teachers of English, 1982.

Chall, J., and Curtis, M. "Children at Risk." In *Handbook of Research on Teaching the English Language Arts,* edited by J. Flood, J. Jensen, D. Lapp, and J. Squire. New York: Macmillan, 1991, pp. 349–355.

Chall, J. S.; Jacobs, V. A.; and Baldwin, L. E. *The Reading Crisis: Why Poor Children Fall Behind.* Cambridge, M.A.: Harvard University Press, 1990.

Cohen, S. A. *Teach Them All to Read.* New York: Random House, 1969.

Corrigan, Dean. *Teaching Excellence.* Paper presented at the meeting of American Association of University Women, College Station, Texas, October, 1983.

Cortes, C. E. "The Education of Language Minority Students: A Contextual Interaction Model." California State Department of Education. *Beyond Language: Social and Cultural Factors in Schooling Language Minority Students.* Los Angeles Calif.: California State University Evaluation, Dissemination, and Assessment Center, 1986, pp. 299–343.

Council on Interracial Books for Children. "Criteria for Analyzing Books on Asian Americans." In *Cultural Conformity in Books for Children,* edited by Donnarae MacCann and Gloria Woodard. Metuchen, N.J.: Scarecrow, 1977.

Crowl, Thomas K., and MacGinitie, Walter H. "The Influence of Students' Speech Characteristics on Teachers' Evaluations of Oral Answers." *Journal of Educational Psychology* 66 (June 1974): 304–8.

Cullinan, Bernice E.; Jaggar, Angela M.; and Strickland, Dorothy. "Oral Language Expansion in the Primary Grades." In *Black Dialects and Reading,* edited by Bernice E. Cullinan. Urbana, Ill.: National Council of Teachers of English, 1974

Cumming, A. "Metalinguistic and Ideational Thinking in Second Language Composing." *Written Communication* 7 (1990): 482–511.

Cunningham, Patricia M. "Teachers' Correction Responses to Black Dialect Miscues Which Are Non-Meaning Changing." *Reading Research Quarterly* 12 (Summer 1977): 637–53.

Daniels, Lee A. "Study Links Academic Skills to Race and Family Income." *New York Times* (October 25, 1987): 15.

de Félix, Judith Walker. "Steps to Second Language Development in the Regular Classroom." In *Non-Native and Nonstandard Dialect Students: Classroom Practices in Teaching English, 1982–1983,* edited by Candy Carter. Urbana, Ill.: National Council of Teachers of English, 1982.

Deutsch, M.; Bloom, R. D.; Brown, B. R.; Deutsch, C. P.; Goldstein, L. S.; John, V. P.; Katz, P. A.; Levinson, A.; Peisach, E. C.; and Whiteman, M. *The Disadvantaged Child.* New York: Basic Books, 1967.

Dixon, Carol N. "Teaching Strategies for the Mexican-American Child." *The Reading Teacher* 30 (November 1976): 141–45.

Early, Margaret. "Enabling First and Second Language Learners in the Classroom." *Language Arts* 67 (1990): 567–75.

Eisenberg, Leon. "The Epidemiology of Reading Retardation and a Program for Preventive Intervention." In *The Disabled Reader,* edited by John Money. Baltimore: Johns Hopkins University Press, 1974.

Ezer, H. "Writing Development in a Bilingual First Grader: A Case Study." *Dissertation Abstracts International,* 51, 04A. (University Microfilms No. 90–15,289), 1990.

Farr, M. "Dialects, Culture, and Teaching the English Language Arts." In *Handbook of Research on Teaching the English Language Arts,* edited by J. Flood, J. Jensen, D. Lapp, and J. Squire. New York: Macmillan, 1991, pp. 365–71.

Freedman, B. M. "Literacy and Cultural Identity." *Harvard Educational Review* 60 (1990): 181–204.

Genishi, C. "Observing the Second Language Learner: An Example of Teachers' Learning." *Language Arts* 66 (1989): 509–15.

Goodman, Y. "Evaluating Language Development: Informal Methods of Evaluation." In *Handbook of Research on Teaching the English Language Arts,* edited by J. Flood, J. Jensen, D. Lapp, and J. Squire. New York: Macmillan, 1991, pp. 502–9.

Greenberg, Judith W., and Davison, Helen H. "Home Background and School Achievement of Black, Urban Ghetto Children." *American Journal of Orthopsychiatry* 42 (October 1972): 803–10.

Hall, MaryAnne. *The Development of Evaluation of a Language Experience Approach to Reading with First-Grade Culturally Disadvantaged Children.* Doctoral dissertation, University of Maryland, 1965.

Harber, Jean R., and Beatty, Jane N. *Reading and the Black English Speaking Child.* Newark, Del.: International Reading Association, 1978.

Hunt, Barbara Carey. "Black Dialect and Third and Fourth Graders' Performance on the Gray Oral Reading Test." *Reading Research Quarterly* 10 (Fall 1974): 103–23.

Hutchinson, June O'Shields. "Reading Tests and Nonstandard Language." *Reading Teacher* 25 (February 1972): 430–37.

Juel, C. "Learning to Read and Write: A Longitudinal Study of 54 Children from First through Fourth Grades." *Journal of Educational Psychology* 80 (1988): 437–47.

Kagan, S., and Madsen, M. "Cooperation and Competition of Mexican, Mexican American, and Anglo American Children of Two Ages Under Four Instructional Sets." *Developmental Psychology* 5 (1971): 32–39.

Kronkosky, Preston C. "Testimony Sponsored by the U.S. Department of Education's Public Hearings on Excellence in Education." Speech presented at Dallas, Texas, October 1982.

Labov, William. *Language in the Inner City: Studies in the Black English Vernacular.* Philadelphia: University of Pennsylvania Press, 1973.

_____. *The Logic of Non-Standard English.* Washington, D.C.: Georgetown Monograph Series on Language and Linguistics No. 22, 1969.

_____. "The Logic of Non-Standard English." In *Language and Poverty,* edited by Frederick Williams. Chicago: Markham Publishing Co., 1971.

_____. *Study of Non-Standard English.* Urbana, Ill.: National Council of Teachers of English, 1970.

Latimer, Bettye. *Starting Out Right—Choosing Books About Black People for Young Children.* Madison, Wis.: Wisconsin Department of Public Instruction Bulletin Number 2314, 1972.

Lewis, Rena B., and Doorlag, Donald H. *Teaching Special Students in the Mainstream.* 2d ed. Columbus, Oh.: Merrill Publishing Co., 1987.

McConnell, B. "Education as a Cultural Process: The Interaction between Community and Classroom in Fostering Learning." In *Risk Makers, Risk Takers, Risk Breakers: Reducing the Risks for Young Literacy Learners,* edited by J. Allen and J. Mason. Portsmouth, N.H.: Heinemann, 1989, pp. 201–21.

Maestas, Leo Carlos. "Ethnicity and High School Student Achievement Across Rural and Urban Districts." *Educational Research Quarterly* (Fall 1981): 33–42.

Malmstrom, Jean. *Understanding Language.* New York: St. Martin's Press, 1977.

Mantell, Arlene. "Strategies for Language Expansion in the Middle Grades." In *Black Dialects and Reading,* edited by Bernice E. Cullinan. Urbana, Ill.: National Council of Teachers of English, 1974.

Marzano, R. "Language, the Arts, and Thinking." In *Handbook of Research on Teaching the English Language Arts,* edited by J. Flood, J. Jensen, D. Lapp, and J. Squire. New York: Macmillan, 1991, pp. 559–86.

National Public Radio. "Morning Edition." (January 9, 1992).

Norton, Donna E. "Changing Attitudes Toward Minorities: Children's Literature Shapes Attitudes." *Review Journal of Philosophy and Social Science* 9 (1984): 97–113.

_____. "The Development, Dissemination, and Evaluation of a Multi-Ethnic Curricular Model for Preservice Teachers, Inservice Teachers, and Elementary Children." New Orleans: International Reading Association, National Conference, April 1981.

_____. *The Impact of Literature-Based Reading.* New York: Merrill/Macmillan, 1992.

_____. "The Rise and Fall of Ethnic Literature." Paper presented at the annual meeting of the National Conference of Teachers of English. Phoenix, Ariz., 1986.

_____. "Teaching Multicultural Literature." *The Reading Teacher* 44 (1990): 28–40.

_____ . *Through the Eyes of a Child: An Introduction to Children's Literature.* 3rd ed. New York: Merrill/Macmillan, 1991.

_____ , and Norton, S. E. *Language Arts Activities for Children,* 3rd ed. New York: Merrill/Macmillan, 1993.

Pikulski, J. J. "The Assessment of Reading: A Time for Change?" *The Reading Teacher* 43 (1989): 80–81.

Piper, David. "Language Growth in the Multiethnic Classroom." *Language Arts* 63 (January 1986): 23–36.

Purves, Alan, and Purves, William. "Viewpoints: Cultures, Text Models, and the Activity of Writing." *Research in the Teaching of English* 20 (May 1986): 174–97.

Quintero, E., and Huerta-Macias, A. "All in the Family: Bilingualism and Biliteracy." *The Reading Teacher* 44 (1990): 306–12.

Ramírez III, Manuel, and Castañeda, Alfredo. *Cultural Democracy, BiCognitive Development, and Education.* New York: Academic Press, 1974.

Ramírez III, Manuel, and Price-Williams, D. R. "Cognitive Styles of Children of Three Ethnic Groups in the United States." *Journal of Cross-Cultural Psychology* 5 (1974): 212–19.

_____ . *The Relationship of Culture to Educational Attainment.* Center for Research in Social Change and Economic Development, Houston, Tex.: Rice University, 1971.

Raspberry, William. "Black America's House Fire." Bryan Texas: *Eagle* (February 19, 1988): p. 6A.

Schon, Isabel. "Recent Detrimental and Distinguished Books About Hispanic People and Cultures." *Top of the News* 38 (Fall 1981): 79–85.

Sealey, D. Bruce. "Measuring the Multicultural Quotient of a School." *TESL Canada Journal/Revue TESL Du Canada* 1 (March 1984): 21–28.

Slavin, R. E., and Madden, N. A. "What Works for Students at Risk: A Research Synthesis." *Educational Leadership* 64 (1989): 4–13.

Taylor, D., and Dorsey-Gaines, C. *Growing Up Literate: Learning from Inner City Families.* Portsmouth, N.H.: Heineman, 1988.

Valencia, S. "A Portfolio Approach to Classroom Reading Assessment: The Whys, Whats, and Hows." *The Reading Teacher* 43 (1990): 420–22.

Van Allen, Roach. *Language Experiences in Communication.* Boston: Houghton Mifflin Co., 1976.

Watson-Thompson, O. B. "An Investigation of Elementary School Teachers' Attitudes toward the Use of Black English in West Alabama." Doctoral Dissertation, Univ. of Alabama, 1985. *Dissertation Abstracts International* 46, 11A. (University Microfilms No. DA 8600778)

Wolfram, Walt. "Sociolinguistic Implications for Educational Sequencing." In *Teaching Standard English in the Inner City,* edited by Ralph Fasold and Roger W. Shuy. Washington, D.C.: Center for Applied Linguistics, 1970.

Wong-Fillmore, Lily. "Research Currents. Equity or Excellence? *Language Arts* 63 (September 1986): 474–81.

ANNOTATED MULTICULTURAL CHILDREN'S LITERATURE REFERENCES

The following books are examples of literature that meet the multicultural criteria listed in this chapter. The books include an interest level designated by age (I:5–8) and a readability level designated by grade (R:3).

African-American Literature

Traditional Tales

Aardema, Verna. *Bringing the Rain to Kapiti Plain: A Nandi Tale.* Illustrated by Beatriz Vidal. New York: Dial Press, 1981. (I:5–8). A cumulative tale from Kenya tells how a herdsman pierces a cloud with his arrow and brings rain to the parched land.

_____ . *What's So Funny, Ketu? A Nuer Tale.* Illustrated by Marc Brown. New York: Dial Press, 1982. (I:5–8, R:6). The repetitive language and African words add authenticity.

_____ . *Who's in Rabbit's House?* Illustrated by Leo and Diane Dillon. New York: Dial Press, 1977.

(I:7+, R:3). A Masai folktale is illustrated as a play performed by villagers wearing masks.

Bryan, Ashley. *Beat the Story-Drum, Pum-Pum.* New York: Atheneum Pubs., 1980. (I:7+, R:6). This text includes five Nigerian folktales.

Faulkner, William. *The Days when the Animals Talked.* Chicago: Follett, 1977. An excellent adult reference includes African-American folktales and interpretations about how they developed.

Grifalconi, Ann. *The Village of Round and Square Houses.* Boston: Little, Brown & Co., 1986. (I:4–9, R:6). This is a folktale from Cameroon.

Hamilton, Virginia. *The People Could Fly: American Black Folktales.* Illustrated by Leo and Diane Dillon. New York: Alfred A. Knopf, 1985. (I:9+, R:6). This book contains animal, fanciful, supernatural, and slave tales.

Harris, Joel Chandler. *Jump Again! More Adventures of Brer Rabbit.* Adapted by Van Dyke Parks, illustrated by Barry Moser. New York: Harcourt Brace Jovanovich, 1987. (I:8+, R:6). Five stories appear in this illustrated version.

Hooks, William H. *The Ballad of Belle Dorcas.* Illustrated by Brian Pinkney. New York: Knopf, 1990. (I: 8+, R:4). This folktale has a theme about love and freedom.

Jaquith, Priscilla. *Bo Rabbit Smart for True: Folktales from the Gullah.* Illustrated by Ed Young. New York: Philomel, 1981. (I:all, R:6). These four tales are from the islands off the Georgia coast.

Knutson, Barbara, retold by. *How the Guinea Fowl Got Her Spots.* Minneapolis: Carolrhoda, 1990. (I: all, R:4). This Swahili folktale is about friendship.

Lester, Julius. *The Tales of Uncle Remus: The Adventures of Brer Rabbit.* Illustrated by Jerry Pinkney. New York: Dial Press, 1987, (I:8+, R:5). This is a new retelling of the Joel Chandler Harris tales.

Walker, Barbara, retold by. *The Dancing Palm Tree and Other Nigerian Folktales.* Illustrated by Helen Siegel. Lubbock, Tex.: Texas Tech University Press, 1990. (I:all, R:5). The text includes eleven Nigerian folktales.

Poetry and Songs

Adoff, Arnold. *All the Colors of the Race.* Illustrated by John Steptoe. New York: Lothrop, Lee & Shepard, 1982. (I:all). These poems are written from the point of view of a child who has a black mother and a white father.

_____ . *Black Is Warm Is Tan.* New York: Harper & Row, 1973. (I:all). This story in poetic form is about an integrated family.

Brown, Marcia. *Shadow* (from the French of Blaise Cendrars). New York: Charles Scribner's Sons, 1982. (I:8+). Poetry and collage paintings evoke the image of African storytellers and shamans.

Bryan, Ashley. *I'm Going to Sing: Black American Spirituals, Volume Two.* New York: Atheneum Pubs., 1982. (I:all). Words and music are complemented by woodcuts.

_____ . *Walk Together Children: Black American Spirituals.* New York: Atheneum Pubs., 1974. (I:all). This book includes twenty-four spirituals.

Davis, Ossie. *Langston: A Play.* New York: Delacorte Press, 1982. (I:10+). Langston Hughes's poetry is used as part of the dialogue in a play about the famous poet.

Feelings, Tom. *Something on My Mind.* New York: Dial Press, 1978. (I:all). Poems and illustrations express hopes and fears associated with growing up.

Contemporary Realistic Fiction

Flournoy, Valerie. *The Patchwork Quilt.* Illustrated by Jerry Pinkney. New York: Dial Press, 1985. (I:5–8, R:4). Constructing a quilt brings a family together.

Greene, Bette. *Phillip Hall Likes Me. I Reckon Maybe.* Illustrated by Charles Lilly. New York: Dial Press, 1974. (I:10+, R:4). A humorous book about a girl's first crush is set in the Arkansas mountains.

Greenfield, Eloise. *Sister.* Illustrated by Moneta Barnett. New York: Thomas Y. Crowell Co., 1974. (I:8–12, R:5). A thirteen year old reviews the memories written in her book.

Grifalconi, Ann. *Darkness and the Butterfly.* Boston: Little, Brown & Co., 1987. (I:5–8, R:6). An African child overcomes her fear of the dark.

Hamilton, Virginia. *The House of Dies Drear.* Illustrated by Eros Keith. New York: Macmillan Co,. 1968. (I:10+, R:4). This contemporary suspenseful story is about a family living in a home that was on the Underground Railroad.

_____ . *M. C. Higgins, the Great.* New York: Macmillan Co., 1974. (I:10+, R:4). A boy dreams of leaving his home and the spoil heap that threatens his security; instead, he builds a wall to protect his home.

_____ . *The Planet of Junior Brown.* New York: Macmillan Co., 1971. (I:10+, R:6). Three outcasts create their own world in a secret basement room.

_____ . *Zeely.* Illustrated by Symeon Shimin. New York: Macmillan Co., 1967. (I:8–12, R:4). A girl discovers Zeely's identity and also discovers her own.

Mathis, Sharon Bell. *The Hundred Penny Box.* Illustrated by Diane Dillon. New York: Viking Press, 1975. (I:6–9, R:3). A penny represents each of the years in the life of a 100-year-old woman.

Myers, Walter Dean. *The Mouse Trap.* New York: Harper & Row, 1990. (I:10+, R:5). A boy describes his summer in Harlem.

Steptoe, Joe. *Stevie.* New York: Harper & Row, 1969. (I:3–7, R:3). A boy is jealous at first but then discovers the importance of friendship.

Historical Fiction

Brenner, Barbara. *Wagon Wheels.* Illustrated by Don Bolognese. New York: Harper & Row, 1978. (I:6–9, R:1). This easy-to-read history book is based on the story of a family who moves from Kentucky to Kansas in 1878.

Collier, James, and Collier, Christopher. *Jump Ship to Freedom.* New York: Delacorte Press, 1981. (I:10+, R:7). A slave obtains his freedom and the freedom of his mother.

Monjo, F. N. *The Drinking Gourd.* Illustrated by Fred Brenner. New York: Harper & Row, 1970. (I:7–9, R:2). An "I can read" history book tells about a family on the Underground Railroad.

Petry, Ann. *Tituba of Salem Village.* New York: Thomas Y. Crowell Co., 1964. (I:11+, R:6). A talented sensitive slave becomes part of the Salem witch trials in the 1690s.

Taylor, Mildred. *The Gold Cadillac.* Illustrated by Michael Hays. New York: Dial, 1987. (I:8–10, R:3). A black family encounters racial prejudice in attempting to drive an expensive car into the segregated South.

———. *Let the Circle Be Unbroken.* New York: Dial Press, 1981. (I:10+, R:6). The author continues the story of the family in *Roll of Thunder, Hear My Cry.*

———. *Roll of Thunder, Hear My Cry.* Illustrated by Jerry Pickney. New York: Dial Press, 1976. (I:10+, R:6). A Mississippi family in 1933 experiences night riders and humiliating experiences but retains their independence.

Nonfiction

Adler, David A. *Martin Luther King, Jr.: Free at Last.* Illustrated by Robert Casilla. New York: Holiday, 1986. (I:7–10, R:5). This book stresses the magnitude of King's work and the reasons he fought against injustice.

Adoff, Arnold. *Malcolm X.* New York: Thomas Y. Crowell Co., 1970. (I:7–12, R:5). This biography of a black leader highlights the changes that took place in his life.

Greenfield, Eloise, and Little, Lessie Jones. *Childtimes: A Three Generation Memoir.* New York: Thomas Y. Crowell Co., 1979. (I:10+, R:5). Three black women tell about their childhood experiences.

Hamilton, Virginia. *Anthony Burns: The Defeat and Triumph of a Fugitive Slave.* New York: Knopf, 1988. (I:10+, R:6). This is a biography of the escaped slave whose trial caused riots in Boston.

Haskins, James. *Black Theater in America.* Thomas Y. Crowell Co., 1982. (I:10+, R:6). The history of the theater proceeds from minstrel shows to contemporary theater.

Patterson, Lillie. *Frederick Douglas: Freedom Fighter.* Champaign, Ill.: Garrard, 1965. (I:6–9, R:3). This is a biography of a great black leader.

———. *Sure Hands, Strong Heart, the Life of Daniel Hale Williams.* Nashville: Tenn.: Abingdon Press, 1980. (I:10+, R:5). This is a biography of a black physician.

Tobias, Tobi. *Arthur Mitchell.* Illustrated by Carol Byard. New York: Thomas Y. Crowell Co., 1975. (I:7–9, R:5). This book describes the life of the founder of the Dance Theatre of Harlem.

Asian-American Literature

Traditional Tales

Asian Cultural Center for UNESCO. *Folk Tales from Asia for Children Everywhere,* Book Three. Weatherhill, 1976. (I:8–12, R:6). This is a collection of folktales from many Asian nations.

Carrison, Muriel Paskin, retold by. *Cambodian Folk Stories.* Rutland, Vt.: Tuttle, 1987. (I:8+, R:6). This book contains tales of scoundrels and rascals, kings and lords, and foolishness and fun.

Clark, Ann Nolan. *In the Land of Small Dragon.* Illustrated by Tony Chen. New York: Viking Press, 1979. (I:7–12, R:7). This is a Vietnamese "Cinderella" story.

Haviland, Virginia. *Favorite Fairy Tales Told in Japan.* Illustrated by George Suyeoka. Boston: Little, Brown, & Co., 1967. (I:8–10, R:5). This is a collection of Japanese folktales.

Ike, Jane, and Zimmerman, Baruch. *A Japanese Fairy Tale.* New York: Warne, 1982. (I:5–8, R:5). A hunchback takes the disfiguration of his future wife, allowing her to be beautiful.

Laurin, Anne. *The Perfect Crane.* Illustrated by Charles Mikolaycak. New York: Harper & Row, 1981. (I:5–9, R:6). A Japanese folktale tells about friendship between a magician and the crane he creates from paper.

Lee, Jeanne M. *Legend of the Milky Way.* New York: Holt, Rinehart & Winston, 1982. (I:5–8, R:4). A Chinese folktale tells about the origin of the Milky Way.

Louie, Ai-Lang. *Yeh Shen: A Cinderella Story from China.* Illustrated by Ed Young. New York: Philomel, 1982. (I:7–9, R:6). This is a Chinese variation of the "Cinderella" story.

Mahy, Margaret. *The Seven Chinese Brothers.* Illustrated by Jean and Mou-sien Tseng. New York: Scholastic, 1990. (I:5–8, R:5). These brothers show unusual qualities.

Newton, Patricia Montgomery. *The Five Sparrows: A Japanese Folktale.* New York: Atheneum Pubs., 1982. (I:5–8, R:6). Kindness is rewarded and greed is punished in this Japanese folktale.

Paterson, Katherine. *The Tale of the Mandarin Ducks.* Illustrated by Leo and Diane Dillon. New York: Dutton, 1990. (I:7–10, R:5). Compassion is rewarded in this Japanese folktale.

Philip, Neil, ed. *The Spring of Butterflies and Other Folktales of China's Minority Peoples.* Translated by He Liyi, illustrated by Pan Aiqing and Li Zhao. New York: Lothrop, 1986. (I:9+, R:6). These tales are from northwestern China.

Sadler, Catherine Edwards. *Treasure Mountain: Folktales from Southern China.* Illustrated by Chen Mung Yun. New York: Atheneum Pubs., 1982. (I:8+, R:6). Six folktales depict values such as kindness and humor and disliked characteristics such as greed.

Stamm, Claus. *Three Strong Women.* Illustrated by Jean and Mousien Tseng. New York: Viking, 1990. (I:6+, R:5). A wrestler is trained by three women in this Japanese folktale.

Yagawa, Sumiko. *The Crane Wife.* Illustrated by Suekicki Akaba. New York: William Morrow & Co., 1981. (I:7–10, R:6). A wife returns to her animal form when her husband breaks his promise.

Yep, Laurence. *The Rainbow People.* Illustrated by David Wiesner. New York: Harper & Row, 1989. (I:8+, R:5). This text includes Chinese folktales collected from Asian-Americans.

Contemporary and Historical Literature

Clark, Ann Nolan. *To Stand Against the Wind.* New York: Viking Press, 1978. (I:10+, R:4). A Vietnamese boy now living in America prepares for the traditional Day of the Ancestors.

Davis, Daniel S. *Behind Barbed Wire: The Imprisonment of Japanese Americans during World War II.* New York: E. P. Dutton, 1982. (I:10+, R:7). The author explores the actions taken against Japanese Americans following the declaration of war.

Friedman, Ina R. *How My Parents Learned to Eat.* Illustrated by Allen Say. Boston: Houghton Mifflin Co., 1984. (I:6–8, R:3). This humorous story tells about trying to eat with chopsticks or with knives and forks.

Levin, Ellen. *I Hate English.* Illustrated by Steve Bjorkman. New York: Scholastic, 1989. (I:6–9, R:4). A girl from Hong Kong is helped by a sympathetic teacher.

Lord, Bette Bao. *In the Year of the Boar and Jackie Robinson.* Illustrated by Marc Simont. New York: Harper & Row, 1984. (I:8–10, R:4). Developing a love for baseball helps a Chinese girl make friends in America.

Nhuong, Huynh Quang. *The Land I Lost: Adventures of a Boy in Vietnam.* Illustrated by Vo-Dinh Mai. New York: Harper & Row, 1982. (I:8–12, R:6). The author tells about his boyhood experiences.

Uchida, Yoshiko. *Journey Home.* Illustrated by Charles Robinson. New York: Atheneum Pubs., 1978. (I:10+, R:5). In a sequel to *Journey to Topaz,* Yuki and her parents return to California after World War II.

Wallace, Ian. *Chin Chiang and the Dragon's Dance.* New York: Atheneum Pubs., 1984. (I:6–9, R:6). A young boy dreams of dancing on the first day of the Year of the Dragon.

Yep, Lawrence. *Child of the Owl.* New York: Harper & Row, 1977. (I:10+, R:7). A Chinese-American girl learns about her heritage when she lives with her grandmother.

⸻. *Dragonwings.* New York: Harper & Row, 1975. (I:10+, R:6). This historical book is set in San Francisco, 1903.

⸻. *Sea Glass.* New York: Harper & Row, 1979. (I:10+, R:6). A boy faces problems as he tries to make his father understand his desires.

Native-American Literature

Traditional Literature

Baker, Betty. *Rat Is Dead and Ant Is Sad.* Illustrated by Mamoru Funai. New York: Harper & Row, 1981. (I:6–8, R:2). This cumulative Pueblo Indian tale stresses the consequences of reaching wrong conclusions.

Baker, Olaf. *Where the Buffaloes Begin.* Illustrated by Stephen Gammell. New York: Warne, 1981. (I:8+, R:7). A Prairie Indian legend tells about the lake in which buffaloes are created and how the buffaloes help a boy who believes.

Baylor, Byrd. *And It Is Still That Way: Legends Told by Arizona Indian Children.* New York: Charles Scribner's Sons, 1976. (I:all, R:3). This is a collection of tales told by children.

⸻. *God on Every Mountain.* Illustrated by Carol Brown. New York: Charles Scribner's Sons, 1981. (I:6–10, R:5). These southwest Indian tales are about sacred mountains.

Cleaver, Elizabeth. *The Enchanted Caribou.* New York: Atheneum Pubs., 1985. (I:6–10, R:6). This is an Inuit tale of transformation.

Coatsworth, Emerson, and Coatsworth, David. *The Adventures of Nana Bush: Ojibway Indian Stories.* Illustrated by Frances Kagige. New York: Atheneum Pubs., 1980. (I:8+, R:6). Sixteen tales are about a powerful spirit.

de Paola, Tomie. *The Legend of the Bluebonnet.* New York: G. P. Putnam's Sons, 1983. (I:all, R:6). In a Comanche tale, unselfish actions are rewarded.

Goble, Paul. *Beyond the Ridge.* New York: Bradbury, 1989. (I:all, R:5). An elderly Indian woman from the Great Plains experiences death and goes to the afterlife.

⸻. *The Girl Who Loved Wild Horses.* Scarsdale, N.Y.: Bradbury, 1978. (I:6–10, R:5). An American Indian girl, who loves wild horses, joins them in a flight during a storm.

⸻. *Iktomi and the Boulder: A Plains Indian Story.* New York: Orchard, 1988. (I:4–10, R:4). This trickster tale is good for choral arrangements.

Grinnell, George Bird. *The Whistling Skeleton: American Indian Tales of the Supernatural.* Edited by John Bierhorst. Illustrated by Robert Andrew Parker. New York: Four Winds, 1982. (I:10+, R:6). Nine mystery tales are told by nineteenth century storytellers from the Cheyenne, Pawnee, and Blackfoot tribes.

Haviland, Virginia. *North American Legends.* Illustrated by Ann Strugnell. New York: Collins, 1979. (I:8+, R:6). This is an anthology of North American tales.

Highwater, Jamake. *Anpao: An American Indian Odyssey.* Illustrated by Fritz Scholder. Philadelphia:

J. B. Lippincott Co., 1977. (I:12+, R:5). A Native American travels across the history of traditional tales in order to search for his destiny.

Robinson, Gail. *Raven the Trickster. Legends of the North American Indians.* Illustrated by Joanna Troughton. New York: Atheneum Pubs., 1982. (I:8–12, R:6). These nine tales are from the Northwest.

Spencer, Paula Underwood. *Who Speaks for Wolf.* Illustrated by Frank Howell. Austin: Tribe of Two Press, 1983. (I:all). This Native American learning story emphasizes the need to consider animals.

Poetry and Songs

Baylor, Byrd. *Before You Came This Way.* Illustrated by Tom Bahti. New York: E. P. Dutton, 1969. (I:all). The Indian petroglyphs of the Southwest are described in poetic form.

_____ . *The Desert Is Theirs.* Illustrated by Peter Parnall. New York: Charles Scribner's Sons, 1975. (I:all). The poetic form captures the life of the Papago Indians.

_____ . *Hawk, I'm Your Brother.* Illustrated by Peter Parnall. New York: Charles Scribner's Sons, 1976. (I:all). A young boy longs to glide through the air like a hawk.

Belting, Natalia. *Whirlwind Is a Ghost Dancing.* Illustrated by Leo and Diane Dillon. New York: E. P. Dutton, 1974. (I:all). The lore of numerous tribes is depicted in poetic form.

Bierhorst, John. *A Cry from the Earth: Music of the North American Indians.* New York: Four Winds, 1979. (I:all). This is a collection of Native American songs.

Contemporary and Historical Literature

Dodge, Nanabah Chee. *Morning Arrow.* Illustrated by Jeffrey Lunge. (New York: Lothrop, Lee, and Shepard, 1975. (I:7–10, R:3). A ten-year-old Navaho boy lives with and helps his partially blind grandmother.

Hudson, Jan. *Sweetgrass.* Edmonton: Tree Frog, 1984. (I:10+, R:4). A Blackfoot girl grows up during the winter of a smallpox epidemic in 1837.

Martin, Bill, and Archambault, John. *Knots on a Counting Rope.* Illustrated by Ted Rand. New York: Holt, Rinehart & Winston, 1987. (I:7+). This is a rhythmic tale of a blind Native American boy who rides in a horse race.

Miles, Miska. *Annie and the Old One.* Illustrated by Peter Parnall. Boston: Little, Brown, & Co., 1971. (I:6–8, R:3). Annie's love for her grandmother causes her to interfere with the completion of a rug she associates with the probable death of her grandmother.

O'Dell, Scott. *Sing Down the Moon.* Boston: Houghton Mifflin Co., 1970. (I:10+, R:6). The 1864 forced march of the Navaho is told through the viewpoint of a young girl.

Paulsen, Gary. *Dogsong.* New York: Bradbury, 1988. (I:10+, R:6). An Eskimo boy journeys 1,400 miles by dogsled as he crosses the ice.

Rockwood, Joyce. *Groundhog's Horse.* Illustrated by Victor Kalin. New York: Holt, Rinehart & Winston, 1978. (I:7–12, R:4). A humorous, warm story tells of a Cherokee boy, who in 1750, rescues his horse.

Sneve, Virginia Driving Hawk. *High Elk's Treasure.* Illustrated by Oren Lyons. New York: Holiday, 1972. (I:8–12, R:6). A dream beginning in 1876 is renewed in the late 1970s.

_____ . *Jimmy Yellow Hawk.* Illustrated by Oren Lyons. New York: Holiday, 1972. (I:6–10, R:5). This is the story of a contemporary boy who lives on an Indian reservation in South Dakota.

White Deer of Autumn. *Ceremony—In the Circle of Life.* Illustrations by Daniel San Souci. Milwaukee: Raintree, 1983. (I:all). A contemporary boy learns about his heritage and the importance of living in harmony with nature.

Nonfiction

Ashabranner, Brent. *Morning Star, Black Sun: The Northern Cheyenne Indians and America's Energy Crisis.* Photographs by Paul Conklin. New York: Dodd, Mead & Co., 1982. (I:10+, R:7). The text traces the history of the Northern Cheyenne Indians and discusses the tribe's fight to save their lands from power companies and strip mining.

Fall, Thomas. *Jim Thorpe.* Illustrated by John Gretzer. New York: Thomas Y. Crowell Co., 1970. (I:7–9, R:2). This is a simple biography about a great athlete.

Freedman, Russell. *Buffalo Hunt.* New York: Holiday, 1988. (I:8+, R:6). Illustrations and text show the importance of the buffalo to Great Plains Indians.

_____ . *Indian Chiefs.* New York: Holiday, 1987. (I:8+, R:7). These are biographies of six native American chiefs; photographs add authenticity.

Hirschfelder, Arlene. *Happily May I Walk: American Indians and Alaska Natives Today.* New York: Charles Scribner's Sons, 1986. (I:10+, R:6). This is an excellent resource book about contemporary life.

McGraw, Jessie Brewer. *Chief Red Horse Tells About Custer: The Battle of Little Bighorn: An Eyewitness Account Told in Indian Sign Language.* New York: Elsevier/Nelson, 1981. (I:8+). The historical background and glossary of Indian terms add to the story based on pictographs.

Morrison, Dorothy Nafus. *Chief Sarah: Sarah Winnemucca's Fight for Indian Rights.* New York: Atheneum, 1980. (I:10+, R:6). Sarah Winnemucca was a leader of the Paiute people.

Tobias, Tobi. *Maria Tallchief.* Illustrated by Michael Hampshire. New York: Thomas Y. Crowell Co., 1970. (I:7–12, R:4). This ballerina was a member of the Osage Indian tribe.

Weiss, Malcolm. *Sky Watchers of Ages Past.* Illustrated by Eliza McFadden. Boston: Houghton Mifflin Co., 1982. (I:10+, R:6). The author introduces readers to some of the astronomers of the past, such as the Anasazi Indians and the Mayans.

Hispanic Literature

Traditional Tales

Aardema, Verna. *The Riddle of the Drum: A Tale from Tizapán, Mexico.* Illustrated by Tony Chen. New York: Four Winds, 1979. (I:6–10, R:3). The man who marries the king's daughter must guess the kind of leather in a drum.

Belpré, Pura. *The Rainbow-Colored Horse.* Illustrated by Antonio Martorell. New York: Warne, 1978. (I:6–10, R:6). Three favors granted by a horse allow Pio to win the hand of Don Nicanoro's daughter.

Bierhorst, John, ed. *Black Rainbow: Legends of the Incas and Myths of Ancient Peru.* New York: Farrar, Straus & Giroux, 1976. (I:10+, R:7). This book contains twenty traditional tales.

_____ . *Doctor Coyote.* Illustrated by Wendy Watson. New York: Macmillan, 1987. (I: all). This fable is from the Indians of Mexico.

_____ . *Spirit Child: A Story of the Nativity.* Illustrated by Barbara Cooney. New York: William Morrow & Co., 1984. (I:8–12, R:6). Pre-Columbian style illustrations accompany an Aztec story.

de Paola, Tomie. *The Lady of Guadalupe.* New York: Holiday, 1980. (I:8+, R:6). This Mexican tale is about the patron saint of Mexico who appeared to an Indian in 1531.

Hinojosa, Francisco, adapted by. *The Old Lady Who Ate People.* Illustrated by Leonel Maciel. Boston: Little, Brown & Co., 1984. (I:all, R:6). These four frightening tales are from Mexico.

Jagendorf, M. A., and Boggs, R. W. *The King of the Mountains: A Treasury of Latin American Folk Stories.* New York: Vanguard, 1960. (I:9+, R:6). This is a collection of tales from twenty-six countries.

Lattimore, Deborah. *The Flame of Peace: A Tale of the Aztecs.* New York: Harper & Row, 1987. (I:all, R:6). This story is based on Aztec mythology.

Rohmer, Harriet; Octavio, Chow; and Viduare, Morris. *The Invisible Hunters.* Illustrated by Joe Sam. Children's Press, 1987. (I:all, R:5). This is a tale about European traders.

Contemporary and Historical Literature

Clark, Ann Nolan. *Year Walk.* New York: Viking Press, 1975. (I:10+, R:7). A Spanish Basque sheep-herder faces loneliness and the challenges of becoming a man when he crosses the desert into the high country.

Ets, Marie Hall, and Labastida, Aurora. *Nine Days to Christmas, A Story of Mexico.* New York: Viking Press, 1959. (I:5–8, R:3). The book includes lovely illustrations of a girl preparing for a Mexican Christmas holiday.

Krumgold, Joseph. *And Now Miguel.* Illustrated by Jean Charlot. New York: Thomas Y. Crowell Co., 1953. (I:10+, R:3). Miguel, a member of a proud sheep-raising family, wishes to go with the sheepherders to the Sangre de Cristo Mountains.

Mohr, Nicholasa. *Felita.* Illustrated by Ray Cruz. New York: Dial Press, 1979. (I:9–12, R:2). A family tries to adjust to a new neighborhood.

O'Dell, Scott, *The Captive.* Boston: Houghton Mifflin Co., 1977. (I:10+, R:6). A Spanish seminarian witnesses the exploitation of the Mayas during the 1500s.

_____ . *Carlota.* Boston: Houghton Mifflin Co., 1977. (I:9+, R:4). A girl fights beside her father in California during the Mexican War.

_____ . *The Feathered Serpent.* Boston: Houghton Mifflin Co., 1981. (I:10+, R:6). The seminarian in *The Captive* witnesses the arrival of Cortés.

Politi, Leo. *The Nicest Gift.* New York: Charles Scribner's Sons, 1973. (I:5–8, R:6). There are many Spanish words in the text and illustrations from the barrio in East Los Angeles.

_____ . *Song of the Swallows.* New York: Charles Scribner's Sons, 1949. (I:5–8, R:4). Illustrations of Spanish architecture appear in a story set in Capistrano.

Soto, Gary. *Baseball in April and Other Stories.* Harcourt Brace Jovanovich, 1990. (I:11+, R:6). This is a collection of stories about Mexican-American youth in California.

Taha, Karen T. *A Gift for Tia Rosa.* Illustrated by Dee deRosa. Minneapolis: Dillon, 1986. (I:5–8, R:3). A young girl faces a neighbor's death and learns about love.

Nonfiction

Ashabranner, Brent. *Children of the Maya: A Guatemalan Indian Odyssey.* Photographs by Paul Conklin. New York: Dodd, Mead & Co., 1986. (I:9–12, R:6). This is a contemporary report about Mayans who settled in Florida after escaping from Guatemala.

Brown, Tricia. *Hello, Amigos!* Photographs by Fran Ortiz. New York: Holt, Rinehart & Winston, 1986. (I:6–9). This photographic essay is about a Mexican-American boy who lives in San Francisco.

Franchere, Ruth. *Cesar Chavez.* Illustrated by Earl Thollander. New York: Thomas Y. Crowell Co.,

1970. (I:7–9, R:4). A biography depicts Chavez's struggles to improve the pay and living conditions for migrant workers.

Martinello, Marian L., and Nesmith, Samuel P. *With Domingo Leal in San Antonio 1734.* The University of Texas, Institute of Texas Cultures at San Antonio, 1979. (I:8+, R:4). The text is based on research on the lives of Spanish settlers who arrived in Texas during the 1730s.

Meltzer, Milton. *The Hispanic Americans.* Photographs by Morrie Camhi and Catherine Noren. New York: Thomas Y. Crowell Co., 1982. (I:9–12, R:6). The author discusses the influence in America of Puerto Ricans, Chicanos, and Cubans.

Wolf, Bernard. *In This Proud Land: The Story of a Mexican American Family.* Philadelphia: J. B. Lippincott Co., 1978. (I:all, R:4). Photographs and text follow a family from the Rio Grande Valley to Minnesota for summer employment.

Chapter Six

After completing this chapter on handwriting, you will be able to:

1. State some of the issues related to handwriting instruction.
2. Describe some informal means for assessing readiness.
3. Describe some instructional activities to help children see the need for good handwriting and to develop their handwriting skills.
4. Describe some instructional activities that develop fine-motor skills and readiness for letter formations.
5. Develop and demonstrate a lesson that teaches manuscript printing to beginning writers.
6. Evaluate handwriting samples for letter formation, slant, spacing, and line quality.
7. Identify the manuscript errors made most frequently by first-grade students.
8. Demonstrate the formation of manuscript and cursive letters.
9. Develop and demonstrate a lesson that introduces students to cursive writing.
10. Describe and use a technique for collecting handwriting samples under the three conditions of normal, best, and fastest writing.
11. Describe some instructional procedures specific to left-handed writers.
12. Describe a kinesthetic approach for teaching handwriting to learning disabled students.

Handwriting

*H*andwriting instruction that emphasizes ornate, consistent penmanship for every student is no longer a part of modern curricula. Modern handwriting instruction, although it does not develop beautiful flourishes, does stress legibility—well-formed letters, consistent slant, and proper spacing of letters and words. Whereas writing was once almost an art form, modern handwriting is viewed as a tool for personal communication. There is now considerable leeway for developing a personal handwriting style, although the writing cannot be so personal that only the writer is able to read it.

In a review of research in handwriting, Hodges (1991) states that "summaries of current practices indicate that handwriting instruction is fairly uniform throughout the United States, typically beginning with manuscript writing in the first grade, with a transition to cursive writing sometime before the third grade" (p. 780). According to Hodges, direct instruction is common in teaching handwriting. He goes on to state: "What appears to be important in the development of handwriting is the amount of emphasis teachers place on legible, neat writing, and also the presence in the classroom of good handwriting models" (p. 780).

Summarizing another review of research in the area of handwriting, Farris (1991) emphasizes the importance of including handwriting instruction: "Without being introduced to and given instruction in the basic handwriting skills such as letter formation, alignment, slant, and size, children are left to discover such skills on their own. As such, they develop inappropriate techniques, and legibility suffers. . . . Teachers in early childhood education should teach handwriting through direct instruction, for it is a basic and important skill for writing. Teachers at both the early and middle childhood levels need to understand handwriting methods and to be able to identify and correct students' problems. The teacher–student conference, a crucial component of whole language instruction, can include direct handwriting instruction just as it serves as a vehicle for improving the content, grammar, and punctuation of a piece of writing" (p. 314).

EFFECTIVE HANDWRITING INSTRUCTION

Fairchild (1987) offers the following guidelines for effective handwriting instruction:

1. Knowing the purpose for the activity increases student participation.
2. Visual demonstrations by teachers and other students help students see what to practice.

3. Students who verbalize the task before performing it show greater improvement.
4. Sessions that are spaced are more effective than very long sessions.
5. Analyzing the motor task to practice and then identifying small, learnable steps permits students to master the activity.
6. Reinforcement encourages continued practice.
7. Giving students knowledge of the results of their practice and teaching them to evaluate their own progress enhances instruction.

Handwriting instruction has three phases. First is readiness for handwriting, which is developed at home, in kindergarten, and in early first grade. Second is the formal teaching of manuscript writing, usually beginning in first grade. Third is the formal teaching of cursive writing, beginning about third grade. However, you may need to give special consideration to left-handed writers and mainstreamed writers. In addition, throughout any handwriting instruction, special care should be taken to provide students with opportunities to apply their handwriting skills in meaningful situations. You must also remember that handwriting is a tool—one of the conventions of writing—that leads to meaningful composition and communication.

WRITING READINESS

Readiness for handwriting requires an interest in writing and a desire to write, adequate visual acuity and fine-motor skills, understanding of left-to-right progression, and understanding of the concept of language. Donoghue (1990) identifies the following six prerequisite skill areas for handwriting: (1) small-muscle development and coordination, (2) eye-hand coordination, (3) ability to hold writing tools properly, (4) ability to form basic strokes, (5) letter perception, and (6) understanding of printed language, including left-to-right progression and language maturity. You can evaluate these readiness skills through simple observation. A child's interest or lack of interest in writing is usually apparent. Does the child ask how to write his or her name or other words? Does the child pretend to be writing?

Informal Assessment

Durkin (1966) found that children who read prior to entering school also show an early interest in learning to print. The learning sequences of these early printers moved from (1) scribbling and drawing to (2) copying objects and letters of the alphabet to (3) asking questions about spelling to (4) reading. It is easy to observe children and assess where they are in this sequence.

Because both reading and writing progress from left to right, it is logical that understanding this sequence benefits handwriting instruction. Observe each child to see whether the child progresses from left to right when trying to read a book. If you place two dots on a chalkboard or paper, does the child connect the dots in a left-to-right sequence? By observing children in such activities as drawing, bead stringing, paper cutting, and pencil holding, you can learn a great deal about their fine-motor coordination. Observation also permits you to ascertain a child's hand preference.

Tracing a raised letter develops a kinesthetic feel for that letter.

De Ajuriaguerra and Auzias (1975) recommend looking at handwriting in a framework that includes both language and motor analysis. They believe that in both drawing and scribbling, children first explore paper by using indiscriminate actions; they then show increased purpose and good use of space. Based on de Ajuriaguerra and Auzias's research, Graves (1978) developed the following six questions that can be used to determine children's level of development of the skills necessary for writing and to evaluate how they explore space in artwork, construction, movement, and writing:

1. Is the child consistent in the use of the thumb and forefinger grip? Children who demonstrate a poor grip when using a crayon in artwork will have difficulty controlling a pencil in writing.
2. Does the child show erratic movement in artwork or handwriting? When children first write, the writing stops and starts because they are not

familiar with the task. Continued erratic movements suggest underdeveloped fine-motor skills.

3. Does the child change the position of the elbow, affecting the stability of
body axis? When children begin to draw or write, they exhibit a great deal
of body and elbow motion. Children who do not reduce this motion will
have a great deal of difficulty with the fine-motor demands of writing.

4. Does the child change the position of the writing surface in relation to the
midline? When children first face paper, they approach it squarely in
relation to the body. Gradually, they come to understand the relationship
of the position of the paper to the position of the body in writing.

5. Does the child vary the applied strength? In writing, children must sup-
press large muscles so that small muscles can gain control. Observe
changes from light to heavy lines on the paper as well as changes in the
body position of the child.

6. How does the child use writing space? Look at how he or she chains
letters together. If children do not have good enough fine-motor control,
angles will be inconsistent and spaces will be uneven. Children who do
not understand the concept of language also show a tendency to run
words and sentences together.

Graves believes that any of the preceding factors can contribute to slowness in
handwriting and thus affect the quality and content of writing.

REINFORCEMENT ACTIVITY

1. Observe children in a nursery school or kindergarten. Using informal assessment techniques, describe some of the relevant characteristics of those children you feel are ready for writing and those who may not be ready.

2. Use Graves's six elements to evaluate children's use of space. Compare samples from children who appear to be ready for writing with samples from
those who do not.

Instruction

Early-childhood educators contend that the readiness phase in handwriting is as important as the readiness phase in reading. Many activities in nursery school, kindergarten, and early first grade contribute to readiness for handwriting. Early readiness
experiences give children opportunities to explore the space provided by paper. As
Graves (1978) suggests, at first—at two or three years of age—there is no difference
between drawing and writing attempts. Later, children differentiate by drawing pictures and making continuous scribbles across pages to represent writing. When children try to write, they are indicating a need for handwriting. A child who does not feel
a need for writing has unusual difficulties with all aspects of writing.

Kindergarten programs that include oral reading and language experience
activities, in which children dictate group or individual chart stories, help children

FIGURE 6–1
Elements needed to make the
manuscript alphabet

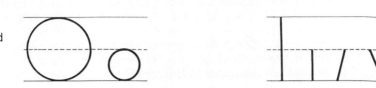

FIGURE 6–2
Fundamental shapes on lined
paper

see relationships between oral language, printed stories, and handwriting. If children do not understand the concepts of word and sentence, handwriting is meaningless to them. Wordless books provide enjoyable instructional sources for language experience stories. Develop many readiness activities to allow children to see that the purpose for handwriting is composition and communication—not isolated drill.

Moving, drawing, painting, and cutting help develop fine-motor skills. Dances, such as looby-loo and hokey pokey, nurture mastery of left and right. Other activities include drawing cars on a road that goes from left to right and moving small cars and trucks on the road in the classroom or on the playground.

A second group of readiness activities helps children with letter formations. The movements needed to form the manuscript alphabet are primarily circles and lines in vertical, horizontal, or angled positions; therefore, have children practice making these strokes on large paper or on the chalkboard. Kindergarten and first-grade teachers often have children make creative pictures from elements such as those shown in Figure 6–1. One first-grade teacher had those students who demonstrated underdeveloped fine-motor control make delightful stick figures and animals using the basic shapes necessary for formal manuscript writing. Thus, the children experimented with space and line dimensions while enjoying art activity. Tompkins (1980) recommends using basic penmanship strokes to create stories and pictures. She develops activities around the language game Let's Go on a Bear Hunt, instructions for making jack-o-lanterns, and a snow-day story.

After children have had opportunities to experiment with shapes and lines on unlined paper, teachers often introduce them to the use of lined paper by having them draw the fundamental shapes between the appropriate lines (see Figure 6–2).

PRINTING

Printing, also called manuscript writing, is taught to first- and second-graders in most American schools. Printing rather than cursive writing is considered preferable for beginners because the printing symbols are similar to reading symbols.

Although manuscript writing is taught in most elementary grades, there is some disagreement about what size pencils and what type of paper should be used. According to Askov, Otto, and Askov (1970), research in this area is too scant to permit any conclusions. They cite one research article reporting that children prefer adult pencils to larger-sized beginner pencils. Many educators recommend allowing each child to use whatever pencil size is most comfortable because the larger pencils have not been proven better for beginning writers.

Yardley (1973), a British educator, points out that unlined paper offers a surface free of restrictions when a child's attempts to write are immature. In England, children spend several years working with unlined paper, whereas most American children use paper that progresses from wider to narrower spaces, even for early instruction.

There are several published instructional programs in the area of handwriting. If your school has approved one of these programs, you should learn the formation of the letters for that program. Children are very observant; they will notice if letters you make are different from those used in the program. Figures 6–3

Writing for personal journals provides an opportunity to practice manuscript in a meaningful context.

FIGURE 6–3
Manuscript alphabet (Used with permission from *Handwriting: Basic Skills and Application.*
Copyright 1987. Zaner-Bloser, Inc., Columbus, Ohio.)

and 6–4 show manuscript alphabets taught in many schools. The first example is
published by the Zaner-Bloser Company. The second is the D'Nealian Handwriting
model published by Scott, Foresman. Compare the two examples for letter shapes
and strokes.

REINFORCEMENT ACTIVITY

Before you proceed with specific instructional techniques for manuscript writing, practice printing the manuscript alphabets shown in Figures 6–3 and 6–4 or the manuscript
alphabet used in the schools in your area. Practice the alphabet on paper and a chalkboard until you feel comfortable with it.

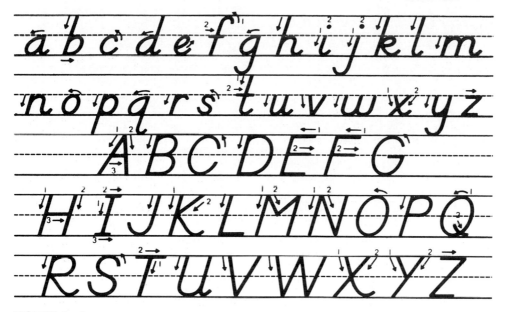

FIGURE 6–4
D'Nealian manuscript alphabet (*D'Nealian*® *Handwriting* by Donald Thurber. Copyright ©
1987 by Scott, Foresman & Co. Reprinted by permission.)

Instruction

Readiness activities help children understand the techniques that contribute to
legible handwriting. Manuscript writing instruction should involve correct sitting
posture, correct letter formation, proper spacing of letters, and uniform slanting of
letters. Several language arts authorities stress the role of teachers in helping
children analyze a letter before writing it. Furner (1969) recommends a perceptual-
motor approach for teaching letter formation. This approach allows children to
identify writing position, letter formation, alignment, and spacing of letters before
they actually print a letter.

In all early writing activities, remember that writing is a difficult and slow
process for many children, so early handwriting practice should not overtire them.
Allow children to practice their handwriting through a functional approach as soon
as possible. Instead of merely having them copy model sentences, let them write
their names and addresses. Let them write diaries, invitations, letters, captions for
artwork, weather charts, autobiographies, and so forth. When children are first
learning to write, supervise them closely so that they will not reinforce incorrect
letter formations. Also, do not waste time repeatedly practicing letter formations
they have already mastered.

FOR YOUR PLAN BOOK
A Handwriting Lesson Using a Letter-Analysis Approach

Teachers should help children analyze a letter by encouraging them to visualize the letter, study its characteristics (beginning stroke, ending stroke, strokes peculiar to the letter, height of the letter, height of various parts of the letter, and width of the letter), and check the quality of the strokes. The following lesson plan uses this letter-analysis approach. The objective is to enable the students to analyze and form the manuscript letter a. The teaching procedures follow.

1. Make lines on the chalkboard similar to the lines on manuscript paper. A musical staff marker with chalk placed in the top, middle, and bottom holders is useful.

2. Ask the children to watch carefully as you make the letter a. Ask, "How am I making the letter a?" "What kinds of strokes do you see?" (Circle stroke and straight-line stroke.) You may discuss the fact that the class has practiced these strokes (see Figure 1).

Figure 1
The letter *a*

3. Emphasize the beginning stroke for the letter a. Ask the class to watch as you make the circle portion of the letter. Ask, "Where does the circle begin?" (Just below the dotted, or middle, line.) "In what direction does the stroke go?" (The circle goes to the left.) A mark and an arrow will help students visualize this formation (see Figure 2).

Figure 2
Beginning the letter *a*

4. Have the students watch you make the letter a again. This time, ask them to watch the straight-line formation. Ask, "Where does the straight line begin?" (The line begins on the dotted, or middle, line.) "Where does the straight line touch the circle?" (On the right side of the circle.) "Where does the straight line end?" (On the bottom line.) (See Figure 3.)

Figure 3
Finishing the letter *a*

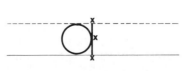

5. Have the students watch again so that they can describe the height of the letter. Ask, "How tall is the circle part of the letter?" (The circle is one space high. It touches the middle line and bottom line, but it does not go over either line.) "How tall is the straight-line part of the letter?" (The straight line is one space high. It touches the middle line and the bottom line, but it does not go over either line.) (See Figure 4.)

Figure 4
Size of the letter *a*

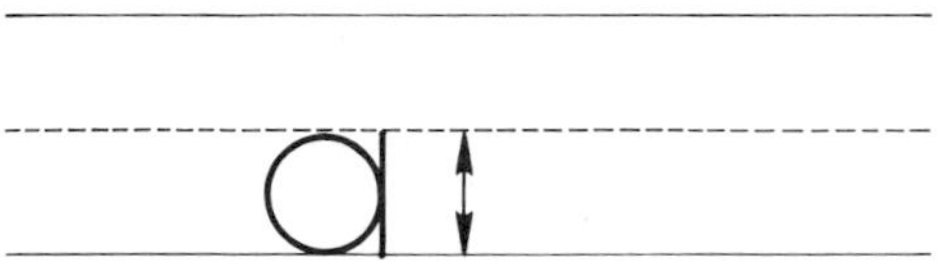

6. Ask the children to describe how the letter is formed. Have them write the letter independently, describing the process to themselves.

After introducing the letter a, teach other letters in a similar manner.

REINFORCEMENT ACTIVITY

Develop a lesson plan for teaching one of the letters of the manuscript alphabet. Use your lesson plan with beginning writers, or try the lesson plan with a small group of your peers.

Assessing Handwriting

After reviewing strategies for writing and evaluating writing, Hodges (1991) states that the critical criteria for determining handwriting quality are legibility (well-proportioned letters and words) and fluency (rate of writing). He finds that the legibility classification system most commonly used includes letter form, uniformity of slant, letter alignment, quality of line, and spacing between letters and words, all of which may be assessed informally. To check letter formation—the most important factor—Burns and Broman (1983) recommend using a card with a circular hole cut in the center. Move this hole, a little larger than a letter, along the line of writing to expose one letter at a time. Thus, you or a child may identify poorly formed or illegible letters (see Figure 6–5).

You can easily observe letter formation when children use lined paper or when you draw lines across the tops of the letters to see if they are uniform. In the example on the left of Figure 6–6, a second-grade child has formed each letter according to his first-grade teaching. In the example on the right, another second-grade child is having considerable difficulty with letter formation.

In both manuscript and cursive writing, the letter slant affects legibility. To evaluate consistency in slant, you or a child can draw straight lines through the letters in words (see Figure 6–7). The lines quickly indicate whether or not the letters are slanted consistently. Posture is the most important factor affecting the slant of handwriting, so observe children while they are writing.

FIGURE 6–5
Cards allowing assessment of
individual letters

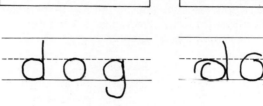

FIGURE 6–6
Good and poor letter formation

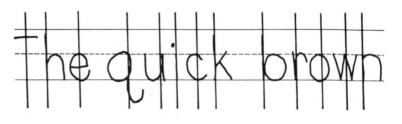

FIGURE 6–7
Letter slant

Consistent slant:

Inconsistent slant:

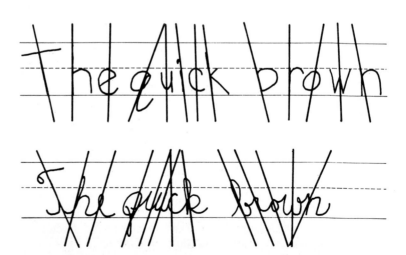

Spacing also affects legibility. Too much spacing between letters can slow the speed of reading. Obviously, if there are no spaces between words, material is hard to read. Some children place their letters so close together that the letters are difficult to decipher, which can affect assessment of spelling ability, too. (See Figure 6–8 for examples of proper spacing and poor spacing.)

When you assess line quality, evaluate the thickness of the lines and their lightness and darkness. For children with well-developed fine-motor skills, the lines will usually reflect consistent pressure. In contrast, for children whose fine-motor skills are not adequately developed, there may be noticeable differences in line quality (see Figure 6–9).

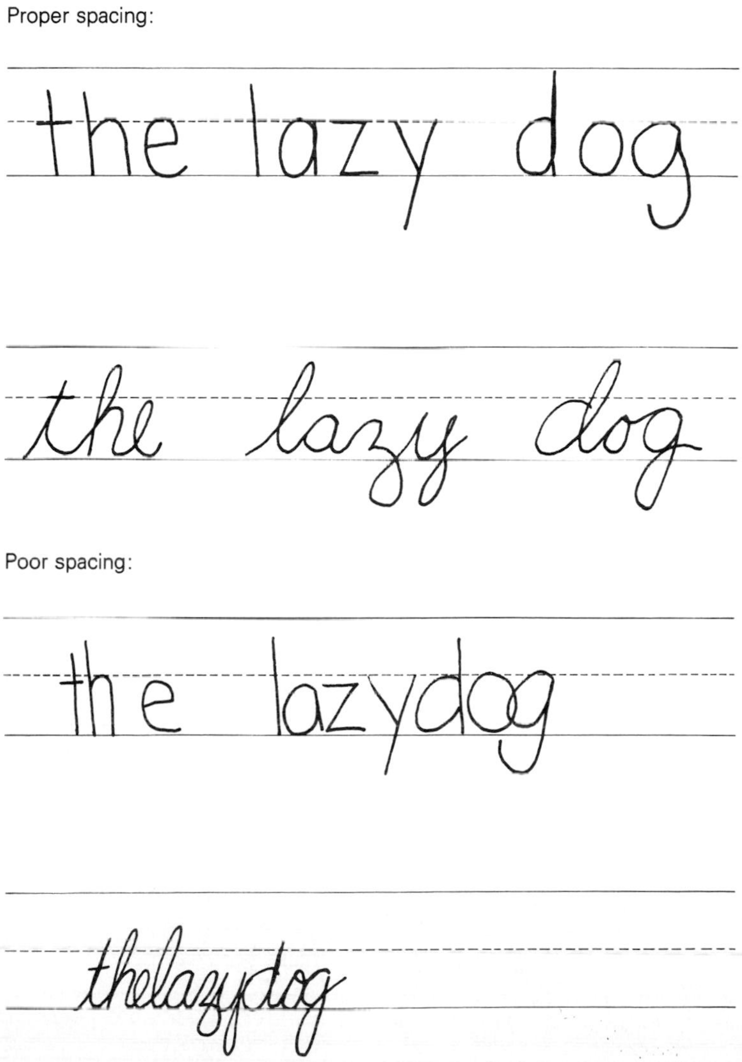

Proper spacing:

FIGURE 6–8
Spacing

Poor spacing:

FIGURE 6–9
Noticeable differences in line
quality

the lazy dog

Name_____
Grade_____

		Sept.	Jan.	May
1.	Formation of letters:			
	a. All correctly formed	___	___	___
	b. Incorrect letters	___	___	___
2.	Slant of letters:			
	a. Consistent slant	___	___	___
	b. Irregular slant	___	___	___
	c. Too much back slant	___	___	___
3.	Posture while writing: (Posture of hand, body, paper)			
	a. Correct	___	___	___
	b. Incorrect	___	___	___
4.	Spacing within words:			
	a. Spaces too wide	___	___	___
	b. Letters crowded	___	___	___
	c. Spaces irregular	___	___	___
5.	Spacing between words:			
	a. Spaces too wide	___	___	___
	b. Spaces too narrow	___	___	___
	c. Spaces irregular	___	___	___
6.	Speed of writing:			
	a. Appropriate for grade	___	___	___
	b. Too slow	___	___	___
	c. Too fast	___	___	___
7.	Overall appearance of writing:			
	a. Neat	___	___	___
	b. Poor appearance due to _____	___	___	___

(Place checks, examples, and comments in appropriate spaces.)

FIGURE 6–10
Progress chart

Informal evaluation provides substantial diagnostic information and a basis for planning to meet individual needs. It also provides opportunities for you to correct errors before they become reinforced. Keep folders of writing examples for each child, so that both you and the child are aware of progress. It is helpful to develop a progress chart for each child in order to evaluate the various aspects of handwriting over a period of time. Figure 6–10 illustrates the type of information that you may keep on a progress chart.

As we have mentioned, most children experience some difficulties when first learning to print. It is quite common for beginners to reverse letters, for example, writing *b* instead of *d*. They also commonly omit letters from words or space letters poorly. If these errors are still apparent after a reasonable period of instruction, however, the child probably has a problem that requires special attention. Identifying children who are unable to write with normal legibility and speed is the goal of diagnostic procedures.

Lewis and Lewis (1964) analyzed both the number and types of errors made by first-grade children. Their findings included common errors, letters that are relatively easy to learn, and letters that are relatively difficult. Following are some conclusions from this first-grade study:

1. Most errors are made in letters that go below the line—*q, g, p, y,* and *j.*
2. Errors are frequent in letters in which curves and vertical lines merge—*J, U, f, h, j, m, n, r,* and *u.*
3. Letters most likely to be reversed are *n, d, q,* and *y.*
4. Errors that are most frequent include improper size, incorrect relationships of parts, and incorrect relationships to lines.
5. Fewest errors are made in the letters *H, O, o, L,* and *l.*

CURSIVE WRITING

As reported by Hodges (1991), most elementary schools require children to change from printing to cursive writing sometime between the end of the second grade and the middle of third grade; however, the transition usually begins in early third grade. Although cursive writing may be more acceptable for some social and business uses, there is no compelling reason to change from printing to cursive writing. Cursive writing, however, is more personal than printing, and usually faster.

Beginning Instruction

Cursive writing is not a new skill that children must memorize in the slow, meticulous way they study printing. By the time children begin cursive writing, they have had several years of practice with printed language and can compare and contrast manuscript and cursive writing. When Furner (1969) introduces her students to cursive writing, she uses two approaches. First, she organizes readiness activities in which she guides the students in recognizing and reading cursive letters. They name the letters, read their own names in cursive writing, and so forth. Next, they examine samples of cursive writing and its formation to compare it with printing.

Cursive writing charts may be used to find the similarities and differences between cursive writing and printing. The cursive alphabets published by Zaner-

Bloser and Scott, Foresman are used in most schools (see Figures 6–11 and 6–12). Following observation and discussion, list printed letters that are similar to those in the cursive alphabet. Also note similarities in direction of strokes, size, and relation to baseline (whether the letters touch or extend below the baseline). Following are some differences to note:

1. The letters are joined in cursive writing, and there are no spaces until the end of a word.

2. Cursive writing has a slant, whereas printing is straight.

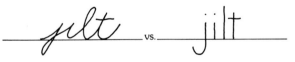

3. The letters *f* and *z* go below the baseline in cursive writing, whereas they do not in printing.

4. When a word is written in cursive, the *t* is crossed and the *i* and *j* are dotted after the word is completed, rather than after the letter is completed, as in printing.

5. The position of the paper may be more slanted for cursive writing than for printing.

Continuing Instruction

Burns and Broman (1983) recommend teaching letters and words having similar strokes at the same time. This procedure progresses from the straight printed to the slanted cursive version of words in the steps shown in Figure 6–13. Lowercase letters that are similar in manuscript and cursive alphabets are *a, d, g, h, i, l, m, n, o, p, q, t, u,* and *y*. Similar capital letters are *B, C, K, L, O, P, R,* and *U*.

Next, teach the letters that are dissimilar, such as *f, k, r, s,* and *z*. Use practical types of writing in instruction. Have the children practice their spelling words or have them write letters. At this level, individualize instruction so that each child will have extra practice with the letter formations and combinations that he or she finds difficult.

FIGURE 6–11

Cursive handwriting alphabet (Used with permission from *Handwriting: Basic Skills and Application.* Copyright 1987. Zaner-Bloser, Inc., Columbus, Ohio.)

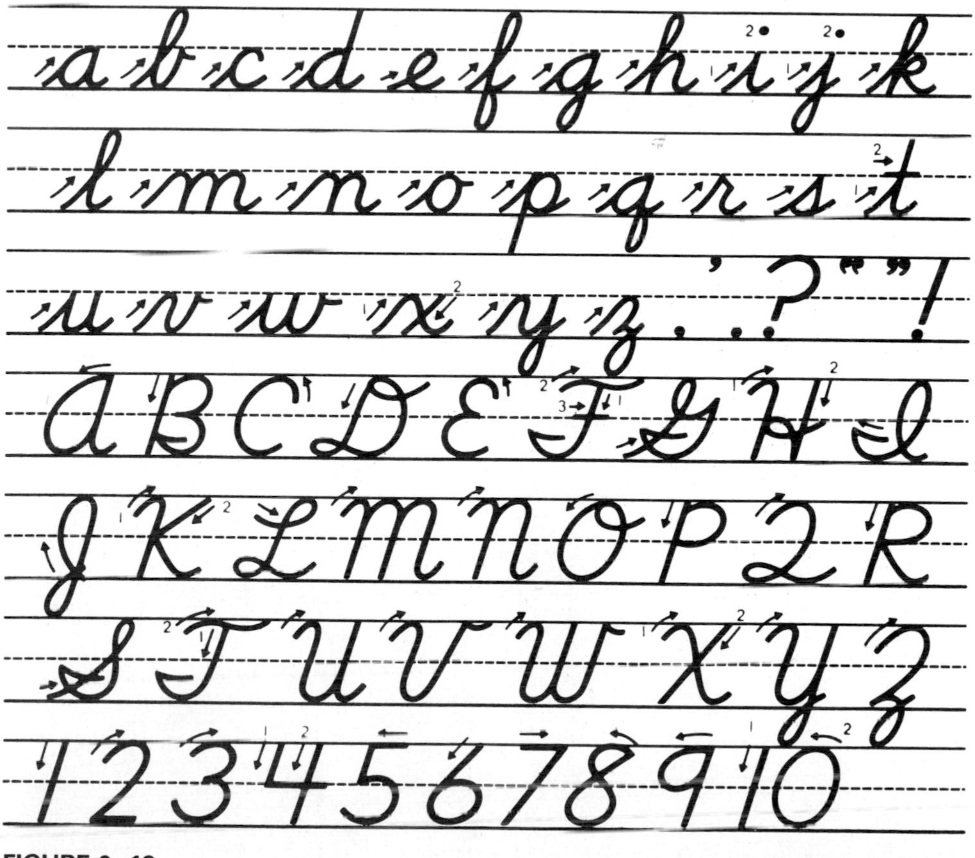

FIGURE 6–12

D'Nealian cursive alphabet *(D'Nealian® Handwriting* by Donald Thurber. Copyright © 1987 by Scott, Foresman & Co. Reprinted by permission.)

FIGURE 6–13
Transition from printing to
cursive writing

1. manuscript

2. dotted manuscript

3. nonslant cursive

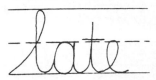

4. cursive slant

*Research has not shown any
great advantage in changing from
manuscript to cursive.*

1. Develop a lesson or series of lessons to demonstrate the transition from manuscript to cursive handwriting. If you are teaching elementary students at the appropriate age, use your lesson plan with them. If you are not teaching, demonstrate your activity to a group of your peers.
2. Investigate the way cursive writing is taught in one of the commercial sets of handwriting materials. Look at suggestions for transition to and development of the cursive alphabet. What skills are stressed? In what order are the letters presented? Are functional practice activities suggested to accompany the instruction? How much time is recommended for handwriting instruction?

Assessing Cursive Handwriting

Handwriting evaluation demands some experience. Consequently, beginning teachers may want to use the *Evaluation Scales for Expressional Growth Through Handwriting* published by the Zaner-Bloser Company (1969). The scales contain five examples each of manuscript printing for grades one and two. These examples represent high, good, medium, fair, and poor quality. The scales also provide five examples of cursive writing for each grade from three through nine. Looking at the various degrees of legibility may help you evaluate formation, slant, and spacing of letters.

There are few standardized tests for assessing handwriting. Teachers must rely on either informal sampling procedures or loosely standardized writing scales to evaluate children's handwriting skills. For the evaluation of handwriting of older students, Otto and Smith (1980) recommend gathering handwriting samples under three conditions: (1) usual writing, (2) best writing, and (3) fastest writing. Legibility may be acceptable when a child is able to work slowly and methodically, but it may deteriorate when the child has to write rapidly to keep up with the demands of school assignments. For gathering handwriting samples, Otto and Smith suggest the following procedures:

1. Use a sentence containing most of the letters of the alphabet; for example, The quick, sly fox jumps over the lazy, brown dog. Write the sentence on the chalkboard (in manuscript or cursive, depending on the grade level) and have the students read it several times to become familiar with it.
2. Ask the students to write the sentence five times. Tell them to write as they normally do. Allow them to write for three minutes. Then, stop the activity.
3. Provide a period of relaxation. Then, tell the students to write the sentence in their very best handwriting. They may take all of the time that they need. Ask them to write the sentence three times, with no time restrictions.
4. Provide a second period of relaxation. Then, tell the students that you want them to write as fast as they are able to write. Allow them three minutes to write the sentence as many times as they can.

5. Compare each child's three writing samples. Use either informal evaluations or an evaluation scale.

You may keep samples of students' handwriting in their portfolios as part of your informal assessment process. Students can also assess changes in their own writing.

REINFORCEMENT ACTIVITY

Collect samples of handwriting from several children using the procedures for gathering a normal sample, the best sample, and the fastest sample. Evaluate the samples using the informal assessment techniques described. After you have evaluated the samples, place the results on a handwriting analysis chart. (Use the categories on the progress chart in Figure 6–10.) Include recommendations for instruction or remediation.

LEFT-HANDED WRITERS

Teachers today do not try to force left-handed writers to be right-handed writers, as was frequently the practice in the past. Although left-handed writers are allowed to retain their hand preference, they do require some specific instruction in handwriting. You may wish to use the following procedures when working with left-handed writers:

1. Have the children assume positions that are the *opposite* of those expected of right-handed children, with the added caution that the position should be one that is most comfortable to them.
2. Have the children reverse the position of the paper (it may be less slanted and more toward a straight up-and-down position for left-handers). Have them reverse the direction of the pencil, too. The grip is basically the same as that for right-handed students.
3. Seat left-handed children so the light comes over their left shoulder.
4. Provide much practice writing on the chalkboard. (It is nearly impossible to use the upside-down hand style on the board.)
5. Furnish left-handed children with pencils that have slightly harder lead than those used by right-handers. Harder lead will not smear as easily, giving less reason for twisting the wrist into the upside-down position. The point should not be so sharp that it will dig into the paper.
6. Encourage left-handed children to grasp their writing instrument at least an inch-and-a-half from the point. At this distance, a child can see over or around his or her hand. You can put a rubber band around the pencil at the point where the child should grasp it.
7. If possible, provide children with individual model charts written by a left-handed teacher or community worker.
8. At the primary levels, seat left-handed writers together near the front of the room, where you can give them constant encouragement. After

their handwriting habits are formed and no further adjustments are needed, you can discontinue this seating.

9. Encourage left-handed children to develop a writing slant that is natural and that "feels good."
10. Avoid any attention that may lead to self-consciousness.
11. Avoid forcing older left-handed pupils to write a certain way. If an awkward position cannot be easily corrected, it is sometimes best to let the child continue.

MAINSTREAMING

Mainstreamed children frequently exhibit problems in handwriting as well as in other areas. Otto and Smith (1980) stress the complexity of these problems. They state that difficulties in handwriting frequently coexist with difficulties in reading and spelling. Both reading and spelling may be influenced by inadequate visual memory, inability or lack of readiness to handle visual symbols, or difficulties with sound-symbol relationships.

Research indicates that a kinesthetic approach to handwriting (one that involves movement of the body and sensations of position) is best for certain learning disabled students (Askov, Otto, & Askov, 1970). Learning disabled students may require extensive pencil tracing activities, as well as tracing of raised letters with the finger. Birch and Lefford (1967) also imply advantages for adding a tracing component to handwriting instruction for such children. These researchers investigated the ability of five through eleven year olds to draw geometric forms by tracing, connecting dots, and freehand copying. The tracing activity was the easiest for younger children, and it also produced the highest accuracy score. Connecting the dots was the next easiest task, whereas freehand drawing was the most difficult and resulted in the greatest number of errors. Tracing provides a kinesthetic component for handwriting. Add a tracing activity to the beginning analysis approach before requiring learning disabled children to form each letter independently.

If adding a kinesthetic activity is still not enough guidance for a student who is having difficulty, Hammill and Bartel (1975) recommend that you teach handwriting with a procedure that encompasses four developmental levels. Reger, Schroeder, and Uschold (1968) also recommend this procedure. In this four-level approach, begin with the first level, and move on to the next level only when the student has mastered the skills at the earlier level.

The first level introduces handwriting movements to the student. Discuss each movement and demonstrate it on the chalkboard. For example, demonstrate the straight-stick movement in manuscript, and say, "We put the chalk on the board and then go down." Demonstrate the movement on the board; then, have the student make the same movement at the board while looking at your model but not at his or her own hand. The student should say "down" when the movement goes down, or "up" when the movement goes up. Have the student practice the movement, verbalizing the directions, for several days. Then have the student remove the auditory clue and make the movement while looking at the model, but not at the hand. Finally, have the student follow the same procedures with crayon, on newsprint or paper. Figure 6–14 illustrates handwriting movements to demonstrate.

FIGURE 6–14
Handwriting movements

The second level requires the student to repeat the same procedures as level one, but this time to look at the paper as he or she forms the movements. At this level, pay attention to correct posture and the slant of the paper. Make lines on the desk with masking tape to guide the student in placing the paper or line paper with three different colors. You might use the colors of traffic lights, with green at the top, yellow in the center, and red at the bottom. This makes it easy for the child to verbalize directions such as, "Put my pencil on the green line, draw it straight down through the yellow line, and stop on the red line."

During the third-level activities, have the student move on to letter formation at the chalkboard, using the procedures described in level 1 for movements. After the student uses the chalkboard, have him or her go to one-inch lined paper, then to regular lined paper. The sequence for this fourth level follows:

1. Name the letter—for example, "The name of this letter is *b*."
2. Discuss the form of the letter while the child looks at it. "How many shapes are there in *b*?" (A straight stick, and a circle or ball.)
3. Make the letter for the student to see. You can use a transparency, and make each part with a different color.
4. Show the student the directions for each movement in the formation of the letter, and discuss the directions.
5. Develop a kinesthetic feel for the letter form by tracing a raised, script letter with a finger. You can make raised letters by placing a few drops of food coloring in a glue dispenser and writing the word in glue on a strip of tagboard. Goodson (1974) recommends a kinesthetic method using a sandpaper board. In this method, 9-by-11-inch pieces of coarse sandpaper are mounted on a piece of board. The student places a sheet of paper over the sandpaper board, and uses a crayon to write the troublesome letter correctly. He or she removes the paper and traces the letter with a finger. Also, you may make alphabets using trays filled with plaster of Paris. While the plaster is still damp, write the letters with a blunt pencil or stick in cursive or manuscript alphabet. The student can use this tray to trace the letters with a pencil or crayon. The tray is reusable and quite inexpensive.
6. Place a model of the letter on each student's paper. (Students with learning problems may have difficulty copying from the chalkboard.) Discuss with the student the letter form and direction. Have the student make the letter while looking at the model instead of at his or her hand.
7. Help each student compare the letter with the model. (Close supervision is necessary.)

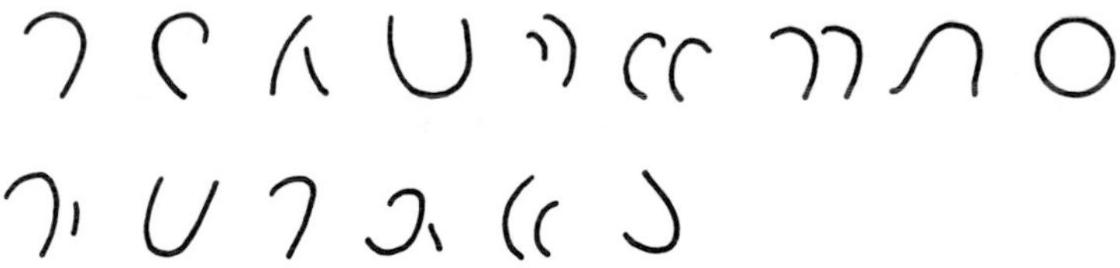

FIGURE 6–15
Some movements in cursive writing

8. You or the student may use auditory clues to help with letter formation. If necessary, also hold the student's hand to help with the formation.
9. Have the student write the letter on the chalkboard without looking at the model.
10. Have the student write the letter on paper without a model and without watching his or her hand.
11. Have the student write the letter on paper while watching the paper.

You can use the same procedures to introduce the writing movements in cursive. These begin with chalkboard activities and progress to newsprint and paper. The movements in Figure 6–15 are suggested for levels 1 and 2.

As you can see, this is a complicated approach to handwriting instruction, and it is not necessary or desirable to use it with every student in a class. It is designed for those who demonstrate difficulties in learning to write by more conventional approaches. You can use the steps for individual instruction, or for small-group instruction of six or seven pupils. It is too difficult to supervise the movements of larger groups in this detailed approach.

You can also create transparencies. One set might have the manuscript alphabet, with the different parts of letters shown in different colors, such as two-space-high straight lines, as in *b, d, h, k, l,* and *t,* in blue and complete circles, as in *a, o, b, d, g, q,* in orange, and so forth. Place these transparencies over the student's letters for checking formation.

Table 6–1 presents characteristics that might interfere with handwriting development of learning disabled children and suggests teaching techniques for handwriting instruction. Table 6–2 presents the same information for mentally handicapped children. The techniques for language arts instruction result from research and authorities who work with mainstreamed children.

SUMMARY

Modern instruction considers handwriting a tool for personal communication. The viewpoint stresses that handwriting should be taught within the broader context of composition rather than as isolated drill. This chapter stresses readiness for formal handwriting, which includes use of space, interest in handwriting, left-to-right progression, and fine-motor control. Research indicates that the most efficient handwriting instruction utilizes an individualized diagnostic approach, but apparently, few elementary schools actually use such procedures.

The chapter discusses handwriting instruction in terms of readiness, printing manuscript writing), and cursive writing. Readiness activities that develop a child's understanding of a need and purpose for writing are necessary, as are activities that develop fine-motor skills and readiness for letter formations.

TABLE 6-1
Mainstreaming and handwriting for learning disabled children

Characteristics of Learning Disabled Children	Teaching Techniques for Language Arts Instruction
1. Deficits in visual perception, visual-motor integration, and fine-motor skills (Harber, 1979; Lyon & Watson, 1981).	1. Trace on acetate (Spache, 1976). Use four developmental levels suggested by Hammill and Bartel (1975). Use directional arrows, color cues, and numbers to help children trace. Cut with scissors, draw outlines of patterns, and try simple paper folding (Lerner, 1976). Use biofeedback training to help children relax their writing forearm and control forearm tension voluntarily (Carter & Russell, 1980). Provide handwriting readiness activities that encourage development of fine-motor control: coloring, painting, finger painting, chalkboard activities. Let children with severe motor difficulties use an electric typewriter (Lerner, 1976).
2. Orientation confusions characterized by rotations and reversals of letters and words (Frith & Vogel, 1980).	2. Add color cues to letter formations (Bracey & Ward, 1980). Analyze the situation and try to identify specific bases for children's rotation and reversal errors: a. Rotation: Point out that the letter may look better rotated, but it is usually written so it looks upside down. Change to a slanted easel so there is a definite top and bottom. b. Reversal: Train children in the importance of left-right orientation of symbols (Frith & Vogel, 1980).

Beginning teachers must become proficient in the manuscript or cursive alphabet taught in area schools. The chapter presents a letter-analysis approach for instruction of printing. It describes evaluative scales and informal means of assessing letter formation, slant, spacing, and line quality. Information on the most frequent types of letter-formation errors is available. An internalized scale developed through training and experience may eventually help a teacher the most.

The transition to cursive writing usually takes place sometime early in the third grade, although research does not point to any advantage in changing from manuscript to cursive writing and indicates that the time of transition is not very important. The chapter describes an approach that helps children understand the similarities and differences between manuscript and cursive writing.

Few standardized tests are available for assessing handwriting. Consequently, you should gather handwriting samples informally under conditions of normal, best, and fastest writing.

Left-handed writers are no longer required to forgo their hand preference; however, they do need specific instruction in developing their handwriting skills. The chapter includes a set of procedures to follow when working with left-handers.

TABLE 6–2
Mainstreaming and handwriting for mentally handicapped children

Characteristics of Mentally Handicapped Children	Teaching Techniques for Language Arts Instruction
1. Visual discrimination deficits that cause difficulty identifying letters (Adams, Taylor, & Glendenning, 1982). 2. Tendency to have motor coordination handicaps (Gearheart, Weishahn, & Gearheart, 1988).	1. Use positive reinforcement during practice to increase letter discrimination capability (Adams, Taylor, & Glendenning, 1982). 2. Provide opportunities for development of motor skills that are prerequisites for writing. Include simplified games and specific motor exercises such as hopscotch, bag throwing, and jumping games to promote eye-hand coordination (Gearheart, Weishahn, & Gearheart, 1988)

Since the inception of mainstreaming, regular classroom teachers have been providing instruction for many children who used to be in self-contained special education classes. Research indicates a kinesthetic approach is effective for teaching handwriting to many learning disabled students. Such an approach begins with teaching the movements of handwriting and extends to teaching the formation of letters.

ADDITIONAL HANDWRITING ACTIVITIES

1. Compile a list of readiness activities appropriate for children who have not developed large-motor and fine-motor coordination.
2. Develop a creative activity that reinforces readiness skills related to basic manuscript strokes.
3. Go to the library and locate language arts curriculum guides published by several school districts. What are the goals for handwriting instruction? What recommendations are included for instructional strategies? How much time is recommended for instruction at various grade levels? Is handwriting taught in isolated drills, or is the subject emphasized during meaningful writing activities?
4. Use ERIC to locate programs designed to improve handwriting capabilities. Describe the program. Do you believe it would be successful? Why or why not? Report your findings to your language arts class.
5. Secure scope and sequence charts from several published handwriting programs. Compare the programs according to expectations at specific levels, pace of instruction, instructional objectives, instructional emphasis, and evaluation.
6. Collect handwriting samples from first-, second-, and third-grade children. Analyze the handwriting at each level. What developmental changes do the writing samples illustrate?

BIBLIOGRAPHY

Adams, Gary L.; Taylor, Ronald L.; and Glendenning, Nancy J. "Remediation of Letter Reversals." *Perceptual and Motor Skills* 54 (June 1982): 1002.

Askov, Eunice; Otto, Wayne; and Askov, Warren. "A Decade of Research in Handwriting." *Journal of Educational Research* 64 (November 1970): 100–111.

Birch, H. G., and Lefford, A. "Visual Discrimination, Inter-sensory Integration, and Voluntary Motor Control." *Monographs of the Society for Research in Child Development* 32 (1967): 2.

Bracey, Susan A., and Ward, Jefflyn. "Dark, Dark Went the Bog: Instructional Interventions for Remediating *b* and *d* Reversals." *Reading Improvement* 17 (Summer 1980): 104–12.

Burns, Paul C., and Broman, Betty L. *The Language Arts in Childhood Education.* 5th ed. Chicago: Rand McNally & Co., 1983.

Carter, John L., and Russell, Harold. "Biofeedback and Academic Attainment in LD Children." *Academic Therapy* 15 (March 1980): 483–86.

de Ajuriaguerra, J., and Auzias, M. "Preconditions for the Development of Writing in the Child." In *Foundations of Language Development,* vol. 2, edited by Eric and Elizabeth Lenneberg. New York: Academic Press, 1975.

Donoghue, M. *The Child and the English Language Arts.* Dubuque, Iowa: Brown, 1990.

Durkin, Dolores, *Children Who Read Early.* New York: Teachers College Press, 1966.

Fairchild, Steven H. "Handwriting as a Language Art." In *Language Arts Instruction and Beginning Teaching,* edited by Carl Personke and Dale Johnson. Englewood Cliffs, N.J.: Prentice-Hall, 1987.

Farris, P. "Views and Other Views: Handwriting Instruction Should Not Become Extinct." *Language Arts* 68 (1991): 312–14.

Frith, Uta, and Vogel, Juliet M. *Some Perceptual Prerequisites for Reading.* Newark, Del.: International Reading Association, 1980.

Furner, Beatrice A. "Recommended Instructional Procedures in a Method Emphasizing the Perceptual-Motor Nature of Learning in Handwriting." *Elementary English* 46 (December 1969): 1021–30.

Gearheart, Bill R.; Weishahn, Mel; and Gearheart, Carol J. *The Exceptional Student in the Regular Classroom,* 4th ed. Columbus, Oh: Merrill Publishing Co., 1988.

Goodson, Roger A., and Floyd, Barbara J. *Individualizing Instruction in Spelling: A Practical Guide.* Minneapolis: Denison & Co., 1974.

Graves, Donald H. "Research Update—Handwriting Is for Writing." *Language Arts* 55 (March 1978): 393–99.

Hammill, Donald D., and Bartel, Nettie R. *Teaching Children with Learning and Behavioral Problems.* Boston: Allyn & Bacon, 1975.

Harber, Jean R. "Differentiating LD and Normal Children: The Utility of Selected Perceptual and Perceptual-Motor Tests." *Learning Disabled Quarterly* 2 (Spring 1979): 70–75.

Hodges, R. "The Conventions of Writing." In *Handbook of Research on Teaching the English Language Arts,* edited by J. Flood, J. Jensen, D. Lapp, and J. Squire. New York: Macmillan, 1991, pp. 775–86.

Lerner, Janet W. *Children with Learning Disabilities.* 2d ed. Boston: Houghton Mifflin, 1976.

Lewis, Edward R., and Lewis, Hilda P. "Which Manuscript Letters Are Hard for First Graders?" *Elementary English* 41 (December 1964): 855–58.

Lyon, Reid, and Watson, Bill. "Empirically Derived Subgroups of Learning Disabled Readers: Diagnostic Characteristics." *Journal of Learning Disabilities* 14 (May 1981): 256–61.

Otto, Wayne, and Smith, Richard. *Corrective and Remedial Teaching.* Boston: Houghton Mifflin Co., 1980.

Reger, R.; Schroeder, W.; and Uschold, K. *Special Education: Children with Learning Problems.* New York: Oxford University Press, 1968.

Spache, George. *Investigating the Issues of Reading Disabilities.* Boston: Allyn & Bacon, 1976.

Tompkins, Gail E. "Let's Go on a Bear Hunt! A Fresh Approach to Penmanship Drill." *Language Arts* 57 (October 1980): 782–86.

Yardley, Alice. *Exploration and Language.* New York: Citation Press, 1973.

Chapter Seven

After completing the chapter on spelling, you will be able to:

1. Define the objectives of elementary spelling programs.
2. Place students on their proper instructional spelling levels.
3. Analyze how standardized spelling tests can help you evaluate a student's spelling skills.
4. Use informal spelling inventories to evaluate a student's spelling strengths and weaknesses.
5. Evaluate a student's application of spelling generalizations.
6. Understand the two most commonly used criteria for selecting spelling words.
7. Use the best developmental approach for spelling instruction, including the corrected-test method and the most efficient self-study method.
8. Design a weekly spelling program.
9. Teach spelling generalizations inductively.
10. Understand the step-by-step procedures needed to instruct students who require an effective remedial approach.
11. Develop accelerated spelling activities for gifted students.
12. Teach a proofreading spelling unit to an elementary class.

Spelling

*L*ike handwriting, spelling is a tool to improve written communication and reading ability. There is an obvious connection between spelling and writing. For example, students frequently begin writing with invented spellings and then progress to more accurate spellings. Young students who are encouraged to use invented spellings in their early writing produce longer or better first drafts. This approach allows them to experiment with words, to explore their thoughts, and to become aware of patterns within words. It is hoped that these experiences will prepare them for conventional spelling instruction. Spelling is also closely related to reading. After reviewing the research pertaining to spelling and reading, Adams (1990) advocates spelling instruction: "In summary, the arguments for including spelling instruction as a major component of the reading program are strong. Learning about spelling reinforces children's knowledge about common letter sequences. It also reinforces their knowledge about spelling–sound relationships and may help children become aware of word parts. Because of this, spelling practice enhances reading proficiency" (p. 102).

Petty and Jensen (1980) maintain that the long-range objectives for spelling programs should be stated in terms of the following attitudes, skills and abilities, and desired habits:

Attitudes

Each child should:

1. Recognize the necessity and responsibility for correct spelling in effective communication.
2. Show a desire to spell all words correctly.
3. Believe that spelling correctly is something he or she can accomplish.

Skills and Abilities

Each child should be able to:

1. Recognize all the letters of the alphabet in capital and lowercase forms in both printed and handwritten materials.
2. Write all the letters of the alphabet in a legible manner in both capital and lowercase forms.
3. Alphabetize words.

4. Hear words accurately as they are spoken
5. Pronounce words clearly and accurately.
6. See printed words accurately.
7. Group and connect the letters of a word properly.
8. Use punctuation elements that are necessary for spelling.
9. Use a dictionary, including diacritical markings and guide words.
10. Pronounce unfamiliar words properly.
11. Use knowledge of sound and symbol relationships.
12. Use knowledge of orthographic patterns that recur in language.
13. Use the most effective spelling rules (generalizations).
14. Use personally effective procedures in learning to spell new words.

Habits

Each child should habitually:

1. Proofread all writing carefully.
2. Use reliable sources to find the spellings of unknown words.
3. Follow a specific study procedure in learning to spell new words.

The major objective of spelling is effective written communication. Mature spellers can correctly write a great number of words without conscious effort. Consequently, to develop effective spellers, a spelling program must enhance the independent spelling skills of students. In addition, the spelling program must include many opportunities for writing for an audience.

DEVELOPMENTAL STAGES

In a review of research pertaining to developmental patterns in spelling, Adams (1990) states: "Over time, children's writing gradually but clearly reflects increasing knowledge of the spelling of particular words and of general orthographic conventions. In addition, it reflects increasing sensitivity to the phonemic structures of words. Of particular interest, young writers have special difficulty in hearing the separate phonemes of consonant clusters, suggesting that the spellings of consonant blends warrant explicit instruction attention" (p. 96).

Researchers in the 1970s and 1980s, such as Read (1971), Henderson and Beers (1980), Gentry (1982), Henderson (1985), and Henderson and Templeton (1986) investigated developmental stages through which children proceed as they acquire spelling ability. Henderson and Templeton (1986) concluded that "developmental theory validates the skills we should teach and provides a rationale for the pacing and maintenance of instruction in a more detailed and clearly stated manner than has been possible before" (p. 314). These researchers used children's inventive spellings to identify the following five stages in developing spelling competence:

1. Stage I—Preliterate stage, in which young children spontaneously use symbols to represent words; there is, however, no knowledge of letter–sound correspondence.
2. Stage II—In approximately first grade, children begin to spell alphabetically, matching sounds and letters systematically. Their spellings reflect errors such as *MAK* = *make*.

3. Stage III—In approximately third and fourth grades, children begin to assimilate word knowledge and conventional alternatives for representing sounds, include vowels in every syllable, use familiar spelling patterns, and intersperse standard spelling with phonetic spelling. Their spellings reflect errors such as *CREME = cream*.

4. Stage IV—In approximately fourth through sixth grades, children increase understanding of word patterns. Their spellings reflect errors such as *INOCENT = innocent*.

5. Stage V—Children understand that words related in meaning are often spelled similarly; children's knowledge of the English orthographic system and the accompanying rules are established; children's knowledge of base and root words is extensively developed.

Henderson and Templeton (1986) provide suggestions for instruction that apply at each of these stages. For example, at stage II, children should begin to systematically examine groups of words that are organized around common features such as short-vowel phonograms, beginning consonant digraphs, and common long-vowel patterns. Use short lists of words that are chosen from reading vocabularies for examination and memorization. At the same time, instruct children in letter formation and provide them with many opportunities for creative and purposeful writing.

At stage III, Henderson and Templeton maintain that spelling instruction should emphasize basic pattern features of words, including review of the long-vowel patterns taught in stage II (for example, /a/:*bait*), introduction of common digraphs (for example, *ow, oi*), study of *r*- and *l*-influenced vowel patterns (for example, *card, fall*), study of relationships between words in compounds, learning of functions of homophones in spelling, examination of common inflections and their joining to base words (for example, *ed, ing, ly*), presentation of base words that can stand alone after prefixes and suffixes are removed, and study of the sounds and meanings of common prefixes and suffixes.

At stage IV, Henderson and Templeton emphasize continued study of common and uncommon vowel patterns, scanning of words syllable by syllable, examination of prefixes and suffixes for meaning rather than sound (for example, when to use *able* or *ible, ant* or *ance, ent* or *ence*), exploration of homophones, and study of consonant doubling as it applies to a broader range of vocabulary.

At stage V, Henderson and Templeton emphasize study of silent and sounded consonant patterns (for example, *resign, resignation*); study of different vowel-alternation patterns sequenced from long to short (for example, *sane–sanity*), long to schwa (for example, *inflame–inflammation*), short to schwa (for example, *excel–excellent*), and predictable alternations in sound and spelling (for example, *explain–explanation*); and examination of contributions of Greek and Latin forms to the spelling and meaning connection in English.

Recent articles related to spelling frequently focus on either developmental stages in children's spelling or on disputes between those who draw implications from children's spontaneous spelling and those who adhere to more traditional approaches. Although the two camps have not resolved their differences, Henderson and Templeton provide the following support for combining implications from both approaches: "Today most list words are selected, as they should be, by frequency counts of their occurrence in the language as a whole and in children's language in particular. Examination of basal spelling programs of the past decade for the primary grades will show a remarkable correspondence between the features derived from the stage theory and the scope and sequence plans for word study. . . . What developmental research has achieved is not a radical revision of traditional spelling instruction but a clarification of those things long practiced, and what is important, an extension of word study principles to the middle and upper grades, where they are presently most crucially needed" (p. 314).

SCHOOL SPELLING PROGRAMS

In this section we will consider recommendations for encouraging invented spellings in young writers and instructional approaches that lead to phonological awareness and finally to spelling mastery.

Encouraging Invented Spellings in Young Writers

Recent research indicates that young children who are encouraged to write words so that they can read them, or to use their own invented spellings, will write longer stories than those children who are encouraged to use only correct spellings. Adams (1990) concludes: "In overview, classroom encouragement of invented spellings and independent writing from the start seems a very promising approach toward the development of phonemic awareness and orthographic skills. Beyond this, early writing seems an incomparable means of developing children's abilities to reflect on their own thoughts, to elaborate and organize their ideas, and to express themselves in print. Moreover, such challenges require children to think actively about print" (p. 99).

Invented spelling is especially important in process writing. According to Cunningham (1991), "children who are allowed and encouraged to 'spell it so you can read it,' write longer and better first drafts than children who only write words they know how to spell" (p. 91). Cunningham maintains that when writing a first draft students should be encouraged to say the words and write down the letters they hear. Many teachers encourage invented spellings during first drafts and then help students spell the words correctly for their final writing. Bob Yukster (personal communication, October 1991), a trainer in the Reading Recovery program, sometimes encourages students to use invented spellings; at other times, he tells them that invented spellings are not acceptable. For example, during early drafts of creative writing, students are encouraged to use their own invented spellings. However, when the students are using their writings to learn to read, invented spellings are not used. Likewise, teachers at a 1991 writing and literature workshop indicated that they allow invented spellings for first drafts, but then encourage the development of correct spellings during the editing process.

You can help young children understand the usefulness of invented spellings by modeling the process for them. Hansen (1985) describes how she introduces invented spelling to kindergarten children. She begins by using an overhead projector and drawing a picture on a transparency. After drawing the picture, she writes a sentence across the top by sounding out the words and writing the letters for the most prominent sounds. She explains that she is writing the way most children write when they begin. Then she writes the same sentence in conven-

Invented spelling is encouraged in free writing activities, but when writing is ''published,'' attention to correct spelling becomes important to clear communication.

tional spelling along the bottom of the page. She explains that this is the kind of writing that adults do, and that is found in books. Next, the children draw a picture and write a story using their own invented spellings. She then talks to each child about his or her story and writes a sentence or two in conventional spelling at the bottom of each page.

Cunningham (1991) describes another strategy to help children experiment with invented spellings. The teacher asks students to suggest words they might use to write a paper on a specific topic. When a student suggests a word, everyone says the word slowly and writes a possible spelling. When the task is completed, the teacher calls on students to tell how they might spell the word. After writing several possibilities on the board, the teacher points out to the students that these are words they could read, which is their goal when writing a first draft; however, if they are writing a finished paper, they would need to edit and correct their spellings. The teacher ends the lesson by writing the conventional spelling above each column and talking about which spellings were closest to the conventional spelling.

Developing Phonological Awareness

Researchers who investigate characteristics of good spellers report the importance of developing students' awareness of words. Barron (1980) found that good spellers seem to depend on sensitivity to patterns of letters within words. Likewise, Sloboda (1980) reports that good spellers seem more sensitive to whether a spelling looks correct. Adams (1990) concludes that difficulty with either phonemic analysis or knowledge of spelling patterns interferes with good spelling.

Several recent studies conducted in Europe indicate the benefits of programs that encourage phonological awareness in students. For example, Lundberg, Frost, and Peterson (1988) developed such a program for Danish preschool children. The children in this program were superior in spelling at the end of both first and second grades. The instruction includes daily sessions in which children take part in listening games that emphasize nonverbal and verbal sounds and in rhyming games that focus on nursery rhymes, rhymed stories, and games for rhyme production. Following the introduction of these games, children respond to syllables in their own names and in other known multisyllabic words by clapping their hands and by dancing, marching, and walking in pace with the various patterns.

A Norwegian study suggests that lower ability students may gain the most from phonological training. Lie (1991) found that spelling achievement of first-grade students was superior when they were involved in a program that encouraged phonemic awareness of the initial, final, and medial sounds in spoken words. As part of this awareness training, teachers and students discuss the meaning of language and the fact that words can be divided into sounds that can be heard when the words are pronounced. Students then identify initial phonemes in words. Lie concludes: "The evidence . . . suggests that a systematic training program for stimulating skills in word analysis in first-grade children facilitates both reading and spelling acquisition" (p. 247).

Adams (1990) reinforces the importance of helping students look for and listen for patterns in words. After reviewing the research in spelling, she concludes:

> Successful spelling improvement depends on getting children to attend to unfamiliar patterns. . . . Research indicates that the experience of seeing a word in print is not only superior to hearing it spelled but, further, is an extremely powerful and effective means of acquiring its spelling. In addition, the experience of seeing or imagining a word's spelling, as contrasted with repeatedly hearing the word or even rehearsing it aloud, has been shown to be a superior means toward remembering its pronunciation, even among first graders. One obvious instructional implication of this evidence is that teachers should habitually encourage students to look at the spellings of words. Teachers should write the words of interest on the board or point to them on the page. Merely spelling words aloud, relatively speaking, is a waste of time. . . . Research demonstrates that the process of copying new words strengthens students' memory for those words. . . . Perhaps this should not be surprising—the writing of a word forces attention to its full sequence of letters. For students, the thought that somebody else might evaluate their products may encourage such attention even more. (p. 102)

Guidelines for Spelling Instruction

In addition to studies conducted by Henderson and Templeton, considerable research in spelling diagnosis, instructional programs, and teaching techniques provides clear guidelines for spelling instruction. Following a review of research spanning more than fifty years, Hillerich (1982) identified the following effective procedures and instructional approaches:

1. Determine the appropriate instructional spelling level for each student.
2. Teach the list of high-frequency words using a research-based approach.

3. Teach generalizations about apostrophes and word endings.
4. Provide experiences with homophones.
5. Teach dictionary skills along with ways of spelling various sounds.
6. Develop a desire to spell correctly when writing for an audience other than an informal group.
7. Encourage considerable writing to help children develop an understanding that writing is the only reason for learning to spell.
8. Provide children with many meaningful writing experiences that reinforce the automatic spelling of their security lists.

These recommendations will be apparent throughout the forthcoming discussions on assessment and instruction.

Using Computers

Computer programs may be especially useful for helping children improve their spelling accuracy and increase their knowledge of spelling patterns. Gustafson (1982) compared spelling achievement scores and spelling retention ability of students who learned to spell with a computer spelling program with the scores of children who learned to spell with a teacher-directed approach. Both achievement and retention were higher in the computer-based group.

Mason (1983) maintains that computer programs are excellent accuracy trainers. When students print in words incorrectly, they must find their errors before continuing. He states: "Teachers using this approach report dramatic improvement in spelling in addition to greater accuracy in reading words. They also report incidents of student jubilation when pesky bugs are found and corrected and programs finally run as they should. This joy in accomplishment is so profound that it often shocks teachers who had thought nothing in school could excite these children" (p. 506).

The ease of changing words in a word processor prior to printing can motivate proofreading for spelling and mechanical errors as well as improvement of other aspects of composition. This potential is not yet reached. Becker, director of the Johns Hopkins classroom-technology study, states that one of the best uses for computers with older children is the teaching of writing (McGrath, 1983). He estimates, however, that less than 7 percent of computer time in high school programs involves word processing activities.

Balajthy (1986) provides the following guidelines to use when selecting spelling software: It should allow teachers to add new words, contain colorful and interesting programs, use voice synthesis to present words, provide feedback, review misspelled words, and assist recordkeeping.

ASSESSMENT

Spelling offers an excellent opportunity for diagnostic teaching. Assessment is necessary to discover at what grade level to begin spelling instruction and to evaluate each student's specific spelling strengths and weaknesses.

Formal Assessment

Because there is no economy in teaching words children can already spell correctly, it is important to determine each child's appropriate spelling level. It is equally important to diagnose the level of students who are having spelling problems. Students will not make adequate gains if they are expected to spell words of an unrealistically high level of difficulty.

Hillerich (1977) believes children should receive instruction in a word list for which they can spell approximately 75 percent of the words; children who are not able to correctly spell 50 percent of a graded word list have not mastered the prerequisite spellings taught at lower grade levels.

It is not difficult to place elementary students on appropriate spelling levels. First, select approximately twenty-five words from each graded spelling list. Do not choose only the most difficult or the easiest words from that level. Many teachers find the best procedure is to choose every tenth word from a list of spelling words for each grade. Table 7–1 illustrates this procedure, using a graded word list from the *Skills in Spelling* series published by the American Book Company.

After compiling the lists, administer the tests to the class to determine spelling levels. Administer the first-grade list to all students. Do not administer a further test to children who spell fewer than 75 percent correctly; you will have discovered their level of spelling ability. Use first-grade instruction for these children.

TABLE 7–1

Word list from the *Skills in Spelling* series

Grade 1	Grade 2	Grade 3	Grade 4
pig	after	Monday	act
pretty	wet	fed	dream
send	win	trip	drove
she	block	week	eight
five	top	name	tip
purple	game	Friday	base
can	five	these	penny
like	boat	sent	cook
there	stay	cent	paid
come	nest	full	all right
not	friend	keep	everywhere
	fall	then	careful
	band	add	everybody
	dinner	bread	country
	girls	where	church
	dress	fight	comb
	there	asked	coal
	when	things	bow
	thanks	tall	busy
	open	use	ocean
	call	with	circus
	our	stopped	hurry
	at	nuts	master
	calling	snowball	lucky
	something	throw	popcorn

SOURCE: From Bremer, Bishop, and Stone, *Skills in Spelling*. (Dallas: American Book Co., 1976). Reprinted by permission of American Book Co.

Test students who have mastered the first-grade list with the second-grade list. If the students have not mastered this list, provide them with second-grade instruction. Then, test students who demonstrate mastery of the list with the third-grade list. Test the children on consecutive days until you have placed all of them in their most efficient instructional level. This diagnostic procedure is not overly time consuming, and assures that each child will receive instruction at the correct spelling level.

REINFORCEMENT ACTIVITY

Compile a spelling test list, using the graded lists from one of the spelling series. Administer the list to a group of children and estimate the spelling instructional level for each member of the group.

Informal Assessment

Informal spelling assessment, including teacher-made tests and observations, will give you the most useful information for designing a spelling program. Informal evaluation techniques are vital when you require specific information about a child's spelling. Moreover, informal diagnosis is essential for designing a program to remediate spelling difficulties. Questions you might consider during informal observation include: Does the child accurately produce letter and sound symbols when writing? Can the child blend sounds together to make words? Does the child reverse letters? Can the child remember words written on the board? Can the child hear minimal differences in words such as *pin* and *pen*?

Maximize informal spelling assessment by systematic study of a child's spelling errors. If a child follows a pattern in misspelling certain words, expect that child to make the same type of error when spelling similar words. Spache's Spelling Errors Test provides a list of types of errors often reflected in children's spelling.

1. A silent letter is omitted—*take–tak.*
2. A sounded letter is omitted—*stand–stan.*
3. A double letter is omitted—*letter–leter.*
4. A single letter is added—*park–parck.*
5. Letters are transposed or reversed—*angel–angle.*
6. There is a phonetic substitution for the vowel—*green–grean.*
7. There is a phonetic substitution for the consonant—*bush–buch.*
8. There is a phonetic substitution for the syllable—*flies–flys.*
9. There is a phonetic substitution for the word—*hare–hear.*
10. There is a nonphonetic substitution for the vowel—*bats–bot.*
11. There is a nonphonetic substitution for a consonant—*camper–canper.*

Use this list to analyze test papers and other written work. Various creative writings and written assignments in content areas provide sources for informal spelling assessment.

Besides observing written work, also analyze a child's oral spelling and speech performance. How does the child approach oral spelling? Does the child

Written assignments from social studies or science provide sources for informal spelling assessment.

sound words one letter at a time, by syllables, or as whole-word units? Are the child's oral errors similar to his or her written errors? Does the child enunciate words carefully? How does the child pronounce the words he or she spells incorrectly? Does the speech of the child reflect a dialect? Does the dialect interfere with spelling patterns? Is the child able to blend sounds orally into a whole word?

You can compile other useful information by observing study skills in regard to spelling. Does the child apply an effective method of study to spelling-word lists? A positive attitude toward spelling is essential. Does the child feel that spelling is important? Does the child carefully proofread his or her papers for spelling errors? Does the child use a dictionary to verify spelling questions? Does the child use new spelling words in other daily assignments?

You can also obtain valuable diagnostic information by questioning children. Ask children to tell you how they spell an unknown word. Question them about their best method for remembering a spelling word. Many children say they must carefully write a word several times before they are able to remember it. One learning-disabled child indicated that he traced words with his hands when his teacher asked him to spell orally. Other children say they benefit from spelling words aloud while writing. One fourth-grade girl explained her method for overcoming a dialect difference between herself and her teacher. She solved her difficulty by whispering each word before writing a dictated word. Children can frequently describe their greatest spelling problems, so make this information a vital part of your informal spelling assessment.

Another useful informal assessment diagnoses a child's ability to apply spelling generalizations. Horn (1963) recommends teaching rules that apply to a large number of words and have few exceptions. Administer a cloze test to assess a child's knowledge of the more reliable generalizations. A cloze test for specific spelling generalizations might include the following examples:

1. Generalization—Words that end with a silent *e* usually drop the *e* before adding a suffix beginning with a vowel.
   Cloze: Jim was rak _____ the leaves. (ing)
2. Generalization—Words ending in silent *e* retain their *e* when adding a suffix beginning with a consonant.
   Cloze: The president lives in a stat _____ mansion. (ely)
3. Generalization—If a word ends with a consonant plus *y*, change the *y* to *i* before adding suffixes except those beginning with *i*. Do not change the *y* to *i* when adding suffixes to words ending in a vowel plus *y*.
   Cloze: The bab _____ were all crying at once. (ies)
   Cloze: The horse was carr _____ a heavy load. (ying)
   Cloze: The boy scouts were enjo _____ the football game. (ying)
4. Generalization—Double the final consonant in one-syllable words or words accented on the last syllable, ending in a single consonant preceded by a single vowel before adding a suffix beginning with a vowel.
   Cloze: The horse was run _____ a very fast race. (ning)
   Cloze: Sunday is the begin _____ of the week. (ning)
5. Generalization—The letter *q* is always followed by the letter *u* in the English language.
   Cloze: At night it is q _____ iet in the house. (u)
6. Generalization—Proper nouns should begin with capital letters.
   Cloze: The dog's name is _____ over. (R)

REINFORCEMENT ACTIVITY

The following examples are excerpts from a third-grade student's daily written work. The first selection is an outlining activity following a reading lesson. The second example is from a social studies assignment. Study the child's papers and find the spelling errors. Classify the errors according to the Spache spelling-error categories and then according to Henderson and Templeton's stages in developmental spelling. How do the errors compare with Henderson and Templeton's stages? At what stage or stages is this student? What proof do you have for your answer? Do you see any consistent errors? Discuss the implications of these errors for remedial instruction.

I. Daytime
  A. a sailor showd Mark around
  B. there was a spider
  C. Mark went to play with his frends
  D. the boys climed around
  E. the sailer toke the spider to a sientest
II. Nighttime
  A. the tarantual was luse
  B. Marks Mother was wered
  C. he wated until 9 o'clock with the spider
  D. Tim quickly looked at the spider
  E. Tin cauld another polece

Fur Seals

Seals are excellent swimers and they spend lots of time in the water. They have fur all over them.

The mail seals are cauld bulls and femail seals are cauld cows. They have there pups on land and they usualy have one pup but sometimes two.

Seals spend much of there time on land or on floating chunks of ice.

Fur seals stay at sea for 6 to 8 months.

They are found along the costes of continents in most parts of the world.

A few kinds live in fresh water lakes and cloes to inland seas.

WORD SELECTION

An examination of the word lists in major spelling books illustrates two different viewpoints on the selection of spelling words. According to some experts, the English language system is irregular; consequently, spelling instruction should emphasize gradual accumulation of the most useful words. In contrast, others believe that the English language is remarkably regular, and that efficient spelling programs should have greater phonetic emphasis.

A Frequency-of-Use Approach

Many spelling programs concur with the philosophy that the English language system is irregular and that instruction should be based on the words most frequently used. Ernest Horn, whose writings and research span the past fifty years in education, is the most influential proponent of this view. As early as 1919, Horn stated: "One must show that a rule can be easily taught, that it can be remembered, and that it will function in the stress of actual spelling. Evidence seems to cast a doubt on all three of these assumptions." In 1954, he said, "The limited success in attempts to teach pupils to learn and apply even a few spelling rules suggests that we should not be too optimistic about the practicality of teaching the more numerous and complicated rules or principles in phonetics," and in 1957, "There seems no escape from the direct teaching of the large number of common words which do not conform in their spelling to any phonetic or orthographic rule." By 1963, Horn believed that some emphasis on phonics should be included in the spelling program. He cautioned, however, that "instruction in phonics should be regarded . . . as an aid to spelling rather than a substitute for the systematic study of the words in the spelling list."

The words Horn believed should compose the spelling list are those most frequently used by children and adults. In selecting these high-frequency words, Horn recommended the following:

1. The easiest words should be taught in the beginning grades and the most difficult words in the advanced grades.
2. Words most frequently used in writing should be taught first.
3. Words commonly used by children in a specific grade should be taught in that grade.
4. Words needed in other content subjects should be taught in the appropriate grades.

Researchers have compiled several spelling lists that can be useful in evaluation and selection of high-frequency spelling words. The first ten words on Horn's list (*I, the, and, to, a, you, of, in, we, for*) constitute 25 percent of the words used in various kinds of writing. The first 100 words in the list account for 65 percent of the words written by children and adults. Encouraging mastery of meaningful lists is appropriate because spelling efficiency increases when children are taught the words they need to spell most frequently.

A Phonetic Emphasis

Some linguists disagree with Horn's opinion that the English language system is irregular; they maintain that there is a high degree of regularity between the graphemic presentation of a written word and its corresponding sounds. In 1965, Hodges and Rudorf investigated the relationship between phonemes (sounds) and graphemes (printed letters) in over 17,000 words; they found a high degree of regularity between the sounds and the written letters.

Hanna and Hanna (1965) recommend that a spelling program reflect the finding of the Hodges and Rudorf investigation; they believe that children should learn to spell words using a phonic approach. In an earlier article, Hanna and Moore (1953) recommended putting aside some time for a concentrated attack on translating sounds into written symbols, during which a child would learn phonic patterns inductively. The simple patterns, such as the consonant-vowel-consonant in *cat*, would be learned first, and the complex phonic patterns later. Hanna and Moore argue the English words that follow a rarely occurring phonic pattern should be memorized.

An Emphasis on Meaning

Chomsky (1970) suggests that words that mean the same tend to look the same, even though they may have different pronunciations. Thus, the words *nation* and *national* have a similar spelling, and the meanings are consistent even though the phonetic pronunciations are different. Likewise, certain spelling patterns are considered consistent because they indicate a specific part of speech. From this perspective, the writing system seems both sensible and systematic.

Some researchers recommend children spend concentrated time learning phonetic patterns, such as consonant-vowel-consonant.

Zutell (1978) suggests that teachers apply linguistic and psycholinguistic findings by helping children develop their understanding of the writing system. To do so, "teachers must consciously construct environments in which children have the opportunity to systematically examine words and to freely generate, test, and evaluate their own spelling strategies" (p. 847). Such a spelling program allows children to examine their own writing; provides experiences for reading and vocabulary development; and provides activities that allow children to compare, contrast, and categorize words according to root words, word origins, and similarities in structural patterns.

INSTRUCTION

In a developmental spelling program, teachers must consider such questions as: How many words should be taught? How many minutes a day should be spent on spelling instruction? What words should be studied? What is the most efficient individual study method? How often should review be included? And how should students receive instruction in spelling generalizations?

Several factors contribute to a decision about how many words to teach during spelling lessons. You must consider the number of words that students can learn efficiently in a specific grade as well as how much emphasis is placed on spelling in other content areas. Most spelling series contain fewer than 4,000 words. One spelling authority describes this accumulation of words in terms of daily tasks. If 2 new words a day are presented in second and third grades, 3 new words a day in fourth and fifth grades, and 4 new words a day in sixth, seventh, and eighth grades, students can master the spelling of 4,180 words. If the words are chosen according to high frequency, this accumulation accounts for 98 percent of the words written by children and adults. It does not seem an impossible task for most students to master the essential spelling lists if spelling is systematically taught. Most authorities believe that students can learn these spelling words during concentrated daily spelling instruction periods of approximately fifteen minutes.

Your problem now is deciding what words each student should master. It would be inefficient to have students work on words that are either too easy or too difficult, so begin the program with assessment procedures to ascertain each student's individual spelling instructional level. After assessment, divide the class into appropriate groupings. The average elementary class will have, perhaps, four spelling groups. Initiate spelling instruction with the corrected-test method.

The Corrected-Test Method

Horn indicates that the single best method for learning to spell is the corrected-test method. Personke (1987) states that the approach "has been reexamined many times and remains the single best method for learning to spell words. The reason for its success is simple: it provides immediate, positive feedback" (p. 79). In fact, Hillerich (1977) indicates that the use of a pretest, with immediate correction by the child, accounts for about 95 percent of all learning that takes place in spelling. In the corrected-test method, the teacher administers a spelling test before the students study the words. This procedure liberates students from systematic study of words they already know.

First, administer the test. Immediately afterward, have the pupils self-correct their tests; they may self-correct from their own spelling lists, typed lists that you provide, or listening to you slowly read the correct spelling. Have the pupils immediately write the correct spelling of any words they have missed. This method gives students essential positive feedback. If you collect the tests, correct them, then return them to the children, they may retain the misspellings rather than the correct spellings. Monitor the corrected-test procedure carefully to ensure that the students are checking accurately, and writing their misspelled words correctly.

Classroom teachers have found two successful techniques for administering more than one spelling list to a class. Some teachers test the various ability groupings simultaneously. These teachers read, in turn, one word from each spelling list. For example, the teacher dictates the first-grade word, *pretty,* to one group, the second-grade word, *block,* to the next group, the third-grade word, *Friday,* to the third group, and the fourth-grade word, *everywhere,* to the last group. After each group receives a word, the teacher returns to the initial group's next word and follows the same sequence until all students have been tested on their lists. Other teachers prefer to test one group at a time, which takes longer but gives a smaller group to monitor. Self-correction and immediate writing of misspelled words follow both methods of administration. Each child's misspelled words form the list of words that the child systematically studies for that week.

The Self-Study Method

The self-corrected test procedure gives students an individualized list of words to master. Now, each student must learn these misspelled words efficiently. Teachers know that students do not automatically use the most effective study methods. In fact, proper study methods should be reviewed at the beginning of each grade.

Horn recommends teaching the following self-study procedure:

1. Pronounce the word correctly. Correct pronunciation is important in learning to spell. Enunciate each syllable distinctly while looking closely at the word.
2. Close your eyes and try to recall how the word looks, syllable by syllable. Pronounce the word in a whisper while you try to visualize the word.
3. Open your eyes and make sure you have recalled the word correctly. Repeat these steps two or three times.
4. When you feel that you have learned the word, cover it and write it without looking. Check your written word with the correct, covered word.
5. Repeat this writing procedure until you have correctly spelled the word three times. Check the correct spelling after each writing.

Students who have a lot of trouble with spelling need to overlearn their spelling words; they may need more than three correct repetitions of each spelling word, and some of these students may benefit from a more rigorous remedial technique.

The Weekly Spelling Plan

A study plan might result in a Monday through Friday arrangement similar to that recommended by Burns and Broman (1983):

1. On Monday, give a pretest to each spelling group. The pretest should consist of all the words that the group is expected to master during the week. Have the children check their own words, using the corrected-spelling approach. Have them study each misspelled word immediately.
2. On Tuesday, have the children continue to study misspelled words. Also, have them work on exercises to expand the meaning of the spelling words. Such exercises might consist of writing phrases with each word, or adding affixes to the words. For example, affixes to the word *decide* produce *decided, deciding,* and *undecided.*

3. On Wednesday, give a midweek test of all the words given on Monday to each spelling group. If children spell the list correctly on Wednesday, do not require them to take an additional test. If children miss words, have them immediately use the self-study method again with their words.

4. For Thursday's spelling lesson, include enrichment activities that use the words in various situations. Unless children use the spelling words they learn, they quickly forget them. Some students will need self-study time before the Friday test.

5. On Friday, have students who missed spelling words on both Monday and Wednesday take a final test. Add words they miss on Friday to the students' spelling lists for periodic review.

Have students keep charts to help them visualize their individual growth in spelling. They should chart their spelling scores from the Wednesday or Friday tests. The charts will resemble that in Figure 7–1.

Horn emphasizes periodic review as an essential aspect of an efficient spelling program. The first review should occur within a day or two after the words are taught; the Wednesday test provides this review. The second review should take place during the following month. Place missed words on a special list and review them regularly. Finally, include words the children find especially difficult during the year on the instructional list for the following grade.

In a developmental spelling program, remember six important factors when planning the spelling curriculum. The initial step is diagnostic testing to find the most efficient spelling level for each student. Second, the weekly program begins with a pretest, followed immediately by the corrected-test procedure. Third, each child should work only on the words that are difficult for him or her, and you should

FIGURE 7–1

Individual pupil spelling progress chart

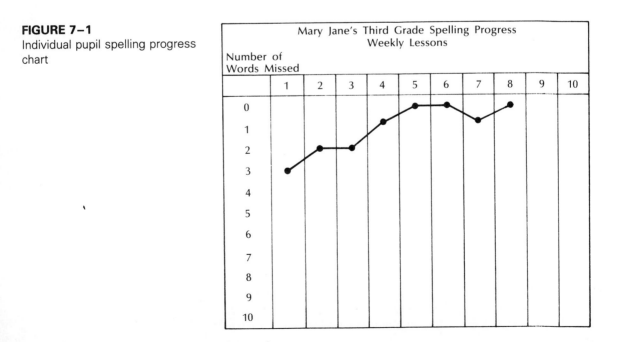

show the child a definite method for learning these words. Fourth, rigorous reviews will emphasize the more difficult words. Fifth, the pupil should chart his or her daily, weekly, monthly, and yearly progress. Finally, students need to apply their spelling words in various contexts.

The Inductive Method

Most spelling authorities believe that the instructional program should include some spelling generalizations. Disagreement over the teaching of spelling generalizations pertains to the number of generalizations considered reliable; you should definitely include the more reliable generalizations in a developmental spelling program. Students will be better able to apply these generalizations if they learn them inductively.

Using an inductive method, initiate the learning experience by writing on the board several words that demonstrate the particular generalization. Then, ask the children to supply more words like those listed, and add them to the list. Write any exceptions to the rule on a separate list. Then, guide the class to look carefully at the words to discover the generalization involved. After they discover the generalization, the children should turn to their spelling books or lists to verify their discovery. Inductive teaching tends to be active and pupil-involved; consequently, it both motivates and provides positive reinforcement.

FOR YOUR PLAN BOOK
A Spelling-Generalization Lesson Using an Inductive Approach

An excellent third-grade teacher developed this lesson plan. Begin by placing the following words on the board in two columns. Put singular forms in the left-hand column, plural forms in the right-hand column.

key	keys
day	days
monkey	monkeys
boy	boys
donkey	donkeys
baby	babies
cherry	cherries
lady	ladies
berry	berries
daisy	daisies

Pronounce all the words with the children. Have individual children say sentences aloud, using the listed words, and then ask the children to add similar words to the list. Put the children's words on the board next to the appropriate list.

Have the class examine the left hand column and decide on a common element for all of the words (all words end with *y*). Next, have the class look at the right-hand column and determine how the first five words were made plural (*s* was added to each word). Ask how the second five words were made plural (*es* was added and the *y* was changed to *i*). Also, ask why the *y* was changed in some words but not in others. The question should lead the children to formulate a generalization similar to the following:

If a word ends in *y,* add *s* to make the plural if a vowel is before the *y.* If a consonant is before the *y,* change the *y* to *i* and add *es* to form the plural.

Then, have the students test their generalization on new words. The following words conform to the above generalizations:

sky	lorry	ferry	penny	play	tray
bay	trolley	body	country	toy	

Finally, ask the class to open their spelling and reading books to find additional words that fit the *y* generalization.

REINFORCEMENT ACTIVITIES

1. Administer a list of appropriate spelling words to an elementary class. Following the corrected-test activity, instruct the class in the most efficient method for self-study. Develop a chart, with student assistance, to remind the students how to use the study procedures.
2. Develop a lesson plan that teaches a spelling generalization step by step. If you are a preservice teacher, demonstrate your activity to a group of peers in your college class. If you are an in-service teacher, instruct a group of children with your lesson plan.

Virginia Smith, a fourth-grade teacher, developed the following unit to teach the proofreading skills associated with spelling improvement. She taught the unit to her class. This unit is based on research by Personke and Yee (1971). They conclude that students must attain an attitude toward spelling that they label "spelling conscience" and must be instructed in the techniques necessary for proofreading their own compositions efficiently. The dictionary is the primary reference tool for such proofreading. Smith's unit begins with an informal diagnostic test, followed by proofreading activities that stress dictionary skill, proofreading spelling lists, proofreading a story, and writing a paragraph from dictation.

FOR YOUR PLAN BOOK
Proofreading Unit—Grade 4

I. Informal Diagnostic Test
   A. Objectives:
      1. Introduce the importance of proofreading for increasing spelling accuracy in compositions.
      2. Discover a student's proofreading skills.

B. Procedures: Give each child a copy of the following letter. Explain that there are spelling errors in the letter, and you want the children to look carefully at the words and draw a line under each incorrect spelling. Explain that the procedure of reading written material and correcting spelling is called proofreading. After children underline the words, have them write the correct spelling above each word, if they know it. Ask the children to write "proofread for spelling" at the end of the letter.

C. Materials:

Deer Tom,	1
Have you playd much basbal	2
lately? I am know on the Red	1
Arows teem. My bruther is two.	4
We both bated Fryday nite. I	3
gut a hit but he diddn't.	2
We are coming to yur town	1
next week to viset. I hope we	1
cen play basbal together then.	2
Yur frend,	2
Tony	19 errors

D. Evaluation: Make a proofreading folder for each child. Check each child's proofreading accuracy, noting the types of errors the child detects, and the types of errors he or she does not correct. Return the papers to the class and discuss the need for proofreading skills.

II. Dictionary Skills—Arranging Words in Alphabetical Order

A. Objective: To review the use of a dictionary in order to improve proofreading skills.

B. Procedures: Explain to the children that the dictionary is used to check all guesses they make in spelling. Review the procedures for arranging words in alphabetical order. First, alphabetize words according to the first letter of the word: *cattle, bottle, safety, another, timber, doctor, meat, laughter.* Next, alphabetize words according to the second letter of the word: *builder, better, brake, battle, blimp, box, bicycle.* Finally, review the practice that if two words begin with the same letters, you alphabetize according to the first letter that is different. Example: *clever, clatter, clergy, climate, cloudy, cloak, clothes, clump, club, claw, click.*

C. Materials: Divide the class into teams. Give each team a set of words written on cards to put into alphabetical order. The first team to put their words into correct order scores a point. Players may move about with the cards, or they can place cards on the chalk tray. The cards should progress from easier to more complicated alphabetizing tasks. Eventually, have the children put lists of words such as these into alphabetical order: *interesting, interested, interests.*

III. Dictionary Skills—Using Guide Words

A. Objective: To learn that speed of dictionary use can be improved through the use of guide words.

B. Procedures: Have the students open their dictionaries to a specific page. Discuss the two words at the top of the page. For example, on page 955 are the words *rally* and *rang.* Have the students look at the page and decide the purpose of the two words. Help them understand that *rally* is the first word on the page and *rang* is the last word. Discuss the benefits of using guide words.

C. Materials: Each team or individual student needs a copy of the same dictionary. Ask the students how rapidly they can find the guide words on the page where the word *horse* is found. Continue this procedure with various words. For another activity with individual dictionaries, provide the guide words for a page and ask the students if certain words would be found on that page. For example, is the word *know* on the same page with the guide words *knight* and *knotting?* Have the students look the words up in the dictionary to verify their answers.

D. Evaluation: Evaluate each student's ability to use guide words accurately. Provide a worksheet on which students must find the pages where specific guide words appear. Informally test the students' ability to find specific words rapidly.

IV. Proofreading Spelling Lists

A. Objective: To learn to apply the proofreading skills to a list of spelling words.

B. Procedures: Have the students write down a list of words that you read to them slowly. Ask the students to pronounce the words carefully to themselves before they write the words. Tell them to underline the words they don't know how to spell. After dictating the list, allow the students about fifteen minutes to check the spellings in their dictionaries. Have them write the correct spellings above misspelled words. When they have made their corrections, have them write "proofread for spelling" on their papers.

C. Materials: Use the following words for dictation. (The words were taken from the fourth-grade text.)

read	glow	alone	nice
case	twice	fool	hour
afraid	noisy	chair	fear
eager	worst	pearl	harbor
seed	collar	thread	cover

D. Evaluation: How well did the students check their guesses? Were they able to distinguish between words that they knew positively and words that they estimated?

V. Proofreading a Story

A. Objective: To improve the students' ability to apply proofreading skills to a written composition.

B. Procedures: Give each child a copy of a poorly written story. Have the children read through the story, then proofread for spelling errors, underlining each incorrect spelling once and writing the corrected word above. Have the children use the dictionary to verify any guesses and ask them to write "proofread for spelling" when they are finished.

C. Materials:

The fat cat ran swiffly across	1
the gras. He was chaseing a mous.	3
Wood he cetch it? The mouse ran bak	3
and fourth by the flower bed.	1
Suddenly the cat jumbd. The mous	2
dashd behind the roze bush, then	2
dizappeared from site. He wuz safe	4
frum the fat cat.	1
	17 errors

   D. Evaluation: Observe how well students are able to find errors and to use their dictionaries to find correct spellings. Go over the corrections in class so the students can see how they have done.
VI. Writing a Paragraph from Dictation and Proofreading It
   A. Objective: To practice the proofreading skills following a dictated paragraph.
   B. Procedures: Dictate a short paragraph to the class. Tell the students to underline any unknown spellings as they write the paragraph. After the dictation, allow time for the class to check their guessed spellings in the dictionary. Have them write the correct spellings above the word. Have them write "proofread for spelling" on the paper when they are finished.
   C. Materials:

   Mary and her brother Tom went to the beach last Thursday. The sun was hot, the sea was cold and the sand was clean. Mary and Tom had fun swimming and playing. When they came home they were both very tired and very happy.

   D. Evaluation: Observe how well the students check their guesses using the dictionary. Have the students state the steps that they should follow when proofreading a story or a list of spelling words. They should practice these steps in every subject area.

Used with permission of Virginia Smith, teacher at St. Michael's Academy, Bryan, Texas.

GIFTED SPELLERS

When you use a diagnostic and pretest approach, accelerated students will not have to waste class periods on words they can already spell. Gifted spellers can thus take part in a spelling period without excessive boredom. Because accelerated students may learn their words very rapidly, they will have time during the spelling period to increase their vocabularies and work on word lists that suit their particular interests. As an example, one gifted third-grade student was especially interested in astronomy and another in dinosaurs. The children learned to spell subject-related words that allowed them to write about their favorite topics. The words are not normally taught in the third-grade spelling curriculum, but these students used them frequently.

Successful spelling programs for gifted spellers are usually individualized. Gifted students should not be punished by having to master a second list of words after they have learned one list. One student who described her spelling experience indicated that her spelling teacher always gave her an additional twenty-five spelling words if she spelled the first twenty-five correctly. The second list proved to be punishment for this girl, rather than an award for accurate spelling. The girl solved her problem by intentionally missing words on the first list so she would not have to write an additional list of words. Obviously, the teacher had not placed this child on the correct spelling level and had not used a pretest to determine the words she did not need to study.

You can enrich the spelling curriculum with vocabulary-building activities. Help students find synonyms for overworked words and discover when the meaning of a sentence would improve with use of a more exact word. For example, the

word *small* has several different meanings. Students who are investigating synonyms would find three categories of words relating to *small:*

Little		Minor		Small-minded	
diminutive	wee	unimportant	trivial	ignoble	narrow
miniature	dwarfish	insignificant	modest	bigoted	petty
Lilliputian	minute	inconsiderable	secondary	stingy	limited
tiny		inconsequential	trifling	provincial	intolerant

Have the students categorize the various synonyms according to their proper
meanings and discuss the context for using each of them. Among other words with
multiple meanings and numerous synonyms are *strong, big, rub, rude, nice, real,
look, safe,* and *fair.*

REMEDIAL APPROACHES

Slower spellers in a class may need remedial consideration. Accurate diagnosis of
spelling ability levels and specific strengths and weaknesses is especially important for effective remedial instruction. You may need to reduce by half the list of
words that you expect remedial spellers to master because a more detailed study
method may be necessary.

The Fernald Approach

Fernald's multisensory approach has been successful with many disabled spellers
(Campbell, 1976). Begin by writing a word on a card in large letters. (Use cursive
writing for older children and manuscript for younger students.)

Next, show this card to the child and name the word. Ask the child to look
carefully at the word and say it with you. Trace the word with two fingers while the
child repeats the word. Next, have the child trace the word with two fingers while
he or she pronounces each syllable; the child does not spell the word. Have the
child repeat this tracing and verbalizing until he or she feels ready to write the
word without copying it.

When the child is ready, have the child turn the card face down and write the
word without looking at it. After writing the word, have the child turn the card over to
verify the spelling. If the child spells the word correctly, have the child go through the
writing and verification procedures three more times without copying either the card
or the previously written words. If unsuccessful, have the child go back to the finger-
tracing and verbalizing experience. Do not permit the child to erase part of the word;
the child must rewrite the whole word if he or she makes an error. The following day,
retest words learned in this manner.

You can use the Fernald approach individually or with small groups. One teacher
who used this approach with severely remedial spellers reported that her pupils increased mastery of their spelling words by 80 percent. They learned fewer words, but
used the words they learned in daily work and remembered them.

Reinforcement Games

Remedial students also need reinforcing spelling activities. Games offer diversion
from the more drill-centered remedial approaches. The tic-tac-toe and the sports
and spelling games enrich and motivate remedial instruction.

The sports section of the newspaper provides an opportunity for children to locate sports-related spelling words.

Tic-tac-toe   In the tic-tac-toe game, print the week's spelling words on one side of tagboard cards. One player shuffles the cards while the second player draws a tic-tac-toe grid. The players decide who is to be X and who is to be O. Player X draws the first card, and asks player O to spell the word on the card. If player O spells the word correctly, he or she places an O on the grid and draws a card for player X to spell. When a player is unable to spell a word, he or she places the card on the bottom of the card pile and is not allowed to place a marker on the grid. The winner is the player who places three of his or her markers in a row.

Sports and spelling   For the sports and spelling game, have the students divide into pairs. Give each pair the sports section from the daily newspaper. The children must find as many words from their spelling list as possible. The winners are the team or teams who find the most words.

REINFORCEMENT
ACTIVITY

Develop a spelling game for reinforcing a weekly spelling list. Play the game with children of the appropriate age. Caution: when you use games to reinforce learning, be sure to supervise the play. Children may circumvent the rules of the game and make up their own. When this happens, the objective for the game is not realized.

MAINSTREAMING

With its demands for visual and auditory perception, short- and long-term memory, attention to details, and fine-motor capabilities, spelling instruction causes considerable problems for learning disabled and mentally handicapped children. Consequently, many teachers provide special instruction in spelling and provide many opportunities for children to dictate their stories to scribes. Table 7–2 presents characteristics of learning disabled children that might interfere with spelling, and corresponding teaching techniques for language arts instruction. Table 7–3 presents the same information for mentally handicapped children. The characteristics and techniques for language arts instruction result from a search of the research literature and recommendations of authorities who work with mainstreamed children.

TABLE 7–2

Mainstreaming and spelling for learning disabled children

Characteristics of Learning Disabled Children	Teaching Techniques for Language Arts Instruction
1. Lower scores than those for normal children on spelling both predictable and unpredictable words (Carpenter & Miller, 1982).	1. Provide extra time for spelling. In-school tutoring in addition to regular classroom instruction may result in gains equal to those made by normal spellers (Bessai & Cozac, 1980). Provide practice and meaningful spelling situations by integrating spelling into the broader curriculum (Cohen & Plaskon, 1980). Try mnemonic aids (Otto & Smith, 1980).
2. Deficiencies in visual perception and visual-motor integration (Harber, 1979).	2. Use informal and formal tests and trial teaching to determine the best method for spelling instruction (Cohen & Plaskon, 1980; Harris and Sipay, 1985; Sapir & Wilson, 1978).
3. Poor visual short-term memory and problems with auditory and/or visual memory (Fisher, 1980; Johnson & Myklebust, 1967; Wallace & McLoughlin, 1988).	3. Try a VAKT approach which emphasizes seeing, saying, hearing, and feeling for learning spelling words (Campbell, 1976; Lerner, 1976; Gearheart, Weishahn, & Gearheart, 1992).
4. Problems with auditory discrimination cause children to have difficulty hearing fine differences of sound within words (Cohen & Plaskon, 1980).	4. Avoid phonics approach and try a linguistic spelling or whole-word system. (Bader, 1980; Sapir & Wilson, 1978). Provide auditory discrimination training (Otto & Smith, 1980). Try the auditory discrimination suggestions on the chart for listening development and learning disabled children.
5. Anxiety created by lack of academic success, which, in turn, may interfere with learning (Frey, 1980).	5. Teach children a self-relaxation technique to decrease anxiety and increase spelling progress (Frey, 1980).

TABLE 7–3
Mainstreaming and spelling for mentally handicapped children

Characteristics of Mentally Handicapped Children	Teaching Techniques for Language Arts Instruction
1. Below-average ability in spelling as well as other academic areas; spelling ability may be even lower than reading ability (Otto & Smith, 1980).	1. Test the student's reading vocabulary with the Dolch Basic Word List or the Johnson Word List. Then test the student's spelling ability on the same list. The initial target words for spelling growth are the words a student can read but cannot spell (Otto & Smith, 1980).
2. Lack of phonic-analysis ability.	2. Try a multisensory approach for spelling instruction (Campbell, 1976). Try an approach emphasizing spelling patterns or word families with high utility value (Otto & Smith, 1980). Use informal and formal tests and trial teaching to determine the best method for spelling instruction (Cohen & Plaskon, 1980; Harris and Sipay, 1985; Sapir & Wilson, 1978). Try color cues (Frostig, 1984).

SUMMARY

In the many articles dealing with the writing crisis in American schools, poor spelling is often cited as a major problem. School programs must proceed from sound diagnosis; help students learn to spell the words they need to know; provide instruction in reliable spelling generalizations; develop an understanding of word meanings; equip spellers with more than one strategy; incorporate spelling into all areas of the curriculum; and provide for motivation, positive attitudes, and sound habits.

Use diagnostic approaches to place students on appropriate instructional levels. Analyze the types of errors each child makes in writing and use this information to individualize your spelling program. You should test to place students at appropriate levels and determine understanding of spelling generalizations. In addition, you should analyze errors.

You may select spelling words according to several different criteria. The frequency-of-use approach bases spelling instruction on the words used most frequently. Consequently, with this approach, you should teach first the words most frequently used in writing. In a specific grade, you should also teach words commonly used by children in that grade, including words from the content areas.

A quite different criterion emphasizes phonic regularity of words. Words in this approach follow consistent spelling patterns. Some linguists and psycholinguists stress consistency of spelling patterns in words of similar meaning. Thus, spelling instruction should allow students to compare, contrast, and categorize words according to root words, word origins, and similarities in structural patterns.

Several techniques are valuable in spelling instruction. The corrected-test method allows immediate feedback, and liberates students from systematic study of words already mastered. The self-study method allows students to master their individualized spelling words. The inductive method allows students to discover and use the reliable spelling generalizations.

Use remedial spelling approaches for disabled spellers. The Fernald approach is useful with learning disabled children. In this multisensory method, children look at the word, say the word, trace the word, then write the word without looking at it. Spelling games are useful for reinforcing and motivating remedial spelling students. However, do not teach spelling as an isolated subject. Students, whether regular, gifted, or remedial, require many opportunities to use spelling in meaningful situations.

ADDITIONAL SPELLING ACTIVITIES

1. Collect writing samples of three to ten year olds. Identify the stages in spelling development according to Henderson and Templeton's five stages.
2. Compare an informal spelling-level test that you compile from one specific spelling program with an informal spelling-level test that you compile from a second spelling program. Evaluate the similarities and the differences between the two tests. What information does each test provide? Is there a difference in word difficulty or word selection?
3. Develop a spelling lesson designed to teach an apostrophe generalization.
4. Interview several good, average, and poor spellers. Determine their perceptions about their spelling ability, their attitudes toward spelling, their study approaches, and their techniques for spelling an unknown word.
5. Develop a spelling unit designed to improve proofreading abilities.

BIBLIOGRAPHY

Adams, M. J. *Beginning to Read: Thinking and Learning About Print.* University of Illinois: Urbana-Champaign, Center for the Study of Reading, 1990.

Bader, Lois A. *Reading Diagnosis and Remediation in Classroom and Clinic.* New York: Macmillan Co., 1980.

Balajthy, E. "Using Microcomputers to Teach Spelling." *The Reading Teacher* 39 (1986): 438–43.

Barron, R. W. "Visual and Phonological Strategies in Reading and Spelling." In *Cognitive Processes in Spelling,* edited by U. Frith. New York: Academic Press, 1980, pp. 195–214.

Bessai, Frederick, and Cozac, Con. "Gains of Fifth and Sixth Grade Readers from In-School Tutoring." *The Reading Teacher* 33 (February 1980): 567–70.

Bremer, Bishop, and Stone. *Skills in Spelling.* Dallas: American Book Co., 1976.

Burns, Paul C., and Broman, Betty L. *The Language Arts in Childhood Education.* 5th ed. Chicago: Rand McNally & Co., 1983.

Campbell, Dorothy. "Mode of Response to Tactual Stimuli and Learning Disabled and Normal Pupils' Learning New Words with Phoneme-Grapheme Equivalence." *Journal of Research and Development in Education* 9 (Winter 1976): 29.

Carpenter, Dale, and Miller, Lamoine J. "Spelling Ability of Reading Disabled LD Students and Able Readers." *Learning Disability Quarterly* 5 (Winter 1982): 65–70.

Chomsky, Carol. "Reading, Writing, and Phonology." *Harvard Educational Review* 40 (1970): 287–309.

Cohen, Sandra, and Plaskon, Stephen P. *Language Arts for the Mildly Retarded.* Columbus, Oh.: Merrill Publishing Co., 1980.

Cunningham, P. *Phonics They Use: Words for Reading and Writing.* New York: Harper Collins, 1991.

Fisher, Dennis F. "Compensatory Training for Disabled Readers: Research to Practice." *Journal of Reading Disabilities* 18 (March 1980): 25–31.

Frey, Herbert. "Improving the Performance of Poor Readers through Autogenic Relaxation Training." *The Reading Teacher* 33 (May 1980): 928–32.

Frostig, Marianne. "Corrective Reading in the Classroom." In *Readings on Reading Instruction*, 3d. ed. Edited by Albert J. Harris and Edward R. Sipay. New York: Longman, 1984.

Gearheart, Bill R.; Weishahn, Mel W.; and Gearheart, Carol J. *The Exceptional Student in the Regular Classroom*. 5th ed. New York: Merrill/Macmillan, 1992.

Gentry, J. Richard. "An Analysis of Developmental Spelling in GNYS AT WRK." *The Reading Teacher* 36 (November 1982): 192–200.

Gustafson, B. "An Individualized Teacher-Directed Spelling Program Compared with a Computer-Based Spelling Program." Doctoral Dissertation, Iowa State University, 1982. *Dissertation Abstracts International* 991A–992A. (University Microfilms No. DA 8221191)

Hanna, Paul R., and Hanna, Jean S. "Applications of Linguistics and Psychological Cues to the Spelling Course of Study." *Elementary English* 42 (November 1965): 753–59.

———, and Moore, James. "Spelling—From Spoken Word to Written Symbol." *Elementary School Journal* 53 (February 1953): 329–37.

Hansen, J. *Breaking Ground*. Portsmouth, N.H.: Heinemann, 1985.

Harber, Jean R. "Differentiating LD and Normal Children: The Utility of Selected Perceptual and Perceptual-Motor Tests." *Learning Disability Quarterly* 2 (Spring 1979): 70–75.

Harris, Albert J., and Sipay, Edward R. *How to Increase Reading Ability*. 8th ed. New York: Longman, 1985.

Henderson, Edmund. *Teaching Spelling*. New York: Houghton Mifflin Co., 1985.

———, and Beers, James W., eds. *Developmental and Cognitive Aspects of Learning to Spell: A Reflection of Word Knowledge*. Newark, Del.: International Reading Association, 1980.

———, and Templeton, Shane. "A Developmental Perspective of Formal Spelling Instruction Through Alphabet, Pattern, and Meaning." *The Elementary School Journal* 86 (January 1986): 305–16.

Hillerich, Robert L. "Let's Teach Spelling—Not Phonetic Misspelling." *Language Arts* 54 (March 1977): 301–7.

———. "Spelling: What Can Be Diagnosed?" *Elementary School Journal* 83 (1982): 138–47.

Hodges, R. E., and Rudorf, E. H. "Searching Linguistics for Cues for the Teaching of Spelling." *Elementary English* 42 (May 1965): 527–33.

Horn, Ernest. "Phonetics and Spelling." *Elementary School Journal* 57 (May 1957): 424–32.

———. "Phonics and Spelling." *Journal of Education* 136 (May 1954): 233–35.

———. "Principles of Methods in Teaching Spelling as Derived from Scientific Investigation." *18th Yearbook of the National Society for the Study of Education, Part II*. Bloomington, Ill.: Public School Publishing Co., 1919, pp. 52–77.

———. *Teaching Spelling*. American Educational Research Association, Department of Classroom Teachers Research Pamphlet. Washington, D.C.: National Education Association, 1963.

Johnson, D., and Myklebust, Helmer. *Learning Disabilities: Educational Principles and Practices*. New York: Grune & Stratton, 1967.

Lerner, Janet W. *Children with Learning Disabilities*. 2d ed. Boston: Houghton Mifflin Co., 1976.

Lie, A. "Effects of a Training Program for Stimulating Skills in Word Analysis in First-Grade Children." *Reading Research Quarterly* 26 (1991): 234–50.

Lundberg, I.; Frost, J.; and Petersen, O. "Effects of an Extensive Program for Stimulating Phonological Awareness in Preschool Children." *Reading Research Quarterly* 23 (1988): 263–84.

McGrath, Ellie. "Education: The Bold Quest for Quality." *Time*, October 10, 1983, 58–66.

Mason, George E. "The Computer in the Reading Clinic." *The Reading Teacher* 36 (February 1983): 504–7.

Otto, Wayne, and Smith, Richard. *Corrective and Remedial Teaching*. Boston: Houghton Mifflin Co., 1980.

Personke, Carl. "Spelling as a Language Art." In *Language Arts Instruction and the Beginning Teacher*, edited by Carl Personke and Dale Johnson. Englewood Cliffs, N.J.: Prentice-Hall, 1987.

———, and Yee, Albert. *Comprehensive Spelling Instruction*. Scranton: Intext Educational Publishers, 1971.

Petty, Walter T., and Jensen, Julie M. *Developing Children's Language*. Boston: Allyn & Bacon, 1980.

Read, Charles. "Pre-School Children's Knowledge of English Phonology." *Harvard Educational Review* 41 (February 1971): 1–34.

Sapir, Selma, and Wilson, Bernice A. *Professional's Guide to Working with the Learning-Disabled Child*. New York: Brunner/Mazel, 1978.

Sloboda, J. A. "Visual Imagery and Individual Differences in Spelling." *Cognitive Processes in Spelling*, edited by U. Frith. New York: Academic Press, 1980, pp. 231–50.

Wallace, Gerald, and McLoughlin, James A. *Learning Disabilities: Concepts and Characteristics*. 3d ed. Columbus, Oh.: Merrill Publishing Co., 1988.

Zutell, Jerry. "Some Psycholinguistic Perspectives on Children's Spelling." *Language Arts* 55 (October 1978): 844–50.

Chapter Eight

After completing this chapter on grammar, usage, and mechanics, you will be able to:

1. Develop a definition of grammar that includes the three parts of grammar.
2. Describe several characteristics of traditional grammar and list several instructional activities included in a study of traditional grammar.
3. Describe several characteristics of structural grammar and list several instructional activities included in a study of structural grammar.
4. Describe several characteristics of transformational grammar and list several instructional activities included in a study of transformational grammar.
5. Define the levels of usage and list the goals for a level of usage appropriate for classrooms.
6. Develop an inductive lesson for helping children understand a usage concept.
7. List the punctuation skills usually taught in the elementary grades.
8. List the capitalization skills usually taught in the elementary grades.

Grammar, Usage, and the Mechanics of Writing

*L*ike handwriting and spelling, grammar is not an end in itself. Rather, it should be viewed as a means to achieve clarity in both oral and written language. Grammar has been an important part of the language arts curriculum for many years, although the emphasis it receives varies from time to time. There have been revolutionary changes in the approaches of educators to grammar and grammar instruction. These innovations, however, have not gone unchallenged. Grammar is frequently mentioned in the back-to-basics movement, and some critics of American education feel that instruction will profit from a return to a more traditional approach to grammar. To be prepared to answer the critics and to provide better instruction, teachers need to understand the different aspects of grammar, as well as appropriate methods for improving the grasp and application of grammar and usage.

Many college students admit, rather sheepishly, that they have forgotten a great deal about grammar, so this chapter starts with a definition. Francis (1964) provides a useful, three-part definition of grammar:

> Grammar 1: The first thing we mean by grammar is the set of formal patterns in which the words of a language are arranged in order to convey larger meanings. It is not necessary that we be able to discuss these patterns consciously in order to be able to use them. In fact, all speakers of any language above the age of five or six know how to use its complex forms of organization with considerable skill. In this sense of the word they are thoroughly familiar with its grammar.

> Grammar 2: The second meaning of grammar is that branch of linguistic science which is concerned with the description, analysis, and formalization of language patterns.

> Grammar 3: The third sense in which people use the word grammar is that of linguistic etiquette. The word in this sense is often coupled with a derogatory adjective; the expression "He ain't there" is "bad grammar." What we mean is that such an expression is bad linguistic manners in certain circles. (pp. 69, 70)

GRAMMAR 1

The first part of this definition includes the intuitive knowledge of sentence structure that most children demonstrate by the time they enter school. This was the major subject of Chapter 2 of this text, "Language and Cognitive Development." Hartwell (1985) builds on Francis's definition when he identifies this first part of grammar as a set of formal patterns that speakers of a language use automatically to construct meaning. Hillocks and Smith (1991) define knowledge of grammar as "the ability to produce and understand a wide range of grammatical structures" (p. 595). Consequently, students have a substantial knowledge of grammar before they receive any formal instruction. Hillocks and Smith add, however, "the fact that students enter school with this knowledge already in place does not imply that they do not develop during their years of formal schooling" (p. 595). This intuitive knowledge is the basis for further grammar instruction in school. You can emphasize grammar 1 by providing many opportunities for children to explore their language through oral language activities. These activities help children discover the flexibility of language and the possibilities of using it for communication.

GRAMMAR 2

Grammar 2, the linguistic branch of grammar, is concerned with the description, analysis, and formalization of language patterns. Traditional grammar, structural grammar, and transformational grammar are various approaches within this branch.

Traditional Grammar

Traditional grammar has its roots in the eighteenth-century works of Joseph Priestly, Robert Lowth, George Campbell, and Lindley Murry. These writers were prescriptive. They based their rules on Latin, which they saw as a perfect language. Baker (1989) states: "These rules owe their place in school grammars to a project that began in the English Renaissance. At that time, it was felt that the best of all possible languages would be one in which the grammatical rules of the language could be identified with the rules of reasoning that humans everywhere use. Classical Greek and Latin appeared to Renaissance thinkers to be the languages that most clearly embodied this idea" (p. 24).

Traditional grammar is called prescriptive because it attempts to tell people how to speak or write. Traditional grammar classifies words as verbs, adjectives, nouns, adverbs, pronouns, prepositions, conjunctions, or interjections. Instructional activities in traditional grammar might require children to underline all the nouns in a sentence, draw an arrow between a pronoun and its antecedent, mark the verb in a sentence, define the classification of the verb, change the verb to passive or active voice, conjugate verbs, identify adverbs in a sentence, indicate the words that adverbs modify, find the prepositions in a sentence, or identify the conjunctions in a sentence.

Structural Grammar

Structural grammar began with the work of Leonard Bloomfield. It was further developed by linguists such as Charles Fries and James Sledd. The structuralists suggested a new way to classify language. Consequently, structural grammar is not prescriptive, as is traditional grammar; instead, it is descriptive.

With the development of structural grammar, structural linguists began to study the structure of individual languages. According to Baker (1989), structural linguistics provided two basic truths that are extremely important: First, contrary

Children need to recognize that each occasion, audience, and purpose requires different language standards or usage.

to what was believed at the time, there are no "primitive" languages. Instead, oral languages are "governed by coherent systems of rules in exactly the same way that the better known written languages were" (p. 13). Second, there is a much wider diversity among different languages than had been suspected. Consequently, "language scholars abandoned the practice of trying to fit the description of every newly encountered language into the mold provided by the rule systems of Latin and Greek. Instead, they increasingly adopted the view that each language deserved to be described in its own terms" (p. 13).

Form classes Structuralists divide words into groups according to the ways in which the words change form, the positions of the words in a sentence, and the structure of the words preceding them. Structuralists identify four form classes, resembling nouns, verbs, adjectives, and adverbs. Consider nouns, for example, for how they might be described in structural grammar:

1. Nouns change form by adding *s* or *es* to show plural and *s* or *'* to show possession. For example:

    father—fathers (plural)—*father's* (possessive)

    Other groups of words, such as verbs, adjectives, and adverbs, cannot be made either plural or possessive.

2. Nouns also occur in certain positions in sentences. For example, in the sentence "This (determiner) boy (noun) ran (verb) away (adverb)," the noun falls after the determiner and before the verb. Any word placed in this specific position is a noun:

    This _____ ran away.

    Nouns also occur after verbs as objects (as in "Jerry mailed *letters*" and after prepositions as objects (as in "We are at *home*").

3. Nouns often appear with structure words called determiners. These determiners frequently precede nouns. For example:

    articles: *an* airplane   possessives: *my* sister
               a story   *your* brother
               the city   *their* wagon

    demonstratives: *this* house
                     that tree
                     these balls

Verbs may also be described in terms of changes in form, positions in sentences, and relationships to certain structure words. For example:

1. Simple verbs may change form by adding *s* for present tense (she walks) and *ed* for past tense (she walked). However, there are many irregular verbs, which are changed to past tense without adding *ed*, as in *ring, rang,* and *rung*.

2. Verbs usually are located after the subject of a sentence (a noun). In the sentence "Jimmy ran to school," only verbs fit into this position:

    Jimmy _____ to school.

3. The structure words that come before verbs are auxiliaries, such as *can, would, were,* and *has been,* as in the sentence "Mother *has been* painting all morning."

Structuralists describe adjectives in the following ways:

1. Adjectives containing one or two syllables usually change form to show comparison by adding *er* and *est*. For example:

    small, smaller, smallest

    Adjectives containing more than two syllables usually change form by adding the structure words *more* and *most*. For example:

    appealing, *more* appealing, *most* appealing

2. Adjectives often occur before the nouns they modify, as in "Let's climb the bigg*est* tree." Only adjectives may be placed in this position:

Let's climb the _____ tree.

Adjectives may also appear after linking verbs, as in the sentence "The sky is *cloudy.*" (Note that nouns, too, may come after linking verbs.)

3. Intensifiers, such as *very* and *quite,* frequently come before adjectives. (In addition, adverbs may come before adjectives.)

The final form class is adverbs.

1. Adverbs, like adjectives, may change form by adding *er* and *est.*
2. Adverbs are often found at the end of a sentence, as in "Call your mother *immediately*!"
3. Adverbs, like adjectives, may also be marked by intensifiers.

Instructional activities in a structural grammar text might require the students to change the forms of verbs by adding *s, ed,* or *ing.* (These may be taught inductively).

Sentence patterns   Structural grammar also describes grammar according to sentence patterns. Roberts (1962) developed a sequence of ten patterns to describe existing sentences. These sentence patterns are frequently used in textbooks that use a structural grammar approach. Pattern 1, for example, follows:

Determiner	*Noun*	*Verb (Intransitive)*	*Adverb*
The	woman	walks	rapidly

Students might identify existing sentences as to their appropriate sentence pattern. Teachers might place on the board a sentence such as "The tree was tall and _____ "and let the children discuss the characteristics of words that fit the empty position and provide examples of appropriate words. Classes might develop similar sentences with empty positions for each of the patterns in the grammar. According to Goodman (1965), patterns are frequently provided as models for the analysis of existing sentences.

Transformational Grammar

Transformational grammar is based on the work of Noam Chomsky (1957). It builds on the work of the structuralists but extends structural grammar into the meaning of language. Whereas structural grammar is concerned primarily with syntax, transformational grammar is concerned primarily with semantics and the generation of sentences. According to Lamb (1977), "transformational grammar purports to provide rules for producing new sentences as well as patterns for the analysis of existing sentences. Although sentence patterns are suggested in transformational grammars, these serve a different function than they do in structural grammars" (p. 100).

The term *transformational* refers to basic sentences and the transforms, or variations, that can be developed from these basic sentences. The basic sentences, or kernel sentences, have several definite characteristics. They are formed by placing words together in certain patterns. The second part of transformational grammar consists of directions or rules for rearranging or combining the kernel sentences into new, more complicated structures.

Kernel sentences   The formula for a kernel sentence is:

Sentence = noun phrase + verb phrase

Diagram this sentence formula as follows:

Noun Phrase	Verb Phrase
The car	is red

Kernel sentences have several definite characteristics:

1. In a kernel sentence, the subject is followed by the predicate.

Subject (The car)   Predicate (is red)

2. A kernel sentence is a statement, not a question. (All questions are transforms.)
3. A kernel sentence is affirmative. (All negative sentences are transforms.)
4. A kernel sentence is in the active voice. (All passive-voice sentences are transforms.)
5. A kernel sentence contains a single predicate.

Sentence patterns   Transformationalists also suggest patterns, or basic-sentence types. Mellon (1964) named five basic-sentence patterns, whereas Kean and Personke (1976) identified four types of sentences, according to the positions or slots that words may fill. Any sentence that does not follow one of the four patterns is considered a transformation:

1. The *be* sentence:

Noun Phrase	Verb (Be class)	Noun Phrase, Adjective, or Prepositional Phrase	Optional Adverb
The squirrel	is	a rodent	
The squirrel	is	lively	today
The squirrel	is	in the tree	

2. The intransitive verb sentence:

Noun Phrase	Verb (Intransitive)	Open Adverb or Prepositional Phrase	Optional Adverb
Jerry	ran		rapidly
Jerry	ran	outside	quickly
Jerry	ran	into the field	

3. The transitive verb sentence:

Noun Phrase	Verb (Transitive)	Noun Phrase (Direct object)	Optional Adverb
The girls	mailed	the package	yesterday

4. The linking verb sentence:

Noun Phrase	Verb (Linking)	Noun Phrase or Adjective	Optional Adverb
Judy	became	the president	
Judy	became	frightened	today

Basic-sentence transformations   Both single-base transformations, which act upon one kernel sentence, and double-base transformations, which combine two kernel sentences, are possible with the rules of transformational grammar (Kean & Personke, 1976). The following single-base transformations are possible:

1. Question transformation—The kernel sentence "The car is red" may be easily transformed into a question by rearranging the words into "Is the car red?" The sentence also becomes a question by changing the intonation to "The car is red?" The words *do, does,* or *did* may transform the kernel into a question; for example, "Did Judy become the president?" Question transforms may begin with *who, what, when, where,* and *why.* Thus, the kernel "Jerry ran into the field" could become "Why did Jerry run into the field?" or "When did Jerry run into the field?"

2. Passive transformation—The kernel sentence must be in the active voice, so this change affects sentences that contain transitive verbs. The sentence must be transformed so that the subject receives, rather than performs, the action expressed in the verb. The kernel sentence "The teacher read the book" would become the transformation "The book was read by the teacher." As you can see, the direct object of the original kernel sentence is now the subject of the transformation.

3. Negative transformation—The original kernel sentence, "The car is red," becomes a transformation merely by inserting *not* or *n't* after the verb. This transformation results in the sentence "The car is not red." *Do, does,* or *did* may be used along with the *not* to transform the sentence "Jerry ran outside quickly" to the negative transform "Jerry did not run outside quickly."

Sentences may also be transformed through double-base transformations, in which the transformations result from combining two kernel sentences into one transformation. More complex sentences result from this transformation. The following double-base transformations are possibilities:

1. Coordinating transformation—Coordinating transformations often use coordinating conjunctions, such as *and, but, or,* or sentence connectors, such as *however, therefore, moreover,* to combine kernel sentences in equal or coordinating positions. For example, the two kernel sentences "Jerry has a bicycle" and "Jerry has a kite" combine in the transform to become "Jerry has a bicycle and a kite."

2. Adjective insert—Two kernel sentences may also be joined to form a more interesting and complex transform by combining a kernel sentence containing an adjective with a kernel sentence containing a noun phrase. For example, the two kernel sentences "The squirrel is a rodent" and "The squirrel is lively today" may be transformed into "The squirrel is a lively rodent today."

3. Subordinating transformation—This transformation is more complex than the coordinating transformation. Subordinating connectors, such as *although, whenever, until,* or *because,* are used to connect the two kernel sentences. For example, the two kernel sentences "The boy was quiet" and "He was happy" might combine in the transform "The boy was quiet, although he was happy," or "Although he was happy, the boy was quiet."

4. Relative clause transformation—A relative clause begins with a relative adverb or relative pronoun and is inserted in or at the end of the sentence. For example, the kernel sentences "The car is red" and "I have a car" may combine to form the transform "I have a car that is red." Similarly the two kernels "The man is old" and "The man lives on our street" may combine to form the transform "The man who lives on our street is old."

Instructional activities in a transformational grammar should relate closely to the descriptive elements of the grammar. Because the basic sentence is *noun phrase plus verb phrase,* instructional activities should help children develop an understanding of noun and verb phrases. The major emphasis of instruction should be to guide children in experiencing and working with grammar by helping them examine their own sentences, as well as those written by others. Children should learn how sentences are formed, changed, combined, and improved.

REINFORCEMENT ACTIVITY

With a group of your peers, select several language arts textbooks designed for elementary and middle-school children. Analyze the texts to see whether they are based on traditional, structural, or transformational philosophy. Find examples of learning activities that represent a particular viewpoint. Compare their similarities and differences. Which do you feel is most teachable? Which do you feel would result in the best understanding of language? Share your findings with the rest of your language arts class and be prepared to support your conclusions about the grammar with which you would feel most comfortable in the classroom.

Assessment

In the chapters on language and cognitive development and oral language development in this text we discuss informal methods for evaluating oral language that encourage the gathering of oral language samples and that provide sources for the analysis of how children use word patterns and how they convey meaning with those patterns.

You may analyze children's knowledge of and application of grammar through informal approaches. Many of the activities suggested later in this chapter may provide source material for this analysis. Test applications only by analyzing actual speech or written samples produced by the individual child. According to Savage (1977):

> Evaluation of grammatical application centers on the sentences that the children themselves produce: whether they can produce individual sentences based on models, the sentence types and sentence variety that are evident in their written work, how ideas are combined into sentences and how sentences are grouped into paragraphs, and how effective the writing is through the use of grammatical constructions. (p. 380)

Topic variance, however, may influence the quality of written samples. Hirsch (1982) maintains that sentences are more varied and coherent, spelling and punctuation are better, and syntax is improved if the topic is easy rather than difficult or unfamiliar. Consequently, he believes that students may need to write on as many as five different topics before one can make valid judgments.

Assessment procedures vary according to state and local requirements. Many local school districts are developing methods of assessment, such as informal assessments of students' writings. Other schools rely on state-developed and mandated tests. In any case, proceed with caution to assure that whatever type of assessment you use matches the goals for instruction and assesses the application of grammar during realistic writing situations. As Lamb (1977) notes, "those responsible for selecting tests should recognize the possible discrepancy between what is taught and what is tested" (p. 114).

One test for evaluating a child's ability to combine sentences is the Syntactic Maturity Test, by Roy O'Donnell and Kellogg Hunt (*Measures for Research and Evaluation in the English Language Arts,* Urbana, Ill.: National Council of Teachers of English, 1975). This test relates to transformational grammar. You may use it before teaching sentence combining, or afterward, to evaluate instructional effectiveness. You can administer the Syntactic Maturity Test to students from beginning fourth-graders to adults. It contains a paragraph of thirty-two very short, three-to-five-word sentences (for example, "Aluminum is a metal. It is abundant."), and asks students to rewrite the paragraph by combining the sentences without omitting any information. The new paragraph is then analyzed for mean T-unit length (independent clauses and their modifiers).

Instruction

Research does not show that teaching formal rules of grammar improves either speaking or writing (Hillocks & Smith, 1991). Educators emphasize the knowledge that children gain from reading literature and from writing because there is a strong correlation between reading and writing. Researchers such as Krashen (1984) and Stotsky (1983), who investigated writing competence, emphasize that reading ability and experience consistently correlate with writing skill and that the abstract knowledge that proficient writers have about text comes "from large amounts of self-motivated reading for interest and/or pleasure" (Krashen, p. 20).

In fact, there is a great deal of argument over the value of teaching grammar and which grammar, if any, to teach. Research reveals no advantage in teaching traditional grammar, but there has been some indication that instruction in sentence combining yields positive results in writing. Mellon (1969) found that a tech-

Children need many opportunities for meaningful writing.

nique using transformational sentence combining and grammar produced beneficial results. O'Hare (1973) also used a sentence-combining approach to improve the quality of students' writing. In a review of research, Hillocks and Smith (1991) conclude that the overwhelming majority of sentence-combining studies have been positive and that sentence-combining activities improve writing quality.

The National Council of Teachers of English (1983) believes that grammar should be taught not only to improve writing but also to increase understanding of the language. According to Kean and Personke (1976), "the only justifiable reason for teaching grammar is to lead children to want to explore their language and discover how it works" (p. 313). They explain that the process of communication is the objective of all language study, and that "grammar can play a significant role in such a program if children are guided to experience and work with grammar directly rather than studying it as a complex system that must be memorized" (p. 313). Krashen (1984) maintains that "conscious knowledge of rules of grammar and usage helps only at the editing stage and is limited to straightforward, learnable aspects of grammar" (p. 27). Lamb (1977) recommends that teachers compare the various grammars, note their similarities and differences, and judge for themselves which is most teachable and will result in better understanding and appreciation of language. She feels each of the newer grammars has merit.

Several authors recommend choosing the best aspects of several grammars. Savage (1977), for example, recommends an eclectic grammar:

> In grammar, eclecticism involves drawing on some of the content and techniques that characterize new grammar in helping children master the grammar they are expected to learn as part of the language arts. It involves, for example, using the signals employed by the structural grammarian as an aid in helping children identify parts of speech, or engaging in some of the sentence-combining activities used by the transformational grammar in helping children generate sentences. It attempts to "plug up" some of the leaks in traditional grammar. (p. 338)

The instructional activities we will describe next use an eclectic approach for helping students understand and use their language. Sentence-combining activities are emphasized.

Activities for Early-Elementary Grades

In the early-elementary grades, use linguistic blocks, cloze sentences, and scrambled sentences to build understanding of sentence patterns. Also, have students change order but retain meaning and have them expand sentences.

Linguistic blocks Use linguistic blocks to help develop and reinforce the basic sentence patterns in English, and help children understand the movable and immovable parts of language. A linguistic block has a different word printed on each of its sides; all of the words on the block belong to the same form class. You can make these blocks out of wooden blocks or even milk cartons. Use words the children have learned in reading or language experience activities. Coding the blocks by color will help children see relationships and patterns within a sentence. For example, you might use blue for nouns, red for verbs, green for adjectives, white for noun determiners, yellow for conjunctions, orange for adverbs, gray for prepositions, purple for pronouns, and brown for punctuation.

You can use linguistic blocks for a great many experiments with sentence construction and meaning. For example, beginning with the simplest noun–verb pattern of a kernel sentence, have students create sentences, such as "Jerry swam." By changing the noun block, students will discover that all the names on the noun blocks fit that same position; for example, "Jane swam," "Tag swam," and "Bill swam." They will also discover they cannot reverse the words in this sentence and still make sense (swam Jerry). Next, have the children try other words in the second position and talk about the words that fit that position; for example, "Jerry sang," "Jerry called," and "Jerry moved." Allow the students to suggest other simple combinations.

Next, have the students try noun blocks that are not people's or pets' names. They can substitute a noun block with the words *dog, cat, man,* and *girl* for the proper-noun block. Look at the resulting sentence, "dog swam." Decide whether it sounds appropriate. By trying each of the common-noun blocks, students will discover that they must add something to make a complete sentence. They usually provide examples such as, "My dog swam," "This dog swam," and "The dog swam." Then, introduce another block marked with determiners, such as *the, my, this, your,* and *these,* and lead the students, inductively, to the realization that certain types of words are used before nouns that are not names.

Allow the children to experiment with other sentence patterns. Can they add more to the simple noun, verb, and noun-determiner blocks? (It is not necessary to use these terms with children.) Encourage the children to expand orally by telling *how* someone ran, swam, sang, moved, and so forth. Having thus introduced the adverb, discuss what this kind of word does and how it adds information to the kernel sentence. The children will develop sentences such as "Jerry swam quickly" and "Jane moved quietly."

In order to help children to understand the changes in meaning that result when some sentence sequences are reversed, introduce, with the linguistic blocks, the transitive-verb sentence. Remember that all the verbs on a given block must belong to the same verb class. Sentences such as "The girls mailed the letter" can be formed with transitive-verb blocks. Then, ask the children to experiment by exchanging the noun blocks, "girls" and "letter," so that the sentence reads "The letter mailed the girls." Finally, discuss how the meaning changed when the two words were exchanged. This activity demonstrates how closely meaning is related to a specific sequence of words.

You also can use linguistic blocks to transform kernel sentences into questions, negatives, and so forth. Linguistic blocks allow students to experiment with expanding sentences and to visualize how expansion changes meaning. Data show that such manipulation activities tend to improve written sentence structures for even young students. In an unpublished doctoral dissertation evaluating children's writing achievement after a special language program using linguistic blocks in first, second, and third grades, Baele (1968) found that children in a reading program that included the language supplement showed a significant increase in language quality in sentence structures compared to students who did not use the supplementary program.

Cloze sentences   You may use a cloze technique for building an understanding of sentence patterns. In this approach, write a model sentence, omitting a specific type of word, and ask the students to suggest words that fill the position. Such an approach inductively builds knowledge of form classes. For example, a second-grade teacher used the following examples to introduce the noun class:

The _____ was in the zoo.

The teacher asked the children to think of words that would fit in the blank. They provided *zebra, monkey, lion,* and so forth. The class read the sentences and discussed the types of words that fit into the blank. You can also introduce another pattern for nouns, in which the noun is the object, as in the following:

I could see the _____ .

Ask the children to offer and discuss words such as *car, train, house,* and *clouds.* Also, have them work with the pattern in which the noun is the object of a preposition:

The man was in the ___ _____ .

You can use the cloze technique for other class forms; for example:

Verbs:	Susan _____ (*ran, walked, limped, hopped*) home.
Adjectives:	The _____ (*big, small, blue*) car was on the street.
	The food tasted _____ (*good, hot, spicy, delicious*).
Adverbs:	The cat ran _____ (*quickly, rapidly, quietly*) after the bird.

Use the various patterns of form class to devise similar exercises.

Sentence transformations   Students in lower-elementary grades can do simple transformations as oral activities and, later, use the same principles in written activities. The sentence transformations described with transformational grammar provide the information for this activity. For example, you might present the coordinating transformation by showing and discussing the following kernel sentences:

> Susan has a ball.
> Susan has a bat.

Next, lead a discussion of how the two sentences could be combined into one better sentence; for example, "Susan has a ball and bat." You and the students may suggest numerous combinations.

Sentence scrambling   Sentences may be scrambled, then rearranged to make sense. This activity is much like a game, because the scrambled sentences can be quite humorous; in fact, you may present it as a game. For example:

> walked the slowly turtle (The turtle walked slowly.)
> hopped rabbit the (The rabbit hopped.)
> her lost Amy game (Amy lost her game.)

Let children scramble their own sentences for another student to unscramble. Their sentences may become quite complex as they progress in ability and grade levels.

Changing word order   Ask students to practice rearranging word order in a sentence without changing the original meaning:

> I ate my breakfast this morning.
> = This morning I ate my breakfast.
> The third grade girls won the race yesterday.
> = Yesterday the third grade girls won the race.

Sentence expansion   Start with a simple sentence and expand it to supply more information. Pantomime and pictures are good introductions to this activity. For example, one second-grade teacher wrote, "Mrs. Brown _____" on the chalkboard, and asked the children to watch her to see if they could fill in the blank. First, she walked to the door. The sentence now became "Mrs. Brown walked." Then, "Mrs. Brown walked to the door." Next, she asked the children, "How did Mrs. Brown walk?" The children watched a second time, and responded, "Mrs. Brown walked slowly to the door." Then, she asked, "When did Mrs. Brown walk slowly to the door?" The class now responded with "Mrs. Brown walked slowly to the door this morning" and "This morning Mrs. Brown walked slowly to the door." The teacher continued the activity by having some of the children pantomime. They expanded each sentence to include not only who, but also what, where, when, how, and why.

Another time, the group looked at large pictures and expanded simple sentences that introduced a subject without telling anything about the subject, such as "Snoopy slept," "The bear ran," and "Mother cooked." The children also drew their own pictures and expanded sentences to describe them.

Activities for Middle- and Upper-Elementary Grades

Many of the preceding activities are useful, also, in the middle- and upper-elementary grades. The normal rate of syntactic development can be hastened with sentence-combining activities such as those developed for fourth graders by Hunt and O'Donnell (1970). Stoddard (1982) found that sentence-combining activities developed for fifth- and sixth-grade students improved both the overall quality of writing and syntactic maturity. Research by O'Hare (1973) showed that seventh-grade children improved their writing when sentence combining appeared in the curriculum.

In addition to improving the quality of written composition, Mackie (1982) improved the reading comprehension of fourth-grade students who used a sentence-combining approach. In a recent review of sentence-combining research, Hillocks (1986) reported that the majority of studies indicate that sentence combining promotes syntactic fluency. Remember, however, that the goals of sentence combining are (1) to improve syntactic control and (2) to make sentence construction more automatic. Syntactic control and automaticity allow students to focus on writing content rather than the mechanics of sentence construction. Hillocks and Smith (1991) conclude that sentence combining is effective for all types of students—from remedial students to those that are above average.

FOR YOUR PLAN BOOK
Improving the Writing of Fourth Graders Using a Sentence-Combining Approach

The series of lessons that Kellogg Hunt and Roy O'Donnell presented to fourth graders required about fifteen minutes per day, about three times a week, over the school year. Hunt and O'Donnell did not use grammatical terms during the classroom activities. They described the instruction only as combining two or more sentences into one. The first lesson required them to show the following two sentences on the chalkboard or a transparency:

> I rode in a boat.
> The boat leaked a little.

They read the two sentences as they presented them, and presented a third sentence that combined the first two:

> I rode in a boat that leaked a little.

Next, they read aloud a similar pair of sentences and called on the children to combine the second pair as demonstrated by the model. They covered twelve such combinations in the first lesson.

The transformation lessons progressed in the following sequence:

1. Relative clause modifying object:
   Judy lost a book.
   The book was red.
     Judy lost a book that (which) was red.
     Judy lost a red book.

2. Relative clause modifying subject:
The girl is selling cookies.
The girl is tall.
    The girl who is tall is selling cookies.
    The tall girl is selling cookies.

3. Relative clause reduced to adverb of place:
The monkey eats bananas.
The monkey is in the tree.
    The monkey that is in the tree eats bananas.
    The monkey in the tree eats bananas.

4. Relative clause reduced to past participle:
The boy won the race.
The boy is named Joe.
    The boy who is named Joe won the race.
    The boy named Joe won the race.

5. Relative clause reduced to present participle:
The lion is scary.
The lion is sitting on the log.
    The lion that is sitting on the log is scary.
    The lion sitting on the log is scary.

6. Relative clause reduced to nonrestrictive appositive:
Mr. Jones directs traffic.
Mr. Jones is a policeman.
    Mr. Jones, who is a policeman, directs traffic.
    Mr. Jones, a policeman, directs traffic.

7. Relative clause with nonsubject relativized:
The sunset was beautiful.
We saw the sunset.
    The sunset that we saw was beautiful.
    The sunset we saw was beautiful.

8. Free combining of sentences (children may combine them however they wish):
Children have Christmas stockings.
The stockings are red.
The stockings hang by the fireplace.
Santa fills the stockings.
Nuts and candy are in the stockings.
(This activity covered several lessons.)

9. Coordination of noun phrase, verb phrase:
Mortimer plays football.
Henry plays football.
    Mortimer and Henry play football.

10. Review of coordination and modifiers of nouns.

11. Free writing, combining three sentences.

12. *That* plus subject as object:
He said something.
His name is John.
    He said that his name is John.
    He said his name is John.

13. Extraposition with *it:*
We lost.
This disappointed me.
    It disappointed me that we lost.

14. Free writing, combining four sentences.

15. Nonembedded yes-no questions:
The cat will play the flute.
    ''Will the cat play the flute?''
Embedded in direct quotation:
    He asked, ''Will the cat play the flute?''
Embedded as indirect question:
    He asked (if, whether) the cat would play the flute.

16. Changing statements to questions by replacing *some* with a
word such as *who, what, which, where, when:*
    Someone will eat the trainer.
     Who will eat the trainer?

17. Adverb clauses: *as, before, after, until, if, unless, because:*
    The game started.
    My friend came in.
     As the game started my friend came in.
     Before the game started my friend came in.
     After the game started my friend came in.

18. A story of twenty-six short sentences.
    The students combined the sentences in free writing.

The complete series of lessons is presented in Hunt and O'Donnell's *An Elementary School Curriculum to Develop Better Writing Skills*. A sentence-combining program for seventh graders, which includes examples of sentences for each lesson, can be found in O'Hare's *Sentence Combining: Improving Student Writing Without Formal Grammar Instruction*.

Sentence combining Sentence-combining activities are found in numerous textbooks designed for use in elementary through college courses. William Strong (1986) provides guidelines and examples that use sentence-combining approaches to teach twenty different types of activities. Some of these activities are similar to the structured sentences developed by Hunt and O'Donnell. In other activities, students generate a range of responses. These activities help students explore, discuss, and evaluate various stylistic options. Strong recommends the following guidelines for developing sentence-combining activities:

1. Discuss purposes for sentence combining. Include creating good sentences, becoming flexible in writing, and exploring ways to transform sentences.
2. Encourage students to try new patterns and to take risks with solutions to sentence-combining problems.
3. Provide a positive environment for risk taking by accepting various solutions. When students offer marginal solutions, refer the solutions to the class for judgment.
4. Use signal exercises, context clues, and oral prompts to help students understand the functions of sentence combining.
5. After modeling sentence-combining exercises, place students in pairs to work through exercises orally.
6. When students are working in pairs, have one student act as scribe for the other; then reverse roles. Have the students discuss problems and work out solutions.
7. Have pairs of students develop options for a sentence-combining activity and then agree on the best solution. Ask the students to explain why they prefer particular sentences.
8. In round-robin combining, encourage students to listen closely and then give as many solutions to a sentence-combining cluster as they can. Ask the students to vote on the solutions and discuss reasons for their choices.

9. Be specific in your praise of good sentences. Tell the students what you like about these sentences.
10. Welcome mistakes as opportunities for group problem solving and use mistakes as bases for skill development in editing workshops.
11. Use transformations handed in by students for in-class workshops.
12. Assign an exercise for homework and then ask several students to put their work on ditto masters. Compare their versions in class.
13. Brainstorm with the class to make an exercise more specific and detailed by adding information. Put these details between exercise sentences or elaborate sentence-combining clusters and then compare results.
14. Have students write out solutions to various sentence-combining clusters on note cards. Shuffle the cards and ask the students to rearrange them into a clear, coherent paragraph.
15. Use sentence combining as a springboard for journal writing. Have the students do an exercise each day and then extend that exercise with sentences of their own.
16. Have students combine sentences in a lean, direct style. Contrast the effects of active and passive voice.
17. Ask students to compare their style with that of professional writers. Rewrite a passage into kernel sentences and ask the students to recombine the kernel sentences and then compare their versions with the original.
18. Analyze a sentence-combining exercise for tone, cohesion, method of development, and logical patterns.
19. Create original sentence-combining exercises for specific transformations, course content, or discourse patterns.
20. Emphasize transfer learning by drawing sentence-combining activities from student texts and literature. Have the students revise their writing with particular sentence-combining techniques. Follow sentence-combining lessons with parallel writing tasks for application.

Open-response exercises   You can structure sentence-combining activities with definite correct responses or with open responses in which students generate a range of acceptable responses. Open responses help students explore, discuss, and evaluate various stylistic options. During sentence-combining exercises, you can challenge writing teams by giving oral prompts. For example, give prompts such as begin with *carefully,* begin with "not wanting to," begin with "the paper," begin with "to keep," use *because* as a connector, use a semicolon and *therefore,* use "so that" as a connector, and use "in order to" as a connector. Use prompts to help teach sentence variety. In addition, help students realize that some sentences sound better than others, and that judgments about quality frequently depend on the surrounding sentences. Have students hand in sentence-combining activities for credit; share them in small groups for proofreading, judging, or comparing; enrich them with details generated during prewriting activities; or use them as springboards for in-class follow-up assignments.

You may choose sentence-combining activities from content areas and literature. For example, sentences to combine might include information from social studies or science, recommendations from writing stylebooks, and kernel sentences rewritten from literature paragraphs. You can cluster kernel sentences into groups, or you can list them without clustering. Clustering provides more structure for young students and students who may require extra guidance. When you use kernel sentences from literary sources, let the students compare their solutions with the source material and discover the impact of various literary techniques.

When introducing open-response exercises, Strong (1986) first explains to students that there are many right answers when combining sentences and that making mistakes is expected because people learn from their errors. Next, he asks students to think of different ways to combine two sentences, such as "Carol was working hard on her test. Sue slipped her a note." Before they do this task, he tells the students that they can (1) add connecting words, (2) take out unnecessary words, (3) move words around, and (4) change word endings. Then, he shows students how to combine sentences by modeling various transformations, such as "Carol was working hard on her test, and Sue slipped her a note," "As Carol worked hard on her test, Sue slipped her a note," and "Carol was working hard on her test when Sue slipped her a note." During this modeling, he presents and discusses several awkward or confusing transformations, such as "Working hard on her test, Carol was slipped a note by Sue," "It was Carol, hard at work on her test, who was slipped a note by Sue," and "A note was slipped from Sue to Carol, who was working hard on her test." Finally, he models and discusses unacceptable sentence transformations, such as "Carol working hard on her test, Sue slip her a note," "On her test Carol was hardly working, and a note Sue slipped to her," and "Slipping a note to Carol was Sue, who was working hard on her test" (p. 26).

Next, Strong leads an oral discussion during which the students try several other examples for sentence combining, such as those found in Figure 8–1. Strong then pairs students as they search for various sentence-combining solutions to additional short sentences from Figure 8–1. After five minutes, the students transcribe two or three transformations on the board. Strong expands this activity by having students combine the sentence transformations into extended text, such as "Carol was hard at work on her test when Sue slipped a note to her. Not wanting her teacher to see, she unfolded it carefully" or "Carol was working hard on her test when Sue slipped her a note, which she carefully unfolded because she didn't want her teacher to see" (p. 27).

REINFORCEMENT
ACTIVITY

1. Develop a series of kernel sentences from the following paragraph selected from Jerome Wexler's science information text *From Spore to Spore, Ferns and How They Grow* (1985):

   Fossils are traces we have found of animals and plants that were once alive. They may be bones or teeth or shells, or imprints left in rocks, or animals and plants preserved in ice, or even insects preserved in amber. A petrified tree trunk is a fossil, and so is a footprint left by a dinosaur. (p. 3)

2. Model the introduction to a sentence-combining activity for your class.
3. Identify materials from literature and social studies. What would you emphasize with each sentence-combining activity? Develop kernel sentences to accompany the materials. Share your activity with a group.

Value Judgment

1.1   Carol was working hard on her test.
1.2   Sue slipped her a note.
2.1   Carol unfolded the paper carefully.
2.2   She didn't want her teacher to see.
3.1   The note asked for help on a question.
3.2   The question was important.
4.1   Carol looked down at her paper.
4.2   She thought about the class's honor system.
5.1   Everyone had made a pledge.
5.2   The pledge was not to cheat.
6.1   Carol didn't want to go back on her word.
6.2   Sue was her best friend.
7.1   Time was running out.
7.2   She had to make up her mind.
8.1   Her mouth felt dry.
8.2   Her mouth felt tight.

Assignment: Finish the story. Explain the reasons behind Carol's judgment.

FIGURE 8–1

Sentence-combining exercise (From William Strong, *Creative Approaches to Sentence Combining.* Urbana, Ill.: National Council of Teachers of English, 1986. Reprinted by permission.)

Cohesive devices   Words such as *he, she, it, we* (personal pronouns); *this, these, those* (demonstrative pronouns); *who, whom, whose* (relative pronouns); *here, there* (location noun substitutions); and *now, then, former,* and *later* (temporal noun substitutions) are used frequently in writing. Such terms reduce redundancy, clarify relationships, and link ideas within the text. These cohesive devices tie together information within sentences, paragraphs, and longer passages. When authors provide clear, logical cohesive devices (for example, referents such as pronouns, conjunctions that link two ideas, substitutions that replace one word with another word to add to the meaning of the first word, and repetitions that restate information), comprehension of a text increases. In contrast, when the connectors are vague or inferred, comprehension decreases for many students. Cox, Shanahan, and Sulzby (1990) found that cohesive harmony characterizes well-written and coherent text. Moe and Irwin (1986) state that teachers must not only be aware of these cohesive devices within texts, but also help students understand and use cohesive devices.

Baumann and Stevenson (1986) recommend the following four-step procedure for teaching cohesive devices. The approach moves from full teacher responsibility to shared student/teacher responsibility to full student responsibility.

1.   Introduce the lesson by telling the students what skill related to cohesive devices you will teach, by providing an example of the cohesive device, and by explaining why the acquisition of that skill is important.

2. .Provide direct instruction, in which you model, show, demonstrate, and lead the instruction in the skill.
3. Provide students with guided application of the skill, but use materials not used during previous instruction.
4. Provide independent practice, in which the students apply the skill in their comprehension of text. Trade books and other primary sources as well as content-area texts are effective materials for this activity and increase the transfer of the skill to additional contexts. Trade books also allow students to practice their skills within passage-length texts rather than isolated sentences that do not consider prior information.

FOR YOUR PLAN BOOK
A Lesson Plan on Cohesive Devices

Objectives

To teach students to comprehend personal pronouns and to apply this knowledge when reading or listening to picture story books.

Introduction

Teacher: When people write they often use words that stand for other words. These words allow writers to repeat an idea without repeating the same words. Look at the following sentences written on the board and read the sentences with me:

> Barbara likes to write stories. She writes funny stories about animals.

In the first sentence, find the word *Barbara*. In the second sentence, find the word *she*. This is an example of a sentence in which one word replaces another word. "She" means the same thing as "Barbara." Words like "she" are called pronouns. Check to see if we are right in our identification of the meaning of the word by reading both sentences, but replacing "she" with "Barbara" in the second sentence. Now read these sentences with me:

> Barbara likes to write stories. Barbara writes funny stories about animals.

Notice that the two sentences still mean the same thing. If we replace "she" with another girl's name, the second sentence has a different meaning. These sentences are examples of what we will learn about today. We will learn that words such as *she, he, we, her, you, they, their,* and *it* stand for other words. This is important because it helps you understand what writers are trying to tell you. It is also important so that you can use this skill in your own writing.

Teacher-Directed Instruction

(Write sentences on the board that include the pronouns to be emphasized. Choose the sentences according to the reading and interest levels of your students.) Teacher: Look at the sentences written on the board:

1. Cinderella lived with her stepmother and her stepsisters. She sat in the ashes in the kitchen, and that is how she got her name.

2. The prince wanted to marry one of the girls in the kingdom. <u>He</u> gave a ball to meet the girls.
3. The stepsisters and the stepmother dressed in <u>their</u> best clothes. <u>They</u> went to the ball.
4. Cinderella was unhappy because <u>she</u> wanted to go to the ball. <u>She</u> was granted a wish by <u>her</u> fairy godmother.
5. A magical carriage took <u>her</u> to the ball. <u>It</u> turned back into a pumpkin at midnight.

Read the sentences in number 1 with me. Look for the words used in place of Cinderella. Notice that the words are underlined. Now, listen as I tell you how I figured out the meanings of the words. First, I noticed that <u>her</u> was used twice in the first sentence. I thought about whose stepmother and whose stepsisters the sentence meant. I replaced both of the <u>hers</u> with <u>Cinderella</u> and the sentence made sense. Then I noticed that <u>she</u> was used twice in the next sentence. I thought about the first sentence and I asked myself if <u>she</u> and <u>her</u> meant Cinderella, the stepmother, or the stepsisters. I knew that <u>she</u> could not mean the stepsisters because the word would have to be <u>they</u>. I used the meaning of the first sentence to help me identify that <u>she</u> meant Cinderella. I knew from the story about Cinderella that Cinderella was given her name because she sat in the cinders and ashes in the kitchen fireplace. Now, let's read the two sentences together and replace <u>she</u> and <u>her</u> with <u>Cinderella</u>. Do the sentences have the correct meaning? Also, notice how much better the sentences sound when <u>she</u> and <u>her</u> replace <u>Cinderella</u>. These sentences also show that we often need to read the sentences before or after a pronoun to understand what the author means.

Now look at the sentences in number 2. Read the sentences with me. I want you to think through the meaning of the sentences. What word is substituted? (He) Good. Who gave the ball? (The prince) Good. How do you know that <u>he</u> refers to the prince? (Students provide evidence and reasoning.) (Continue with a teacher-led discussion for the sentences in numbers 3 through 5. Add additional sentences if the students do not master this portion of the lesson.)

Teacher: We are now going to read some examples of these pronouns used by authors of the books in our school library. I have written several paragraphs on transparencies. Look at these paragraphs from *Millions of Cats* (Gág, 1928, 1956):

> "But <u>we</u> can never feed them all," said the very old woman, "<u>They</u> will eat <u>us</u> out of house and home."
> "I never thought of that," said the very old man, "What shall <u>we</u> do?"
> The very old woman thought for a while and then <u>she</u> said, "<u>I</u> know! <u>We</u> will let the cats decide which one <u>we</u> shall keep."
> "Oh yes," said the very old man, and <u>he</u> called to the cats, "Which one of <u>you</u> is the prettiest?"
> "<u>I</u> am!"
> "No, <u>I</u> am!" (p. 20 unnumbered)

In the Cinderella example, we discovered that we sometimes have to read sentences before a pronoun or sentences after a pronoun to know what the pronoun means. In this example from *Millions of Cats* we will need to read into the paragraph before we know what the first pronoun means. Read the first sentence with me. What is the first word that is underlined? (We) Good. Can anyone tell me what <u>we</u> refers to? In this example, we need to read beyond the word. Now, let's read the whole selection together. Then, we'll go back and try to identify what each underlined word means. Who can tell me what <u>we</u> means and how you know what <u>we</u> means? (Student response and reasoning) Now who can write the words that mean <u>we</u> on the right place on the transparency? (Student writes <u>woman</u> and <u>man</u> above <u>we</u> on the transparency or on the board if board work is preferred to a transparency.) Good. Now who can read the sentence by replacing <u>we</u> with the words that mean the same as <u>we</u>? (Student response) Good. (Continue with the remainder of the story, stopping at each underlined word to discuss the meaning and to write the word above the pronoun. Reread the total selection to verify the meaning of the underlined words. Discuss how the use of pronouns improves the beauty of the text.)

Teacher-Guided Application

Teacher: We are going to look at different paragraphs taken from library books. The words that you need to identify are underlined. I want you to read the paragraphs, think about the meanings for the pronouns, and write the correct meaning over each underlined word. We'll do the first one together to make sure that we all understand what to do. Then, I want you to do the rest of the sentences by yourself. Be sure to read the whole selection to make sure that your choice makes sense and is accurate. When you are finished, we'll read the paragraphs together and discuss your answers.

The Mother's Day Mice (Eve Bunting, 1986)

Biggest Little Mouse wakened first. It was early in the morning and still almost dark. <u>He</u> tugged gently on the whiskers of Middle Mouse, who slept next to <u>him</u>. "It's Mother's Day," <u>he</u> whispered. "Time to get up and go for our presents."

Middle Mouse tugged gently on the whiskers of Little Mouse, who slept between <u>him</u> and the wall. "Mother's Day," <u>he</u> whispered.

<u>They</u> crept out of bed and tiptoed past Mother's room. (p. 1)

The Man Who Could Call Down Owls (Eve Bunting, 1984)

By day the man worked in <u>his</u> owl barn. There were wings to be mended and legs to be splinted.

"How do <u>you</u> find the owls that need your help?" the boy asked.

The man smiled. "<u>They</u> find me." <u>He</u> held a screech owl. "When an owl is sick and frightened <u>you</u> must hold <u>it</u> firmly. Then <u>it</u> can't hurt <u>itself</u> or <u>you</u>. Always remember that." (p. 7)

(After the students complete this activity independently, conduct a guided discussion of this phase of the lesson. Encourage discussion that looks at the reasons for the replacements as well as at the correct answers.)

Independent Practice

Teacher: We have completed several paragraphs in which authors use pronouns to replace other words in the stories. I have a selection of books in which I want you to find examples of pronouns. When you find an example of a pronoun, write the sentence on your paper. Leave space to write the meaning of the word above the pronoun. We'll share these examples in class tomorrow. Be ready to read your selection to the class and to tell the class what each pronoun means.

Following are examples of books that you may use for this activity:

■ Ann Durell and Marilyn Sachs's *The Big Book for Peace* (1990)
■ Lisa Campbell Ernst's *Ginger Jumps* (1990)
■ Valerie Flournoy's *The Patchwork Quilt* (1985)

- Florence Parry Heide and Judith Heide Gilliland's *The Day of Ahmed's Secret* (1990)
- Pat Hutchins's *What Game Shall We Play?* (1990)
- Emily Arnold McCully's *The Evil Spell* (1990)
- Cynthia Rylant's *Henry and Mudge and the Happy Cat* (1990)
- Jean Van Leeuwen's *Oliver Pig at School* (1990)

REINFORCEMENT ACTIVITY

Develop a cohesive comprehension lesson plan appropriate for older students. To identify an area for instruction, analyze several books written for middle- and upper-elementary students. What cohesive devices do the authors use? For example, Patricia Lauber's 1987 Newbery Honor book *Volcano: The Eruption and Healing of Mount St. Helens* uses the referent "*it*" nine times in the first two paragraphs. "It," however, may refer to volcano, Mount St. Helens, earthquake, rock, molten rock, or magma. The meanings of the referents are clear as long as you read the text carefully.

Include in your lesson plan the following four titles: introduction, direct instruction, teacher-guided application, and independent practice. Whenever appropriate, include modeling in the lesson plan.

GRAMMAR 3 (USAGE)

Language usage concerns the various language standards considered appropriate for different occasions, audiences, and purposes. Usage instruction should help children make proper decisions both in speaking and in writing.

Discussions related to usage generate considerable controversy. According to DeHaven (1983), "the controversy stems from a lack of agreement in (1) defining an acceptable level of usage and (2) setting instructional goals" (p. 69). People make usage choices in response to forces external to the language. Everyone's language varies, depending on the formality of the occasion. For example, you would use words differently when conversing casually or when writing to a friend than you would when presenting a formal speech or when writing a letter of inquiry to a prospective employer.

The number of usage levels differs according to which grammarian is speaking. Lodge and Trett (1968) postulate three levels of usage: (1) nonstandard English, (2) general English, and (3) formal English. Language standards change from one group to another and with time. What was considered almost illiterate a number of years ago may be virtually ignored today; for example, when to use *may* and *can,* or *shall* and *will.* According to Savage (1977), "In the final analysis, the 'correctness' or appropriateness of usage must be judged in the social context in which the language is used" (p. 369). Elementary schools usually design usage instruction to help children move from one usage situation to another because different levels are appropriate for different audiences and purposes. Instead of teaching that some form is incorrect, modern usage instruction stresses appropriateness for

Crossword puzzles can be tools for helping students apply their knowledge of grammar, especially identifying how affixes change the part of speech or form classes of words.

certain purposes and audiences. Modern usage instruction, then, is flexible, and tries to increase the range of levels of usage available to children.

Tiedt and Tiedt (1975) recommend that "we teach educated forms of standard English without undue stress on picayune points that really achieve little" (p. 30). What are these educated forms of English? According to Kean and Personke (1976), "among the many attempts to sort out the more important usage 'violations' for teachers who guide children's language development, perhaps the most noteworthy to date is a list of twenty-five goals for elementary language instruction prepared by English educator Robert Pooley" (p. 290). Pooley compiled his list in 1960 and warned at the time that some of the goals would eventually require modification. Read and decide which are still valuable for classroom usage:

1. The elimination of all baby talk and "cute" expressions.
2. The correct uses in speech and writing of *I, me, he, him, she, her, they, them.* (Exception: It's me.)
3. The correct uses of *is, are, was, were,* with respect to number and tense.
4. Correct past tense of common irregular verbs such as *saw, took, brought, bought, stuck.*
5. Correct uses of past participles of the same verbs and similar verbs after auxiliaries.

6. Elimination of the double negative: "We don't have no apples," etc.
7. Elimination of analogical forms: *ain't, hisn, hern, ourn, theirselves,* etc.
8. Correct use of possessive pronouns: *my, mine, his, hers, theirs, ours.*
9. Mastery of the distinction between *its,* possessive pronoun, and *it's, it is.*
10. Placement of *have* or its phonetic reduction to *ve* between *I* and a past participle.
11. Elimination of *them* as a demonstrative pronoun.
12. Elimination of *this here* and *that there.*
13. Mastery of use of *a* and *an* as articles.
14. Correct use of personal pronouns in compound constructions: as subject (Mark and I), as object (Mary and me), and object of preposition (to Mary and me).
15. The use of *we* before an appositional noun when subject; *us* when object.
16. Correct number agreement with the phrases *there is, there are, there was, there were.*
17. Elimination of *he don't, she don't, it don't.*
18. Elimination of *learn* for *teach, leave* for *let.*
19. Elimination of pleonastic (redundant) subjects: *my brother he, my mother she, that fellow he.*
20. Proper agreement in number with antecedent pronouns *one, anyone, everyone, each, no one.* With *everybody* and *none* some tolerance of number seems acceptable now.
21. The use of *who* and *whom* as references to persons. (But note, "Who did he give it to?" is tolerated in all but very formal situations. In the latter, "To whom did he give it?" is preferable.
22. Accurate use of *said* in reporting the words of a speaker in the past.
23. Correction of *lay down* to *lie down.*
24. The distinction between *good* as adjective and *well* as adverb: "He spoke well."
25. Elimination of *can't hardly, all the farther* (for "as far as") and *Where is he (she, it) at?"*

In addition, Pooley listed eight items that are no longer considered "incorrect," and that may even be in quite general use:

1. Any distinction between *shall* and *will.*
2. Any reference to the split infinitive.
3. Elimination of *like* as a conjunction.
4. Objection to the phrase "different than."
5. Objection to "He is one of those boys who is . . . "
6. Objection to "the reason . . . is because . . . "
7. Objection to *myself* as a polite substitute for *me,* as in "I understand you will meet Mrs. Jones and myself at the station."
8. Insistence upon the possessive case standing before a gerund.[1]

Assessment

To evaluate usage, look at a child's ability to use appropriate forms of grammar according to occasion, audience, and purpose. Listen to the child's speech in several different situations and analyze the writing that the child produces for various purposes. An informal checklist (see, for example, Figure 8–2) may be the most valuable evaluation guide. Base your checklist on the understanding and demonstrated use of several levels of usage and on Pooley's list of appropriate usage for classrooms.

---

[1] From Robert Pooley, "Dare Schools Set a Standard in English Usage?" *English Journal* 49 (March 1960): 176. Copyright © 1960 by the National Council of Teachers of English. Reprinted by permission of the publisher.

Name_____

Grade_____

	Yes	Some-times	No
1. Understands that there is more than one level of appropriate usage	___	___	___
2. Is able to change level of spoken usage according to occasion, audience, and purpose	___	___	___
3. Is able to change level of written usage according to occasion, audience, and purpose	___	___	___
4. Has eliminated baby talk	___	___	___
5. Uses correct form of *I, me, he, him, she, they, them*	___	___	___
6. Uses correct form of *is, are, was, were*	___	___	___
7. Uses correct past tense of irregular verbs	___	___	___
8. Uses correct past participle	___	___	___
9. Does not use double negative	___	___	___
10. Does not use *ain't, hisn, hern,* etc.	___	___	___
11. Uses correct possessive pronouns	___	___	___
12. Uses *it's* and *its* correctly	___	___	___
13. Does not use *them* as a demonstrative pronoun	___	___	___
14. Does not use *this here* and *that there*	___	___	___
15. Uses *a* and *an* correctly	___	___	___
16. Uses correct personal pronouns in compound constructions	___	___	___
17. Uses *we* (subject) and *us* (object) correctly	___	___	___
18. Does not use *he don't, she don't, it don't*	___	___	___
19. Uses number agreement in *there is, there are, there was, there were*	___	___	___
20. Uses *learn* and *teach* and *leave* and *let* correctly	___	___	___
21. Does not use *my brother he,* etc.	___	___	___
22. Uses proper agreement with antecedent pronouns	___	___	___
23. Uses *said* in past tense	___	___	___
24. Uses *good* as adjective and *well* as adverb	___	___	___
25. Most critical usage problems are:			

_____

_____

_____

FIGURE 8–2
Informal checklist for usage

Instruction

Instruction in usage usually emphasizes that there are several appropriate levels of usage for oral or written communications depending on the purposes and the audiences. For example, what is appropriate on the playground may not be appropriate when addressing the principal or mayor, or when writing a formal letter requesting a job interview. Activities such as role playing, inductive teaching of usage, and analyzing levels of usage exemplified by characters in books or on television help students improve their understanding of usage.

Role playing   Role-playing activities can help children improve their understanding of various levels of usage. Role playing also allows children opportunities to think about and discuss the roles of speaker or writer, audience, and subject matter in regard to appropriate levels of usage. You and the students can suggest a number of situations requiring different levels of usage. A middle- or upper-elementary class might try the following roles:

1. Jerry's friend Jimmy has joined a neighborhood softball team. Jimmy has invited Jerry to go with him to meet the team, because the team needs a pitcher. Jerry wants them to accept him as the newest member of the team. Pretend Jerry and Jimmy are talking on their way to a vacant lot or park. Make up the conversation that might occur between Jimmy, Jerry, and the rest of the team.
2. You have just found out that your school will have a science fair. The winner of the science fair will receive a microscope that you have wanted for a long time. In addition, the winner will represent the school in the regional science fair. You have an idea for a project and want to talk about it with the science teacher. You want to convince him that you have thought about your ideas, and you want him to give you some additional out-of-school help.

After role playing, have the students discuss the appropriateness of the communication according to subject matter and audience. What are the consequences of an inappropriate level of usage?

Inductive teaching   Inductive approaches that help children analyze their problems are more helpful than isolated drills, in which the children merely underline choices on a worksheet. As an example, look at a lesson built around one of the appropriate usages recommended by Pooley—the correct use of *is, are, was,* and *were* in number agreement (singular and plural) and tense (present tense, past tense).

FOR YOUR PLAN BOOK

An Inductive Approach to **Was** and **Were**— *Singular and Plural Forms in Past Tense*

First, write the following sentences on the chalkboard:

1. Carol *was* at the movie last night.
2. Jane and Julie *were* also at the movie last night.

3. They *were* at the movie together.
4. Jim *was* at home last night.
5. I *was* also at home.
6. We *were* at home together.
7. You *were* at the park.

Next, read the sentences (use numbers 1–6 first) to the students, asking them to listen carefully. Then ask the students to read the sentences to you. Now, tell the students to look carefully at the underlined words in sentences 1–6. Then ask, "When did the activity in each sentence take place?" The students should conclude that it was last night, which is in the past, and not something that is happening right now, in the present. Next ask, "How many people were in each of the sentences?" The students should conclude that sentences 1, 4, and 5 concern one person, and that sentences 2, 3, and 6 concern more than one person. Write just this portion of each sentence on the board, in two columns:

One Person	*More Than One Person*
Carol *was*	Jane and Julie *were*
Jim *was*	They *were*
I *was*	We *were*

Now, ask the students if they can think of a guiding suggestion to help them remember when to use *was* and when to use *were.* They will usually produce a generalization like this:

> When we are talking about something that happened in the past, we use *was* if we are talking about one person and we use *were* if we are talking about more than one person.

Now, ask the students to look at sentence 7. "Does this sentence follow our guide? What is wrong?" The students should conclude that the word *you* refers to only one person, but uses *were* in the past tense as if the word *you* referred to more than one person. Ask the students where to place the sentence on the list. They will usually suggest that, because it is an exception, placing it in a third column will help them remember. Now, ask if there is anything the students need to add to their guiding rule. The fact that *were* follows the word *you* can be added as an exception. Finally, ask the students to create additional sentences that conform to the same patterns. Remember that they will need frequent opportunities to practice with oral and written activities rather than with worksheet drills.

Analyzing usage in literature   What levels of usage are exemplified by characters in literature or on television? Are the levels formal or informal? Do characters change their level of usage depending on their purposes and audiences? Use tape-recorded examples from television to show various levels of usage. Older students may make discoveries about changing levels of usage by comparing books written during different time periods. For example, students might compare the language usage in contemporary writings of such authors as Betsy Byars, Barbara Corcoran, and Walter Dean Myers with language usage in the classic writings of Frances Hodgson Burnett, Kenneth Grahame, and Lucy M. Montgomery.

REINFORCEMENT ACTIVITY

Select one of the recommendations for classroom usage on pages 296–301. Develop an inductive lesson (on something other than *was* and *were*) that will help children understand the usage level. Also, provide suggestions for ways of reinforcing the lesson.

THE MECHANICS OF WRITING

The mechanics of writing includes punctuation and capitalization. Remember, as with other aspects of composition, children learn punctuation and capitalization most effectively in conjunction with meaningful writing activities.

Hodges (1991) emphasizes the need for writers to be familiar with graphic features, such as punctuation, segmentation, and capitalization: "Punctuation sets apart syntactic units, and provides intonational cues and semantic information. Segmentation (the spaces between words in print) identifies word boundaries. In conjunction with periods, capital letters have both semantic and syntactic uses in indicating proper names and sentence boundaries" (p. 779).

Punctuation

Punctuation is important because it clarifies meaning. During oral interchanges, listeners hear signals—pauses, speech stops, rising and falling voice tones—that help them comprehend meaning. Writers replace these vocal signals with punctuation. The early activities in which children dictate short stories or sentences to place under pictures provide readiness for and instruction in punctuation.

Studies show that punctuation—particularly with commas and periods—is frequently a problem for elementary-age children (Hazlett, 1972; Porter, 1974). The punctuation usually taught in the elementary grades is listed in Table 8–1.

REINFORCEMENT ACTIVITY

Look at a scope-and-sequence chart in a language arts textbook. Make a punctuation chart to use with a specific elementary-school level. Design your chart to show the signal given by the punctuation mark and its placement. For example, you might finish the following chart:

Name	*Example*	*Signal*	*Where Used*
Period		Come to a full stop	At the end of a sentence that tells something

TABLE 8–1

Punctuation taught in elementary grades

Punctuation Rule	Example
1. A period is used at the end of a sentence.	1. We went to the zoo.
2. A period is used after numbers on a list.	2. 1. Show and Tell 2. Reading
3. A period is used after abbreviations.	3. Sun. Mon. Tues. Mr. Mrs.
4. A question mark is used after a sentence that asks a question.	4. What was the name of Billy's dog?
5. A comma is placed between the day of the month and the year.	5. Today is October 1, 1980.
6. A comma is used between the names of a city and a state.	6. We live in Ithaca, New York.
7. A comma is used after the salutation in a letter.	7. Dear Sandy,
8. A comma is used after the closing of a letter.	8. Your friend, Jimmy
9. Commas divide items in a list.	9. Susan brought an acorn, a colored maple leaf, and an ear of Indian corn.
10. A comma is used before a coordinating conjunction (upper elementary).	10. He wanted to eat the whole pie, but he knew he would be sick.
11. A comma is used to signal the subject of the sentence (upper elementary).	11. Even though the day was hot, we all decided to go on a picnic.
12. A comma is used when a slight interruption offers additional information (upper elementary).	12. Jim Black, our basketball coach, is a very nice man.
13. A comma is used between two equal adjectives that modify the noun (upper elementary).	13. That swimmer is a strong, healthy athlete.
14. An exclamation mark follows a statement of excitement.	14. Help! Help! Jimmy is chasing me with a snake!
15. An apostrophe shows that letters have been omitted in a contraction.	15. I will = I'll
16. An apostrophe is used to show possession.	16. This is Judy's basketball.

Learning about punctuation can be fun.

Capitalization

Capitalization is another signal that clarifies meaning. Writers signal the beginning of a sentence with a capital letter and the end of a sentence with a period, question mark, or exclamation mark. Writers also signal important titles and names by capitalization. If a writer capitalizes Northeast, he or she is referring to a specific section of the country; if the writer does not capitalize northeast, the reference is to a direction.

Most children seem to have fewer problems applying capitalization rules than applying punctuation rules. The National Assessment of Educational Progress concluded: ''Capitalization errors tended to appear less frequently in the 9-year-old papers than most of the other kinds of errors'' (Hazlett, 1972, p. 12). The National Assessment found that most high-quality papers were free of capitalization errors; this was also true of middle-quality papers. The low-quality papers were, however, inconsistent; the first word in a sentence was often left uncapitalized, and many common nouns, such as *deer* and *tree,* were capitalized. The judges concluded that children who wrote the low-quality papers had some idea of when

TABLE 8–2
Capitalization taught in elementary grades

Capitalization Rule	Example
1. Capitalize the first word in a sentence.	1. The first grade is planning a puppet show.
2. Capitalize the first and last names of people.	2. Sandy Smith
3. Capitalize the pronoun "I".	3. I do not think I will go.
4. Capitalize the name of a street.	4. Our school is on Southwest Parkway.
5. Capitalize the name of the city and state.	5. We live in San Francisco, California.
6. Capitalize the names of months, days, holidays.	6. Today is Monday, June 1. Christmas Hanukkah
7. Capitalize the first word and other important words in titles.	7. We are reading A Snowy Day.
8. Capitalize a title such as Mr., Mrs., Miss, or Ms.	8. Our teacher is Mrs. Chandler.
9. Capitalize the greeting in a letter.	9. Dear Martin,
10. Capitalize the first word in the closing of a letter.	10. Your friend,
11. Capitalize the titles of persons (upper elementary).	11. Doctor Erickson General Washington
12. Capitalize all cities, states, countries, continents, and oceans (upper elementary).	12. United States North America Pacific Ocean
13. Capitalize proper adjectives (upper elementary).	13. French
14. Capitalize the names of organizations (upper elementary).	14. Girl Scouts Boy Scouts
15. Capitalize the names of sections of the country but not directions (upper elementary)	15. The Northeast has many large cities. Lake Superior is northeast of Minneapolis.
16. Capitalize words referring to the Bible and the Deity (upper elementary).	16. The Bible God

to use capitals and when not to, but their ideas were incomplete. It thus appears that most children learn about and apply appropriate capitalization in their writing, while a few will require more concentrated assistance.

Introduce children to capitalization in their early, dictated stories. A teacher who writes a sentence on the board or chart can point out the capital letter at the beginning of each sentence. When writing names of people, cities, states, or holidays, teachers can again indicate the importance of the capital letter. Capitalization rules usually taught in the elementary grades are listed in Table 8–2.

Instruction

Both punctuation and capitalization clarify written communication. Children need to understand why mechanical skills are necessary, but they must also be aware that writing is primarily concerned with the development of content and ideas. In this context, punctuation and capitalization are very important during the editing process.

How can you maintain balance without overemphasizing one aspect of writing to the detriment of the other? Kean and Personke (1976) offer three general guidelines for instruction in mechanics:

1. Several of the mechanics of written language are learned as children write, read, and observe, making formal classroom presentations unnecessary in many cases. Students who did not naturally learn them may require individual help.

2. Individual variation in readiness makes it likely that learning will be most efficient when instruction is conducted among small groups of children who are at similar stages of readiness. [This means small-group instruction of children who demonstrate similar needs, rather than whole-class instruction.]

3. Instruction in mechanics needs to begin and culminate in a real writing situation; if isolated practice is necessary, it should be in the intermediate learning stage.[2]

If you follow these guidelines, you will call the children's attention to various punctuation and capitalization items as they encounter them in reading or in dictating charts and stories. This provides readiness for a skill they will need in writing and may enable some children to apply the skill accurately in their own writing. For example, many children are able to begin sentences with capital letters and end them with periods after a teacher has pointed out these mechanics during frequent language experience activities. Some children, however, require additional direct teaching of these skills before they can apply them consistently. When direct teaching is necessary, it should take place in groups, with children who show the same readiness or need for a new or reviewed skill. Table 8–3 shows one method for teaching the separation of words in series with a comma.

Activities

Some children need visual assistance with punctuation and capitalization. Charts that show various writing conventions are helpful. For example, use the colors of traffic signals to mark sentences written on charts. Mark the capital letters at the beginning of sentences, which also signal go, in green; commas, signaling a short pause, in yellow; and periods at the end of sentences, signaling stop, in red.

Let children work with a paragraph written without punctuation, without capitalization, or without both punctuation and capitalization (depending on ability level). As you read the paragraph, ask the children to mark the punctuation according to the verbal signals of your voice.

Upper-elementary children can take dictation from kindergarten and first-grade children. To produce a short, written story that expresses what the younger child means, the older child will have to supply appropriate punctuation and cap-

---

[2] From John M. Kean and Carl Personke, *The Language Arts: Teaching and Learning in the Elementary School* (New York: St. Martin's Press, 1976). Reprinted by permission.

TABLE 8–3
Steps in instruction for "a comma separates words in series"

Guideline	Example
1. Call attention to the rule in reading or dictated stories.	1. Find sentences that contain words in series in reading. Point them out in language experience. Example: Oranges, grapefruit, and lemons grow in Florida.
2. Observe a mechanical need in an actual writing situation.	2. Students are writing series of words without using the appropriate punctuation.
3. Develop individual or small-group instruction designed to eliminate the problem.	3. Have the students read four or five sentences with words in series. Ask the students to inductively state the rule. Write new sentences on chalkboard without commas. Have the students put in the commas, using colored chalk. Reinforce the principle with games.
4. Assign a real writing task that requires application of the skill.	4. "Write a sentence telling us what you had for breakfast." "Write a sentence listing the members of your family."
5. Observe to see if the mechanical problem has been eliminated.	5. Observe future writing. Are the students using the skill? If not, provide further direct teaching.

italization signals. The older child should then read the selection back to make sure the meaning is what the younger child intended.

Proofreading symbols are often effective with upper-elementary students. Ask someone connected with a newspaper to talk to the children and show them proofreading symbols. Children are usually impressed to learn that adult writers also need to proofread and correct their writing before it is published in a paper. Children can also create their own classroom proofreading symbols, or use the standard symbols, which can be found in a dictionary.

Ideas for Teachers from Teachers: Elementary Language Arts published by the National Council of Teachers of English (1983) describes several activities developed by classroom teachers. For example, you can make punctuation pins from clip-on clothespins. (Paint a punctuation mark on each clothespin.) Print sentences without punctuation on tagboard strips. Ask the children to clamp the correct clothespin markers, in the correct locations, onto the sentences. Another effective activity is based on dialogue created to accompany pictures students bring to class. Each student brings a picture of a character, teams with another student, creates dialogue between the pictured characters, and transcribes the resulting dialogue.

REINFORCEMENT ACTIVITY

1. Identify a mechanics-of-writing need, such as use of quotation marks or capitalization of proper nouns. Design a small-group instructional activity for appropriate use of that skill.
2. Design a writing-mechanics game that reinforces understanding of a punctuation or capitalization rule.
3. Develop a proofreading lesson for use with older-elementary children. You may wish to refer to the "Proofreading" unit in the spelling chapter. Use a similar approach for introducing the proofreading of punctuation or capitalization.

MAINSTREAMING

Grammar, usage, and mechanics are not ends in themselves. As with handwriting, the major purpose is effective communication. All students need many opportunities to use language in meaningful context. This is especially true for mainstreamed children who have difficulty using syntactic information and generalizing limited grammatical knowledge in a variety of settings. If children demonstrate restricted language ability and vocabulary development, give them many meaningful learning opportunities designed to broaden their language experiences. Table 8–4 presents characteristics of learning disabled children that might interfere with learning grammar and suggests techniques for language arts instruction. Table 8–5 presents the same information for mentally handicapped children.

SUMMARY

This chapter discusses a three-part definition of grammar: grammar 1, a set of formal patterns; grammar 2, the linguistic science concerned with description, analysis, and formalization of formal language patterns; and grammar 3, the use of language according to language standards for different occasions, audiences, and purposes.

Grammar 2 includes the various systems developed to describe and analyze sentence patterns and to classify words, and it is the grammar taught in most school systems. Traditional grammar is prescriptive; it provides a series of rules for constructing sentences and for classifying parts of speech. In contrast, structural grammar is descriptive; it describes words according to form classes, and describes sentence patterns or positions of words in sentences. Transformational grammar is built on the work of the structuralists but extends grammar into the meaning of language. Whereas structural grammar is concerned primarily with syntax, transformational grammar is concerned primarily with semantics and the generating of sentences. The term *transformational* refers to the division of sentences into kernel sentences and the transforms, or variations, that can be developed from these basic sentences.

Grammar instruction should expand a child's understanding of language; consequently, the best aspects of the newer grammars are often included in instructional programs. Activities using linguistic blocks, cloze sentences, sentence

TABLE 8–4

Mainstreaming and grammar for learning disabled children

Characteristics of Learning Disabled Children	Teaching Techniques for Language Arts Instruction
1. Deficit in use of grammatical form class and syntactic information (Fay, Trupin, & Townes, 1981; Henderson & Shores, 1982).	1. Have students read aloud materials in which words ending in *ed* and *ing* are underlined. Have the pupils chart errors, identify correct forms necessary to complete sentences (Henderson & Shores, 1982). Provide systematic training in the arrangement of inflectional forms of verbs (Cartelli, 1980). Prepare activities developed around generative-transformational grammar and context (Knott, 1979). Generate transformations of kernel sentences and encourage children to experiment with sentence-pattern variations. Encourage many meaningful oral language activities, such as role playing, show and tell, puppetry, choral speaking, interviewing, and storytelling (Lerner, 1976).
2. Disability in comprehending information signaled by grammatical morphemes (McClure, Kalk, & Keenan, 1980).	2. Emphasize comprehension available through function words, word endings, and word stem changes (McClure, Kalk, & Keenan, 1980). Use pictures to help build morphological generalizations (Lerner, 1976).

transformations, sentence scrambling, changing word order, sentence expansion, sentence combining, open-response exercises, and cohesive devices help develop understanding of language and improve spoken and written grammar.

Grammar 3, or usage, refers to appropriate choices of words, phrases, and sentences. Usage deals with attitudes and language standards rather than meaning. Consequently, a level of usage appropriate for one subject and audience might not be appropriate for another. Instead of teaching that a particular form is incorrect, modern usage instruction stresses appropriateness for certain purposes and audiences, and helps children increase their range of usage.

Instruction in usage helps children understand that there is more than one level of usage, although one level may be more appropriate for a specific occasion. Activities such as role playing help develop this understanding. Inductive approaches help children understand and apply a classroom level of usage. Modern usage instruction helps children move appropriately from one usage situation to another.

The mechanics of writing, including capitalization and punctuation, relate to the understanding of language and grammar. Both capitalization and punctuation are signals that help readers understand written communication.

TABLE 8–5
Mainstreaming and grammar for mentally handicapped children

Characteristics of Mentally Handicapped Children	Teaching Techniques for Language Arts Instruction
1. Below-average language ability, restricted vocabulary (Gearheart, Weishahn, & Gearheart, 1992).	1. Provide many opportunities to broaden language experience. Provide structured, concretely oriented experiences consistent with the students' interests and level of language development (Gearheart, Weishahn, & Gearheart, 1992). Help the children develop sentence sense through easy reading materials, listening activities, and reading their writing orally (Otto & Smith, 1980). Provide opportunities to improve language clarity by rearranging grammatical elements, deleting grammatical elements, substituting grammatical elements, and adding grammatical elements (Otto & Smith, 1980).
2. Difficulty generalizing and conceptualizing in a variety of settings (Gearheart, Weishahn, & Gearheart, 1992).	2. Provide many opportunities for functional writing. Diagram letter formats and establish a classroom post office to encourage using writing and punctuation skills (Cohen & Plaskon, 1980).

ADDITIONAL GRAMMAR AND USAGE ACTIVITIES

1. Locate language arts/English textbooks that represent each of the major philosophies of grammar: traditional, structural, and transformational. Identify sentence-combining activities located in each text. Compare the similarities and differences found in the sentence-combining activities. Why might the activities differ according to the philosophy?

2. Locate several language arts/English journals such as *Language Arts, Research in the Teaching of English,* and *College English.* Read any journal articles pertaining to grammar. What are the issues and concerns? Do these issues and concerns vary according to the audience for the journal?

3. Develop a lesson plan that allows children to experiment with sentence-pattern variations and understand that various sentence patterns are possible and beneficial when writing.

4. Develop a lesson plan that develops ability to expand sentences.

5. Tape-record several examples of children's oral language. Listen for the levels of usage. Are the children able to vary their levels of usage depending on their audience and purpose? What instructional strategies, if any, would you recommend?

BIBLIOGRAPHY

Baele, Ernest R. *The Effect of Primary Reading Programs Emphasizing Language Structure as Related to Meaning upon Children's Written Language Achievement at Third Grade Level.* Doctoral dissertation, University of California, Berkeley, 1968.

Baker, C. L. *English Syntax.* Cambridge, Mass.: MIT Press, 1989.

Bauman, James, and Stevenson, Jennifer. "Teaching Students to Comprehend Anaphoric Relations." In *Understanding and Teaching Cohesion Comprehension,* edited by Judith W. Irwin. Newark, Del.: International Reading Association, 1986.

Cartelli, Lora M. "Reading Comprehension: A Matter of Referents." *Academic Therapy* 15 (March 1980): 421–30.

Chomsky, Noam. *Syntactic Structures.* The Hague: Mouton & Co., 1957.

Cohen, Sandra B., and Plaskon, Stephen P. *Language Arts for the Mildly Handicapped.* Columbus, Oh.: Merrill Publishing Co., 1980.

Cox, B. E.; Shanahan, T.; and Sulzby, E. "Good and Poor Readers' Use of Cohesion in Writing." *Reading Research Quarterly* 25 (1990): 47–65.

DeHaven, Edna P. *Teaching and Learning the Language Arts.* Boston: Little, Brown & Co., 1983.

Fay, Gayle; Trupin, Eric; and Townes, Brenda D. "The Young Disabled Reader: Acquisition Strategies and Associated Deficits." *Journal of Learning Disabilities* 14 (January 1981): 32–35.

Francis, W. Nelson. "Revolution in Grammar." In *Readings in Applied English Linguistics.* 2d ed., edited by Harold Allen. New York: Appleton-Century-Crofts, 1964.

Gearheart, Bill R.; Weishahn, Mel; and Gearheart, Carol J. *The Exceptional Student in the Regular Classroom.* 5th ed. New York: Merrill/Macmillan, 1992.

Goodman, Ralph. "Transformational Grammar." In *An Introductory English Grammar,* edited by Norman Stageburg. New York: Holt, Rinehart & Winston, 1965.

Hartwell, P. "Grammar, Grammars, and the Teaching of Grammar." *College English* 47 (1985):105–127.

Hazlett, James A. *A National Assessment of Educational Progress. Report 8, Writing: National Results.* Washington, D.C.: U.S. Government Printing Office, 1972.

Henderson, Ann J., and Shores, Richard E. "How Learning Disabled Students' Failure to Attend to Suffixes Affects Their Oral Reading Performance." *Journal of Learning Disabilities* 15 (March 1982): 178–82.

Hillocks, George, Jr. *Research on Written Composition: New Directions for Teaching.* Urbana, Ill.: ERIC Clearinghouse on Reading and Communication Skills and the National Conference on Research in English, 1986.

———, and Smith, M. W. "Grammar and Usage." In *Handbook of Research on Teaching the English Language Arts,* edited by J. Flood, J. Jensen, D. Lapp, and J. Squire. New York: Macmillan, 1991, pp. 591–603.

Hirsch, E. D. "Some Principles of Composition from Grade School to Grad School." In *The English Curriculum under Fire: What Are the Real Basics?,* edited by George Hillocks. Urbana, Ill.: National Council of Teachers of English, 1982, pp. 39–52.

Hodges, R. "The Conventions of Writing." In *Handbook of Research on Teaching the English Language Arts,* edited by J. Flood, J. Jensen, D. Lapp, and J. Squire. New York: Macmillan, 1991, pp. 775–86.

Hunt, Kellogg, and O'Donnell, Roy. *An Elementary School Curriculum to Develop Better Writing Skills.* Washington, D.C.: U.S. Department of Health, Education, and Welfare, Bureau of Research, 1970.

Kean, John M., and Personke, Carl. *The Language Arts, Teaching and Learning in the Elementary School.* New York: St. Martin's Press, 1976.

Knott, Gladys P. "Developing Reading Potential in Black Remedial High School Freshmen." *Reading Improvement* 16 (Winter 1979): 262–69.

Krashen, Stephen D. *Writing: Research, Theory, and Applications.* Oxford: Pergamon Press, 1984.

Lamb, Pose. *Linguistics in Proper Perspective.* 2d ed. Columbus, Oh.: Merrill Publishing Co., 1977.

Lerner, Janet. *Children with Learning Disabilities.* 2d ed. Boston: Houghton Mifflin Co., 1976.

Lodge, Helen C., and Trett, Gerald L. *New Ways in English.* Englewood Cliffs, N.J.: Prentice-Hall, 1968.

Mackie, B. C. *The Effects of a Sentence-Combining Program on the Reading Comprehension and Written Composition of Fourth-Grade Students.* Doctoral Dissertation, Hofstra University, 1982 (University Microfilms No. DA 8207744)

McClure, Judith; Kalk, Michael; and Keenan, Verne. "Use of Grammatical Morphemes by Beginning Readers." *Journal of Learning Disabilities* 13 (May 1980): 34–49.

Mellon, John. *The Basic Sentence Types and Their Simple Transforms.* Culver, Ind.: Culver Military Academy, 1964.

———. *Transformational Sentence Combining: A Method for Enhancing the Development of Syntactic Fluency in English Composition.* Champaign, Ill.: National Conference of Teachers of English, 1969.

Moe, Alden J., and Irwin, Judith W. "Cohesion, Coherence, and Comprehension," in *Understanding and Teaching Cohesion,* edited by Judith W. Irwin. Newark, Del.: International Reading Association, 1986.

National Council of Teachers of English. *Ideas for Teachers from Teachers: Elementary Language Arts.* Urbana, Ill.: National Council of Teachers of English, 1983.

O'Hare, Frank. *Sentence Combining: Improving Student Writing without Formal Grammatical Instruction.* Urbana, Ill.: National Council of Teachers of English, 1973.

Otto, Wayne, and Smith, Richard J. *Corrective and Remedial Teaching.* Boston: Houghton Mifflin Co., 1980.

Pooley, Robert. "Dare Schools Set a Standard in English Usage?" *English Journal* 49 (March 1960): 176–81.

Porter, Jane. "Research Report." *Elementary English* 51 (January 1974): 144–51.

Roberts, Paul. *English Sentences.* New York: Harcourt Brace Jovanovich, 1962.

Savage, John F. *Effective Communication.* Chicago: Science Research Associates, 1977.

Stoddard, E. P. "The Combined Effect of Creative Thinking and Sentence-Combining Activities on the Writing Ability of Above Average Ability Fifth and Sixth Grade Students." Doctoral Dissertation, University of Connecticut, 1982. *Dissertation Abstracts International,* 1982. (University Microfilms No. DA 821 3235)

Stotsky, Sandra L. "Research on Reading/Writing Relationships: A Synthesis and Suggested Directions." *Language Arts* 60 (1983): 627–42.

Strong, William. *Creative Approaches to Sentence Combining.* Urbana, Ill.: National Council of Teachers of English, 1986.

Tiedt, Iris, and Tiedt, Sidney. *Contemporary English in the Elementary School.* Englewood Cliffs, N.J.: Prentice-Hall, 1975.

CHILDREN'S LITERATURE REFERENCES

Bunting, Eve. *The Man Who Could Call Down Owls.* Illustrated by Charles Mikolaycak. New York: Macmillan Co., 1984.

———— . *The Mother's Day Mice.* Illustrated by Jan Brett. New York: Clarion, 1986.

Durell, Ann, and Sachs, Marilyn, edited by. *The Big Book for Peace.* New York: Dutton, 1990.

Ernst, Lisa Campbell. *Ginger Jumps.* New York: Bradbury, 1990.

Flournoy, Valerie. *The Patchwork Quilt.* Illustrated by Jerry Pinkney. New York: Dial Press, 1985.

Gág, Wanda. *Millions of Cats.* New York: Coward-McCann, 1928, 1956.

Heide, Florence Parry, and Gilliland, Judith Heide. *The Day of Ahmed's Secret.* Illustrated by Ted Lewin. New York: Lothrop, Lee & Shepard, 1990.

Hutchins, Pat. *What Game Shall We Play?* New York: Greenwillow, 1990.

Lauber, Patricia. *Volcano: The Eruption and Healing of Mount St. Helens.* New York: Bradbury, 1986.

McCully, Emily Arnold. *The Evil Spell.* New York: Harper & Row, 1990.

Rylant, Cynthia. *Henry and Mudge and the Happy Cat.* Illustrated by Sucie Stevenson. New York: Bradbury, 1990.

Van Leeuwen, Jean. *Oliver Pig at School.* Illustrated by Ann Schweninger. New York: Dial, 1990.

Wexler, Jerome, *From Spore to Spore: Ferns and How They Grow.* New York: Dodd, Mead & Co., 1985.

Chapter Nine

After completing the chapter on composition, you will be able to:

1. *Discuss several viewpoints on the teaching of writing.*
2. *Describe the theoretical bases for the writing process.*
3. *Identify classroom procedures related to the processing approach to writing.*
4. *Describe and develop prewriting activities.*
5. *Describe and develop activities that focus on writing the first draft.*
6. *Describe and develop activities that focus on revision.*
7. *Describe and develop methods for evaluating writing.*

Composition: The Writing Process

W ritten composition is receiving increasing attention in research studies and in nontechnical publications as well. For example, Hillocks's (1986) text *Research on Written Composition: New Directions for Teaching* reviews research studies, selects the most effective approaches to teaching writing, and adds strategies for teaching within the writing process. Professional organizations such as the National Council of Teachers of English are publishing texts that examine the role of teachers in the writing process, the various stages in the process, and activities to help improve writing.

Some writing improvements are so spectacular that newspapers are providing detailed coverage. For example, the *Dallas Morning News* (Kruh, 1988) proudly reported that elementary students significantly improved their writing through an approach called RADAR writing. Using this approach, teachers introduce specific ways to approach various writing tasks, teach transitions in development, provide guidance during independent writing, and encourage students to share their writing with peers who provide critical feedback and incentive to revise and improve their writing. The article included interviews with teachers and students, examples of students' writing, and test results.

This chapter and Chapter 10 explore the writing process and develop activities that enhance the writing of children. These two chapters consider the development of narrative, expository, descriptive, and persuasive writing. Chapter 9 focuses on the writing process and outlines each of the steps in detail. In addition, it discusses assessment of composition, research on effective modes of instruction, teacher–pupil and peer-editing-group conferencing, and sharing of students' work. Chapter 10 deals with specific strategies that are useful for children in the upper grades. Expressive, imaginative, and expository writing are featured.

According to the National Council of Teachers of English (1983), students should learn to write clearly and honestly; to recognize that writing is a way to learn and develop personally, as well as a way to communicate with others; to find ways to generate ideas for writing, select and arrange them, express them in appropriate ways, and evaluate and revise what they have written; to adapt expression to various audiences; to master techniques to make their writing appealing and persuasive; to develop their talents for creative and imaginative expression; and to recognize that precision in punctuation, capitalization, spelling, and other elements of manuscript form is part of the total effectiveness of writing. Careful analysis of these recommendations suggests both demands for numerous competencies and requirements for varied writing experiences.

VIEWPOINTS

There is no one favored approach to teaching writing. Some educators recommend approaches that emphasize the process of writing, whereas others recommend those that emphasize the goals of writing. Applebee (1984) argues for an approach that considers both the process and the resulting products of writing: "We must develop models of writing that more explicitly take account of topic knowledge and of interaction between the writing process and the goals of the writing event. The separation of process and product, though perhaps a needed step in the development of our research, seems now to be a major stumbling block to future progress" (p. 591).

Following a review of the findings gained from the National Writing Project, Myers and Gray (1983) state that teachers use writing activities that include processing (problem-solving that includes specific stages, such as prewriting, writing, and postwriting), modeling (imitating written samples); and distancing (focusing on the relationships between writer and subject and between writer and audience). Effective writing practices frequently include elements from processing, modeling, and distancing. According to Myers and Gray,

> writing to an audience has both a processing function (the words often flow more easily in social interaction) and a distancing function. Imitation of texts has a modeling function (the student is modeling the pattern in the text) and a distancing function (the student is adopting a particular point of view). The best classroom techniques probably include all three approaches. Writing groups and a classroom publication program are two ways to combine approaches. Both techniques encourage discussion of the ideas (processing), provide an actual audience that one can study (distancing), and generate a variety of student models that other students can imitate (modeling). (p. 43)

It is interesting to note that the most effective mode of instruction identified by Hillocks (1986) accounts for topic knowledge and interaction between the writing process and the goals of the writing event. This effective mode may also include components from processing, modeling, and distancing.

Hillocks's comprehensive review of research on composition is one of the most frequently cited studies related to effective approaches and implications for the types of activities that should be included in the writing process. A brief review of Hillocks's findings illustrates the importance of many of the activities and principles discussed in this chapter. First, Hillocks found that the least effective mode of instruction was characterized by teacher lectures and teacher-dominated discussions. The next most effective mode was characterized by considerable free writing about personal interests, by writing for audiences of peers, and by teachers' responses to whatever students write. The most effective mode was characterized by instruction emphasizing (1) processes such as prewriting, composing, and revising; (2) prewriting activities that help develop the skills to be applied during the ensuing writing; (3) specific objectives for learning; (4) activities that help students learn the procedures for using those forms during the writing process; and (5) interaction with peers and feedback during the total writing process rather than primarily at the end of a composing activity.

In summary, according to Hillocks, the most effective instruction is characterized by specific objectives (for example, to increase the use of figurative language in writing), materials and problems selected to engage the students in the processes important for that specified aspect of writing, and activities such as small-group problem-centered discussions. In effective instruction, teachers frequently give brief introductory lessons about the principles to be studied and applied during small-group activities and then during independent work. It is worthwhile to note Hillocks's assumptions about the most effective composition approaches:

1. Teachers should actively seek to develop identifiable writing skills in students.
2. Students develop skills by using them orally before using them in writing.
3. One major function of prewriting activities is to develop writing skills.
4. The use of skills such as generating criteria to define a concept are complex, and therefore may require collaboration with and feedback from others.

THEORIES

Current practice in written composition is shifting away from total emphasis on the products of writing to concern for the processes of writers during the act of writing. The information-processing model for written composition is based on the work of cognitive psychologists such as Bruner (1956), Gagné (1970), and Ammon (1977). Researchers in this area ask what the act of writing involves, how skilled and unskilled writers approach the different tasks faced in a writing project, and how educators can assist writers as they perform various writing tasks.

Cognitive psychologists view the brain as a system for processing and storing information that is very much like a computer. In this view, a computer program is a map or an internal hierarchy (Simon, 1981). Cognitive research focuses on the writer's mind and researchers identify, analyze, and describe steps that writers go through during various phases of the writing process. Researchers also try to identify and describe the qualities of mental maps that writers use to organize information into meaningful units.

Researchers have identified and analyzed the processes involved in writing by observing writers and asking them to think aloud as they approach various writing tasks. The writing process model defined by Flower and Hayes is one of the most frequently cited. Flower and Hayes (1978) define writing as a problem-solving cognitive process that includes making plans, operating, searching memory, using procedures that get things done, and testing or evaluating the results of the plans and operations. Figure 9–1 shows the structure of the Hayes and Flower (1980) model. Notice the interactions of the processes as writers approach the problem and then engage in planning that emphasizes generating ideas, organizing, and setting goals. At the same time, writers draw from their memories to obtain knowl-

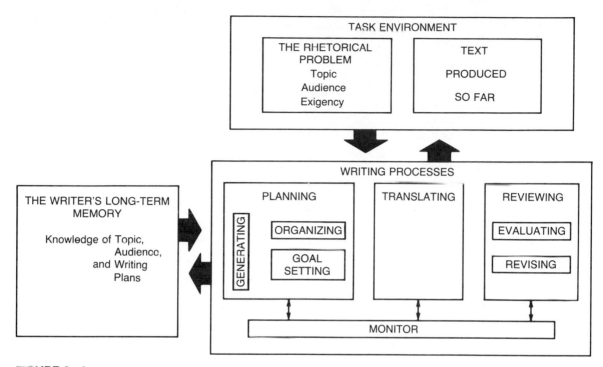

FIGURE 9-1

Stages in the writing process (from "Writing and Problem Solving" by J. Hayes and L. Flower, 1980, *Visible Language, 14,* pp. 388–390. Reprinted by permission.)

edge of the topic, audience, and writing plans. As the process continues, writers compose or translate with interactions still taking place. Finally, they review, evaluate, and revise their writing. Again interactions take place because the reviewing stage requires information considered during other stages in the writing process.

Many researchers who observe the writing process have developed definitions and models that differ only slightly from the one envisioned by Hayes and Flower. For example, following the observation of primary-age students, Graves (1981) defined the writing process as "a series of operations leading to the solution of a problem. The process begins when the writer consciously or unconsciously starts a topic and is finished when the written piece is published" (p. 4).

Britton, Burgess, Martin, McLeod, and Rosen (1979) identify the stages in the writing process as (1) conception, which is a long or a brief time during which a specific incident provokes the decision to write; (2) incubation, which is the preparatory period; and (3) production, which includes the actual writing. In addition, they identify memory, influences of written and printed sources, and revision as other important aspects of the writing process. Glatthorn (1982) identifies four similar phases of the writing process: (1) exploring, (2) planning, (3) drafting, and (4) revising. Notice that the terms used may be different, but the actual stages or phases are very similar.

INSTRUCTION

Instruction for processing emphasizes the steps in the writing process. Many of the effective procedures used during this sequence of events were developed as a result of large writing projects, such as the Bay Area Writing Project and The National Writing Project. For example, Proett and Gill's (1986) sequence of events and recommended activities resulted from information compiled during the Bay Area Writing Project and the University of California Project.

Proett and Gill sequence the steps in the writing process according to activities that teachers and students should do before students write, while students write, and after students write. The before-writing activities encourage students to discover and explore, choose a focus for writing, gather and record ideas, classify information, structure information, and apply general truths to specific cases. The during-writing activities encourage students to record ideas into a tentative, first-draft shape; make choices depending on the audience, purpose, and desired form of writing; and consider such concerns as choice of words and sentence structure. The after-writing activities encourage students to scrutinize their first drafts, get peer responses from editing groups, rethink, revise, polish, and proofread. Finally, students share their writings through various activities. Figure 9–2 shows this process as envisioned by Proett and Gill and presents activities appropriate for each phase.

In addition to the steps in the writing process, Proett and Gill identify the following principles to guide the selection of activities under the process approach:

1. Neither guided composition on an occasional basis nor frequent unguided writing produces marked growth in writing skill. Experience strongly argues for frequent, clearly purposeful, guided writing experience.
2. Students need to produce more writing than a teacher of classes of twenty-five to thirty can possibly evaluate carefully. Some compromise with the practice of thoroughly marking every paper is necessary.
3. Students can profitably practice the steps in the writing process (brainstorming, focused timed writing, sentence combining, small-group editing, and so forth) one at a time, but they also need to experience the entire process on a single writing project in order to develop a sense of working from start to finish on a paper on their own. When the steps in the process are undertaken separately, you must connect them to understanding of the whole process so that students can see how each step is independent but also integral in the production of a final written piece.
4. Although writing is a legitimate homework activity, all elements of the writing process should be undertaken at some time during class so that teachers can coach and monitor progress. Real teaching must continue after the assignment is given, through all stages of the process.
5. Writing is a tremendously complex activity. It involves the simultaneous application of a series of intellectual and physical activities. In the classroom, teachers must break these activities into manageable segments to give learners a chance to handle them successfully in some consecutive fashion (for example, clustering of ideas, then seeking coherence through some logic of organization, then identifying controlling elements of stance, then drafting paragraphs for peer review, and finally revising in light of valid criticism).

	Content and Idea Building		
Before	Observing	Brainstorming	Dramatizing
	Remembering	Clustering	Reading
	Researching	Listing	Mapping
	Imagining	Detailing	Outlining
	Experiencing	Logging	Watching films and other media

Before Students Write

Development and Ordering

Developing with details, reasons, examples, or incidents

Ordering by chronology, space, importance, logic

Classifying

Applying a general truth to a specific case (deductive)

Generalizing from supporting details (inductive)

Structuring by cause and effect

While Students Write

Rhetorical Stance

Voice: Who am I? How do I feel? What do I know? How sure am I?

Audience: Who's listening? What are they ready for? What help do they need? How are they feeling?

Purpose: What do I want to happen? What is likely to result? What effect do I seek? What am I willing to accept?

Form: What form fits this message?

Linguistic Choices

Specific, concrete word choice

Figurative language

Sentence structure: length, opener, verb structure

Sentence type: simple, expanded, complex, compound, cumulative

Syntax: phrase and clause structures, word order; connections and transitions; modification and subordination

After Students Write

Revision

Getting responses: editing groups, read-arounds

Raising questions, expanding, clarifying

Testing against criteria; using a rubric

Proofreading and polishing

Highlighting

Sharing	Posting	Mailing
Publishing	Filing	Reading

FIGURE 9–2

The writing process (Jackie Proett and Kent Gill, *The Writing Process in Action: A Handbook for Teachers.* Copyright © 1986 by the National Council of Teachers of English. Reprinted with permission.)

6. Teachers and curriculum experts have long sought the ideal linear sequence for the writing program, asking what logically must precede what in a course or a series of grade levels. However, there has been no clearly accepted linear sequence for writing-skill development, either in textbooks or in curriculum guides. Because writing is a holistic act, requiring application of the whole range of skills to every writing project, a recursive model seems more appropriate. It gives students experience with most of what a writer does early on, but then circles back periodically to give maturing learners another, perhaps more sophisticated, experience with the skill employed earlier.

ACTIVITIES

In this section we consider some of the activities that take place during the writing process (presented in outline form in Figure 9–2) and try to develop an understanding of the writing process. We include both unstructured and structured activities as students and teachers progress through the stages of prewriting, composing, and postcomposing. Before we begin developing specific aspects of the writing process for instruction, we should consider Suhor's (1984) warning: "The sequence in the Writing Process Model, as flexible as it is, cannot be followed slavishly. The sequence is not a stairway progression. . . . It should be thought of as 'looped,' not tightly linear, since certain aspects—discussion, conferencing, note-taking, revising, proofreading—may take place at several points, not just in the slots assigned on the visual model" (p. 101).

Before you try to teach writing to students, develop your own understanding of the writing process. Hayes and Flower's model in Figure 9–1 developed by asking experienced writers to describe what they did as they approached and completed a writing task. Proett and Gill developed their model (Figure 9–2) through various writing workshops and research with students. Daniels and Zemelman (1985), who developed workshops for training teachers in the writing process, state that asking adults to create their own models of the writing process is "one of the main mechanisms by which participants formalize the discoveries they have made from their own writing experiences" (p. 78).

REINFORCEMENT ACTIVITY

Before you proceed with this chapter, try one or two approaches for developing your own model of the writing process. Remember that your model does not need to be identical to one presented in this text. Your model may vary somewhat, depending on your purpose for writing, your topic, your background knowledge, and your audience.

1. Assuming you have a writing assignment in one of your classes, keep a log describing your activities and actions as you approach the writing assignment, write various drafts, and finish the paper in the form to be handed in to the professor.

2. Within your language arts class, complete a writing task that is to be eventually shared with a group of your peers through your college or university

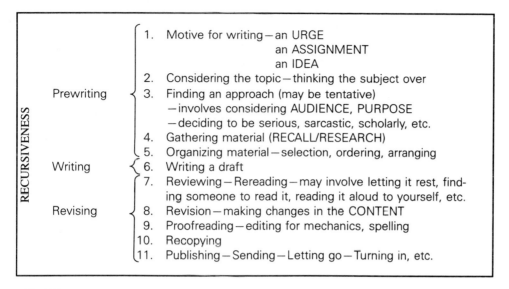

FIGURE 9–3
Writing process model (From Harvey Daniels and Steven Zemelman, *A Writing Project: Training Teachers of Composition from Kindergarten to College.* Copyright 1985 by Heinemann Educational Books. Reprinted with permission.)

newspaper. Choose an issue of concern on your campus. You may share your writing with your language arts class to gain recommendations before you submit your article to the newspaper.

3. After you have completed either one of the preceding tasks, form groups within your language arts class. On large sheets of paper or the chalkboard, list the steps you went through as you approached and completed your writing task. You may find it helpful to first list all of your actions, then categorize them into types of activities, and finally put them into a chronological order. Like Hayes and Flower, you may find that you performed various interactions and repetitive actions during different stages in your writing process.

4. Share and discuss your model of the writing process in your language arts class. Are there any commonalities among the models? Look especially at what you did before writing, while writing the first draft, and while revising and reviewing before you were satisfied with your paper.

5. Finally, compare your model of the writing process with the one developed by a group of teachers during Daniels and Zemelman's writing workshop (see Figure 9–3). What are the similarities and differences?

6 After you have compared your model with the one by Daniels and Zemelman, compare the Hayes and Flower model, and the Proett and Gill model. What are the commonalities across models? Why do you believe there are such similarities? Do all of the models have categories that take into account prewriting, writing, and postwriting activities? Are these stages important when you teach writing composition to a group of students? Why are they important? How could this knowledge influence your teaching?

Before Writing

This first stage in the writing process includes activities that motivate students to write, generate ideas for writing, and focus the attention of students on the subject or objective of the writing. This phase allows students to become engrossed in a topic, extend their knowledge, heighten their awareness, and develop appropriate thinking skills. Proett and Gill (1986) include in this prewriting phase activities such as semantic mapping and webbing, brainstorming, dramatizing, experiencing, observing, reading, and watching films. These activities help students build ideas and create content. They frequently stimulate students to pull knowledge from long-term memory and apply it to the writing experience. They include developing details and reasons, ordering by chronology or space, classifying, applying, generalizing, and structuring cause–effect relationships.

Prewriting activities vary according to the age of the students and the objectives for the writing. Activities may include going on a class excursion and then talking about the experience, planning and then drawing a picture, or reading and then discussing a model story or poem written around a specific structure that students identify, try to duplicate, and evaluate in their own writing. Prewriting activities also may be extensions of ongoing school work, such as a science or social studies unit. They may result from common experiences, such as birthdays or family vacations. They may be new experiences created by the teacher. It is at this point in the writing process that you should question and interview students to clarify their ideas, assist them in thinking about procedures for gathering information, and help them make plans for future writing. Whatever activities you include, planning is extremely important. Carey (1989) found a positive relationship between the amount of initial planning and the quality of the finished writing. Blohm and Benton (1991) showed that generating questions prior to writing enhances the quality of informative writing. Haas (1990) found that note taking and predraft planning are critical when writing technical reports. Extensive oral exchanges of ideas during such activities as brainstorming and semantic mapping help students clarify and extend their ideas.

Drawing In an analysis of the written products of kindergarten children, Medearis (1985) found that writing occurred most frequently in the art center. Artwork created by students is one of the earliest motivators used to stimulate writing and to help young students plan written compositions. Prewriting activities include planning the artwork, creating it, and talking about it. As students draw something that interests them, they have opportunities to think about the details in the picture, the person or the object in the picture, and the things they want to disclose. Stories develop naturally from such experiences. In addition, students enjoy sharing both their artwork and their dictated or individually written stories.

Semantic mapping Semantic maps are good for idea building and organizing ideas during the prewriting phase of composition. Heimlich and Pittelman (1986) state that semantic mapping helps students identify main ideas and supporting details of a topic of interest, organize prior knowledge, and write paragraphs.

You may use semantic mapping or webbing prior to writing as a total-class, small-group, or individual activity. For a total-class or small-group activity, write the desired topic in the center of the chalkboard or large sheet of paper. Next, lead

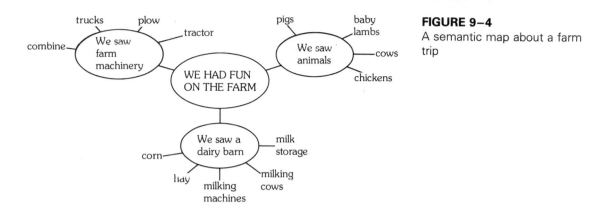

FIGURE 9–4
A semantic map about a farm trip

a discussion in which you elicit main ideas or categories from the students and draw in circles that extend from the center. Add supporting ideas and details as the discussion continues. Then, let the students review the information and write or dictate their stories.

The first processing experience with mapping and writing is usually a group activity. Demonstrate how easily ideas developed during the brainstorming may be charted and expanded, and how easily writing may be organized. For example, a writing activity in first or second grade might be generated from a group trip to a farm. Ask for a logical title, such as "We Had Fun on the Farm," and then begin the map. Ask questions to help students remember important events during the visit: "What machinery did we see?" Figure 9–4 illustrates this semantic map.

After developing the map, the class wrote a group story following the organization presented on the chalkboard. Through this procedure, the mapping and the group-written story acted as models for future group and individual activities. The students learned a great deal about organization, grouping ideas into paragraphs, and supporting main ideas with important details. The teacher extended individual writing, asking students to write descriptive accounts of each of the main ideas. Students could choose to write about the animals, the buildings, or the machinery. Each of these areas can be further extended using a mapping and discussing process.

The semantic mapping technique is equally helpful before an individual writing activity. Figure 9–5 was generated by an older student whose assignment was to write a humorous story about her summer vacation.

Brainstorming   Brainstorming activities emphasize quick-paced responses from students without initial evaluation of what they say. Such activities are especially good during prewriting because they act as brain teasers, avenues for generating numerous ideas, and ways of retrieving information from long-term memory. You may structure brainstorming activities to obtain specific types of responses and encourage certain types of thinking. For example, Suhor (1984) recommends a two-part brainstorming/language game involving comparison and contrast. The teacher first writes the following sentences on the board: "How is a _____ like a _____ ? How are they different?" In the first step, the teacher provides five to eight pairs of nouns, such as *oak tree, rabbit; tricycle, jet plane; zoo, schoolyard;*

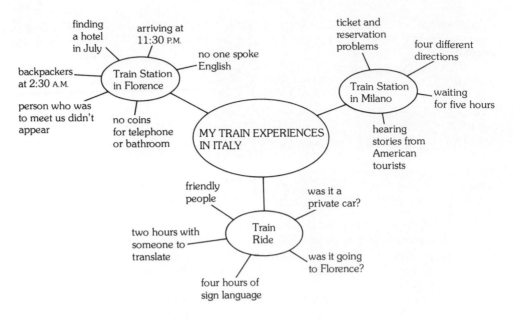

FIGURE 9–5
A semantic map that helped an older student develop her story

jogging, studying. The students then provide rapid responses to the initial question. In the second step, the students write single nouns on slips of paper that they place in a grab bag, from which a volunteer randomly picks two slips. They apply the questions on the chalkboard to the randomly selected pairs. Then, they use their imaginations for more ingenious comparisons and contrasts. This warmup activity leads to the discussion of comparison and contrast topics that interest students, such as two television shows, two cities, two countries, or two poems. Then, paragraph writing that compares and contrasts two subjects follows naturally.

Brainstorming is especially good before writing certain types of poetry. Students might brainstorm rhyming words before writing limericks or brainstorm contrasting nouns, describing words, and action words before writing poetry in the diamante formation.

Modeling   Many of the activities listed under Proett and Gill's development and ordering phase of prewriting (see Figure 9–2) lend themselves to brief instruction in which a teacher models certain kinds of paragraph development, plot structure, or figurative language. The students then apply what they have learned as they go through the writing phase and use it to provide criteria during the revision process as they share their writing with peer groups, editing groups, and teachers, and then revise their first drafts.

The structure of a limerick or diamante illustrates the need for models during some prewriting activities. To understand this requirement, stop and write a limerick or a diamante. Can you do it without referring to either a model or a specific definition for each type of poetry form? Unless you have been studying and writing these forms of poetry recently, you probably cannot accomplish the task. This is equally true for elementary students.

Use the following models for limericks, cinquains, and diamantes with elementary students. First, read numerous examples of limericks to students. Edward Lear's *Nonsense Omnibus* (1943, 1846), David McCord's *One at a Time: Collected Poems for the Young* (1977), and N. M. Bodecker's *A Person from Britain Whose Head Was the Shape of a Mitten and Other Limericks* (1980) provide excellent examples for this activity. Next, discuss the form of the limerick as shown below. Then, lead a brainstorming activity, during which the students list words that rhyme with several possible key words to use in their own writing. Have the students write their own limericks, share them with the class, and make any revisions after this initial exchange. Then have the students place their limericks into their own class book of limericks.

Limericks are short, funny, five-line poems in which the first, second, and last lines rhyme with each other. The third and fourth lines are shorter and rhyme only with each other. This form results in a poem that looks approximately like this:

Line 1. _____ *a*	*a* lines rhyme
Line 2. _____ *a*	
Line 3. _____ *b*	*b* lines rhyme
Line 4. _____ *b*	
Line 5. _____ *a*	

The following limerick was written by a fifth-grade student:

> *There once was a computer named Zeke*
> *Who turned out to be quite a freak.*
> *When you told him to add,*
> *He would call for his Dad*
> *So his outlook in life was quite bleak.*

During other class periods, follow the same reading, modeling, brainstorming, writing, and sharing formats with the cinquain and diamante formats for poetry. In the cinquain, the lines are not difficult to write, and they stress certain types of vocabulary. Unlike the limerick, the cinquain does not use rhyming words. The cinquain is composed of five lines that meet the following requirements:

1. A word for a title
2. Two words to describe the title
3. Three words to express action
4. Four words to express feeling
5. The title again, or a word like it

A diagram of the cinquain looks like this:

```
                      title
              describe      title
          action    action    action
        feeling   about   the    title
                     title
```

The cinquain offers a chance for inductive teaching of such language concepts as descriptive words and action words. Students can improve their cinquains if they talk about the kinds of words that make up each line and brainstorm examples. The following cinquains were written by fourth-grade students:

Clouds

Fluffy, white
Floating, moving, falling
Clouds are pillowy soft
Clouds

Scrubbrush

Low, brown
Tumbling, scratching, dying
Scrubbrush is painfully ugly
Scrubbrush

The diamante is another form of poetry that has certain requirements for each line. Deborah Elkins (1976) described this poetry:

line 1: noun
line 2: two adjectives
line 3: three participles
line 4: four nouns or phrase
line 5: three participles indicating change
line 6: two adjectives
line 7: contrasting noun (p. 222)

Elkins believes that teachers should help students with this format by drawing it and illustrating the types of words used, rather than merely using the terminology of the parts of speech. Thus, in line one, you will have to present examples of a noun; in line two, examples of adjectives related to the first-line noun; in line three, of participles, as verb forms ending in *-ing, -ed, -en.* The nouns or phrase in the fourth line provide a transition from the subject of the first noun to the subject of the contrasting noun on line seven. The fifth line contains three participles that correspond with the seventh-line noun and indicate change from the first noun. The sixth line contains two adjectives that correspond with the final noun and, thus, contrast with line two. The final noun contrasts with line one. A diagram of the diamante looks like this:

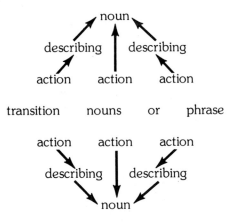

Besides illustrating the parts of speech used in the diamante, you must make clear the concept of contrasts. Contrasting nouns are necessary, in addition to contrasting adjectives and contrasting verb forms that correspond with the appropriate nouns. An instructional activity leading up to this form of poetry begins with identifying the form and suggesting contrasting nouns, such as *war–peace, freedom–slavery,* and *giant–dwarf.* The class should also discuss contrasting descriptive words and contrasting action words. The students will find a thesaurus helpful when working with this form of poetry.

The following diamante was written by a fifth-grade student:

> *fantasy*
> *magical, mysterious*
> *dreaming, fooling, inventing*
> *An Unidentified Flying Object*
> *proving, trying, testing*
> *genuine, true*
> *reality*

As you can see, *fantasy* and *reality* are opposites. *Magical* and *mysterious* describe *fantasy,* and contrast with *genuine* and *true.* The participles *dreaming, fooling,* and *inventing* show action related to fantasy, and contrast with *proving, trying,* and *testing.* This student chose for the middle line the phrase "An Unidentified Flying Object," which might be either fantasy or reality and thus provides transition between the two words.

Listing and categorizing   Activities that encourage students to list and categorize, classify, or order information provide opportunities for content building and idea building. For example, a third-grade teacher used this strategy to help students identify and categorize the incidents that occurred before, during, and after a field trip. The class decided that division by time would be most appropriate. It developed the following three categories of events:

1. Things we did to get ready for our train ride.
2. Things we did on the day of our train ride.
3. Things we did for several days after the train ride.

Next, the class changed these categories into questions, and wrote each question on a separate section of the chalkboard:

1. What did we do to get ready for our train ride?
2. What did we do on the day of our train ride?
3. What did we do for several days after the train ride?

In the next step, the children answered the three questions by listing information under the appropriate question. They developed the following sentence outline:

A Ride on the Train

I. What did we do to get ready for our train ride?
    A.   We studied about railroads.
    B.   We called the railroad depot to get train times and ticket cost.
    C.   We wrote a note to our parents asking permission to go on the train ride.
    D.   We called the school bus company to get a bus to pick us up at school, take us to the depot, and pick us up at the next train depot.
II. What did we do on the day of our train ride?
    A.   We rode on the bus to the train depot.
    B.   We bought our train tickets.
    C.   We each got a seat on the train.

       D. The conductor took our tickets.
       E. The conductor told us about the train.
       F. We saw the dining car, the observation car, and the Pullman cars.
       G. When we got off the train we looked at the engine.
       H. We rode the bus back to school.
III. What did we do for several days after the train ride?
       A. We drew pictures of the train and the depot for a bulletin board.
       B. We wrote thank-you notes to the train conductor.
       C. We wrote a story so we could remember the train ride.
       D. We read more books about trains.
       E. We learned some songs about trains.

    After developing this outline, the students wrote individual stories about their trip. The children used the outline, but added their own details to make the story personal. As you can see, this activity also became an introduction to outlining and writing a longer factual report.

    Another way to motivate interest and help students categorize ideas, know what references they need from library sources, and organize materials is to list some questions that the children want answered about a general topic. One grad-

Listing and categorizing are excellent prewriting activities because they stimulate ideas.

uate student, who also teaches fourth grade, used this approach before her students wrote reports about Native Americans. The students first listed a number of questions they would like to have answered. Then, they grouped the questions into categories. Part of the list appears in Figure 9–6 (the full list contained over 100 questions). When the students selected a category they wished to investigate, the questions on the list provided both a starting point for the information search and a topic for writing.

Writing

Prewriting experiences allow students to explore, imagine, consider initial structure, and think about details to go into their writing. Writing, however, demands some additional considerations. Proett and Gill (1986) state:

> The writing stage needs to be viewed in two very different ways. Seen in one way, it is the flowing of words onto the page, easily, naturally, rapidly. But it is also a time of making decisions, of choosing what to tell and what to leave out, or thinking about who is speaking and who is listening, of determining what order, what structure, what word works best. In some ways these functions even seem contradictory; the first needs to be fluid and fast while the other calls for deliberation and reason. The teaching task is to help the writer coordinate these two functions. (p. 11)

Native Americans

1. Clothing
   a. What did Native Americans wear?
   b. How did they get their materials?
   c. How did they sew?
   d. Did all Native Americans dress alike?
2. Education
   a. Did Native Americans have to go to school?
   b. What did they need to learn?
   c. Who taught the Native American children?
   d. What did they write on?
3. Houses
   a. What were tepees made from?
   b. How did they cook and wash?
   c. Did all Native Americans live in the same kinds of houses?
4. Medicine
   a. Did Native Americans get sick?
   b. Why did the medicine men dance?
   c. Did Native Americans take medicine?

5. Food
   a. What did the Native Americans eat?
   b. Where did they get their food?
   c. Was their food tasty?
   d. How did they store their food?
   e. What else did they use for hunting besides bows and arrows?
6. Tribes
   a. How did you get to be a chief?
   b. Where did the different Native American tribes live?
   c. How were they alike or different?
7. War and Peace
   a. Why did the Native Americans fight the settlers?
   b. Were any Native Americans friendly with the settlers?
   c. How did the settlers treat the Native Americans?
   d. What would happen if you went on a reservation today?

FIGURE 9–6
Outline of questions asked by fourth-grade students about Native Americans

This section begins with ways of helping students make decisions about audience, purpose, form, organizational pattern, and linguistic style. Next, it considers ways of helping students write a first draft rapidly.

Audience and purpose   To entertain an audience or to inform the audience about a new scientific development, would you write a composition in the same way? Should you write a composition for a second-grade audience using the same words you would use for an adult audience? The answer to both of these questions is an obvious no. To help students realize the importance of audience and purpose, you must provide them with many opportunities to write for different types of real audiences, ranging from themselves, to their peers, to you, to other known audiences, to unknown audiences. (This concern is important in both processing and distancing approaches to writing.)

Unfortunately, studies in both Britain and the United States show that the audiences and the purposes for student writing are very narrow. For example, Britton, Burgess, Martin, McLeod, and Rosen (1979) analyzed 2,122 pieces of writing by British students ages eleven to eighteen. They found that 95 percent of the writing was allocated to writing for the teacher. Writing in which the writer must consider the requirements of an unknown reader accounted for 1.8 percent of the writing; writing to known nonexperts or peer groups accounted for 0.3 percent; writing for oneself as audience accounted for 0.5 percent. Unfortunately, much of the writing for the teacher audience was for examination purposes rather than interaction.

Similar audiences for student writing were reported in Applebee's (1984) survey of writing in American schools. Applebee found that the teacher-examiner was the primary audience for student writing in all subjects. About one third of those papers resulted in some type of teacher–learner dialogue. The rest were addressed to the teacher as an examiner. Only 10 percent of the teachers reported that student writing was read regularly by other students. The findings suggest that students need many opportunities to write for varied real audiences, for purposes other than to be examined on their knowledge, and for audiences that respond to the writing in ways that go beyond the examination.

There are many opportunities in school to encourage students to write for real audiences and for different purposes. For example, students can write letters or stories to and for their families. They can have pen pals in other classrooms and even other school districts. They can write stories and other types of articles to be displayed in the library, on bulletin boards, and in a school or classroom newspaper. They can write diaries and autobiographies for their own pleasure. They can send reports to and correspond with local historical societies, newspapers, television stations, government officials, and businesses. They can develop their own books, literary magazines, comic books, newspapers, and other types of journals. Then, they can share these products with larger audiences. Students themselves will think of many additional ways to create real audiences for their writing.

Students need to realize the importance of audience characteristics and purposes when they are making decisions about writing. To help them realize the importance of audience and purpose, encourage students to list questions they need to answer about the characteristics of the audience and the purpose of the composition. A group of fifth graders developed the following list:

1. How old is my audience?
2. How much knowledge of the subject does my audience have?

3. Is the subject going to be interesting to my audience?
4. Would the subject add new knowledge to my audience?
5. Does the audience want to be informed or entertained?
6. How do I want the audience to react? Do I want them to be persuaded to my viewpoint? Do I want them to laugh? Do I want them to follow directions? Do I want them to have new ideas? Do I want them to have new information? Do I want them to be sad?

After they developed the questions, they discussed why and how the answers to the questions would influence their writing.

Another processing and distancing activity that helps students understand requirements for audience and purpose is having the students list several different types of writing and then discuss the purpose of that type of writing, the requirements for it, and the intended audience. One group of fourth-grade students put this information into table form, shown in Table 9–1.

Form   After discussing information similar to that shown in Table 9–1, students have clearer ideas about possible content for each type of writing, as well as about purpose and audience. They also understand that writing can take on numerous forms. You can expand this list to include other forms of writing, such as poetry, cartoons, picture storybooks, nonfictional textbooks, essays, interviews, reviews, songs, and sketches. Next, bring to class examples of these various forms for writing. Share the forms with students as they consider the differences and why certain forms may be more appropriate for specific purposes and audiences.

It is also interesting to try to change forms and then compare the content and impact on the audience. For example, after reading historical fiction about early British heroes, some college students wrote book reports in the form of ballads and then asked fifth- and sixth-grade students to complete a similar task. The students learned that ballads were appropriate for sharing heroic character information during the colonial time period, discovered information about the ballad as a form of writing, determined that content might be similar or different depending on the form, and recognized that the influence on an audience may depend on the form chosen to deliver the message. Other interesting activities with form include writing telegrams from news articles, science fiction from scientific factual information, diary entries from novels, letters from biographies, and cartoons from any type of literature. Whatever the motivation, students conclude the activity by comparing information, characteristics of form, and appropriateness of different forms for different purposes and audiences.

Organizational pattern   Students frequently pay little attention to the organizational patterns used in their own writing or the writing of others. The organizational patterns in limericks, cinquains, and diamantes are obvious and must be followed for authenticity. However, there are other, less obvious and less structured organizational patterns that provide logical order. Writers frequently use several of these patterns within the same paper or book. As shown by the titles, these major organizational patterns lend themselves to writing in many of the content areas. You may introduce these forms through activities in which you model the identification of various organizational approaches, diagram paragraphs according to the organizational pattern, and lead discussions in which students identify and describe the organizational pattern. Then, the students should write compositions using organizational patterns that they believe are

TABLE 9-1

Writing activity, purpose, requirements, and audience

Writing	Purpose	Requirements	Audience
1. Weather and temperature charts	1. Compare conditions over a nine-month period.	1. Thermometer to take temperature. Observe clouds at same time of day. Accuracy.	1. Science class.
2. Personal letters	2. Exchange accounts of experiences with friend.	2. Interesting personal information. Informal writing level.	2. A friend who knows me.
3. Invitations	3. Inform and invite audience to a program, party, etc.	3. What, who, why, when, where. (Proofreading is important.)	3. Parents, neighbors, friends.
4. Puppet plays	4. Entertain.	4. Original story that entertains. Puppets.	4. Class, parents, other invited guests.
5. Diaries	5. Record daily experiences and feelings.	5. Short notes on things important to me.	5. Me.
6. News stories	6. Inform about news, events, sports, etc.	6. Accuracy—who, what, when, where. Clear, brief reporting. (Editing and proofreading are important.)	6. Whole school. If city paper, large unknown audience that wants information.
7. Forms	7. Obtain social security card, driver's license. Send for information.	7. Accurate information, clear handwriting. (Proofreading is important.)	7. People who don't know me, government.
8. Imaginative	8. Entertain, enjoy.	8. Fresh ideas, imagination, feelings.	8. Class. If published, a large, unknown audience.
9. Autobiographies	9. Tell others about myself. Compile class book.	9. Facts about myself, feelings, wishes. (Proofreading is important.)	9. Class and parents. If published, a large, unknown audience.
10. Book reports	10. Report author, title information, summary, and personal reactions.	10. Careful reading and writing for summary. Outlining important information. (Proofreading is important.)	10. Class. If book review in a paper, people who might want to read the book.
11. Reports and projects in social studies, science, etc.	11. Share new facts and information.	11. Research from several sources, data, main ideas, and details. Accuracy of facts, best order for ideas. (Proofreading and rewriting are important.)	11. Class. If journal or magazine article, people wanting that information.
12. Biographies	12. Report knowledge about well-known person.	12. Research from several sources. Comparisons of information. Accuracy. (Proofreading is important.)	12. Class. If published, a large, unknown audience.
13. Editorials	13. Persuade someone to my viewpoint.	13. Knowledge of ways to persuade and use facts. Rewriting to clearly persuade.	13. People who read the newspaper. Some will agree with the writer, some will disagree.
14. Minutes for meetings	14. Keep a record of what happened.	14. Accurate listening and reading.	14. Class, group, or organization.

appropriate. Our example of the train ride used a chronological order of events. Compositions such as those reporting historical events or autobiographies lend themselves to ordering in which the earliest events are reported first.

A second method of organization is through spatial concepts. The order might proceed from inside to outside, from right to left, or from bottom to top. Such a pattern might look like this:

Bottom   The Old Man in the Park
  ↓   ↓ New and shiny black shoes
Top   ↓ Bare white ankles
             ↓ Cuffed, baggy, and torn pants
             ↓ Faded flannel shirt
             ↓ Expression of contentment and satisfaction

Or this:

Inside   Water distribution
  ↓   On the inside of the earth.
Outside   ↓ On the earth's surface.
             ↓ In the atmosphere.

A third method starts with the simplest or most familiar ideas and progresses to the most complex or unfamiliar ideas. A writer may begin by reviewing information or concepts the audience already knows and then progress to new information that is harder to understand without background information. Following is a diagram of this order:

Familiar   Wind energy
  ↓   Trees swaying
Unfamiliar   ↓ Kites flying
               ↓ Windmill pumping water
               ↓ Wind turbine connected to a generator

Social studies and science writers often use two other patterns of organization to develop main ideas and supporting details. A report might first identify a problem, continue by suggesting causes for the problem, and conclude with possible solutions. A diagram would look like this:

Problem   Air pollution
  ↓ Cause of problem   ↓ Automobiles—Industrial waste
  ↓ Possible solutions of the problem   ↓ Catalytic converters—Filtering
                                           smoke in factories

After identifying a problem, a report might discuss its effects rather than its causes. This report form also concludes with possible solutions to the problems, for example:

Problem   Air pollution
  ↓ Effect of problem   ↓ Lung diseases—Plant diseases
  ↓ Possible solutions to the problem   ↓ Catalytic converters on cars—
                                           Filtering smoke in factories

A final useful arrangement is question and answer. In this pattern, a writer asks a question and answers it, asks another question and answers it, and so forth; for example:

Question	What clothes should you take to
↓ Answer	↓ keep dry when camping:
Question	Discuss characteristics of a
↓ Answer	good raincoat or poncho

Most professional authors use a combination of several organizational patterns. The patterns help authors develop their ideas and readers follow the ideas. Understanding the advantage of various organizational patterns helps students write their own compositions. You can provide many opportunities for students to identify organizational patterns used by authors and analyze the effectiveness of the patterns for the particular content. For example, ask students to search for and identify examples of chronological order in Russell Freedman's *Franklin Delano Roosevelt* (1990) as the author describes the life of the former president from boyhood through his experiences as commander in chief. In Judith St. George's *The White House: Cornerstone of a Nation* (1990), the author uses chronological order to trace the history of the White House. The chronological order in Rhoda Blumberg's *The Incredible Journey of Lewis and Clark* (1987) is reinforced with maps that trace the journey from east to west and then from west to east.

An organizational pattern based on a spacial concept is evident in the following example from James Cross Giblin's *The Riddle of the Rosetta Stone: Key to Ancient Egypt* (1990):

> What makes this stone so special? Step closer, and you'll see. Spotlights pick out markings carved into the surface of the stone, and close up you can tell that these markings are writing. At the top are fourteen lines of hieroglyphs—pictures of animals, birds, and geometric shapes. Below them you can make out thirty-two lines written in an unfamiliar script. And below that, at the bottom of the slab, are fifty-four more lines written in the letters of the Greek alphabet. (p. 7)

In Patricia Lauber's *The News About Dinosaurs* (1988), the author presents familiar information about dinosaurs and follows with new and unfamiliar information. Various patterns that begin with problems and include solutions are evident in Laurence Pringle's *Global Warming: Assessing the Greenhouse Threat* (1990), Charlotte Wilcox's *Trash!* (1988), and Carole Vogel and Kathryn Goldner's *The Great Yellowstone Fire* (1990). A question-and-answer organizational pattern is used by Seymour Simon in *New Questions and Answers About Dinosaurs* (1990).

Because authors use many different organizational patterns within the same book, students can analyze the effectiveness of each pattern. After students have identified and analyzed the effectiveness of the various organizational patterns, have them write their own stories and reports based on one or more of these patterns.

Linguistic style   The sentence-combining and modeling activities developed in Chapter 8 help students explore various linguistic styles, develop fluency in writing, and develop a variety of appropriate solutions to linguistic choices. You may use these approaches during group lessons, introductory activities, or individual conferences when students need help making linguistic decisions. Teachers frequently use examples from students' writing to show how sentence combining, other transformations, and word choices can improve fluency and clarity. You may write your own compositions to reflect any student problems, place the compositions on transparencies or handouts, and lead discussions during which students identify and use various sentence-combining strategies to improve the writing.

Literature provides good sources for observation and discussion. Through models, students can discover various techniques used by authors to create interest and achieve fluency and clarity. For example, have the students observe how Armstrong Sperry develops vivid descriptions of setting and conflict in *Call It Courage* (1940). In the following passage, Sperry decreases the length of his sentences as the tension rises and the conflict increases. This changing of sentence length not only stresses developing tension, it also reflects the rhythm of the angry ocean:

> There was a wave lifting before the canoe. Many the boy had seen, but this was a giant—a monster livid and hungry. Higher, higher it rose, until it seemed that it must scrape at the low-hanging clouds. Its crest heaved over with a vast sigh. The boy saw it coming. He tried to cry out. No sound issued from his throat. Suddenly the wave was upon him. Down it crashed. Chaos! Mafatu felt the paddle torn from his hands. Thunder in his ears. Water strangling him. Terror in his soul. The canoe slewed round into the trough. The boy flung himself forward, wound his arms around the mid-thwart. It was the end of a world. (p. 24)

Literary models are especially important for demonstrating the importance of carefully chosen words. Authors Paula Fox and Jan Hudson, for example, develop strong characterizations through the use of similes, metaphors, and other types of figurative language. In *One-Eyed Cat* (1984), notice how Fox uses a simile to describe the main character's guilt: "When there was a splinter in his foot, it was all he could think about; he would forget that every part of his body except where the splinter was felt fine. That's the way it was now with the attic. The gun was like a splinter in his mind" (p. 90). Later, Fox compares Ned's secret to a mountain of snow: "All the lies he had told, the subterfuge, were piled up over the gun like a mountain of hard-packed snow. He felt his secret had frozen around him. He didn't know how to melt it" (p. 162).

The author's choice of language in Hudson's *Sweetgrass* (1989) is especially appropriate for a story about a Blackfoot Indian girl who lived on the northern prairies in the 1800s. Students can discuss the carefully chosen words for this character's thoughts: "When thinking about her life, Sweetgrass thinks: 'All things moved as they should. Our lives seemed fixed as in a beaded design or the roundness of an old tale told on winter nights' " (p. 10).

First draft The objective of this phase of the writing process is the fairly rapid writing of ideas generated, developed, and refined during the prewriting phase. The objective is not to produce finished compositions; that objective takes place in the postwriting, or revision, phase. (All writing, however, does not need to lead to a finished composition.)

Your students may find it helpful if you show them how you write your own first drafts. For example, my own first drafts are written with pencil on legal-size pads. I leave enough space between lines to make changes in word choices or to rewrite sentences. I draw arrows if I change my mind about the ordering of sentences in paragraphs or the ordering of paragraphs. I frequently insert ideas between sentences, on the next page, or even on the back of the page. Again, arrows show me where to locate and place this material. I erase and cross out words, sentences, and even paragraphs. If I cannot think of a specific word or need to add a specific reference, I draw a line. The word will come later; the reference must be found and added. I draw lines if I need to check spelling or a convention in punctuation or grammar. In this case, I draw a line under the questionable word or punctuation, place an abbreviation (*sp., gr.,* or *pn.*) above the line, and continue with my flow of ideas. The lines and abbreviations are cues for areas to check during revision. From an example such as this, students should see that first drafts are frequently tentative and messy. They require editing and revisions. Students should also understand some of the techniques they may use in developing their first, or rough, drafts.

I use semantic mapping to develop my ideas and organize my writing, so I frequently go back and forth between the map and the first draft. As I write, I ask myself questions such as: Did I include those ideas and develop those points? What should come next in the development of the writing? Do I have more information on my map than I can develop thoroughly in a paper? Would it be better if I omitted this portion? If I omit this portion, do I need to change my introduction or my conclusions? A semantic map helps jog memory, improves organization, and provides key evaluators for the revision process. Working with the map and the written composition in this way may also suggest that the original ideas are not working, that major modifications are necessary, and that it is necessary to start over. As we all know, writing is not easy.

Using computers Computer-assisted programs may help students organize their ideas before writing, compose their stories, and revise and edit their selections. Computers with various software programs for writing and word processing motivate writing because the children can focus on content rather than penmanship, easily edit their ideas, interact with peers, see what the finished product looks like before it is printed, and produce attractive final drafts. At the prewriting stage, Gomez (1987) recommends three prewriting modules published by Milliken. These modules allow students to brainstorm and organize their ideas on disks, print the results, and either write with pen and paper or merge ideas with their files on word processors. Other programs that have prewriting capabilities include *The Writers Helper* published by Conduit, *Bank Street Writer Activity Files* published by Scholastic, and *Quill* published by D. C. Heath.

At the composing level, various word processor programs encourage students to compose first drafts and then revise without recopying. Some programs have unique motivating capabilities: *That's My Story,* published by Learning Well, includes story starters; *Kidwriter,* published by Spinnaker, includes pictures that children may choose to write about; and *Story Tree,* published by Scholastic, has a choose-your-own adventure format.

Several studies emphasize the advantages of student interaction during the composing process. For example, Dickinson (1986) used computer teams and encouraged children to talk with each other about their writing plans, discuss their actual writing, and consider their teammates' reactions and feedback when they made their revisions. The capabilities of the *Quill* program extend to the

Using computers promotes longer compositions and motivates children to do careful editing.

composing level. Describing students' interactions while using this program, Bruce, Michaels, and Watson-Gegeo (1985) state: "Students' writing is public and available to be read as it is entered into the computer (looking over the writer's shoulder as it appears on the screen). Later, using an information storage and retrieval system, students can retrieve their own or someone else's writing stored in the computer. Writing comes off the printer typed and formatted like published print (newspapers, magazine ads). It can then be seen on the wall (where its neatly typed format makes it easier to read and hence more accessible to classmates and outside visitors)" (p. 148). Interactions during this observation occurred as students wrote on the computer, read and discussed other students' writing and revisions, and used the computers to send messages to each other.

At the revising and editing levels, word processing programs allow students to respond to the text of others, encourage spelling checks, and make it easier for students to revise and edit their own writing. Texts by Selfe (1986) and Wresch (1984) provide detailed directions for using computers in all stages of the writing process.

Educators also emphasize computer applications to teach sentence combining and to increase and improve the writing skills of children with special needs. Bradley (1982) helped students improve their sentence structures by teaching them sentence combining through a computer program. Rubenstein and Rollins (1978) developed a letter-writing project with deaf children. Over a year's time, forty previously reluctant writers used computers to generate more than 1,500 letters to each other. The authors concluded that electronic mail is a powerful motivator for children's writing. Likewise, Kleiman and Humphrey (1982) found that learning disabled children ranging in age from seven to sixteen enthusiastically increased their writing when encouraged to use word processors.

Although many educators are enthusiastic about using computer programs for writing, there are several potential problems that warrant consideration. If children are to make full use of the capabilities of computers during the writing process, they must have numerous opportunities to use the computers. This means they must have frequent access to computers. In addition, they must learn how to type on a computer keyboard, use a word processor, use various software packages, and use a printer. The greatest need may be for students and teachers to understand that word processing programs will not magically solve writing problems and provide instruction in all phases of writing. In a study of the quality and writing capabilities of seventh- through ninth-grade students, Dauite (1986) emphasizes this point: "This study suggests that word processing features for revising are most useful for writing development when combined closely with cognitive and instructional aids that draw students into reading their texts and developing revising strategies such as self-questioning. Experienced writers who have benefited from the basic processing features already know what good writing looks like and how to evaluate their texts critically. If our students are to benefit from automatic recopying and reformatting, we have to continue to help them learn what good writing is and how to improve their own draft texts" (p. 158).

After Writing

After the writing phase, major portions of the writing process still remain. During the final phase, help students develop self-evaluative skills as they reread, review, and revise their compositions. Provide opportunities to share the writings with peer editing groups and with you during teacher conferences. Encourage the students to proofread their writings and share their finished examples orally or through various publishing and presentation techniques.

Revising   Schebell (1988) found that without teacher influence students are not likely to write more than one draft. Working with older writers, Wallace and Hayes (1991) found that students who are given instruction in revision produce superior compositions when compared to students who are simply asked to make the text better.

Experienced writers use several techniques that are equally effective with less experienced student writers. Experienced writers may reread their compositions aloud to check for fluency. They frequently put their writing aside and try to approach it later from the viewpoint of the intended audience. They may share it with a critical audience whom they ask to respond to the clarity of ideas and give suggestions about areas or points that need clarification or change. Through this process, experienced writers may add, delete, change, or rearrange ideas. If the written project is very important to an experienced writer, the writer may go through this revision process several times before the paper is ready for the final proofreading and sharing with the intended audience.

You can duplicate the areas of the revision process in the classroom. Sharing your own writing experiences with students will place you in the role of a model. Demonstrate to the students how you changed a written project because you read it aloud to yourself and then shared it with another individual or group. This activity helps students understand the importance of this phase of writing.

Teacher–student conferencing   Conferencing with peers and teachers is important during the revision process. Tompkins and Hoskisson (1991) identified and briefly described various types of conferences used during this stage, as illustrated in Figure 9–7.

Research indicates that conferences and editing groups are beneficial at all grade levels. In an investigation of the revision process of first-grade students, Fitzgerald and Stamm (1990) found group conferences to be most helpful for those students who had the least knowledge about revision and who needed the most assistance in their writing. Gibbs (1990) found fifth-grade peer response groups to be especially effective when the members provided specific statements and suggestions about the needs of each others' stories. Olson (1990) found peer feedback to exert a positive influence on the writing of sixth-grade students. Nelson (1990) found that peer response between drafts produces better quality final drafts.

Three types of teacher–student conferences are frequently mentioned in the literature: (1) informal conferences, in which teachers provide immediate help for students who require assistance; (2) regularly scheduled conferences for individual students; and (3) scheduled conferences, in which groups of students are given lessons on writing conventions. Graves (1983) recommends both informal conferencing (teachers moving around the room, stopping at individual desks) and regularly scheduled conferencing (individual students coming to teachers prepared to discuss their work, ask and answer questions, and receive motivation and guidance). Graves believes that teachers should have regularly scheduled conferences with students at least once a week.

You may structure conferences on general, open-ended questions or on questions dealing with specific details, paragraph organization, and purpose for the writing. General, open-ended questions include: What do you like best about this piece of writing? What questions would you like to ask me? What surprised you as you were writing this draft? Are you having any problems? Which part is giving you problems? In a conference dealing with more specific elements, you might say, "I like the way you described the dog in your story. I could really see and hear him. I knew he was unhappy because he was lost. How do you think you could make your readers know more about his master, Davey? How do you think you could make your readers understand how Davey is feeling because his dog is lost?" Similar comments and questions may lead to discussions on ways to work with setting and plot.

Other possible topics for discussion are paragraph development, vocabulary choices, transitional phrases or sentences, story conclusions, and literary form. You could focus on the objectives of the lesson and refer to specific lessons taught as part of the prewriting phase, such as lessons on organizational patterns. You could use poetry forms to help students focus on their writing. You could use questions asked about the audience or the relationship between semantic maps and the various stages of the revision drafts. If the conference is focusing on proofreading, you and the student could explore whether or not he or she checked the underlined words for spelling or checked particular writing conventions.

During these conferences, you should keep in mind that teachers who are supportive are likely to be the most effective. An experiment by Spaulding (1989) underscores the importance of teacher interaction during the writing process. One group of students was given a writing assignment without having had any class

1. *On-the-Spot Conferences*
    The teacher visits briefly with a student at his or her desk to monitor some aspect of the writing assignment or to see how the student is progressing. The teacher begins by asking the student to read what he or she has written and then asks a question or two about the writing. Usually the teacher has several questions in mind before having the conference with the student. These conferences are brief; the teacher spends less than a minute at a student's desk before moving away.

2. *Drafting Conferences*
    Students bring their rough drafts and meet with the teacher at a table set up in the classroom specifically for that purpose. Students bring to the conference examples of specific writing problems that they would like to talk to the teacher about. These short, individual conferences often last less than 5 minutes so it is possible for a teacher to meet with 8 to 10 students in 30 minutes. Often students sign up for these conferences in advance.

3. *Revising Conferences*
    A small group of students and the teacher meet together in writing group conferences. Students read what they have written and ask for specific suggestions from classmates and the teacher about how to revise their compositions. These conferences offer student writers an audience to provide feedback on how well they have communicated. These small-group conferences last approximately 30 minutes or as long as necessary for each student to share his or her writing. Many elementary teachers schedule these conferences periodically in place of reading groups. After all, the purpose of reading and writing groups is virtually the same: to read and react to a piece of writing.

4. *Editing Conferences*
    Students meet with the teacher for an editing conference. In these individual or small-group conferences, the teacher reviews students' proofread compositions and helps them to correct spelling, punctuation, capitalization, and other mechanical errors. The teacher takes notes during these conferences about the problems students are having with mechanical skills in order to plan individual, special instruction conferences.

5. *Instructional Conferences*
    Ten- to fifteen-minute conferences are scheduled with individual students to provide special instruction. Teachers prepare for these conferences by reviewing students' writing folders and by planning instruction on one or two skills (e.g., capitalizing proper nouns, using commas in a series) that are particularly troublesome for individual students.

6. *Conferences with Classmates*
    Students meet with one or two classmates to ask for advice, to share a piece of writing, or to proofread a composition in much the same way that they hold a conference with the teacher. In these student conferences, students are expected to maintain a helpful and supportive relationship with their classmates.

7. *Class Conferences*
    Conferences with the entire class are held periodically to write and revise class collaboration compositions, to practice new conferencing strategies, and to discuss concerns relating to all students. Sometimes, these conferences are planned, and at other times they occur spontaneously as the need arises.

FIGURE 9–7
Types of writing conferences (From Gail E. Tompkins, and Kenneth Hoskisson, *Language Arts: Content and Teaching Strategies,* 2d. ed. [New York: Merrill/Macmillan, 1991].)

lessons on the assigned topic. Another group was first provided a lecture on the topic and then assigned a writing task in which the students used their notes to write about the topic. Spaulding's findings showed that those students who were given the lecture first were more engaged with their writing tasks than the students who had not been provided with instruction. She concluded: "The students generally manifested greater persistence, more reflective behaviors, and less self-doubt in the lecture condition than they did in the no instruction conditions. . . . The importance of instructional support, both content-related and procedural, in explaining the students' task-related engagement is evident throughout this study" (p. 157).

As suggested by the variety of questions and discussion topics, teachers play a variety of roles during writing conferences. According to Harris (1986), teachers encourage student writers by playing the role of coach, commentator, counselor, listener, and diagnostician. As coach, a teacher uses such comments as "You've done a good job describing the boy in the picture. Can you do the same thing when you describe the girl?" The coach, Harris states, "uses comments to help writers identify what they have to watch out for, what they have to work harder on, what has been working well for them, and what to build on" (p. 35).

In the commentator role, a teacher helps students see where they are in the writing process and where they need to move in the next draft. Comments may include statements such as "Good. The first draft helped you focus your subject on _____ . You are now ready to try your idea to add more detail about _____ ." In the counselor role, a teacher considers the whole person, including previous experience, motivation, prior learning, attitudes, and interests. This role is especially important when a teacher is trying to help students counteract writing blocks or other problems that are interfering with writing.

As a listener, a teacher plays several changing roles (Murray, 1979). At prewriting conferences, the teacher is a friendly listener who is interested in each student as an individual with ideas to express. As students develop drafts, the teacher becomes a fellow writer who tries to focus, shape, and form the written composition. As the writing progresses, the teacher listens closely to the language of the paper. Throughout this sequence, the teacher listens carefully to discover what the student needs to know.

As diagnostician, a teacher probes, asks questions, engages in exploratory conversations, and encourages students to make final decisions about their writing. Harris warns, however, that in this role, a teacher should not "unwittingly assume total control, wresting from the student all responsibility for what happens and closing off all avenues for student participation. When this happens, chances for students to improve their writing decrease dramatically" (p. 40). This final role may be the most difficult. Students may expect teachers to provide the major input. The purpose of a teacher–student conference is to encourage writers to participate in the discussion and develop independent writing skills. This role is not met when students respond passively to teacher comments without becoming involved in the process.

Peer editing   Peer editing groups are effective in the revision process because groups of three to five students provide a known audience for student writers. They encourage writers to sense the impact of their work, answer questions about their writing, clarify points, and revise writing to meet the needs of real audiences. Moreover, they allow student editors to hone their own editing and revising techniques, ask clarifying questions about content, and apply their new skills to their own writing.

Before peer editing groups can function, students need to develop trust. They must be willing to share their work with others and provide critical dialogue when it is their turn to respond to writing. The teacher should model the first editing group as a participant to help the students understand that the role of the editing group is to respond to specific things that they like about the paper, to ask questions about parts that are unclear, and to consider what could be added or changed to clarify or increase enjoyment and understanding. You may use sample papers to encourage this interaction and show students how to respond effectively as both presenter and editor. The complexity of the tasks expected of the peer editing groups and even the length of such activities depends on the ages, writing capabilities, and understandings of the students. Younger elementary students may focus on what they like about a paper, ask questions to clarify details in the paper, and respond to the effectiveness of revisions. Older students may become much more involved in the connections between the objectives of the lesson, form of the writing, and evaluation of the drafts during stages in the revision process.

From their work with older students during the National Writing Project, Daniels and Zemelman (1985) generated many useful suggestions for peer editing groups. They recommend that you form peer editing groups by tentatively ranking students from 1 (best prepared for writing) to 25 or whatever number is in the total class (least prepared for writing). Then, list students numerically in three columns. Form groups by selecting students across columns. In this way, each group includes above-average, average, and poor writers. You may alter these groups to balance students according to sex or to make changes because of inability to work together. You may keep the groups intact for long periods or re-form them monthly.

Several guidelines improve the function of these groups. First, peer editing groups are most effective when writers read their papers aloud so that both the writers and listeners hear the effect of the language. In addition, group members as well as writers should sign the drafts presented and discussed in the peer editing groups. These signatures show that both the author and the group members share responsibility for the writing. Furthermore, peer editing groups may benefit from checklists of criteria or forms that relate to the specific writing assignment being revised. Forms may be as simple as spaces to show examples of what the editing group liked about the writing and where clarification could take place to improve the writing, or they may consider such elements in a writing project as characterization, plot development, settings, or cause-effect relationships. The Holistic Scoring Scale (Table 9–2) and other such scales may help editing groups focus on important aspects of the writing task.

Daniels and Zemelman suggest that editing groups should meet for three different purposes. First, they should meet to discuss the assignment. Second, they should meet to edit each other's rough drafts. Finally, they should meet to proofread the final drafts. Daniels and Zemelman propose the weekly schedule in Figure 9–8. It incorporates the three functions of the peer editing groups and includes focus lessons on particular elements in writing.

Point Score	Characteristics
6	Has a thesis Concrete details used effectively Fluent in words and ideas Varied sentence structure Satisfactory closing statement Generally clear mechanics
5	Has a central idea Specific facts, details, or reasons Consistent development Less insightful, imaginative, concrete, or developed than a 6 Generally clear mechanics, errors do not interfere with overall effectiveness
4	Has several clear ideas Relevant and specific details Evidence of fluency, but not of unified development May be overly general or trite May have simple sentence structure or vocabulary Mechanical errors do not affect readability
3	Has at least one idea, few, if any supporting details Less fluent, developed, or detailed than a 4 Sentences, vocabulary, and thought may be simplistic Mechanical errors do not affect readability
2	No thesis Has a sense of order, but order may be only that of plot summary Fluency and thought are minimal Has at least one relevant idea May have many mechanical errors but paper is readable
1	No thesis and, of course, no support for thesis No sense of organization Simplistic or vague language May be unreadable due to spelling, handwriting, or other mechanical problems

TABLE 9–2
Holistic scoring scale for writing

SOURCE: "Effects of Student Writing of Teacher Training in the National Writing Project Model by R. J. Pritchard, 1987, *Written Communication, 4,* p. 58. Printed with permission.

Mondays
1. Rough drafts are due for assignment given the previous Friday.
2. Groups meet immediately and begin work. Each paper is read aloud by its author. The other group members ask questions about the content of the paper, which the author records on his rough draft, without actually answering any of them at this time. Both positive comments and constructive suggestions are expected at this time. Students have the entire period for this purpose and are instructed to think over the questions that were asked and make any changes that seem appropriate before coming to class on Tuesday.

Tuesdays
1. "Final" drafts are due.
2. Ten-minute free writing.
3. Groups meet again, this time actually exchanging papers and looking over them silently. Their focus today is on content and grammar/mechanics. No marks are made on another person's paper; instead, group members are to point the problems out and allow the author to decide what he/she wants to do about them.
4. Papers are turned in, signed by the author, and cosigned by the readers. Those who wish to do further rewriting simply sign a list on the teacher's desk and are automatically granted an extension.

Wednesdays
1. Ten-minute free writing.
2. People who have done further rewriting may have their group members go over their new "final" drafts instead of doing the ten-minute free writing on this day.
3. Focus lesson subject matter, writing process, or grammar item.

Thursdays
1. Ten-minute free writing.
2. Complete the focus lesson.

Fridays
1. Student evaluation (alternating between self-evaluation and group evaluation).
2. Vocabulary due.
3. Students are allowed to work independently, reading their novels, working on the next paragraph, or revising papers. Individual conferences are held at this time. (pp. 167–68).

FIGURE 9–8
Weekly schedule for writing activities (From Harvey Daniels and Steven Zemelman, *A Writing Project: Training Teachers of Composition from Kindergarten to College.* Copyright 1985 by Heinemann Educational Books. Reprinted with permission.)

A group of peers can help a young author revise her writing by asking clarifying questions.

Simpson (1986), a seventh-grade language arts teacher, discusses the roles she plays while her students are involved in the writing process. Read the following roles and decide during which phase or phases of the writing process she assumes each of these roles and describe her actions as if you could observe her classroom:

1. Serving as students' most ardent admirer and astute critic.
2. Teaching writers to internalize the reading role so that they communicate their intended meaning to others.
3. Aiding students so that they write in a tone that readers recognize as genuine.
4. Protecting authors as they offer their writings to the audience for comments and helping them screen suggestions and comments as to the appropriateness of the suggestions.
5. Modeling appropriate group responses, questions, and techniques.
6. Helping students focus their attention on the task that is appropriate for their stage in the writing process.
7. Integrating skill instruction within the context of revision.
8. Monitoring individual progress.
9. Maintaining the human connection.

Sharing   Students should share their writing with a genuine audience. They should mail letters, editorial comments, and reactions to books. They should read poetry and short stories to peers. They should place stories in the library or post them on the bulletin board. They should publish class newspapers and magazines. Although it is not necessary to extend writing to any other activity, students often enjoy using their own writing for choral-reading and reader's theater arrangements, art interpretations, or dramatizations.

Students enjoy making permanent collections of their poems and stories. One teacher had each child develop an accordion-pleated poem book. To construct the books, the students folded large sheets of heavy drawing paper in half, connected several sheets with tape, and printed their poems and an accompanying illustration on each page. Other classes made their own books by constructing covers in various appropriate shapes, cutting paper to match the shapes, and binding the cover and pages together. A group of second graders placed Halloween stories inside a jack-o-lantern book, fourth graders wrote city poems and stories inside a book resembling a skyscraper, and third graders placed humorous mythical animal stories and poems inside a book resembling a Dr. Seuss beast.

Many teachers use a study of newspapers as an introduction to creating a classwritten newspaper or to introduce editing and proofreading of a child's own writing. Newspapers can motivate almost limitless writing activities and are also useful for developing learning centers.

FOR YOUR PLAN BOOK
Learning Center Activities Based on Newspapers

Meet the Press
Purpose: To increase reading and writing ability through use of newspapers.

Grade level: Intermediate upper elementary. Appropriate for individual, small-group, and large-group activity. Suggested limit: 30

General materials: Newspapers, paper, pencil, manila folders, typewriter (optional), picture file. More specific materials are listed for each activity.

Plan to progress: Give the students a mimeographed handout with their assignments, determining level placement (for example, Reporter One). Allot space for "Extra, Extra" activities to meet individual needs. The handout should indicate the activities that the students will complete as they progress through the learning center. Post these general instructions and explain them orally to the students:

> Dear Reporter,
> I have given you some assignments for our next newspaper. You may do the assignments in any order you wish. When you complete each assignment, check your answers. Then place your finished work in the "Ready for Print" box. When all of the assignments are completed, sign up for an activity in the school newspaper. (The following categories are suggested: Lifestyle, Dennis the Menace, Editorials, Sports, News, Dear Abby, and Wedding.) In order to write your activity, interview a person in your field of interest. Place the article in the "Ready for Print" box. When all of your work is completed, you may begin work on the "Extra, Extra" box.
>
> Good Luck,
> The Editor

Instructions: Besides the general instructions, write specific instructions for each activity on its manila envelope.

Evaluation: Provide an answer box or envelope so the students can easily locate the answer keys they need. Keep the students' work in a class file. Have the students indicate by a check mark the activities they have completed. Observe the students' work and initial each student's handout upon approval.

Activities:

Reporter One (low-level)

DEAR ABBY

Objective: To match the advice column with the correct solution.

Materials: Glue "Dear Abby" advice columns to a manila envelope with the problems separated from the solutions. Number the problems and letter the solutions.

Activity: Have the students match the correct solution with the problem by writing their answers on a sheet of paper.

Evaluation: Answer key.

CAPTURE THE CAPTION

Objective: To match pictures with the correct captions.

Materials: Manila folders, each containing several pictures and captions. Number the pictures and letter the captions.

Activities: Have the students choose one of the manila folders. Have them match pictures with the captions and write their answers on paper.

Evaluation: Answer key.

HEADLINE SCRAMBLE

Objective: To match each article with the correct headline.

Materials: Manila folders, each containing several articles with matching headlines. Place the articles separately from the headlines in the manila folders. Number the articles and letter the captions.

Activity: Have each student choose one of the folders, place the words in a line, and then classify each picture under the appropriate word.

Evaluation: Student self-check.

FEELINGS, FEELINGS

Objective: In one word, to describe how each person feels.

Materials: A manila folder with several pieces of construction paper. Each piece of construction paper has a picture of a person glued to it. Number each picture.

Activity: Have each student choose three of the sheets of construction paper with the pictures. In one word, each student must describe how each person feels. The students must use a different word for each person.

Evaluation: Pupil self-check.

GETTING THE MEANING

Objective: To match the article with the main idea.

Materials: A manila folder with numerous low-level, high-interest articles. Each article should contain strips of paper with three possible main ideas.

Activity: Have the students choose four articles from the manila folder. Have them match the strip of paper that contains the main idea with the appropriate article.
Evaluation: Answer key.

SEQUENCING CARTOONS

Objective: To sequence cartoon frames.
Materials: Five multiframed cartoons, each backed with different-colored construction paper. Cut these into separate frames, and number them in the correct order on the back.
Activity: Have the students group the cartoon frames according to color and then sequence them.
Evaluation: The students will check their answers by turning them over. The correct order is indicated by the numbers on the back.

Reporter Two

HEADLINES

Objective: To write an article to go with a specific headline.
Materials: Headlines placed in a manila folder.
Activity: Have each student choose one headline from the manila folder and then write an article in journalistic form.
Evaluation: Rating scale (see Figure 1).

MAIN IDEAS

Objective: To write out the main idea of an article students have read.
Materials: Articles without the headlines. Manila folders.
Activity: Have the students read the articles and write out the main idea of each.
Evaluation: Rating scale.

ARTICLE ARTISTRY

Objective: To write an article and a caption from a photograph.
Materials: A picture file.
Activity: Have the students choose a picture from the picture file and then write an article for the picture and a caption for the article.
Evaluation: Rating scale.

CATCHY CARTOONS

Objective: To write one caption for each of several pictures.
Materials: A picture file.
Activity: Have the students choose several pictures from the picture file and then write one caption for each of the pictures.
Evaluation: Rating scale.

DON'T BE CONNED

Objective: To identify propaganda techniques contained in advertisements.
Materials: Several advertisements illustrating propaganda techniques.
Activity: Have the students read the advertisements and identify in writing the propaganda techniques used.
Evaluation: Answer key.

Rating Scale

Student's name:_____

		Low . . . . .High				
1.	Originality	1	2	3	4	5	NA*
2.	Creativity	1	2	3	4	5	NA
3.	Expressive	1	2	3	4	5	NA
4.	Form or Style-(Newspaper)	1	2	3	4	5	NA

    a. who _____
    b. what _____
    c. when _____
    d. where _____
    e. why _____

5.	Sentence Structure	1	2	3	4	5	NA
6.	Paragraph Structure	1	2	3	4	5	NA
7.	Consistency in Theme	1	2	3	4	5	NA
8.	Grammatical Structure	1	2	3	4	5	NA

    a. Spelling
    b. Punctuation
    c. Capitalization

Notes_____

_____

*NA means nonapplicable for this assignment.

FIGURE 1

CARTOON TALK
Objective: To fill in cartoon balloons with appropriate words.
Materials: Liquid paper; several cartoons, each mounted on construction paper with their ballooned message opaqued out.
Activity: Have the students fill in the cartoon balloons with appropriate dialogue.
Evaluation: Rating scale.

ARTICLE SEQUENCING
Objective: To sequence an article.
Materials: Several articles cut into sections and mounted on colored construction paper.
Activity: Have the students group article pieces according to color and then sequence them.
Evaluation: Self-checked; answers on the back.

ADVICE EDITOR
Objective: To write advice to a given problem.
Materials: A variety of advice columns mounted on tagboard.
Activity: Have each student choose one problem and write an original solution.
Evaluation: Rating scale.

Extra, Extra

WRITING CARTOONS
Objective: After drawing a cartoon, to write a script to accompany it.
Materials: Blank cartoon frames, colored pencils.
Activity: Have each student create a cartoon sequence using his or her favorite cartoon character. The students should write scripts to go along with their drawings.
Evaluation: Rating scale.

JUNIOR JUMBLE
Objective: To unscramble words.
Materials: Several junior jumbles mounted on poster board.
Activity: Have the students choose three junior jumbles, unscramble the words, and solve the puzzle.
Evaluation: Answer key.

TV QUIZ
Objective: Using the *TV GUIDE*, to answer several questions.
Materials: *TV GUIDE,* typed questions mounted on tagboard.
Activities: Have the students read the questions on the tagboard and skim the magazine to answer them.
Evaluation: Answer key.

BRAIN TWISTERS
Objective: To solve the problem in the brain twister.
Materials: Several brain twisters mounted on construction paper.
Activity: Have the students read the brain twisters and then solve each problem.
Evaluation: Self-checked; answers on the back.

ADVERTISING
Objective: To write an original advertisement using some propaganda technique.
Materials: Various pictures of products mounted on tagboard.
Activity: Have the students choose at least one of the pictures and write an advertisement for it using one of the propaganda techniques.
Evaluation: Rating scale.

FACT OR OPINION GAME
Objective: To classify headlines into fact or opinion.
Materials: Game board made from construction paper. On it, a definition of fact and a definition of opinion. Under each definition, staple a pocket to the construction paper. Provide twenty headlines, some of which are facts, the remainder of which are opinions.
Activity: Have each student choose a headline and read it. Then have the student decide whether it is a fact or an opinion and place the headline into the correct pocket on the game board.
Evaluation: Self-checked; answers on the back.

FUN FACTS FOR BROWSING
Objective: To read fun facts for enjoyment.

Materials: An envelope that contains fun facts items, such as facts from *Ripley's Believe It or Not,* Wrigley's "Fun Fact" and *Guinness Book of World Records* excerpts.
Activity: This activity is merely for the enjoyment of reading. Let the students read these materials during free time.
Evaluation: None

Used with permission of Nancy Mangano, Debra Penkert, and Jacqueline Thurston, graduate students at Texas A&M University.

ASSESSMENT

Studies that analyze the composing process of skilled and unskilled writers provide important insights for language arts teachers. In addition, the studies identify characteristics of writers who might benefit from activities stressing the writing process.

Glatthorn (1982) synthesized the results from several studies and reached several conclusions about the writing processes of skilled and unskilled writers. The following observable characteristics describe the actions of skilled and unskilled writers during each of Glatthorn's four stages of the writing process:

1. Exploring—the beginning stage, in which writers think about a topic, discover what they know, collect information, consider audience, and reflect about approaches.

Skilled Writers	*Unskilled Writers*
Take time to explore the topic and use many strategies.	Do little exploring and do not consider it important or useful.

2. Planning—the stage in which writers make tentative decisions. Writers make preliminary choices about content, organization, and proportion.

Skilled Writers	*Unskilled Writers*
Take time to plan and use a variety of techniques, such as listing, sketching, and diagramming.	Do little planning either before writing or while writing.

3. Drafting—the psychomotor process by which writers choose the words and craft the sentences.

Skilled Writers	*Unskilled Writers*
Write in ways that are less like speech and show sensitivity to the reader. Usually, they spend more time drafting than do unskilled writers.	Write in ways that imitate speech show little concern for readers, and seem preoccupied with spelling and punctuation.

4. Revising—the stage in which writers evaluate what they wrote and make changes in the form and content.

Skilled Writers	*Unskilled Writers*
Either revise very little or revise extensively. When they make extensive revisions, they examine larger issues, such as content and reader appeal.	Either revise very little or revise only at the word level. They see revising as error hunting and copying over in ink.

Students who exhibit the characteristics of unskilled writers might benefit from a processing approach to composition. In addition, Myers and Gray (1983) state that writers who lack fluency and have difficulty generating or expanding ideas should engage in processing activities. One of the most effective ways to assess growth is accumulation of writing samples. You may keep each child's examples in a folder, compiled over long periods of time, so that both you and the child can look at and evaluate changes in the writing. If changes are not occurring, you should suspect that the instruction is probably not appropriate for that particular child. Phelps (Gleason and Mano, 1986), an advocate of teaching the writing process, emphasizes that writing instructors should analyze drafts in terms of potential for writing development, not in terms of errors. Such an analysis looks for clues to changes going on within the writing and considers ways to help students proceed toward the next step in writing development.

Effective evaluation considers the purpose for each writing activity. For example, if the objective of a poetry-writing lesson is for children to become aware of their uniqueness through self-expression, the instruction is effective to the degree that children write their own thoughts and emotions in poetic form. You should evaluate poetic originality by comparing a child's poetry with the previous poetry for that child, not some standard for all children. Rupley (1976) suggests that if a teacher's purposes are to develop interest in writing and foster creative thought, evaluation should also relate to these purposes.

In order to analyze the influence of both audience and purpose, Goodman (1985) recommends that teachers keep copies of children's letters written to different audiences for different purposes. You should analyze the letters according to the following considerations: the appropriateness of the language for the specific purpose, the degree to which children change their language and style to meet the needs of the specific audience, the increase in conventional spellings, the changes in grammatical complexity of the sentences, and the concern for legibility.

In an evaluation of teaching composition in open classes in England, Williams (1978) concluded that merely dating the children's materials allows them to see their own improvement over a period of time. As she put it, "the teacher could not have developed a more motivating feedback system than this chronological record of the student's composition efforts. Handwriting and quantity and quality of work had all improved noticeably" (p. 3). A writing folder should include samples of many types of writing. You may compile a checklist of some of the areas to observe for written composition. Such a checklist would look something like Figure 9–9.

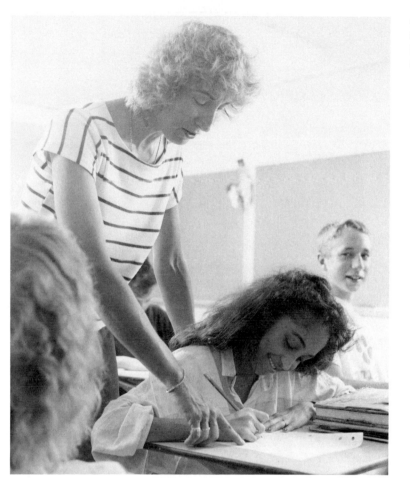

Effective teachers analyze writing in terms of its strengths and weaknesses rather than merely circle errors.

Collect several written compositions from the same child and evaluate the writing using the Holistic Scoring Scale (Table 9–2) and the checklist for informal evaluation of writing (Figure 9–9). Tabulate your findings.

	Yes	Sometimes	No
Ideas:			
1. Sentences express his or her ideas.	_____	_____	_____
2. Ideas flow from one sentence to another.	_____	_____	_____
Purpose and Audience:			
3. Understands the purpose for an audience when writing.	_____	_____	_____
4. Age, knowledge, and interest of audience influence the composition.	_____	_____	_____
5. Purpose of the composition influences the writing.	_____	_____	_____
Organizing Ideas—Paragraphs:			
6. Groups and classifies related ideas.	_____	_____	_____
7. Understands need for and chooses main idea that unifies a paragraph.	_____	_____	_____
8. Supports main ideas with necessary facts and details.	_____	_____	_____
9. Puts main idea and supporting details into logical order.	_____	_____	_____
Organizing Ideas—Longer Compositions:			
10. Narrows subject to one that can be realistically covered.	_____	_____	_____
11. Gathers ideas and information before trying to write composition.	_____	_____	_____
12. Understands and develops important questions on the topic.	_____	_____	_____
13. Organizes important questions and supporting data into logical sequence.	_____	_____	_____
14. Demonstrates progress in ability to write composition with interesting introduction, main ideas, supporting details, and logical conclusion.	_____	_____	_____
Rewriting:			
15. Reads orally while developing composition and makes changes to improve clarity of writing.	_____	_____	_____
16. Responds to teacher questions and makes appropriate writing changes.	_____	_____	_____
17. Reads composition silently while developing it and makes changes.	_____	_____	_____
Vocabulary:			
18. Has extensive writing vocabulary.	_____	_____	_____
19. Uses context clues to develop new vocabulary understanding.	_____	_____	_____
20. Uses precise vocabulary in factual writing.	_____	_____	_____
21. Uses few slang expressions in factual writing.	_____	_____	_____
22. Does not rely on trite expressions.	_____	_____	_____

FIGURE 9–9
Checklist for informal evaluation of writing

SUMMARY

Current research in written composition analyzes approaches to teaching written composition. Studies of the writing process and corresponding models examine the tasks of writers as they identify the topic for a writing project, generate ideas, plan and organize their writing, write rough drafts, review and evaluate their writing, and revise their writing.

You can develop composition skills through the writing process by emphasizing activities that help students during each phase. During the prewriting phase, activities can motivate students to write, generate ideas, and focus their attention on desired subjects or objectives. Prewriting activities include drawing, semantic mapping, brainstorming, and listing and categorizing. Activities designed to improve progress during the writing phase include deciding on audience and purpose, deciding about form, deciding about organizational pattern, deciding about linguistic style, and writing the first draft. After-writing activities include revising, teacher-student conferencing, peer editing, and sharing writing with an audience.

ADDITIONAL WRITING PROCESS ACTIVITIES

1. Observe an elementary student. Identify the activities of the student in approaching and completing a writing task.
2. Interview an elementary, a middle-school, and a high-school language arts or English teacher. Ask how often the students should write, the purpose for writing, and the appropriate audience for writing. Share your findings in your language arts class. How do these results compare with both the American and the British studies discussed in this chapter?
3. Develop a file of ideas and resources to use during the prewriting stage of the writing process.
4. Develop a modeling activity appropriate for the prewriting or writing stage. Share your activity with your language arts class.
5. Lead a prewriting activity in which you help a group of children or an individual child develop a semantic map or web for a writing assignment.
6. Collect examples of various forms of writing, such as diaries, editorials, and short stories, that are appropriate for writing projects. List the characteristics of each form and identify writing assignments in which the forms would be appropriate.
7. If possible, visit a classroom during a teacher–student conference or during peer editing groups. What is the focus of the activity? How do teachers or peers respond to papers? How do students respond when they present or discuss their writings? What questions do they ask? Can you identify where the students are in the writing process? What are the major writing problems experienced by the students? How are the students receiving help with those writing problems?
8. Develop a file of different ideas for sharing writing with an audience. Your file might include directions for making books, developing writing bulletin boards, and making oral presentations that emphasize original work.

BIBLIOGRAPHY

Ammon, Paul. "Cognitive Development and Early Childhood Education: Piagetian and Neo-Piagetian Theories." In *Psychological Processes in Early Education,* edited by H. L. Hom and P. A. Robinson. New York: Academic Press, 1977.

Applebee, Arthur N. "Writing and Reasoning." *Review of Educational Research* 54 (Winter 1984): 577–96.

Blohm, P. J., and Benton, S. C. "Effect of Prewriting Interventions on Production of Elaboration in Informative Writing." *Journal of Research and Development in Education* 24 (1991): 28–32.

Bradley, Virginia N. "Improving Students' Writing with Microcomputers." *Language Arts* 59 (October 1982): 732–43.

Britton, James; Burgess, Tony; Martin, Nancy; McLeod, Alex; and Rosen, Harold. *The Development of Writing Abilities (11–18).* Schools Council Research Studies, London: Macmillan Co., 1979.

Bruce, Bertram; Michaels, Sarah; Watson-Gegeo, Karen. "How Computers Can Change the Writing Process." *Language Arts* 62 (February 1985): 143–49.

Bruner, Jerome; Goodnow, Jacqueline; and Austin, G. A. *A Study of Thinking.* New York: John Wiley & Sons, 1956.

Carey, L. *Differences in Writers' Initial Task Representation.* 1989. (Technical Report No. 35). Center for the Study of Writing. ERIC Document Reproduction Service No. ED 310 403.

Daniels, Harvey, and Zemelman, Steven. *A Writing Project: Training Teachers of Composition from Kindergarten to College.* Portsmouth, N.H.: Heinemann, 1985.

Dauite, Colette. "Physical and Cognitive Factors in Revising: Insights from Studies with Computers." *Research in the Teaching of English* 20 (May 1986): 141–59.

Davis, B. H. "The Effects of Expressive Writing on Social Studies Achievement, Writing Fluency, and Learning Retention of Fourth-Grade Students." 1990. *Dissertation Abstracts International,* 51, 09A. (University Microfilm No. 91-04, 761)

Dickinson, David K. "Cooperation, Collaboration, and a Computer: Integrating a Computer into a First-Second Grade Writing Program." *Research in the Teaching of English* 20 (December 1986): 357–78.

Elkins, Deborah. *Teaching Literature: Designs for Cognitive Development.* Columbus, Oh.: Merrill Publishing Co., 1976.

Fitzgerald, J., and Stamm, C. "Effects of Group Conferences on First Graders' Revision in Writing." *Written Communication* 7 (1990): 96–135.

Flower, Linda, and Hayes, John. "The Dynamics of Composing: Making Plans and Juggling Constraints." In *Cognitive Processes in Writing,* edited by Lee W. Gregg and Erwin R. Steinberg. Hillsdale, N.J.: Lawrence Erlbaum Associates, 1978.

Gagné, Robert. *The Conditions of Learning.* 2d ed. New York: Holt, Rinehart & Winston, 1970.

Gibbs, E. B. "Peer Response Groups: Implications for Writing Development in a Fifth-Grade Classroom." 1990. *Dissertation Abstracts International,* 51, 05A. (University Microfilms No. 90-11, 331)

Glatthorn, Allan A. "Demystifying the Teaching of Writing." *Language Arts* 59 (October 1982): 722–25.

Gleason, Barbara, and Mano, Sandra. "Issues in Development: An Interview with Wetherbee Phelps." *The Writing Instructor* 5 (Winter 1986): 45–50.

Gomez, Mary Louise. "Using Microcomputers in the Language Arts." In *Language Arts Instruction and the Beginning Teacher,* edited by Carl Personke and Dale Johnson. Englewood Cliffs, N.J.: Prentice-Hall, 1987.

Goodman, Yetta, "Kidwatching: Observing Children in the Classroom." In *Observing the Language Learner,* edited by Angela Jaggar and M. Trika Smith-Burke. National Council of Teachers of English, 1985, pp. 9–18.

Graves, Donald. *A Case Study Observing the Development of Primary Children's Composing, Spelling, and Motor Behaviors during the Writing Process.* Final Report, NIE Grant No. G-78-0174. Durham, N.H.: University of New Hampshire, 1981. ED 218 653.

———. *Writing: Teachers and Children at Work.* Exeter, N.H.: Heinemann, 1983.

Haas, C. "Composing in Technological Contexts: A Study of Note-Making." *Written Communication* 7 (1990): 512–47.

Harris, Muriel. *Teaching One-to-One: The Writing Conference.* Urbana, Ill.: National Council of Teachers of English, 1986.

Hayes, John, and Flower, Linda. "Writing as Problem Solving." *Visible Language* 14 (1980): 388–90.

Heimlich, Joen E., and Pittelman, Susan D. *Semantic Mapping: Classroom Applications.* Newark, Del.: International Reading Association, 1986.

Hillocks, George. *Research on Written Composition: New Directions for Teaching.* Urbana, Ill.: National Conference on Research in English, 1986.

Kleiman, Glenn, and Humphrey, Mary. "Word Processing in the Classroom." *Compute* 22 (March 1982): 96–99.

Kruh, Nancy. "The Challenge: Teach Two Classes of Kids How to Write." *Dallas Morning News.* Sunday, May 22, 1988, section F, pp. 1, 10. Additional news articles on subject, F, pp. 8–9, 8, and 11.

Medearis, L. "The Written Production of Four Kindergarten Children in a Whole Language Classroom." Doctoral Dissertation, North Texas State University, 1985. *Dissertation Abstracts International,* 46, 09A. (University Microfilms No. 85–25,570)

Murray, Donald. "The Listening Eye: Reflections on the Writing Conference." *College English* 41 (1979).

Myers, Miles, and Gray, James. *Theory and Practice in the Teaching of Composition: Processing, Distancing, and Modeling.* Urbana, Ill.: National Council of Teachers of English, 1983.

National Council of Teachers of English. *Language Arts* 60 (February 1983): 244–48.

Nelson, R. R. "The Revision Processes of Male Tenth Graders: Qualitative Differences in Revision Activities in Expository Modes." 1990. *Dissertation Abstracts International,* 51, 90-08, 005.

Olson, U. C. "The Revising Processes of Sixth-Grade Writers with and without Peer Feedback." *Journal of Educational Research* 84 (1990): 22–29.

Pritchard, Ruie Jane. "Effects on Student Writing of Teacher Training in the National Writing Project Model." *Written Communication* 4 (January 1987): 51–67.

Proett, Jackie, and Gill, Kent. *The Writing Process in Action: A Handbook for Teachers.* Urbana, Ill.: National Council of Teachers of English, 1986.

Rubenstein, R., and Rollins, A. *Demonstration of the Use of Computer Assisted Instruction with Handicapped Children: Final Report.* Cambridge, Mass.: Bolt Beranek & Newman, 1978.

Rupley, William H. "Teaching and Evaluating Creative Writing in the Elementary Grades." *Language Arts* 53 (May 1976): 586–90.

Schebell, R. A. "Influences of Writing Instruction and Teacher Response on the Revising Practices of Seventh Grade Writers." 1988. *Dissertation Abstracts International,* 49, 05A. (University Microfilms No. 88-12, 382)

Selfe, Cynthia. *Computer-Assisted Instruction in Composition: Create Your Own.* Urbana, Ill.: National Council of Teachers of English, 1986.

Simon, Herbert A. *The Sciences of the Artificial.* 2d ed. Cambridge, Mass.: The M.I.T. Press, 1981.

Simpson, Mary K. "What Am I Supposed to Do While They're Writing?" *Language Arts* 63 (November 1986): 680–84.

Spaulding, C. "The Effects of Ownership Opportunities and Instructional Support on High School Students' Writing Task Engagement." *Research in the Teaching of English* 23 (1989): 139–62.

Suhor, Charles. "Thinking Visually about Writing: Three Models for Teaching Composition, K–12," in *Speaking and Writing, K–12,* edited by Christopher Thaiss and Charles Suhor. Urbana, Ill.: National Council of Teachers of English, 1984, pp. 74–103.

Tompkins, Gail, and Hoskisson, Kenneth. *Language Arts: Content and Teaching Strategies.* 2d ed. New York: Merrill/Macmillan, 1991.

Wallace, D., and Hayes, J. R. "Redefining Revision for Freshmen." *Research in the Teaching of English* 25 (1991): 54–66.

Williams, Laura E. "Methods of Teaching Composition in Open Classes—England, Canada, and the United States." *Innovator* 9 (January 1978): 1–3.

Wresch, William, ed. *The Computer in Composition Instruction: A Writer's Tool.* Urbana, Ill.: National Council of Teachers of English, 1984.

CHILDREN'S LITERATURE REFERENCES

Blumberg, Rhoda. *The Incredible Journey of Lewis and Clark.* New York: Lothrop, Lee & Shepard, 1987.

Bodecker, N. M. *A Person from Britain Whose Head Was the Shape of a Mitten and Other Limericks.* London: Dent, 1980.

Fox, Paula. *One-Eyed Cat.* New York: Bradbury, 1984.

Freedman, Russel. *Franklin Delano Roosevelt.* New York: Clarion, 1990.

Giblin, James Cross. *The Riddle of the Rosetta Stone: Key to Ancient Egypt.* New York: Harper Collins, 1990.

Hudson, Jan. *Sweetgrass.* New York: Philomel, 1989.

Lauber, Patricia. *The News about Dinosaurs.* New York: Bradbury, 1988.

Lear, Edward. *Nonsense Omnibus.* New York: Warne, 1943 (from earlier editions dating from 1846).

McCord, David. *One at a Time: Collected Poems for the Young.* Boston: Little, Brown & Co., 1977.

Pringle, Laurence. *Global Warming: Assessing the Greenhouse Threat.* New York. Little, Brown, 1990.

Simon, Seymour. *New Questions and Answers about Dinosaurs.* Illustrated by Jennifer Dewey. New York: Morrow, 1990.

Sperry, Armstrong. *Call It Courage.* New York: Macmillan, 1940.

St. George, Judith. *The White House: Cornerstone of a Nation.* New York: Putnam's, 1990.

Vogel, Carole G., and Goldner, Kathryn A. *The Great Yellowstone Fire.* Boston: Sierra Club and Little, Brown, 1990.

Wilcox, Charlotte. *Trash!* Photographs by Jerry Bushey. Minneapolis: Carolrhoda, 1988.

Chapter Ten

After completing this chapter on expressive, poetic, and expository writing, you will be able to:

1. Define terms related to expressive, imaginative, and expository writing.
2. Identify and develop writing approaches that encourage expressive writing.
3. Identify and develop writing approaches that encourage imaginative writing.
4. Describe the importance of the environment for developing creative writers.
5. Describe and develop writing approaches that improve ability to create plots, settings and characters.
6. Describe how creative writing is enhanced through an understanding of symbolism.
7. Identify writing approaches to encourage poetic expression.
8. Describe writing approaches that develop and improve expository writing.
9. Develop a unit that focuses on a composition approach to the study of biography.

Composition: Expressive, Imaginative, and Expository Writing

*T*his chapter emphasizes expressive, imaginative, and expository writing. In the expressive function, writers, especially young children, write as they speak. In the imaginative function, writers use language as an art medium to simultaneously inform and entertain. In the expository function, writers inform, record, report, and explain. Yet, there are no absolute divisions between expressive, imaginative, and expository writing. As you approach this chapter, remember that the ideas for stimulating writing are more important than the divisions.

EXPRESSIVE WRITING

Expressive writing is very close to speech and, consequently, very close to the writer. It is relaxed and intimate. It reveals the writer and verbalizes the writer's consciousness. According to Britton, Burgess, Martin, McLeod, and Rosen (1975), writing is important because "not only is it the mode in which we approach and relate to each other in speech, but it is also the mode in which, generally speaking, we frame the tentative first drafts of new ideas: the mode in which, in times of family and national crisis, we talk with our own people and attempt to work our way towards some kind of resolution" (p. 82).

Expressive writing, with its close relationship to speech, is the most accessible form of writing for young children. Children come to school with knowledge of speech and are used to speaking to known audiences on intimate terms. Britton et al. maintain that in the early stages, writing should be in the form of expressive speech. From this starting point, children can proceed into the imaginative and expository forms.

Expressive writing is frequently characterized as thinking aloud on paper. Expressive writing activities encourage writers to explore their reactions and to express their moods, feelings, and opinions. The form for this personal expression may be a diary, journal, or letter written to a friend. Shared beyond oneself, the writing is addressed to a known audience, or at least to an audience that shares the values, opinions, and interests of the writer. On the adult level, such writing may take the form of gossip columns or special-interest articles.

Journals can be used to begin and extend the writing process.

Journals and Diaries

Journal writing is recommended at all levels of education. Even adult writers keep journals in which they write or draw. When Maurice Sendak was a boy, he drew pictures of other students playing. Later, he used these pictures to get ideas for his books.

Watson (1987) describes a kindergarten journal activity in which teachers first prepare journals for each student by folding eight sheets of 12-by-18-inch paper in half, adding a cover of heavier paper, and stapling the pages so that they lie flat when the journal is opened. You may introduce the journal to students by explaining to them that they will be keeping a journal in which they will write stories, personal anecdotes, or summaries of and reactions to various school activities. They will be using inventive spellings or dictating the entries to you or an aide. Volunteers will be able to publish their entries by reading them aloud to the class. The students will be writing in a different journal during each month of the year. These journals will remain in school until the end of the year, at which time the students may take them home. However, the journals will be available to the students and may be used for parent–teacher conferences. You may also use them to extend the writing process by asking students to select short entries to expand and refine. Kept on a monthly basis, the journals provide a means of assessing individual growth.

Teachers use journal writing to encourage students to express ideas and to react in personal ways. For example, Armstrong (1990) found that journals show how students think about literature and composition. Some teachers have students write about topics of their choosing during short daily writing periods. For example, Bromley (1985) describes a technique called sustained spontaneous writing (SSW), in which students write for five to fifteen minutes on subjects of their choice. This writing, in the form of a personal journal or diary, is dated, but it is not shared with anyone unless the student volunteers to share it. Bromley recommends dating so that students can review their entries from different time periods.

Journal writing may be more structured and encourage students to think about what they already know or feel about a subject. Ideas for journal writing may include listing pleasant smells or sights, describing wishes, identifying favorite colors or music and explaining why they are favorites, listing memorable characters from books and explaining why they are memorable, and recording impressions following a walk.

Dialogue journals (see Gambrell, 1985) are specifically designed to increase the interaction between students and teachers. As the name implies, students write questions and comments about something happening in their personal lives or in school with the knowledge that the teacher will read their entries. The teacher then writes brief responses directly in the journal. Due to time constraints, teachers frequently read and respond to journals on a rotating basis.

Learning Logs

Learning logs focus on specific content. Students respond to what they learned in a lesson, project, or unit of study. They make their entries at the end of the class, although perhaps not every day. In many ways, learning logs form bridges between expressive writing and expository writing. From the expressive viewpoint, students can respond to what they liked best about a lesson or how the lesson could be improved. They can explain why they think the lesson is important, how they will use it in the future, and what they would like to know more about. From the expository viewpoint, students can respond to the main points of the lesson, state what they learned during the lesson, and list questions about content that they would like answered.

You may use learning logs to help students retain material and develop understanding. MacVaugh (1990) found that journal writing facilitates learning in the content areas. The logs may also generate ideas for writing projects and help students realize that their viewpoints and responses are worthwhile. This format, as we will discuss later, is especially appropriate for responding to literature.

Writer's Journals

A writer's journal forms a natural bridge between expressive and imaginative writing. The information in a writer's journal provides a source for story ideas, characterizations, language choices, and sensory experiences. Although a few students may create writer's journals on their own, most need to be encouraged to do so.

In *The Young Writer's Handbook: A Practical Guide for the Beginner Who Is Serious About Writing* (1984), Susan and Stephen Tchudi provide ideas for students and teachers who are developing writer's journals. The Tchudis recommend that writers of all ages use journals to explore their experiences, their world, and their language. The descriptions and reactions frequently become bases for fictional stories, poetry, and other forms of writing. Writers should probe their memories and record early experiences. Then, they should think about how the experiences shaped their lives. When exploring their experiences, they should record their dreams, daydreams, and nightmares, as well as their opinions about various topics. Finally, they should sit in various places and record everything around them. They should describe in detail what they see, hear, smell, feel, and taste. They should also compare things in their environment; these comparisons may later be used as similes and metaphors in their writings.

In exploring their world, writers should move beyond their own experiences and day-to-day events and seek new ideas and new ways of looking at things. They should describe impressions of new experiences and analyze broad concepts, such as fear and friendship. They should extend their experiences through newspapers and write their reactions to news stories and editorials, as well as to feature and sports articles.

To explore language, writers should listen for and record unusual or interesting expressions. They can write down dialects and word choices to later add authenticity to characterizations in their writings. They can collect interesting expressions and quotes to add vitality to stories.

The Tchudis recommend that writers set aside a few pages of their journals to list areas of special interest (hobbies, reading interests, locations); landmarks in their lives (first day of school, trip to a dentist, ride on an airplane); people who are important in their lives and imaginary characters of interest; places that are real or imaginary; memories of pleasant and unpleasant experiences; things they would like to change; and questions that fascinate them.

Letters

Writing letters to friends, relatives, teachers, authors, or even imaginary people is an excellent way to encourage expressive writing in children. Numerous experiences motivate such writing. For example, stories that include situations in which characters write letters can be used to motivate children to write letters of their own. Younger students could be introduced to letters through Janet and Allan Ahlberg's *The Jolly Postman* (1986). In this book, the postman delivers letters to fairy-tale characters, such as Cinderella and The Three Bears. Several books use trips or moving as reasons for letter writing. For example, in *Your Best Friend, Kate* (1989), Pat Brisson develops a story in which Kate writes letters to her best friend describing her experiences as she takes a car trip with her family. In *Stringbean's*

Trip to the Shining Sea (1988), Vera Williams bases her story on a series of postcards written during a camping trip across the western United States. In *Jenny's Journey* (1991), Sheila Sampton's character writes a letter to a friend and fantasizes about sailing to the friend's new island home. In *Little Dog Lost* (1991), Inga Moore develops a character who discovers that letter writing helps when she moves away from her friends.

There are many excellent stories in which characters write to relatives. For example, in Marc Brown's *Arthur Goes to Camp* (1982), Arthur tells of his adventures in letters to his mother and father. In Judith Caseley's *Dear Annie* (1991), the author uses letters to develop the relationship between Annie and her grandfather. In Philippe Dupasquier's *Dear Daddy* (1985), a girl writes to her father who is away at sea. Nancy Winslow Parker's *Love from Aunt Betty* (1983) is written in the form of a letter. Patricia MacLachlan's *Sarah, Plain and Tall* (1985) begins with a series of letters written by a woman who later becomes mother to the children. This book is especially good for letter writing because students can compose the missing letters.

Some books that include letters are based on comical or exaggerated situations. These books may motivate humorous letters. For example, Simon James's *Dear Mr. Blueberry* (1991) involves a series of letters that explores the improbable situation of finding a whale in a backyard pond. In Nathan Zimelman's *Please Excuse Jasper* (1987), a series of letters explains the fantastic events that prevent Jasper from attending school. Crescent Dragonwagon's *Dear Miss Moshki* (1986) includes letters that explain how and why trouble began in a classroom.

There are also many stories in which characters write letters based on historical events. Leong Va's *A Letter to the King* (1991) is set in ancient China and revolves around a letter that a girl delivers to persuade the king to release her father. Patricia Reilly Giff's *The War Began at Supper: Letters to Miss Loria* (1991) includes letters written about the Persian Gulf war to a former student teacher. Yoshiko Uchida's "Letter from a Concentration Camp" in *The Big Book for Peace* (Durrell & Sachs, 1990) is a fictional letter written by a Japanese American boy from an American internment camp during World War II.

Students frequently enjoy writing letters to their favorite authors. Such books as Beverly Cleary's *Dear Mr. Henshaw* (1983) may be used to interest students in writing to authors.

REINFORCEMENT ACTIVITY

1. Choose an area in which learning logs are appropriate. What questions would you use to heighten expressive writing? Try keeping a learning log for one week in one of your college classes. Include both expressive and expository reactions.

2. Reread the description of a writer's journal. How would you modify the journal for younger elementary students? What would you emphasize in upper-elementary and middle school? Begin a writing journal of your own observations. Include entries that encourage you to explore your experiences, world, and language. What topics could stimulate you to write a paper using details and information from your journal?

IMAGINATIVE WRITING

Terms such as *poetic writing, creative writing,* and *imaginative writing* describe fictional prose, poetry, or drama. In Horace's terms, the purpose for such writing is "to inform and delight." A similar belief is expressed by contemporary author and Pulitzer Prize winner Donald Murray (1973) who states that this type of writing "not only communicates information, it makes the reader care about that information, it makes him feel, it makes him experience, it gets under his skin" (p. 523). Creativity, Murray believes, cannot be taught; rather, it must be developed by encouraging students to discover who they are and what they have to say. The creative process involves awareness of all aspects of life, as well as discovery of meaning in life. Good writers use these perceptions to create meaning through words, and communicate both their feelings and information.

Poetic and imaginative writing, then, includes original writing that uses both imaginative and experimental thinking. The child writing an original poem, a fairy tale, a puppetry script, or developing a personal experience, is engaging in this creativity. Unfortunately, creativity does not develop without a great deal of nurturing. Through experiences that lead to creative writing, a child's creative expression can be stimulated. Vocabularies can be enriched when children describe experiences related to sight, touch, smell, hearing, and taste. Vocabularies can be refined when they search for and discover the most appropriate word to express an idea. Writing poetry and original drama allows experimentation with the sounds and impact of well-chosen words. Writing an original story helps students understand the development of plot and characterization. As we will see in this chapter, writing can be improved by teaching students to respond to story structure and to elaborate on descriptive details. Finally, writing improvement can be taught in the context where it actually belongs—in the process of meaningful writing.

Developing the Creative Writer

In this section we present some of the factors that encourage creative writing development. We discuss the environment; the role of the teacher in creative development; useful types of stimulation; an example of a creative writing activity, including a motivational period, discussion time, a writing period, and a sharing experience; and the development of the creative poetry writer. You will see that the previously discussed stages related to the writing process apply in the development of the poetic imaginative writer. The prewriting phases may include stimulation of creative processes, models for literary forms, and lessons designed to teach various conventions that may be applied and evaluated during writing and revision (Hillocks, 1986).

The environment Just as a rich environment is necessary for the development of oral language skills, so, too, does the development of creative writing depend on such an environment. Oral expression flourishes in an atmosphere that allows many opportunities for purposeful communication; this is true as well with creative writing. The environment should offer opportunities to write for many different purposes and many different audiences. You would not, for example, write in the same way when composing an informal note as you would when writing an original story for publication. Thus, development of an audience sense, or distancing, is clearly important for skillful writing.

According to Murray (1973), an educational environment that fosters creativity allows children to progress through seven stages of development at their own pace. First, children need to develop an awareness of life. This means developing sensitivity through activities in which they experience visual stimulation, sounds, smells, tastes, movements, and feelings. Take the children outside to experience a tree or a busy city street. Have them look, listen, feel, and then share descriptive language about their sensations. Developing descriptive vocabularies requires this type of activity. Fine literature, poetry, and music also expand sensitivity. Art and building materials also allow children to manipulate and feel before they discuss and write.

Second, the environment should encourage children to care about others. Many awareness experiences help children develop empathy for the feelings and experiences of others. Role-playing activities allow children to experience what it would be like to be in another's position. Role playing often leads to exciting creative writing.

Third, the environment should allow time for children to consider new awareness. Murray called this an "incubation period." It allows the mind to think both consciously and unconsciously. Many of you have had the experience of thinking about an almost impossible task, until all of a sudden, the solution seemed very clear. This is applicable to writing. It often requires longer than half an hour for a child to create a product that he or she feels is satisfactory. Some children may need much longer awareness periods than others. Some children need many awareness and oral language experiences before they tentatively dictate or write a piece that demonstrates feeling and originality.

Fourth, the environment should allow children to make their own discoveries. Children need opportunities to ask questions and find answers. Children need opportunities to be involved in discussions in which there is not one correct answer but from which many questions arise and many answers appear.

Fifth, the environment should stimulate writers to create meaning with words. You must provide many opportunities to try various types of writing in all content areas. You must be involved in the students' writing during writing conferences and other phases of composing. When necessary, provide guidelines for writing that children can apply during writing and revision. This is especially important when introducing certain types of poetry writing and literary elements.

Sixth, after children have created meaning by writing, the environment should allow for the development of detachment, so the authors can involve themselves in the evaluation process through reexamination and rewriting of the creations until they most effectively portray the feelings and meanings.

Finally, the environment should allow writers opportunities to test the effectiveness of their communication. Do the compositions convey both the intended information and the feelings when they are presented to an audience? Children need many opportunities to write and evaluate their work with specific audiences in mind and to present their writings to these audiences. Something wonderful happens when a child's finished product expresses the child's feelings effectively and meets with awe and pleasure from an audience.

Topics   Many topics provide motivation for writing. If students are already involved in a unit or study of a topic, they have in-depth experience and information on which to base their writings. Caprio (1986) found that kindergarten and first-

Happiness is going ice skating.
Happiness is having your own bike.
Happiness is having your own puppy.
Happiness is having your own bedroom.
Happiness is learning how to ride a bike.
Happiness is jumping in a pile of leaves.
Happiness is getting your allowance every week.
Happiness is catching a frog in a swimming pool.
Happiness is being nice to your brother and sister.
Happiness is sharing your jelly beans with no fighting.
Happiness is going snake hunting and finding big snakes.
Happiness is having your own swimming pool in your backyard.
And best of all, happiness is being alive.

Another topic close to the everyday experience of children is recess. The following imaginative writing resulted when a third-grade teacher asked each child to imagine that he or she was a ball and to write a story from the ball's point of view:

The Life of a Ball

Hi, I am a ball. And you know what balls are used for, bouncing. Well, I'm not. I just sit in the closet all day long.

Hey, here comes somebody and they're taking me outside. Ouch! You kicked me. I'm not going to make a basket for you. Oh no, they're going inside and that was the last recess. Now they're getting on the bus and going home.

Burrr. It's starting to snow. Ouch! A big hunk of ice hit me. I wish I had a set of ball muffs and a jacket. It's starting to rain and I wish I had some galoshes and a raincoat. Oh. Here comes some wind and I'm blowing under the car. Ouch! I hit the tire. I'm going to try to get into the school.

At last I got inside with my friends the football, and the baseball and my mom the basketball. It was so warm that I went to sleep.

Something just woke me up. Oh no, it's those kids again. I'm being taken outside, but last night was so hard on me that I'm flat and I won't bounce. They say I'm dead and they are putting me back in the closet. I guess I'll just have to stay here until someone blows me up again. But there are worse places than this closet.

New experiences   Another stimulation is new experiences. These experiences may be in the form of short lessons such as those described in Hillocks's environmental mode for teaching composition. They may include models of writing and literature to be applied during writing experiences. Many sense awareness activities fall into this category: going for a walk; listening to, smelling, and touching the environment; discussing sensations and writing descriptive phrases; and finally, composing stories or poems about the experience. You may also bring in unique objects, or use music, literature, or pictures and photographs for stimulation.

Many of the research studies that Hillocks (1986) identifies as the most effective approaches for teaching writing fall under teacher-introduced approaches: the teacher first introduces a concept in a short structured lesson and then the students apply that concept during the writing and revision stages of the writing process. Hillocks refers to Sager's study. In this study, Sager increased the abilities of sixth-grade students to elaborate details. For example, Sager (1973) asked students working in small groups to read the following story:

The Green Martian Monster

The Green Martian monster descended on the USA. He didn't have a mouth. "Who goes?" they said. There was no answer. So they shot him and he died.

grade students wrote both longer and higher-quality compositions if their writing originated from firsthand experiences rather than textbook assignments. Science, social studies, and literature units are excellent sources for stimulation. If students are already reading, talking about, and listening to the topic, it is logical to have them write about it as well.

For example, one second-grade student teacher developed a unit on the post office and mail service. As the unit progressed, students constructed a classroom mailbox, learned about zip codes, went to a post office, and investigated mail transportation from the pony express days to the present. This unit stimulated a great deal of writing. The children wrote and mailed letters in the real and class-room post offices, wrote creative stories about what happened to letters when Mr. Zip was ignored, wrote diaries from the viewpoint of a pony express rider crossing dangerous mountains and traversing Indian territory, and wrote stories depicting the journey of a letter down the Mississippi on a riverboat. Some children wrote about the adventures of pilots in the early airmail service, and other students looked into the future to write fanciful versions of mail service in the year 3000. Instead of conducting a unit that was dull and ordinary, this teacher provided many opportunities for creative writing and stimulated further study and investigation. In turn, that study motivated still more writing. The children wrote from a back-ground rich in knowledge, and the classroom activities provided enough diversity that all of the students were motivated by at least a portion of the topic. (Early planes, the pony express, and futuristic travel especially appealed to the boys.)

Everyday experiences   Stimulation can come from everyday experiences. These are the common things that children know best: their neighborhood, their street, shop-ping, their family, their hopes and fears, and their likes and dislikes. For example, some fanciful stories came out of a reading of Dr. Seuss's *And to Think That I Saw It on Mulberry Street*. After hearing the story, the children discussed their own streets. They talked about what they saw every day and how the street and the things on it might appear to a person with a vivid imagination. Finally, they wrote stories from this new perspective.

Personal feelings also stimulate creative writing. A third grader lets you know very clearly what he considers trouble (the spelling is as in the original):

Trouble Is

Trouble is runing in the hall becase the principal will cach you.
Trouble is I can't wright a poem becase its hard.
Trouble is getting a tooth pulled becase it hurts.
Trouble is when someone yells at you becase you get punished.
Trouble is ending a poem becase its hard.

Happiness is another emotion close to children. Following is a dictated poem, created by a group of five first-grade students:

Happiness Is

Happiness is having pets.
Happiness is having a cat.
Happiness is going skiing.
Happiness is riding a horse.
Happiness is loving a snake.
Happiness is having food to eat.

After reading the story, which the students had been told scored 0 on elaboration, Sager asked the students to do the following:

1. Quickly list all the reasons why a mouthless green Martian monster might land in the USA.
2. List all the places the Martian could have landed.
3. Who could "they" have been? List all possibilities.
4. List all the thoughts "they" could have been thinking when they saw the Martian.
5. What could have happened between the time the Martian was shot and the time he died? List all possibilities.
6. Look at your lists. To be interesting and easy to understand, a story needs details such as you have written. Add some of these details to the story and take turns reading the story the way you would have written it. (p. 95)

Hillocks emphasizes the importance of this example because students did far more than rate a composition. He says: "They found problems with the writing, generated ideas which would help to correct those problems, and synthesized those problems with the existing frame. Finally, they considered the principles underlying what they had done. Using such materials as the above composition, the experimental groups in the study worked with scales dealing with vocabulary, elaboration, organization, and structure" (p. 123).

As a result of her research, Sager (1977) identifies the following four factors that contribute to effective writing in the upper-elementary grades:

1. A rich and varied vocabulary that allows a writer to hold the reader's interest. A rich vocabulary uses exact words, synonyms, words that appeal to the senses, descriptive words and expressions, and word combinations and comparisons.
2. An organizational ability that presents ideas in a logical arrangement, stays with the subject, and follows an effective sequence.
3. The ability to elaborate and fully develop ideas so that they flow smoothly from one to the next. The ability to elaborate reveals itself in an abundance of related ideas and vivid details.
4. The ability to use a variety of sentences and thus state ideas both accurately and fluently.

Cartoons are especially reliable for developing narrative writing with young children. Cartoons featuring Charlie Brown and Snoopy are excellent. In one, Charlie says, "Get a hit or there'll be no dessert." In another, Charlie runs into some waves shouting, "Snoopy! Stop teasing that porpoise." In still another, Charlie looks perplexed and says, "I always pick myself up, dust myself off, and fall right down again." Charlie Brown coloring books are also highly motivating, especially for reluctant readers.

Harpin (1976) offers guidelines for using photographs with children from ages seven to ten. Harpin found that photographs are effective if children can identify with them. He cautions, however, that you must make sure the photographs are open-ended enough to allow different interpretations but unambiguous enough so as not to confuse the children. Use individual pictures or series of pictures to stimulate discussion and develop dictated or individually written stories. Laminate pictures that you wish to use many times. Pictures are effective with even seventh and eighth graders in remedial programs.

Another stimulus is music. Harpin warns that too much of a musical selection may have a numbing effect on subsequent writing. A few bars are often enough to stimulate creative response, although the whole selection may be required with narrative records such as *Peter and the Wolf.* One university student used "Night on Bald Mountain," by Mussorgski, which stimulated an imaginative sixth grader to write the following description:

Night on Bald Mountain

It is midnight, everyone is asleep, except, bald mountain! As the church bell strikes, the devil of mountaintops opens his wings and smiles evily onto the small graveyards, the evil gleaming of his eyes seems to say, "Thou shalt come out of hiding and appraise the devil of bald mountain!" As if in answer, ghostly shadows and skeletons begin to float up. When seeing this he cackles in delight, and suddenly thrusts his fingers at a huge boulder, and where the boulder had been, there was a fiery pit of flame.

Still another stimulus involves objects that provoke discussion and speculation. Several that Harpin found especially provocative are a Tibetan prayer wheel, a collection of hats, a stuffed fox with one leg missing, a model stagecoach, a boomerang, and a small nineteenth-century writing case with a hidden compartment. Harpin concludes that the key to success in using objects is developing questions and discussion prior to the writing. Children need opportunities to think about what an object is, who made it, how and why it was used, who owned it, and so forth. As an example of this type of stimulation, you might bring into a class that is studying frontier America, a collection of dolls and other toys characteristic of the period. Some might be handmade, such as a cornhusk doll, whereas others might be replicas of period toys. The children would have background and knowledge of the period. They could look at the toys and describe them, discuss the adventures the toys might have shared with their owners, and the feelings the owners might have had about their toys. They could talk about which toy they would choose if they could take only one on a covered-wagon journey. After discussion, they could write their stories, from the viewpoint of either the toy or the child.

Literature is not only an excellent stimulus for creative writing but also a model for writing improvement. One fourth-grade teacher used a study of fables to stimulate creative writing. Because a child cannot write a fable without understanding what it is, the teacher first did a modeling activity in which she read a number of Aesop's fables to the class. Good adaptations of Aesop's works for elementary students include *The Aesop for Children* (1919, 1947), Heidi Holder's *Aesop's Fables* (1981), Tom Paxton's *Aesop's Fables Retold in Verse* (1988), Michael Hague's *Aesop's Fables* (1985), Charles Santore's *Aesop's Fables* (1988), and Mitsumasa Anno's *Anno's Aesop* (1989). John Bierhorst's *Doctor Coyote: A Native American Aesop's Fables* (1987) shows students how fables can be adapted to a different culture and environment. Several picture storybook versions of fables, such as Lorinda Bryan Cauley's *The Town Mouse and the Country Mouse* (1984) and Janet Stevens's *The Tortoise and the Hare* (1984) and *The Town Mouse and the Country Mouse* (1987), illustrate how authors use the fable idea to develop longer stories by expanding the original fables.

The students learned that fables have the following characteristics: (1) they are fictional, (2) they are meant to entertain, (3) they are poetic, (4) they have a double or an allegorical meaning, and (5) they are moral tales, usually about animal characters who behave and act like human characters (Norton, 1991).

The class developed their own criteria for fables: They are short tales in which animals talk as humans; the animals represent human nature (for example, a fox is sly and cunning); and fables have a moral. The class read and discussed many fables. Finally, the teacher had the children write their own fables. The teacher typed and reproduced the finished fables in a booklet so that each student had the accumulated class collection. Following is an example from this fourth-grade collection.

The Cat and the Birds

Once there was a cat that picked on all the birds in his neighborhood because they were smaller than he was. One afternoon the cat was chasing a bird when suddenly he felt a striking pain in his back. He turned around and saw a little sparrow on his back. From that day on he never judged anyone by his size.

For creative writing, the instructional sequence is as important as the type of stimulation. Therefore, you must place stimulation activities within the framework of the writing process discussed in Chapter 9.

Vocabulary development   Choice of words is extremely important in creative writing. Mason, Herman, and Au (1991) state that students who have extensive vocabularies have a vast array of concepts about meaning-related connections among words. These students use vocabulary skills appropriately in numerous situations as they write, listen, speak, and read. As mentioned previously, creative writing is often termed visual writing. Consequently, students must make readers visualize a character, scene, or incident without using trite expressions. Vocabulary is the key, and students need practice in describing objects, scenes, and people. To develop descriptive vocabulary, have children reach into a bag containing a ball, a penny, a pencil, a rubber band, sandpaper, and a glass. Each child describes an item without looking at it. The description may include the texture, size, shape, and firmness of the item. The rest of the group then guesses what the item is.

One class listed a number of phrases that they thought were too vague. These included "a beautiful scene," "a handsome man," "a big dog," "a lovely girl," and "an exciting moment." "A beautiful scene" conjured up as many different images as students in the group. The activity showed a need for precision if readers are to perceive the visual images that writers intend. Strunk and White (1979), in their popular *The Elements of Style*, state that one of the elementary principles of composition is to use definite, specific, and concrete language: "If those who have studied the art of writing are in accord on any one point, it is on this: the surest way to arouse and hold the attention of the reader is by being specific, definite, and concrete. The greatest writers . . . are effective largely because they deal in particulars and report the details that matter. Their words call up pictures" (p. 21).

Overuse of adjectives and adverbs is a common problem in writing. For example, "The great green expanse of meadow was filled with stately, brown, soft-eyed deer eating their sweet-smelling breakfast" is a description so overdone that it is ineffective. To avoid this pitfall, children need a variety of descriptive techniques. An important technique is use of vivid action words, in both story writing

Children can expand their vocabularies by producing word "banks" on charts.

and poetry. Strunk and White (1979) state that writers should write with nouns and verbs rather than with adjectives and adverbs.

How can you help children learn to choose more descriptive verbs? If you look at children's writing, especially in the early-elementary grades, you will find certain words used over and over. One such word is *said.* You see "Mother said," "Father said," and so forth repeatedly. But does "said" describe how a person is saying anything? One class compiled a list of over 100 words to use in place of *said.* They decided that *argued, yelled, growled, whined, declared,* and so forth were much more descriptive of how a person talked and felt than the overused *said.* The children became aware of visual verbs, looked for them in their reading, and used them in their writing.

The children talked about other verbs that do not communicate as well as they should. They read sentences, such as "The boy walked down the street," and they discussed why and where he might be walking. Then, they substituted other, more visual verbs. For example:

The boy *strolled* down the street.   (He was not in a hurry and just wanted to go for a walk.)

The boy *strutted* down the street.   (He had just won a baseball game and was very proud.)

The boy *tramped* down the street.   (He was angry because his father told him he couldn't go to a movie.)

The children worked with other verbs, such as:

The girl *drank* a large glass of lemonade.

The girl *sipped* a large glass of lemonade.   (She was at a party and wanted to be polite.)

The girl *gulped* a large glass of lemonade.   (She had been running and was very hot and thirsty.)

Jim *sat* in the large chair.

Jim *sprawled* in the large chair.   (He was tired and by himself and he wanted to relax.)

Jim *crouched* in the large chair.   (Jim was ready to leave the chair in a hurry.)

This kind of exercise helps students use visual verbs and makes them more observant when they read literature.

Story Writing

There is a strong connection between reading and listening to literature and writing stories. Schema theory supports reading and telling stories to children and helping children understand such literary elements as plot, setting, and characterization. To apply schema implications to creative writing, read literature to children. Literature provides models for the literary elements and helps children increase their understanding and appreciation of them.

Plot   Use very simple stories to introduce the concept of plot. Stories that have strong, logical sequence are good for this beginning activity. For example, one teacher used the following sequence of instruction with a fifth-grade class. First, the teacher read a simple story, "The Three Billy Goats Gruff." He asked the children to listen carefully to identify the characters and incidents in the story. After listening to the story, the children identified its four characters: (1) the littlest billy goat, (2) the middle-sized billy goat, (3) the great big billy goat, and (4) the troll. Next, the class listed the incidents that occur in the story:

1. The goats want to eat the grass on the other side of the bridge, but there is a terrible troll under the bridge.
2. After being threatened by the troll, the littlest goat crosses successfully.
3. The middle goat crosses successfully, also after being threatened by the troll.

4. The largest billy goat is confronted by the troll and knocks the troll off the bridge.
5. The three goats eat grass on the other side of the bridge.

The teacher had the class investigate the order of the five incidents by acting them out. Then, he asked whether the action had to be in that specific order. The students rearranged the order in several ways and tried to act out each new order. The five incidents were written on strips of cardboard and arranged in the order being demonstrated. The students concluded that if the story is to retain logical development, the incidents cannot be presented in a different order. Some of their reasons follow: (1) the beginning must start with the goats on one side of the bridge and a need to cross the bridge; (2) the littlest goat must cross the bridge first, so that he can tell the troll to wait for his middle-sized brother, who is fatter and will taste better; (3) the middle-sized goat must come next, so that a larger goat will remain; (4) the biggest goat must cross in order to eliminate the troll; and (5) the goats must eliminate the troll in order to eat happily on the other side. The group also concluded that if the biggest goat eliminates the troll in the beginning, the story is not interesting, because there is too little conflict.

Through this activity, the students realized that plot connects actions in a logical sequence. The students listened to other short stories and identified the sequence of events, from which they began to realize that many stories develop their plots through conflict.

In the next activity, the class looked again at "The Three Billy Goats Gruff." They identified which characters were in conflict: the three goats against the ugly old troll. They identified the reason for the conflict: the goats wanted grass on the other side of the bridge, but the troll lived under the bridge and wanted to eat the goats. They identified the series of conflicts: first, the little goat against the troll; next, the middle-sized goat against the troll; and finally, the biggest goat against the troll.

The teacher then read Alexander Nikolayevich Afanasyev's folktale, *The Fool and the Fish* (1990). The students listened for the major characters: a lazy man named Ivan, an enchanted fish, a tsar, and a princess. They listened for the source of conflict: the furious tsar tries to eliminate Ivan and the princess. They identified the series of incidents that develop the plot:

1. Ivan draws an enchanted fish out of the stream.
2. The fish offers Ivan unlimited wishes in return for freedom.
3. Ivan asks the fish for help carrying water, fetching wood, and beating off angry villagers.
4. Ivan is transported to the tsar's palace.
5. The angry tsar orders Ivan and the princess placed in a barrel and thrown into the sea.
6. The fish saves Ivan and the princess and grants Ivan a fine palace.
7. The tsar accepts Ivan as his son-in-law and they all live in peace.

The teacher introduced the concept that a plot has beginning incidents, middle incidents, and ending incidents. With the teacher's assistance, the class drew a diagram to show the progress of a plot (see Figure 10–1). After they drew the diagram and discussed plot development, they placed the incidents from *The Fool and the Fish* on the diagram (see Figure 10–2).

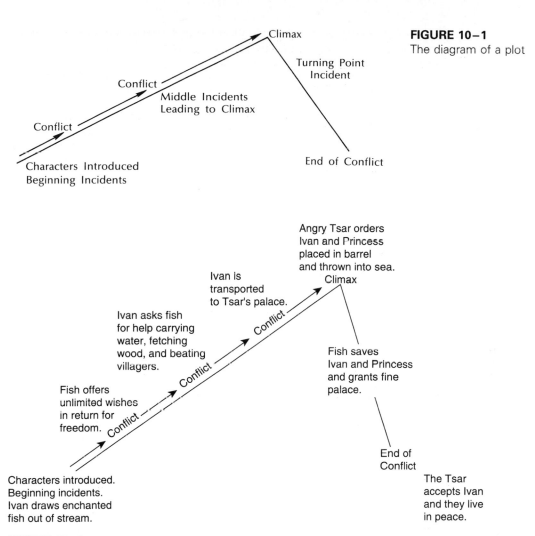

FIGURE 10–1
The diagram of a plot

FIGURE 10–2
Plot diagram with incidents from *The Fool and the Fish* included

Finally, students wrote their own stories, using beginning, middle, and ending incidents. The teacher interacted with each student during the composing phases, and the children shared their finished products. The class used the plot-development model during different phases of the writing process. During prewriting, students listened to stories, developed a model, and applied the model to other stories. During the writing phase, the students referred to the model to develop stories with beginning, middle, and ending incidents and to include rising action. After writing their first drafts, the students referred to the model during teacher conferences and peer editing groups. The model helped the students determine areas that were well developed as well as those that needed to be revised for clarity. The model encouraged self-evaluation because the students were able to refer to specific components and analyze whether their writings included those components.

Additional plot structures that are useful in writing are illustrated in Chapters 11 and 12. The plot structure in person-versus-self conflicts (problem → struggle → struggle → self-realization → achievement of peace and truth) is diagrammed in Figure 11–11. Three other patterns of action are used in plot structures: (1) the action moves from one incident to another incident (final climax leaves the reader with a sense of uncertainty); (2) the action moves with a tension that does not develop a climax (minimal suspense); and (3) the action moves in a lifeline that does not have one dramatic climax, but may have several dramatic episodes. These additional plot structures are especially interesting when working with older students. Literature written for younger students usually follows the plot structure shown in Figures 10–1 and 10–2.

REINFORCEMENT ACTIVITY

1. Develop a writing lesson that follows the plot development shown in Figures 10–1 and 10–2. Develop a model using examples other than the two presented in this chapter. Develop a list of children's literature selections that follow that specific plot development. What types of children's books develop this plot structure?

2. Choose another plot structure. Identify several literature selections that follow that specific plot structure and place the incidents from the story on the plot structure. Develop a writing lesson that helps students understand and apply the plot structure.

Setting   Several of the ideas for entries in a writer's journal emphasize describing a specific location or new experience by writing vivid details related to sight, sound, smell, and touch. Similar activities provide valuable prewriting experiences before students write settings for stories. For example, ask students to jot down details as they are walking through a park, looking at a busy city street, or looking at the sky during different weather conditions.

The RADAR approach to writing (Davis, 1988) uses a structured approach to help students describe both settings and characters. In this approach, students look at a picture, divide the picture into three parts, and then circle each part. For example, if the picture includes a dog chasing a cat into the woods, the students circle the dog, the cat, and the woods. Next, the students number each part and describe it in detail. They start with the first part and write their descriptions moving from top to bottom. The students also use terms to indicate location, such as *beside, over,* and *under,* in writing their descriptions.

Picture storybooks are among the best classroom sources for developing observational and writing skills related to setting. Introduce the books, read the stories while encouraging the students to look carefully at the settings, and then ask the students to describe the settings in detail. Emphasize the students' words and phrases that they believe describe the settings. Encourage them to make comparisons through simile and metaphor. Finally, ask them to write their own descriptions, incorporating what they learned during the discussion. It is advisable to develop the first setting description as a group activity in which you use descriptive words and phrases and highlight various things the students should look for.

Books that have familiar settings are excellent for younger students. If the settings are within their experiential backgrounds, the students may even compare the settings in the illustrations with similar settings in their own environments. At least some of the following settings should be familiar to many children: Bruce McMillan's *One Sun: A Book of Terse Verse* (1990) — a beach in summer; Jane Yolen's *Owl Moon* (1987) — rural woods in winter; Dayal Khalsa's *I Want a Dog* (1987) — city neighborhood and home; Lois Lenski's *Sing a Song of People* (1987) — city environment; Merle Peek's *The Balancing Act: A Counting Song* (1987) — an amusement park; Marc Brown's *Arthur's Baby* (1987) — family home, preparing for a baby; and Valerie Flournoy's *The Patchwork Quilt* (1985) — a close, three-generation black family.

After students master writing simple descriptive settings, let them describe and write settings that have specific purposes. For example, many settings create the mood of a story. Students may try to match the feeling of a setting through their choice of words. Marcia Brown's illustrations for Cendrar's *Shadow* (1982) are excellent for exploring how setting can create a frightening, spooky mood. The illustrations in sharp collage seem to reach out menacingly. After students try to describe the settings in their own words, have them analyze how the author creates the mood as the shadow staggers, grabs, and teems like snakes and worms. Cynthia Rylant's *When I Was Young in the Mountains* (1982) creates a warm, gentle, nostalgic mood. Descriptions of grandfather's kiss on a front porch and grandmother's holding a child's hand in the dark enhance the mood. Pictures of country kitchens, country stores, and swimming holes suggest a leisurely, secure, and happy way of life for children. In Catharine O'Neill's *Mrs. Dunphy's Dog* (1987), the illustrations that show lampposts and fenceposts at angles, animals in caricature, and literal interpretations of the news create a humorous mood.

Students can explore how both illustrations and text create moods. They can brainstorm lists of words and phrases that suggest different moods and try to match the mood of the illustrations in their own writings. You may share only the illustrations in books and ask students to describe the mood they think the illustrations suggest, write descriptions reflecting this mood, and then compare their descriptions with those developed by the author. After completing several writing activities of this sort, a fifth-grade class listed and categorized words that reflected specific moods in books and in their own writings that accompanied the illustrations. The students included words that depicted mood in both setting and characterizations. Table 10–1 illustrates part of this activity.

Books with illustrations that show setting as the antagonist include the previously mentioned *Shadow*. In Margaret Hodges's *The Wave* (1964), Blair Lent creates a large, dark swirl of a tidal wave. Robert McCloskey's *Time of Wonder* (1957) shows the destructive force of a hurricane as it bends the lines of the trees. Students can use these illustrations to write settings that reflect danger.

Picture books that you may use to stimulate historical setting include Donald Hall's *Ox-Cart Man* (1979) — early nineteenth-century New England; John Goodall's *The Story of a Main Street* (1987) — England from the medieval period through con-

TABLE 10–1
Words that suggest moods for settings

Frightening Mood	Warm, Happy Mood	Funny Mood
Cendrar's *Shadow:* prowler, stolen like a thief, body dragging, teeming like snakes	McPhails's *The Dream Child* moon like warm breath, Tame Bear, Dream Child, drift, sleepy, hugs, licks	Small's *Imogene's Antlers* Imogene had grown antlers antlers decked with doughnuts antlers drying towels
Our Words: squirming black fingers, clawing branches, ghostly white silent shapes	Our Words: cuddly little bear, secure in mother's lap, cradling boat, drifting in sky	Our Words: silly, preposterous unbelievable, stupefied, speechless

temporary time; Tomie de Paola's *An Early American Christmas* (1987) — New Hampshire, early 1800s; Byrd Baylor's *The Best Town in the World* (1983) — nineteenth-century rural Texas; Reeve Lindbergh's *Johnny Appleseed* (1990) — frontier America from Massachusetts to Indiana; and Diane Stanley's *Peter the Great* (1986) — Russia, late 1600s through early 1700s. These books provide excellent sources because students can see how an illustrator provides authenticity through illustrations. Then, students can try to make readers see the same historical settings through words.

Characterization   Another problem emerges for young authors when they try to write stories by weaving incidents together to form a plot. The characters in a story are intrinsic to the incidents that occur. The characters may be people or animals, but young authors often have problems developing their characters so they seem real. Again, you may use literature to help students. How do authors of some of the children's favorite books make the characters seem so real? Most authors use the following methods to develop characters:

1. Tell about the person through narration.
2. Record the character's conversation with others in the story (dialogue).
3. Describe the person's thoughts.
4. Show others' thoughts about the character.
5. Show the character in action.

You can use these five methods to explore characterization and add new dimensions to students' writing. In preparation, have the students read books about memorable characters with whom they are familiar and notice how the authors develop the characters. They will undoubtedly discover basically the same techniques listed previously.

One class, for example, developed large charts, each of which depicted one of the methods of characterization. On the charts, the class described each method in greater detail and recorded examples from various pieces of literature. Finally, the students experimented with that type of character writing. Figure 10–3 gives examples of this activity as it was conducted with a fifth-grade group of accelerated students. The charts and examples provided references throughout the writing process, as the students wrote character sketches using the various techniques. Students can choose undeveloped characters from literature, such as Snow White or Cinderella. It is interesting to take an in-depth look at Cinderella through her thoughts and the thoughts of her stepsisters, her stepmother, and the prince. Older students can read Robin McKinley's *Beauty* (1978) to discover how an author developed a full-length novel from the characters and plot of a folktale. Character sketches may also come from people students know or people they read about in the newspapers or see on television. It is interesting to speculate about what two sports stars are thinking as they shake hands or what two world leaders are like.

The Author Tells About the Character

Look for:
1. The author tells you what he thinks about the character.
2. The author describes what the character looks like.
3. The author describes the setting to let you know more about the character.

Example: Little Town on the Prairie (Laura Ingalls Wilder) A description of Mary, after she becomes blind—"Even in the days before scarlet fever had taken the sight from her clear blue eyes, she had never liked to work outdoors in the sun and wind. Now she was happy to be useful indoors." (p. 8)

The Author Records Conversations with Other Characters (Dialogue)

Look for:
1. Speech lets you know about attitudes, dialect (where the character lives), education, mood, wisdom, etc.
2. What does the character actually say?
3. How does the character say it?

Example: Little Town on the Prairie
Ma's attitude toward drinking—" 'It's a pity more men don't say the same,' said Ma. 'I begin to believe that if there isn't a stop put to the liquor traffic, women must bestir themselves and have something to say about it.'
    Pa twinkled at her. 'Seems to me you have plenty to say, Caroline. Ma never left me in doubt as to the evil of drink, nor you either.' " (p. 55)

FIGURE 10–3
Methods of developing characters (Excerpts from *Little Town on the Prairie* by Laura Ingalls Wilder. Copyright, 1941, as to text, by Laura Ingalls Wilder. Renewed 1969 by Roger L. MacBride. By permission of Harper & Row, Publishers, Inc.)

The Author Describes the Person's Thoughts

Look for:
1. The thoughts describe the person's inner feelings.
2. Do they agree with the dialogue, or does the character have a hidden side?

Example: Little Town on the Prairie
Laura is not sure that there is always something to be thankful for—"Laura thought, 'Ma is right, there is always something to be thankful for.' Still, her heart was heavy. The oats and the corn crop were gone. She did not know how Mary could go to college now. The beautiful new dress, the two other new dresses, and the pretty underwear, must be laid away until next year. It was a cruel disappointment to Mary." (p. 106)

The Author Shows Others' Thoughts About the Character

Look for:
1. How do other people react to the character? Do they like him or her? Do they trust him or her? Do all people react the same way?
2. How does your reaction change after you read another's reaction?

Example: Little Town on the Prairie
Laura's various reactions to her sister Mary—"Mary had always been good. Sometimes she had been so good that Laura could hardly bear it." (p. 11)

" 'Oh, Mary,' Laura said. 'You look exactly as if you'd stepped out of a fashion plate. There won't be, there just can't be, one single girl in college who can hold a candle to you.' " (p. 96)

The Author Shows the Character in Action

Look for:
1. Actions suggest what the character is really like, what he or she is doing, and what he or she is planning.
2. Do the actions agree with the dialogue?

Example: Little Town on the Prairie
Laura is very conscientious and trustworthy—"Laura stopped, aghast. Suddenly she had realized what she was doing. Ma must have hidden this book, Laura had no right to read it. Quickly she shut her eyes, and then she shut the book. It was almost more than she could do, not to read just one word more, just to the end of that one line. But she knew that she must not yield one tiny bit to temptation." (p. 141)

FIGURE 10–3, *Continued*

REINFORCEMENT
ACTIVITY

Select plot, setting, or characterization. Develop a series of lessons to improve under-standing of the components of plot, the purposes for setting, or the methods authors use to show character. Use your lessons with children, and share the results with your language arts class, or present your lessons to a small group of your peers.

Symbolism and allusion Both creative writing and literature appreciation profit from an understanding of symbolism and allusion. Research with gifted children shows that the creative writing of fifth-grade children improved when they were taught to symbolize their personal characteristics using concrete objects. Andressen (1973) believes that if children look at themselves symbolically, they are stimulated to more profound internalization, and, consequently, a higher degree of creativity in writing. In his study, Andressen had children discuss symbolism in places of worship and advertisements. Next, they discussed and wrote about pos-sible symbols for classmates. Then, they chose and wrote about symbols that would apply to themselves.

Greek and Roman mythology present heroes and gods as symbols for certain human characteristics. Jane Yolen (1977) believes that study of mythology is im-portant for building an understanding of ancient cultures and for acquiring the background necessary to understand many of the allusions in writing. For exam-ple, a child cannot fully understand why some mountains are called volcanoes, or what "as strong as Atlas" or "as swift as Mercury" mean if he or she has no experience with mythology.

FOR YOUR PLAN BOOK
A Mythology Unit to Develop Symbolic Writing

The following series of lessons allows children to study mythology, understand the symbolism in mythology, relate the mythological characters to well-known present-day or historical people, and relate the characteristics portrayed by the mythological charac-ters to their self-images. The activities were developed with sixth-grade students who had been studying Greek and Roman mythology in reading/language arts; thus, the les-sons were a natural outgrowth of a classroom activity. First, the students reviewed characters from Greek mythology, discussed the characteristics, and looked at what they symbolized:

Poseidon	god of the sea; Greeks prayed to him to protect them when they took a sea voyage.
Ares	god of war, symbolized by the vulture; Hades liked him be-cause he increased the underworld population.
Heracles	extremely strong Greek hero; accomplished such tasks as kill-ing the nine-headed Hydra.

Zeus	ruler of Mount Olympus, supreme ruler, god of the wealthy.
Apollo	god of the sun, truth, music, medicine, and prophecy.
Aphrodite	goddess of love and beauty; presided over girlish babble and tricks.
Hermes	swift messenger of the gods; god of commerce, orators, and writers.
Demeter	goddess of crops.
Artemis	goddess of the moon; guardian of cities, young animals, and women.
Athena	goddess of wisdom.
Dionysus	god of wine, symbol of revelry; he gave Greece the gift of wine; driven mad by Hera.
Hephaestus	god of fire and artisans; an inventor.

The students then searched for advertisements that used mythological characters and discussed why they were good symbols. For example, Why is Mercury a good symbol for a car? Why is Atlas used as a symbol for a tire company? Why has a camera company chosen the name Argus? (Argus was a giant with a hundred eyes.) They then described what products might use names such as Heracles, Hermes, Apollo, and Poseidon as advertising symbols, and wrote advertisements for their created products.

In the next part of the sequence, the students discussed well-known personalities from the present and past. Each chose a personality and listed the characteristics that they felt described the person. As a final activity in that session, they wrote short descriptions of a person in terms of Greek heroes. One of the students wrote the following symbolic description of Hitler:

> Characteristics of Hitler: paranoid, insane, greedy, hated the Jewish people, powerful speaker, influential, a killer, an egotist, thought his was the master race.

Hitler and Mythology

> Since Hitler was a madman who envisioned conquering the world, I would say that Ares and Dionysus would describe Hitler well. Ares was the god of war; since Hitler started World War II, Ares would be a good mythical symbol. I believe that Hades would have also liked Hitler because the war would have sent so many new people to the underworld. Dionysus also is an excellent symbol for Hitler because Dionysus caused a great deal of revelry with his gift of wine but he later went insane. Hitler also caused revelry when he first influenced the German people, but he went insane and his actions caused a great deal of misery.

Finally, the students thought about themselves and identified characteristics that might be used to describe them. They wrote short symbolic descriptions of themselves in terms of mythology. One boy wrote:

The Way I See Myself and Mythology

> I personally think that the Greek gods who closely resemble my beliefs are Apollo, Athena, and Hephaestus. Apollo was the god of music and medicine. I hopefully will become a doctor and an accomplished musician. Apollo was also the patron of truth, which is essential for friends to have between one another. Athena was the goddess of wisdom. I always want to know more about everything. Hephaestus was the god of fire and the artisans. He was a great engineer. Hopefully I'll be able to invent patentable items.

1. Read several selections from mythology. (Do not use Greek mythology.) Make a chart showing the characteristics of the heroes and what they might symbolize. Describe yourself in terms of these characteristics.
2. Make a collection of current advertisements that use symbols from mythology. Are they appropriate? Why or why not?

Poetic Writing

Why do some children produce quality poetry, while others do not? According to Duffy (1973), the answer lies primarily with a teacher's dedication to the development of poetic self-expression. Just as in presenting other forms of creative writing, teachers must structure the environment so that children are not punished for novel and creative thinking. The school experience is often criticized because many children apparently learn to conform, and thus, they learn at an early age not to express themselves. If children are to develop imagination, Khatena (1975) believes that someone must teach them to break away from the usual and commonplace, restructure, and synthesize.

What are some instructional approaches that you can use to develop creative poetry writers? First, stimulate an interest in and a love for poetry. Nobody can write poetry without first developing a feel for it. Duffy (1973) maintains that no stimulation technique is as important as reading good poetry to children. He believes that teachers should begin by reading humorous poems, which establish a positive image, and simple free-verse poems, which serve as models for beginning writing. Popular humorous poets include Jack Prelutsky, Shel Silverstein, William Jay Smith, John Ciardi, and Laura Richards. Sources for poetry selections include textbooks by Huck (1987), Norton (1991), and Sutherland and Arbuthnot (1990).

Awareness and observation   In addition to reading poetry to children, teachers must structure activities that nurture both awareness and powers of observation in children. For example, one third-grade student teacher planned a lesson around an orange. He began by asking the children where oranges came from, what oranges are used for, and whether they liked oranges. Then, he gave an orange to each child and explained that the children were to take their time discovering all they could about an orange through touch, taste, sight, and smell. He told them: "Discover all you can about the outside of your orange by looking at it; look at the pores, the color, the shape, the scars, and the soft spots. Now feel it. Roll it in your hands and on the table, squeeze it, rub your fingers over the pores, close your eyes and feel it. Smell it. Slowly begin to peel it; how does it smell? Contrast the feel and sight of the outside of the skin to the inside; taste the inside of the skin. Now look at the inside of the orange. What shape is it? What color is it? Feel the inside, gently squeeze it, taste the inside of the orange. What is inside some of the sections? Put one in your hand. What color is it? What shape is it? Is it hard or soft?"

After the students talked about all the things they had discovered about an orange, the teacher asked them to write a poem, beginning each line with "An orange." Following are some observations that resulted from this activity.

Effective teachers provide an
environment to encourage
creative thinking.

An Orange

An orange is round like a ball
An orange is the color of the sun
An orange is bumpy on the outside
An orange is squeezy and yummy
An orange rind is bitter as a lemon
An orange has squishy pulp
An orange has tough, slippery seeds

This type of observation and poetry development was influenced by Kenneth Koch's (1971) *Wishes, Lies, and Dreams,* in which he describes his experiences teaching poetry to children in New York City. The book describes such techniques as developing wish poems, noise poems, and color poems, and it includes examples of poetry written on these themes by first- through sixth-grade children. Listening to poetry written by other children stimulates enthusiasm in elementary students. Koch found that the theme of wishes is one that all children are able to relate to. The same format used in "An Orange" can help children develop their wishes into poems. The following poem developed after a teacher read a number of "Wish" poems from Koch's book. After hearing the poems, the students talked about various wishes of their own, then wrote their own wish poems.

I Wish . . .

I wish I was a towering giraffe
    So I could see everything
I wish I was a swift cheetah
    So I could run like the wind
I wish I was a majestic tree
    So all the birds could rest on me
            —*A fourth-grade wish*

In another type of observation lesson, the students were to write a visually descriptive piece about a fall afternoon. But the teacher did not just tell them to take out paper and pencil and write a page about a fall day; instead, she began in a field. The students made lists of sight, sound, and smell words and word clusters (distinguishing between insect, plant, and mechanical life). They listed the images that they saw in the clouds. They investigated their surroundings—finding, catching, and describing daddy longlegs, crickets, and katydids. This activity resulted in observations that later took a poetic form. After observing a cricket, one student wrote the following poem:

Cricket

creeping, putting
    one leg first,
    then another,
    and another,
till all six
    have moved
  and he starts
    again.

      ing, le
    p   *a*
   m   *p*
  u   *i*
 j   *n*
            g

flying through
    the air
and then
    Bump
he lands
    and
    jumps
    again.

Notice how this sixth-grade student has captured the essence of the cricket. Another student used her powers of observation to watch an eagle in the sky. She jotted down her feelings as she watched and later put her observations and feelings into this poetic form:

Eagle

I like to watch an eagle soar,
How he just glides alone,
I wonder what it's like,
gliding freely through the air,
his wings spread widely,
and, he looks so nice and proud
but, pretty soon he'll be extinct,
and he'll glide and soar no more.

Imagery   Much of poetry revolves around imagery. Poets often create word pictures by comparing their thoughts to experiences and likenesses and differences in life. The following third-grade author uses various comparisons to describe a giggle:

Giggles

Giggles are good-tasting fellows
They smell like brownies
Just coming out of the oven
They feel like a new Bugs Bunny doll
Giggles look like a red clown at the circus
Giggles are shaped like bubbles

Another child developed the image of a gulp:

Gulps

A gulp is very heavy,
especially on rainy days.
A gulp tasks like chocolate,
smells like coffee,
and feels like a magnet.

In order to develop imagery, children must practice describing objects in terms of other objects. One teacher introduced color description through a brainstorming activity in which the class rapidly provided associations with a color. For example,

It is as red as—a stop sign, blood, a valentine, danger, a lobster, a sunset, an apple, a strawberry

And, similarly, with another concept:

As quick as—drinking a glass of lemonade on a hot day, a shooting star, a mongoose

Children can also make comparisons with the following expressions: as tired as, as hungry as, as thin as, as quiet as, as silly as, as sneaky as, as soft as. After this kind of practice, one student described a house as "so empty, you could hear the spiders spin webs."

The experiences of these classes demonstrate the interaction of a stimulation activity and the brainstorming of ideas and concepts prior to writing. Stimulation and discussion activities not only develop creative awareness but also the descriptive vocabularies necessary for creative writing. Student teachers as well as classroom teachers report that their creative writing activities are not very successful when they ignore the oral exchange of ideas.

Poetry forms   Several of the student poems presented in this chapter use a basic form, such as starting each line with "Happiness is," or ending each line with a rhyming word. Children enjoy several other forms of poetry and find them not too difficult to write. Such forms may also provide some children with a little more guidance and structure. Chapter 9 presents forms for limericks, cinquains, and diamantes as examples of poetry forms that you could use as models during the writing process.

EXPOSITORY WRITING

Britton et al. (1975) and Applebee (1984) report that expository writing is the most common writing used in classrooms. According to Frye, Baker, and Perkins (1985), expository writing is "explanatory writing, the presentation of facts, ideas, or opinions, as in short forms like the article or essay, or in longer nonfictional forms like the history, scientific treatise, travel book, biography, or autobiography. Expository writing is often treated as a larger category including exposition as a major element, but making use also of argument, description, and narration. It is contrasted with imaginative writing or creative writing" (p. 184).

There is currently renewed interest in the role of expository writing in all areas of the curriculum. Ideas for developing writing to learn are found in current journals as well as books published by the National Council of Teachers of English. For example, NCTE publications such as Gere's *Roots in the Sawdust: Writing to Learn Across the Disciplines* (1985) includes ideas for all content areas, Golub's *Activities to Promote Critical Thinking: Classroom Practices in Teaching English* (1986) includes ideas for speaking and writing across the curriculum, and Fleming and McGinnis's *Portraits. Biography and Autobiography in the Secondary School* (1985) includes both reading and writing activities, many of which may be adapted to upper-elementary and middle-school classrooms.

Some activities use content-area sources to improve understanding of writing and the writing process, whereas other activities emphasize the writing process as a way to learn in the content areas. Many writing activities reflect both goals, although one or the other may be more important for a specific teacher and a specific content area. Writing-to-learn strategies should develop writing fluency, foster abstract thinking, and guide students in their quest for knowledge. There are numerous ways that you may accomplish learning through writing.

Research Reports

The third-grade students who wrote an outline of their class trip, using questions and answers, were actually developing a report (see Chapter 9). The structure of the report included a central theme: the train ride. Each paragraph had a main idea relating to the central theme. The answers to the main-idea questions provided supporting ideas, which developed the three main ideas under the central theme. This exercise was an excellent readiness activity for the time when the students would have to produce individual, well-planned reports or other expository compositions. As elementary students progress into longer expository writing, they must decide on the audience and purpose for the writing. Once they have chosen their subject, they must narrow it to one they can cover realistically in a short composition, gather ideas and information, organize the ideas and information, write the report, and revise it.

Audience and purpose   Activities that focus on expository writing requirements include charting weather and temperature; filling out forms; and writing news stories, autobiographies and biographies, book reports, editorials, class minutes, and reports for projects in science and social studies. Audiences range from known class members, teachers, parents, and friends to wider, unknown audiences. The purposes for most of these projects are to inform, compare, compile, convince, and report.

Subject   Students will be more motivated to write if they find a subject that is both interesting and important to them. In addition, students must be able to uncover information about the subject. They should look for information in textbooks, journals, magazines, encyclopedias, newspapers, and so forth. Students should look through class, school, and public libraries to see how much information is available to them on various subjects.

Many subjects are just too broad for elementary students. For example, energy, transportation, air travel, and the Revolutionary War are obviously too broad to approach in a short composition. Students should narrow the scope of these subjects. There are several ways to help students narrow a subject. Brainstorming helped a group of fifth graders look at the general subject of water and find specific

The writing process will help young writers focus on audience and purpose.

topics and main ideas to develop in short compositions. The fifth graders developed a web of interest, narrowing the broad subject of water to four topics: (1) sports, (2) energy, (3) sea life, and (4) weather. Each specific topic had several main ideas that students could use in organizing a composition. This technique is successful with elementary students, but you can use it with various grade levels by changing the subject matter.

Students can also narrow topics by studying the tables of contents in several books on a general subject. For example, the subject of camping is interesting to many elementary children because they often go camping with their families or scout troops. After looking through books on camping, a fourth-grade class developed the list in Figure 10–4. This search yielded many specific, interesting topics that the students could turn into meaningful compositions. The approach also teaches students how to use tables of contents for locating information. Many students need such practice in reference skills.

Camping

1. Camp cooking
   a. campfires
   b. camping stoves
   c. cooking utensils
   d. food
   e. recipes
2. Equipment for sleeping
   a. tents
   b. sleeping bags
   c. cots and air mattresses
   d. pickup campers
   e. trailers
   f. motor homes
3. Special clothes
   a. hiking shoes and clothing
   b. raincoats or ponchos
   c. cold-weather wear
   d. clothing for horsepacking
4. Skills
   a. using an ax
   b. using knives
   c. using a rope—knots, hitches, splices
   d. reading a map and compass
   e. building a fire
   f. packing a backpack
   g. setting up and taking down camp

5. Safety in camp
   a. first aid
   b. pure water
   c. water safety
   d. insects
   e. snakes
   f. wild animals
6. Survival
   a. navigation
   b. getting help
   c. emergency food
   d. emergency shelter
   e. water
7. Transportation
   a. backpacking
   b. canoes
   c. bicycles
   d. horsepacking
   e. boats
   f. trailers
8. Where to camp
   a. national parks
   b. state parks
   c. wilderness areas
   d. private campgrounds

FIGURE 10–4
A list of camping topics

Another way to narrow a subject is to have children list some questions they want answered about a general topic. For example, a group of fourth graders became concerned because a stream near their homes was cluttered with bottles, cans, and other offensive garbage. They investigated the dangers of this kind of pollution and what other communities had done in similar circumstances. Then, they recommended ways to improve their stream. They developed good reports from their study, and they even wrote some letters to the editor of the local newspaper and to community groups to generate community interest.

Ideas and information   The methods for narrowing a topic proceed naturally into the next step: searching for ideas and information to include in the composition. For example, after students who were studying Native Americans changed or added questions to the categories they had chosen, the teacher explored the library with them. They looked through card files, tables of contents, indexes, and so forth, to discover sources of information. From these resources, the students compiled information to answer each of their questions.

After narrowing the subject and developing important questions, students should write each of their questions on a separate index card or sheet of paper. Then, when they find information that pertains to the question, they should write it, in their own words, on the appropriate card or paper. Placing the items on separate cards helps students rearrange their questions and information into the most logical order. They find it easier to deal with one main idea at a time rather than a disorganized pile of information. For example, a card asking a main-idea question about camping might look like Figure 10–5.

Organization   After students finish gathering information and ideas on cards, they are ready to start analyzing, selecting, and ordering their information. Webbing, discussed previously, is a good way to accomplish this task. Students may

---

How can you make an emergency shelter if you are lost?

Start looking for your shelter in the day.
Shelter should protect from cold, wind, and rain.
Build a lean-to from about 1-inch-thick poles tied together with vines or fishline.
    Draw a picture to show this in my report.
Put evergreens or leaf branches on poles to protect yourself from rain.
    Draw a picture to show this in my report.
Make the lean-to very steep.
A cave or overhanging rock makes a shelter.
Build a fire in front of the shelter.
A fire will make you warm and be a signal.
If you are in snow, dig a cave in the side of a drift.
Put pine boughs on the floor of the snow cave.
A snow cave is a good insulator.
Leave air holes in the cave.
Mark the outside of the cave so searchers will know you're there.
    Draw a picture to show this in my report.

FIGURE 10–5
A card asking a main-idea question about camping

find they have too little or too much information about one main idea. Some information may be important, whereas other information may be trivial. Some information may require verification from sources other than those they have already used. As students arrange and rearrange their information cards, they frequently discover the best organizational patterns to use. The various organizational patterns include chronological, spatial, familiar to unfamiliar, problem to cause of problem to possible solutions, problem to effect of problem to possible solutions, and question to answer. These formats provide logical organizations for reports in many content areas.

Writing   Now, the students must develop the main ideas and important details into a closely related unit. In literature, the plot has a beginning, a middle, and an end. The same progression appears in factual writing, but it does not build the action to a climax. Instead, the beginning introduces readers to what the writing will be about and catches attention, the middle develops the main ideas and supporting information, and a summary or concluding paragraph pulls together the ideas in the composition and gives readers the feeling that the composition is finished.

The introductory paragraph is important. When you pick up a magazine, how do you choose the articles that you read? The author may ask a question that arouses your interest, make a startling statement, or present an interesting, little-known fact. The author may show how important something is to you personally. Questions such as "Would you like to save $100 a month on your grocery bill?" or "Do you know that the new_ _____ cars are considered unsafe and are being recalled?" usually attract attention because the subject matter of the article affects you in a highly personal way. You would expect the introductory paragraph of the first example to introduce a piece about various ways to save money in the grocery store, and that of the second article to introduce a critical report on the dangers of a specific new car. The writer has presented the issue, and you expect the remainder of the article to develop facts and information that will help solve the problem. No matter how attention-getting an opener, it is a poor introduction if it raises false expectations about the content of the composition that follows.

The body of a work develops the main ideas related to the introductory paragraph. If students grasp the concept of a paragraph, writing the body is not too difficult. If students understand the need for rational sequencing of ideas, they can move logically from one point to the next. Some vocabulary terms help writing move from one idea to another. If students are writing in chronological order, for example, they may use such words as *first, second, third, before, during, after, yesterday, today, tomorrow, next,* and *last.* Or they may use dates, such as "in 1990," "in 1992," and "in 1993." These words signal the developing order of ideas. If students organize their thoughts according to problem, causes, effects, and solutions, they can show relationships between ideas. Words such as *because, therefore, since, too,* and *when* signal relationships in this kind of organization.

Certain phrases signal that a composition is drawing to a close. Phrases such as "in conclusion" and "to summarize" indicate that the writer is going to end a report.

To review the three parts of the composition, look at them in diagram form in Figure 10–6. This diagram is quite different from the diagram for a story. A written report presents an introduction that quickly interests readers and develops ideas that move toward a conclusion or summary.

FIGURE 10–6
A diagram identifying the major
parts of a composition

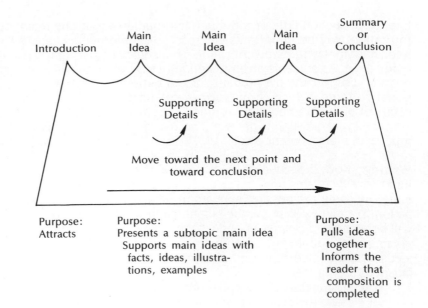

Revision   In teaching composition skills, you should help students develop clear ideas, organize them, and elaborate on them. Consequently, teacher feedback, student evaluation of writing, and any rewriting should emphasize these aspects. Schwartz (1977) defines the rewriting connected with composition in this way: "Rewriting is not just recopying neatly, minus a few punctuation errors. It is not just fixing what is wrong. Rewriting is finding the best way to give your newly discovered ideas to others; it's a finishing, a polishing up, and it should be creative and satisfying as any job well done" (p. 757).

Interact with students during the entire writing process. Provide both positive feedback and opportunity to make improvements during each step of the process. Do not wait for the finished product. Writing conferences can provide opportunities to interact with students when they select a topic, narrow the topic, gather information, organize information, develop an outline, and write the final composition. React as students discuss and write during each part of the process.

Writing and the Content Areas

As we have already stated, some activities use content-area sources to improve understanding of writing and the writing process; other activities emphasize using writing to learn in the content areas. To show the differences in the two goals, Gere (1985) states that writing-to-learn approaches are designed to do more than develop writing fluency; the writing-to-learn strategies are designed to foster abstract thinking, encourage learning, and guide students in their quest for knowledge. There are numerous ways that you may accomplish learning through writing. According to Gere, "there is no 'right way' to use writing to learn. Although the general approach is solidly grounded in theory, there are no quick fixes or rigid

Writing-to-learn strategies foster abstract thinking.

systems for implementing writing to learn. Rather, as is true in all good teaching, it is the responsibility of the individual instructor to select from a wide range of approaches those which seem best suited to accomplish course goals'' (p. 5).

Informational text (nonfiction)   Hairston (1986) uses simulation activities with older students to place them in the role of a specific professional writer and to have them consider how that author may have responded during the writing process. For example, Hairston selects a good example of nonfictional literature and then helps students construct scenarios in which they try to reconstruct the writer's actions, both mental and physical, from the time of the initial idea to the time of the completed product. Within these scenarios, the students consider what motivated the author to write the text; how and why the author chose a certain approach to attract attention and gain sympathy or understanding; what techniques the author used to substantiate the specific point of view, including examples, experiences, comparisons, details, and images; why the author chose those techniques; and how the author shaped the text to develop that specific point of view.

During this analysis and simulation, students should discover that good professional authors of nonfiction support their writing with facts and specific details rather than with generalizations and unsupported opinions. In addition, students should discover how professional authors deal with some of the same problems that cause them difficulty. To extend understanding of specific writing techniques used by authors, develop files of examples that illustrate solutions to various writing problems, such as gaining attention, developing support for positions, shaping articles to develop positions, using figurative language and images to persuade, and developing conclusions. Then, ask the students to apply these techniques in their own writing.

The following books are useful in helping students discover how authors use various organizational patterns to shape their ideas and improve their writing (Norton, 1992): Seymour Simon's *New Questions and Answers About Dinosaurs* (1990)—question and answer; Laurence Pringle's *Global Warming: Assessing the Greenhouse Threat* (1990)—problem–effect—cause–solution; Peter and Connie Roop's *Seasons of the Cranes* (1989)—chronological order; and Helen Roney Sattler's *Giraffes, the Sentinels of the Savannas* (1990)—main idea to supporting details.

Additional authors of nonfictional information literature that may be used for extending understanding of specific writing techniques include Franklyn Branley, Joanna Cole, Patricia Lauber, Hershell and Joan Nixon, Dorothy Patent, Jack Denton Scott, Millicent Selsam, and Jerome Wexler.

FOR YOUR PLAN BOOK
Using **Lincoln: A Photobiography** to Analyze Writing Techniques

The 1988 Newbery Award winner, Russell Freedman's *Lincoln: A Photobiography* (1987) provides an excellent source for analyzing various writing techniques used by authors. The American Library Association selected this book as the most distinguished contribution to children's literature for 1987. A group of fifth-grade students chose the following techniques in *Lincoln: A Photobiography* as among their favorites:

1. Freedman uses examples from Lincoln's own speeches to introduce each chapter. This gains the readers' attention and makes Lincoln seem like a believable person. A good example of this technique is the introduction to ''This Dreadful War'':

   > When I think of the sacrifice yet to be offered and the hearts and homes yet to be made desolate before this dreadful war is over, my heart is like lead within me, and I feel at times like hiding in a deep darkness. (p. 93)

2. Freedman separates fact from fiction by letting readers know when information cannot be proven. A good example of this technique is Freedman's discussion of Lincoln and Ann Rutledge:

   > He also fell in love—apparently for the first time in his life. Legend tells us that Lincoln once had a tragic love affair with Ann Rutledge, daughter of the New Salem tavern owner, who died at the age of twenty-two. While this story has become part of American folklore, there isn't a shred of evidence that Lincoln ever had a romantic attachment with Ann. Historians believe that they were just good friends. (p. 28)

3. Freedman uses chronological order to develop the story of Lincoln's life. First, Lincoln is described as a poor backwoods farm boy. Next, his life in law and

politics is explored. Then, Freedman discusses Lincoln's life as president in Washington, D.C.

4. Freedman increases interest in Lincoln's life by including photographs of Lincoln's own writings. For example, there is a photograph of a page from Lincoln's copybook and one of Lincoln's handwritten Gettysburg Address. This brings readers closer to Lincoln and also shows them that Freedman did a lot of research.

5. Freedman presents and discusses photographs of newspaper drawings and posters from Lincoln's time period. Included in these photographs are a cartoon ridiculing Lincoln's secret arrival in Washington; a cartoon showing Lincoln, General McClellan, and Jefferson Davis fighting over the Union; a poster about *Uncle Tom's Cabin;* and a poster offering a $100,000 reward for the murderer of Lincoln.

6. Freedman includes many photographs of places, people, and battles. This helps readers understand the events that took place. Freedman lists where he obtained the photographs at the back of the book. This also suggests careful research.

Carnes (1988) developed units in which remedial students write nonfictional books modeled after content-area textbooks. The units incorporate the writing process as the students proceed from prewriting activities through printing and book binding. At the prewriting stage, they study nonfictional works; list characteristics of nonfictional literature; develop standards for their own books; choose their topics; determine structure for their books; brainstorm ideas and questions related to their topics; arrange categories into topics, subtopics, and important details; and read materials to gain more knowledge about their topics. During the research and notetaking phase, Carnes models such skills as finding key words and concepts and summarizing material before the students collect their own notes. During the writing phase, Carnes guides the students in integrating their notes, determining headings, sequencing information, and including specific facts. It is at this phase that the students begin to make use of a word processor. During the revision phase, the students refer to the original standard. After several rough drafts, the writings are ready for final printing and binding in book form. Then, the students share their books orally, compare them with the books of previous classes, and place second copies in the class library.

Summaries

Identifying a main idea in a book is often difficult for elementary students. Taylor (1986) found that fourth- and fifth-grade students had difficulty finding and expressing main ideas when they were asked to write summaries. Teaching children to write summaries integrates reading, writing, listening, and speaking with the various content areas. Hidi and Anderson (1986) found that effective summary writing teaches students how to discover information important to the author and how to analyze and paraphrase this information. Key elements in this approach require identification of topic sentences, main ideas, and important details; identification of key phrases, such as "in summary"; identification of text clues, such as underlining, italics, and boldface print; and ability to supply synonyms and para-phrase text.

Hidi and Anderson recommend that teachers begin with short passages and gradually increase passage length as students improve their summarizing skills. In addition, early experiences should use simple narratives and texts that are well organized so that important text elements are obvious to students.

Teaching summary writing is enhanced by modeling and by approaches that proceed from introduction of the skill, to direct instruction by the teacher, to teacher-guided application, and finally to independent practice. Notice how this sequence is incorporated into the following effective strategies identified by Bromley and McKeveny (1986) for teaching summary writing: (1) establish purposes and provide rationales for using summary writing; (2) use demonstrations and simulations to develop understandings and to provide opportunities to study such topics as paragraph organization and location of main ideas; (3) use verbal practice to help students to identify key words, supply synonyms, and paraphrase text; (4) try group composition of summaries before expecting students to write individual summaries; (5) use models of acceptable summaries to help students compare, evaluate, and revise their own summaries; (6) use folders in which students keep their summaries for review and study; and (7) provide study time during which students can use their summaries to review important information from various content areas. Bromley and McKeveny emphasize the importance of long-term instruction in summary writing. Their research showed that "using precise writing twice weekly over an entire semester was more effective than daily 45-minute lessons for three or four weeks" (p. 393).

Writing that requires paraphrasing and summarizing may take place within any content area and may emphasize various types of activities. Shugarman and Hurst (1986) provide the following additional suggestions for paraphrasing and summarizing:

1. Have students elaborate on paraphrasing and summarizing by creating captioned cartoons, graphs, or maps that reflect the information in the text.
2. Ask students to paraphrase and summarize compositions written by other students. Then, have them share and discuss their summaries with the original authors.
3. Divide the class into teams and choose a panel of experts. Assign text passages to be read and paraphrased by each team. Have the panel select the best paraphrased text.
4. Have students bring in relevant text from library materials, newspapers, and magazines. Ask them to write summaries of the materials and to compare and discuss the various solutions.

Book Reports

Almost every elementary teacher uses book reports, whether oral or written. Through the creative use of book reporting, you can provide opportunities for many types of writing as well as strengthen the connections between writing, reading, and literature. Literature includes books from all content areas; thus, book reporting also heightens learning in the content areas.

For expressive book reports, instruct students to:

1. Write a personal response to a book in your journal. Include in your reaction to the book what you liked or did not like about a character, the plot of the story, or the language. How would you change any of these elements if you could rewrite the book?
2. Choose one of the characters in the book and keep a dialogue journal with that character. Write questions you would like to ask that character about feelings, reactions, beliefs, motives, or actions. Exchange your dialogue journal with someone else in the class who has read the same book. Ask the other person to write the answers to your questions as if he or she were that person.
3. Keep a learning log about a piece of nonfictional literature. Write reactions to the author's ability to interest you in the subject and to present information so that you believed it was true. What points was the author trying to make? Did he or she accomplish this task?
4. Keep a diary as if you were one of the characters in a book. Include personal reactions to things that happened to you in the story.
5. Pretend that you are the author of the book you just finished and that you were motivated to write the book because of entries in your writer's journal. Write entries that might have motivated you to develop the setting, characters, plot, or theme of the book.
6. Pretend that you are the author of a book you have read. Write an inventory of experiences from your writer's journal that you would need before you wrote the book.

For imaginative and poetic writing, instruct students to:

1. Write sequels to books you have read or tell stories of your own about characters in books. Choose a book that could have a next installment. Choose one of the characters from the book and tell what happens after the first story ends.
2. Choose a character from your book. Write a letter that character might write to another character in the story. Be sure that you write the letter from the viewpoint of that character. You might choose a problem that your character must solve and have the character write to a friend or relative in the book asking for advice or explaining why your character responded in a certain way.
3. Write a limerick about one of the characters in your book. (This activity should follow writing limericks in class.)
4. Identify the main theme in your book. Write a cinquain about that theme. For the title, select one word that expresses that theme. On the next line, write two words that describe the theme. On the third line, write three action words that express the theme. On the fourth line, write four words that express your feelings about the theme. Complete your cinquain with the title or a word that has the same meaning as the title. (This activity should follow writing cinquains in class.)
5. Identify the major conflicting forces in your book (for example, good versus evil). Write a poem in the diamante format that expresses the conflict in your book. Line 1 should be one of the conflicting forces. Line

2 should have two words that describe the force. Line 3 should have three action words related to the force. Line 4 should have four transitional nouns or a phrase about the conflict. Line 5 should have three action words related to the opposite force. Line 6 should have two words that describe the opposite force. Line 7 should be the opposite force. (This activity should follow the writing of diamante formats in class.)

6. Draw and label the plot development in your book.

7. Pretend that you are the set designer who will construct the set when your book becomes a stage play. Divide the book into three acts. Write detailed descriptions of the settings for each of the acts. Make your readers ''see'' the stage settings.

8. Choose a picture book and describe the setting as if you could not use illustrations in the book. Make your readers ''see'' and ''feel'' the settings through your choice of words.

9. Create a dictionary of words and phrases that suggest the mood of the story. Add words and phrases that you believe would be appropriate in addition to those chosen by the author.

10. Choose a character from your book and write a character sketch showing how the author feels about the character, how the character feels about him- or herself, and how other characters feel about that character.

11. Choose an incident in the book in which you would like to interact with the character. Pretend that you are one of the new characters introduced into the story. Write the incident in which you interact with the character. You may use your incident to clarify information or to try to persuade the character to do something. You may not, however, change the character from the characterization developed by the author.

12. Create a postcard that one of the characters might have sent in the story. Select one of the scenes from the book to draw on the front. Write the postcard as if you are that character.

For expository writing, instruct students to:

1. Write an appropriate weather report for several scenes in the book or for each chapter in the book.

2. Pretend you are the author of an informational book or a biography you have just read. Write a paragraph describing the audience for your book. How old is your audience? How much information on your subject does your audience have? How did you obtain information about your audience? How did this information influence the way you wrote your book?

3. Pretend you are the author of an informational book or a biography you have just read. Write a paragraph about your purpose for writing the book. What decisions did you have to make in order to write for that purpose? After you read your completed book, did you still think you were successful in presenting your purpose? How would you know if you were successful?

4. Pretend that you are the author of an informational book or a biography. Write three paragraphs about your book: (a) a paragraph describing how you decided on your subject, (b) a paragraph describing how you narrowed your subject to one that could be covered in your book, and (c) a paragraph describing how you conducted research on your book.

5. Pretend you are the author of an informational book. Draw a web of interest that you might have developed to help you organize the book.

6. Choose an exciting incident in the story. Write the incident as a news article. Include accurate information on who, what, when, where, and why.

7. Choose an incident in the book that could be controversial. Pretend you are one of the characters in the book and write a letter to the newspaper editor to persuade readers that your point of view is correct.

8. Write a summary of your book in the form of a cartoon, graph, or map. Write a caption explaining your content.

9. Diagram your book according to the major organizational patterns that the author used. The organizational patterns include chronological; spatial; familiar to unfamiliar; problem, to cause of problem, to possible solutions for the problem, problem, to effect of problem, to possible solutions for the problem; and question/answer.

REINFORCEMENT
ACTIVITY

1. Select a content area and develop a lesson plan for teaching beginning summarizing skills within that content area. Include in your lesson a rationale for teaching summarizing, a modeling in which you write a summary, a guided application, and an independent practice that encourages students to apply the summary skills within the content area. (Note: This lesson may require several days to complete.)

2. Develop a file of examples of expository writing to share with students who are having difficulties with writing introductions, substantiating facts, organizing information, presenting arguments, or drawing conclusions.

FOR YOUR PLAN BOOK
A Composition Approach to the Study of Biography

This unit is based on evaluative criteria and teaching suggestions in Norton (1991) and on recommendations by Johnson (1986) and Fleming and McGinnis (1985). This approach to biography first analyzes short biographies to discover characteristics of biographical writing and then encourages students to conduct interviews and to complete research in order to write their own biographies. Discussion and other activities related to the approach encourage students to read reflectively, analyze the impact of the writing, consider the types of information that make biographies interesting, develop interviewing skills that obtain interesting biographical information, complete research to obtain biographical information, and write factual and interesting biographies. The approach emphasizes the interaction of reading, writing, oral language, and listening. As you develop the unit, place it in the framework of the writing process.

Unit Objectives

1. To develop an appreciation for biographical literature.
2. To identify characteristics of the biography genre.
3. To differentiate between biography and fictional literature.
4. To analyze techniques that successful biographical writers use to make their subjects seem real.
5. To develop interviewing and research skills needed to complete biographical writing.
6. To develop and reinforce composition skills and to apply information gained from biographical literature to writing.

Procedures

1. Read and analyze the content of several shorter biographies such as Lillian Gish's *An Actor's Life for Me!* (1987). Discuss the answers to the following questions:

   a. What characteristics make this literature biographical? Are all of the characters people who actually lived? How do you know? Are the dialogue, thoughts, and actions authentic? Did the author support them with research, facts, and interviews? Is the setting authentic for the time? (As you lead this discussion, ask students to support their answers with evidence.)

   b. What differences are there between a fictional story and this nonfictional work? Read Jean Fritz's foreword to her fictionalized autobiography, *Homesick: My Own Story* (1982). How does Fritz differentiate between fictionalized and nonfictionalized work in the following quote?

   > Since my childhood feels like a story, I decided to tell it that way, letting the events fall as they would into the shape of a story, lacing them together with fictional bits, adding a piece here and there when memory didn't give me all I needed. I would use conversation freely, for I cannot think of my childhood without hearing voices. So although this book takes place within two years from October 1925 to September 1927, the events are drawn from the entire period of my childhood, but they are all, except in minor details, basically true. (unnumbered foreword)

   c. Who is the biographical subject? What period in the subject's life does the biographer emphasize? What techniques does the author use to make you believe that the subject is real? Is the biographer successful? Why or why not?

   d. What types of information does the author include? Are any types of information left out of the biography? What is the impact of this information? Why do you believe the author included or left out specific information? Do you believe that the age of the intended audience influenced the author? What other factors might influence the author?

   e. Who most influenced the life of the subject? How important are these people in the development of the subject's character? Are they positive or negative influences? What techniques does the author use to make you believe that these people are real? Is the author successful? Why or why not?

   f. How does the author authenticate the biography? What documentation is included? What research information is included or inferred in the text?

How does the author get to know the biographical subject? What other ways could an author authenticate this subject and this period? (The Lillian Gish biography provides interesting discussion material because the biographical subject told her own story to the author. Consequently, interviewing skills were necessary. The biographical subject seems very real. Numerous personal anecdotes reveal her emotions, dreams, times of happiness and sadness, and interactions with her family and theatrical friends. The biography includes enough references to famous actors and directors that students may do additional research about the time period and the people who influenced Lillian Gish.)

2. Choose a biographical subject or other people from a biography. Give a short oral presentation to the class. Make the class believe that the person is real. For example, choose one of the anecdotes developed in the Gish biography. Tell this anecdote as if you were either Lillian Gish or one of the other people involved in the incident.

3. Choose a scene in the biography in which the subject interacts with one or two other people. With a classmate, prepare the interaction as a presentation for the class. Make the class believe that the interaction is real.

4. Choose an incident in the life of the biographical subject or an emotion expressed by the subject. Pretend that you have the opportunity to interact with the person. What additional questions would you ask? What information do you think you would learn? Write this incident as if it were an anecdote in the life of the person. For example, you might be interested in having Lillian Gish expand on the following thoughts:

> Our greatest fear was of being separated from Mother. She gave us security. Father brought us insecurity. As I grew older, I often wondered which was the most valuable gift. Insecurity taught me to work as if everything depended on me, and to pray as if everything depended on God. Somehow, given enough insecurity, I learned to do for myself, never counting on others to do things for me. Wherever Mother was, we had love, peace, and sympathy. Yet, without the insecurity Father brought, the blessings Mother provided might have left us weak, dependent, and helpless. (p. 10)

5. Choose one of the other people developed in the biography. Find out more information about the person and write a short biography from the viewpoint of that person. Include the original biographical subject in your biography, but make the biographical subject a supporting character. For example, in the life of Lillian Gish, try to find information about her sister Dorothy Gish, actress Mary Pickford, film director D. W. Griffith, or someone else involved in the early melodramas that played in small theaters across the country.

6. Read a review of your biography, such as "Taking It Like Little Troupers" in the *New York Times Book Review*. What techniques and incidents does the reviewer emphasize? Do you agree with this evaluation of the book? Why or why not? If you were going to write a review of the biography, what would you emphasize? Write a paragraph that develops your own evaluation of the biography.

7. List all of the ways that authors and class members made their biographical subjects seem real and allow readers or listeners to learn the facts about the person and the time period. Include an example of each technique.

8. Choose a person you know, such as a family member, a neighbor, or a class-mate. Consider how you would gather information to write a biography about that person. How do you think the biographer of Lillian Gish encouraged her subject to reveal the interesting anecdotes and other factual information? Brainstorm with the class to identify questions and questioning techniques to gather information about someone that you know. After you identify the questions and techniques, role-play your interviewing experiences. Consider other sources of information, such as school yearbooks, newspaper articles, photograph albums, journals, courthouse documents, and people who know the person. Select an interesting anecdote, a personal characteristic, or an experience for an interesting short biography. Compose a rough draft of your biographical subject. Share the rough draft with a group of your peers. How did you make the person seem real? Could you use any other techniques to improve understanding of the person? Organize your introduction, body, and conclusion. Does each part reinforce the qualities or the experiences you are emphasizing? Continue the rewriting process until the biographies seem like biographies of real and interesting people.

9. Write a biography about a person you do not know. Choose a person whose biography requires library research and other documentation. Consider possible sources of information and decide how you will gather that information. Choose a person about whom there is sufficient source material. Choose an interesting period in that person's life. Accumulate as many reference materials as you can find; for example, speeches and writings by the person, biographies and autobiographies, newspaper and magazine articles about the person, letters, and diaries. Write a biography that uses the facts to support a person's possible thoughts, actions, associations, concerns, and so on. Make your readers believe that the person is real. As you are writing your biography, share it with your editing group and with your teacher during conferences.

SUMMARY

This chapter looks at three specific types of writing: (1) expressive writing; (2) imaginative writing, including stories and poetry; and (3) expository writing. Expressive writing is very close to speech. It is relaxed and intimate. It is personally relevant to the writer and reveals the writer's feelings. Expressive writing encourages personal responses and emotional reactions. Such writing includes journals and diaries, learning logs, writer's journals, and letters.

Imaginative writing includes fictional prose and poetry. You can develop creative writers by stimulating fictional story writing. Develop students' vocabularies. Study plots, settings, and characterizations. Also explore symbolism and allusions to mythology. For poetic writing, encourage students to observe and to study imagery and poetic forms.

Expository writing presents facts, ideas, or opinions. Researchers show that expository writing is dominant in the schools. For research reports, students should consider their audience and purpose for writing. They should determine their topic, making sure that it is narrow enough to be appropriate for the length of the report. In addition, they should gather and organize their ideas and information. After writing their reports, students should revise. In the content areas, specific activities can help students understand the process of writing and learn the subject matter. Within expository writing, summary writing is an important skill.

Book reporting can take on an expressive, a poetic, or an expository function. A biography unit that integrates the language arts through reading, literature, writing, and oral language concludes the chapter.

ADDITIONAL ACTIVITIES TO ENHANCE UNDERSTANDING OF EXPRESSIVE, IMAGINATIVE, AND EXPOSITORY WRITING

1. Develop a lesson in which you introduce journal writing, learning logs, or writer's journals to students. Explain why these writing sources are important and how students might be able to use them to expand and enhance other types of writing.
2. Interview a student about imaginative writing. What subjects does the student like to write about? How does the student approach a creative writing task? Ask to see examples of writing that the student would like to share with you.
3. Diagram several books according to plot development.
4. Develop a characterization reference file in which you include examples of how authors tell about a character through narration, record the dialogue of a character, describe the thoughts of a character, show the thoughts of others about a character, and show a character in action. Choose references to model characterization with students in the grade levels in which you teach or would like to teach.
5. Write a lesson plan for story or poetry writing. Account for the various stages in the writing process.
6. Interview a teacher about how he or she teaches poetry writing. How often does the teacher ask students to write poetry? How does the teacher stimulate students' interests? What instructional techniques does the teacher consider effective? How does the teacher encourage students to share poetry?
7. Develop a file of poetry sources that you could use to stimulate poetry writing.
8. Develop a file of ideas that encourage expressive, poetic, and expository book reports.
9. Read an article from Gere's Roots in the Sawdust: Writing to Learn Across the Disciplines (1985). Use the article to develop or adapt a lesson for a writing-to-learn activity designed for elementary or middle-school students.

BIBLIOGRAPHY

Andressen, Oliver. "Creativity in Children's Writing." In *A Forum for Focus,* edited by Martha L. King, Robert Emans, and Patricia J. Cianciolo. Urbana, Ill.: National Council of Teachers of English, 1973.

Applebee, Arthur N. "Writing and Reasoning." *Review of Educational Research* 54 (Winter 1984): 577–96.

Armstrong, D. B. "A Teacher Reflects on a High School English Class: The Dialogue Journal's Contributions to Learning and to Interpersonal Relations." 1990. *Dissertation Abstracts International,* 51, 02A. (University Microfilms No. 90-04,261)

Brand, A. G., and Chibnall, J. "The Emotions of Apprentice Poets." *Empirical Studies of Arts* 7 (1989): 45–49.

Brand, A. G. and Leckie, P. A. "The Emotions of Professional Writers." *Journal of Psychology* 122 (1988): 421–39.

Britton, James; Burgess, Tony; Martin, Nancy; McLeod, Alex; and Rosen, Harold. *The Development of Writing Abilities* (11–18). Schools Council Research Studies. London: Macmillan Co., 1975.

Bromley, Karen. "SSW: Sustained Spontaneous Writing." *Childhood Education* 62 (1985): 23–29.

_____ , and McKeveny, Laurie. "Precis Writing: Suggestions for Instruction in Summarizing." *Journal of Reading* 29 (February 1986): 392–95.

Bugeja, M. J. "Poetry: Stay in Line." *Writer's Digest* (February 1992): 14–16.

Caprio, J. "The Influences of First-Hand Experiences on Children's Writing." Doctoral Dissertation, Univ. of New Jersey at New Brunswick, 1986. *Dissertation Abstracts International,* 47,02A. (University Microfilms No. 86–09, 228)

Carnes, E. Jane. "Teaching Content Area Reading Through Nonfiction Book Writing." *Journal of Reading* 31 (January 1988): 354–60.

Daniels, J. P. "Reading and Writing to Learn: The Effects of a Literature Program and Summary Writing Strategies on Achievement in and Attitude toward Social Studies Content among Fourth-Grade Students." 1990. *Dissertation Abstracts International,* 50, 11A. (University Microfilms No. 90–00, 793)

Davis, Stephanie. "How Radar Writing Works." *Dallas Morning News.* (May 22, 1988): 8F.

Duffy, Gerald G. "Crucial Elements in the Teaching of Poetry Writing." In *A Forum for Focus,* edited by Martha L. King, Robert Emans, and Patricia J. Cianciolo. Urbana, Ill.: National Council of Teachers of English, 1973.

Fleming, Margaret, and McGinnis, Jo, editors. *Portraits: Biography and Autobiography in the Secondary School.* Urbana, Ill.: National Council of Teachers of English, 1985.

Frye, Northrop; Baker, Sheridan; and Perkins, George. *The Harper Handbook to Literature.* New York: Harper & Row, 1985.

Gambrell, L. B. "Dialogue Journals: Reading-Writing Interaction." *The Reading Teacher* 38 (1985): 512–15.

Gere, Anne Ruggles, editor. *Roots in the Sawdust: Writing to Learn across the Disciplines.* Urbana, Ill.: National Council of Teachers of English, 1985.

Golub, Jeff, Chair. *Activities to Promote Critical Thinking: Classroom Practices in Teaching English,* 1986. Urbana, Ill.: National Council of Teachers of English, 1986.

Hairston, Maxine. "Using Nonfiction Literature in the Composition Classroom." In *Convergencies: Transactions in Reading and Writing,* edited by Bruce T. Petersen. Urbana, Ill.: National Council of Teachers of English, 1986, pp. 179–88.

Harpin, William. *The Second "R," Writing Development in the Junior School.* London: George Allen & Unwin Ltd., 1976.

Hidi, Suzanne, and Anderson, Valerie. "Producing Written Summaries: Task Demands, Cognitive Operations, and Implications for Instruction." *Review of Educational Research* 56 (Winter 1986): 473–93.

Hillocks, George. *Research on Written Composition: New Directions for Teaching.* Urbana, Ill.: National Conference on Research in English, 1986.

Huck, Charlotte; Hepler, Susan; and Hickman, Janet. *Children's Literature.* New York: Holt, Rinehart & Winston, 1987.

Johnson, Scott. "The Biography: Teach It from the Inside Out." *English Journal* (October 1986): 27–29.

Khatena, Joe. *Creative Imagination and What We Can Do to Stimulate It.* Paper presented at the National Association of Gifted Children. Chicago, 1975.

Koch, Kenneth. *Wishes, Lies, and Dreams.* New York: Vintage Book/Chelsea House Publishers, 1971.

MacVaugh, P. Q. "Writing to Learn: A Phenomenological Study of the Use of Journals to Facilitate Learning in the Content Areas." 1990. *Dissertation Abstracts International,* 51, 04A. (University Microfilms No. 90–24, 465)

Mason, J.; Herman, P.; and Au, K. "Children's Developing Knowledge of Words." In *Handbook of Research on Teaching the English Language Arts,* edited by J. Flood, J. Jensen, D. Lapp, and J. Squire. New York: Macmillan, 1991, pp. 721–31.

Murray, Donald M. "Why Creative Writing Isn't—or Is." *Elementary English* 50 (April 1973): 523–25, 556.

Norton: Donna E. *The Impact of Literature-Based Reading.* New York: Merrill/Macmillan, 1992.

_____ . *Through the Eyes of a Child: An Introduction to Children's Literature,* 3d ed. Merrill/Macmillan, New York: 1991.

Rothman, John. "Taking It like Little Troupers." *The New York Times Book Review.* (November 8, 1987)

Sager, Carol. "Improving the Quality of Written Composition in the Middle Grades." *Language Arts* 54 (October 1977): 760–62.

_____ . "Improving the Quality of Written Composition through Pupil Use of Rating Scale." Doctoral

Dissertation, Boston University, 1973. *Dissertation Abstracts International* 34, 04A.

Schwartz, Mimi."Rewriting or Recopying: What Are We Teaching?" *Language Arts* 54 (October 1977): 756–59.

Shugarman, Sherrie L., and Hurst, Joe B. "Purposeful Paraphrasing: Promoting a Nontrivial Pursuit for Meaning." *Journal of Reading* 29 (February 1986): 396–99.

Strunk, William, Jr. and White, E. B. *Elements of Style*, 3d ed. New York: Macmillan, 1979.

Sutherland, Zena, and Arbuthnot, May Hill. *Children and Books*. Glenview, Ill.: Scott, Foresman & Co., 1990.

Taylor, K. K. "Summary Writing for Young Children." *Reading Research Quarterly* 21 (1986): 193–208.

Tchudi, Susan, and Tchudi, Stephen. *The Young Writer's Handbook*. New York: Charles Scribner's Sons, 1984.

Watson, Dorothy, ed. *Ideas and Insights: Language Arts in the Elementary School*. Urbana, Ill.: National Council of Teachers of English, 1987.

Yolen, Jane. "How Basic Is Shazam?" *Language Arts* 54 (September 1977): 645–51.

CHILDREN'S LITERATURE REFERENCES

Aesop. *Aesop's Fables*. Illustrated by Heidi Holder. New York: Viking, 1981.

———. *Aesop's Fables*. Selected and illustrated by Michael Hague. New York: Holt, Rinehart & Winston, 1985.

———. *Aesop's Fables*. Illustrated by Charles Santore. New York: Jelly Bean, 1988.

———. *Aesop's Fables Retold in Verse*. Retold by Tom Paxton. Illustrated by Robert Rayevsky. New York: Morrow, 1988.

Afanasyev, Alexander Nikolayevich. *The Fool and the Fish*. Retold by Lenny Holt. Illustrated by Gennady Spirin. New York: Dial, 1990.

Ahlberg, Janet, and Ahlberg, Allen. *The Jolly Postman*. Boston: Little, Brown, 1986.

Anno, Mitsumasa. *Anno's Aesop*. New York: Orchard, 1989.

Baylor, Byrd. *The Best Town in the World*. Illustrated by Ronald Himler. New York: Charles Scribner's Sons, 1983.

Bierhorst, John. *Doctor Coyote: A Native American Aesop's Fables*. Illustrated by Wendy Watson. New York: Macmillan, 1987.

Brisson, Pat. *Your Best Friend, Kate*. Illustrated by Rick Brown. New York: Bradbury, 1989.

Brown, Marc. *Arthur's Baby*. Boston: Little, Brown & Co., 1987.

———. *Arthur Goes to Camp*. Boston: Little Brown, 1982.

Caseley, Judith. *Dear Annie*. New York: Greenwillow, 1991.

Cauley, Lorinda Bryan. Retold by. *The Town Mouse and the Country Mouse*. New York: Putnam, 1984.

Cendrars, Blaise. *Shadow*. Illustrated by Marcia Brown. New York: Charles Scribner's Sons, 1982.

Cleary, Beverly. *Dear Mr. Henshaw*. Illustrated by Paul Zelinsky. New York: Morrow, 1983.

de Paola, Tomie. *An Early American Christmas*. New York: Holiday, 1987.

Dragonwagon, Crescent. *Dear Miss Moshki*. Illustrated by Diane Palmisciano. New York: Macmillan, 1986.

Dupasquier, Philippe. *Dear Daddy*. New York: Bradbury, 1985.

Durrell, Ann, and Sachs, Marilyn, eds. *The Big Book for Peace*. New York: Dutton, 1990.

Flournoy, Valerie. *The Patchwork Quilt*. Illustrated by Jerry Pinkney. New York: Dial Press, 1985.

Freedman, Russell. *Lincoln: A Photobiography*. New York: Clarion, 1987.

Fritz, Jean. *Homesick: My Own Story*. New York: G. P. Putnam's Sons, 1982.

Giff, Patricia Reilly. *The War Began at Supper: Letters to Miss Loria*. Illustrated by Betsy Lewin. New York: Delacorte, 1991.

Gish, Lillian. *An Actor's Life for Me!* As told to Selma G. Lanes. New York: Viking Press, 1987.

Goodall, John. *The Story of a Main Street*. New York: Macmillan Co., 1987.

Hall, Donald. *Ox-Cart Man*. Illustrated by Barbara Cooney. New York: Viking Press, 1979.

Hodges, Margaret. *The Wave*. Illustrated by Blair Lent. Boston: Houghton Mifflin Co., 1964.

James, Simon. *Dear Mr. Blueberry*. New York: Macmillan, 1991.

Khalsa, Dayal. *I Want a Dog*. New York: Potter, 1987.

Lenski, Lois. *Sing a Song of People*. Illustrated by Giles Laroche. Boston: Little, Brown & Co., 1987.

Lindbergh, Reeve. *Johnny Appleseed.* Boston: Little, Brown, 1990.

MacLachlan, Patricia. *Sarah, Plain and Tall.* New York: Harper Collins, 1985.

McCloskey, Robert. *Time of Wonder.* New York: Viking Press, 1957.

McKinley, Robin. *Beauty.* New York: Simon & Schuster, 1978.

McMillan, Bruce. *One Sun: A Book of Terse Verse.* New York: Holiday, 1990.

McPhail, David. *The Dream Child.* New York: E. P. Dutton, 1985.

Moore, Inga. *Little Dog Lost.* New York: Macmillan, 1991.

O'Neill, Catharine. *Mrs. Dunphy's Dog.* New York: Viking Press, 1987.

Parker, Nancy Winslow. *Love from Aunt Betty.* New York: Putnam, 1983.

Peek, Merle. *The Balancing Act: A Counting Song.* New York: Clarion, 1987.

Pringle, Laurence. *Global Warming: Assessing the Greenhouse Threat.* New York: Arcade, 1990.

Roop, Peter, and Roop, Connie. *Seasons of the Cranes.* New York: Walker, 1989.

Rylant, Cynthia. *When I Was Young in the Mountains.* Illustrated by Diane Goode. New York: E. P. Dutton, 1982.

Sampton, Sheila. *Jenny's Journey.* New York: Viking, 1991.

Sattler, Helen Roney. *Giraffes, the Sentinels of the Savannas.* New York: Lothrop, Lee & Shepard, 1990.

Seuss, Dr. *And to Think That I Saw It on Mulberry Street.* New York: Vanguard, 1937.

Simon, Seymour. *New Questions and Answers about Dinosaurs.* Illustrated by Jennifer Dewey. New York: Morrow, 1990.

Small, David. *Imogene's Antlers.* New York: Crown Pubs., 1985.

Stanley, Diane. *Peter the Great.* New York: Four Winds, 1986.

Stevens, Janet. Retold by. *The Tortoise and the Hare.* New York: Holiday House, 1984.

_____ . Retold by. *The Town Mouse and the Country Mouse.* New York: Holiday House, 1987.

Va, Leong. *A Letter to the King.* New York: Harper Collins, 1991.

Wilder, Laura Ingalls. *Little Town on the Prairie.* New York: Harper & Row, 1941.

Williams, Vera B. *Stringbean's Trip to the Shining Sea.* Illustrated by Vera B. Williams and Jennifer Williams. New York: Greenwillow, 1988.

Yolen, Jane. *Owl Moon.* Illustrated by John Schoenherr. New York: Philomel, 1987.

Zimelman, Nathan. *Please Excuse Jasper.* Illustrated by Ray Cruz. Nashville: Abingdon, 1987.

Chapter Eleven

After completing this chapter on literature, you will be able to:

1. Describe an environment that stimulates interest in literature.
2. Select literature that considers appropriateness, balance, and children's interests.
3. Prepare and tell an appropriate story.
4. List benefits of reading aloud to children, discuss selection of books for reading aloud, and read a selection aloud to children.
5. Describe how art adds to appreciation of literature.
6. Describe methods and develop lessons that increase students' understanding of literary elements through webbing, modeling, and plot diagramming.
7. List the instructional possibilities for a children's book.
8. Describe ways for developing students' understanding of and appreciation for literary genres.
9. Describe how to increase world understanding through folktales.

Literature

*T*he many books written especially for children open up new and wonderful worlds. Through books, children experience the enchantment of Cinderella, the adventure of Huckleberry Finn, and the loneliness and challenge of living on the Island of the Blue Dolphins. Most adults have favorite books from childhood that remain vivid in their memories. Mary Poppins, Pooh Bear, or Caddie Woodlawn may seem like personal friends. Not all children, however, regard literature as a source of pleasure and as a way of meeting new friends. The goal of this chapter is to show you how to help children develop a love of reading and an appreciation for a variety of literary genres. In addition, the chapter stresses using literature in the language arts curriculum and suggests ways to integrate literature and language arts objectives into other subject areas. Chapter 12 continues this emphasis with approaches that bring literature into the reading curriculum.

Using literature in the curriculum and teaching about literature in the classroom are two exciting yet complex areas. Choosing literature that motivates students to read requires knowledge about literature, awareness of the interests of students, and knowledge about instructional approaches that motivate and stimulate interest. Likewise, teaching about literature requires knowledge about literature and instructional approaches that encourage understanding of various genres, story structures, and such literary elements as style, characterization, and theme.

As you approach literature and methodologies related to literature, keep in mind Fishel's (1984) warning for English and language arts teachers: "Of the content areas, English is one of the most demanding in terms of the reading skills required to understand the various genres. In addition, appreciation of genres is a teaching goal" (p. 9). This chapter considers the selection of literature from various genres, identification of students' interests, stimulation of interest and appreciation of literature, and methodologies that help students understand particular genres and literary elements. Remember, however, that the roles of enhancing appreciation and increasing understanding cannot be separated. Methodologies should never turn children off to the excitement of reading literature.

The dual role of enhancing appreciation and increasing understanding is emphasized by endorsements of educational groups, by various state goals and objectives, and by curriculum documents in public schools. For example, the National Council of Teachers of English (1983) states that students should gain the following objectives from literature:

1. Realize the importance of literature as a mirror of human experience, reflecting human motives, conflicts, and values.
2. Be able to identify with fictional characters in human situations as a means of relating to others; gain insights from involvement with literature.
3. Become aware of important writers representing diverse backgrounds and traditions in literature.
4. Become familiar with masterpieces of literature, both past and present.
5. Develop effective ways of talking and writing about varied forms of literature.
6. Experience literature as a way to appreciate the rhythms and beauty of language.
7. Develop habits of reading that carry over into adult life. (p. 246)

State goals and objectives may also include literature objectives within the language arts curriculum. For example, the literature goal for language arts in the Illinois *State Goals for Learning and Sample Learning Objectives: Language Arts* (1985) states: "As a result of their schooling, students will be able to understand the various forms of significant literature representative of different cultures, eras, and ideas" (p. 43). The sample objectives identified to encourage students to meet this goal emphasize developing appreciation, understanding genres of literature, and understanding literary elements. For example, at the appreciation level the third-grade objective states that students will read and enjoy appropriate literary works. At the same grade level, objectives related to genre state that children will recognize the nature of poetry, prose, and biography, and will compare versions of folktales.

Curriculum documents from various school districts frequently develop this multifaceted nature of the literature curriculum. For example, a kindergarten through sixth-grade literature curriculum may have the following goals: (1) to introduce children to their literary heritage; (2) to encourage children to read for pleasure and knowledge; (3) to provide children with knowledge about literary elements and structure; (4) to allow children to give creative responses to literature; (5) to develop children's ability to evaluate literature; and (6) to develop independent readers and learners.

Literature programs have broad educational and personal goals. Folklore from around the world, the writings of Mark Twain and Robert Louis Stevenson, and the poetry of Langston Hughes and Edward Lear, for example, help children understand and value cultural and literary heritage. Historical fiction and nonfiction chronicling early explorations and frontier expansion allow children to vicariously live through history. Books on outer space and scientific breakthroughs open doors to new knowledge and expand interests. Fantasy and science fiction nurture and expand imaginations and allow children to visualize worlds that have not yet materialized. Biography and autobiography allow children to explore human possibilities while promoting their personal and social development. Interactions with many types of literature allow children to expand their language and to develop their cognitive skills. The time spent with literature is among the most rewarding. Smith (1991) argues that a variety of genres are necessary to promote emotional growth as the children learn to appreciate literature and identify with fictional characters. In addition, the analysis of different literary genres promotes cognitive development as children identify themes discussed in one genre and find similar themes in other genres.

THE ENVIRONMENT

A strong literature program includes an environment in which children can easily locate and read books. A key factor in the environment is a teacher who loves books, shares them daily with students, and encourages interaction with a variety of books. Research provides support for this type of environment. Galda (1988) reports that students' responses to literature are extended and heightened when the students have opportunities to read and respond to a variety of genres, styles, and authors and when the environment encourages individual differences, provides opportunities to explore and compare responses, and utilizes various approaches, such as writing, discussing, acting out, and drawing. Interaction through language is extremely important. Spinner (1990) found that adults who enjoy reading and writing poetry had childhoods in which language was a vital part of their environments.

Provide time for children to listen to, read, and discuss books. In a survey of 520 elementary students ranging in age from five to thirteen, Mendoza (1985) found that children like to be given information about books. Tell them about the authors and summarize plots, characters, and settings. Provide opportunities for children to select books themselves. Children throughout the elementary grades enjoy having books read to them, so read to children frequently. Also, provide opportunities for them to read to other children. Encouraging children to read outside of school is also very important. Anderson, Wilson, and Fielding (1988) found that reading books outside of school was the best predictor of students' future reading achievement.

Educators who use or recommend literature-based programs emphasize a dynamic environment. Taxel (1988) describes a literature-based classroom as "fluid and dynamic, . . . a place where educators see literature as central to the curriculum, not as an occasional bit of enrichment undertaken when the 'real' work is completed" (p. 74).

Understanding and enjoying literature are the major goals in a first- through sixth-grade program that May (1987) describes. May's program for exploring different literature genres begins in kindergarten, where students and teachers explore books containing personification and compare these books to other fantasy stories and folktales. At this level, students consider how the characters and their actions seem real. First graders explore literary patterns within folktales, look at variances among folktales found in different cultures, and examine different versions of the same folktale. They also explore realistic fiction and relate the literature to a unit on the family. Second graders discuss repeated patterns, magical numbers, and settings in folktales. They compare additional versions of folktales and explore folktale adaptations. Third graders read E. B. White's *Charlotte's Web* (1952) and discuss animal characters, personification, fantasy, and point of view. They compare fantasy and realistic stories about animals. Fourth graders explore literature around a social studies unit on India. Fifth graders explore literature as part of a social studies unit on medieval Europe and discuss historical fiction as literature and interpretation of history. They also consider the importance of setting, symbolism, and stereotypic characters in legends and work with myths and fables. Sixth graders explore differences between autobiography and biography, conduct oral interviews, write short biographies, and share them with the class.

May is enthusiastic about this literature program and shares the following response from a teacher: "By the end of the first year the children were reading more library books than before. They were also talking about literature and were 'borrowing' an author's style or symbolism when they admired it. They were more appreciative of an author's writing style. All of the students, even the slow learners, were writing and reading for enjoyment" (p. 136).

The teacher of a fifth-grade literature program shows equal enthusiasm. Five (1988) describes a literature-based program in which she begins each session with a mini-lesson on an element of fiction: "Often I use the books that I read aloud to them each day as the basis for my mini-lessons, allowing time for discussions, for making predictions, and interpretations, and for discovering characteristics of a particular author's style that students may wish to apply to their own writing. Different genres are also introduced during these lessons" (p. 105). Some of the mini-lessons involve discussing, some involve direct teaching, and some include sharing specific activities. Mini-lessons focus on such topics as book selection, copyrights, plot structures, and time lines of characters. After the mini-lessons, students read related books of their own choosing, discuss the books, and write about their choices. Five enthusiastically evaluates her program: "Today my reading program is dramatically different and so are the results. Today my students read between 25 and 144 books a year. Children listen to each other and seek recommendations for their next book selections. They wonder about authors and look for feelings, for believable characters, for interesting words, and they are delighted with effective dialogue. And my students and I always talk books before school, during school, at lunch and after school, something we never did in my 'workbook' days" (p. 104).

Both programs emphasize an environment that is rich with literature, encourages children to explore various literary devices in a number of ways, and includes both teacher- and student-directed activities with literature. The programs also show that teachers may use literature to combine reading, writing, and other content areas.

LITERATURE IN THE CURRICULUM

The previously described literature-based language arts programs illustrate the importance of including a variety of genres of literature in the curriculum. Smith (1991) identifies a conceptual shift in education that requires numerous books: "Many educators [now] view the curriculum as more personalized and less mandated. Teachers and children can pursue themes or topics of personal interest. In that kind of environment, a multiplicity of books, resources, and mass media is needed to encourage individuals to learn what is important to them" (p. 516). Literature selections must include books that can be read to and by children and books that meet the goals for developing literary appreciation and understanding. A language arts curriculum should include picture books, folklore, modern fantasy, poetry, contemporary realistic fiction, historical fiction, biography, autobiography, and informational literature selected to help students develop an understanding of and an appreciation for specific genres. The literature within these genres should reflect varied cultural and literary heritage, as well as provide insights into personal and social development. Questions related to appropriateness, balance, resources to help teachers choose literature, and children's interests are basic to achieving these objectives.

What Is Appropriate?

Much concern surrounds contemporary realistic fiction. During times of changing values, such concern is not surprising. Current controversy regarding realistic fiction centers around issues related to literary merit and appropriate content. The heroes and heroines in today's realistic fiction face problems related to sexism, racism, violence, drugs, sexual activities, and such family disturbances as separation, divorce, and abuse. Quan's (1990) analysis of social values in adolescent literature published between 1940 and 1980 indicates a shift from social conservatism to a more liberal interpretation of traditional values. Such shifts cause some groups to question the appropriateness of the literature read in schools.

Certain groups believe in censoring books or authors they suspect are capable of subverting children's religious, social, or political beliefs. According to a survey by People for the American Way, censorship attempts "increased by 20 percent during the 1986–87 school year and by 168 percent in the last five years" (Wiessler, 1987, sec. 1, p. 1). A report by Dronka (1987) indicates that organized groups are increasingly advocating censorship. In 1982–83, 17 percent of censorship incidents were linked to organizations; by 1985–86, 43 percent were associated with organized efforts. As more publishers develop literature-based textbooks, they too face the challenges of censorship. For example, Meade (1990) quotes advocates who view a literature-based series as "a blend of sophistication and wholesomeness" and opponents who detect "a not-so-subtle emphasis on violence, death, and the occult" (p. 38).

Educators and librarians frequently caution against the dangers of censorship. For example, McClenathan (1979) suggests that wholesale avoidance, in addition to encouraging overt censorship, is inappropriate because (1) books about a relevant sociological or psychological problem can give young people opportunities to grow in their thinking process and to extend experiences; (2) problems in books can provide children with opportunities to identify with or sympathize with their peers; and (3) problems in books invite decisions, elicit opinions, and afford opportunities to take positions on issues. In an article in *Education Week,* Rothman (1990) states that "school districts can protect their literature curriculum by having in place procedures that ensure that the materials selected are educationally sound" (p. 5). (For guidelines for evaluating literature and meeting problems related to censorship, see Norton [1991].)

The controversy surrounding Margot Zemach's *Jake and Honeybunch Go to Heaven* exemplifies different reactions to the same book. A review in the *New York Times Book Review* suggests literary merit. In contrast, book-selection committees in Chicago, San Francisco, and Milwaukee found the book weak and/or racially stereotyping. The March 1983 issue of *American Libraries* examines both sides of this controversy (Brandehoff, 1983).

Sexism in children's literature is frequently denounced by critics. Frasher (1982) found that literature published after 1970 reflects a heightened sensitivity toward women. Literature published prior to 1970 not only includes more male main characters, but also more negative comments about females than the more recent literature. School libraries should certainly offer books that portray women and girls in nonstereotyped roles. They should offer biographies of famous women to provide models for girls, just as they offer biographies of well-known men. Libraries should also offer stories about girls who are active and inventive and who do not always follow the initiative of boys.

As mentioned previously, many contemporary books deal with real problems many children face, such as divorce, death, special needs, and various difficulties associated with growing up. Books based on specific problems include the following:

- Divorce—Beverly Cleary's *Dear Mr. Henshaw* (1983): Corresponding with his favorite author helps a sixth-grade boy overcome problems associated with his parents' divorce. Gary Paulsen's *Hatchet* (1987): Surviving in the Canadian wilderness helps a boy face problems associated with his parents' divorce.
- Death—Eleanor Cameron's *That Julia Redfern* (1982): A girl develops a close relationship with her father and then accepts his death. Marion Dane Bauer's *On My Honor* (1986): A boy faces both his own disobedience and the death of his best friend. Norma Fox Mazer's *After the Rain* (1987): A girl develops a close relationship with her grandfather and then mourns his death.
- Special needs—Ellen Howard's *Edith Herself* (1987): A girl faces and solves her problems associated with epilepsy in a story set in the 1890s. Jane Madsen and Diane Bockoras's *Please Don't Tease Me* (1983): A physically disabled girl asks for understanding. Jeanne Lee's *Silent Lotus* (1991): A young mute girl learns to perform the story dances of Cambodia.
- Growing up—Jean Little's *Different Dragons* (1986). A boy and a girl discover that they both have fears that they must overcome.

Literature selections should take into account the needs of children of different ages and abilities. Although many books are geared to the varied interests of children with average or above-average reading ability, there are not so many designed for children with beginning skills or children whose reading ability is several years below grade level. The interests of students who are below grade level are similar to those of children who read at grade level, but teachers must select easier-to-read books for the slower children. Sources such as Agee's *High Interest, Easy Reading* (1984), published by the National Council of Teachers of English, provide guidance in selecting materials for older readers who have reading difficulties.

Literature collections should include books on science, art, social studies, and music topics. Nat Segaloff and Paul Erickson's *A Reef Comes to Life: Creating an Undersea Exhibit* (1991) and Seymour Simon's *Earthquake* (1991) enrich the science curriculum. Jan Greenberg and Sandra Jordan's *The Painter's Eye: Learning to Look at Contemporary Art* (1991), Nancy Willard's *Pish, Posh, Said Hieronymus Boseh* (1991), and Zheng Zhensun and Alice Low's *A Young Painter: The Life and Paintings of Wang Yani—China's Extraordinary Young Artist* (1991) are excellent for increasing appreciation for art. The social studies curriculum is enriched by such books as *Brother Eagle, Sister Sky: A Message from Chief Seattle* (1991) and Jean Fritz's *Bully for You, Teddy Roosevelt* (1991). Books such as Violette Verdy's *Of Swans, Sugarplums, and Satin Slippers: Ballet Stories for Children* (1991) add interest to the study of music.

Materials on specific topics should be available at a wide range of reading levels, even when they are studied at only one grade level. The reason for this is obvious from the test results of several sixth-grade classes. Reading levels in six classrooms ranged from second through twelfth grade. In addition, because specific musical selections can enhance the study of a period of history, and because filmstrips or sets of pictures can promote understanding of written content in the subject areas, library materials should reflect the needs of the overall curriculum.

A Comprehensive Collection

Literature selections for libraries, as well as for individual children, should include picture books, traditional literature, modern fantasy, poetry, contemporary realistic fiction, historical fiction, biography, and nonfiction. Picture books, alphabet books, and storybooks that develop plot and characters afford children their earliest encounters with literature. Teachers and parents usually read these books to younger children because picture-storybook reading levels are usually at least for third grade. Excellent alphabet books include Betsy Bowen's *Antler, Bear, Canoe: A Northwoods Alphabet Year* (1991), Chris Van Allsburg's *The Z Was Zapped* (1987), Suse MacDonald's *Alphabatics* (1986), and Isabel Wilner's *A Garden Alphabet* (1991). These books expand language and encourage interaction with the text. Picture storybooks should include old favorites, such as Dr. Seuss's *The 500 Hats of Bartholomew Cubbins* (1938), Robert McCloskey's *Make Way for Ducklings* (1941), and Maurice Sendak's *Where the Wild Things Are* (1963). As new books are published, you can select titles to add to the collection. Faith Ringgold's *Tar Beach* (1991), Chris Van Allsburg's *The Polar Express* (1985), Audrey Wood's *King Bidgood's in the Bathtub* (1985), and Arthur Yorinks's *Hey, Al* (1986) encourage children to interact with both the illustrations and the text. Picture storybooks, such as Denys Cazet's *A Fish in His Pocket* (1987), show children that even young characters can solve problems in satisfying and creative ways.

A well-balanced collection includes picture storybooks illustrated in a variety of ways. The collection should include photographs, woodcuts, collages, painted pictures, ink drawings, and crayon illustrations. Children frequently enjoy creating their own collages as well as viewing those of professional artists. The following books are illustrated through collage: Gene Baer's *Thump Thump, Rat-a-Tat-Tat* (1989), Lois Lenski's *Sing a Song of People* (1987), Susan Roth's *We'll Ride Elephants through Brooklyn* (1989), Sara's *Across Town* (1991), Laura Whipple's *Eric Carle's Animals Animals* (1989), and David Wisniewski's *The Warrior and the Wise Man* (1989).

A collection should also include well-loved traditional literature—folktales handed down from earlier generations, such as "Little Red Riding Hood," "The Three Billy Goats Gruff," and "Cinderella," along with mythology and stories of epic heroes, such as King Arthur and Robin Hood. Traditional literature should include folklore from numerous cultures. Olaf Baker's *Where the Buffaloes Begin* (1981), Van Dyke Parks's adaptation of Joel Chandler Harris's *Jump Again! More Adventures of Brer Rabbit* (1987), and Momoko Ishii's *The Tongue-Cut Sparrow* (1987) are excellent selections.

Children should be introduced to classics in modern fantasy, such as E. B. White's *Charlotte's Web* (1952), C. S. Lewis's *The Lion, the Witch and the Wardrobe* (1950), A. A. Milne's *Winnie-the-Pooh* (1926), and Beatrix Potter's *The Tale of Peter Rabbit* (1902). Authors such as Lloyd Alexander, Hans Christian Andersen, Michael Bond, Lucy Boston, Lewis Carroll, Susan Cooper, Kenneth Grahame, Rudyard Kipling, Ursula LeGuin, Madeleine L'Engle, and Margery Williams bring excitement to this genre of literature. In addition to these, collections should include newer fantasies, such as Bill Brittain's *The Wish Giver* (1983), Robin McKinley's *The Hero and the Crown* (1984), and Brian Jacques's *Redwall* (1986).

Study of the past might be very dull without historical fiction. Such stories allow children to live vicariously in the past and to understand important themes and values. Children can learn about the Revolutionary War by reading Esther Forbes's *Johnny Tremain* (1943), visit the Pilgrims by reading Patricia Clapp's *Constance: A Story of Early Plymouth* (1968), be persecuted as a witch in Elizabeth Speare's *The Witch of Blackbird Pond* (1958), live in the pioneer wilderness in Laura Ingalls Wilder's *Little House in the Big Woods* (1932), discover Victorian London in Philip Pullman's *The Ruby in the Smoke* (1987) and Leon Garfield's *The December Rose* (1986), or feel what it might be like to be a slave in Belinda Hurmence's *A Girl Called Boy* (1982).

Biographies add another dimension to literature programs by allowing children to learn more about past and present heroes and heroines. You can introduce children to biographies in the early grades with picture storybook biographies, such as Alice Dalgliesh's *The Columbus Story* (1955) and David Adler's *Martin Luther King, Jr.: Free at Last* (1986). Middle-elementary students can read autobiographies such as Lillian Gish's *An Actor's Life for Me!* (1987) and biographies such as Jean Fritz's *Make Way for Sam Houston* (1986). Encourage older children to read biographies such as Russell Freedman's *Lincoln: A Photobiography* (1987) and Polly Brooks's *Queen Eleanor: Independent Spirit of the Medieval World* (1983).

Informational books are available in all areas of knowledge. There are books about the history and culture of the ancient and the modern worlds. Books about the laws of nature encourage children to learn about their own bodies, observe nature, explore the life cycles of animals, consider the impact of endangered species, experiment with plants, and explore the geology of the earth. Informational books answer children's questions about discoveries of the past and present or explain how many kinds of machines work. Informational books also allow children to learn more about their hobbies and interests. Such books often include directions, provide guidelines for choosing equipment or other materials, and give interesting background information.

Sources of Information

Many resources are available to help teachers select literature. Children's literature textbooks are the best source of information for genre-specific literature. *Through the Eyes of a Child: An Introduction to Children's Literature* (Norton, 1991), *The Impact of Literature-Based Reading* (Norton, 1992), *Children and Books* (Sutherland & Arbuthnot, 1986), and *Children's Literature* (Huck, Hepler, & Hickman, 1987) discuss literature according to genre and recommend hundreds of titles useful for literature programs. These texts list Caldecott and Newbery award-winning books. Specialized books, such as Cianciolo's *Picture Books for Children* (1990), present criteria for evaluation and recommend specific books. For example, Cianciolo recommends books that are categorized according to the themes of "Me and My Family," "Other People," "The World I Live In," and "The Imaginative World."

Literature journals are excellent resources for new books and for specialized collections and topics. For example, the *School Library Journal, Booklist,* and *Hornbook* contain book reviews and starred reviews for excellent books. *Booklist* publishes yearly lists of "Notable Children's Books" and "Children's Editors' Choice." In addition, *Booklist* publishes specialty lists, such as "Popular Reading—Chapter Books" (Bennett, 1987); "Popular Reading—After Henry Huggins" (Cooper, 1986); "Storytelling Sources" (Corcoran, 1986); "Picture Books for Older Children" (Kiefer, 1986); "Poetry for Young Children" (Phelan, 1988); and "Contemporary Issues—Intergenerational Relationships" (Wilms, 1986). The *School Library Journal* publishes the "Best Books" list for each year, as well as specific recommendations for literature and media, such as "Modern Classics" (Breckenridge, 1988) and "Cultural Diverse Videos: African-Americans" (Mandell, 1992).

Book Links also publishes lists of recommended books, such as "Book Links Salutes 'A Few Good Books' of 1991" (Elleman, 1992), as well as lists that relate to specific themes, such as "Our Emerging Nation—The Late 1800s" (Chatton, 1992). The *Children's Literature Association Quarterly* publishes articles on specific genres of literature, authors, literary criticism, and issues. It also lists "Touchstone" books—books the editors consider so good that they provide the criteria by which all other books are evaluated. *Language Arts, The Reading Teacher,* and *The New Advocate* also review children's literature. Each October, *The Reading Teacher* publishes a list of books that children from across the United States select as their favorites for the year.

REINFORCEMENT ACTIVITY

1. Visit an elementary classroom in which literature is an important part of the curriculum. Describe the environment, the teacher's attitude toward literature, and the interactions of the children with books.
2. Choose a resource for selecting literature. Review the information about books that you gain from the resource.

Children's Interests

Understanding why and what children read is necessary to help the children select books that stimulate interests and provide enjoyment. You can learn about children's interests by reviewing studies of children's interests and preferences and by talking to children and evaluating their responses on interest inventories.

Each year, a joint project of the International Reading Association and the Children's Book Council allows approximately 10,000 children from around the United States to evaluate children's books published during a given year. Each year, the council records the reactions and a research team uses this information to compile a list of "Children's Choices." These lists of children's favorites give teachers a better understanding of the characteristics of books that appeal to children. Sebesta (1979) evaluated books listed and came to the following conclusions:

1. Plots of the Children's Choices are faster paced than those of books not chosen as favorites.
2. Young children enjoy reading about nearly any topic if the information is presented in specific detail. The topic itself may be less important than

What types of books will interest children at the grade level you will teach?

interest studies indicate; specifics rather than topics seem to underlie children's preferences.

3. Children like detailed descriptions of settings. They want to know exactly how the place looks and feels before the main action occurs.

4. One type of plot structure does not dominate Children's Choices. Some stories have carefully arranged cause-and-effect plots; others have plots that meander, with unconnected episodes.

5. Children do not like sad books.

6. Children seem to like some books that explicitly teach a lesson, even though critics usually frown on didactic books.

7. Warmth is the most outstanding quality of books children prefer. Children enjoy books in which characters like each other, express their feelings in things they say and do, and sometimes act selflessly.

Sebesta believes that teachers and parents should use this information to help children select books and to stimulate reading and discussions. For example, you can draw children's attention to the warmth, pace, or descriptions in a story in order to encourage involvement with the story.

The various lists of children's choices also suggest particular types of stories that appeal to young readers. For example, in a recent list, the "beginning independent reading" category contains comical stories about more or less realistic family situations, humorous animal stories, stories that develop emotional experiences, action-filled fantasies, traditional stories, counting books, rhymes, and riddles. The "younger reader" category includes realistic stories about families, friends, school, and personal problems; animal stories; fantasies; fast-paced adventures; folktales; and humorous stories. Stories that children chose in the middle grades include realistic stories about sibling rivalry, peer acceptance, fears, and lack of conformity to stereotypes; fantasies; suspense stories; and humorous stories. Popular information books include factual and nonsensical advice about human health, factual information about animals, and biographical information about sports stars. Popular poetry includes collections by Judith Viorst, Shel Silverstein, and William Cole. The choices include books from a wide variety of genres.

Research also indicates that reading ability influences the reading interests of children. Swanton's (1984) survey comparing gifted students with students of average ability reports that gifted children prefer mysteries (43 percent), fiction (41 percent), science fiction (29 percent), and fantasy (18 percent). In contrast, the top four choices for students of average ability are mysteries (47 percent), comedy/humor (27 percent), realist fiction (23 percent), and adventure (18 percent). Gifted students indicated that they like science fiction and fantasy "because of the challenge . . . [and] its relationship to Dungeons and Dragons" (p. 100). Gifted students listed Judy Blume, Lloyd Alexander, J. R. R. Tolkien, and C. S. Lewis as favorite authors. Average students listed Judy Blume, Beverly Cleary, and Jack London. As you can see, there are similarities and differences within these favorites. Many additional types of literature may become favorites if understanding and knowledgeable teachers provide opportunities for students to listen to, read, and discuss literature.

Although information from research and children's choices provides general ideas about what subjects and authors children of certain ages and reading abilities prefer, do not develop stereotyped views about children's preferences. Without asking questions about interests, there is no way to know about children's specific and unusual interests. Informal conversation is one of the simplest ways to uncover children's interests—ask a child to describe what he or she likes to do and read about. You will need some way of recording the information when you work with a number of children. Develop interest inventories in which students answer questions about their favorite hobbies, books, sports, television shows, and other interests. Write down young children's answers. Older children can read the questionnaire themselves and write their own responses. Such an inventory might include some of the questions asked in Figure 11–1. (Make changes according to age levels, and add information if children tell why they like certain books.) After the interest inventory is complete, use the findings as the basis for helping children select books and extend their enjoyment of literature.

1. What do you like to do when you get home from school?
   _____
2. What do you like to do on Saturday?
   _____
3. Do you like to watch television? _____ If you do, what are the names of your favorite
   programs? _____
4. Do you have a hobby?_____ If you do, what is your hobby?_____
   _____
5. Do you like to make or collect things?_____ If you do, what have you made or collected?
   _____
6. What is your favorite sport?_____
7. What games do you like best?_____
8. Do you like to go to the movies?_____
   If you do, what is your favorite movie?_____
   _____
9. Do you have a pet?_____ If you do, what is your pet?_____
10. Where have you spent your summer vacations?_____
    _____
11. Have you ever made a special study of rocks?_____ space?_____
    plants? _____ animals? _____ travel? _____ dinosaurs? _____
    other?_____
12. What are your favorite subjects in school?
    art? _____ handwriting? _____ social studies? _____ English? _____
    physical education? _____ science? _____ music? _____ creative
    writing? _____ spelling? _____ arithmetic? _____ other? _____
13. What subject is the hardest for you?_____
14. What kinds of books do you like to have someone read to you?
    animal stories?_____ fairy tales?_____ true stories?_____
    science fiction?_____ adventure?_____ mystery stories?_____
    sports stories?_____ poems?_____ humorous stories?_____
    other kinds of stories?_____
15. What is your favorite book that someone read to you?_____
16. What kinds of books do you like to read by yourself?
    animals?_____ picture books?_____ fairy tales?_____
    true stories?_____ science fiction?_____ adventures?_____
    mystery stories?_____sports stories?_____ poems?_____
    funny stories?_____ other kinds of stories?_____
17. What is your favorite book that you read by yourself?_____
18. Would you rather read a book by yourself or have someone read to you?
    _____
19. Name a book that you read this week.
    _____
20. What books or magazines do you have at home?
    _____
21. Do you ever go to the library?_____
    How often do you go to the library?_____
    Do you have a library card?_____

FIGURE 11–1
An informal interest inventory

STORYTELLING

Have you ever sat around a campfire and listened to a storyteller take you to all kinds of magical places? Have you watched as children become entranced listening to a story? What makes storytelling more effective than merely reading the story aloud? A great deal of magic results from the amount of preparation that goes into the activity.

John Stewig (1978) offers three significant reasons for including storytelling in the curriculum:

1. It promotes understanding of the oral tradition in literature. Young children in many societies have been initiated into their rich heritage through storytelling. Today, however, few children have such experiences.
2. It provides the opportunity to actively involve the children in the storytelling. A teacher who has learned the story is free from dependence on the book and can use gestures and action to involve children in the story.
3. It provides the stimulus for children's storytelling. Seeing a teacher engage in storytelling helps children understand that storytelling is a worthy activity, and it motivates them to tell their own stories.

This last point was made clear to one of my college classes when we invited a group of kindergarten and first-grade children to our class to take part in a story time. One child was particularly delighted with the stories, but was apparently too shy to become involved in any activity or discussion. Her mother informed us a few days later that the child was so stimulated by the experience that when she went home, she told her family all the stories she had heard. She also made flannelboard and puppet figures to accompany some of the stories. Then, she started to practice new stories, and wanted to tell them to anyone who would take a few minutes to listen. Any activity with the power to motivate a child this way is certainly worth the effort.

Selection

When you select a story for telling, choose one that is appropriate for the age of the audience and the time allotted. Choose a story that has a strong beginning, to capture your listeners' attention quickly. Also, choose something suspenseful. Your story should have a lot of action; children enjoy an active plot. Usually three or four characters are enough because both you and the children may have difficulty keeping track of a greater number. Rapunzel, for example, has a wicked witch, a beautiful maiden, and a rescuing prince. In addition, be sure that the dialogue in the story appears natural. As with all stories for young children, choose a story with a

Sometimes teachers will involve children in storytelling.

climax that both you and the children can recognize. Finally, choose a story with a satisfactory conclusion.

Consider both the age and experience of the children. Robert Whitehead (1968) suggests that preschool- through kindergarten-age children need stories that are short and to the point. The stories should include familiar things—animals, children, homes, machines, and people. Humorous and nonsense stories and cumulative tales are good choices, including "The Three Little Pigs," "The Three Billy Goats Gruff," and "Henny Penny." Ancient and modern fairy tales usually appeal to children ages six through ten; therefore, consider "The Elves and the Shoemaker," "Rumpelstiltskin," and "The Bremen Town Musicians." Animal tales and stories of children from other lands are also appropriate. Older-elementary children usually like true stories, hero tales, and stories that teach something about personal ideals.

Such children also enjoy adventure, so myths, legends, and epics are popular. Consider, for example, ''Aladdin,'' ''How Thor Found His Hammer,'' ''Robin Hood,'' ''Pecos Bill,'' and ''Paul Bunyan.''

Some storytellers enjoy telling several stories around a specific theme. For example, a Hans Christian Andersen storytelling festival could include ''The Steadfast Tin Soldier,'' ''The Nightingale,'' ''The Tinderbox,'' and ''The Swineherd.'' The theme of forgetfulness could include ''Soap, Soap, Soap'' in Richard Chase's *Grandfather Tales* (1948), the story of a boy who can't remember what he is shopping for, and ''Icarus and Daedalus,'' a Greek legend, in which Icarus forgets that his wings are attached with wax. If you are interested in choosing several stories about a certain subject, Caroline Bauer's *Handbook for Storytellers* (1977) includes an annotated bibliography of stories by subject as well as recommendations for single stories. Anne Pellowski's *Hidden Stories in Plants* (1990) and *The Family Story-Telling Handbook* (1987) also include recommended stories and suggestions for how to use them.

Preparation

An experienced storyteller, Patti Hubert, recommends the following sequence, which has proven successful for her:

1. Read the story completely through about three times.
2. List mentally the sequence of events. You are giving yourself a mental outline of the important happenings.
3. Reread the story, noting the events you didn't remember.
4. Go over the main events again and add the details you remember. Think about the meaning of the events and ways to express that meaning, rather than memorize the words in the story.
5. When you feel you know the story, tell the story to a mirror. (You will be surprised at how horrible the story sounds the first time.)
6. After you have practiced two or three more times, the wording will improve, and you can change vocal pitch to differentiate characters.
7. Change your posture or hand gestures to represent different characters.
8. Don't be afraid to use pauses to separate scenes.[1]

Introduction

Many storytellers set the mood for story time with a symbol. One librarian uses a small lamp. When the lamp is lit, it is also time to listen. If you have a certain place in your classroom for storytelling, movement to that corner may prepare the children and set the mood. Your storytelling corner might include an easel on which to place a drawing from the story or a motivating question written on cardboard. Some storytellers create a mood with a record or a piano. One student teacher successfully used a guitar for this purpose. As soon as he went into the storytelling corner and played a specific song on the guitar, the students came over, anticipating an enjoyable activity.

---

[1] This sequence is used with permission of Patti Hubert, drama teacher, San Antonio.

There are numerous ways to introduce your story. Ask a question, or tell the students why you enjoy a particular story. Offer something interesting about the author. Give background information about a country or a period of history to add interest to a folktale. Display prominently the book from which your story is taken, along with other stories by the same author and other stories on the same subject. One of the reasons for storytelling is to motivate children to tell stories themselves, so a display adds visual interest.

Many student teachers effectively introduce a story with objects. One student used a stuffed toy rabbit to introduce *The Velveteen Rabbit* by Margery Williams (1922). You could use a toy or figure of a cat with *Puss in Boots* by Charles Perrault (1952). Use a lariat to introduce a tall tale about Pecos Bill. Use artifacts from a country to introduce folktales. One of my favorite objects is a small, painted jewelry case from Japan. I often bring out the case when I am telling stories to young children, and we talk about the magic of stories that is contained in the case because it has been to so many story hours. Then, I open the box slowly while the children catch the magic in their hands. This magic is wonderful, so they hold it carefully while they listen to the story. When the story ends, each child carefully returns the magic to the box until it is time to use it for another story.

Actual Telling

Once you have prepared your story and developed ways to introduce it or to set a mood, you are ready to face your expectant students. Patti Hubert offers the following suggestions for telling your story:

1. Find a place in the room where all the children can see and hear you.
2. Either stand in front of the children or sit with them.
3. Select an appropriate introduction. Use a prop, tell something about the author, discuss a related event, or ask a question.
4. Maintain eye contact with the children. This engages them more fully in the story.
5. Use your voice rate and volume for effect.
6. Take a short step or shift your weight to indicate a change in scene or character or to heighten the suspense. If you are sitting, lean toward or away from the children.
7. After telling your story, pause to give the audience a chance to soak in everything you have said.

Pictures and Objects

Effective storytelling does not require props, but you may want to add variety with felt boards, flip charts, roll stories, objects, or chalk talks.

Felt boards For visual interest, cut out representations of the main characters from felt, flannel, or pellon, and put them on a board covered with felt or flannel. Figures provide cues to the story and give beginning storytellers added security. It is better to tell a felt-board story rather than read it because manipulating both figures and a book at the same time is awkward.

It is easy to make a flannel or felt board. Cover an artist's cardboard portfolio with felt or flannel. Make a firmer felt board by covering a rectangle of lightweight wood, such as fiberboard or plywood, with a large piece of felt or flannel. Hinge two smaller squares of board together if you will need to transport the board. You can make backdrops for different scenes and locations by chalking in scenery on a loose piece of flannel large enough to cover the board. These scenic flannel pieces are easy to store, and they add interest without cluttering the appearance of a felt story.

Certain types of stories are more suitable for felt boards than others. Stories with a great deal of physical action or detailed settings are inappropriate. Simple stories with only a few major figures and definite scenes are easy to handle. Cumulative tales, which add elements throughout the story, are extremely good. Some stories that meet these requirements are ''Goldilocks and the Three Bears,'' ''The Three Little Pigs,'' ''The Three Billy Goats Gruff,'' ''Jack and the Beanstalk,'' and ''The Emperor's New Clothes.'' You can show these traditional favorites with a few simple characters.

When you tell a story, place the board so the whole group can see it. An easel is a good place to position the board for a large group. Place the figures in proper order before you begin the story, and keep the figures out of the children's sight until you place them on the board. You will need to practice several times so you will be talking to the children, not to the board.

Felt stories allow the students to become involved. Children can retell the felt stories, reinforcing oral language and comprehension skills. After they have seen one or two such stories, many children want to make their own. These stories are excellent means of giving oral book reports or illustrating creative writing stories. If you leave the felt board in a room so the children have easy access to it, you will find they use it frequently. (A felt board is also an excellent visual aid for developing concepts in math and science.)

Flip charts   Another technique that adds visual interest to storytelling is illustrating a story on several large sheets of poster board (see Figure 11−2). As with felt

FIGURE 11−2
A flip-chart picture

boards, use flip charts with stories in which you can develop the main ideas with a series of pictures. Draw the charts by hand or with the aid of an opaque projector. The most successful flip charts use three-dimensional materials. Yarn, fabric, sandpaper, small stones, bark, and straws add tactile dimensions to flip charts, and invite children to touch the pictures.

One student teacher drew a flip-chart story entitled "Freddie's Private Cloud." She used rice for shingles on a house, cloth for clothing, real feathers on birds, nylon net for clouds, sandpaper for a lawn-mower engine, spaghetti for a ladder, bark for tree trunks, rolls of real paper for newspaper, beans for stones, sponge for waves, and felt for animals.

Roll stories Roll stories are also sequentially illustrated. Draw the pictures on a large roll of paper, then unroll them as you tell the story. Place the completed roll story inside a box with an opening cut out like a television screen. The roll should have dowels at either end so that it is easy to roll and unroll (see Figure 11–3).

Roll stories are excellent culmination activities after you have read or told a story. Children can form groups to draw pictures and retell a story with their own pictures. Roll stories reinforce reading skills as well as storytelling skills. For example, after one first-grade teacher told "Peter and the Wolf" to her students, the students listed the scenes from the story, and each of them chose two sequential scenes to illustrate. The teacher cut a long roll of paper into sections that fit the length of the work tables in the classroom, and the children, with the teacher's assistance, measured the distance needed for each picture. Then, the children drew their illustrations, in correct sequence, onto the roll. When each child had completed his or her illustrations, the child dictated to the teacher the part of the story that corresponded to the illustrations. Then, the teacher used these individually dictated stories for reading instruction. The children practiced reading their own contributions so they could present a "movie" of "Peter and the Wolf." Next, the class taped together the table-length rolls and attached dowels to each end. They placed the long roll inside a box with a rectangular viewing area, and the children practiced reading their parts as they unrolled the story. They added background music from "Peter and the Wolf," and invited another grade to come in and view their presentation. This is an excellent motivating activity for remedial reading instruction.

FIGURE 11–3
A picture for a roll story

Object stories   Certain stories lend themselves to showing objects from the story. For example, while telling Marcia Brown's *Stone Soup* (1947), a teacher or students can place the ingredients in a soup kettle.

Chalk talks   It is fascinating to watch someone illustrate a story while telling it. One student teacher invited a cartoonist to visit her fourth-grade class. The cartoonist quickly sketched cartoon figures while telling a corresponding story. This highly motivating activity led many students to try the technique with simple figures. Although you may not have this cartoonist's rapid drawing ability, you might enjoy trying the activity with stick-figure characters or simple shapes. Figure 11–4 shows simple sketches to accompany familiar nursery rhymes. One teacher made up a story about the adventures of an Easter egg, with simple shapes that could be sketched quickly on the chalkboard.

REINFORCEMENT ACTIVITY

Choose a story to prepare for storytelling according to the suggestions in this section of the chapter. Use pictures or objects if you wish. Tell your story to a group of children or a group of your peers.

FIGURE 11–4
Chalk figures

Peter, Peter pumpkin eater
Had a wife and couldn't keep her
He put her in a pumpkin shell
And there he kept her very well.

Humpty Dumpty sat on a wall
Humpty Dumpty had a great fall
All the king's horses
And all the king's men
Couldn't put Humpty Dumpty
   together again.

Reading aloud is not only pleasurable but also teaches children about story structure.

READING ALOUD

Walmsley and Walp (1989) found that reading aloud to students is the activity teachers use the most to involve students in literature. There is probably no better way to interest children in the world of books than to read to them. This is one way for children to learn that literature is a source of pleasure. For children who are just struggling to learn to read, a book may not yet be a source of happiness. In fact, the sight of books may actually arouse negative feelings in some children. Thus, instructional techniques that improve attitudes are highly desirable. Is there a better way for children to see the pleasure they can derive from books than by sharing books in a relaxed environment with a teacher who obviously enjoys good literature?

In addition to deriving pleasure, students learn about story structures from the books they hear. They hear language patterns and words that may be unfamiliar to them. These listening experiences increase appreciation for and understanding of different story and sentence structures and prepare children for when they will encounter them in their own reading. Herrell (1990) found that interactive reading aloud to kindergarten children had positive effects on the children's reading. In *Becoming a Nation of Readers: The Report of the Commission on Reading,* Anderson, Hiebert, Scott, and Wilkinson (1985) state: "The single most important activity for building the knowledge required for eventual success in reading is reading aloud to children" (p. 23).

Another important benefit of reading aloud is that it motivates children to do their own reading. After children are excited by hearing a selection, they usually want to read it to themselves; thus, interaction between an enthusiastic teacher and interested peers is especially important.

Style and illustrations are both considerations when choosing books to read aloud. The language in Michael Rosen's *We're Going on a Bear Hunt* (1989) stimulates interaction between the reader and the listeners. Other good choices for young listeners include A. A. Milne's *Winnie-the-Pooh* (1926, 1954) and Dr. Seuss's *The 500 Hats of Bartholomew Cubbins* (1938). Young children also enjoy the illustrations that are part of a story, such as those in Maurice Sendak's *Where the Wild Things Are* (1963) and those in Arthur Yorinks's *Hey, Al* (1986).

Age, attention span, and level of reading ability are important considerations when selecting stories to read aloud. The books should challenge children to improve their reading skills as well as increase their appreciation of literature. Leave the numerous easy-to-read books for children to read independently. Younger children respond to short stories that you can finish in one reading. Books such as Faith Ringgold's *Tar Beach* (1991), Kevin Henkes's *Chrysanthemum* (1991), Amy Schwartz's *Oma and Bobo* (1987), and Ann Grifalconi's *Darkness and the Butterfly* (1987) are favorites with children in first and second grade. Graham Oakley's *The Church Mice in Action* (1982) and Katherine Paterson's *The Tale of the Mandarin Ducks* (1990) have sufficiently developed plot to appeal to second graders. By the time children reach third grade, you can read continued stories, although you should complete a chapter during each story time rather than leave a segment unfinished. Third graders usually enjoy E. B. White's *Charlotte's Web* (1952) and Laura Ingalls Wilder's Little House series. Fourth and fifth graders often respond to Madeleine L'Engle's *A Wrinkle in Time* (1962) and C. S. Lewis's *The Lion, the Witch and the Wardrobe* (1950). Armstrong Sperry's *Call It Courage* (1940) and Esther Forbes's *Johnny Tremain* (1946) often appeal to sixth and seventh graders.

Enthusiasm is a vital ingredient during story time. If you are uninterested and unprepared, you will spoil the story time for the children. Preparation requires reading the story silently so that you understand the sequence of events, the mood, the subject, the vocabulary, and other concepts. Next, read the story aloud to practice pronunciation, pacing, voice characterizations, and so forth. Beginning oral readers should listen to themselves on a tape recorder before they read to an audience. Enunciation, pacing, and volume are especially important for young children's understanding. Finally, consider how to introduce the story using such techniques as those mentioned previously under storytelling.

An appropriate environment for story time is also essential. Children in the early elementary grades need to sit close to you, especially if the story is a picture book that you will show as you read. Also, prepare the children for the listening experience by getting their attention and providing appropriate goals for the experience. If necessary, clarify a concept or a vocabulary word to help the children understand the story. Introduce the story with a question, a discussion about the title, a prediction about the story, or background information about the author. As you read the story aloud, encourage the students to interact with the story.

Just as you should draw on a variety of categories of literature, you should also use various methods for sharing stories with groups—recordings; films; storytelling; and visual techniques, such as puppets, felt boards, and chalk talks. Keep records of the stories you share with the children, and note their reactions. These records will help you balance the types of books you select and understand the interests of the children.

REINFORCEMENT
ACTIVITY

Choose a book and prepare it for reading aloud. Read the book to a group of children or a group of your peers.

ART

Strange and curious worlds, imaginary kingdoms, animal fantasies, space explorations, and historical settings lend themselves to artistic interpretations. Coody (1979) states that "creative art–literature experiences occur in the classroom when boys and girls are moved by a good story well told or read, when art materials are made available, and when time and space are allowed for experimenting with the materials" (p. 92). Illustrated books using various artistic media and containing descriptive passages stimulate artistic expression, encourage enjoyment of literature, enhance aesthetic development, and stimulate understanding of various literary elements, such as setting and plot. (A word of caution: art should allow children to expand their enjoyment of a story through self-expression. Do not force an art activity with every story.)

Use illustrated books to show children that artists see their subjects in different ways and use different media to interpret mood and setting. Help children discover that artistic interpretations are individual qualities. For example, share and discuss Trina Shart Hyman's illustrations for Grimms' *Little Red Riding Hood* (1983), James Marshall's illustrations for *Red Riding Hood* (1987), and Sarah Moon's photographs for Perrault's *Little Red Riding Hood* (1983). In these three examples, illustrations reinforce a "once upon a time" traditional setting, develop a humorous mood, and create a stark, terrifying mood.

Use books illustrated with a particular artistic medium to stimulate students to try that medium in their own illustrations. For example, in collage, any object or substance that can be attached to a surface can be used to develop a design. Artists and student artists may use paper, cloth, cardboard, leather, wood, leaves, flowers, or even butterflies. They may cut up and arrange their own paintings or use paint and other media to add background. When photographically produced in a book, collages still communicate texture. Children's literature selections that show children how adult authors use collage include Ezra Jack Keats's *Peter's Chair*

(1967), *The Snowy Day* (1962), and *The Trip* (1978); Eric Carle's *The Very Hungry Caterpillar* (1971), *Twelve Tales from Aesop* (1980), and *The Honeybee and the Robber* (1981); Marcia Brown's illustrations for Blaise Cendrars's *Shadow* (1982); and Jeannie Baker's *Grandmother* (1978). Giles Laroche's illustrations for Lois Lenski's *Sing a Song of People* (1987) exemplifies the drama of three-dimensional paper constructions.

Books that are filled with descriptive passages and vivid characters entice children to try their own artistic explorations and interpretations. For example, vivid settings from Beatrix Potter's *The Tale of Squirrel Nutkin* (1903, 1986), Kenneth Grahame's *The Wind in the Willows* (1908, 1940), and E. B. White's *Charlotte's Web* (1952) encourage individual drawings or group-developed murals. Monica Hughes's *The Dream Catcher* (1987) can motivate depiction of a science fiction setting in a world yet to materialize. Likewise, Janet Lunn's *Shadow in Hawthorn Bay* (1986) can motivate pictorial comparisons between the hills of Scotland around Loch Ness and Hawthorn Bay, Ontario, in the early 1800s.

Many stories encourage students to hypothesize about what could happen next and to create visual interpretations. Let younger students expand on one of the nursery rhymes in Tomie de Paola's *Mother Goose* (1985). For example, how do Peter, Peter, Pumpkin Eater and his wife live in the pumpkin shell? Students can extend Tejima's *Fox's Dream* (1987) by illustrating the same forest in the spring rather than winter. Older students can extend Robert O'Brien's *Mrs. Frisby and the Rats of NIMH* (1971) by drawing Thorn Valley, the colony that the intelligent rats want to develop. Then, they can compare their drawings with the written descriptions in Jane Leslie Conly's sequel, *Rasco and the Rats of NIMH* (1986). Mythology can inspire students, like illustrators of picture books, to depict the settings for mythological places, such as the sacred lake where a Native American boy waits for the buffalo to appear (Olaf Baker's *Where the Buffaloes Begin,* 1981) or the foaming sea that produces the goddess Aphrodite (Doris Gates's *Two Queens of Heaven: Aphrodite and Demeter,* 1974).

Reading stories aloud, storytelling, and artistic interpretations of literature are stimulating ways to develop appreciation for and understanding of literature. These activities also motivate students to read literature.

LITERARY CRITICISM

At one time in the history of education, choosing selections from a wealth of children's literature was not a problem. Rather the problem was finding anything at all for children. In 1800, only 270 books were published for the juvenile market. Fortunately, this situation has changed dramatically. Currently, almost 3,000 books for children are published annually. This increase in quantity, however, has led to concern for the quality of literature that students read. Quality is important for several reasons. For example, Dressel (1990) found that children who read and discuss higher quality literature produce higher quality written stories. Likewise, Lehr (1988) reported that children's ability to identify theme correlates with their exposure to quality literature. This section discusses ways to help students become critical of the books they read.

Literary Elements

Literature is usually evaluated in terms of plot, conflict, characterization, setting, theme, and style. Consequently, you need to recognize these literary elements in the books you share with students. We will review them quickly here because they are usually covered in detail in children's literature courses.

Plot   The plot of a story develops the action. Plots should provide excitement, suspense, and conflict. The development of events usually follows a chronological order, although flashbacks may answer questions about a character's background or reveal information about the past. The plots of most children's stories follow a structure in which characters and problems are introduced at the beginning of the story, conflict builds until a climax is reached, a turning point occurs, and then the conflict is resolved.

Of more than 3,000 books published for children each year, how will you help children select books to read?

Conflict   Excitement in a story occurs when the main character experiences a struggle or overcomes conflict. Conflict is the usual source of plots in literature. Children's literature includes four kinds of conflict: (1) person versus person, (2) person versus society, (3) person versus nature, and (4) person versus self. Authors must describe and develop conflicts so as to make them believable. A good plot lets children share the action, feel the conflict, recognize the climax, and respond to a satisfactory ending.

Characterization   Characters should seem believable and should develop throughout the course of a story. The credibility of characters depends on the author's ability to reveal their natures, including both strengths and weaknesses. Characters are developed through descriptions of their thoughts and actions and records of their conversations. The most memorable characters usually have several sides—like real people, they are not all good or all bad. Characters who are developed well, so that readers understand their many sides, are called "round." Characters that remain unchanged in a story are called "flat" or "static."

Setting   Setting refers to the geographic location of the story and the time—past, present, or future—in which the events take place. If a location is identifiable as a real place, the author should present it accurately. Authors of historical fiction, for example, must make the backgrounds for their stories as authentic as possible. In addition to a complete historical background, settings may provide instantly recognizable backgrounds, such as "a certain kingdom" or "deep in the forest." Settings can create a mood, develop conflict, or provide symbolic meaning.

Theme   The theme of a story is the underlying idea that ties the plot, characters, and setting together into a meaningful whole. Themes are frequently implied rather than directly stated. They are revealed by studying the actions of the characters, analyzing the central conflict, and considering the outcome of a story. When looking for theme, it is important to consider how the main character changes in the story, what types of conflict exist, what actions are rewarded or punished, and what the main character learns as a result of the conflict. Even the title may provide clues to the theme.

Style   Style refers to the way in which an author uses language to develop a story. Style, of course, should be appropriate for the characters, setting, and plot. Does the language seem in keeping with what the characters would really say? If there is figurative language, will the children be able to grasp the meaning? Reading aloud is a good way to see if the author has a pleasing and appropriate style.

Format

Format refers to the physical aspects of the book—cover, printing and binding, illustrations, and size. Illustrations should help the story come alive. The printing should be clear and easy to read. Some bindings are more appropriate for school libraries than others. Although paperbacks are more readily affordable, hardcover editions last longer and usually appear in permanent collections.

FOR YOUR PLAN BOOK
An Evaluation-of-Literature Unit—Sixth-Grade Level

A sixth-grade teacher introduced her students to this unit by having the children interview their parents and other adults to find out what favorite books the adults remembered reading when they were in elementary school. On a large chart, the children listed the books and the adults who chose them. Then, the students checked book awards, such as the Newbery and Caldecott, to see how many of the books appeared on these lists. Next, each student read a book his or her parents had mentioned and discussed the book with the parents in terms of what made it special. The teacher introduced the concepts of plot, characterization, setting, theme, and style, and the students examined the books they had read for examples of each of these elements. Finally, the sixth graders listed questions to ask in evaluating a book:

1. Is this a good story?
2. Is the story about something I think could really happen?
3. Did the main character overcome the problem, but not too easily?
4. Did the climax seem natural?
5. Did the characters seem real?
6. Did the characters grow in the story?
7. Did I find out about more than one side of the characters?
8. Did the setting present what is actually known about that time or place?
9. Did the characters fit into the setting?
10. Did I feel that I was really in that time or place?
11. What did the author want to tell me in the story?
12. Was the theme worthwhile?
13. When I read the book aloud, did the people sound like real people actually talking?
14. Did the rest of the language sound natural?

As a follow-up activity, the students wrote stories and asked these questions about their own writing. Use this type of activity to introduce a more extensive study of literature.

Instruction

Developing understanding of literary elements is both a challenge to the teacher and an exciting approach to literature. Several strategies may be used to help students appreciate the importance of literary elements in the stories they encounter. Activities such as webbing, modeling, and drawing plot structures are especially effective.

Webbing   When you use webbing during guided book discussions, not only do you help students understand important characteristics of the story, you also help them appreciate literature and improve their reading and writing competencies. Prior to the webbing experience, introduce the literary elements. Then, draw simple webs that include each of these components while leading discussions that help the students identify the important ideas associated with the components. For example, place "The Three Billy Goats Gruff" in the center of a web and then draw

Webbing of a concept during a guided book discussion improves children's reading and writing competence.

each of the literary elements from the center. As you read the story, ask the students to listen for the components. After completing the story, lead a discussion in which the students fill in the main ideas on the web. If necessary, reread sections to help the students identify specific elements. You may also ask students to focus on one element. This technique is effective when you first introduce literary elements and webbing. A short story may require rereading several times to complete all of the literary elements.

Another approach is to ask groups of students to be responsible for specific elements on a web. Each group then listens for specific information and webs a specific element before oral discussion takes place. This approach frequently leads to in-depth analysis as students listen attentively for their own areas of concern.

After completing this activity with several simple books and webs, you and the students may progress to webbing of more complex books. John Steptoe's *Mufaro's Beautiful Daughters: An African Tale* (1987) is a logical next choice. The story is short enough to read several times within one class session and the basic literary elements are easy to identify. First, introduce the story. Next, draw a web on the board with *Mufaro's Beautiful Daughters* in the center. Extend the terms *setting, characters, conflict, plot,* and *theme,* as shown in Figure 11–5. Now, read the story

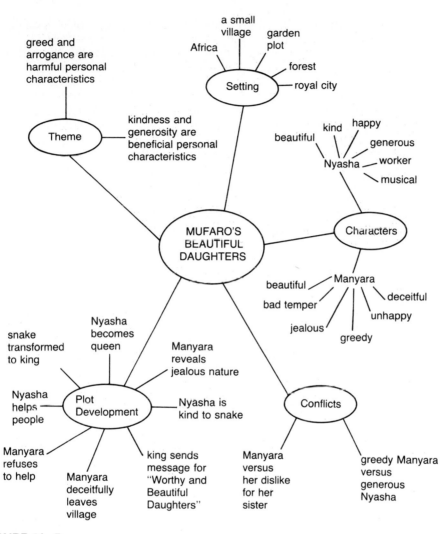

FIGURE 11–5
A literary-discussion web for a folktale

to the students and have them listen for information to place on the web. Following this reading, either reread the story, stopping at appropriate places to consider information that should go on the web, or lead a discussion in which the students fill in the web. If you do not reread the total book before filling in the web, you may need to reread parts of the story to help students decide what should be placed on the web. The choice of approach will depend on the students' listening capabilities and experiences with literary elements. Whichever approach you use, have the students develop a web on their own papers as you complete the web on the board using the information they supply. Some webs become quite large and may cover several chalkboards. In another class period following the development of the web, ask the students to write their own stories about the book using information on the web to help them construct the stories. They may experiment with changing certain literary elements and writing the story to match those changes.

Figure 11–5 shows only the first level of information. When this web was completed with third- and fourth-grade students it extended to several chalkboards. Students supplied additional information for each of the settings. The webbing activity stimulates considerable discussion about literary elements when students must support their ideas with evidence from the text, discuss relationships between the identified elements, and discuss their reasons for certain inferences. For example, the author does not directly state the themes shown on the web in Figure 11–5. The text, however, provides clues to these themes by describing characteristics of people who are rewarded and people who are punished. Also, some of the terms describing the characters are words that the students derived from descriptions of the characters' actions.

You may also develop webs to provide structure for a literary discussion or to identify specific books or poems that exemplify certain literary elements, specific feelings, or literary techniques of special significance to the story. For example, Figure 11–6 is a semantic web developed by a student teacher, Pam Buster. It

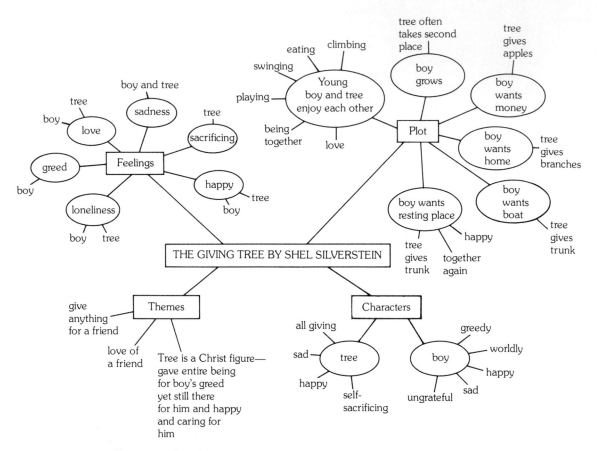

FIGURE 11–6

A semantic web summarizing plot, characters, themes, and feelings

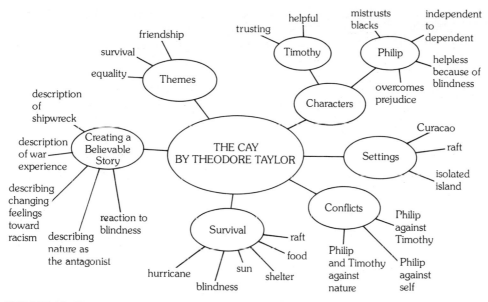

FIGURE 11–7
A web summarizing literary qualities in *The Cay*

summarizes the plot, characters and theme in Shel Silverstein's *The Giving Tree*. Feelings are so important in this book that Pam and the students wanted to emphasize them as a special element on the web. Another student teacher, Karen Wisher, developed the web in Figure 11–7. It summarizes literary qualities of Theodore Taylor's *The Cay*. This time the students also wanted to emphasize how the author created a believable story. The web in Figure 11–8 identifies various literary techniques in Judith Viorst's book on poetry, *If I Were in Charge of the World*. Specific poems are associated with each of the techniques.

*REINFORCEMENT
ACTIVITY*

Choose a book that would be good for a literary discussion. Make a web according to the literary elements found in the book.

Modeling   Modeling was introduced in Chapter 3 as a way of teaching students how to become actively involved in and aware of their thought processing. The example used in Chapter 3 described the steps in modeling inferencing of characterization with Patricia MacLachlan's *Sarah, Plain and Tall* (1985). Review the in-depth lesson plan described for that book on pages 77–82. Notice how the teacher in that example is guiding the students through understanding of characterization. The same approach may be used to model the understanding of any of the literary

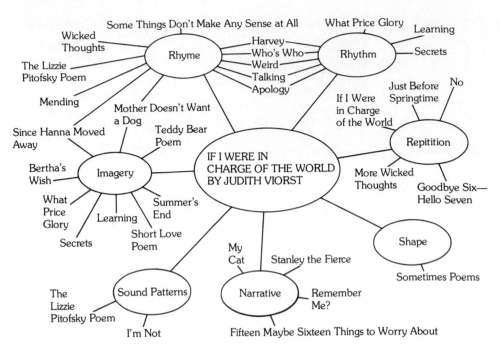

FIGURE 11–8
A web identifying appropriate poems in a book of poetry

elements. This chapter considers how to use modeling to help students understand author's style. A lesson plan format similar to that introduced in Chapter 3 is used in the following example.

FOR YOUR PLAN BOOK
Modeling for the Understanding of Similes

*Level: Lower Elementary   Book: **Swimmy** (1963), Leo Lionni.*

Requirements for Effective Reasoning

1. Going beyond the information the author provides in the text.
2. Knowing that similes are comparisons that authors make between something in the text and something that is not in the text.
3. Knowing that similes are introduced with the clue words *like* and *as*.
4. Knowing that authors use similes to develop vivid descriptions and characterizations.
5. Thinking about how one object is like another object.

Introduction

1. Introduce similes through a dialogue like this: "Sometimes when authors write, they use a special kind of writing called figurative language. This kind of

language is a way for authors to use fewer words but to write more vividly. Similes are a form of figurative language. In similes, authors compare one thing with another thing. Today, we will listen for ways that authors use similes to encourage us to see pictures in our minds."

2. Provide examples and nonexamples of similes: "Similes are stated comparisons in which an author tells us how two things are alike. We say a simile is a stated comparison because the author uses the clue words *like* or *as* to signal the comparison. Many times, an author will compare one object you know and one object that you do not know. For example, in 'Sandy is as quiet as a mouse,' the author is using *as* to clue the comparison. A mouse is shy around people, so I can visualize that Sandy is a very shy person. She does not talk very much. In another example, 'Giraffes have ears like giant leaves,' the author is using *like* to clue the comparison. Even without seeing a giraffe, I know that the ears are shaped like big leaves. I can almost 'see' the giraffe with big, pointed, leaf shaped ears that stick up above its head. We must listen carefully, however, because *as* or *like* in a sentence does not always signal a comparison. For example, in 'We will watch as the moon rises' are there any comparisons? Likewise, in 'I like hamburgers' is there a comparison?"

3. Provide a rationale for why similes are important to students: "We need to know about similes and what they can tell us as we read or listen to stories so that we can understand what we read. Similes help us appreciate the story. Authors use similes to paint vivid pictures with words just as artists paint vivid pictures with paints. We can use similes to make our own writing more vivid and more meaningful. Today, I am going to read a story about a fish. Listen for the similes, tell what you think the comparison means, and explain how you reached the answer. Listen carefully as I do the first one for you. By listening to how I thought through the meaning of the simile, you will know what I expect of you when it is your turn."

Example One:

Read page 1 but do not show the illustration. Ask the question: "What does Swimmy look like?" Answer the question: "Swimmy is shiny and deep black." Provide the evidence: "The author uses the simile clue *as*. The author compares one of the fish to the black of a mussel shell." State the reasoning that you used to reach the answer: "The author is telling me to think about more information. The comparison is between Swimmy's color and the black of a mussel shell. There are many shades of black. I also know from seeing mussel shells at the beach that a mussel shell is dark black and shiny. If I close my eyes, I can see a small, black, shiny fish swimming among many other fish who are not black." (After modeling the simile, ask the students to listen to the page again with their eyes closed. Can they see Swimmy's color? Then share the illustration and compare their visualized pictures with that in the illustration.)

Example Two:

Read pages 4 through 10, stopping with the sentence, "One day . . . a lobster, who walked like a water-moving machine." (Show the illustrations *after* modeling, or the students will use the illustrations to gain visual images rather than the words and their imaginations.) Ask the question: "How does a lobster move? Answer the question: "A lobster walks mechanically through the water, pushing the water ahead of it." Provide evidence: "The author uses the simile clue *like*. The author compares the lobster and a water-moving machine." Provide the reasoning for reaching the answer: "The machine that I see in my mind would move mechanically through the water rather than darting and gliding like a fish. This machine would have to push forward against the water. I imagine it moving like a robot, with its claws moving the water and its feet plodding along. I am also impressed with how many words the author saved and how vivid a picture he depicted by using just the right comparison."

At this point, make sure that all of the students understand the process involved in answering questions, giving evidence, and providing reasoning used to reach the answer. Follow the same procedures, but change the involvement as you ask the questions but the students enter into the discussion with answers, evidence, and reasoning.

Example Three:

Read pages 11–17, stopping with "sea anemones . . . pink palm trees swaying in the wind." Ask the question: "What do the sea anemones look like?" Ask the students to answer the question: "The sea anemones are pink and have thin bodies (trunks). The top of an anemone has thin stringy arms that wave in the water." Continue the discussion, letting the students provide the evidence for the answer and discuss the reasoning that they used to reach the answer. Continue this procedure, reading and stopping at page 18 after the simile comparing the new school of fish to Swimmy's school. Read to the end of the text, where the comparison is with the biggest fish in the sea. Encourage looking for evidence and using the reasoning process. Students' visualizations of the similes may be different from the artist's illustrations, so let the students draw their own interpretations. They frequently decide that their own interpretations are more exciting than are the artist's.

Modeling may be used to improve the understanding of any of the literary elements. Modeling is effective at any grade level because of the wide selection of books available. The following books and literary elements suggest some of the modeling activities that you may develop:

- Setting—Armstrong Sperry's *Call It Courage* (1940), setting as antagonist; Jean Craighead George's *Julie of the Wolves* (1972), setting as antagonist; Joan Blos's *A Gathering of Days* (1979), setting as historical background; Jean Fritz's *Make Way for Sam Houston* (1986), setting as historical background; Kate Seredy's *The White Stag* (1937), setting as mood; Marcia Brown's illustrations and Blaise Cendrars's poetry in *Shadow* (1982), setting as mood.
- Conflict—Byrd Baylor's *Hawk, I'm Your Brother* (1976), person-versus-person and person-versus-nature conflicts; Barbara Cohen's *Molly's Pilgrim* (1983), person-versus-society conflict; Katherine Paterson's *Bridge to Terabithia* (1977), person-versus-society and person-versus-self conflicts.
- Style—Virginia Lee Burton's *The Little House* (1942), personification of objects; Kenneth Grahame's *The Wind in the Willows* (1908, 1940), personification of nature and animals; Sharon Bell Mathis's *The Hundred Penny Box* (1975), symbolism through music and pennies; Cynthia Voigt's *Dicey's Song* (1982), symbolism through music and boat; Kathryn Lasky's *Sugaring Time* (1983), similes; Hugh Lewin's *Jafta and Jafta's Mother* (1983), similes.

- Theme—Margery Williams's *The Velveteen Rabbit: Or How Toys Become Real* (1922), love is powerful and can make the impossible possible; Byrd Baylor's *Hawk, I'm Your Brother* (1976), it is important to have a dream and freedom; Valerie Flournoy's *The Patchwork Quilt* (1985), families can share happy memories while establishing bonds across the generations; Ann Grifalconi's *Darkness and the Butterfly* (1987), we all have fears that cause us problems, but we must overcome our fears; Denys Cazet's *A Fish in His Pocket* (1987), personal problems can be solved if we work on their solutions.

Plot diagramming   As we have mentioned, in most stories for younger readers the characters and problems are introduced at the beginning, the conflict builds until a climax is reached, a turning point occurs, and then the conflict ends. This type of structure is usual in stories in which the main character faces problems caused by external forces. Help students understand this plot development by having them place key incidents from a story on a plot diagram such as that shown in Figure 11–9. Stories ranging from "The Three Billy Goats Gruff" to the high fantasy of Lloyd Alexander follow this type of structure.

To develop an activity around plot diagramming using John Steptoe's *Mufaro's Beautiful Daughters: An African Tale,* draw the plot diagram shown in Figure 11–9 on the board. Introduce the book and ask students to listen for the conflict and the characters in the story. Encourage them to discuss their reactions to the conflict and the characters. Next, have the students diagram the story according to the plot diagram. Ask, "Did each of the characters respond in the same way to the major incidents in the story?" "Why do you believe the greedy, selfish sister and the generous, kind sister reacted differently?" "What do we call this type of conflict in literature?" Be sure that they understand that this is a person-versus-person conflict because the two main characters have different motives and desires that are in conflict. Ask the students to not only plot the major incidents in the story, but also to identify how each of the two characters responded to the incidents. This activity will allow the students to better understand the motivation of the characters and how the characters' motives relate to the conflict. You can reread the story to the children or allow them to reread it themselves. The diagram in Figure 11–10 (Norton, 1992) was completed with middle-elementary students. Notice how the students identified both the common plot structures and the different character responses to each incident.

Additional books that are excellent for this type of plot diagram include Ed Young's *Lon Po Po: A Red-Riding Hood Story from China* (1989) and Arthur Ransome's *The Fool of the World and the Flying Ship* (1968).

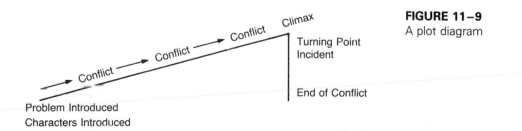

FIGURE 11–9
A plot diagram

When characters try to overcome problems caused by inner conflicts, use the same type of diagram but change the terminology. Cohen (1985) identifies four major components in the development of person-versus-self conflicts: (1) problem, (2) struggle, (3) realization, and (4) achievement of peace or truth: "The point at which the struggle wanes and the inner strength emerges seems to be the point of self-realization. The point leads immediately to the final sense of peace or truth that is the resolution of the quest. The best books are those which move readers and cause them to identify with the character's struggle" (p. 28). Place Cohen's components on a plot diagram, such as that in Figure 11–11, and let the students record major incidents on the diagram. Books such as Paula Fox's *One-Eyed Cat* (1984) and Marion Dane Bauer's *On My Honor* (1986) are examples of person-versus-self struggle.

Listing possibilities   Explore various ways to use a book for instructional purposes. Categories include art interpretation, drama, clarification of values, personal response, characterization, plot development, symbolism, and related literature. A group of college students used this technique to identify the instructional

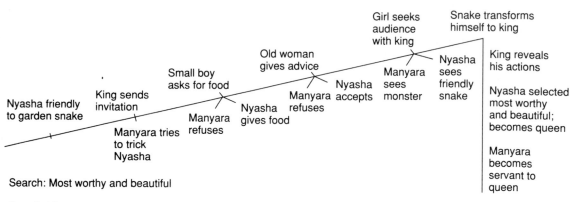

Search: Most worthy and beautiful

Greedy Manyara

Generous Nyasha

FIGURE 11–10
Plot Diagram for *Mufaro's Beautiful Daughters: An African Tale*

FIGURE 11–11
A person-versus-self plot diagram

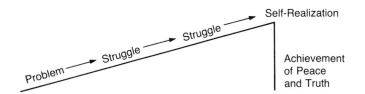

potential of several children's books. The following example illustrates the many activities that arise from Scott O'Dell's *Island of the Blue Dolphins:*

Art Interpretation
a. Make a model of Karana's weapons.
b. Make a shadowbox of Karana's home on the island.
c. Make a model of the Aleuts' ship.
d. Make a salt map of the Island of the Blue Dolphins and mark the places Karana went.

Drama
a. Make masks and dramatize the opening scene between Karana's father and the Aleuts.
b. Pantomime Karana's attempts to make weapons.
c. Pantomime the meeting between Karana and Tutok.

Clarification of Values
a. What took more courage for Karana—to stay on the boat, or to jump off the boat and stay with her brother?
b. Should Karana have broken the tribal taboos about weapons?
c. Was Karana's judgment about the Aleutian otter killing a fair one?

Personal Response
a. Have you ever felt as alone as Karana did? Explain.
b. How did Karana respond after her brother died and after Rontu died? Compare her responses in terms of the loneliness she felt.
c. What factors would have persuaded you to go or to stay on the island?

Characterization
a. How did Tutok see Karana?
b. How did the missionaries see Karana?
c. How did Rontu see Karana?
d. How do you see Karana?

Plot Development
a. What are the major incidents or decisions that influence the plot development?
b. How do each of these decisions influence the story?
   to leave or to stay at the beginning of the story.
   to make weapons.
   to trap Rontu.
   to talk to Tutok.
   to leave or to stay at the end of the story.

Symbolism
a. To reveal a secret name causes it to lose its magic.
b. The island is the shape of a dolphin.
c. Blue clay is symbolic of eligibility for marriage.
d. Dolphins are protectors.

Related Literature
a. Tests of Courage Today:
   Profiles in Courage (Kennedy)
   Rosa Parks (Greenfield)

My Side of the Mountain (George)
Hatchet (Paulsen)
b. Kinds of Courage:
The Cay (Taylor)
Where the Red Fern Grows (Rawls)
The Yearling (Rawlings)
Old Yeller (Gipson)
c. Incredible Journeys:
A Wrinkle in Time (L'Engle)
A Wind in the Door (L'Engle)

REINFORCEMENT ACTIVITY

1. Develop a modeling activity in which you identify a literary element and provide instruction in the understanding of that literary element.
2. With a group of your peers, select a book appropriate for children and identify its possibilities for instructional activities. Share your suggestions with the entire class.

DEVELOPING AN UNDERSTANDING OF PICTURE BOOKS

Picture books are excellent choices for initial analysis of literature. According to Lacy (1986), they may be used to stimulate visual exploration, interpretation, and reflection. Although most children's books are illustrated, not all illustrated books are classified as picture books. Activities such as looking at illustrations, discussing the importance of text and illustrations within a book, comparing picture books and illustrated books, and classifying books as either picture books or illustrated books foster an appreciation of picture books. These activities also stimulate cognitive development.

Picture Books versus Illustrated Books

In their discussion of picture books, Schwarcz and Schwarcz (1991) state: "One must take a close look in order to discover what can be found in, and culled from a picture book. Further, the careful scrutiny of one particular book will aid in the analysis of others" (p. 14). A logical progression for this activity begins by defining picture books, continues by analyzing examples and examining criteria, and finishes by comparing picture books and illustrated books and justifying why particular books are placed within either category. This progression emphasizes discussion, analysis, and support for various decisions. It also shows students that there are no right or wrong answers. Some books lend themselves to lively discussions because students may justifiably classify them in more than one way.

Introduce picture books by asking students to define a picture book. Next, share several definitions developed by either children's literature authorities or

Picture books and stories with large illustrations are not only for the very young child.

illustrators/authors of picture books and discuss the implications of those definitions. For example, Sutherland and Hearne (1984) define a picture book as one in which the illustrations are either as important as the text or more important than the text. Illustrator Uri Shulevitz (1985) states that picture books are closely related to theater and film because picture books are dramatic experiences that include "actors" and "stages." In picture books, the characters, settings, and actions are shown through the pictures.

Next, share and discuss examples of picture books. Begin your discussion with wordless books such as Pat Hutchins's *Changes, Changes* (1971), Emily Arnold McCully's *Picnic* (1984), John Goodall's *The Story of a Main Street* (1987) and David Wiesner's *Free Fall* (1988). Ask the students to tell you the story from the illustrations and to describe the setting, characters, and conflict (if any) that they find in the stories. They should conclude that all of these elements are revealed through the illustrations. Consequently, these books meet the previously stated definitions for picture books.

Proceed from wordless books to books that have minimal texts, such as Maurice Sendak's *Where the Wild Things Are* (1963), David Wiesner's *Tuesday* (1991), and Audrey Wood's *King Bidgood's in the Bathtub* (1985). Ask the students to note that the illustrations present information that the written text does not. For example, the illustrations in Sendak's book portray the magnitude and type of mischief of the wild things, as well as their appearance. In addition, the illustrations provide drama as they increase in size until finally the land of the wild things appear in double-page spreads, without text. This book clearly matches Shulevitz's definition for a picture book, which includes both actors and stages. Likewise, the illustrations in Wood's book provide maximum detail for minimal text. For example, the text states, "Today we lunch in the tub!" (p. 11, unnumbered). The double-page illustrations show an elegant luncheon with a cake centerpiece that is a model of the king's castle. Ask the students to describe the illustrations, either orally or in writing. They will discover that without the illustrations, pages of descriptive material would be required. Furthermore, the author would have to create a humorous and exaggerated mood through words alone. Students should conclude from this discussion that picture books with minimal text contain numerous details in the illustrations that are essential to the meaning of the story.

Next, proceed to picture books in which the illustrations and the text play equal roles, such as Wanda Gág's *Millions of Cats* (1928) and Arthur Yorinks's *Hey, Al* (1986). Gág's book is an excellent choice because the written text complements the illustrations and repetitive style by creating a feeling of movement. Even though there is more written text in *Hey, Al* than in *Where the Wild Things Are,* the illustrator of *Hey, Al,* Richard Egielski, uses some of the same techniques as Sendak. The illustrations become larger as the conflict develops, cover a double-page spread at the height of the interest, and include considerable information about setting and characters. After reading the texts and looking at the illustrations, students should discover that the illustrations and the written text are equally important.

Next, proceed to highly illustrated books that are not classified as picture books. For example, Mildred Taylor's *The Gold Cadillac* (1987) contains an illustration on about every third page and Russell Freedman's *Lincoln: A Photobiography* (1987) contains a photograph or other type of illustration on about every second page. After the students listen to or read the texts and analyze the illustrations in relation to the text, they should discover that although the illustrations add both information and interest, they cannot stand alone or are not so important as the written text.

Finally, ask the students to develop a list of activities and questions to help them decide if a book is a picture book or an illustrated book. For example:

1. Try to retell the story without looking at the words. Does the sequence of illustrations allow me to understand the story? (picture book)
2. Read the text. Is the story self-sufficient without the illustrations? (illustrated book)
3. Compare the illustrations and the text. Are the illustrations so important that they provide information about the setting, actions, and characters that the written text does not provide? (picture book)

Additional examples that you may use for this final comparison include the following picture books: Chris Van Allsburg's *The Z Was Zapped* (1987), David Macaulay's *Black and White* (1990), Nancy Tafuri's *Have You Seen My Duckling?* (1984), Margaret Mahy's *17 Kings and 42 Elephants* (1987), and Marc Brown's *Arthur's Baby* (1987). These may be compared with the following illustrated books: Cynthia Rylant's *Children of Christmas* (1987) and Michael Foreman's illustrated versions of Rudyard Kipling's *Just So Stories* (1987) and *The Jungle Book* (1987).

Books such as Mavis Jukes's *Like Jake and Me* (1984) and Joel Chandler Harris's *Jump Again! More Adventures of Brer Rabbit* (1987) show how important it is to emphasize support for categories rather than right and wrong answers. Lively discussions accompany these books because students can support them as either picture books or illustrated texts.

REINFORCEMENT ACTIVITY

1. Develop a lesson plan in which you teach students to differentiate between picture books and illustrated books.
2. Read Bruce McMillan's article "Photographer or Photo-Illustrator: What's the Difference?" (1991). Select books that you would classify under each category. Develop a lesson in which you help students compare and contrast the categories.

LITERARY GENRES

Children's literature is often categorized as traditional literature, modern fantasy, poetry, contemporary realistic fiction, historical fiction, biography and autobiography, and informational books. Each of these genres has special characteristics related to characters, settings, plots, and techniques the authors use to create believable stories. Discussing and comparing various genres helps students appreciate an author's ability to write within a genre and enhances their understanding of the nature of that genre. Table 11–1 compares several genres with respect to characters, setting, plot development, and believability.

To develop an understanding of and appreciation for differences and similarities, introduce one genre and help students identify its characteristics. After thoroughly investigating this genre by having the students listen to and read literary examples and identify and discuss the characteristics of the genre, continue the same type of listening, reading, and discussing activities with the next genre. Then, ask the students to compare and contrast the genres.

There are numerous, clearly defined differences between modern fantasy and contemporary realistic fiction; this is a logical place to begin the study of literary genres. First, share and discuss several modern fantasy selections and encourage students to identify characteristics of modern fantasy that are similar to those listed in Table 11–1. Within any genre, read texts or portions of texts to students and then identify and discuss various characteristics and examples of those characteristics from the literature. After this initial activity, either you or the students may read additional books from the genre and add them to the charts.

Modern Fantasy

Modern fantasy is fiction in which the author transports readers into a time period and setting where the impossible becomes convincingly possible. Authors of modern fantasy create their settings by altering one or more of the literary elements

TABLE 11–1

Characteristics of literary genres

	Modern Fantasy	Contemporary Realistic Fiction	Historical Fiction	Biography
Characters: Literature selections: Literary evidence:	Personified toys. Little people. Supernatural beings. People who have imaginary experiences. Animals who behave like people.	Fictional human characters who behave like real people. Fictional animal characters who behave like real animals.	Fictional humans who behave like real people and express understanding of historical period.	Real people.
Setting: Literature selections: Literary evidence:	Past, present, or future. Imaginary world created by the author. May travel through time and space.	Contemporary world as we know it. May have fictional location but must be possible in the contemporary world.	Authentic for historic time period. Supported by facts.	True for time the person actually lived. Supported by facts.

that would be expected in the real world. Authors of modern fantasy frequently choose to have their characters depart from known possibilities. The characters themselves may be contrary to reality or may experience preposterous situations (Norton, 1991).

Modern fantasy selections should include stories that reflect the various types of characters in the modern fantasy genre, such as personified toys (Margery Williams's *The Velveteen Rabbit: Or How Toys Become Real,* 1922, 1958, and A. A. Milne's *Winnie-the-Pooh,* 1926, 1954); little people (Mary Norton's *The Borrowers,* 1952, and Carol Kendall's *The Gammage Cup,* 1959); supernatural beings (Lucy Boston's *The Children of Green Knowe,* 1955); people who have imaginary experiences (C. S. Lewis's *The Lion, the Witch and the Wardrobe,* 1950, Lewis Carroll's *Alice's Adventures in Wonderland,* 1866, 1984, and Madeleine L'Engle's *A Wrinkle in Time,* 1962); and animals who behave like people (Beatrix Potter's *The Tale of Peter Rabbit,* 1902, Robert Lawson's *Rabbit Hill,* 1944, and E. B. White's *Charlotte's Web,*

TABLE 11-1
Continued

	Modern Fantasy	Contemporary Realistic Fiction	Historical Fiction	Biography
Plot development: Literature selections: Literary evidence:	Conflict may be against supernatural powers. Problems may be solved through magical powers.	Author creates plot as fictional characters face contemporary situations, such as growing up, survival, family problems.	Author creates plot as fictional characters cope with problems that are authentic for the historical time.	Plot follows life of a real person. Conflict follows real problems and dates.
Creating believable stories: Literature selections: Literary evidence:	Authors encourage readers to suspend disbelief.	Authors rely on relevant subjects, everyday occurrences, or realism.	Authors use research to create historically authentic settings and problems.	Authors use research and documentation. Objectivity.

1952). (Notice how many of these recommendations are considered classics in children's literature.)

Modern fantasy selections should show students that settings may be in the past, present, or future. Settings may also be in worlds that are totally created by the author, such as Narnia in *The Lion, the Witch and the Wardrobe,* Prydain in Lloyd Alexander's *The Book of Three* (1964), and Demar in Robin McKinley's *The Hero and the Crown* (1984). Characters may also go through time warps as the settings shift from present to past (Janet Lunn's *The Root Cellar,* 1983, Ruth Park's *Playing Beatie Bow,* 1982, and David Wiseman's *Jeremy Visick,* 1981) or from present to future (Margaret Anderson's *The Mists of Time,* 1984).

Likewise, conflict may be against supernatural powers, as in *The Lion, the Witch and the Wardrobe* or *The Hero and the Crown.* The problems in modern fantasy may be solved through magical or supernatural powers as they are in both of these books. Supernatural powers may also help in gentler plots, such as *The Velveteen Rabbit: Or How Toys Become Real.*

The books should help students understand and appreciate that authors of modern fantasy must make readers believe in worlds, characters, and actions that are not possible in the world as they know it. In literary terms, an author must encourage readers to suspend disbelief. The key questions for students to consider are: Did the author make me believe that the characters, settings, and conflicts were possible? and How did the author create the world, the people, and the conflict so that I believed they were possible?

Contemporary Realistic Fiction

After students develop a clear understanding of modern fantasy, extend the study of genres into contemporary realistic fiction. In contemporary realistic fiction, everything in the story, including characters, setting, and plot, could happen to real people or animals living in the contemporary world. Contemporary realistic fiction does not mean that the story is true; it means only that it could have happened (Norton, 1991).

Use an instructional approach for the study of contemporary realistic fiction similar to that for modern fantasy. Select books such as the following to help students identify and develop characteristics of contemporary realistic fiction: Beverly Cleary's *Dear Mr. Henshaw* (1983) and *Ramona Quimbly, Age 8* (1981); Judy Blume's *The One in the Middle Is the Green Kangaroo* (1981) and *Tales of a Fourth Grade Nothing* (1972); Betsy Byars's *Cracker Jackson* (1985); Lois Lowry's *Anastasia's Chosen Career* (1987); Katherine Paterson's *Bridge to Terabithia* (1977); Gary Paulsen's *Hatchet* (1987); Virginia Hamilton's *Zeely* (1967); and Dennis Haseley's *The Scared One* (1983).

After identifying and developing the characteristics of contemporary realistic fiction, encourage students to compare modern fantasy and contemporary realistic fiction.

Historical Fiction

Continue with an analysis of historical fiction. Historical fiction is fiction written about an earlier time, in which the setting is authentic in every respect; the actions, beliefs, and values of the characters are realistic for the time period; and the conflicts reflect the historical time period. Although the characters did not actually live, they could have lived during that time period (Norton, 1991).

Follow the sequence of events described under modern fantasy. Select books to help students develop an appreciation for and understanding of the characteristics shown in Table 11–1: Barbara Brenner's *Wagon Wheels* (1978), Patricia MacLachlan's *Sarah, Plain and Tall* (1985), F. N. Monjo's *The Drinking Gourd* (1970), Uri Orlev's *The Island on Bird Street* (1984), Philip Pullman's *The Ruby in the Smoke* (1987), Mildred Taylor's *Roll of Thunder, Hear My Cry* (1976), and Laura Ingalls Wilder's *Little House in the Big Woods* (1932).

After analyzing the literature and identifying and discussing characteristics, compare similarities and differences between historical fiction, contemporary realistic fiction, and modern fantasy.

Biography

Finally, extend the study of genre into biography. A biography is a book written about a real person, living or dead. A biography must be a true story about the person and the other people and the incidents that influenced that person's life.

The characters, their actions, and the settings reflect what actually happened and not what could have happened. Biographies that you may use to help students identify and develop characteristics of the genre include Russell Freedman's *Lincoln: A Photobiography* (1987), David Adler's *Martin Luther King, Jr.: Free at Last* (1986), Lillian Gish's *An Actor's Life for Me!* (1987), Jean Fritz's *Where Do You Think You're Going, Christopher Columbus?* (1980), Joe Lasker's *The Great Alexander the Great* (1983), Betsy Lee's *Charles Eastman, the Story of an American Indian* (1979), Polly Brooks's *Queen Eleanor: Independent Spirit of the Medieval World* (1983), and Tobi Tobias's *Maria Tallchief* (1970).

After you and the students find examples from biographies to support the characteristics and you conclude discussions about biographies, compare characteristics of biography as a genre with the characteristics of other genres.

REINFORCEMENT ACTIVITY

Choose another genre of children's literature, such as poetry, traditional literature, or informational literature, and develop an activity that encourages students to develop appreciation and understanding of the characteristics of that genre.

Traditional Literature

Folklore is that wonderful part of literature handed down by the storytellers of many cultures. Folktales enable teachers to instill an understanding of other cultures and an appreciation for cultures that differ. Folklore is the mirror of a culture and looks at that culture from the inside instead of the outside.

Ruth Kearney Carlson (1972) identifies nine ways in which the study of folklore contributes to world understanding. It encourages (1) understanding of the cultural traditions of the nonscientific mind, through folktales that deal with the mysteries of creation; (2) understanding of the relatedness of story types and motifs among peoples of the world, through such universal tales as Cinderella, which has variations in many cultures; (3) aesthetic appreciation for the music, art, literature, and dance of other cultures; (4) understanding about cultural diffusion, through observation of how different versions of the same tale or hero appear in different world settings; (5) the desire to learn about unfamiliar places around the world; (6) understanding of the dialects and languages of other countries; (7) imaginative identification with people in other times and places; (8) understanding of the conditions of other times and cultures through study of heroes shaped by those conditions; and (9) understanding of the inherent qualities of goodness, mercy, courage, and industry, which folktale heroes possess, and consequently, an intuitive grasp of the better qualities of the human spirit. These insights are certainly worth imparting to children.

See Norton's *Through the Eyes of a Child: An Introduction to Children's Literature* (1991) for additional ways to involve children in traditional literature. The text includes ways of comparing different versions of a folktale and investigating folktales from a single country.

Folklore contributes to a child's understanding of cultural traditions.

REINFORCEMENT ACTIVITY

1. Select a group of folktales from a particular country. Read the folktales and note the information you find about values, beliefs, occupations, transportation, animals, and agriculture.
2. Select a story type or motif from folktales, such as the various Cinderella stories. Find as many folktales as you can from different cultures that tell basically the same story. Compare the different versions. How are they alike? How are they different? How do you account for the similarities?

FOR YOUR PLAN BOOK
A Folktale Unit

General Objectives

1. To encourage children to appreciate a literary form, the folktale, and to realize that they share common interests, attitudes, and values with their counterparts in other lands.
2. To have children verbalize generalizations — such as the strongly contrasted values of good and evil — regarding the nature of folktales.
3. To share enthusiasm for folktales by reading certain selections aloud.
4. To develop listening skills by asking children to listen for specifics in each story.
5. To motivate children to search for more folktales to read and enjoy.
6. To provide opportunity for children to enjoy silent reading of the folktales of their choice.
7. To encourage children, once they are acquainted with the folk literature of a country, to learn more about the people and customs of that country.
8. To encourage children to share what they learn with one another.
9. To have children, individually and as a group, demonstrate their knowledge of and appreciation for folktales to their classmates by creating a bulletin board display and presenting a puppet play, thereby inviting others to read and share in the enjoyment of such stories.

Folktales from India

To motivate interest in Indian folktales, greet the children with a Hindi word, *namaste,* which means both help and good-bye. Display Indian objects — jewelry, metal plates, metal pitchers, a sari, a statue of an elephant — and pictures of musical instruments, such as the sitar (a long-necked guitar) and the banshri (a bamboo flute), as well as pictures of people and buildings. Include a record of music from India as part of the motivational preparation. Let the students talk about the display and list questions about some of the objects and the people. Ask the students to locate India on a globe or a map of Asia. Next, read numerous folktales to the children. Include tales from the following sources:

> Asian Cultural Centre for UNESCO's *Folk Tales from Asia for Children Everywhere,* Books Four and Five (1976, 1977)
> David Conger's *Many Lands, Many Stories: Asian Folktales for Children* (1987)
> Nancy DeRoin's *Jataka Tales* (1975)
> Virginia Haviland's *Favorite Fairy Tales Told in India* (1973)

After reading several stories, ask the children if they think American children can understand and enjoy stories intended for Indian children, and whether or not Indian children would appreciate American stories. As soon as they have a number of stories to draw from, ask them to look for such things as similarities in plot, style, and motifs. Then tell them there are many other interesting folktales in the books they are using. To motivate independent reading, read the titles and show pictures.

While the students read other tales, ask them to pretend that the folktales are the only way that they can learn about the country. Have them look for information about the animals, food, climate, occupations, music, beliefs, and values of the culture.

Next, discuss ways to determine whether their information about India and its cultural heritage is accurate. Have the students compare their information with reference materials, *National Geographic,* and other books and pictures about India. Invite a visitor from India to come to the classroom. Have each child choose some aspect of Indian life on which to prepare a short research report.

Because the class will be reading folktales from countries besides India, begin a bulletin-board display entitled, "Read Around the World." At the base of the bulletin board, put a large world map over a dark-blue background. Each time you read a folktale, attach a symbol representing the story to the appropriate country on the map. Position an annotation of the story against the background and connect it to the symbol with a length of yarn. Place unusual objects from that culture on a table below the bulletin board.

Folktales from Japan and Russia

Also include in this unit folktales from Japan and Russia. Introduce each country with examples of its language, objects, music, and art. Draw on the following sources for folktales:

Japan

Molly Bang's *The Paper Crane* (1985)
Claude Clement's *The Painter and the Wild Swans* (1986)
Virginia Haviland's *Favorite Fairy Tales Told in Japan* (1973)
Jane Hori Ike and Baruch Zimmerman's *A Japanese Fairy Tale* (1982)
Momoko Ishii's *The Tongue-Cut Sparrow* (1987)
Anne Laurin's *The Perfect Crane* (1981)
Nancy Luenn's *The Dragon Kite* (1982)
Arlene Mosel's *The Funny Little Woman* (1972)
Patricia Newton's *The Five Sparrows: A Japanese Folktale* (1982)
Sumiko Yagawa's *Momotaro, the Peach Boy* (1986)
Sumiko Yagawa's *The Crane Wife* (1981)

Russia

Aleksandr Nikolaevich Afanasev's *Russian Folk Tales* (1980)
R. Nisbet Bain's *Cossack Fairy Tales and Folktales* (1976)
Elizabeth Isele's *The Frog Princess* (1984)
Michael McCurdy's *The Devils Who Learned to Be Good* (1987)
Charles Mikolaycak's *Babushka* (1984)
Alexander Pushkin's *The Tale of Czar Saltan or the Prince and the Swan Princess* (1975)
Arthur Ransome's *The Fool of the World and the Flying Ship* (1968)
Arthur Ransome's *Old Peter's Russian Tales* (1916, 1984)
Maida Silverman's *Anna and the Seven Swans* (1984)
Leo Tolstoy's *The Fool* (1981)
Boris Zvorykin's *The Firebird and Other Russian Fairy Tales* (1978)

With the students, read the folktales of each country and record the information that you gain from them about the people, their beliefs, and values. Have the children use the information they learn from the folktales to make travel posters of each country, which can form another colorful bulletin board. Also, let the children construct mobiles depicting various aspects of Japanese life. Encourage the students to use other re-sources to find out more about the cultures of the two countries. Children especially enjoy studying Japanese music, dance, and theater. Ask a visitor from Japan to share experiences with the children, and introduce the children to samples of Japanese cooking and the practice of eating with chopsticks.

Culmination Activities

Choose a favorite folktale from each of the countries: India, Russia, and Japan. Divide the students into three groups according to which story and country they want to repre-sent. Help each group decide on a method for sharing their story (for example, a puppet show, a felt-board story, a play). Have the students prepare and practice the stories, and invite another class to see the presentations. Let each group also share information they learn about their particular country. Continue to maintain the "Read Around the World" bulletin board so that the children can add to their folktale collection whenever they read a story from another country.

SUMMARY

Teach students that they can read literature for both pleasure and understanding. The foundations for a good literature program include an environment in which books are easy to locate and read. Teachers should love books, share them daily with students, and encourage interaction with a variety of books. This chapter includes suggestions for judging appropriateness of books, balancing literature selections, using various sources to find out about books, and identifying the interests of students.

To develop enjoyment of literature through storytelling, consider story selection, preparation, introduction, and the actual telling. Also consider using pictures and objects along with your storytelling. When reading aloud to children, consider their interests, ages, and experiences with literature. Pick books of high quality—worthy of the time spent both by reader and listeners.

This chapter includes techniques to increase understanding of literature. Develop understanding of literary elements through webbing, modeling, and plot diagramming. List various instructional possibilities for the books you consider using. Also, explore the various literary genres. These include modern fantasy, contemporary realistic fiction, historical fiction, biography, and traditional literature.

ADDITIONAL LITERATURE ACTIVITIES

1. Ask a librarian about the literature that children enjoy during story time and the literature that they check out of the library. Are there any differences or similarities between these two groups? Speculate about reasons for either differences or similarities.
2. If possible, visit a library or classroom during story time. Note any effective techniques the storyteller uses to obtain students' interest, introduce the story, and interact with listeners during the story presentation.

3. Read a journal article about the use of literature in the classroom or in the library, such as those found in *The New Advocate, Children's Literature in Education,* and *The School Library Journal.* What is the main emphasis of the article? Share the article and your review of the article with your class.

4. Referring to the journals listed in activity 3, review the articles published during one year. What are the major topics covered during that time period? Are there any recurring issues or themes? What are the recommendations for using literature in the curriculum?

5. Choose a grade level. Develop a list of books that you believe to be appropriate for that grade level. Be sure to balance the selections to include the major genres of literature.

6. Refer to a journal, such as *Booklist, Hornbook,* or *School Library Journal,* that includes critical reviews of literature and recommends children's books. Locate three books that received starred reviews within the journal. Read the books and consider why the journal board of reviewers recommended the books. Do you agree with the reviews? Share the books, your reviews, and the journal reviews with your language arts class.

7. Interview a student about his or her interests. Then develop a list of books that you would recommend to that student.

8. Patricia Wilson (1985) studied the preferences of fifth- and sixth-grade students for literature that is both highly recommended and considered classic in children's literature. She found that the students' favorites included *Charlotte's Web; Little House in the Big Woods; The Hobbit; The Secret Garden; The Lion, the Witch and the Wardrobe; Heidi;* and *The Borrowers.* Either lead a discussion with a student about one of these books or read one of the books to a group of students. What is the reaction of the students to the book? Why do you believe Wilson's subjects chose these books as favorites? If one of these books is also your favorite children's book, why is it your favorite book?

9. Develop a file of books appropriate for stimulating students' enjoyment through art. Include ways to use the books to stimulate enjoyment.

10. Using Table 11–1, identify books for each genre of literature and identify the literary evidence that places the books within that genre. (Choose books that are not discussed in this chapter.)

11. Develop a modeling lesson to help students understand and appreciate one of the literary elements.

12. Using either of the plot diagrams in Figures 11–9 and 11–11, choose a book and place the key events from the book on the diagram.

BIBLIOGRAPHY

Agee, Hugh. *High Interest, Easy Reading.* Urbana, Ill.: National Council of Teachers of English, 1984.

Anderson, R. C.; Hiebert, E. H.; Scott, J. A.; and Wilkinson, I. A. *Becoming a Nation of Readers: The Report of the Commission on Reading.* Champaign, Ill.: Center for the Study of Reading, 1985.

Anderson, R. C.; Wilson, P. T.; and Fielding, C. G. "Growth in Reading and How Children Spend Their Time Outside of School." *Reading Research Quarterly* 23 (1988): 285–303.

Bauer, Caroline. *Handbook for Storytellers.* Chicago: American Library Association, 1977.

Bennet, Kathleen. "Popular Reading—Chapter Books." *Booklist* (November 1, 1987): 488–90.

Brandehoff, Susan E. "Jake and Honeybunch Go to Heaven: Children's Book Fans Smoldering Debate." *American Libraries* 14 (March 1983): 130–32.

Breckenridge, Kit. "Modern Classics." *School Library Journal* 34 (April 1988): 42–43.

Carlson, Ruth Kearney. *Folklore and Folktales Around the World.* Newark, Del.: International Reading Association, 1972.

Chatton, B. "Our Emerging Nation—The Late 1800s." *Book Links* 1 (1992): 48–53.

Cianciolo, P. J. *Picture Books for Children,* 3d ed. Chicago: American Library Association, 1990.

Cohen, Caron Lee. "The Quest in Children's Literature." *School Library Journal* 31 (August 1985): 28–29.

Coody, Betty. *Using Literature with Young Children.* Dubuque, Iowa: William C. Brown Co., 1979.

Cooper, Ilene. "Popular Reading—After Henry Huggins." *Booklist* (November 1, 1986): 415–16.

Corcoran, Frances. "Storytelling Sources." *Booklist* (April 15, 1986): 1234–35.

Dressel, J. H. "The Effects of Listening to and Discussing Different Qualities of Children's Literature on the Narrative Writing of Fifth Graders." *Research in the Teaching of English* 24 (1990): 397–414.

Dronka, P. "Forums for Curriculum Critics Settle Some Disputes: Clash Persists on Students' Thinking about Controversy." *Update* (March 1987): 1, 6, 7.

Elleman, B. "Book Links Salutes 'A Few Good Books' of 1991." *Book Links* 1 (1992): 4–8.

Fishel, Carol T. "Reading in the Content Area of English." In *Reading in the Content Areas: Research for Teachers,"* edited by Mary M. Dupuis. Newark, Del.: International Reading Association, 1984.

Five, Cora Lee. "From Workbook to Workshop: Increasing Children's Involvement in the Reading Process." *The New Advocate* 1 (Spring 1988): 103–13.

Frasher, Ramona. "A Feminist Look at Literature for Children: Ten Years Later." In *Sex Stereotypes and Reading: Research and Strategies,* edited by E. Marcia Sheridan. Newark: International Reading Association, 1982.

Galda, Lee. "Readers, Texts and Contexts: A Response-Based View of Literature in the Classroom." *The New Advocate* 1 (Spring 1988): 92–102.

Herrell, A. L. "A Child and an Adult Interact with a Book: The Effects on Language and Literacy in Kindergarten." 1990. *Dissertation Abstracts International,* 50, 10A. (University Microfilms No. 90-04,995)

Huck, Charlotte; Hepler, Susan; and Hickman, Janet. *Children's Literature.* New York: Holt, Rinehart & Winston, 1987.

Kiefer, Barbara. "Picture Books for Older Children." *Booklist* (September 15, 1986): 138–39.

Lacy, Lyn. *Art and Design in Children's Picture Books.* Chicago: American Library Association, 1986.

Lehr, S. "The Child's Developing Sense of Theme as a Response to Literature." *Reading Research Quarterly* 23 (1988): 337–57.

Mandell, P. L. "Cultural Diverse Videos—African-Americans." *School Library Journal* 38 (1992): 49–51, 54–56.

May, Jill P. "Creating a School Wide Literature Program: A Case Study," *Children's Literature Association Quarterly* 12 (Fall 1987): 135–37.

McClenathan, Day Ann. "Realism in Books for Young People: Some Thoughts on Management of Controversy." In *Developing Active Readers,* edited by Dianne Monson and Day Ann McClenathan. Newark, Del.: International Reading Association, 1979.

McMillan, B. "Photographer or Photo-Illustrator: What's the Difference?" *School Library Journal* 37 (1991): 38–9.

Meade, J. "A War of Words." *Teacher* (November/December 1990): 37–45.

Mendoza, Alicia. "Reading to Children: Their Preferences." *The Reading Teacher* 38 (February 1985): 522–27.

National Council of Teachers of English. "Forum: Essentials of English." *Language Arts* 60 (February 1983): 244–48.

Norton, D. E. *The Impact of Literature-Based Reading.* New York: Merrill/Macmillan, 1992.

———. *Through the Eyes of a Child: An Introduction to Children's Literature,* 3d ed. New York: Merrill/Macmillan, 1991.

Pellowski, Anne. *The Family Story-Telling Handbook.* New York: Macmillan, 1987.

———. *Hidden Stories in Plants.* New York: Macmillan, 1990.

Phelan, Carolyn. "Poetry for Young Children." *Booklist* (January 1, 1988): 790–92.

Quan, N. A. "Social Values in Popular Adolescent Literature, 1940–1980." 1990. *Dissertation Abstracts International,* 50,10A. (University Microfilms No. 90-06,480)

Rothman, R. "Experts Warn of Attempts to Censor Classic Texts." *Education Week,* (February 1990): 5.

Schwarcz, J., and Schwarcz, C. *The Picture Book Comes of Age.* Chicago: American Library Association, 1991.

Sebesta, Sam. "What Do Young People Think about the Literature They Read?" *Reading Newsletter,* No. 8. Rockleigh, N.J.: Allyn & Bacon, 1979.

Shulevitz, Uri. *Writing with Pictures.: How to Write and Illustrate Children's Books.* New York: Watson-Guptill, 1985.

Smith, C. "The Role of Different Literary Genres." *The Reading Teacher* 44 (1991): 440–41.

Spinner, B. T. "A Study of Academic and Nonacademic Experiences that Promote and Sustain Adult Interest in the Reading and Writing of Poetry." 1990. *Dissertation Abstracts International*, 51,02A. (University Microfilms No. 90-19,762)

State of Illinois. *State Goals for Learning and Sample Learning Objectives: Language Arts.* Illinois, 1985.

Stewig, John. "Storyteller: Endangered Species?" *Language Arts* 55 (March 1978): 339–45.

Sutherland, Zena, and Arbuthnot, May Hill. *Children and Books.* Glenview, Ill.: Scott, Foresman & Co., 1986.

_____ , and Hearne, Betty. "In Search of the Perfect Picture Book Definition."In *Jump Over the Moon,* edited by Pamela Barron and Jennifer Burley. New York: Holt, Rinehart and Winston, 1984.

Swanton, Susan. "Minds Alive: What and Why Gifted Students Read for Pleasure." *School Library Journal* 30 (March 1984): 99–102.

Taxel, Joel. "Notes from the Editor." *The New Advocate* 1 (Spring 1988): 73–74.

Walmsley, S. A., and Walp, T. P. *Teaching Literature in Elementary School: A Report on the Elementary School Antecedents of Secondary School Literature Instruction.* Report Series 1.3. Albany, N.Y.: Center for the Teaching and Learning of Literature. University at Albany, State University of New York. (ERIC No. ED 315 754), 1989.

Whitehead, Robert. *Children's Literature: Strategies of Teaching.* Englewood Cliffs, N.J.: Prentice-Hall, 1968.

Wiessler, J. "Book Censorship Attempts Are Soaring, Group's Survey Says." *Houston Chronicle.* August 28, 1987, Section 1, p. 8.

Wilms, Denise. "Contemporary Issues—Intergenerational Relationships. *Booklist* (May 1, 1986): 1318–20.

Wilson, Patricia Jane. "Children's Classics: A Reading Preference Study of Fifth and Sixth Graders." Doctoral Dissertation, University of Houston, 1985. *Dissertation Abstracts International* 47:454A.

CHILDREN'S LITERATURE REFERENCES

Adler, David. *Martin Luther King, Jr.: Free at Last,* Illustrated by Robert Casilla. New York: Holiday, 1986.

Afanasev, Aleksandr Nikolaevich. *Russian Folktales,* New York: Random House, 1980.

Alexander, Lloyd. *The Book of Three.* New York: Holt, Rinehart & Winston, 1964.

Anderson, Margaret. *The Mists of Time.* New York: Alfred A. Knopf, 1984.

Asian Cultural Center for UNESCO. *Folktales from Asia for Children Everywhere.* Books Four and Five, Weatherhill, 1976, 1977.

Baer, Gene. *Thump Thump, Rat-a-Tat-Tat.* New York: HarperCollins, 1989.

Bain, R. Nisbet. *Cossack Fairy Tales and Folktales.* Santa Cruz, Calif.: Mitchell, 1976.

Baker, Jeannie. *Grandmother.* New York: Deutsch, 1978.

Baker, Olaf. *Where the Buffaloes Begin.* Illustrated by Stephen Gammell. New York: Warne, 1981.

Bang, Molly. *The Paper Crane.* New York: Greenwillow, 1985.

Bauer, Marion Dane. *On My Honor.* New York: Clarion, 1986.

Baylor, Byrd. *Hawk, I'm Your Brother.* Illustrated by Peter Parnall. New York: Charles Scribner's Sons, 1976.

Blos, Joan. *A Gathering of Days.* New York: Charles Scribner's Sons, 1979.

Blume, Judy. *The One in the Middle Is the Green Kangaroo.* New York: Bradbury, 1981.

_____ . *Tales of a Fourth Grade Nothing.* New York: E. P. Dutton, 1972.

Boston, Lucy. *The Children of Green Knowe.* San Diego: Harcourt Brace Jovanovich, 1955.

Bowen, Betsy. *Antler, Bear, Canoe: A Northwoods Alphabet Year.* Boston: Little, Brown, 1991.

Brenner, Barbara. *Wagon Wheels.* Illustrated by Don Bolognese. New York: Harper & Row, 1978.

Brittain, Bill. *The Wish Giver.* Illustrated by Andrew Glass. New York: Harper & Row, 1983.

Brooks, Polly. *Queen Eleanor: Independent Spirit of the Medieval World.* Philadelphia: J. B. Lippincott Co., 1983.

Brother Eagle, Sister Sky: a Message from Chief Seattle. Illustrated by Susan Jeffers. New York: Dial, 1991.

Brown, Marc. *Arthur's Baby.* Boston: Little, Brown & Co., 1987.

Brown, Marcia. *Stone Soup.* New York: Charles Scribner's Sons, 1947.

Burton, Virginia Lee. *The Little House.* Boston: Houghton Mifflin Co., 1942.

Byars, Betsy. *Cracker Jackson.* New York: Viking Press, 1985.

Cameron, Eleanor. *That Julia Redfern.* Illustrated by Gail Owens. New York: E. P. Dutton, 1982.

Carle, Eric. *The Honeybee and the Robber.* New York: Philomel, 1981.

_____ . *Twelve Tales from Aesop.* New York: Philomel, 1980.

_____ . *The Very Hungry Caterpillar.* New York: Thomas Y. Crowell Co., 1971.

Carroll, Lewis. *Alice's Adventures in Wonderland.* Illustrated by John Tenniel. Macmillan, 1866, New York: Alfred A. Knopf, 1984.

Cazet, Denys. *A Fish in His Pocket.* New York: Watts, 1987.

Cendrars, Blaise. *Shadow.* Illustrated by Marcia Brown. New York: Charles Scribner's Sons, 1982.

Chase, Richard. *Grandfather Tales.* Boston: Houghton Mifflin Co., 1948.

Clapp, Patricia. *Constance: A Story of Early Plymouth.* New York: Lothrop, Lee & Shepard, 1968.

Cleary, Beverly. *Dear Mr. Henshaw.* Illustrated by Paul O. Zelinsky. New York: William Morrow & Co., 1983.

_____ . *Ramona Quimby, Age 8.* New York: William Morrow & Co., 1981.

Clement, Claude. *The Painter and the Wild Swans.* Illustrated by Frederic Clement. New York: Dial Press, 1986.

Cohen, Barbara. *Molly's Pilgrim.* New York: Lothrop, Lee & Shepard, 1983.

Conger, David. *Many Lands, Many Stories: Asian Folktales for Children.* Ruthland, Vt.: Tuttle, 1987.

Conly, Jane Leslie. *Rasco and the Rats of NIMH.* New York: Harper & Row, 1986.

Dalgliesh, Alice. *The Columbus Story.* New York: Charles Scribner's Sons, 1955.

de Paola, Tomie. *Mother Goose.* New York: G. P. Putnam's Sons, 1985.

DeRoin, Nancy. *Jataka Tales.* Boston: Houghton Mifflin Co., 1975.

Flournoy, Valerie. *The Patchwork Quilt.* Illustrated by Jerry Pinkney. New York: Dial Press, 1985.

Forbes, Esther. *Johnny Tremain.* Illustrated by Lynd Ward. Boston: Houghton Mifflin Co., 1943.

Fox, Paula. *One-Eyed Cat.* New York: Bradbury, 1984.

Freedman, Russell. *Lincoln: A Photobiography.* New York: Clarion, 1987.

Fritz, Jean. *Bully for You Teddy Roosevelt.* Illustrated by Mike Wimmer. New York: Putnam, 1991.

_____ . *Make Way for Sam Houston.* Illustrated by Elise Primavera. New York: G. P. Putnam's Sons, 1986.

_____ . *Where Do You Think You're Going, Christopher Columbus?* Illustrated by Margot Tomes. New York: G. P. Putnam's Sons, 1980.

Gág, Wanda. *Millions of Cats.* New York: Coward-McCann, 1928.

Garfield, Leon. *The December Rose.* New York: Viking Press, 1986.

Gates, Doris. *Two Queens of Heaven: Aphrodite and Demeter.* Illustrated by Trina Schart Hyman. New York: Viking Press, 1974.

George, Jean Craighead. *Julie of the Wolves.* New York: Harper & Row, 1972.

_____ . *My Side of the Mountain.* New York: Dutton, 1959.

Gipson, Fred. *Old Yeller.* New York: Harper & Row, 1956.

Gish, Lillian. Told to Selma Lanes. *An Actor's Life for Me!* New York: Viking Press, 1987.

Goodall, John. *The Story of a Main Street.* New York: Macmillan Co., 1987.

Grahame, Kenneth. *The Wind in the Willows.* Illustrated by E. H. Shepard. New York: Charles Scribner's Sons, 1908, 1940.

Greenberg, Jan, and Jordan, Sandra. *The Painter's Eye: Learning to Look at Contemporary Art.* New York: Delacorte, 1991.

Greenfield, Eloise. *Rosa Parks.* Illustrated by Eric Marlow. New York: Crowell, 1973.

Grifalconi, Ann. *Darkness and the Butterfly.* Boston: Little, Brown & Co., 1987.

Grimm, Brothers. *Little Red Riding Hood.* Retold and Illustrated by Trina Schart Hyman. New York: Holliday, 1983.

_____ . *Red Riding Hood.* Retold and illustrated by James Marshall. New York: Dial Press, 1987.

Hamilton, Virginia. *Zeely.* New York: Macmillan Co., 1967.

Harris, Joel Chandler. *Jump Again! More Adventures of Brer Rabbit.* Adapted by Van Dyke Parks. Illustrated by Barry Moser. San Diego: Harcourt Brace Jovanovich, 1987.

Haseley, Dennis. *The Scared One.* New York: Warne, 1983.

Haviland, Virginia. *Favorite Fairy Tales Told in India.* Boston: Little, Brown & Co., 1973.

_____ . *Favorite Fairy Tales Told in Japan.* Boston: Little, Brown & Co., 1967.

Henkes, Kevin. *Chrysanthemum.* New York: Greenwillow, 1991.

Howard, Ellen. *Edith Herself.* New York: Atheneum Pubs., 1987.

Hughes, Monica. *The Dream Catcher.* New York: Atheneum Pubs., 1987.

Hurmence, Belinda. *A Girl Called Boy.* Boston: Houghton Mifflin Co., 1982.

Hutchins, Pat. *Changes, Changes.* New York: Macmillan Co., 1971.

Ike, Jane, and Zimmerman, Baruch. *A Japanese Fairy Tale.* New York: Warne, 1982.

Isele, Elizabeth. *The Frog Princess.* Illustrated by Michael Hague. New York: Crowell, 1984.

Ishii, Momoko. *The Tongue-Cut Sparrow.* Illustrated by Suekichi Akaba. New York: E. P. Dutton, 1987.

Jacques, Brian. *Redwall.* New York: Philomel, 1986.

Jukes, Mavis. *Like Jake and Me.* Illustrated by Lloyd Bloom. New York: Alfred A. Knopf, 1984.

Keats, Ezra Jack. *Peter's Chair.* New York: Harper & Row, 1967.

_____ . *The Snowy Day.* New York: Viking Press, 1962.

_____ . *The Trip.* New York: Greenwillow, 1978.

Kendall, Carol. *The Gammage Cup.* San Diego: Harcourt Brace Jovanovich, 1959.

Kipling, Rudyard. *The Jungle Book.* Illustrated by Michael Foreman, New York: Viking Press, 1987.

_____ . *Just So Stories.* Illustrated by Michael Foreman. New York: Viking Press, 1987.

Lasker, Joe. *The Great Alexander the Great.* New York: Viking Press, 1983.

Lasky, Kathryn. *Sugaring Time.* Photographs by Christopher Knight. New York: Macmillan Co., 1983.

Laurin, Anne. *The Perfect Crane.* New York: Harper & Row, 1981.

Lawson, Robert. *Rabbit Hill.* New York: Viking Press, 1944.

Lee, Betsy. *Charles Eastman, the Story of an American Indian.* Minneapolis: Dillon, 1979.

Lee, Jeanne. *Silent Lotus.* New York: Farrar, Straus, & Giroux, 1991.

L'Engle, Madeleine. *A Wind in the Door.* New York: Farrar, Straus, & Giroux, 1973.

_____ . *A Wrinkle in Time.* New York: Farrar, Straus & Giroux, 1962.

Lenski, Lois. *Sing a Song of People.* Illustrated by Giles Laroche. Boston: Little, Brown & Co., 1987.

Lewin, Hugh, *Jafta.* Illustrated by Lisa Kopper. Minneapolis: Carolrhoda, 1983.

_____ . *Jafta's Mother.* Illustrated by Lisa Kipper. Minneapolis: Carolrhoda, 1983.

Lewis, C. S. *The Lion, the Witch and the Wardrobe.* New York: Macmillan Co., 1950.

Lionni, Leo. *Swimmy.* New York: Pantheon, 1963.

Little, Jean. *Different Dragons.* New York: Viking Press, 1986.

Lowry, Lois. *Anastasia's Chosen Career.* Boston: Houghton Mifflin Co., 1987.

Luenn, Nancy. *The Dragon Kite.* Illustrated by Michael Hague. San Diego: Harcourt Brace Jovanovich, 1982.

Lunn, Janet. *The Root Cellar.* New York: Charles Scribner's Sons, 1983.

_____ . *Shadow in Hawthorn Bay.* New York: Charles Scribner's Sons, 1986.

Macaulay, David. *Black and White.* Boston: Houghton Mifflin, 1990.

McCloskey, Robert. *Make Way for Ducklings.* New York: Viking Press, 1941.

McCully, Emily Arnold. *Picnic.* New York: Harper & Row, 1984.

McCurdy, Michael. *The Devils Who Learned to Be Good.* Boston: Little, Brown, 1987.

MacDonald, Suse. *Alphabatics.* New York: Bradbury, 1986.

McKinley, Robin. *The Hero and the Crown.* New York: Greenwillow, 1984.

MacLachlan, Patricia. *Sarah, Plain and Tall.* New York: Harper & Row, 1985.

Madsen, Jane, and Bockoras, Diane. *Please Don't Tease Me . . .* Illustrated by Kathleen Brinko. Valley Forge, Penn.: Judson, 1983.

Mahy, Margaret. *17 Kings and 42 Elephants.* New York: Dial Press, 1987.

Mathis, Sharon Bell. *The Hundred Penny Box.* Illustrated by Leo and Diane Dillon. New York: Viking Press, 1975.

Mazer, Norma Fox. *After the Rain.* New York: William Morrow & Co., 1987.

Mikolaycak, Charles. *Babushka.* New York: Holiday House, 1984.

Milne, A. A. *Winnie-the-Pooh.* Illustrated by Ernest Shepard. New York: E. P. Dutton, 1926, 1954.

Monjo, F. N. *The Drinking Gourd.* Illustrated by Fred Brenner. New York: Harper & Row, 1970.

Mosel, Arlene. *The Funny Little Woman.* Illustrated by Blair Lent. New York: E. P. Dutton, 1972.

Newton, Patricia. *The Five Sparrows: A Japanese Folktale.* New York: Atheneum Pubs., 1982.

Norton, Mary. *The Borrowers.* San Diego: Harcourt Brace Jovanovich, 1952.

Oakley, Graham. *The Church Mice in Action.* New York: Atheneum Pubs., 1982.

O'Brien, Robert. *Mrs. Frisby and the Rats of NIMH.* New York: Atheneum Pubs., 1971.

O'Dell, Scott. *Island of the Blue Dolphins.* Boston: Houghton Mifflin, 1960.

Orlev, Uri. *The Island on Bird Street.* Boston: Houghton Mifflin Co., 1984.

Park, Ruth. *Playing Beatie Bow.* New York: Atheneum Pubs., 1982.

Paterson, Katherine. *Bridge to Terabithia.* New York: Thomas Y. Crowell Co., 1977.

_____ . *The Tale of the Mandarin Ducks.* Illustrated by Leo and Diane Dillon. New York: Dutton, 1990.

Paulsen, Gary. *Hatchet.* New York: Bradbury, 1987.

Perrault, Charles. *Little Red Riding Hood.* Illustrated by Sarah Moon. Mankato, Minn.: Creative Education, 1983.

_____ . *Puss in Boots.* Illustrated by Marcia Brown. Charles Scribner's Sons, 1952.

Potter, Beatrix. *The Tale of Peter Rabbit.* New York: Warne, 1902.

_____ . *The Tale of Squirrel Nutkin.* New York: Warne, 1903, 1986.

Pullman, Philip. *The Ruby in the Smoke.* New York: Alfred A. Knopf, 1987.

Pushkin, Alexander. *The Tale of Czar Saltan or the Prince and the Swan Princess.* New York: Crowell, 1975.

Ransome, Arthur. *The Fool of the World and the Flying Ship.* New York: Farrar, Straus & Giroux, 1968.

_____ . *Old Peter's Russian Tales.* London: Jonathan Cape, 1916, 1984.

Rawlings, Marjorie K. *The Yearling.* New York: Macmillan, 1988.

Rawls, Wilson. *Where the Red Fern Grows.* New York: Bantam, 1974.

Ringgold, Faith. *Tar Beach.* New York: Crown, 1991.

Rosen, Michael, retold by. *We're Going on a Bear Hunt.* Illustrated by Helen Oxenbury. New York: Macmillan, 1989.

Roth, Susan. *We'll Ride Elephants through Brooklyn.* New York: Farrar, Straus & Giroux, 1989.

Rylant, Cynthia. *Children of Christmas.* New York: Watts, 1987.

Sara. *Across Town.* New York: Orchard, 1991.

Schwartz, Amy. *Oma and Bobo.* New York: Bradbury Press, 1987.

Segaloff, Nat, and Erickson, Paul. *A Reef Comes to Life: Creating an Undersea Exhibit.* New York: Watts, 1991.

Sendak, Maurice. *Where the Wild Things Are.* New York: Harper & Row, 1963.

Seredy, Kate. *The White Stag.* New York: Viking Press, 1937, Puffin, 1979.

Seuss, Dr. *The 500 Hats of Bartholomew Cubbins.* New York: Vanguard, 1938.

Silverman, Maida. *Anna and the Seven Swans.* Illustrated by David Small. New York: William Morrow & Co., 1984.

Silverstein, Shel. *The Giving Tree.* New York: Harper & Row, 1964.

Simon, Seymour. *Earthquake.* New York: Morrow, 1991.

Speare, Elizabeth. *The Witch of Blackbird Pond.* Boston: Houghton Mifflin Co., 1958.

Sperry, Armstrong. *Call It Courage.* New York: Macmillan Co., 1940.

Steptoe, John. *Mufaro's Beautiful Daughters: An African Tale.* New York: Lothrop, Lee & Shepard, 1987.

Tafuri, Nancy. *Have You Seen My Duckling?* New York: Greenwillow, 1984.

Taylor, Mildred. *The Gold Cadillac.* Illustrated by Michael Hays. New York: Dial Press, 1987.

_____ . *Roll of Thunder, Hear My Cry.* New York: Dial Press, 1976.

Taylor, Theodore. *The Cay.* New York: Doubleday, 1969.

Tejima, Keizaburo. *Fox's Dream.* New York: Philomel, 1987.

Tobias, Tobi. *Maria Tallchief.* New York: Crowell, 1970.

Tolstoy, Leo. *The Fool.* New York: Schocken, 1981.

Van Allsburg, Chris. *The Polar Express.* Boston: Houghton Mifflin Co., 1985.

_____ . *The Z Was Zapped.* Boston: Houghton Mifflin Co., 1987.

Verdy, Violette. *Of Swans, Sugarplums, and Satin Slippers: Ballet Stories for Children.* Illustrated by Marcia Brown. New York: Scholastic, 1991.

Viorst, Judith. *If I Were in Charge of the World.* Illustrated by Lynne Cherry. New York: Atheneum, 1981.

Voigt, Cynthia. *Dicey's Song.* New York: Atheneum Pubs., 1982.

Whipple, Laura, compiled by. *Eric Carle's Animals Animals.* Illustrated by Eric Carle. New York: Philomel, 1989.

White, E. B. *Charlotte's Web.* Illustrated by Garth Williams. New York: Harper & Row, 1952.

Wiesner, David. *Free Fall*. New York: Lothrop, Lee & Shepard, 1988.

_____ . *Tuesday*. Boston: Clarion, 1991.

Wilder, Laura Ingalls. *Little House in the Big Woods*. Illustrated by Garth Williams. New York: Harper & Row, 1932, 1953.

Willard, Nancy. *Pish, Posh, Said Hieronymus Bosch*. Illustrated by Leo and Diane Dillon. Orlando: Harcourt Brace Jovanovich, 1991.

Williams, Margery. *The Velveteen Rabbit: Or How Toys Become Real*. New York: Doubleday & Co., 1922, 1958.

Wilner, Isabel. *A Garden Alphabet*. Illustrated by Ashley Wolff. New York: Dutton, 1991.

Wiseman, David. *Jeremy Visick*. Boston: Houghton Mifflin Co., 1981.

Wisniewski, David. *The Warrior and the Wise Man*. New York: Lothrop, Lee & Shepard, 1989.

Wood, Audrey. *King Bidgood's in the Bathtub*. Illustrated by Don Wood. San Diego: Harcourt Brace Jovanovich, 1985.

Yagawa, Sumiko. *The Crane Wife*. Illustrated by Suekichi Akaba. New York: William Morrow & Co., 1981.

_____ . *Momotaro, the Peach Boy*. Illustrated by Linda Shute. New York: Lothrop, Lee & Shepard, 1986.

Yorinks, Arthur. *Hey, Al*. Illustrated by Richard Egielski. New York: Farrar, Straus & Giroux, 1986.

Young, Ed. *Lon Po Po: A Red-Riding Hood Story from China*. New York: Philomel, 1989.

Zemach, Margot. *Jake and Honeybunch Go to Heaven*. New York: Farrar Straus & Giroux, 1982.

Zhensun, Zheng, and Low, Alice. *A Young Painter: The Life and Paintings of Wang Yani—China's Extraordinary Young Artist*. Photographs by Zheng Zhensun. New York: Scholastic, 1991.

Zvorykin, Boris. *The Firebird and Other Russian Fairy Tales*. New York: Viking Press, 1978.

Chapter Twelve

After completing this chapter on reading and literature, you will be able to:

1. *Identify and describe reading–literature approaches that are supported by research.*
2. *Describe and develop reading–literature approaches that are supported by schema theory.*
3. *Describe and develop approaches that increase students' opportunities to read literature.*
4. *Describe and develop approaches that encourage readers to use the whole text to create meaning.*
5. *Describe and develop approaches that help students improve their comprehension.*
6. *Develop a series of lessons that proceed from a web, to a guided discussion, and finally to a plot diagram.*
7. *Develop a semantic map or web to accompany a book.*
8. *Develop questioning strategies that focus on literary elements.*
9. *Describe and develop approaches that encourage students to make predictions about what they read.*
10. *Develop a unit focusing on literature and reading.*

Reading and Literature

T The following statement from a lead article in *Reading Today* emphasizes the national thrust to include more literature in reading programs: "Everywhere you look, there seems to be renewed interest in the use of children's literature in the reading program. This trend is evident in increased coverage of the topic in conference presentations, journal articles, and books" (Miller & Luskay, 1988, p. 1). Newspapers and popular journals also emphasize this need to make literature a dominant force in reading programs. For example, an article released by the New York Times Service (Hechinger, 1988) reported the following conclusion of recent studies on reading achievement: "Children's literature must be the core of every reading program because real literature touches the lives of children. It makes children want to read and to think about and comprehend what they have read" (p. E16).

Miller and Luskay (1988) attribute the interest in literature to community concern that children are not learning to read and are not reading; realization that literature is important to children; support for activities that promote the fun and enjoyment of reading; and realization that basal readers are limited in that they ignore classic children's literature, provide few good contemporary literature selections, and limit children's interactions with books. Miller and Luskay emphasize that teachers can use literature to introduce children to a wide variety of reading experiences as well as to support the reading curriculum.

Interest in literature in the reading curriculum is not merely an American phenomenon. May (1987) describes a literature program based on a Canadian curriculum structure. Sawyer (1987) reviews Australian and British studies that support a strong literature-based reading curriculum. Arguing that it is no longer acceptable to separate learning to read and reading to learn, he states: "Researchers have been unable to study how and why children learn to read through literature without at the same time addressing the question of how they acquire competence in dealing with literary structures" (p. 33). Sawyer contends that the story structures chosen to teach reading are important because the structures themselves teach the rules of narrative organization. According to this argument, the materials chosen to be read or listened to are just as important as the processes being used. Meeks (1983) provides additional strong support for using literature in the reading curriculum. From her experience as a British educator, she concludes that students who fail to learn to read have not learned "how to tune the voice on the page, how to follow the fortunes of the hero, how to tolerate the unexpected, to link episodes'' (p. 214). Interaction with literature is viewed as one of the most important ways to develop these capabilities in students.

THE READING–LITERATURE CONNECTION

In the literature-based view, reading is not the ability to perform a set of isolated skills. Rather, reading encompasses understanding, appreciating, and enjoying all types of literature. In this view, literature can be used to develop or support the reading curriculum, to teach or reinforce reading skills, and to introduce students to a variety of good and enjoyable books. Students discover that reading is more than skill lessons, workbook pages, and disconnected short stories. Through literature, students discover that reading can become a lifelong pursuit that offers both knowledge and enjoyment. This belief in the power of literature is reinforced by a study by Freppon (1990) investigating students' feelings about the purposes and nature of reading. Findings indicated that students in literature-based programs view reading as language- and meaning-based. An appreciation of language and an emphasis on meaning are certainly two of the goals of any reading and language arts curriculum.

Many published reading programs now contain entire selections of children's literature, some of which are reproduced in a "big book" format ideal for group sharing.

Educators who use and recommend literature-based reading instruction emphasize its dynamic nature. For example, according to Taxel (1988), the literature-based classroom is "fluid and dynamic, . . . a place where educators see literature as central to the curriculum, not as an occasional bit of enrichment undertaken when the real work is completed." (p. 74)

Instructional Formats

The instructional formats of effective literacy programs that focus on children's literature are varied. They range from small- or large-group instruction to independent work (Hiebert & Colt, 1989). One form of literature activity is led by the teacher using teacher-selected materials that relate closely to specified objectives. These lessons provide guidance in such critical strategies as reading for the theme or main idea, evaluating the author's development of characters, understanding the author's point of view, and understanding the characteristics of particular genres. During teacher-led instruction, students can read or listen to the same text or they can read different texts. In both cases, the students find and discuss examples relevant to the instruction. Teachers can also develop mini-lessons in which they model or demonstrate how to approach a difficult concept or passage. Instruction includes considerable discussion as students explore various strategies and try them out with the teacher's guidance.

Another form of instruction includes considerable teacher- and student-led interaction with materials selected by both teachers and students. Instruction usually takes place in small groups, with students having many opportunities to share their new understandings and to respond individually to the literature. In small groups, students can practice strategies presented during teacher-led instruction. Students can be grouped according to interests and needs.

A third instructional format relies on independent reading of student-selected literature. At this stage, students apply their reading abilities independently, and they develop their evaluation skills by choosing their own books. Teachers can include sustained silent reading, recreational reading, and reading for various content projects and units.

Hiebert and Colt (1989) emphasize the desirability of including all three formats in a literature program: "When teachers focus only on independent reading of student-selected material, they fail to consider the guidance that students require for becoming expert readers. A focus on teacher-led instruction fails to develop the independent reading strategies that underlie lifelong reading. A total reading program should contain various combinations of teacher and student interaction and selection of literature so that children develop as thoughtful, proficient teachers" (p. 19).

Instructional formats frequently make reference to three types of literature: core literature, extended literature, and recreational literature (Norton, 1992). *Core literature* refers to books selected for in-depth analysis. Students read and discuss these books as they analyze literary elements, identify genres, and discuss their responses. Core books are selected because they represent the best examples for the specific instructional purpose. They may be used to introduce various units because they are likely to stimulate writing and discussion.

Extended literature includes works that teachers can assign to individuals or to small groups of students. In studying these books, students apply knowledge gained during the analysis of core books. The extended books may be used for literature units, small-group interaction, or independent activity. For example, after students discover the characteristics of a fable during a teacher-directed lesson, they can read other fables and discuss how their extended books meet or do not meet the criteria for fables. During this second phase, students can meet in small groups as they consider specific qualities of fables, or they can receive more individualized guidance. Thus, extended reading can involve both teacher- and student-led interaction, as well as independent application.

Recreational literature refers to the literature recommended for enjoyable independent reading. Recreational literature includes books students select from classroom, school, and community libraries. Teachers, librarians, and parents can also recommend titles to ensure that students are reading literature that allows them to apply specific skills and broaden their understandings. For example, after students complete a unit on historical fiction, many of them want to continue reading books in this genre. If a unit has focused on the pioneer family through Laura Ingalls Wilder's *Little House in the Big Woods* (1932, 1953) and other "Little House Books," students frequently enjoy continuing with books such as Carol Ryrie Brink's *Caddie Woodlawn* (1935, 1963), Patricia MacLachlan's *Sarah, Plain and Tall* (1985), and Louise Moeri's *Save Queen of Sheba* (1981).

Along with emphasizing the importance of varied instructional formats, Five (1988) recommends mini-lessons that focus on such literary elements as characterization, setting, flashbacks, and book selection. After each lesson, the students read related literature, discuss the books, and complete writing activities. According to Five, the program dramatically increases independent reading, peer discussion of literature, and student evaluation in areas such as believability of characters and effectiveness of language and dialogue. The sequence—a mini-lesson followed by reading, discussing, and writing—is similar to that recommended by Hiebert and Colt (1989) for effective literature-based programs. The sequence also has much in common with Zarrillo's (1989) recommended use of core books that emphasize teacher-led instruction, literature units that include small-group discussions and independent work, and self-selected literature.

Responding to Literature

Developing students' comprehension of literature is a complex process. Calfee and Drum (1986) identify three essential components for reading comprehension: "A text, a reader of the text, and an interpretation of the text by the reader" (p. 834). Literature texts range from fairly simple narrative structures in folktales to elaborate novel-length plots with interwoven themes; detailed characterizations; and vivid, complex language styles. Reading requirements vary with the complexity of the text. In addition, each of the genres of literature has unique requirements: the form of poetry is different from that of biography, expository texts require unique reading skills and have different purposes than realistic fiction, and mythology is different from fantasy with respect to its fundamental belief system. Even within expository texts, the writing varies from simple descriptive material to structures and concepts that develop complex ideas, such as cause–effect relationships.

Readers add another dimension as they bring their emotional, cultural, and scholastic backgrounds to the reading task. Readers approach literature with their previous knowledge of a subject and their unique purposes for reading the literature. They derive quite different meanings from the same literature. Rewarding interpretations of literature require personal responses that allow readers to connect experiences, emotions, and text; to understand and appreciate the unique requirements of different literary elements and genres; and to apply various strategies to derive meaning from what they read.

When literary critics discuss meaning related to literature, they frequently emphasize at least two types of meaning—efferent and aesthetic. Rosenblatt (1985) distinguishes between the two. In her view, efferent reading focuses attention on "actions to be performed, information to be retained, conclusions to be drawn, solutions to be arrived at, analytic concepts to be applied, propositions to be tested" (p. 70). In contrast, aesthetic reading focuses on "what we are seeing and feeling and thinking, on what is aroused within us by the very sound of the words, and by what they point to in the human and natural world" (p. 70). A worthy literature-based program should include both efferent and aesthetic responses to literature.

Purves and Monson (1984) emphasize the relationships between text and reader as the reader draws meaning from a text. They describe two important functions of literature programs in preparing readers through a transactional approach. First, the program provides a literary schema that allows students to discuss books using words such as *plot, metaphor, characterization, theme, style,* and *tone.* The program enables students to explain their reasons for deciding that one book is better than another. Second, the program exposes students to a variety of critical questions to consider; for example, How does the literature or character affect me? What does it mean? How good is it?

Purves and Monson also stress both efferent and aesthetic responses to literature:

> It would seem . . . that students should be exposed to a variety of critical questions, including those which are personal and affective, those which are analytic, those which are interpretive, and those which are evaluative. Each of these questions can be answered intelligently and answering each can help a student learn to read and think and feel. And you can teach students how to answer them. (p. 189)

According to Probst (1989), students must learn not only to extract information from texts, but also to derive their own unique meanings from the experience of reading. When reading poetry, for example, most readers seek experience, not information; individual meaning, not facts. Probst argues that students should be encouraged "to attend not only to the text, but to their own experience with it as well—the emotions, associations, memories, and thoughts that are evoked during the reading of the work" (p. 180). Probst recommends the following types of questions to help students respond personally to literature:

1. Questions about initial emotional and intellectual responses: What was your first response or reaction to the literature? What emotions did you feel as you read the literature? What ideas or thoughts were suggested by the literature? Did you feel involved with the literature or did you feel distanced from it?

2. Questions involving attentiveness: What did you focus on as you were reading? What word, phrase, image, or idea caused this focus? If you were to write about your reading, on what would you focus? Would you choose an association or memory, an aspect of the text, something about

the author, or something else about the literature? How would you describe an image that was called to your mind by the text? What caused you the most trouble in reading the literature? Do you think this is a good piece of literature? Why or why not?

3. Questions about the context in which the literature was encountered: What memories were evoked from reading the literature—memories of people, places, sights, events, smells, feelings, or attitudes? What sort of person do you think the author is? How did your reading differ from that of your classmates? How was your reading similar? What did you observe about others in the class as they read or discussed the literature? Does this text remind you of another piece of literature—a poem, a play, a film, or a story? If it does, what connection do you see between the two works?

These questions can be easily included in a discussion of any literary work. Many literature authorities stress that students' first responses to a literary work should be personal ones. For example, Cianciolo (1990) recommends that teachers encourage personal responses during the first sharing of a picture storybook before introducing any other activities related to the literature. You can ask students to share their personal responses by discussing them, writing about them, or drawing pictures or creating other artwork. They can even select music that reflects their responses to the mood or content of the literature.

Applying Reading Research to Literature-Based Programs

Reading research provides support for teaching literature and guidelines for how to teach it. Studies show that certain approaches enhance reading comprehension, understanding of story structures, and appreciation of literature. For example, Feitelson, Kita, and Goldstein (1986) found that first graders who were read to for twenty minutes each day outscored comparable groups in decoding, reading comprehension, and active use of language. Their findings also indicated, however, that adults need to help students interpret the literature by elaborating beyond the text. Feitelson, Kita, and Goldstein attribute the first graders' success to an enriched information base; an introduction to unfamiliar language; exposure to various story structures and literary devices, such as metaphor; and an increased attention span.

Research with fifth- through eighth-grade students indicates that a literature-based reading program combining children's literature and teaching strategies that emphasize cognitive processes, story structures, and modeling significantly improves reading comprehension and attitudes toward reading (Norton, 1987).

Early and Ericson (1988) identify nine findings from reading research that should influence how you teach literature in the reading curriculum. As you read these findings, notice that you can emphasize both efferent and aesthetic responses in many of the approaches recommended for developing comprehension:

1. Readers use their knowledge of texts and contextual cues to create meaning during reading. (Schema theory also suggests that successful readers use their knowledge of various kinds of texts, the world, and contextual cues to create meaning.) Literature provides one of the best sources for gaining and reinforcing this knowledge.

Reading while young increases the likelihood of children becoming lifelong readers.

2. Readers learn to read by reading. This finding implies that students need opportunities to read a variety of literature.

3. Readers need to experience whole texts to increase understanding. Literature is an obvious choice for encouraging students to derive meaning from longer texts.

4. Good readers understand when their reading makes sense. They also are aware when their reading processes break down. Reading different genres that include several literary elements encourages students to use a variety of corrective strategies.

5. Readers improve their comprehension if teachers use modeling, direct explanation, and questioning. These strategies work especially well with literature.

6. Good readers use textual cues and their prior knowledge to make predictions. Again, literature is an excellent source for making predictions.

7. Students benefit from direct teaching of reading strategies. Discussions about literature help to develop reading strategies.
8. Students need help in looking for details from which to draw inferences. Strategies such as modeling for inferring characterization are especially valuable with literature.
9. The range of students' reading achievement grows at each successive grade level. A variety of literature helps meet their growing needs.

By applying these findings to specific literature approaches, you also meet the requirements for effective literature-based instruction (Norton, 1992). Within the activities are teacher-led lessons that can be related to the core curriculum. Many activities also encourage broad reading and responding to literature through teacher and student interaction in small groups, as well as through independent reading. Some approaches highlighted by the research findings emphasize self-selection of recreational reading materials.

SCHEMA THEORY

Schema theory has valuable implications for teachers of literature within a reading curriculum. According to schema theory, the basis for comprehending and remembering ideas in stories and other types of texts is a reader's schema, or organized knowledge. A reader uses prior knowledge of various kinds of texts, knowledge of the world, and the clues supplied by a text to create meaning. According to Anderson (1985), "in schema-theoretic terms, a reader comprehends a message when he is able to bring to mind a schema that gives a good account of the objects and events described in the message" (p. 372).

Prior knowledge and past experiences are extremely important for comprehending and appreciating all types of stories. Afflerback (1990) found that readers automatically construct main ideas when they have prior knowledge of the content. Likewise, Gauntt (1990) showed that prior knowledge of both text structures and content improves comprehension of expository text. Reading stories to students helps them develop schemas for story structures, vocabulary, language patterns, and other literary elements. These sets of knowledge and expectations are valuable when the students face similar structures, vocabularies, and literary elements in their independent reading. Consequently, teachers and parents should read, tell stories, and talk about a wide variety of literature. To provide the maximum knowledge base, make sure that the literature includes a wide variety of genres and language patterns.

Schema theory emphasizes the importance of activating relevant prior knowledge and helping students fill in gaps in knowledge before they read. Valuable instructional strategies include prereading discussions that review prior knowledge, provide information to help students use their prior knowledge, and identify any gaps in knowledge. If you identify any gaps, or if prerequisite knowledge is lacking, remedy this situation before the students approach the literature. Make use of maps, pictures, films, and historical time lines.

As an example, prior to reading Patricia MacLachlan's *Sarah, Plain and Tall* (1985), focus prereading discussions on prairie life in the 1800s to activate previous knowledge and identify knowledge gaps. You can ask the students to close their eyes and pretend they are living in the 1800s. They are sitting on the front steps of a pioneer house located in one of the prairie states. Ask them to use their imaginations and describe what they see when they look toward the prairie. (They should see prairie grass on gently rolling plains, wheat fields, dirt roads, and expanses of space in which the prairie meets the sky. If there are vehicles on the road, they should be drawn by horses.) Next, ask the students to turn around and describe the house. They can see inside because the door is open. The author of *Sarah, Plain and Tall* frequently contrasts the prairie setting and Sarah's familiar Maine coast. Ask the students to close their eyes and pretend they are on the Maine coast. When they look toward the ocean, what do they see? When they look toward the land, what do they see? Such prereading discussions will help the students understand the settings, conflicts, characters, and comparisons in the story.

Illustrated books are especially good for activating prior knowledge or introducing a time or place. For example, Kathy Jakobsen's paintings of the frontier setting in Reeve Lindbergh's *Johnny Appleseed* (1990) provide details of life in the late 1700s and early 1800s. Wendell Minor's paintings for Diane Siebert's *Heartland* (1989) develop the rural nature of a more contemporary Middle West. Ted Lewin's illustrations for Florence Heide and Judith Gilliland's *The Day of Ahmed's Secret* (1990) provide an excellent introduction to Cairo, Egypt, while Catherine Stock's illustrations in *Armien's Fishing Trip* (1990) introduce students to an African village and the life of people who earn their living from the sea. Alice Provensen's *The Buck Stops Here: The Presidents of the United States* (1990) provides a pictorial representation of the personal and political facts and historical events associated with the presidents of the United States. This book is especially good as an introduction to the time frames of historical fiction selections.

You may also use picture books and easier stories to activate students' prior knowledge or prepare them for story structures of more difficult texts. For example, use Selina Hastings' *Sir Gawain and the Loathly Lady* (1985) and Margaret Hodges's *Saint George and the Dragon* (1984) to activate prior knowledge or introduce new information about legends, quests, and chivalry before students read longer legends about King Arthur.

LEARNING TO READ BY READING

Students who demonstrate mastery of higher level reading skills do considerable reading; choose books from a variety of genres, including both fiction and nonfiction; and select books beyond required reading (National Assessment of Educational Progress, 1981). Reading widely and frequently allows students to develop knowledge about the world and literature that helps them comprehend new experiences. Students who read widely and frequently also develop appreciation for literature and increase the likelihood that they will become lifelong readers. This section considers four approaches to reading and literature: uninterrupted sustained silent reading, recreational reading groups, computer-assisted reading programs, and focus units.

Uninterrupted Sustained Silent Reading (USSR)

Cline and Kretke (1980) found that students who had been in a three-year USSR program had more positive attitudes about reading and going to the library than

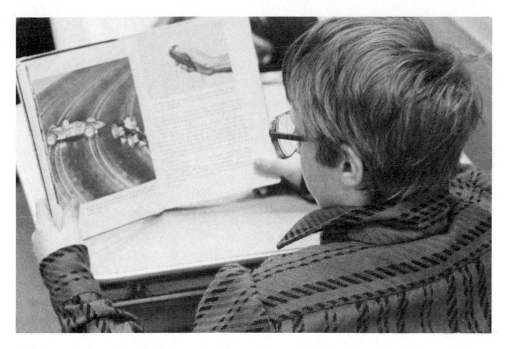

Uninterrupted sustained silent reading is an approach that works with all age groups.

students who had no experience with USSR. The USSR group also considered reading to be an important activity. Classes or whole schools that motivate students to read through the USSR approach provide about a thirty-minute period in the school day or several periods during the week in which students silently read self-selected books. If the total school is involved, the principal, the secretaries, and the custodians stop their normal duties and also read. Within the classroom, everyone reads, including the teacher. For this approach to succeed, students must have access to a wide selection of literature and teachers must have information about the interests and reading levels of the students. In addition, teachers must have knowledge of books that they can recommend to their students.

This approach is applicable to all reading levels. Even kindergarten students can "read" the pictures in picture storybooks and wordless books. Easy-to-read books allow first- and second-grade students to practice their reading skills. High-interest/easy-reading books allow low-ability older readers to extend their knowledge and increase their appreciation of many genres of literature. The book *High Interest–Easy Reading* (Matthews, 1988) suggests sources for older students. The literature available for this activity should include various genres.

Students and teachers can self-select books from the school, classroom, or public libraries, or they can bring selections from home. Students in one school read books selected from the local Reading Is Fundamental (RIF) program. This activity was especially popular because the books became the private property of the students and formed the beginnings for private collections. Some teachers introduce USSR prior to a visit to the public library. Students then get library cards and their first books from the library at the same time. These books become the sources for USSR. The relationship between the library cards and USSR can be beneficial; students learn about the library and the various library services, such as story hours and summer reading programs.

Recreational Reading Groups

Recreational reading groups have some of the characteristics of USSR, but usually contain more structure, encourage students to self-select literature around a specific theme or topic, and include opportunities for the students and teachers to respond verbally to their reading experiences. Students may select books from a wide range of literature or focus on a narrower range of topics, genres, or characteristics. If topics are the focus, form groupings according to interests rather than achievement levels, and include a range of literature to meet the reading levels of all of the students in the group. If the materials are totally self-selected, divide the class into about three groups. Designate a leader for each group. Have the students bring their books to one of these three reading circles and read for about thirty minutes. (Vary the time according to attention spans and reading interests.) Then, have the students relate something interesting about the books they have been reading.

The first time that you form recreational reading groups, have one large group with you as leader. Model independent reading behavior for the total group and begin the discussion by relating something interesting about the book you are reading. After students understand the procedures, more interaction develops in smaller groups. Place competent readers next to less-efficient readers to help with unknown words. Groups may stay together until their books are finished, or the groups may change from one session to the next.

Recreational reading groups structured around specific topics encourage reading of a wider variety of materials and genres than students might otherwise select. They also encourage literary appreciation, as students and teachers consider why they enjoy or dislike the selected literature. For example, the topic humor appeals to students. As they read humorous books, they learn to appreciate the various ways in which authors develop humor. Have the students begin by selecting, reading, and sharing humorous incidents in picture books. These books are excellent choices for stimulating aesthetic responses. Have the students share their enjoyment of the humor developed by both author and illustrator. For example, the various books by Theodore Geisel (Dr. Seuss) develop humor through nonsensical characters and word play. Surprising and unexpected situations provide the humor in Grace Chetwin's *Box and Cox* (1990), Reeve Lindbergh's *The Day the Goose Got Loose* (1990), Audrey Wood's *King Bidgood's in the Bathtub* (1985), and Catharine O'Neill's *Mrs. Dunphy's Dog* (1987). Exaggeration provides the humor in Patricia Polacco's *Meteor!* (1987) and in James Stevenson's *Could Be Worse* (1977). Caricature and ridiculous situations provide the humor in James Marshall's illustrations for Grimm's *Red Riding Hood* (1987). The language and situations provide the humor in Mem Fox's *Hattie and the Fox* (1987) and Paul Galdone's *The Three Wishes* (1967).

Recreational reading groups may explore preposterous characters and situations in such modern fantasy selections as Carl Sandburg's *Rootabaga Stories* (1922), Astrid Lindgren's *Pippi Longstocking* (1950), and Richard and Florence Atwater's *Mr. Popper's Penguins* (1938). Other groups may experience and explore humor in contemporary realistic fiction; for example, in the humorous person-versus-person conflict in Beverly Cleary's *Ramona and Her Father* (1977), in the preposterous situations in Beverly Keller's *No Beasts! No Children!* (1983), in the exaggerations in Helen Cresswell's various "Bagthorpe Saga" books, and in the role reversals in Lois Lowry's *Anastasia on Her Own* (1985). After reading and responding to numerous humorous books in the recreational reading groups, students can read or listen to stories selected by Pamela Pollack in *The Random House Book of Humor for Children* (1988). Now, they can decide why these books might have been chosen to exemplify humor. The students may also choose to develop their own book of humor.

Authors who interest students may also be the focus of recreational reading groups. Maurice Sendak, Beverly Cleary, Virginia Hamilton, Lloyd Alexander, and Tomie de Paola are authors who have numerous books in print. Likewise, poets such as Myra Cohn Livingston, Byrd Baylor, Edward Lear, and Jack Prelutsky have sufficient poetry collections in print to serve as choices for recreational reading groups. A search through the index of a children's literature text will help you identify numerous authors and their books (for example, Norton, 1991).

Computer-Assisted Reading Programs

Computer applications in reading receive mixed evaluations. Kinzer, Sherwood, and Bransford (1986) point out: "Reading appears to be a difficult instructional area to computerize. Much reading software is little more than a high-technology workbook, although software which merely imitates a workbook format is generally a poor use of resources. Much of the software available and being used in schools is of the drill-and-practice variety. Although there is much that reading researchers still do not know about reading, most would agree that no one learns to read from an instructional diet of drill and practice alone" (p. 215). In contrast, these computer experts identify promising reading approaches, including simulation activities that encourage planning and decision making; language experience approaches that allow teachers to type in a story, quickly print and distribute the story, develop lessons from the story, and keep records of students' vocabularies for individualized word banks; tutorial programs; and data management programs that allow teachers to record test scores and other vital information.

Likewise, other computer experts identify both poor and good types of computer-assisted reading programs. Attitudes toward computer-assisted reading programs are also changing. In 1983, Mason, Blanchard, and Daniel were extremely critical of reading software because the programs overemphasized drill and practice activities. In their latest text, Blanchard, Mason, and Daniel (1987) are more optimistic. They state: "The microcomputer reading software of the late eighties promises to fulfill many of the unmet promises made about earlier computer-based instruction programs. Reading software is improving and will continue to improve, but we have a long way to go" (p. 23).

Many of the same advantages cited for using computers during the writing process are also cited for computer-assisted instruction in reading. Bradley (1982), for example, uses a microcomputer to develop language experience lessons with first graders. She types the children's stories into the computer rather than printing them on a chart. She believes that the approach has the following advantages: (1) it is highly motivating, (2) it is easily transcribed, (3) stories are easily changed, and (4) printed copies are ready for immediate distribution. Disadvantages relate

Group teaching using computers can be efficient for the teacher and motivating for students.

to limitations in various programs. Likewise, both Grabe and Grabe (1985) and Smith (1985) state that computers aid teachers and students during language experience activities. Whitaker, Schwartz, and Vockell (1989) also recommend using computers during the language experience approach. They state: "The computer has the potential to help overcome some of the difficulties that have accompanied the language experience approach. In particular, the speech synthesizer and the word processor offer new opportunities for using the LEA to teach beginning reading. The computerized word processor enables students to play with their own ideas and to integrate the reading and writing process" (p. 31). Two programs that combine word processing and speech synthesis are Dr. Peet's Talk/Writer (Hartley) and My Words (Hartley).

Numerous software programs reinforce sight words, expand vocabularies, provide drill in phonics, analyze words according to structural analysis, and test comprehension. Software reading programs are not the only choices for language arts teachers. Reading clinicians who teach children with reading and/or motivational problems recommend some computer games. If games require reading of words or printed descriptions, comprehending written text, and responding to questions or directions, they may enhance reading.

Children with special educational needs seem to benefit from computer-assisted instruction in reading, just as they do from using computers to aid writing. Harper and Ewing (1986) found that having children read passages and answer questions on computer was more effective than having them complete similar tasks in workbook format.

Some educators use children's interests in technology to encourage reading. For example, Sharp (1985) used graphics programs such as Logo to have children create their own designs for a memory quilt as depicted in Ann Jonas's literature selection, *The Quilt* (1984). She used word processing programs and various books that contain specific language patterns, such as Margaret Wise Brown's *The Important Book* (1949). For this activity, she typed the recurring pattern into the word processor, leaving blanks for the main ideas. Children created their own stories, as follows:

The important thing about _____ is that it is _____ . It is _____ and _____ , and _____ . But the most important thing about _____ is that it is _____ .

Other ideas include creating original concrete poems after reading concrete poems in poetry anthologies and creating flowcharts illustrating major decisions or actions in a story. The software program *Story Tree* published by Scholastic allows students to develop cognitive maps or flowcharts related to literature selections.

Following a review of research related to computer-assisted instruction, Balajthy (1989) presents the following conclusions:

1. The effectiveness of computer-assisted instruction increases as the grade level or ability of students decreases.
2. Computer-assisted instruction is consistently more effective than traditional instruction, but the amount of improvement is low to moderate and the cost-effectiveness is uncertain.
3. Structured computer-assisted instruction, with emphasis on direct instruction, is more effective for achievement gains than is unstructured computer-assisted instruction.
4. Computer-assisted instruction results in savings of learning time.
5. Computer-assisted instruction generates favorable attitudes toward computers.

Focus, or Thematic, Units

Focus units help teachers and students focus on specific reading skills and literary attributes. They also encourage considerable individual reading, as students choose literature for either unit-related projects or enjoyment. If one of the objectives of a unit is to provide opportunities for students to expand their reading, then include independent reading activities and expanded reading lists. Moss's (1984) publication *Focus Units in Literature: A Handbook for Elementary School Teachers* provides guidelines for developing units for first through sixth grades. The guidelines include objectives, teacher-directed group sessions, individualized and independent activities, culminating projects, annotated bibliographies of literature for teacher-directed sessions, and extensive bibliographies of literature designed for independent reading. Norton's (1992) publication, *The Impact of Literature-Based*

Reading, develops units on topics entitled "Comparing Different Versions of the Same Folktale," "Developing Understanding and Appreciation for the Native American Culture," "Developing Understanding and Appreciation of the Black Culture," "Responding to Contemporary Issues Through Science Fiction," "Friendship Themes in Literature," "Survival Themes in Literature," and "Overcoming Obstacles and Hardships." At the conclusion of this chapter, there is a unit for teaching reading skills and literary appreciation associated with biography.

You may develop focus topics or themes that include one genre of literature or several genres. You may also combine knowledge from various content areas within your unit. For example, Norton and Kracht (1991) developed a unit combining literature and the following themes from geography: (1) location: position on the Earth's surface; (2) place: landscape and people; (3) relationships within places: cultural and physical relationships and how relationships develop; (4) movement: movement of people, movement of materials, and movement of ideas; and (5) regions: how they form and change. Books were identified that exemplified the themes and a series of activities was developed in which students used their knowledge of geography to locate and analyze each of the themes in literature. The literature included a wide range of genres, including folklore, contemporary realistic fiction, biography, and informational literature.

A fifth-grade teacher developed a "Pioneer Spirit" unit to help students consider the personal, psychological, physical, spiritual, and social qualities that fostered early exploration. The literature included historical fiction, biographies, autobiographies, informational materials, and poetry. Teacher-directed lessons helped students read the literature, gain insights, and draw possible conclusions from the past and present. Smaller group activities encouraged students to consider the kind of pioneer spirit that would be required to explore universes of the future or to restructure environments on planet Earth. Other activities required independent reading and considerable research. The teacher, librarian, and students identified literature from as many genres as possible related to the topic.

WHOLE-TEXT APPROACHES

Literature is an excellent resource for encouraging students to read further before making judgments about what they have read so far. Characters change over the course of a story, themes develop throughout a book, and conflicts develop until problems are overcome or personal conflicts are resolved. Good readers use a number of effective strategies to make these connections. Poor readers have fewer effective strategies from which to choose.

Short picture storybooks are ideal for introducing the concept of reading a whole text to develop understanding. The stories can be read, and reread if necessary, to see how characters, conflicts, and themes are developed throughout a total text.

Help students search for themes of a story and then support those themes through specific examples from the book. First, use an entire short text to derive meaning. Second, use details from the text to support the generalizations arrived at from reading the whole text. Read the text to the students so that they see how important it is to consider the whole book. Then, reread the book to help the students search for support for the theme. Following this activity, provide oppor-

Rereading text helps students search for themes.

tunities for students to read additional stories, identify themes, support these themes with evidence, and respond to the themes. You may use this activity with any grade level, but use simplified terms with younger students. Older students may search for deeper symbolism or higher level relationships between themes, characters, and conflicts.

Before introducing a specific book, tell the students that they will be searching for important themes in a story by answering the question, What is the author trying to tell us that would make a difference in our lives? Tell them that the author may have more than one important message. After the students have identified what the author is trying to tell them, follow with, "How do we know that the author is telling us _____ ?" To answer the second question, have the students search for clues and think about all of the ways in which the author makes readers believe that something is important. Evidence from the book may include illustrations, a character's actions, a character's thoughts, or the story ending. Or, the author may tell the reader directly.

Introduce Ann Grifalconi's *Darkness and the Butterfly* (1987). Tell the students that this is a story about Osa, a young African girl who has a problem to solve. Ask them to listen carefully to the story to discover what the author is saying that will make a difference to Osa and that may even make a difference in their lives. (This is a good book for personal response because many children have had similar feelings.) Now, read the whole book, showing the pictures as you proceed. After you finish the book, allow the children to share their personal responses to the book and then lead a discussion in which the students identify the following themes:

1. It is all right to have fears. We all have fears that cause us problems.
2. We can and must overcome our fears.

Write each of these themes on the chalkboard, allowing room to place evidence under each one. (You may choose to word the themes differently.) Read the story a second time. Encourage the students to identify as much evidence for each theme as possible. Your themes and evidence should include lists similar to the following:

1. It is all right to have fears. We all have fears that cause us problems:
   a. The illustrations show contrasts between the beauty of the world in the daytime without fear and the monsters that haunt Osa's mind at night.
   b. The actions of the mother show that she understands Osa's fear. She gives Osa beads to help Osa feel less afraid.
   c. The actions of Osa show her fear when she contrasts day and night.
   d. The wise woman tells Osa that she too was once afraid, "specially at night!"

2. We can and must overcome our fears:
   a. The story of the yellow butterfly, the smallest of the small, that flies into the darkness suggests that even small beings must and do overcome fear. (The story is based on an African proverb: "Darkness Pursues the Butterfly.")
   b. The wise woman tells Osa, "You will find your own way." (She compares Osa to a butterfly.)
   c. The dream sequence allows Osa to face the night and discover new characteristics of the night.
   d. The actions of the butterfly show need to overcome fear.
   e. Osa expresses self-realization: "I can go by myself. I'm not afraid anymore."
   f. The author states that Osa, the smallest of the small, "found the way to carry her own light through the darkness."
   g. The butterfly symbolizes the author's belief that the smallest, most fragile being in nature can light up the darkness, trust the night, and not be afraid.

Notice that the support for the theme occurs at several levels. Young readers can discuss concrete examples found in illustrations and characters' actions. Older readers may extend discussion into symbolism and the proverb used by the author to develop the theme.

This technique of searching for themes and supporting themes with evidence from the total book is successful with almost any piece of literature. This example was chosen because the themes are reinforced in multiple ways and students can discover the desirable interrelationships between theme, setting, characterization, conflict, and illustrations. Show students that there are several ways to approach the problem. Poor readers may benefit especially from pointing out the reinforcement found in illustrations.

Following this teacher-directed activity, provide opportunities for students to read additional short stories, identify the themes found in the whole text, and then support these themes with evidence.

Other approaches that encourage students to acquire meaning from the whole text include using plot structures to develop understanding of conflict and plot development described in Chapter 11. When developing plot structures, students must use the total story to develop understanding.

COMPREHENSION APPROACHES

Comprehension of text is usually identified as one of the major goals for reading instruction. Yet, critics of comprehension instruction frequently claim that students are not taught the processes required for comprehension and that comprehension questions do not encourage students to develop higher thought processes. This section considers three major approaches to comprehension: semantic mapping or webbing, modeling, and questioning.

Semantic Mapping or Webbing

Many of the approaches for using semantic maps or webs were introduced elsewhere in this text. These approaches are equally beneficial for the reading class. For example, the webbing of literature elements for *Mufaro's Beautiful Daughters,* developed in Chapter 11, is an excellent way to improve understanding and stimulate discussion in the reading class.

To develop a semantic web around the relevant vocabulary in a piece of literature, place the title of the book in the center of the chalkboard. On arms extending from the center, place the important words from the story. Use a brainstorming session to help the students fill in synonyms and definitions. You may use this activity as a prereading vocabulary introduction. You may also use it to extend understandings. Ask the students to consider exact meanings for the words while reading the story. Have them select terms that seem closest to the meaning developed in the story, add new words or even phrases obtained from the story, and use the words identified in the semantic web for story comprehension.

The following example uses a semantic web with the vocabulary from Tomie de Paola's *The Legend of the Bluebonnet* (1983). Notice the progression from a vocabulary web, to discussion of context clues that relate to the vocabulary words, and finally to a plot diagram that reinforces the vocabulary words and places them in the context of the total book. This lesson was developed and taught with lower achieving fifth- and sixth-grade students (Norton, 1987). However, you can use the procedure for all grades with students reading at all ability levels. In addition, you can use the procedure with many other books.

Semantic maps or webs are a tool to help extend understanding of story structure or to introduce vocabulary.

Before reading *The Legend of the Bluebonnet,* draw a web on the chalkboard similar to that shown in Figure 12–1. Place the title of the book in the center and extend the vocabulary words *drought, famine, selfish, healing, plentiful, restored, valued,* and *sacrifice.* Before reading, introduce the words and brainstorm with the students to define the words and find synonyms. However, do not complete the extended vocabulary during this first experience. Add meanings after reading and discussing the book. (Note that your final web may be larger. During and following the reading, you may wish to add words. For example, you and the group may consider *Comanche, shaman,* and *miraculous* important for understanding.)

Following the introductory brainstorming, read the story and discuss the vocabulary words within the context of the story. In this story, cause–effect relationships as well as opposite meanings are important. For example, write the first paragraph on the chalkboard with the vocabulary word *drought* underlined:

‘Great Spirits, the land is dying, your People are dying, too’ the line of dancers sang. ‘Tell us what we have done to anger you. End this drought. Save your people. Tell us what we must do so you will send the rain that will bring back life.’ (p. 1, unnumbered)

After reading the paragraph, ask the students to identify, circle, and discuss the words that mean *drought:* "land is dying." Next, have them identify, circle, and discuss the words that indicate why the drought must end and show the dangerous consequences of the drought: "Save your people," "bring back life." Now, have them discuss the consequences of drought if something that would save the people and bring back life was requested by the most powerful person in the tribe. Discuss

FIGURE 12–1
Vocabulary web for a book

picture clues that show the hot, yellow sun, and the dry, brown earth. As the reading of the story proceeds, extend the meaning of *drought* to include cause–effect relationships:

drought → famine, starving
rain → grass, plenty

and opposite meanings:

drought → rain; earth will be green and alive

Continue this procedure until all the vocabulary words are discussed in context. Now view the web again, add terms if necessary, and identify words previously considered for their meanings.

Finally, draw a plot diagram and encourage students to use as many of the vocabulary words as appropriate when they place the important incidents from the

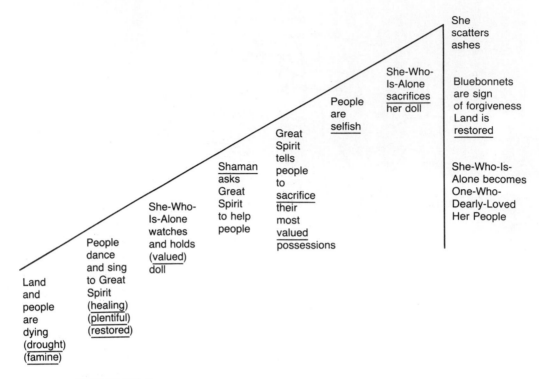

FIGURE 12–2
Plot development highlighting vocabulary

story on this structure. Figure 12–2 shows a plot diagram developed with sixth-grade students. The underlined words were identified by the students during this teacher-led activity. The words in parentheses are vocabulary words drawn out by the teacher during the plotting experience. For example, when the group did not identify *drought* in the beginning problem, the teacher said: "What words did you use for the land and the people are dying?"

This approach develops comprehension of vocabulary, emphasizes the importance of context and picture clues in deriving meaning from text, and relates the vocabulary back to the plot of the story. These interrelationships are especially important for poor readers, who may not make the connections.

You may use webs to identify various types of activities associated with books. This type of web is useful for the teacher who is exploring how books might be used in the curriculum. Figure 12–3 shows the many different activities that could accompany a picture-book version of a folktale. Notice especially the applications of the book in reading, cognitive development, and language development. Also notice that the book is especially good for using stimulating approaches to literature such as storytelling and creative drama. Keep a file of webs showing book possibilities for future reference.

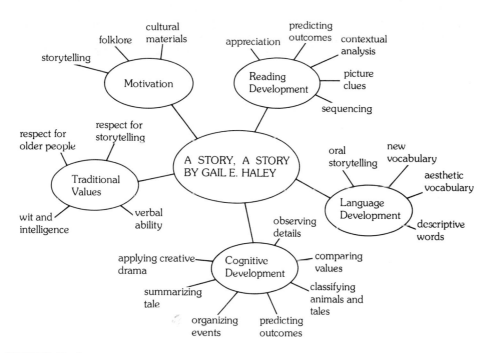

FIGURE 12–3
A web illustrating various activities that might accompany a book

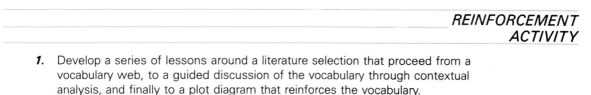

1. Develop a series of lessons around a literature selection that proceed from a vocabulary web, to a guided discussion of the vocabulary through contextual analysis, and finally to a plot diagram that reinforces the vocabulary.
2. Develop a semantic map or web to lead a literary discussion of the book.
3. Develop a semantic map or web that shows the various activities that might accompany the book.

Modeling

Dole, Duffy, Roehler, and Pearson (1991) identify modeling as one of the most effective strategies for developing students' comprehension. Pearson and Camperell (1985) state: "If teachers want students to get the author's message, they are well advised to model for students how to figure out the author's general structure" (p. 338). According to Early and Ericson (1988), research findings indicate that modeling and explaining or describing what students should do during a comprehension lesson is often ignored. They argue that modeling strategies are especially important in teaching students how to draw inferences because failure to make inferences frequently results in poor comprehension.

A modeling approach based on research conducted by Roehler and Duffy (1984) and Gordon (1985) is detailed elsewhere in this text. Chapter 3 presents modeling for inferring characterization using Patricia MacLachlan's *Sarah, Plain and Tall* (1985). Chapter 11 describes a modeling activity designed to develop understanding of similes using Leo Lionni's *Swimmy* (1963). We will now illustrate how you can develop a modeling lesson plan using the 1992 Newbery Medal winner, Phyllis Reynolds Naylor's *Shiloh* (1991).

FOR YOUR PLAN BOOK
Modeling for Inferring Characterization

Core Book: **Shiloh** (1991), Phyllis Reynolds Naylor

Objectives:

1. To be involved in a modeling activity to show how to analyze evidence from the text and speculate about characters.
2. To understand the requirements for effective reasoning.
3. To appreciate and understand how the author implies characterization.
4. To write a response that reflects understanding of the author's implications.

Procedures:

1. Identify the requirements for effective reasoning so that the students will understand those requirements. For this lesson, students must be aware that effective inferring of characterization requires them to go beyond the information an author provides in a text. They must use clues from the text to hypothesize about a character's emotions, beliefs, actions, hopes, and fears. Students must also be aware that authors develop characters through dialogue, narrative, a character's thoughts or the thoughts of others about the character, and a character's actions.

2. Develop an introduction to the process of inferring characterization. Share with students examples of each type of characterization. You may draw these examples from literature or create your own. Ask the students to show how they can make discoveries about characters through dialogue, narration, a character's thoughts, thoughts of others about the character, and a character's actions.

    Explain to students that in this modeling activity they will first listen to you read an excerpt from a book, ask a question, answer the question, provide evidence from the story that supports the answer, and provide the reasoning you used to reach the answer. Tell the students that after they have listened to you proceed through the sequence, they will use the same process to answer questions, identify evidence, and explore their own reasoning. As part of this introduction, discuss the meanings of the terms *evidence* and *reasoning*. Encourage the students to identify evidence about a character in literature and to share how they would use this evidence. They should realize that their own experiences, emotions, and reactions are important aspects of the reasoning process. (This sequence and discussion encourages students to draw on both efferent and aesthetic responses to literature.)

3. Stress the importance of inferring. Ask the students to explain why it is important to be able to make inferences about characters in literature. Encourage them to discuss how understanding characterization makes a story more exciting, enjoyable, and believable. They also should understand that they can infer characterization in their own writing.

4. Provide an introduction to the story. *Shiloh* takes place in the hills of West Virginia and focuses on a boy who tries to save a dog from a cruel owner. The author develops both a strong theme that cruelty to animals is wrong and a personal conflict as the boy tries to save the dog without telling his parents. The boy, Marty, the dog Shiloh, and Shiloh's owner, Judd, are all well-defined characters.

   To introduce the setting, you might use pictures of mountains in the eastern United States. Books such as Cynthia Rylant's *When I Was Young in the Mountains* (1982) allow students to visualize the rural setting. You can ask students how they might respond if they found a dog they believed had been mistreated. How would they try to solve the problem and save the dog? Tell the students they will be reading a book in which a boy tries to save a dog. But, the boy discovers, this is not always easy.

5. Provide the first modeling example. Read from the beginning of the book through the paragraph, "I take the .22 rifle Dad had given me in March on my eleventh birthday and set out up the road to see what I can shoot. Like to find me an apple hanging way out on a branch, see if I can bring it down. Line up a few cans on a rail fence and shoot 'em off. Never shoot at anything moving, though. Never had the slightest wish" (p. 12). Ask, "What do Marty's actions and thoughts reveal about him?" Answer, "I think that Marty likes to practice shooting his gun, but he would never shoot something that is alive. I think Marty cares a great deal for living things and might not like to hunt, hurt, or kill." Provide the evidence from the text: "Marty's actions show that he takes out his gun to practice, but everything that he wants to shoot—the apple and the cans—is not alive. He thinks to himself that he has never shot anything that moves." Provide the reasoning you used to reach your answer. For example: "As I read this story I could see a boy who was comfortable with his rifle. As the author describes Marty's wish to practice his shooting, he refers to harmless actions. I feel that Marty is going out to have a good time with his gun. I also noticed 'never' twice in Marty's thoughts about shooting things that moved. I know from my own experience that when I think 'never,' I really mean what I am thinking. When I read this description, I feel Marty's sadness when he thinks about using the rifle for anything other than hitting cans and apples. I also remember Marty's earlier reactions when he could not eat the rabbit his father had killed with a gun."

6. Provide the second modeling example. At this point, verify that the students understand the procedure. If they do not, model another example completely. When the students understand the process, let them join the discussion by providing answers, evidence, and reasoning. Have the students jot down brief answers to the questions, noting their evidence and reasoning. These notes will improve the quality of the discussion that follows each question.

7. Continue reading the book until you come to the next logical discussion point. Interesting inferences can be drawn from the way in which Marty meets the beagle and responds to the beagle's actions: "I look, and about fifteen yards off, there's this shorthaired dog—white with brown and black spots—

not making any kind of noise, just slinking along with his head down, watching me, tail between his legs like he's hardly got the right to breathe. . . . The dog gets up and backs off. He don't even whimper, like he's lost his bark. Something really hurts inside you when you see a dog cringe like that. You know somebody's been kicking at him. Beating on him, maybe" (p. 14). Ask, "What do these actions imply about the characters of the dog and Marty? What do we know about each of these main characters in the story?" Ask the students to answer the question. They will probably provide answers similar to this one, although you should encourage a range of speculation and ideas: The dog may be shy around people, or maybe he has been hurt and is afraid of people; The dog does not act like a normal, happy dog. Something is wrong; Marty's feelings reveal that he is a very sensitive person and would probably never hurt an animal. Ask the students to provide evidence for their answers. For example: The author tells us that the dog was slinking and watching the boy, but he did not come to the boy; The dog did not bark—he put his tail between his legs and cringed; Marty's thoughts and feelings show that the cringing dog is very disturbing to him. Ask the students to provide reasoning. For example: The author gave a very sad description of the dog. I have seen dogs that act like that. I believe that the dog was telling us that he had been hurt by someone and that he was afraid of people; I reacted to the words that the author used; The picture of the dog made me so sad that I thought something was wrong; I know from my own experience what a young dog should look and act like if he is happy. This dog is not happy; I could feel Marty's sadness. I know what it feels like to hurt inside.

8. Continue this process, having the students discuss the many instances of implied characterization in the book. There are numerous examples, such as the following:

Text: After Marty reveals that he would like to become a veterinarian and his father tells him that it would take a lot of money, Marty responds with a simile: "My dream sort of leaks out like water in a paper bag. 'Could be a veterinarian's helper,' I suggest, my second choice" (p. 22). Question: "What is the author telling us about Marty's dream and his character? What are his feelings?"

Text: When Marty thinks about why he does not like Shiloh's owner, Judd Travers: "The reason I don't like Judd Travers is a whole lot of reasons, not the least is that I was in the corner store once down in Friendly and saw Judd cheat Mr. Wallace at the cash register. Judd gives the man a ten and gets him to talking, then—when Mr. Wallace gives him change—says he give him a twenty. I blink, like I can't believe Judd done that, and old Mr. Wallace is all confused. So I say, 'No, I think he give you a ten' " (p. 22). Question: "What do Judd's actions reveal about his character and what does Marty's response reveal about Marty?"

Text: When Marty's father insists that he must return Shiloh to Judd: "We're in Shiloh now. Dad's crossing the bridge by the old abandoned gristmill, turning at the boarded-up school, and for the first time I can feel Shiloh's body begin to shake. He's trembling all over. I swallow. Try to say something to my dad and have to swallow again" (p. 24). Questions: "What do Shiloh's reactions reveal about his feelings? What do Marty's reactions reveal about Marty? At this point, do you believe that Marty is correct about Judd's treatment of the dog? Why or why not?"

Longer stories, such as *Shiloh,* lend themselves to discussions according to chapters. Students can read and discuss several chapters each day. After each session, ask the students to summarize what they know about Marty, Shiloh, and Judd. Ask, "What do you want to know about these characters?"

While the students are reading this book, or after they have completed the book, ask them to describe their personal responses to Marty, Shiloh, and Judd in writing.

REINFORCEMENT ACTIVITY

Develop a modeling lesson and share it with your class. You may complete the book, *Shiloh,* or select a new book.

Questioning

Critics of comprehension instruction emphasize that questions too frequently encourage students to respond at the lowest levels of thinking. Ambrulcvich (1986) found that questions in literature anthologies focus on the two lowest types of thinking on Bloom's Taxonomy. Reading textbooks emphasize the need for developing questioning strategies that require higher level thought processes, and basal readers usually identify the taxonomy level of comprehension questions.

Do not accompany all literature selections with questioning. Nevertheless, develop a framework for designing questions that help students focus on certain aspects of a story and use their higher level thought processes.

You can develop questioning strategies by using Barrett's Taxonomy of Comprehension (1972), or you can focus on developing appreciation of the literary elements of setting, plot, characterization, theme, and style. Both approaches have merit. The following examples are based on Beverly Cleary's *Dear Mr. Henshaw* (1983). As you read the questions, consider the advantages or disadvantages of each approach. How would the development of both series of questions help students improve their questioning strategies and their ability to focus on important elements in literature?

The first series of questions illustrates how questioning strategies can be developed around Barrett's four levels of reading comprehension: literal recognition or recall, inference, evaluation, and appreciation. The questions listed exemplify each level of the taxonomy. More questions or fewer might be advisable, depending on the book and the instructional purpose.

Literal recognition requires students to identify information provided in the literature. You may require students to recall information after reading or listening to a story, or to locate information while reading. Literal questions often include such words as *who, what, where,* and *when:*

1. *Recall of details:* How old was Leigh Botts when he first wrote to Mr. Henshaw? What is the name of Leigh's dog? What is Leigh's father's occupation? Where does the story *Dear Mr. Henshaw* take place?

2. *Recall of sequence of events:* What sequence of events caused Leigh to place an alarm on his lunch box? What sequence of events caused Leigh to write to Mr. Henshaw and to write in his diary?
3. *Recall of comparisons:* Compare the way that Leigh thought of his mother and the way that he thought of his father.
4. *Recall of character traits:* Describe Leigh's response to Mr. Henshaw when Mr. Henshaw asks Leigh to answer ten questions about himself.

When children infer an answer to a question, they go beyond the information the author provides and hypothesize about such things as details, main ideas, events that might have led to an occurrence, and cause–effect relationships. Inference is usually considered a higher level thought process; the answers are not specifically stated within the text. Examples of inferential questions include the following:

1. *Supporting details:* At the end of the book, Leigh says that he "felt sad and a whole lot better at the same time." What do you think he meant by this statement?
2. *Main idea:* What is the theme of the book? What message do you think the author is trying to express?
3. *Comparisons:* Think about the two most important characters in Leigh's life, his mother and his father. How are they alike and how are they different? Compare Leigh at the beginning of the book, when he is writing to Mr. Henshaw, with Leigh at the end of the book, when he is writing in his diary and writing true stories for school.
4. *Cause–effect relationships:* If you identify any changes in Leigh, what might have caused those changes?
5. *Character traits:* On page 73, Leigh decides that he cannot hate his father anymore. What does this tell you about Leigh and about his father? Why do you think Leigh's father sent him $20.00?
6. *Outcomes:* At one point in the story, Leigh wishes that his mother and father would get back together. What do you think would have happened to the story if that happened? How would Leigh's life have changed? How would his mother's life have changed? What might have been the outcome of the writing contest at school if Leigh had not had the advantages of his advice from Mr. Henshaw?

Evaluation questions require children to make judgments about the content of the literature by comparing it with external criteria, such as what authorities on a subject say, or internal criteria, such as the reader's own experience or knowledge. Following are examples of evaluative questions:

1. *Adequacy or validity:* Do you agree that an author would take time to write to a child and to take such an interest in him? Why or why not?
2. *Appropriateness:* Do you believe that Leigh's story, "A Day on Dad's Rig" was a good story for the *Young Writers' Yearbook?* Why or why not?
3. *Worth, desirability, or acceptability:* Do you believe that Leigh had the right to feel the way he did toward his father? Why or why not? Do you believe that Leigh was right in his judgment that his father did not spend enough time with him? Why or why not? Was Leigh's mother's judgment right at the end of the book? What would you have done?

Appreciation of literature requires a heightening of sensitivity to the techniques that authors use in order to create an emotional impact. Questions can encourage students to respond emotionally to the plot, identify with the characters, react to an author's use of language, and react to an author's ability to create visual images through words. Following are examples of questions that stimulate appreciation:

1. *Emotional response to plot or theme:* How did you respond to the plot of *Dear Mr. Henshaw?* Did the author hold your attention? If so, how? Was the theme of the story worthwhile? Why or why not? Pretend you are either recommending this book for someone else to read or recommending that this book not be read; what would you tell that person?

2. *Identification with characters and incidents:* Have you ever felt like Leigh? Have you ever known anyone who felt like Leigh? What caused you or the person to feel that way? How would you have reacted to the theft of an excellent lunch?

3. *Imagery:* How did the author encourage you to see Leigh's home, neighborhood, and school? Close your eyes and try to describe your neighborhood or town. How would you describe it so that someone else could "see" it?

The preceding examples are not organized according to any sequence for presentation to students, but they do indicate the range of questions to consider when strengthening students' reading comprehension abilities. The next series of questions was written about the same book, *Dear Mr. Henshaw,* but examines specific literary elements within the text.

1. *Setting:* How have Leigh's living conditions changed as a result of his parents' divorce? What are some of the positive and some of the negative aspects of where he is now living? Leigh's mother describes their new home by saying, "At least it keeps the rain off, and it can't be hauled away on a flatbed truck." How does this statement reflect her opinion of their past living conditions? What is the importance of having a stable environment in which to live?

2. *Plot:* What problem is causing conflict for Leigh and his family? Why does Leigh write his first letter to Mr. Henshaw? Why does he continue to write letters even after the assigned letter is completed? What does Mr. Henshaw suggest that Leigh do? How do Mr. Henshaw's suggestions help Leigh accept the divorce? What causes Leigh to stop writing "Dear Mr. Pretend Henshaw"? What was the significance of this title when he first began his journal? Why does Leigh have such a problem with his lunch box? What plan does he devise to overcome the thief? Does the plan work? What happens as a result of his plan? What does Mrs. Badger say to Leigh that makes him feel good? What does Leigh learn from Mrs. Badger? What helps Leigh understand his mother's point of view about the divorce? How do we know that he understands his mother's point of view? What happens to help Leigh understand his father's point of view? What does Leigh do to show that he understands his father's point of view? How does Leigh feel about himself and his family at the end of the story?

3. *Characterization:* How does Leigh view himself in comparison to the other children in his school? What three events help improve Leigh's self-

image? How does Leigh's self-image change as a result of these events? How does the following passage reflect changes in Leigh's character and reflect his growth: "I don't have to pretend to write to Mr. Henshaw anymore. I have learned to say what I think on a piece of paper. And I don't hate my father either. I can't hate him. Maybe things would be easier if I could" (p. 73). How does Leigh's real father differ from the father of his dreams? In what ways does Leigh's father disappoint him? How do we know that Leigh's father still cares about Leigh and Leigh's mother? How does the character of Leigh's mother differ from that of his father? What actions show that Leigh's mother wants to care for and to provide for her son?

4. *Theme:* Why did Beverly Cleary write *Dear Mr. Henshaw* in a diary and letter format? Why is this an effective way to present this book? What important messages do the letters and the diary reveal about Leigh and the problems that he faces within himself and his family? How does either the real or the imaginary exchange of letters and ideas with Mr. Henshaw allow the author to develop this message? How does Leigh change because of these exchanges? At what point do you think Leigh starts to accept his parents' divorce? At what point in the story does Leigh begin to understand that his parents are not going to get back together? How do we know that divorce is difficult for everyone involved? How do we know that divorce may not be blamed on one person in the family? Based on the theme, what do you think would be another good title for this book?

5. *Style:* From whose point of view is this story told? How do you know that the story is written from the point of view of a young boy? How does the format of *Dear Mr. Henshaw* differ from that of most other fictional books? How does this diary and letter format allow the author to develop the theme, the conflict, and the characters? Does the author's style make you believe that you are or are not reading the writing of a real boy who is facing believable problems? This book deals with some painful and serious emotions. At the same time, the author is able to make readers laugh. How does she accomplish this?

REINFORCEMENT ACTIVITY

1. Analyze the two series of questions. Are there any overlapping topics? What are the strengths and the weaknesses of each questioning framework? Do you agree that students gain more literary understanding by focusing on the literary elements of setting, plot, characterization, theme, and style but they gain insights about balancing questions so that they include all levels of thought processes from the taxonomy of comprehension?

2. Choose a book and develop questioning strategies to accompany that book. Try to include the strengths from a focus on literary elements and the taxonomy of comprehension.

Literature card files Files of questioning strategies, book summaries, difficult words or concepts, and other activities that can accompany a book are beneficial. You will need to know a great deal about specific children's books to use them effectively in recreational reading, individualized instruction, storytelling, or social studies. College students should begin to read a number of children's books from the various categories of literature. It is easier to file pertinent information about a book when you read it than to try to remember it months or even years later. The following format is valuable to many students:

1. Title
2. Author, publisher, date
3. Reading level
4. Interest level
5. Category
6. Difficult words or concepts
7. Short summary
8. Questions to ask during a conference. Include factual, inferential, evaluative, and appreciative, with possible answers to each question.
9. Several follow-up activities to use with the book
10. Other books on same subject or by same author

Put the information on a large filing card or a separate page in a loose-leaf notebook, and group the cards or pages by grade level or category. Some students also code their files by color so they can easily choose an appropriate card from a file box. Figures 12–4 through 12–6 are examples of cards developed by preservice teachers.

You can use literature files with summaries, questions, and activities in numerous ways. The questions provide a framework for discussion for extending understanding of a book, with individual children or during small-group discussions with several children who have read the same book. You can use the activities for enrichment experiences after a child or a group of children have read the book. At times, you may use the files only to find books to recommend for recreational reading. If you have listed other books, you can recommend additional books to a child who has a specific interest or wants to explore a topic further.

PREDICTION APPROACHES

Good readers use textual cues and prior knowledge to make predictions. You may stimulate and enhance predictive skills at any level. Books such as John Ivimey's *The Complete Story of Three Blind Mice* (1987) and Scott Cook's *The Gingerbread Boy* (1987) encourage students to join in during repetitive phrases. Predictable story structures such as "The Three Billy Goats Gruff" and "The Three Little Pigs" encourage students to hypothesize about plot developments. Teaching students to identify foreshadowing, a device in which an author suggests plot development before it occurs, is another method for helping students use cues in the text to predict outcomes. A detail in an illustration, the mood of the story, the author's choice of words, a minor episode, or a symbol presented early in the story may foreshadow later action.

Horton Hears a Who   Second Grade/Lower Elementary
Dr. Seuss. New York: Random House   Fantasy: Animals

Difficult words: *murmured, nonsensical, vigor, vim, hullabaloo*

Summary: Horton the elephant hears a cry from a small dust speck flying by him. He decides there must be a small creature on the dust speck, and proceeds to save the small "Who." He puts the small "Who" on a clover and carries it with him everywhere. The other characters make fun of him and think he has gone crazy. At the end of the story, the other characters hear the small Who and Whoville is saved by the smallest of all.

Questions (F = Factual, I = Inferential, E = Evaluative, A = Appreciative):

(F) **1.** Where did the eagle drop Horton's clover? (In a field of clover.)
(I) **2.** What do you think this story is trying to tell you about small people? (Small people are important even though they are small.)
(I) **3.** What do you think made Horton decide to take care of the small Who? (Answers will vary: He wanted to have some new friends; he did not want the Whos to get hurt.)
(E) **4.** Was it important for the other creatures to hear the Whos? Why or why not? (Yes, because every little Who was important and they would not be saved if they could not be heard.)
(A) **5.** How would you have felt if you lived in Whoville? (Answers will vary: I would have been glad that Horton took care of us and made us feel important.)

Activities:

1. Have the students role-play an experience with a younger brother or sister to see how it would feel to be small. Have them discuss how they would want people to treat them.
2. Have the students write a creative story telling what they would do to protect the small Whos.

Other Books by Dr. Seuss:
Horton Hatches the Egg, How the Grinch Stole Christmas, And to Think That I Saw It on Mulberry Street, The Sneetches and Other Stories, Scrambled Eggs Super!

FIGURE 12–4
A card for a book for early-elementary grades

Picture storybooks are good introductions to foreshadowing because the illustrations frequently include details that suggest later actions. For example, one of Don Wood's illustrations for Audrey Wood's *Heckedy Peg* (1987) shows the young girl feeding a friendly blackbird through the window; the same blackbird later helps the children by leading their mother to the witch who has transformed them into food. Another illustration shows the boisterous children playing within their cottage, while through the window the witch is approaching. Later, the witch arrives at the door, the children disobey their mother, and the children allow the witch to enter the cottage. Students may try to search for such clues while they read a book, or they may reread a book, searching for clues that foreshadow later developments. You may use many other books in the same way. For example, Richard Egielski's illustrations of a bird with hands in Arthur Yorinks's *Hey, Al* (1986) foreshadow the fate of Al and his dog Eddie.

Bill Cosby: *Look Back in Laughter*   Third–Fourth Grade
James T. Olsen   Biography

Summary: Bill Cosby lived his childhood years in a black ghetto. He got his first job shining shoes at age six. He later worked in a grocery store for eight dollars a day; he gave this money to his mother. His brother James died and his father, heavily in debt, left home. Bill did not do well in school and dropped out to join the Navy. He got his high school diploma in the Navy and later enrolled at Temple University. He earned money as an entertainer by telling jokes about his childhood. He first became popular during his television series *I Spy.* Since then, he has acquired millions of fans, but he tries to help everyone he comes in contact with. He gives heavily to charities and is also concerned with education. He wants to work with children because ''the one child who could have gone the other way but who changed his mind is worth everything.''

Factual Questions:
1. How old was Bill when he got his first job? What was it? (6; shining shoes)
2. Did Bill have a happy home life when he was growing up? (No; his father left his family and his brother died.)
3. What was Bill's first television show? (*I Spy*)
4. Who starred with Bill on his first show? (Robert Culp)
5. What are some charities Bill contributes to? (Boy Scouts, American Cancer Society, United Fund)

Inferential Questions:
1. Do you think Bill uses his money in a good way? Why? (Yes, he helps others.)
2. Why did Bill become a medic in the Navy? (They did not have to fight at the battlefront.)
3. Why did Bill use his childhood as a subject for jokes? (Everyone has some pleasant childhood memories and can relate to children.)

Evaluative Questions:
1. Is this a true story? How do you know?
2. Do you think Bill should have given all the eight dollars he made at the grocery store to his mother? Why or why not?
3. Do you think entertaining is a job that is well-suited to Bill Cosby? Explain.
4. Do you think Bill's wife's parents were right in not wanting her to marry him when he was working in a bar? Why or why not?

Appreciative Questions:
1. Have you ever seen or heard Bill Cosby? Did his life story sound like you thought it would? Explain.
2. Did you feel sorry for Bill as a child? Why or why not?
3. What does this story tell you about people who work hard for what they want?

Activities:
1. Write a script with jokes that Bill Cosby might use in a television show.
2. Write about the things a charity would do with the money Bill gave them.
3. Make a time line of important events in Bill Cosby's life.
4. Write a review of this book. Illustrate it, and show it to the class.
5. Compare this biography with others you have read. How are they alike? How are they different?

Other Books About the Lives of People:
Louis Braille: The Boy Who Invented Books for the Blind by Margaret Davidson
The Golda Meir Story by Margaret Davidson
Franklin D. Roosevelt, Gallant President by Barbara Silberdick
Arthur Mitchell by Tobi Tobias
Lincoln: A Photobiography by Russell Freedman

FIGURE 12–5
A card for a book appropriate for third or fourth grade

Across Five Aprils Sixth Grade and Up
Irene Hunt Historical Fiction: Civil War

Summary: This is the story of the Creighton family and the Civil War as seen through the eyes of Jethro, the youngest member of the family. Jethro never fought in the war, but he saw all his brothers, cousins, and his only surviving sister leave home to fight for either North or South. The book opens in April 1861, and gradually, all of Jethro's brothers go to war. Tom, Eb, and John go to fight for the North, while Bill, Jethro's favorite brother, goes to fight for the South. Jethro is left with his parents to work on the farm. Two families in the community blame the Creightons for Bill's view on the war, and one night their barn is burned and their well filled with kerosene. Jethro's sister leaves to marry her fiance, who was wounded while fighting for the North. Jethro keeps up with the war through newspaper reports provided him by the newspaper editor, Ross Milton. Jethro becomes lonely for the past and comes to realize how horrible war is. He has to make many decisions and grows up in many ways during the five Aprils in this book.

Factual Questions:
1. In what part of the country does this book take place? (Illinois)
2. Why is the book called *Across Five Aprils*? Is the title appropriate? (The book covers five Aprils of the Civil War.)
3. Why was Jethro the only one who did not go to war? (He was too young.)
4. Why was the Creighton's barn burned and their well contaminated? (One of their sons was fighting for the South.)
5. Why did Jethro want to keep up with his studies? (He idolized Shad, his schoolmaster, and knew study would help him in life.)

Inferential Questions:
1. Why was Ross Milton so special to Jethro? (He was an understanding adult; he understood Jethro's need for education.)
2. If Jethro had spare time, what do you think he would spend it doing? (Educational projects, reading, etc.)
3. How did Jethro feel about the men of the community helping them so much to rebuild their barn? (Very grateful; he felt how good it was to have understanding friends.)

Evaluative Questions:
1. Do you think the author portrays the feelings and problems of the Civil War accurately, even though it is through the eyes of a young boy? Explain.
2. Do you think Jethro should have helped the man who burned down the barn? Why or why not?
3. Do you think Jethro had a right to feel overburdened? Did he?

Appreciative Questions:
1. How did the author present historical facts in an interesting and real way?
2. Did the Civil War seem more interesting to you? In what way?
3. Did you learn more about the Civil War than just the names and dates of the battles? Explain.

Activities:
1. Make a time line of the five years covered by the book. Include on the time line the important things that happened in Jethro's life.
2. Draw a map of the United States and have students code the Union and Confederate States by color.
3. Write a letter that Jethro might have written to Shad in Washington, D.C., after Shad had been injured fighting for the North.
4. Write a letter to a history teacher and recommend the book for teaching about the Civil War. List several reasons why the book would be a good instruction book about the war.

Other Historical Fiction Books or Books About the Civil War:
The Drinking Gourd by F. N. Monjo
The Slave Dancer by Paula Fox
Zoar Blue by Janet Hickman
Rifles for Watie by Harold Keith

FIGURE 12–6
A card for a book appropriate for upper-elementary grades

Illustrations in picture storybooks frequently foreshadow the ending, the type of story, and plot development by creating appropriate moods. For example, Marcia Brown's delicate lines and soft colors suggest a magical setting and foreshadow a fairy-tale ending in Charles Perrault's *Cinderella* (1954). In contrast, Charles Keeping's stark, black lines create ghostly, terrifying subjects and foreshadow the tale's sinister and disastrous consequences in Alfred Noyes's *The Highwayman* (1981). John Schoenherr's illustrations for Jane Yolen's *Owl Moon* (1987) and Marcia Brown's illustrations for Blaise Cendrars's *Shadow* (1982) allow students to look at the illustrations, analyze the mood that the illustrations create, and predict the type of story, type of conflict, and possible ending.

Terms that authors use to describe characters may provide clues to plot changes and even foreshadow themes and endings. For example, students may predict plot development, changing characters, and possible themes as they trace the significance of name changes in Sid Fleischman's historical fiction *The Whipping Boy* (1986). For example, the book uses the following names in reference to the Prince and to his whipping boy, Jemmy. The names in parentheses indicate who is using the specific name:

Prince	**Jemmy**
p. 1 Prince Brat (King, royalty)	p. 2 Common boy (narrator)
p. 4 Your Royal Awfulness (Jemmy)	p. 6 Jemmy-from-the-Streets (Prince)
p. 5 You fiddle-faddle scholar (tutor)	p. 6 Contrary rascal (Prince)
p. 8 No friends (Jemmy)	
p. 18 Empty-headed prince (Jemmy)	p. 20 My whipping boy (Prince)
p. 21 His Royal Highness (Prince)	p. 21 That ratty street orphan (Prince)

Changing Roles:

p. 21 Witless servant boy (Jemmy)	
p. 28 Whipping boy (Hold-Your-Nose Billy)	
p. 31 Jemmy-from-the-Streets (Jemmy)	
p. 32 Contrary as a mule (Jemmy)	
p. 33 Prince Blockhead (Jemmy)	p. 33 Imposter (Prince)
	p. 42 Unfaithful servant (Prince)
p. 53 A wounded bird (Jemmy)	
p. 53 Friend (Jemmy)	
p. 61 A brave one (Jemmy)	p. 61 Jemmy (Prince)
p. 61 Friend-O-Jemmy's (Prince)	
p. 70 Heir to the throne (Jemmy)	p. 74 My friend (Prince)
p. 88 Friend (Jemmy)	

In this example, notice how the changes in names and references to the main characters follow the plot, suggest changes in relationships, and even develop one of the themes of the book. Students and teachers both enjoy this searching for clues provided by the author to help them predict the story line.

Books for older students may use complex symbolism to foreshadow. In such books, students may identify symbols and hypothesize how the symbols foreshadow. For example, in Cynthia Voigt's *A Solitary Blue* (1983), students may trace

Jeff's changing attitudes toward the heron and predict how these gradual changes in attitude reveal Jeff's growing self-esteem. Likewise, in Voigt's *Dicey's Song* (1982), students may trace, discuss, and predict the importance of the author's reference to musical selections, a dilapidated boat, and a tree.

REINFORCEMENT ACTIVITY

1. Select a grade level and develop a list of books to encourage students to make predictions.
2. Develop a lesson in which you lead students in a search for clues that will help them predict plot development, character development, theme, or story ending.

FOR YOUR PLAN BOOK
A Literary Approach to the Study of Biography

This unit includes activities to enhance students' appreciation of biography as literature, encourage students to read carefully, and help students evaluate critically what they read. The unit objectives come from all of the language arts, including reading, speaking, listening, and writing. The bibliography includes books for a range of ability levels—from picture biographies to biographies appropriate for upper-elementary and middle-school students. The literary approach to biography emphasizes understanding of and appreciation for the techniques that authors use to tell about real people. The approach is concerned primarily with character development, but it also involves plot, setting, theme, and style.

Choose the literature and activities that are appropriate for your specific grade level. Use teacher-directed activities with the class and a specific book, and use other activities with individual students to encourage them to read widely and independently. Also include content and concepts from the social studies, history, and geography. Fleming and McGinnis's *Portraits: Biography and Autobiography in the Secondary School* (1985) contains additional ideas. Although the activities are designed for secondary students, you may adapt many of the excellent ideas for younger children.

Unit Objectives

1. To develop an appreciation for biography.
2. To analyze and critically evaluate plot in biography.
3. To analyze and critically evaluate characterization in biography.
4. To analyze and critically evaluate setting in biography.
5. To analyze and critically evaluate theme in biography.
6. To analyze and critically evaluate style in biography.
7. To integrate the language arts and English skills of reading, speaking, listening, and writing within a literature focus.

Biographies Discussed in This Approach

Adler, David. *Martin Luther King, Jr.: Free at Last* (1987)
Brooks, Polly. *Queen Eleanor: Independent Spirit of the Medieval World* (1983)
Coerr, Eleanor. *Sadako and the Thousand Paper Cranes* (1977)
Dalgliesh, Alice. *The Columbus Story* (1955)
D'Aulaire, Ingri, and D'Aulaire, Edgar. *Columbus* (1955)
Fido, Martin. *Oscar Wilde: An Illustrated Biography* (1987)
Fido, Martin. *Rudyard Kipling: An Illustrated Biography* (1987)
Freedman, Russell. *Lincoln: A Photobiography* (1987)
Fritz, Jean. *Where Do You Think You're Going, Christopher Columbus?* (1980)
Goodnough, David. *Christopher Columbus* (1979)
Goodsell, Jane. *Eleanor Roosevelt* (1970)
Grimble, Ion. *Robert Burns: An Illustrated Biography* (1987)
Hamilton, Virginia. *W. E. B. Du Bois* (1972)
Hamilton, Virginia (ed.). *Writings of W. E. B. Du Bois* (1975)
Roosevelt, Elliot. *Eleanor Roosevelt, with Love* (1984)
Ventura, Piero. *Christopher Columbus* (1978)
Whitney, Sharon. *Eleanor Roosevelt* (1982)
Yates, Elizabeth. *Amos Fortune, Free Man* (1950)
Yates, Elizabeth. *My Diary, My World* (1981)
Yates, Elizabeth. *My Widening World* (1983)

Procedures

Read, analyze, and discuss a biography according to the following literary elements:

1. Plot Development
   a. What is the order for the plot development? Does author use chronological order? flashbacks? How does the author present important information from the past that influences the biographical character?
   b. What time frame does the author emphasize? Why do you believe the author chose that time period in the character's life?
   c. What types of conflict does the biographer develop? Find examples of these conflict types. Why do you believe the biographer chose to emphasize these types of conflict?
      (1) Person versus self
      (2) Person versus person
      (3) Person versus society
      (4) Person versus nature
   d. What pattern of action does the author develop?
      (1) Rising action with identifiable climax and end of conflict.
      (2) Action moves from one incident to another incident. (There is a final climax but author leaves reader with a sense of uncertainty.)
      (3) Action moves with a tension that does not develop a climax. There is minimal suspense.
      (4) Action moves in a line that does not have one dramatic climax but may have several dramatic episodes.
   e. How does the author develop readers' interest in the plot?

(1) Find examples of interest-creating introductions. For example, how does Brooks attract your attention in this introductory paragraph to *Queen Eleanor: Independent Spirit of the Medieval World:*

> The French King, Louis the Fat, lay dying in his hunting lodge where he had been taken to escape the summer heat, the flies, the stench of Paris. His hands shook with palsy, and his bleary eyes could hardly see. Recently he had grown so fat that he could no longer mount a horse or bend over to tie his shoes. (p. 7)

(2) Find examples of direct quotes from the biographical character or photographs that the author uses to stimulate interest. For example, how does Freedman attract attention in the introduction to Chapter 1 in *Lincoln: A Photobiography:*

> If any personal description of me is thought desirable, it may be said, I am, in height, six feet, four inches, nearly; lean in flesh, weighing, on average, one hundred and eighty pounds; dark complexion, with coarse black hair and grey eyes—no other marks or brands recollected. (p. 1)

(3) Find examples of any other techniques, such as foreshadowing of events to come.

f. Additional activities can help students analyze plot development in biography:

(1) Draw and label the life-line of a character such as Yates's *Amos Fortune, Free Man.* Draw and label the pattern of action developed by the author. Compare the two drawings. How are they alike, and how are they different? Try to account for any differences.

(2) Compare the pattern of action for two biographies written about the same person but written by two different authors. For example, choose two of the biographies listed about Christopher Columbus or about Eleanor Roosevelt. Try to account for any differences.

(3) Compare introductory paragraphs in several biographies. Choose the example that you think is the most effective. Prepare the paragraph as an oral reading, share it with your class, and tell why you believe the introduction is effective.

(4) Develop a class chart of types of conflict found in biographies. Categorize the biographies according to their predominant conflict. Are there any similarities among biographies in a specific category? For example, are person-versus-society conflicts found more often in biographies about civil-rights leaders?

2. Characterization

a. How does the author reveal the character of the biographical person? Find and discuss examples of any of the following ways that authors can reveal character:

(1) Actions of the character.

(2) Dialogue that reveals the speech of the character.

(3) Thoughts of the character.

(4) Thoughts of others toward the character.

(5) Narrative—comments about the character made by the author.

b. Using each of the aforementioned examples, what did you learn about the character? Was each technique appropriate for the biography? Could

Cover photograph of Russell Freedman's book **Lincoln: A Photobiography** *(from* **Lincoln: A Photobiography** *by Russell Freedman, copyright © 1987 by Russell Freedman. Reprinted by permission of the Chicago Historical Society and Clarion Book/Ticknor & Fields, a Houghton Mifflin Company)*

the author substantiate that each way of revealing character was authentic? (Look for references in the biography and for sources used by the author.)

c. How did the person change over the course of the biography? What caused any changes? How did the author show the changes?

d. Who influenced the biographical subject? How did the author develop these supporting characters?

e. Who is telling the biographical story? What is the relationship of the author to the biographical subject? How does this relationship influence the tone of the biography and the attitude toward the biographical subject? For example, answer these questions for Elliot Roosevelt's *Eleanor Roosevelt, with Love.*

f. Additional activities can help students analyze characterization in biography:

(1) Identify scenes in the biography that include dialogue between characters. Dramatize the scenes using the dialogue presented in the literature. Discuss the impact of the dialogue with the class.

(2) Compare the characterizations developed in two biographies written about the same person but by different authors.

(3) If possible, read something written by the biographical subject. How does the viewpoint in the writing compare with the viewpoint developed in the biography? For example, compare Hamilton's *W. E. B. Du Bois: A Biography* and *Writings of W. E. B. Du Bois,* which were written by Du Bois but edited by Hamilton.

(4) Rewrite a scene from a biography but choose to write the scene from a different point of view. Discuss how this different point of view changes the presentation of the character. How do the tone and the attitude change?

3. Setting

a. How important is the setting in biography? Why is the setting important or not important?

b. What role does the setting have in biography? Locate examples, if used, and discuss the importance of each of these purposes for a biography:

(1) Providing historical background.

(2) Setting the mood.

(3) Providing an antagonist.

(4) Providing symbolic meanings.

(5) Providing illumination for character and clarifying conflict.

c. What are the various settings developed in a biography? How much detail is included?

d. Is the setting in the past or present? How does the author inform readers of the time period?

e. How much influence does the setting have on character?

f. Additional activities that help students understand and evaluate setting in biography:

(1) Locate the specific locations mentioned in a biography. Find these locations on a map and locate descriptions of these places in geography texts or other nonfictional sources. How do the descriptions compare with the settings in the biography?

(2) Locate the specific dates and historical happenings identified in a biography. Check the accuracy of these dates and happenings in other nonfictional sources.

(3) Choose a specific setting described in a biography. Draw the setting as if the setting were a backdrop for a stage production. Is there enough detail to complete the drawing? If not, what information would improve your drawing?

4. Theme

    a. There may be one primary theme in a biography and several secondary themes. Search for and identify any primary and secondary themes in a biography. How are these themes integrated into the biography? Does the title of the biography reflect the theme? For example, what could Adler's title *Martin Luther King, Jr.: Free at Last* imply?

    b. An author may literally state a theme or merely imply it. Search for evidence of themes that the author states and themes that the author implies. Why do you believe the author used each approach? What was the impact?

    c. Themes in biographies frequently depict the biographical person's ability to triumph over obstacles or to struggle for identity. Search for evidence of either of these themes.

    d. Additional activities can help students analyze theme in biography:

        (1) The themes in biographies frequently include didacticism, or instruction. The lives of great people often provide models for readers and suggest proper values, attitudes, and actions. Analyze several biographies to identify any instructional purposes. Why do you believe the author chose that specific person's life to teach a lesson?

        (2) Compare biographies written for younger children with biographies written for young adults. Analyze any differences in themes. Are any themes more consistently developed at either level?

        (3) Identify and compare the themes developed in several biographies written about the same person. If the themes are not the same, how do you account for the differences? Could the differences relate to the author's purpose for writing the biography or the age level of the readers?

5. Author's Style

    a. Author's style refers to how an author says something rather than what the author says. Authors may vary sentence length, repeat words, or choose descriptive words to suggest mood and create interest. For example, in her biography *The Columbus Story,* written for younger readers, Alice Dalgliesh repeats words to create interest and excitement. The waves beckon Columbus, "Come, Come, Come!" White sails chant, "Adventure, adventure, adventure!" "day after day after day." Excitement is enhanced by "Land! Land! Land" and "Climbing, climbing, -higher-higher-higher." By repeated words, such as "Nothing but sea—and—sea—and sea" Dalgliesh lengthens the days and creates an image of vast open sea. Identify examples in which an author's choice of words enhances the mood of a biography.

    b. Symbolism is a complex literary technique. It allows authors to suggest deeper meanings. For example, a dove may symbolize peace and a flag may symbolize patriotism. Authors of biographies, especially those for older readers, may choose symbols that relate to the people, conflict, and theme. For example, Eleanor Coerr uses considerable symbolism in her biography, *Sadako and the Thousand Paper Cranes.* The cranes are an ancient Japanese symbol for honor, humility, respect, hope, and protection. An ancient Japanese myth reveals that the gods will grant a long and happy life to a sick person who can make one thousand paper cranes. Coerr uses both the symbolic meaning for crane and belief in the myth to develop Sadako's character and the plot, as Sadako tries to overcome the personal ravages caused by the atomic bomb. The symbolism of the crane also suggests and reinforces themes. Search for examples of symbolism in a biography. How does the symbolism relate to the people, plot development, and theme? Do you believe the symbolism is appropriate? Why or why not?

c. Authors may use figurative language, such as similes and metaphors, to clarify and enhance descriptions of settings and people. For example, in *Sadako and the Thousand Paper Cranes,* Coerr uses a simile when she states, "There was a flash of a million suns. Then the heat pricked my eyes like needles" (p. 18). She uses a metaphor to imply a comparison between the atomic bomb and a thunderbolt. In *The Columbus Story,* Dalgliesh uses numerous similes to describe the setting in which the sea is smooth and "quiet as a river," the colors are as beautiful "as feathers of birds," and the trees are "as green and beautiful as the trees of Spain in the month of May." Search for examples of similes and metaphors. How do the comparisons relate to the setting or the people? Are they appropriate? Why or why not?

d. Additional activities can help students understand style in biography:

(1) Many biographies are about individuals who are authors. Read a biography about an author. Then, read several works written by that author. Think of the work as revealing information about and emotional responses of the author. Analyze whether or not the biography develops the style, character, emotions, and beliefs of the real person. Examples for this activity include Grimble's *Robert Burns: An Illustrated Biography* and various collections of Robert Burns's poetry; Fido's *Rudyard Kipling: An Illustrated Biography* and Kipling's *Just So Stories* and *The Jungle Books;* and Fido's *Oscar Wilde: An Illustrated Biography* and Wilde's "The Happy Prince" and "The Selfish Giant."

(2) Authors of biographies are frequently prolific writers. Identify a biographer who has written numerous books, including, if possible, nonfictional materials that reveal information about the author. Analyze the works according to any similarities in style, themes, and characterizations. Elizabeth Yates is an excellent example. Her 1950 biography *Amos Fortune, Free Man* won the Newbery award for literature; her autobiographies *My Diary, My World* and *My Widening World* received critical acclaim. Her many other books are available in libraries, and her biographical profile and acceptance speech for the Newbery award are available in the *Horn Book* magazine.

(3) Reviews of biographies usually emphasize the author's literary style and ability to develop accurate characters. Search in sources such as *Horn Book, Booklist, School Library Journal,* and the *New York Times*

Book Review to find reviews of biographies that you have read. What do the critics who wrote the reviews emphasize? Do you agree or disagree with the book critic? Why or why not?

(4) Attitudes toward some biographers and biographies differ. Attitudes toward a biography and the author's writing style may also change over time. Yates's *Amos Fortune, Free Man,* which won the Newbery award for excellence in literature, illustrates such diversity and changing attitudes. The book is still highly acclaimed by numerous critics. For example, Zena Sutherland (1986) describes the book as "written with warmth and compassion. . . . The details are grim, but Amos Fortune carried suffering lightly because his eyes were on the freedom of the future. It is this characteristic of Fortune's, so clearly depicted by Yates, that causes some modern critics to disparage the book. They disapprove of the quiet way Amos Fortune bore his enslavement with courage and dignity, forgetting the circumstances under which he achieved his own personal integrity and offered the chance to live free to other blacks" (p. 459). In contrast, Donnarae MacCann (1985) states that the book is written with a "white supremacist attitude" (p. 169) and that "the author's descriptions are condescending, but beyond that they make the African appear almost subhuman" (p. 170). Read a book such as *Amos Fortune, Free Man* and decide for yourself which viewpoint you endorse. Defend your reasons for this viewpoint.

SUMMARY

There is currently a renewed interest in using children's literature in reading programs. Educators and community leaders recognize that the content of what children read is as important as the reading approach. This chapter reviews the literature–reading connection. It describes and develops approaches and methodologies supported by reading research.

First, the chapter reviews schema theory and discusses the importance of literature in providing a basis for comprehension, learning, and remembering ideas in stories. The chapter describes approaches that help teachers use literature to develop understanding of story structures, activate relevant prior knowledge, and help students fill in gaps in their knowledge before they read. The chapter also describes approaches that increase students' opportunities to learn to read by reading. It describes approaches such as uninterrupted sustained silent reading (USSR), recreational reading groups, computer-assisted reading and focus, or thematic, units because these approaches motivate students to read widely and independently.

The chapter describes approaches that encourage readers to use a whole text to create meaning. Examples include methodologies for helping students use the whole text to search for important themes and then support those themes through specific information in the book.

The chapter also describes approaches that help students improve their comprehension. The chapter develops specific lesson plans and descriptions of methodologies for semantic mapping or webbing, modeling, and questioning.

In addition, the chapter describes approaches designed to encourage students to make predictions. It discusses predictable books for younger students. Teaching students to identify foreshadowing is a way to help them find clues in the text and predict plot development, character development, and theme. The chapter concludes with a unit on teaching biography.

ADDITIONAL READING AND LITERATURE ACTIVITIES

1. Read an article in a current journal such as *The Reading Teacher, The Journal of Reading,* or *Language Arts* that describes a reading program developed around literature or approaches for using literature in the reading curriculum. Report your findings to the class.
2. Develop an introduction to a book that helps students activate prior knowledge or provides important background information before the students read the book.
3. Analyze how you use prior knowledge of texts, knowledge of the world, and clues supplied by text to create meaning (schema theory). Read several pieces of unfamiliar literature chosen from different genres, such as traditional literature, poetry, modern fantasy, and nonfictional information. Keep a journal account of how you created meaning during your reading.
4. Conduct a recreational reading group with a group of students or a group of your peers.
5. Develop a lesson plan in which students must use the whole text to find and support a theme or trace the developing conflict in the story.
6. Develop a file of semantic webs or questioning to accompany specific books. Emphasize the development of higher comprehension skills.
7. Develop a file of books and accompanying activities to encourage students to make predictions.
8. Develop a thematic unit around reading and literature.

BIBLIOGRAPHY

Afflerbach, P. P. "The Influence of Prior Knowledge on Expert Readers' Main Idea Construction Strategies." *Reading Research Quarterly* 25 (1990): 31–46.

Ambrulevich, A. K. "An Analysis of the Levels of Thinking Required by Questions in Selected Literature Anthologies for Grades Eight, Nine, and Ten." Doctoral Dissertation, Univ. of Bridgeport, 1986. *Dissertation Abstracts International* 47,03A. (University Microfilms No. 86-13,043)

Anderson, Richard C. "Role of the Reader's Schema in Comprehension, Learning, and Memory." In *Theoretical Models and Processes of Reading.*

3d ed., edited by Harry Singer and Robert Ruddell. Newark, Del.: International Reading Association, 1985.

Balajthy, E. *Computers and Reading: Lessons from the Past and the Technologies of the Future.* Englewood Cliffs, N.J.: Prentice-Hall, 1989.

Barrett, Thomas. "Taxonomy of Reading Comprehension." In *Reading 360 Monograph.* Lexington, Mass.: Ginn, 1972.

Blanchard, Jay S.; Mason, George E.; and Daniel, Dan. *Computer Applications in Reading.* 3d ed. Newark, Del.: International Reading Association, 1987.

Bradley, Virginia N. "Improving Students' Writing with Microcomputers." *Language Arts* 59 (October 1982): 732–43.

Calfee, R., and Drum, P. "Research on Teaching Reading." In *Handbook of Research on Teaching*, 3d ed., edited by M. C. Wittrock. New York: Macmillan, 1986, pp. 804–49.

Cianciolo, P. *Picture Books for Children*, 3d ed., Chicago: American Library Association, 1990.

Cline, R. K., and Kretke, G. L. "An Evaluation of Long-Term Sustained Silent Reading in the Junior High School." *Journal of Reading* 23 (1980): 503–6.

Cress, S. W. "Journal Writing in Kindergarten." 1990. *Dissertation Abstracts International,* 51, 03A. (University Microfilm No. 90-21 840)

Curry, J. E. "Improving Secondary School Students' Inferential Responses to Literature." 1987. *Dissertation Abstracts International,* 48, 11A.

Dimino, J.; Gersten, R.; Arnine, D.; and Blake, G. "Story Grammar: An Approach for Promoting At-Risk Secondary Students' Comprehension of Literature." *Elementary School Journal* 91 (1990): 19–32.

Dole, J.; Duffy, G.; Roehler, L.; and Pearson, P. D. "Moving from the Old to the New: Research on Reading Comprehension Instruction." *Review of Educational Research* 61 (1991): 239–64.

Early, Margaret, and Ericson, Bonnie O. "The Act of Reading." In *Literature in the Classroom: Readers, Texts, and Contexts,* edited by Ben F. Nelms. Urbana, Ill.: National Council of Teachers of English, 1988, pp. 31–44.

Feitelson, Dina; Kita, Bracha; and Goldstein, Zahava. "Effects of Listening to Series Stories on First Graders' Comprehension and Use of Language." *Research in the Teaching of English* 20 (December 1986): 339–55.

Five, C. L. "From Workbook to Workshop: Increasing Children's Involvement in the Reading Process." *The New Advocate* 1 (1988): 103–13.

Fleming, Margaret, and McGinnis, Jo, eds. *Portraits: Biography and Autobiography in the Secondary School.* Urbana, Ill.: National Council of Teachers of English, 1985.

Freppon, P. A. "An Investigation of Children's Concepts of the Purpose and Nature of Reading in Different Instructional Settings." 1990. *Dissertation Abstracts International,* 50, 10A. (University Microfilms No. 85, 08-451)

Gauntt, H. L. "The Process of Prior Knowledge of Text Structure and Prior Knowledge of Content in the Comprehension and Recall of Expository Text." 1990. *Dissertation Abstracts International,* 50, 11A. (University Microfilms No. 90-10, 405)

Gordon, Christine J. "Modeling Inference Awareness Across the Curriculum." *Journal of Reading* 28 (February 1985): 444–47.

Grabe, M., and Grabe, C. "The Microcomputer and the Language Experience Approach." *The Reading Teacher* 38 (1985): 508–11.

Harper, J., and Ewing, N. "A Comparison of the Effectiveness of Microcomputer and Workbook Instruction on Reading Performance of High Incidence Handicapped Children." *Educational Technology* 26 (1986): 40–45.

Hechinger, Fred M. "Study Blames Boring Texts for Students' Poor Comprehension." Austin, Texas: *Austin American-Statesman.* (April 9, 1988): p. E16.

Henderson, J. L. "An Analysis of the Responses to Community College Freshman to Three Short Stories before and after Class Discussion." 1990. *Dissertation Abstracts International,* 51, 02A. (University Microfilms No. 90-16, 895)

Hiebert, E., and Colt, J. "Patterns of Literature-Based Instruction." *The Reading Teacher* 43 (1989): 14–20.

Kinzer, Charles K.; Sherwood, Robert D.; and Bransford, John D. *Computer Strategies for Education: Foundations and Content-Area Applications.* Columbus, Oh.: Merrill Publishing Co., 1986.

MacCann, Donnarae. "Racism in Prize-Winning Biographical Works." In *The Black American in Books for Children: Readings in Racism,* edited by Donnarae MacCann and Gloria Woodard. Metuchen, N.J.: Scarecrow Press, 1985, pp. 169–79.

Mason, George E., Blanchard, Jay S.; and Daniel, Danny B. *Computer Applications in Reading.* Newark,Del.: International Reading Association, 1983, 1987.

Matthews, Dorothy, and Committee to Revise High Interest-Easy Reading. *High Interest-Easy Reading.* Urbana, Ill.: National Council of Teachers of English, 1988.

May, Jill P. "Creating a School Wide Literature Program: A Case Study." *Children's Literature Association Quarterly* 12 (Fall 1987): 135–37.

Meeks, Margaret. *Achieving Literacy: Longitudinal Case Studies of Adolescents Learning to Read.* London: Routledge & Kegan Paul, 1983.

Miller, Marilyn, and Luskay, Jack. "School Libraries and Reading Programs: Establishing Closer Ties." *Reading Today* 5 (January 1988): 1, 18.

Moss, Joy F. *Focus Units in Literature: A Handbook for Elementary Teachers.* Urbana, Ill.: National Council of Teachers of English, 1984.

National Assessment of Educational Progress. *Three National Assessments of Reading: Changes in Performance, 1970–1980.* Report 11-R-01. Denver: Education Commission of the States, 1981.

Norton, Donna E. "An Evaluation of the BISD/TAMU Multiethnic Reading Program." Research Report, College Station: Texas A&M University, 1987.

_____ . *The Impact of Literature-Based Instruction.* New York: Merrill/Macmillan, 1992.

_____ . *Through the Eyes of a Child: An Introduction to Children's Literature,* 3d. ed. New York: Merrill/ Macmillan, 1991.

_____ , and Kracht, J. "Developing Understanding of Geography Themes through Literature." Washington, D.C.: National Conference for Social Studies, 1991.

Pearson, P. David, and Camperell, Kay. "Comprehension of Text Structures." In *Theoretical Models and Processes of Reading,* edited by Harry Singer and Robert Ruddell. Newark, Del.: International Reading Association, 1985, pp. 323–42.

Probst. R. "Teaching the Reading of Literature." In *Content Area Reading and Learning: Instructional Strategies,* edited by D. Lapp, J. Flood, and N. Varnum. Englewood Cliffs, N.J.: Prentice-Hall, 1989, pp. 179–186.

Purves, A., and Monson, D. *Experiencing Children's Literature.* Glenview, Ill.: Scott, Foresman, 1984.

Roehler, Laura, and Duffy, Gerald G. "Direct Explanation of Comprehension Processes." In *Comprehension Instruction,* edited by Gerald G. Duffy, Laura R. Roehler, and Jana Mason. New York: Longman, 1984, pp. 265–80.

Rosenblatt, L. "Language, Literature, and Values." In *Language, Schooling, and Society,* edited by S. N.

Tchudi. Upper Montclair, N.J.: Boyton/Cook, 1985, pp. 64–80.

Sawyer, Wayne. "Literature and Literacy: A Review of Research." *Language Arts* 64 (January 1987): 33–39.

Sharp, Peggy Agostino. "Children's Books and Computers—A Perfect Team." *The Computer Teacher.* June 1985, pp. 9–11.

Skillings, M. J. "Exploring the Interrelationships between Literature-Based Instruction in Expository Text Structures and Third-Grade Students' Writing Behaviors and Products and Reading Selectons." 1990. *Dissertation Abstracts International,* 51, 03A. (University Microfilms No. 90-22, 557)

Smith, N. "The Word Processing Approach to Language Experience." *The Reading Teacher* 38 (1985): 556–59.

Sutherland, Zena, and Arbuthnot, May Hill. *Children and Books.* Glenview, Ill.: Scott, Foresman, 1986.

Taxel, J. "Notes from the Editor." *The New Advocate* 1 (1988): 73–74.

Whitaker, B. T.; Schwartz, E.; and Vockell, E. L. *The Computer in the Reading Curriculum.* New York: McGraw-Hill, 1989.

Zarrillo, J. "Teachers' Interpretations of Literature-Based Reading." *The Reading Teacher* 43 (1989): 22–28.

CHILDREN'S LITERATURE REFERENCES

Adler, David. *Martin Luther King, Jr.: Free at Last.* Illustrated by Robert Casilla, New York: Holiday, 1987.

Atwater, Richard, and Atwater, Florence. *Mr. Popper's Penguins.* Boston: Little, Brown & Co., 1938.

Brink, Carol Ryrie. *Caddie Woodlawn.* Illustrated by Trina Schart Hyman. New York: Macmillan, 1935, 1963.

Brooks, Polly. *Queen Eleanor: Independent Spirit of the Medieval World.* Philadelphia: J. B. Lippincott Co., 1983.

Cendrars, Blaise. *Shadow.* Illustrated by Marcia Brown. New York: Charles Scribner's Sons, 1982.

Chetwin, Grace. *Box and Cox.* Illustrated by David Small. New York: Bradbury, 1990.

Cleary, Beverly. *Dear Mr. Henshaw.* Illustrated by Paul O. Zelinsky. New York: William Morrow & Co. 1983.

_____ . *Ramona and Her Father.* New York: William Morrow & Co., 1977.

Coerr, Eleanor. *Sadako and the Thousand Paper Cranes.* New York: G. P. Putnam's Sons, 1977.

Cook, Scott. *The Gingerbread Boy.* New York: Alfred A. Knopf, 1987.

Cresswell, Helen. "The Bagthorpe Saga" *Ordinary Jack* (1977), *Absolute Zero* (1978), *Bagthorpes Unlimited* (1978), and *Bagthorpes Abroad* (1984). New York: Macmillan Co.

Dalgliesh, Alice. *The Columbus Story.* New York: Charles Scribner's Sons, 1955.

D'Aulaire, Ingri, and D'Aulaire, Edgar. *Columbus.* New York: Doubleday & Co., 1955.

de Paola, Tomie. *The Legend of the Bluebonnet.* New York: G. P. Putnam's Sons, 1983.

Fido, Martin. *Oscar Wilde: An Illustrated Biography.* New York: Harper & Row, 1987.

_____ . *Rudyard Kipling: An Illustrated Biography.* New York: Harper & Row, 1987.

Fleischman, Sid. *The Whipping Boy.* New York: Greenwillow, 1986.

Fox, Mem. *Hattie and the Fox.* New York: Bradbury, 1987.

Freedman, Russell. *Lincoln: A Photobiography.* New York: Clarion, 1987.

Fritz, Jean. *Where Do You Think You're Going, Christopher Columbus?* Illustrated by Margot Tomes. New York: Putnam, 1980.

Galdone, Paul. *The Three Wishes.* New York: McGraw-Hill Book Co., 1967.

Goodnough, David. *Christopher Columbus.* Mahwah, N.J.: Troll, 1979.

Goodsell, Jane. *Eleanor Roosevelt.* New York: Thomas Y. Crowell Co., 1970.

Grifalconi, Ann. *Darkness and the Butterfly.* Boston: Little, Brown & Co., 1987.

Grimble, Ion. *Robert Burns: An Illustrated Biography.* New York: Harper & Row, 1987.

Grimm brothers. *Little Red Riding Hood.* Retold and illustrated by James Marshall. New York: Dial Press, 1987.

Hamilton, Virginia. *W. E. B. Du Bois: A Biography.* New York: Thomas Y. Crowell Co., 1972.

_____ . *Writings of W. E. B. Du Bois.* New York: Thomas Y. Crowell Co., 1975.

Hastings, Selina. *Sir Gawain and the Loathly Lady.* New York: Lothrop, Lee & Shepard, 1985.

Heide, Florence, and Gilliland, Judith. *The Day of Ahmed's Secret.* New York: Lothrop, Lee & Shepard, 1990.

Hodges, Margaret. *Saint George and the Dragon.* Boston: Little, Brown & Co., 1984.

Hunt, Irene. *Across Five Aprils.* Chicago: Follett, 1964.

Ivimey, John. *The Complete Story of the Three Blind Mice.* Illustrated by Paul Galdone. New York: Clarion, 1987.

Keller, Beverly. *No Beasts! No Children!* New York: Lothrop, Lee & Shepard, 1983.

Lindbergh, Reeve. *The Day the Goose Got Loose.* Illustrated by Steven Kellogg. New York: Dial, 1990.

_____ . *Johnny Appleseed.* Illustrated by Kathy Jakobsen. Boston: Little, Brown, 1990.

Lindgren, Astrid. *Pippi Longstocking.* New York: Viking Press, 1950.

Lowry, Lois. *Anastasia on Her Own.* Boston: Houghton Mifflin Co., 1985.

MacLachlan, Patricia. *Sarah, Plain and Tall.* New York: Harper & Row, 1985.

Moeri, Louise. *Save Queen of Sheba.* New York: Dutton, 1981.

Naylor, Phyllis Reynolds. *Shiloh.* New York: Atheneum, 1991.

Noyes, Alfred. *The Highwayman.* Illustrated by Charles Keeping. New York: Oxford, 1981.

O'Neill, Catharine. *Mrs. Dunphy's Dog.* New York: Viking Press, 1987.

Perrault, Charles. *Cinderella.* Illustrated by Marcia Brown. New York: Charles Scribner's Sons, 1954.

Polacco, Patricia. *Meteor!* New York: Dodd, Mead & Co., 1987.

Pollack, Pamela, selected by. *The Random House Book of Humor for Children.* Illustrated by Paul O. Zelinsky. New York: Random House, 1988.

Provensen, Alice. *The Buck Stops Here: The Presidents of the United States.* New York: Harper & Row, 1990.

Roosevelt, Elliot. *Eleanor Roosevelt, with Love.* New York: E. P. Dutton, 1984.

Rylant, Cynthia. *When I Was Young in the Montains.* New York: Dutton, 1982.

Sandburg, Carl. *Rootabaga Stories.* San Diego: Harcourt Brace Jovanovich, 1922.

Seuss, Dr. *Horton Hears a Who.* New York: Random House, 1954.

Siebert, Diane. *Heartland.* Illustrated by Wendell Minor. New York: Crowell, 1989.

Stevenson, James. *Could Be Worse!* New York: Greenwillow, 1977.

Stock, Catherine. *Armien's Fishing Trip.* New York: Morrow, 1990.

Ventura, Piero. *Christopher Columbus.* New York: Random House, 1978.

Voigt, Cynthia. *Dicey's Song.* New York: Atheneum Pubs., 1982.

_____ . *A Solitary Blue.* New York: Atheneum Pubs., 1983.

Whitney, Sharon. *Eleanor Roosevelt.* New York: Watts, 1982.

Wilder, Laura Ingalls. *Little House in the Big Woods.* Illustrated by Garth Williams. New York: Harper & Row, 1932, 1953.

Wood, Audrey. *Heckedy Peg.* Illustrated by Don Wood. San Diego: Harcourt Brace Jovanovich, 1987.

_____ . *King Bidgood's in the Bathtub.* Illustrated by Don Wood. San Diego: Harcourt Brace Jovanovich, 1985.

Yates, Elizabeth. *Amos Fortune, Free Man.* New York: E. P. Dutton, 1950.

_____ . *My Diary, My World.* Philadelphia: Westminster, 1981.

_____ . *My Widening World.* Philadelphia: Westminster, 1983.

Yolen, Jane. *Owl Moon.* Illustrated by John Schoenherr. New York: Philomel, 1987.

Yorinks, Arthur. *Hey, Al.* Illustrated by Richard Egielski. New York: Farrar, Straus, & Giroux, 1986.

Chapter Thirteen

After completing this chapter about library and reference skills, you will be able to:

1. *Describe the composition of print and nonprint items recommended for school libraries.*
2. *Describe several methods for acquiring minimal-cost materials for classrooms or school libraries.*
3. *Evaluate a student's use of library skills.*
4. *Describe the library skills taught in the primary, intermediate, and upper-elementary grades.*
5. *Develop a learning activity for teaching reference skills in the primary, intermediate, and upper-elementary grades.*

Library and Reference Skills

*T*he school library and media center are becoming increasingly important in schools that emphasize literature-based instruction. In *Becoming a Nation of Readers: The Report of the Commission on Reading,* Anderson, Hiebert, Scott, and Wilkinson (1985) emphasize that quality books, the nature of instruction, and opportunities for meaningful practice are all essential factors in improving literacy in our schools. They conclude that ready access to books is extremely important.

This access to books is important at all levels. For example, Cullinan, Greene, and Jaggar (1990) describe an innovative program in the New York Public Library to teach librarians how children become literate, to develop collections of materials for young children, and to provide services for young children and their caretakers. The librarians study research on language learning, early literacy learning, and child development. They develop criteria for selecting print and nonprint materials and explore ways to work with both children and parents. The library literacy program for young children is shaped around three aspects of practice developed in New Zealand and Australia: reading to, reading with, and reading by children. The librarians read to children, so that the children learn book language and discover story patterns, story conventions, and concepts about their world. Reading with children, also called shared reading or lap reading, occurs with an individual child or a small group of children. Now, the children see the print and take part in the storytelling and reading process. Reading by children emphasizes independent practice. Children select such materials as board books, picture books, and easy-to-read books and are praised for their early attempts at reading. In this program, librarians learn to interact with children during reading. Cullinan, Greene, and Jagar conclude: "There is no one right way to read a book with a child. The key is to keep reading aloud embedded in a social and cultural context and to keep children involved and interested" (p. 754). The program also shows the benefits of developing relationships between librarians, early childhood educators, and parents.

Interrelationships between teachers, librarians, and libraries become increasingly important as teachers integrate more literature into their reading programs. Dales (1990) describes new visions for access to information: "[Librarians can] view themselves more as teachers, and teachers can view libraries as their own classrooms. Both need to see each other as team-teachers" (p. 734). Hiebert, Mervar, and Person (1990) point out that guidance in classrooms and libraries is crucial for both students and teachers in selecting and sharing books. They found that children who are involved in literature-based programs are more apt to give elaborate reasons for their selections and indicate specific books, illustrators, or authors when they go to the library than children in textbook-based classrooms. The latter require more guidance in book selection from librarians.

Lamme and Ledbetter (1990) describe library media centers in which children frequent the library before, during, and after school as they search for books to read during sustained silent reading. They look for specific genres of books, books by particular authors or illustrators, and books recommended by other students. In this same center, teachers in the media production room bind their students' writing, publish newsletters to keep parents involved and informed, and read and discuss articles. The teachers help students select good books and find resources that relate to their classroom studies.

The close relationship between librarians and teachers is also emphasized by the American Association of School Librarians (1988). This organization recommends that librarians provide information and service whenever it is needed, rather than on a fixed schedule. In this situation, librarians and teachers work together to provide instruction in research skills, help students locate materials, and recommend new books. Furthermore, the library becomes a genuine media center that includes multimedia materials and word-processing programs.

MEDIA CENTER RESOURCES

School libraries no longer contain only books. If you visit a well-developed library, you will find children using encyclopedias, dictionaries, newspapers, magazines, films, filmstrips, and recordings. To provide adequately for a full range of learning possibilities and activities, a library must contain materials covering varied reading levels and subjects.

Research shows that children who have access to a well-staffed, well-stocked school library read more books and have higher verbal test scores. (Merchant, Broadway, Robinson, & Shields, 1984). They read more than twice as many books and a greater variety than do children who have access only to a classroom library or a centralized, school-district library. Both a school library and a classroom library are essential for easy and frequent access to materials. Lamme and Ledbetter (1990) identify the following resources that characterize an effective school library:

1. Materials that relate to thematic studies—anthologies of poetry and humor; indices to poetry by topic; indices to songs by topic; and files of community volunteers and guest speakers categorized according to topics of study.
2. Materials that relate to authors—information files about individual authors and illustrators and filmstrips and videos featuring particular authors and illustrators.
3. Materials that relate to literature—lists of books by genre, including ideas for student involvement, and literature sets that may be checked out by teachers.

4. Materials that relate to activities to accompany stories—collections of stories that are good for storytelling; collections of flannelboard patterns; information on how to make puppets and perform puppet skits; tape recordings of good storytellings; and packaged storyhour ideas, with book titles and matching flannelboard sets or filmstrips.

If you are teaching in a school that does not yet have an outstanding library and you want to augment your classroom library, there are a number of creative ways to do this at minimal cost. In one school, for example, a program was initiated to teach communication and language arts skills to fifth- and sixth-grade students of lower reading ability. The teachers needed motivating reading materials in the classrooms and recreational reading materials that students could keep. The teachers used two methods to acquire the paperback books many of the students preferred. First, they sent a letter to parents of children in the school district explaining the new educational program. They asked the parents to donate children's books, especially paperbacks, so that other children could enjoy them. The response was excellent. They set up an attractive book corner and had enough books left over to start a paperback reading center in the school library as well. The students could use the books in the classroom or check them out. The teachers also established a paperback book exchange. Students who found books they especially wanted to keep had only to bring in other paperback books to trade.

The teachers used several methods to augment the reference materials in the classroom. The letter asking for paperbacks also asked for donations of periodicals, such as *National Geographic, Smithsonian, Life Magazine,* hobby magazines, *Popular Science, Popular Mechanics,* sports magazines, and so forth. The periodicals served as reading materials for special interests and provided materials for a picture-information file. The students compiled the file, and thus learned such library skills as classifying materials, alphabetizing, and developing a card index.

As a final means for collecting additional reference information, the students wrote for free or inexpensive materials. This activity required them to use their letter-writing skills. When the materials arrived, the students had to file them for easy retrieval, thus reinforcing their library skills. If the materials contained advertising, the children critically evaluated it for bias and propaganda techniques.

In addition to literature, multimedia material, and reference material, libraries also contain materials designed to instruct students in the use of the library media center. According to Hart (1985), "since 1978, twice as many items have been developed for instructing students in the use of a library media center as had been developed previously" (p. 1).

Criteria for Evaluating Materials

Spiegel (1990) provides the following criteria for evaluating resources for developing reference and study skills:

1. Does the material have content validity? Does it develop activities or lessons that focus students' attention on performing some research or real study? After completing the activity, will the students be able to identify the process used to complete the task?
2. Does the material have transfer potential? Are the skills and strategies practiced with the specific material of value when using other materials, in other settings, and for real purposes?

3. Does the material include adequate reinforcement? Do students get enough, but not too much, practice in the target skill or strategy?
4. Does the material contain clear and complete directions? Do the directions enable the students to use the materials independently? Are sufficient examples given? Is the language at an appropriate level?
5. Is the material adaptable and flexible so that it is appealing to and appropriate for many types of learners?
6. Is the material free from any content bias? For example, are minority groups, including females, represented in the examples?

REINFORCEMENT ACTIVITY

1. Use the preceding criteria to evaluate reference and study-skill instructional materials in a school library. For example, evaluate Mealy's (1989) *Biography Reports Without Copying, Childcraft Dictionary* (1989), Foster's *Looking It Up* (1989), and Kaplan's *Study Skills for Success* (1988).
2. Choose several selections from Hart's *Instruction in School Library Media Center Use (K–12)* (1985) and use Spiegel's criteria to evaluate the materials. Categories include interest rousers, orientation, and alphabetization; citizenship; listening and interpreting; using parts of a book, including the table of contents and index; publication terminology; location and arrangement of materials, including picture books, nonfiction, periodicals, fiction, biography, vertical files, newspapers, and nonbooks; classification, including Dewey decimal system and guide words; card catalogs, including special rules, fiction arrangement, nonfiction arrangement, and subject cards; methods of research; reference tools, including source materials, language dictionaries, biographical dictionaries, encyclopedias, thesauruses, maps, yearbooks, almanacs, subject indices, readers' guides, newspapers, handbooks, and nonprint sources; and equipment operation, including filmstrip projectors, filmstrip viewers, projectors, slides, video recorders, cameras, record players, tape recorders, microforms, and microcomputers.

LIBRARY SKILLS

Library skills are essential for locating information. They also help students develop positive attitudes toward research, stimulate their interest in functional and recreational reading, and increase their knowledge about how libraries can enrich their lives.

Instruction in library skills cannot be left to incidental learning. Usually, a librarian and classroom teacher teach these skills cooperatively. According to Hart (1985), research indicates that "instruction in the use of library media resources needs to be correlated with classroom instruction" (p. 1). Certain skills are taught as early as kindergarten, when teachers introduce children to the proper care of books—how to hold a book, how to turn pages, how to use a bookmark, how to put a book back on the shelf, how to put a book down on a desk or a table, and how to care for a book when taking it home. Kindergarten teachers also introduce children to school and classroom libraries. Teachers and librarians should cooperatively teach children where to find the picture books and easy-to-read books, as well as other materials. Students also need to learn how to check out books and return them.

During the primary grades, children learn to find specific types of materials, to refer to books by author and title, and to use some of the reference materials. Introduce skills such as alphabetizing; using an index; using a table of contents; and categorizing items according to subject, title, or author. Acquaint children with picture dictionaries, primary school dictionaries, thesauruses, and encyclopedias.

In the intermediate and upper-elementary grades, teach library skills more formally, so that children become competent in locating books on the shelves from information in card catalogs, preparing new books for shelves, and creating bulletin boards and displays of colorful books.

Children need to know where to find and how to use different types of books.

1. Visit an elementary school library. What print and nonprint materials are included? Observe what learning activities are going on in the library. Are the activities vital extensions of the classroom?
2. Interview a school librarian. Find out what instructional tasks he or she performs. What does the librarian feel is the most important aspect of the job? How does this librarian cooperate with classroom teachers?

Evaluation of Library Skills

Formal instruction in library skills does not usually begin until the intermediate grades, although the readiness skills are taught in the primary grades. Evaluate attainment of these skills by observing students as they use the library and its various print and nonprint reference materials. Instead of using paper-and-pencil tests, use checklists to evaluate a student's skills, and discuss learning activities that are prerequisites for assignments requiring library skills.

The primary grades   This is the time to develop positive attitudes toward books, teach the children where to find and how to use specific types of books, and introduce other prerequisites for using a library to its fullest. Table 13–1 illustrates the library skills you might evaluate for primary-grade children.

TABLE 13–1
Checklist of library skills—primary grades

Skill	Evaluation		
	Yes	Some-times	No
1. Care of Books—Is able to			
a. hold book correctly	____	____	____
b. turn pages correctly	____	____	____
c. care for book when taking it home	____	____	____
2. Library Orientation—Is able to			
a. find specific types of books and other media in the library	____	____	____
b. refer to books by author and title	____	____	____
c. check out books	____	____	____
3. Miscellaneous Skills—Is able to			
a. manage the classroom library	____	____	____
b. make simple author-card for classroom library	____	____	____
c. make simple title-card for classroom library	____	____	____
d. make simple subject-card for the classroom library	____	____	____
e. alphabetize a short list of words by first letter	____	____	____
f. use a primary picture dictionary	____	____	____
g. make and use a class telephone directory	____	____	____
h. use a class-made encyclopedia	____	____	____

Reference skills become more important in intermediate grades.

The intermediate grades   Instruction in library skills becomes more formal in the intermediate grades. Consequently, there are more opportunities to evaluate a student's attainment of certain skills. Table 13–2 indicates the skills to evaluate in the intermediate grades.

The upper-elementary grades and middle school   As the various subject areas begin to demand greater involvement with library references, upper-elementary and middle-school children must be able to find and use library materials efficiently and effectively. You should review their skills every year, so that

TABLE 13–2
Checklist of library skills—intermediate grades

Skill	Evaluation		
	Yes	Some-times	No
1. Library Orientation—Is able to			
a. find specific books and media	_____	_____	_____
b. check out materials independently	_____	_____	_____
2. Library Use—Is able to			
a. understand and demonstrate appropriate uses for library at different times	_____	_____	_____
b. use librarian for appropriate reasons	_____	_____	_____
c. explain how books are arranged	_____	_____	_____
d. select materials at an appropriate level of difficulty	_____	_____	_____
3. Dictionary Skills—Is able to			
a. alphabetize words according to 2nd, 3rd, and 4th letters	_____	_____	_____
b. use guide words	_____	_____	_____
c. locate correct meaning for a word from multiple definitions	_____	_____	_____
d. locate synonyms and antonyms	_____	_____	_____
4. Other Reference Materials—Is able to			
a. use a children's encyclopedia	_____	_____	_____
b. use a telephone directory	_____	_____	_____
c. understand importance of various reference materials	_____	_____	_____
d. use card catalog to find books on shelves	_____	_____	_____
5. Parts of a Book—Is able to			
a. use the table of contents and the index to find information in a reference book	_____	_____	_____
b. refer to the copyright date, and use it to evaluate information	_____	_____	_____

the students feel comfortable and secure in their library searches. Especially crucial times for teaching and diagnosing library skills are when students proceed from elementary to middle school (at the end of fifth grade) or when they proceed from elementary to junior high school (at the end of sixth grade). The students not only change schools but change from a self-contained teaching environment to one in which classes are completely departmentalized. Teacher expectancies may also be different. Elementary teachers usually provide considerable guidance in library searches, but this is not necessarily the case with middle-school content-area teachers. In middle schools, any language arts skills, including library skills, are usually the responsibility of the language arts, or English, teacher. Often, however, students lack the skills they need to do reports in the content areas, so a major instructional shift is required. Introduce students to an appropriate skill before and at the time it is needed. Do not assume that students have mastered adequate library skills before coming to class. Table 13–3 indicates library skills to evaluate for upper-elementary or middle-school students.

TABLE 13–3

Checklist of library skills—upper-elementary or middle school

Skill	Yes	Some-times	No
1. Dictionary Usage—Is able to			
a. alphabetize words by 5th or 6th letters, if necessary	_____	_____	_____
b. use guide words	_____	_____	_____
c. find spellings for phonetically regular words	_____	_____	_____
d. find spellings for phonetically irregular words	_____	_____	_____
e. find the correct meaning from multiple meanings	_____	_____	_____
f. find synonyms and antonyms	_____	_____	_____
g. use pronunciation symbols to find correct pronunciation	_____	_____	_____
2. Library Orientation—Is able to			
a. locate specific items in the library (e.g., check-out desk, card catalog)	_____	_____	_____
b. locate different categories of books	_____	_____	_____
3. Card Catalog—Is able to			
a. demonstrate how and when to refer to a subject card	_____	_____	_____
b. demonstrate how and when to refer to an author card	_____	_____	_____
c. demonstrate how and when to refer to a title card	_____	_____	_____
d. understand the need to use, and uses, a cross-reference card	_____	_____	_____
4. Classification Systems—Is able to			
a. use the Dewey decimal or Library of Congress classification system	_____	_____	_____
b. locate books by call numbers	_____	_____	_____
5. Encyclopedia—Is able to			
a. find and use the index of an encyclopedia to locate related articles on a subject	_____	_____	_____
b. use the cross reference in an encyclopedia	_____	_____	_____
c. use guide words in an encyclopedia	_____	_____	_____
d. check copyright date of an encyclopedia	_____	_____	_____
e. choose an encyclopedia on an appropriate level of reading difficulty	_____	_____	_____
f. use more than one encyclopedia to compare information	_____	_____	_____
6. Other Tools—Is able to			
a. understand the purposes for, and use, other reference materials	_____	_____	_____
biographical dictionaries	_____	_____	_____
atlases	_____	_____	_____
almanacs	_____	_____	_____
specialized encyclopedias (e.g., science and social studies)	_____	_____	_____
7. Finding Information in Periodicals—Is able to			
a. understand that periodicals can provide the most recent information on a subject	_____	_____	_____
b. identify subject headings that might provide references	_____	_____	_____
c. use the *Reader's Guide to Periodical Literature*	_____	_____	_____
d. understand abbreviations in the *Reader's Guide*	_____	_____	_____
e. find the correct periodicals after locating references in the *Reader's Guide*	_____	_____	_____

1. If you are now teaching students, use the appropriate checklist to evaluate a student's library skills. What skills have reached the level of independence? What skills require further instruction?
2. Look at language arts textbooks used in elementary or middle schools. Choose a specific series and grade level, and design a checklist of library skills to correspond with that series.

FOR YOUR PLAN BOOK
A Unit for Teaching Library Skills
(Upper-Elementary Grades and Middle School)

An effective way to supplement initial orientation visits to a library is to prepare a series of classroom tape presentations. Use the tapes to:

1. Introduce students to library facilities at the beginning of the year.
2. Reinforce the location of materials and facilitate their use when they are needed.
3. Introduce the library to students who transfer into class later in the year.
4. Organize an effective learning center on library skills.
5. Provide reinforcement and additional study for students who need more time to assimilate the necessary information.

In addition, make the tapes to fit the available library facilities, and to present necessary information in a sequence the teachers and libraries consider most appropriate.

Lesson One: Introduction to the Library

Overview: Lead the students on a walking tour of the library that includes:

1. The location and a brief explanation of the most important physical facilities
2. A discussion of the rationale behind the usual behavior expected in libraries
3. An outline of regulations specific to the library the students will use

Activities:

To encourage students to reinforce the introductory information they have received from the tape, include some application activities. Put these activities on the tape or put them on cards and incorporate them into a learning center.

1. Draw a sketch of our school library, locating the following:
   a. Circulation desk
   b. Card catalog
   c. Shelves
      (1) Fiction
      (2) Nonfiction
      (3) References
      (4) Periodicals
      (5) Audiovisual materials

2. Using your own materials and imagination, make a bookmark suitable for use in any book.

3. Using your own materials and imagination, make a cartoon or drawing that shows an important library regulation or encourages use of the library. You may use pictures cut from magazines and other periodicals. This cartoon or drawing can be notebook size.

4. Using your own materials and imagination, make a poster suitable for display in the library or a classroom illustrating a library regulation or encouraging use of the library.

5. Interview one of the librarians to find out what librarians do besides checking out books, and how one prepares to become a librarian. Here are some questions you might ask (you can probably think of others):
   a. Who chooses books for the library and how are they chosen?
   b. What steps does the librarian go through to get a book on the shelf?
   c. What other tasks does a librarian do?
   d. How does a librarian learn what to do?
   e. What are the advantages and disadvantages of being a librarian?

Lesson Two: Arrangement of Books in the Library

Overview: This lesson is designed to:

1. Enable students to become proficient in locating books of fiction and biography.
2. Introduce students to the general arrangement of nonfiction books.
3. Introduce students to library classification systems.

Outline: By following this general outline, you can provide your students with the necessary information to become proficient in finding books in the library.

   I. Books of fiction
      A. General information
         1. Definition of fiction
         2. Distinction between full-length books of fiction and story collections
         3. Symbols often used on the spine to indicate a book of fiction and those often used to indicate a story collection
      B. How fiction books are arranged on shelves
         1. Alphabetically by author's name
         2. Alphabetically by title when several books are available by the same author (*a, an,* and *the* are disregarded in alphabetizing)
      C. How to use the card catalog to locate a book of fiction
         1. Use of the title card to find out the author
         2. Use of the subject index to select a book of interest
   II. Biography and autobiography
      A. General information
         1. Definitions of biography and autobiography
         2. Distinction between individual biographies and collective biographies
      B. How biographies are arranged on shelves
         1. Biographies and autobiographies
         2. Collective biography
      C. How to use the card catalog to locate a biography

III. Nonfiction books
   A. Distinction between fiction and nonfiction
      1. Definition of nonfiction
      2. Contrast with fiction. Often, teachers falsely assume that students have a clear concept of the distinction between fiction and nonfiction. Actually, many students have translated these two terms into "false" and "true." As a result, their concept of fiction is limited to books of fantasy, while their concept of nonfiction includes all books about "real life." To have a common reference base, use popular television shows as examples to explore your students' concept of these two terms.
      3. Examples of nonfiction books
IV. Library classification systems
   A. Rationales behind library classification systems
      1. Need for order to provide easy access
      2. Desire to organize knowledge
   B. Two major classification systems used
      1. Library of Congress—formerly used with large libraries, such as universities, but now becoming popular in public libraries
      2. Dewey decimal system—still the most popular in school libraries
   C. General divisions of the Dewey decimal system. Avoid any temptation to get too detailed here. Students are to be users of a library, not librarians. However, many students are fascinated by learning what the numbers mean. You may wish to include an explanation of the interrelationship of the broad classifications of the Dewey system, as well as prepare a handout for the students.

Activities:

1. Put the following books of fiction in the order they would appear on the shelf. Put author's name first.

The Call of the Wild—London
The Witch of Blackbird Pond—Speare
The Bronze Bow—Speare
The Secret Garden—Burnett
The Voyages of Dr. Dolittle—Lofting
Charlotte's Web—White

Mary Poppins Comes Back—Travers
And Now Miguel—Krumgold
It's Like This, Cat—Neville
Mary Poppins—Travers
The Big Road—Clarke

2. Find the answers to these questions about our school library and write them on notebook paper.
   a. How are fiction books marked?
   b. How are biographies marked?
   c. How are collective biographies marked?
   d. How are story collections marked?
3. On the plan of our library you made for Lesson One, locate the biography shelves. Using the card catalog, get the title, author, and mark whether biography or autobiography, about the following:
   a. a president of the United States
   b. a sports figure
   c. a famous woman

4. Survey the biography shelves in the library to locate:
   a. three books about one famous person.
   b. a collective biography that contains an article on that person.
   c. any three biographies.
      List the title and author of each book and write a short identification of the subject of each book. Arrange your list in the order these should be found on the shelves.

5. Making the Dewey system work for you:
   a. Make a chart of the ten main classifications.
      List two types of books you would find in that category.
      Example: 000–009   General Works:
                                                      encyclopedias, dictionaries
   b. Using your chart, give the general numbers (for example, 500) for the following types of books:
      (1) American history
      (2) Basketball
      (3) Poetry
      (4) Chemistry
      (5) How to build a house
      (6) Teenage problems
      (7) Greek gods
   c. Give the general numbers (for example, 500) of sections where you would expect to find the following titles:

   John Paul Jones
   Alligators and Crocodiles
   History of South America
   The Yellow Fairy Book
   Mathematics Made Easy

   Stars for Sam
   Pioneer Art in America
   Poems Every Child Should Know
   Myths of Greece and Rome
   America Sings

6. Use the card catalog to find a biography or autobiography of each of the following persons, and list the titles and authors of the books. Look through the book to answer these questions:
   a. Approximately when did this person live?
   b. What nation claims this person?
   c. What was this person's main occupation?

   Louisa May Alcott
   Hans Christian Andersen
   Louis Armstrong
   John James Audubon
   Benedict Arnold
   Johann Sebastian Bach
   P. T. Barnum
   Clara Barton

   Richard Byrd
   Cleopatra
   Coronado
   Bob Cousy
   Althea Gibson
   G. Marconi
   Jim Thorpe

7. Make a set of posters illustrating the classifications of the Dewey decimal system.

Used with permission of Mary Russell, an English professor who teaches courses in English and language arts methods.

REFERENCE SKILLS

Why is it so important for students to develop effective reference skills? Think for a moment about the last time you were required to write a factual report or research paper. Where did you look for information? What sources did you use? Did you read an entire reference book? How did you know where to find what you needed? How did you pull together ideas from various sources to write your final report? As a college student, the task was probably fairly easy for you. The first time you had to write a report, however, you probably found the assignment anything but easy. You may have been confused about where to locate information or what to do with the reference books after you finally found them.

To use a library successfully, students must know which references to use and where they are located. There are also prerequisite skills for using dictionaries, encyclopedias, and card catalogs. Have you ever watched children grope through a dictionary when they do not have sufficient skills in alphabetizing? Alphabetizing is equally important for locating information in encyclopedias and card catalogs. Furthermore, to find information in encyclopedias, card catalogs, and reader's guides, students must be able to identify categories under which to look. Whereas formal dictionary, encyclopedia, and card-catalog instruction may not begin until about fourth grade, readiness for these sophisticated skills begins earlier.

The Primary Grades

Even first-grade children can use the easy picture dictionaries published for them. In these dictionaries, a picture is used to define each word entry. Introduce these books when children are discussing the meaning of a new word in a reading class or during early writing activities to help them see how to use a dictionary to find the proper spelling of a word. The pictures and words are alphabetized, so you can also introduce the concept of alphabetizing.

Language experience word banks Word cards, normally used in the primary grades, may be used to develop alphabetizing skills. A word card contains a word that a child should know. A collection of word cards forms a word bank for individualized instruction. As the number of word cards increases, the children experience more difficulty in locating specific words for their writing activities. Therefore, the need for an efficient way of grouping word cards becomes apparent. First, alphabetize the word cards according to the first letters, then according to the second and third letters (see Figure 13–1).

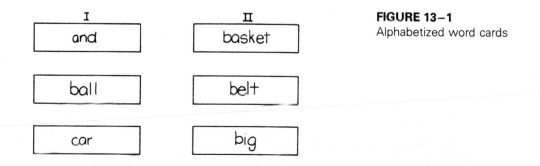

FIGURE 13–1
Alphabetized word cards

Alphabetizing skill-building needs to precede effective dictionary use.

Class-made picture dictionaries   Another activity that allows children to practice alphabetizing skills is constructing individual and class picture dictionaries. Picture dictionaries can center around specific categories, such as animals or famous people. Have the children start with one page for each letter (for example, ant, bee, cat) and later add pages that require alphabetical arrangement according to second letter (for example, ladybug, lion, lobster, lynx) and third letter (for example, ladybug, lamb). They can draw the accompanying pictures or cut them from newspapers and magazines. Real photographs also add interest to picture dictionaries.

Class telephone books   The telephone directory is another source that requires understanding of alphabetical order. Have the students examine real telephone directories to see how they are organized. Then, have them assemble a class telephone directory that contains the same kind of information.

Manipulative objects   Alphabet blocks allow children to practice putting the letters in sequential order. Children can also string wooden beads with printed letters in alphabetical order. To make an inexpensive alphabet tray, fill an old cookie sheet with damp sand or plaster of paris. Carve the letters into the sand or plaster of paris with a blunt object, such as a tongue depressor. Let the students use the tray to trace the letters with their fingers as they recite the alphabet.

Encyclopedias   Primary-grade children are not too young to be introduced to encyclopedias. Show them how to develop their own encyclopedia by creating a picture file and arranging subject words in alphabetical order. Have them list categories, such as animals, cities, families, farms, holidays, houses, seasons, transportation, and weather, on dividers. Then, have them place pictures and other information under the appropriate subject. As the encyclopedia gets larger, materials will fall into more than one category. The need for an index will then become apparent.

Card catalogs   To use a card catalog effectively, children must eventually understand three classifications: title, author, and subject. Primary children can begin to understand the card catalog by constructing a simple catalog for the books in their classroom library. Class discussion will lead to several suggestions for arranging the books, and usually someone will mention alphabetical order by author's name or by title. Children should first concentrate on one kind of classification, and put the necessary information for each book on a 3-by-5-inch index card, then arrange the finished cards by alphabetical order in a file box. Whichever method they begin with, children soon realize that more than one arrangement of categorizing and filing can be useful. If the library is using a computer system for cataloging, students will require instruction in use of the computer.

An integrated approach   Keel (1985) identifies the following practices to improve the instruction of library media skills:
1. Teach children only the skills they need, at the time they need them.
2. Make instruction specific, simple, practical, brief, and entertaining.
3. Involve as many senses as possible in the presentation.
4. Lead children to discover conclusions for themselves.
5. Give them opportunities to use new skills as soon as possible.
6. Give each child praise, encouragement, and guidance. (p. 51)

Keel teaches library skills lessons that coincide with the beginning of various social studies units. To meet a multimedia goal and involve as many senses as possible, she uses filmstrips, pictures, charts, posters, transparencies, tape recordings, records, and slides. For example, when introducing the reference skills for a third-grade study of Mexico, she uses Mexican folk music and a narrated slide presentation showing children how to locate the subject heading "Mexico," where to find books about Mexico in the library, and how to find books most useful in answering specific questions about Mexico. Later, she teaches children how to find and use other materials about Mexico, such as those found in filmstrips, picture files, vertical files, and recordings.

The Intermediate Grades

Formal instruction in reference skills usually begins about fourth grade. At this point, children have developed enough reading skills to use easy-to-read dictionaries and encyclopedias. Some children are already quite proficient, whereas others require considerable formal instruction.

Alphabetizing   Intermediate-grade teachers should have children progress from simple to more demanding alphabetizing skills in order to discover which students still require assistance in alphabetizing. Have the students begin by alphabetizing a list of words by initial letters: *frog, count, vine, round, light, antler, water, peace.* Students who have difficulty with this task may need to work on the readiness activities suggested for primary grades, especially the alphabet tray and other manipulative devices.

Next, ask students to alphabetize a list of words according to second letters: *after, avenue, apple, air, able, amount, acrobat, attic.* Then, have them alphabetize according to the third letter of a word: *dew, death, deck, detail, debate, defend, design, delight.* Finally, have them alphabetize according to the fourth letter of a word: *stress, strong, stray, struggle, stride.* Similar lessons can require students to alphabetize in different combinations of difficulty. Use envelopes filled with word cards of different combinations for alphabetizing according to first letter, second letter, and so forth, for individualized instruction and additional practice.

Dictionaries   To find words quickly in a dictionary, a student must understand the function of and be able to use guide words. Even when students know how to alphabetize, they often ignore the guide words at the top of dictionary pages. Approach this understanding inductively. For example, have the students open their dictionaries to a specific page and ask them to examine it carefully to see how it is organized. After they have discovered the organization, have them look at the tops of the pages to see what is printed at the left and the right sides of each. Next, have them try to decide how the two words at the top of the page were chosen. They will usually deduce quickly that the word on the left is the first word on the page and the word on the right is the last word on the page. Then, have them look at other pages to see if this generalization is true for all pages and also for other dictionaries. Tell the students that these words are called guide words. Guide words help dictionary users locate a word quickly because all words on the page must come after the left-hand guide word and before the right-hand guide word.

You may use a skeleton dictionary to focus attention on guide words. The skeleton dictionary lessons come after an introduction to a dictionary and demonstration of its organization. A skeleton dictionary consists of several pages containing only guide words and page numbers; the pages should correspond to a classroom dictionary used for instruction. Figure 13–2 is an example of a skeleton dictionary page. Students should compare the skeleton pages with the real dictionary and then indicate where certain words would appear in the skeleton dictio-

ground	318	guard

FIGURE 13–2
A skeleton dictionary page

Are these words on this dictionary page? grumble, green, guess, gruff, gypsy, great, growl. Why or why not?

nary, explain why they would be on a certain page, and verify the location with the real dictionary. Finally, from another list of words, the students should locate the guide words that appear on the page containing a specific word and verify that the word is actually on that page.

Another dictionary skill that needs practice is locating the correct definition for a word from the multiple definitions presented. Some students have a tendency to read only the first definition after a word and ignore the remaining information. One student interpreted the sentence, "John will fast all day Friday," as "John will be held firmly to some object all day Friday, because fast means to fasten firmly." This problem results from dictionary practice in which students find the meanings of words presented in isolation. To stress multiple meanings, list several sentences using the same word with different meanings:

1. The clock is *fast;* it shows 5:00.
2. The boat was tied *fast* to the dock.
3. The Olympic runner was very *fast.*
4. It was a holy day, so the monk had to *fast.*

Ask for a definition of the word *fast.* Then, discuss with the students whether that definition makes sense in each sentence. Next, ask the students to look up *fast* in the dictionary, notice how many meanings are given, and find the correct definition as it applies to each sentence.

Dictionary races give children practice in finding words. For a dictionary race, write a sentence on the board with one word underlined. Allot points to each team that finds a word first, gives the correct guide words on the page, gives the correct meaning, pronounces the word correctly, gives the correct part of speech, and gives correct synonyms and antonyms.

Encyclopedias   In the intermediate grades, children begin using an encyclopedia for reference. The encyclopedias available in libraries are written for different levels of ability. Thus, it will be helpful to both teacher and students to know what reading level each encyclopedia requires. Following are encyclopedias identified for different ability groups:

1. Upper-elementary (fourth grade and higher):
   Britannica Junior (Chicago: Encyclopedia Britannica).
   The World Book Encyclopedia (Chicago: Field Enterprises Educational Corp.).
2. Upper-elementary and middle school:
   Compton's Encyclopedia (Chicago: F. E. Compton & Co.).
3. Middle school and high school:
   Collier's Encyclopedia (New York: Crowell Collier & Macmillan).
   Encyclopedia International (New York: Grolier).
4. High school, college, and adult:
   Encyclopedia Americana (New York: Americana Corp.).
   The Encyclopedia Britannica (Chicago: Encyclopedia Britannica).

Card catalogs   If intermediate-grade children have made classroom card catalogs, they already understand the function of author, title, and subject cards. Some intermediate children may have been using a library card catalog since early primary grades, whereas other children have no understanding of the system.

There are three things to teach intermediate-grade children about a card catalog: (1) the abbreviations used on the cards (for example, © 1988 means copyright, 1988; 127 pp. illus. means the book has 127 pages and contains illustrations); (2) cross-reference cards direct users to other sources of information; and (3) call numbers indicate where to find a book in the library. Instruction in these three areas may take only a few lessons for some children, but it is extremely important that all children digest the information thoroughly, however long it takes. One fourth-grade teacher, for example, introduces her students to the card catalog by having them put on a play about the card catalog, adapted from a play printed in *Instructor* (Sister Mary Denis Tompkins, 1971). The play introduces Charlie Catalog, Art Author, Terry Title, Sam Subject, Dewey Decimal, Ruthie Reference, Dottie Dictionary, Al Atlas, Amy Almanac, and Ed Encyclopedia.

After presenting the play, the students make an author card, a title card, and a subject card for the same book. Next, they use the card catalog in the library to search for answers to questions such as the following:

Who is the author of _____ ?
What books has _____ written?
How many pages does the book _____ have?
What books might help us find out more information about Mars?

This teacher gives the children many opportunities to use the card catalog and guides them while they use the references.

The Upper-Elementary Grades and Middle School

In the upper-elementary grades and in middle school, review and refine reference skills through instruction requiring students to use encyclopedias, card catalogs, and other references designed for specific content areas.

FURTHER REFERENCE INSTRUCTION

Once you have introduced your students to the library, you may want to encourage them to use the library facilities to find information. One of the most useful tools is the card catalog. The following activities and exercises may prove helpful in designing instruction on the card catalog.

1. On manila folders or cardboard notebook covers, prepare sample author, title, and subject cards that contain only essential information, so the students can learn the location of the information they will use.
2. Prepare exercises that will give students practice in interpreting the information on cards. For example, using a sample subject card, have them answer the following questions:

What is the title?
What is the call number?
Who is the author?
When was the book published?
Where was it published?
Who published it?

How many pages?
What does *illus.* mean?
What kind of card is this one?
Under what letter of the alphabet would this card be filed?

Then, from the information on the sample subject card, have them pre-pare sample author and title cards.

REINFORCEMENT
ACTIVITY

Develop an instructional lesson plan to teach a reference skill at the primary, intermediate, upper-elementary, or middle-school level. If you are now teaching, present the lesson to a group of children. If you are not teaching, present the lesson to a group of your peers.

USING LITERATURE SELECTIONS
TO TEACH LIBRARY SKILLS

Not only are books a major feature of a library, they are also resources for introducing children to the multifaceted nature of a library. Books can introduce children to bookmaking processes, to the various functions of a library, and even to the history of a library. Books and literature review journals can be used to teach children the particulars of reviewing books and writing their own reviews.

Books That Teach About Books and the Library

Elleman (1990) points out that many specific titles celebrate books in general, libraries, and reading: "While a first grader will chuckle through Eric Kimmel's *I Took My Frog to the Library* (1990), fourth graders can use the story as a springboard to writing about their own imagined capers. And fifth graders making their own books will find Aliki's *How a Book Is Made* (1986) as instructive as a second grader will" (p. 622).

You will find many books in the library that inform readers about how to make books. For example, in addition to Aliki's *How a Book Is Made*, children can read Michelle Edwards's *Dora's Book* (1990) to discover how a boy sets the type and prints a book by hand after his friend writes a story about her grandparents. From reading Howard Greenfeld's *Books: From Writer to Reader* (1988), children will learn about the process of professional book publishing and printing as the author proceeds from the conception of an idea to the completion of the bound book. Michael Kehoe's *The Puzzle of Books* (1982) provides a photo essay about book production.

Several books focus on using the library. For example, Gail Gibbons's *Check It Out! The Book About Libraries* (1985) shows people using libraries throughout history. She covers such details as using card catalogs, tracking titles by computer, and checking out books. Nancy Levinson's *Clara and the Bookwagon* (1988) is the story of America's first bookmobile, a horse-drawn library in Hagerstown, Maryland, in 1905. Lisl Weil's *Let's Go to the Library* (1990), another history of libraries, encourages children to get a library card. Ruth Radlauer's *Molly at the Library* (1987) is the story of a girl who discovers that she can check out ten books from the library. Anne Rockwell's *I Like the Library* (1977) is the story of a small boy who describes his delightful trips to the public library.

Becoming Reviewers of Books

Jenks and Roberts (1990) describe a collaborative project in which a teacher and a librarian involved fourth- and fifth-grade students in a project that included reading literature and writing reviews about the books. First, the librarian asked the students to identify what they wanted to know about a book in order to decide whether or not to read it. Then, the students listened to book reviews from sources such as the *School Library Journal* and the *Horn Book Magazine*. After listening to the reviews, the students listed the elements of these reviews, such as brief summaries, comments about the writing, and recommendations. Next, the students chose their books, read them, and wrote first drafts of their reviews. Students shared their final edited and illustrated copies the following week. Finally, the illustrated reviews were displayed in the library. The following lesson plan shows how this approach can be used in a classroom.

FOR YOUR PLAN BOOK
A Lesson Plan for Book Reviewing

I. Purposes for the lesson:
    A. To increase students' appreciation of literature.
    B. To introduce students to the reviewing process.
    C. To write a book review.
II. Materials needed: Book reviews from sources such as the *Horn Book Magazine* and the *Bulletin of the Center for Children's Books*.
III. Procedures:
    A. Read several book reviews to the students. You may select book reviews that represent different genres. Or have the class identify several favorite books and then search for book reviews. One fifth-grade class identified Bill Martin and John Archambault's *The Ghost-Eye Tree* (1985) as a read-aloud book that they enjoyed when they were younger and Virginia Hamilton's *The People Could Fly: American Black Folktales* (1985) as a favorite folklore collection. As you read reviews, keep in mind that they are written for adults; consequently, you may need to help students understand some of the meanings. Following is a book review of *The Ghost-Eye Tree:*

A top-notch hair-raiser that will do for any old night of the year but will really spike a Halloween story hour. It's poetry, too, the kind that reaches out to grab you. The narrator remembers one autumn eve when his mother asked him and his sister "to take the road/to the end of the town/to get a bucket of milk." His problem is dread of a haunted old oak tree. Both his fears and his old hat draw teasing from his big sister, until, lugging their milk home, she sees the oak ghost, too. They both run pell-mell home, and, in a touching finale, his sister courageously retrieves the hat he has dropped. This is very real in capturing both the siblings' tit-for-tat talking and childhood terrors in general. The language and sound patterns beg for oral presentation, and the watercolor paintings for group viewing. They give full play to light/dark contrasts, the yellows and white startling against black shapes and deep-blue skies. The focus of the compositions is arresting, too, with faces central to shadowy backgrounds. Evocative for adults and immediate for children'' (p. 114, *Bulletin of the Center for Children's Books,* 1986).

The book review for *The People Could Fly: American Black Folktales* is found in the March/April, 1986 issue of the *Horn Book Magazine,* pages 212–13. The book reviews and the books chosen can be related to various content areas. For example, students can read and review biographies about scientists, historical fiction about a time period studied in history, and nonfiction about any subject matter.

B. Discuss the reviews and list elements such as brief summaries, comments about the authors' language and the impact of the illustrations, and recommendations about the literature.

C. Ask the students to select a book and write a book review that includes the preceding elements. Follow the writing process approach, in which the students write and edit first drafts and develop completed reviews that are ready to share with classmates.

D. Share the reviews and the books the reviews are about. Students may first share them orally and then display the reviews and books in the library.

SUMMARY

School libraries no longer house only books. They have become media centers emphasizing both nonprint and print media. Access to a good school library increases both the number and variety of books students read. Methods for acquiring free or inexpensive materials for classrooms include (1) asking parents for donations of used children's books, (2) paperback book exchanges, (3) requesting donations of used reference periodicals, and (4) writing letters to request free or inexpensive materials.

Library skills are essential for finding materials efficiently. Such skills are necessary for the development of independent study skills, positive attitudes toward investigation, interest in functional and recreational reading, and knowledge about libraries that will last a lifetime. Do not leave library skills to incidental learning.

Students need to know which references to use, where the references are located, and how to use them efficiently. Instruction in the primary grades emphasizes readiness and prerequisite skills, such as alphabetizing, class-made picture dictionaries, class telephone directories, manipulative objects, learning centers, encyclopedias, and card catalogs. Formal instruction in reference skills usually begins in the intermediate grades and includes dictionary skills, such as alphabetizing; using guide words; locating correct definitions for multiple definitions; determining pronunciation; and finding synonyms, antonyms, and parts of speech. Students are also taught to use encyclopedias, the card catalog, and other library references. The upper-elementary and middle-school grades review and refine these skills.

ADDITIONAL LIBRARY AND REFERENCE SKILLS ACTIVITIES

1. Visit several school, public, and/or university libraries. Interview the librarians. What reference skills do the librarians believe students and adults require?
2. Look at an elementary language arts scope and sequence. What library and reference skills are included? At what grade levels is instruction recommended?
3. Look at several journals such as *Book List* and *School Library Journal* that review literature. If possible, find references to nonprint media. Compile a current list of recommended nonprint media and share it with your language arts class.
4. Interview a media center specialist at your university. What changes does the specialist believe will occur during the next ten years? How will these changes affect the language arts program?
5. Select several dictionaries or encyclopedias designed to be used with early elementary grades, middle-elementary grades, and upper-elementary grades. Compare the readability levels, content, and illustrations.
6. Hart's *Introduction in School Media Center Use (K–12)* (1985) provides descriptions of numerous instructional activities and includes references to a wide range of approaches for teaching various library-related skills. Read about several of these approaches and describe the ones that you believe are the most interesting or beneficial. Share your findings with your class.

BIBLIOGRAPHY

American Association of School Librarians. *Information Power: Guidelines for School Library Media Programs.* Chicago: American Library Association, 1988.

Anderson, R.; Hiebert, E.; Scott, J.; and Wilkinson, I. *Becoming a Nation of Readers: The Report of the Commission on Reading.* Washington, DC: National Institute of Education, 1985.

Bulletin of the Center for Children's Books. The University of Chicago, Vol. 39, p. 114, 1986.

Childcraft Dictionary. Chicago: World Book, Inc, 1989.

Cullinan, B.; Greene, E.; and Jaggar, A. "Books, Babies, and Libraries: The Librarian's Role In Literacy Development." *Language Arts* 67 (1990): 750–55.

Dales, B. "Trusting Relations between Teachers and Librarians." *Language Arts* 67 (1990): 732–34.

Elleman, B. "Celebrating Books and Libraries." *Book Links* 622 (1990): 625–27.

Foster, M. P. *Looking It Up.* Belmont, Calif.: Fearon Teacher Aids, 1989.

Hart, Thomas L. *Instruction in School Library Media Use (K–12).* Chicago: American Library Association, 1985.

Hiebert, E.; Mervar, K.; and Person, D. "Research Directions: Children's Selection of Trade Books in Libraries and Classrooms." *Language Arts* 67 (1990): 758–63.

Horn Book Magazine. (March/April 1986), pp. 212–13.

Jenks, C., and Roberts, J. "Reading, Writing, and Reviewing: Teacher, Librarian, and Young Readers Collaborate!" *Language Arts* 67 (1990): 742–45.

Kaplan, D. *Study Skills for Success.* Pleasantville, N.Y.: Sunburst Communications, 1988.

Keel, Helen. "Library Skills." In *Instruction in School Library Media Center Use (K–12)*, edited by Thomas L. Hart. Chicago: American Library Association, 1985.

Lamme, L., and Ledbetter, L. "Libraries: The Heart of Whole Language." *Language Arts* 67 (1990): 735–41.

Mealy, V. *Biography Reports without Copying.* O'Fallon, Mo.: Book Lures, Inc, 1989.

Merchant, Maurice P.; Broadway, Marsha D.; Robinson, Eileen; and Shields, Dorothy. "Research into Learning Resulting from Quality School Media Service." *School Library Journal* 30 (April 1984): 20–22.

Spiegel, D. L. "Content Bias in Reference and Study Skills." *The Reading Teacher* 44 (1990): 64–66.

Tompkins, Sister Mary Denis. "A Friend in Need." *Instructor* 81 (November 1971): 90–91.

CHILDREN'S LITERATURE REFERENCES

Aliki, *How a Book Is Made*. New York: HarperCollins, 1986.

Edwards, Michelle. *Dora's Book*. Minneapolis: Carolrhoda, 1990.

Gibbons, Gail. *Check It Out! The Book about Libraries*. Orlando: Harcourt Brace Jovanovich, 1985.

Greenfeld, Howard. *Books: From Writer to Reader*. New York: Crown, 1988.

Hamilton, Virginia, retold by. *The People Could Fly: American Black Folktales*. Illustrated by Leo and Diane Dillon. New York: Knopf, 1985.

Kehoe, Michael. *The Puzzle of Books*. Minneapolis: Carolrhoda, 1982.

Kimmel, Eric. *I Took My Frog to the Library*. Illustrated by Blanche Sims. New York: Viking, 1990.

Levinson, Nancy S. *Clara and the Bookwagon*. Illustrated by Carolyn Croll. New York: HarperCollins, 1988.

Martin, Bill, and Archambault, John. *The Ghost-Eye Tree*. Illustrated by Ted Rand. Orlando: Holt, 1985.

Radlauer, Ruth. *Molly at the Library*. New York: Simon & Schuster, 1987.

Rockwell, Anne. *I Like the Library*. New York: Dutton, 1977.

Weil, Lisl. *Let's Go to the Library*. New York: Holiday, 1990.

Name Index

Subject Index

ISBN 0-02-388310-3

DATE DUE